Third Edition **An Introduction to Contemporary Business**

An Introduction to
to

William Rudelius
University of Minnesota

W. Bruce Erickson
University of Minnesota

William J. Bakula, Jr.
Anne Arundel Community College

Jeanne Hanson
University of Minnesota

Contemporary Business

Third Edition

Harcourt Brace Jovanovich, Inc.

New York   San Diego   Chicago   San Francisco   Atlanta

London   Sydney   Toronto

An Introduction to Contemporary Business, Third Edition
Rudelius/Erickson/Bakula/Hanson

DECIDE acronym © 1981, 1973 by William Rudelius.

Cover credit: H. Armstrong Roberts, Inc.
Art by Joyce Kitchell, Ralph Mapson, and Carol Schwartzback.

Printed in the United States of America
Library of Congress Catalog Card Number: 80-84607
ISBN: 0-15-541655-3

Preface

You are about to start on what we believe is an absorbing and valuable journey through the realm of American business. AN INTRODUCTION TO CONTEMPORARY BUSINESS, Third Edition, is about *real* people, whose problems, decisions, mistakes, and successes offer important lessons about the everyday world we live in. The people you will encounter—whether starting their own small retail shop or looking into million-dollar investment opportunities—have had experiences that will afford you a practical view of business. A study of these experiences will also help you to apply the fundamental principles and methods of business. This integrated approach to the study of modern American business is intended to help prepare you to meet the special challenges of the 1980s.

Business is a fundamental and inseparable part of our society. If you consider that nearly 90 percent of all goods and services in the U. S. economy are produced by business, you can see that your chances of making a career somewhere within this broad area are very good. But even if you choose to work outside of business, your life will be affected by the decisions that business makes. If you aren't selling television sets or manufacturing clothes or growing produce, you are certainly buying them. To study business is also to gain an understanding of history and to develop a framework for anticipating the shape of tomorrow. Most new ideas—from the modern assembly line to the microcomputer—have been born out of the needs of business. So a thorough knowledge of the basic principles and practices of business not only makes good sense but has real dollars-and-cents value, both for you and our future society.

Many practical features of AN INTRODUCTION TO CONTEMPORARY BUSINESS, Third Edition, will help you gain this knowledge. Here are some examples:

Your Next Job. Within each chapter is a section describing business careers related to the subject matter of that chapter. This section, called "Your Next Job," gives specific information on career opportunities for your future, including educational requirements, advancement possibilities, salary ranges, and where to write to obtain more information. If you are especially attracted to the material of a given chapter, you may be a good candidate for that set of career choices.

Boxes. Each chapter includes several boxed inserts, set off in color. They describe people or situations relevant to the chapter's content. Some are humorous, some serious, and some will engage your active participation; but all have high human-interest appeal.

Critical Business Decision. At the end of each chapter is a special section called "A Critical Business Decision," which describes a real-life business person and a problem he or she is facing. Each is relevant to its chapter's subject matter, and questions at the end of the box challenge you to apply what you have learned to determine the best course of action.

Functional Framework. The main functional areas of business—management, production, marketing, accounting, finance, and data processing—are presented early in the book and in some detail. This arrangement enables you to grasp key business concepts quickly and to apply them to the later discussions of small business and franchising, government and business law, unions, and international business.

Logical Flow. Within each chapter and throughout the text as a whole, there is a clear and logical progression of ideas. No concept is presented before you have the background to understand it, yet nowhere is there so much background that the main themes become clouded. And the two-color design allows you to clearly distinguish text from supplemental material so that the flow of thought as you read need not be interrupted.

We hope that AN INTRODUCTION TO CONTEMPORARY BUSINESS, Third Edition, will teach and even entertain you . . . and perhaps launch you into a challenging and rewarding career.

William Rudelius

W. Bruce Erickson

William J. Bakula, Jr.

Jeanne Hanson

Acknowledgments

Any book that covers a subject as diverse as American business cannot help but require contributions from a large number of people. Like its previous editions, AN INTRODUCTION TO CONTEMPORARY BUSINESS, Third Edition, could not have been written without the assistance of the many scholars and business executives we consulted.

The academics who helped us—in some cases both with textbook content and teaching approach—include the following:

Professors Bengt A. Anderson, S.U.N.Y., Farmingdale

W. Gary Bacon, Northlake Community College

Peter J. Boone, Tidewater Community College

James Bowman, Stephen F. Austin State University

Sonya Brett, Macomb County Community College

Robert W. Doty, Saddleback College

John W. Ernest, Los Angeles City College

Thomas W. Faranda, Inver Hills Community College

Judith Furrer, Inver Hills Community College

Joyce L. Grahn, University of Minnesota

R. A. Johannsen, Miami-Dade Community College

Warren Keller, Grossmont College

Iris B. Kohler, Palomar College

Patrick Kroll, University of Minnesota

Fritz Lotze, Southwestern College

Sheldon Mador, Los Angeles Trade Technical College

Carmen L. Marinella, Los Angeles Harbor College

Donald R. McCauley, McLennan Community College

Frank D. Mitchell, Inver Hills Community College

Jack Partlow, Seminole Community College

Robert Ripley, San Diego City College

Joseph F. Salamone, Erie Community College

Barry Shane, Oregon State University

Mary K. St.John Nelson, University of Minnesota.

We are also grateful to our colleagues in the College of Business Administration at the University of Minnesota with whom we consulted. In addition to those who contributed to the first and second editions, we would like to acknowledge the special contributions of Professors Gary W. Dickson, James M. Gahlon, Paul F. Jessup, and Timothy J. Nantell.

Since 1973, when the first edition of AN INTRODUCTION TO CONTEMPORARY BUSINESS was published, the field of business has seen considerable change. Updating the material for students whose careers will span the 1980s, 1990s, and beyond, has involved writing almost an entirely new book. We could not have completed this task without the editorial help of Gretchen Lindstrom and Sandra Whelan, whose assistance with the main text and the supplements proved invaluable. Our secretaries—Joyce Hegstrom, Pamela DeMink, and Char Duncan—patiently dealt with draft after draft. We would also like to acknowledge the contributions of the many people at Harcourt Brace Jovanovich, Inc., who contributed to the third edition—in particular designer Geri Davis and art editor Sue Lasbury, who worked to provide layouts, drawings, and pictures that have lent the book a fresh and exciting appearance; and, finally, our editor—Barbara Rose—who displayed great ingenuity in dealing with the foibles of authors.

Because of the extensive revisions involved in producing a truly up-to-date business text, we cannot honestly say that "many hands made light work." But all these contributors did make the work lighter, and for this we are truly grateful.

Contents

Part One

*The American
Business System*

1 American Business: An Overview 5

1-3 Test
4-7
8-10
12-14
18,19,20 Last

2 Private Enterprise and Its Social Responsibility 29

3 Business Ownership: You, Your Partners, Your Corporation 57

Part Three   Marketing

Part Four   Accounting, Finance, and Management Information

Part Five   *Small Business and Franchising*

16   *Small Business: Your Own Franchise*   **387**

17   *Small Business: On Your Own*   **409**

Part Six   *The Environment of Business*

18   *Government and Business Law*   **431**

19 Unions and the American Worker   453

20 International Business   479

Third Edition An Introduction to Contemporary Business

1 The American

Business System

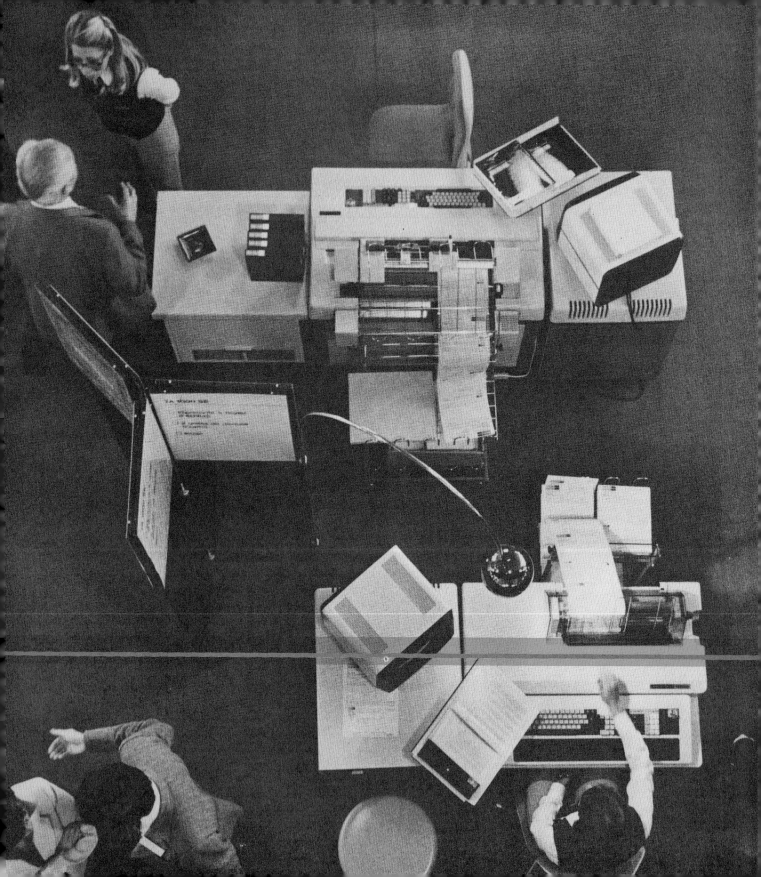

American Business: An Overview

1

6

People can be divided into three groups: those who make things happen, those who watch things happen, and those who wonder what happened.

JOHN A. NEWBORN

avid Dornbush found *the* product and his future job while watching a third-rate TV program—when he should have been studying. He and Chad Erickson, both in their 20's, were college friends. They had talked about starting a manufacturing business but couldn't find the right product.

What caught Dornbush's eye on TV was a "home food dehydrator." A crude wooden model, it was designed by an Oregon do-it-yourselfer to dry garden fruits and vegetables. It was being sold mostly to the designer's friends and whoever could be reached through a few cheap TV ads.[1]

Dornbush and Erickson knew that hobby gardening was growing like a weed as people became more energy-conscious, health-conscious, and money-conscious. Wouldn't a lot of people want to buy a practical appliance to dry food? The two young men liked the idea of producing something technical. And they felt they could improve the product shown on TV enough to gain sales before large competitors jumped into the business.

They made mistakes at first, like the motor that had five times the power it needed. "And we were too dumb to realize the odds against us," said Dornbush. But it has paid off. Dornbush and Erickson's firm, called Alternative Pioneering Systems, Inc., now is producing several models of home food dehydrators (see Figure 1–1), has hit $2,400,000 in annual sales, and just moved into a new 26,000 square foot facility for its thirty employees. But Dornbush and Erickson aren't free of all problems yet, as you'll see in the Critical Business Decision at the end of the chapter.

All businesses are made up of an endless array of fascinating ingredients: unusual people, creative ideas, precise plans, and—as David Dornbush showed—occasional flashes of insight.

In the chapters that follow, you'll see what leads to business success and failure. And you'll learn how some enterprising business people transformed their unusual ideas into products that are now household words. You'll hear about some astounding failures, too. And you just might discover your own future career in the process.

**FIGURE 1–1
The Home
Food Dehydrator.**

WHAT IS BUSINESS?

Business is both an economic activity and a way of life for over 72 million Americans. In its broadest sense, **business** refers to all profit-producing activities that provide goods and services to customers.

Business as an Economic Activity

To be successful, a business (1) must provide value to its customers, (2) be profitable, and (3) be managed efficiently.

Customer Satisfaction

The product or service offered by a business must have utility for customers to want to buy it. Customers find *utility,* or satisfaction, in items whose benefits are available when and where they are wanted. A high-quality stereo, a useful computer-repair service, or a very average late-night pizza parlor all have utility if they are in the right place at the right time.

As a corporation, International Business Machines (IBM) has succeeded in satisfying its customers extremely well. Most experts agree that IBM computers are not the most technically advanced in the industry. But IBM has succeeded brilliantly in adapting its computers to the needs of its diverse customers, whether giant banks or small retailers. And IBM service is unexcelled—from setting up computers on floating oil rigs to 2 A.M. repair jobs in downtown Chicago to get a customer's payroll out on time.

The relationship between a business firm and its customers appears in Figure 1–2. The figure emphasizes that both parties are better off after the exchange than before. The relationship applies equally well to IBM or a local stereo store or a basement inventor, because the idea of both parties benefiting from an exchange underlies the entire business process. One inventor's hairbrained idea (see the box on page 10) ultimately satisfied customer needs so well it created a billion-dollar-a-year business that didn't exist two decades ago.

Profit

If a business succeeds at identifying and meeting customer needs through the products or services it markets, it is likely to earn a profit. **Profit** is the difference between the revenues earned by a business and the costs it incurs in providing the product or service.

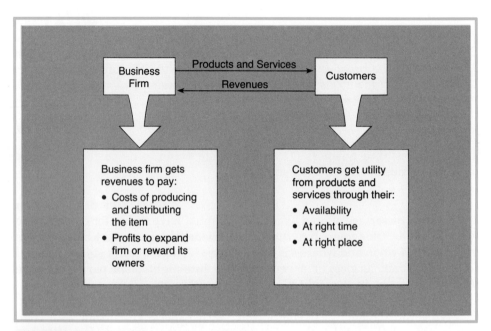

FIGURE 1-2
What Business Firms and Customers
Get from Each Other.

General Motors (GM) is an example of how profits affect business. In the late 1970s, when gasoline prices skyrocketed, GM introduced its new line of fuel-efficient "X-cars"—the Chevy Citation, Buick Skylark, Pontiac Phoenix, and Oldsmobile Omega. Revenues from the X-cars included dollars from car sales, interest income from car loans made to customers, and funds obtained by selling worn-out machinery. General Motors' costs included dollars paid out for employee wages, raw materials, machinery, and taxes. Revenues exceeded costs, so GM made a profit.

Without products that customers like, there is no profit. With profit, the business can be maintained and expanded and the owners, or shareholders, paid dividends. General Motors correctly anticipated customers' wants on the X-cars. Even when sales slumped for its larger cars, GM dealers sold all of the X-cars they could get. The result: GM made enough profit on the X-cars to cover losses on some of its other lines. It paid dividends to shareholders. And it stepped up X-car production.

Managerial Efficiency

Rock groups like the Beatles can be an immense success and their records and personal appearances tremendously profitable. But their business can be a financial disaster. The Beatles nearly went bankrupt because their incompetent and dissension-ridden managers frittered away the group's earnings on a series of bad businesses.

So managerial efficiency is essential. A business may produce a good or service that satisfies customers and earns some profit. But unless it is as efficient as its major competitors, these aggressive rivals will serve customers better, make more profit, and eventually drive it out of business.

A good location, large size, quality people, and other factors like luck help a business remain efficient. But the most important component of efficiency is good management. So an effective management must:

- Set realistic goals for the firm.
- Identify the key markets and types of customers for its main production and marketing efforts.
- Use the resources of a business (its men and women, materials, machinery, and money) efficiently.
- Adapt to outside factors, such as government regulations, ethical standards, and economic and technological trends.

In short, management must direct the resources of the business toward realizable objectives. In the process, management must consider both (1) the firm's own strengths and weaknesses and (2) the opportunities and threats posed by outside factors in determining what the business actually can achieve. The ways in which management accomplishes these tasks are the subjects of this book.

Business as a Way of Life

For those who own or manage businesses, work is not simply a job—it is a life style. The decisions they make, the people they deal with, the ideas they have are not confined to a 9:00 A.M. to 5:00 P.M. day. Faced with great demands and responsibilities, the product manager of Duncan Hines cake mixes or the president of a new solar energy company often "work" even when they are "playing." But, for them, the challenges and rewards can be great.

A Man, an Idea, and a Business

J.H. Dessauer, C.F. Carlson, and J.C. Wilson of Haloid (later Xerox) with early dry-copying machine. Rochester, New York, 1948.

Nothing ever came easily for Chester F. Carlson. There were no flashes of genius, no thunderbolts of brilliant inspiration. His success was the result of dogged determination in the face of repeated failures.

Part of grade school Carlson spent in a one-room schoolhouse. At 12, Chester F. "Chet" Carlson—along with the county welfare board—became the main support of his family. Chet's father had crippling arthritis, and both his parents had tuberculosis. The jobs Chet found in San Bernardino, California, were the family's main source of income.

When Chet was 17, his mother died. At 20, he entered the California Institute of Technology and emerged four years later—exhausted from studying, working at odd jobs, and nursing his father—with a B.S. degree in physics. It was 1930, the start of the Great Depression. Chet wrote over 80 letters applying for work. He received only two replies, both saying no.

After his father died, Chet moved to New York and found a job in the patent department of a large firm. One night he worked until midnight on a patent application with a colleague. The big problem was the long time spent copying the drawings. Chet

Carlson turned wearily from his desk to say, "There must be a quicker, better way to make these copies!"

"Sure," the colleague agreed. "But nobody has ever found it."

"Maybe nobody ever tried," Chet responded.

So Chet tried—in his Astoria, New York, "lab," a dingy room behind a beauty parlor. After many failures he tried a process in which a powder adhered to spots on a surface charged with static electricity. On October 22, 1938, he used this process to transfer the inscription *10-22-38 Astoria* from a glass slide to a piece of waxed paper. Seeing this meager result, his assistant quit. But Carlson patented his invention, knowing he needed a company to improve, manufacture, and market it. During the next six years, he showed his invention to 21 major companies, including IBM, RCA, Remington Rand, A.B. Dick, and General Electric.

No one was interested.

Then the tiny Haloid Company in Rochester, New York, heard about Carlson's patent. After talking to Carlson and to other scientists, Haloid decided to work on the idea—against the dire warnings of experts who predicted that it would take ten years and tens of millions of dollars to produce a marketable machine. And Haloid's profits at that time were a mere $138,000 per year.

What became of the man, the idea, and the company in this American business drama?

The man, Chet Carlson, became wealthy. He quietly donated fortunes to charitable and public service organizations, including millions of dollars to the California Institute of Technology. The idea of using photoelectrical principles to provide paper copies was given a name. It was called "xerography," which is Greek for "dry writing" or "dry copying." The firm was renamed. The Haloid Company became Haloid-Xerox, Inc., and then simply the Xerox Corporation. Today Xerox has over 100,000 employees scattered in 40 plants around the world and is considered one of the best managed and most socially responsible firms in American business.[2]

Three different types of business people that work within society's framework to make a business successful are the *entrepreneur,* the *professional
manager,* and the *functional specialist.*

The Entrepreneur

Most businesses start as a dream in somebody's mind. An **entrepreneur** is a
person with an idea. He or she also is someone with the energy and drive to
turn that idea into a business. An entrepreneur needs these characteristics
because in a young firm he or she must often do everything at once—manufacture the product, sell it, find enough money to keep going, and manage a
few employees.

The entrepreneur must be willing to take great risks, too, for most new
businesses fail within a year. The odds against success are stiff, partly because
many business ideas simply are not very good. After all, whoever wanted to
buy paper dresses or quadraphonic sound? As it turned out, almost no one.
Factors that create special risks for new businesses are those over which
entrepreneurs have little control. For example, large, well-established organizations would rather deal with each other than with a tiny new company.
Also, technology has become highly complex and many new products—a filter
to remove the salt from sea water, for example—require many years and teams
of scientists and engineers to develop. Then, too, a vast array of government
regulations creates additional burdens of time, energy, and expense for owners
of new businesses.

But successful entrepreneurs can overcome these risks. And we owe them
a great debt. From the earliest colonial days, their ideas and daring have been
the major force for economic growth and change in this country.

The Professional Manager

Once an entrepreneur's business is established, growth can be rapid. The task
is to produce the product in quantity and market it to consumers effectively. To
do this, the firm must add employees. And if it is successful, it quickly becomes
too large for casual working relationships and unstructured organization.
What it needs is a **professional manager** to organize employees into specific
units, set up rules and procedures, and make operations more efficient.

This manager is not necessarily the original entrepreneur, who may or
may not be suited to this type of work. Entrepreneurs usually like to be on
their own, whether manufacturing an improved moped or opening a new

Chinese restaurant. Ordinarily their concerns are with ideas and with overseeing their implementation.

Managers, on the other hand, usually assume the more concrete tasks of organizing people and other resources and solving specific types of problems. For instance, they may work with a company task force to design a new kind of breakfast cereal, or they may figure out a better way to move Alaskan oil from the West Coast to the Midwest. The activities of planning, organizing, leading, and controlling that are used by all professional managers will be discussed in detail in Part II of the text.

The Functional Specialist

Businesses hire millions of people who are neither entrepreneurs nor managers. Ranging from clerks to nuclear physicists, these employees are called **functional specialists.** Usually they are trained in a specialized field of business, such as accounting, finance, marketing, or production. One of their primary duties is to advise management in their areas of expertise. Functional specialists may combine this expertise with some managerial skills and supervise a department of other functional specialists. Today, Levi's jeans, for

Levi's Jeans: From Entrepreneurs . . .

Jeans are everywhere. More than 500 million were sold last year in this country—over two pairs for every man, woman, and child. And almost 400 million more were sold abroad.[3]

The brand that leads the way—Levi's—was launched by two entrepreneurs. Levi Strauss went West in the days of the California Gold Rush with a stock of canvas cloth to sell to miners for tents and wagon covers. But the miners needed work pants, not tents. So Strauss used the canvas to stitch some pants. They were so comfortable and durable that miners asked for more, and Strauss went into the pants business.

Later, in 1872, Strauss got a letter from a Russian immigrant, Jacob Davis, who was living in Nevada and couldn't keep up with the demand for his own work pants. He wanted a partner and a patent for his design, which featured copper rivets at stress points.

The next year Strauss and Davis put their needles and talents together and made history. Modern Levi's—the straight-legged, cotton-denim, copper-riveted jeans—vary only slightly from the design originally patented in 1873.

example, are sold throughout the world because the skills of professional managers and functional specialists extended those of the original entrepreneurs (see box).

These specialists normally have no direct responsibility for profits and so may work under less pressure than the typical professional manager. Their standing in their own profession is sometimes as important to them as the success of the business for which they work. But they must have a good general knowledge of how business operates because they work closely with people from other areas and departments. Parts III and IV of the text discuss the functional specialists in production, marketing, accounting, finance, insurance, and computers.

A Business Career for You?

Because people differ in their abilities, interests, and goals, they need to consider carefully whether their primary aim in a business career is to become an entrepreneur, a professional manager, or a functional specialist. To help

... to Professional Managers and Functional Specialists

Today, Levi Strauss & Co. is the largest clothing manufacturer in the world. With about $2 billion in annual sales, it ranks among the 200 largest corporations in the United States.[4]

Supervising 41,000 employees in 70 countries is a big job. And although descendants of the first Levi Strauss still run the company, they must employ hundreds of professional managers and thousands of functional specialists to handle day-to-day operations in such areas as accounting, finance, marketing, and production.

The Levi's name is so popular that the company now also employs full-time investigators who search the world trying to track down counterfeit producers who use its brand name. And in the U.S., truckloads of Levi's are prime targets for hijackers.

Fortunately, Levi Strauss & Co. has an advantage in finding talented employees: young people tend to extend their liking for Levi's jeans to the company that makes them—and they are eager to work for an organization whose products they believe in.

The Critical Business Decision at the end of Chapter 20 takes a closer look at this dynamic company.

Your Next Job

It's Not Too Early to Start Thinking

After spending thousands of hours in school, many young men and women are still basically unprepared for a career, and they select a job in a rather hit-or-miss fashion. As a result, their talents may be misused—or never realized—and their goals unformulated. It doesn't have to be this way. When approached systematically, career selection can lead to a lifetime of personal satisfaction and financial rewards, and a chance to make a meaningful contribution to society.

Five Steps in Choosing a Career

1. *Assess your personal characteristics.* Think about your strengths, weaknesses, aptitudes, interests, mental abilities, manual dexterity, and personality. Ask yourself such questions as: "Would I prefer to work with things, with ideas, or with people?" "Do I need to see the physical results of my work?" "Would I rather work independently or as part of a team?" "Could I handle a job that requires physical stamina?" "Would I be suited to a supervisory position?" Answers can be found through self-appraisal, career-guidance testing, and counseling.
2. *Assess employment and industry trends.* No one can predict future employment opportunities exactly. But knowing the projected demand for various skills can help. Occupation and industry trends are discussed in the Your Next Job boxes in Chapters 2 and 3.
3. *Match career and personal characteristics.* People who like to work with numbers may want to become engineers, accountants, statisticians, market researchers, or computer programmers. Opportunities for people who enjoy direct public contact include such jobs as personnel counseling, selling, and industrial buying. Consider a variety of jobs that complement your personal characteristics. The Your Next Job sections in Chapters 4 through 19 discuss career opportunities in various fields, including the nature of the work, education, and experience requirements, salary, expected employment outlooks, and sources of additional information.
4. *Make sure you have the necessary education and training.* Some jobs are open to high-school graduates; others require two-year or four-year college degrees. And still others are open only to those with graduate degrees. Some require no work experience, and others require years of prior training. To plan your career effectively, you must know the education and training it requires and make sure you are on the right course.
5. *Find the position.* "Selling yourself" effectively involves developing a good resume (to be discussed in Chapter 5) and knowing how to ask and answer questions in a job interview. Work through your college placement office and solicit interviews on your own, too. Some tips are found in the Your Next Job section in Chapter 20.

Good luck!

Basic career references:

- *Occupational Outlook Handbook, 1980–81 Edition,* Bulletin 2075 (Washington, D.C.: U.S. Government Printing Office, 1980).
- Bolles, Richard N., *What Color Is Your Parachute?* (Berkeley, Calif.: Ten Speed Press, 1977).

you in thinking about your career, each chapter in this text will contain a boxed page titled Your Next Job. These boxes cover everything from career planning and descriptions of specific jobs to interviewing for the job. The first of these boxes appears on the opposite page.

AMERICAN BUSINESS: A BRIEF HISTORY

Business came to America with the Pilgrims. In fact, the boats that brought the Pilgrims to the New World were paid for by joint stock companies in England, the forerunners of modern American corporations. Colonial businesses soon were producing one-seventh of the world's iron; whaling, fur trading, banking, and land speculation were other major business activities.

The Industrial Revolution

In the **Industrial Revolution,** which began in the United States in about 1790, factories with machinery were used to produce goods formerly made individually with hand tools. This change led to the development of large-scale production. Typical of the early stages of the Industrial Revolution was widespread use of the power loom, the spinning jenny (which could spin several yarns of wool at the same time), the machine lathe, and the steamboat.

The Industrial Revolution produced an unprecedented application of scientific technology to everyday life, and inventor-entrepreneurs shaped history. Samuel Morse, who invented the telegraph, founded a company that was the forerunner of today's Western Union. Cyrus McCormick created the mechanical harvester, the first of International Harvester's line of farm implements. I. M. Singer developed the sewing machine and formed the Singer Company.

The use of *standardized* or *interchangeable parts* was an essential ingredient in the Industrial Revolution, for it enabled even unskilled workers to make complex products with equipment like lathes and drill presses. The result was **mass production**—the manufacturing of large quantities of identical or similar products with the assistance of power-driven machinery. Standardized parts and mass production began with Eli Whitney. In 1799, Whitney, who also invented the cotton gin, was given an Army contract to produce 10,000 rifles. Normally, Army rifles were painstakingly built—one at a time—by highly skilled gunsmiths. And the Army was concerned about Whitney's failure to deliver the first rifles on time. When the Army inspectors paid a surprise visit to Whitney's plant, they couldn't find one completed rifle. But Whitney pulled ten different pieces from ten boxes and proceeded to assemble ten rifles before the eyes of his astounded visitors. The inspectors were impressed and Whitney kept the contract.

Along with mass production came **mass marketing,** the distribution of goods and services among large numbers of customers. Improved roads, canals, and, most importantly, the spread of railroads made it possible to sell the vast quantities of products that poured from the new factories. The joining of the East with the West in 1869, when the railroads met in Utah, was the beginning of a truly national economy. National markets were opened to manufacturers for the first time in the nation's history.

The rise of "money power" and **finance capitalism** after the Civil War, and the growth of financial centers in such cities as New York, Philadelphia, Boston, and Chicago, ushered in a new era in American history. Powerful financiers like the aloof J. Pierpont Morgan and Jay Gould, a notorious stock-market manipulator, ruled many businesses through the money they con-

Declaration of
Independence
(1776)

Start of Industrial
Revolution in the
United States
(1790)

Eli Whitney produces
Army rifles using
interchangeable parts
(1799)

Mass markets open because
of spread of railroads and
improved roads and canals
(after 1830)

Growth of U.S. "money
centers" in New York,
Boston, Chicago, and
Philadelphia
(after 1865)

1750   1800   1850

Rapid growth of
factory system
(after 1870)

trolled. Although the era of finance capitalism was short (about 1880 to 1910), it financed many manufacturing plants and speeded up the factory system of production. It also demonstrated that American business was no longer dependent on Europe for capital.

The Modern Era

By the end of World War II in 1945, the Industrial Revolution was complete. The need for war goods required the development of new forms of production and technology, which later were used to produce consumer goods. Inventiveness was at a high peak. Synthetic plastics and chemicals replaced natural substances as the basis for many products. Better machinery made it possible to manufacture products to precise specifications. (This type of precision is what led eventually to the Apollo moon shot, which required components that were accurate to several one-hundred thousandths of an inch.) Reflecting the United States' changing world economic role, most large businesses became international in scope.

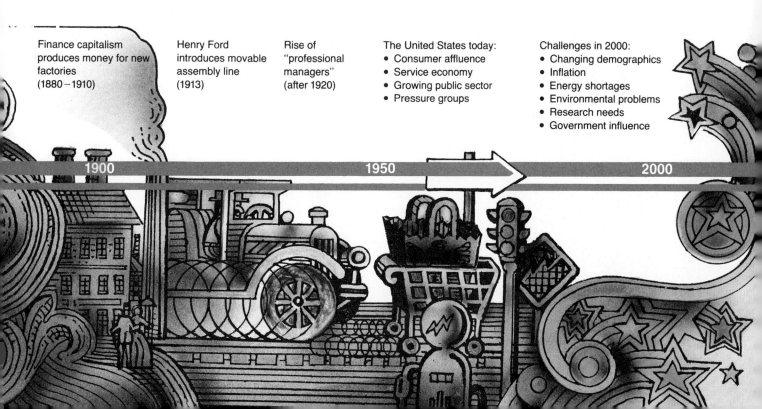

Finance capitalism produces money for new factories (1880 – 1910)

Henry Ford introduces movable assembly line (1913)

Rise of "professional managers" (after 1920)

The United States today:
- Consumer affluence
- Service economy
- Growing public sector
- Pressure groups

Challenges in 2000:
- Changing demographics
- Inflation
- Energy shortages
- Environmental problems
- Research needs
- Government influence

1900   1950   2000

In the 1970s, widespread use of computers enabled management to process large quantities of data. Factories could be *automated,* with computer-controlled machinery carrying out many routine activities that could previously be completed only by time-consuming human labor.

By 1980, more than 80 percent of this country's 500 largest businesses were multinational, operating facilities in five or more foreign countries. And even for smaller companies and individual consumers, the world has become more like a large neighborhood than a huge, unknowable planet. High-speed computers, orbiting satellites, fluctuating exchange rates, and worldwide scarcities of natural resources bind us together with common needs, concerns, and goals.

AMERICAN BUSINESS TODAY

Today, professional managers run most of the nation's 10 million businesses, which produce a startling array of new products that range from synthetic fabrics to electronic TV games. And although sales of certain energy-consuming products are down, our society still enjoys amazing wealth.

The most common measure of a country's wealth is its **gross national product (GNP)**—the money value of all goods and services produced, usually in a period of one year. In 1980, GNP for the United States was about $2.5 trillion. Even when the effects of inflation are subtracted, *real GNP* has still grown by about 3 percent a year since 1945. In 1980, if the GNP were to have been divided equally among all members of the population, *per capita GNP* would have been about $11,000.

Although GNP is not the only measure of a successful society, it is an important yardstick of the standard of living of that society. Figure 1–3 shows how the standard of living of an average American compares with that of people in five other highly developed countries. If the standard for the Ameri-

FIGURE 1-3
Living Standards,
Based on the Per Capita Consumption
of Goods and Services.

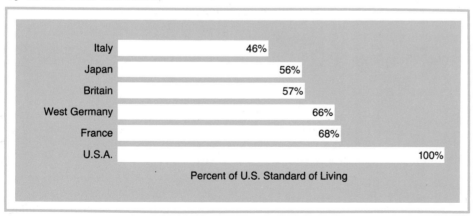

Italy — 46%
Japan — 56%
Britain — 57%
West Germany — 66%
France — 68%
U.S.A. — 100%

Percent of U.S. Standard of Living

Source: Reprinted with permission of *The Wall Street Journal,* © Dow Jones & Company, Inc. 1977. All rights reserved.

can is 100 percent, the figure shows that a Frenchman is 68 percent as well off and an Italian only 46 percent as well off as the American.

The Service Economy

The economy today is oriented more toward services than products. **Products**—material items from chewing gum to nuclear reactors—now account for less than 40 percent of the GNP. **Services,** ranging from Xerox repair to garbage collection, now employ a full two-thirds of all workers. Virtually all transportation, communication, public utilities, finance, and government activities are considered to be part of the service economy.

The growth of services presents several challenges. Many services cannot use mass-production techniques; productivity is hard to increase; and labor costs are rising fast. You can't produce more efficient music by transferring some orchestra members to other projects and using a machine to play Chopin's "Minute Waltz" in 40 seconds. So prices rise more easily in the service economy. However, those services that *can* employ automation—for example, vending machines and automatic bank tellers—are generally well-rewarded.

The Public Sector

The **public sector**—which includes all federal, state, and local government activities—now accounts for more than 30 percent of the nation's GNP. Although the public sector does not produce any products, it does purchase them—from paper clips to space probes. And it transfers income from group to group, through such activities as social security, income taxes, and a system of laws and regulations.

The **private sector**—which includes all economic institutions not owned by the government—does not exist entirely apart from the public sector. Managers now find that activities such as selling to the government, paying taxes to the government, and filling out forms for the government take massive amounts of time and energy. Business managers must follow books full of government regulations, covering rules dealing with everything from heart pacemakers to clothes hooks for factory workers.

Pressure Groups

Big business, big labor, and big government are giants on the economic scene. As a *pressure group* or *interest group,* each tries to achieve its own objectives. And, of course, the major objective of a business is to earn profits. Some are more successful than others. In fact, seven businesses—General Motors, Ford, American Telephone and Telegraph, Exxon, Texaco, Gulf Oil, and IBM—now earn one-fourth of all U.S. corporate profits. To become—and stay—this successful, these businesses employ full-time representatives to fight for and protect their interests with government and consumers alike.

Labor is big, too. It has been ever since millions of workers were unionized in the days of President Franklin Roosevelt's New Deal. Unions like the International Brotherhood of Teamsters, the nation's largest, increase their ranks both by signing up new members and by annexing smaller unions. The pressuring power of unions is evidenced by such accomplishments as minimum-wage laws and 40-hour work weeks, and, more recently, by the massive government loans to Chrysler Corporation.

Big government now employs more than 25 percent of all workers in its agencies, departments, and programs. The federal budget alone exceeds $600 billion. Pressure from government is felt through such actions as taxes, environmental-protection laws, and antitrust legislation.

There is a wide variety of other types of pressure groups such as the media, professional organizations like the American Medical Association and the National Education Association, neighborhood organizations, and dissident stockholder groups. Large and small pressure groups like these work vigorously to influence business, labor, and government in directions favorable to their own interests.

THE FUTURE OF AMERICAN BUSINESS

No one has a clear crystal ball in which to see the future. But past trends and current research point out a number of probabilities about what we might expect in the remainder of this century. Following are some predictions for the areas of demographics, inflation, energy, the environment, management, research and development, and government.

Changing Demographics

Business people typically keep a close watch on *demographics*—the age, sex, income, education, and other key characteristics of the nation's consumers. The reason is that any significant change in demographics can dramatically alter consumer purchases. The rest of this century will see an increasingly larger middle-aged and elderly population as those who were born in the postwar "baby boom" in the late 1940s reach maturity. As you might expect, this demographic change will have a big effect on a number of different businesses, including the recording and motion picture industries, hospitals, apparel, and so forth. The expected slowdown in U.S. population until 2000 has caused Procter and Gamble to search for products besides those bought by consumers (see the accompanying boxed insert).

Procter and Gamble: Past . . .

Procter and Gamble (P & G) is one of the nation's largest firms. But it may not have been here today were it not for an accident. As long ago as 1878 the company had already perfected its pure white soap. But one day an employee took a long lunch break and his vat stirred too long. Extra air got into the soap. When he came back, he shipped out the batch anyway, hoping no one would notice the difference. But customers discovered the error in their bathtubs—and liked it. They wrote in for more of "that soap that floats." So Ivory Soap, "99 and 44/100ths percent pure," was discovered. And it is still floating. In fact, in the past 100 years, P & G has sold 30 billion bars of Ivory—the equivalent of 5½ times the weight of the Washington Monument.[5]

This success helped provide the money P & G needed to increase its research and development of new products. That this research has paid off is evidenced by such popular brand names as:

- Tide, Joy, and Comet—cleaning products.
- Crest, Scope, and Prell—personal-care products.
- Crisco oil, Duncan Hines cakes, Pringle's potato chips, and Folger's coffee—grocery products.

Inflation

Inflation, an increase in the nation's price level, has been a serious problem since 1968. It is usually measured by the **consumer price index (CPI),** an average of all prices paid by consumers for the goods they purchase. Inflation is difficult to control because many government actions designed to reduce inflation also create unemployment. But its effects can be partially offset by improved technology, which results in price decreases for some types of products—like TVs, computers, and calculators. For example, digital watches were unveiled in 1972 at $400 apiece. By 1978, some were priced at $9.95—about $3.00 less than the cheapest Timex mechanical watch.

Inflation harms consumers, and it also hurts businesses. Long-range planning is harder when future costs cannot be accurately predicted. It is also more

. . . and Future

Procter and Gamble is still looking for new products. In fact, in 1980 P & G visited or phoned 1.5 million people on about 1,000 research projects to find out what they liked or disliked in old products and what they wanted in new ones. And many of the items P & G is developing are far removed from the familiar household names that boosted past sales. Consider the following list:

- Artificial cocoa butter, to replace natural cocoa butter in chocolate bars and foods. Already developed, it is being improved.

- "Boundary" disposable surgical gowns. Introduced in 1976, they are now being distributed nationally.

- Sucrose polyester. A cholesterol-reducing drug that is still being developed. Within this decade it may also appear as a cooking oil.

- Didronel, a prescription drug. Now prescribed to stop abnormal bone growth, it may ultimately be used for arthritis.

Board chairman of P & G, Edward G. Harness, says surprisingly that all of these innovations have stemmed directly or indirectly from the company's soap-making technology. So P & G might consider drinking an artificial cocoa toast to Ivory Soap and to the workman who took the long lunch break.[6]

costly to borrow money: lenders demand high interest rates so that the purchasing power of their own savings doesn't deteriorate. Virtually no one, though, thinks that the United States in the 1980s and 1990s will see the annual inflation rates of 200–300 percent common in some countries.

Energy Shortages

In the future, businesses and consumers will be increasingly challenged to conserve oil, natural gas, and coal. Consumers' organizations, governments, and research institutions will need to cooperate to develop alternative energy sources. Energy shortages will affect what consumers buy, too. Fewer recreational vehicles and reduced driving will undoubtedly increase the demand for home entertainment products.

Environmental Problems

Managers in the next two decades will need to be increasingly sensitive to environmental issues—from smokestack pollution to chemical and nuclear wastes. Costs of such cleanup programs can be enormous: under pressure from the states of Wisconsin, Michigan, and Minnesota, the Reserve Mining Company in 1980 stopped dumping 67,000 tons of iron ore tailings a day into Lake Superior—at a cost to the company of $370,000,000. And through the year

You, Business, and the Year 2000

In 1970, no one had heard of a hand calculator, a computer-on-a-chip, or gasoline for $1.50 a gallon. Yet in the period of one decade, these things have become commonplace. What changes will another decade or two bring?

By 2000, you will probably be driving a car that will automatically avoid crashes and sense and program the best fuel mixture. You will listen to music on noise-free digital records. You will "talk" to your refrigerator to report items out of stock, so that it can make a shopping list and automatically order it from the supermarket. You may substitute potatoes for meat because the nutritional value of plants will have been altered.

Business changes will be equally dramatic. Once, two human researchers won a Nobel Prize for isolating insulin. Today, computers are being taught to isolate such hormones. Tomorrow, they may be able to synthesize them, with the help of gene splicing, in laboratory dishes. Researchers believe that new nitrogen-fixing bacteria will make chemical fertilizers and cancer treatments unnecessary.

2000, individuals, as well as institutions, can expect to be asked to make increasing sacrifices in both convenience and money in order to help assume the responsibility for protecting the environment.

Productivity and People-Management Problems

Productivity—real output per working hour—is not rising as quickly as it did in the mid-1970s. This does not necessarily mean that workers are becoming lazier. What it does mean is that in an uncertain economy, U.S. businesses are not investing enough in the machinery needed to help workers accomplish more. For example, our steel plants are so obsolete that Japan and Germany are taking over the international steel markets. Too, as our economy becomes more service-oriented, productivity tends to slow down. The reason is that services—such as family counseling—tend to be able to increase productivity only by reducing their quality.

Managing people and resources on all levels of organizations will continue to be a major managerial challenge. Future managers have to be more sensitive to people's needs and more flexible in resolving problems. Early retirement and part-time work programs are likely to become common in the near future.

Research and Development Needs

In a country thick with large organizations and bureaucratic red tape, the opportunities for innovation are increasingly threatened. Managers in the last part of this century will try to create a better climate for research and development that leads to new and better products and services.

Government Influence

In 1980, there were about 90 government agencies issuing 7,000 new regulations a year. Although there is political pressure to limit government's influence over the private sector, future managers will surely deal with an even bigger roll of government red tape. The long-term challenge to business, government, and consumers will be to work together in ways that best utilize the country's talents and resources to solve its social, economic, and environmental problems.

Chapter Review & Applications

Key Points to Remember

1. Business is all profit-producing activity that provides goods and services to customers. Profit is the difference between the revenues earned by a business and the costs it incurs.

2. Managerial efficiency requires realistic goals, identification of the market, efficient use of resources, and adaptation to the environment.

3. Entrepreneurs are people with ideas and with the energy and drive to carry them out. Professional managers have the ability to organize people, procedures, finances, and production. Functional specialists are professionals trained in specialized areas of business.

4. The Industrial Revolution used technology, mass production, and transportation to transform the country. Factories with machinery were used to mass-produce goods formerly made by hand.

5. After the Civil War, business and society were changed forever by electricity, big money, professional management, and mass markets.

6. The contemporary American economy is affluent, service-oriented, and strongly influenced by government. Big business, big labor, and big government are important pressure groups.

7. Gross national product (GNP) is the money value of all goods and services produced in a nation during a designated time period, usually a year.

8. Future business people face these key challenges: changing demographics, inflation, energy shortages, environmental problems, productivity- and people-management issues, research and development needs, and continued government influence on business.

Questions for Discussion

1. Why must a business serve its customers? Why must it make a profit?

2. Have you ever bought a product without much utility—a "lemon" car or a junky tape deck? Should ads for such products be controlled by the government? How would you feel about that question if you were an entrepreneur experimenting with a new product?

3. Mass-production concepts are often difficult to apply to the service sector. For example, have mass-production techniques been applied to your education so far? If so, in what ways? What characteristics of education make it difficult to use mass-production techniques effectively?

4. Critics of the Industrial Revolution and of the role of business in it focus their attacks on five areas: (a) the disadvantages of mass production; (b) the "exploitation" of workers, including long hours, child labor, and low pay; (c) the unequal distribution of wealth; (d) the mistreatment of minorities, especially blacks; and (e) the destruction of natural resources through such practices as strip mining. What is your assessment of each of these criticisms?

5. What is productivity? Can you think of a service industry that *could* benefit from increased productivity? How might it be achieved?

Short Case

The following data for the years 1977–1979 are taken from official government reports:

STATISTIC	1977	1978	1979
Money GNP (in billions of current dollars)	1,887	2,128	2,369
Consumer price index (1967 = 100)	181.5	195.3	217.7
U.S. population (in millions)	216.9	218.7	220.6

(a) Using the consumer price index when appropriate, calculate real GNP, per capita money GNP, and per capita real GNP for 1977–1979. What do these calculations tell you about what is happening to U.S. output and to money available for an individual to spend?

(b) Make the same calculations for each year between 1980 and the last calendar year. (*Hint:* You can find the recent data in *Statistical Abstract of the United States, Survey of Current Business,* and *Economic Report of the President.*)

A Critical
Business Decision

—made by David Dornbush and Chad Erickson
of Alternative Pioneering Systems

The Situation

More than luck was involved when David Dornbush
and Chad Erickson found *the* right product—home
food dehydrators—for the manufacturing business
they wanted to start.

They had been looking for something that would
enjoy steady growth, a long life cycle, and wide
demographic appeal. It also needed to be practical in
an energy-hungry, inflation-rocked country, and to
involve low technology, but be patentable. "The patentable part is important," Dornbush says, "because
we want some protection if we develop the market
and General Electric and Sunbeam try to jump in."
As for the practical part: "We weren't interested in
being the first of sixteen companies to make a new
kind of popcorn popper—or a gift hot dogger that
would be used only twice a year," he explains.

So when Dornbush saw a home food dehydrator
on TV (see page 6), he and college-friend Chad
Erickson formed Alternative Pioneering Systems,
Inc., and went into business.

But it was a long way from seeing a crude home
food dehydrator on TV to manufacturing and marketing a better one. As Erickson puts it, "We went
through our own Industrial Revolution." However,
their first model, developed only two weeks after
Dornbush saw the TV ad, successfully dried the food
he took with him on a camping trip.

"From there our expectations took off," Erickson
says. They glued a few models together in their
college's carpentry shop, took them around in the
back of their cars to a couple of trade shows, and
predicted sales of $186,000 in five months.

But the two entrepreneurs were too optimistic.
The product was overengineered and cost too much.
So they only sold 300 units the first year when they
expected to sell 1,000. This meant they had to redesign the product, which required more money.
They put their cars up for collateral to get a bank
loan, made countless presentations to potential investors, and persuaded one of their parents to mortgage a lake home.

The Decision

With their newly acquired funds, Dornbush and
Erickson began to redesign their dehydrator. An
industrial designer agreed to produce a more attractive model, and they found a manufacturer who had
the machinery to produce key parts in the new design to their specifications. They applied for patents
on unique features in the improved model, obtained
Underwriters Laboratory approval on it, and gave it
the "Harvest Maid" brand name.

Dornbush and Erickson analyze the advantages
of their home food dehydrator this way: It has the
ability to dry a variety of fruits, vegetables, and
meats that can be "rehydrated" by adding water. It
preserves good nutrition in dried food that has a
long shelf life and requires little storage space. It
also saves energy compared with the alternatives of
freezing or canning. Still, most Americans know almost nothing about food dehydration—a major
stumbling block that they feel must be overcome.
They are now asking such questions as, Who are our
prospective buyers? and How do we get the dehydrators into places where they can be seen and
bought? The future of Alternative Pioneering Systems, Inc., depends on the answers they get.[7]

Questions

1. What groups of consumers might be prospective
   purchasers of the home food dehydrator?
2. What is the best way of reaching them with
   enough information about food drying and dehydrators to get them to consider buying one?
3. What kind of retail outlets should be sought to
   carry the dehydrators, and how can retail managers be made interested in the idea?

Private Enterprise and Its Social Responsibility

In this chapter you will learn . . .

- *how America's mixed private enterprise system works.*
- *how ethical considerations enter into business decisions.*
- *about the social responsibility of business.*
- *how business is taking actions to benefit consumers, employees, and the physical environment.*

Paul Austin has a radical dream. Use plastic bubbles and a bottle of pop to stop world hunger.

He is no idle dreamer. As chief executive officer of Coca-Cola, Austin has achieved some dramatic breakthroughs. Four days after the United States resumed diplomatic relations with China, Austin announced that China had granted Coke the exclusive marketing rights for cola throughout the country.

Working with the Universities of Arizona and Sonora (in Mexico), Coke uses inflatable plastic domes to grow shrimp on a fifty-acre fish farm in the Mexican desert. These same bubbles are used to grow plump tomatoes, cucumbers, and beans in the deserts of Abu Dhabi—for 10 cents a pound.[1]

But what excites Austin most is even simpler: a soft drink with one-third of an adult's daily vitamin and mineral requirements and 10 percent of the adult's protein needs. It's called "Samson" and it's already being sold in Mexico and Brazil. Samson is made from the protein-rich whey left over from cheese production and can be given virtually any taste and color—from orange to split pea. Before Samson was developed, the whey was dumped into streams, where it caused algae growth. So Samson's not only nutritious, but it also fights pollution. Furthermore, tests show Samson increases learning among poorly nourished school children.

When will Samson arrive for all of us? About 1985. It will cost about a penny more a bottle than Coke or Tab. Austin wants to go slowly because Samson costs more to make than Coke. And consumers may be suspicious about a good-for-you drink. Also, to stay in business, the company must make a profit on Samson. So Coca-Cola Company is a good example of a socially responsible firm working within the private enterprise system to make profits. For more about the Coca-Cola Company and its expansion into other beverage markets, see the color section at the end of the text.

HOW PRIVATE ENTERPRISE WORKS

Private, or **free, enterprise** is the economic system used in this country. It means that most of the country's goods and services are provided by privately owned firms that compete with a minimum of government controls. The 220 million consumers and 13 million businesses in this country make many of the economic decisions. Will you buy a scratch-and-sniff T-shirt this year? Or join a sun-lamp club next year? You are free to decide.

A **mixed economy** is a system in which many of society's goods and services are provided by private enterprise, but others are provided by government. We have evolved into this system, and so has Great Britain, but to a much greater degree. In Britain, the government provides such important things as transportation, steel, coal, and health insurance, with private industry providing nearly everything else. In the United States, about four-fifths of the goods and services are produced by private industry, about one-fifth by government. The following section describes how our mixed private enterprise system works.

Key Aspects of Private Enterprise

The private enterprise system in the United States has six key characteristics, described below.

Private Ownership of Property

Most businesses, land, minerals, buildings, machinery, and personal goods are owned by people, not by governments. Americans consider this ownership their right. We also think of it as an incentive to work hard to acquire and care for our own property. This sort of incentive contributes to the economic growth of the country.

Freedom of Choice and Limited Government

Freedom of choice allows businesses to select the products they produce, hire and fire employees, compete for customers and supplies, and make and dispose of profits. Freedom of choice also allows consumers to buy whatever products and services they are willing and able to buy from whichever firms they choose.

Freedom of choice implies a limited amount of government intervention in the area of private enterprise. In a free enterprise system, government sets the "economic rules of the game" by establishing basic laws and regulations that ensure society's welfare. But within that context, individuals and organizations are left largely free to pursue their own interests and inclinations.

Consumer Sovereignty

We consumers rule. And the more carefully we make our decisions, the more clearly the American economy will reflect our needs. The more dollar "votes" you spend in the marketplace, the greater your influence. If you have $15—or 15 votes—available to spend on entertainment, you can "vote" for a rock concert, several movies, a couple of tape cassettes, or any number of other alternatives. Buying the tapes will stimulate the tape manufacturer to produce more tapes, but it will discourage the rock promoter slightly. Thus, **consumer sovereignty** means that you can affect what is produced.

Profits

Profits make businesses responsive to consumer wants. If a lot of people want to buy a scratch-and-sniff T-shirt, businesses will make them—and quickly—until the demand is met.

Profits are also a good indicator of where to expand and how to compete better. If your jeans boutique is doing very well with designer jeans, you'll probably stock more. As a shopowner you can also compare the overall profits of the boutique with past results or with profits of other businesses to gauge how well your shop is doing. Profits are the clearest standard of performance available to a business.

But consumers often misinterpret business profits. They also don't always understand how profits direct a business' efforts. And consumers usually substantially overstate how high business profits actually are.

---

*H*ow much of the average sales dollar actually ends up as profit in a company's coffer? How much <u>should</u> end up there?

Pollsters like Louis Harris ask Americans these questions periodically, and the answers they receive are always far too high. On average, people think that profits are 28 percent of the typical sales dollar and that they should be "only" 10 percent.

The truth is that the average profit is actually 4 percent.

Competition

Most business leaders believe their industries are highly competitive. But the term "competitive" has many meanings. **Pure,** or **perfect, competition** exists in an industry when (1) there are many firms of about equal size, (2) all firms produce the same product, (3) each firm can enter or leave the industry when it wants, and (4) all firms and customers are well-informed about prices and availability of products. No American industry completely satisfies all these conditions, although some—like wheat and cotton producers—come close. Most industries in the United States operate under conditions of **imperfect competition.** This means they satisfy some but not all the conditions of pure competition.

Oligopoly is another form of competition. Here, there are only a few firms in an industry, so their actions affect each other closely. The auto industry—which includes General Motors, Ford, Chrysler, American Motors, and foreign firms—is a good example. Another is the tobacco industry. Under oligopoly, firms compete with one another by lowering prices, advertising heavily, or changing their product design.

Monopoly occurs when there is only one firm in the industry and there are no close substitutes for its product or service. Local utilities that supply water, gas, electricity, and telephone service are examples. A typical monopolist like the local electric utility can set prices without regard to competition because there is none. Its prices are limited only by customers' willingness to pay its prices and by its fear of government intervention—for example, a utility commission may refuse to approve a proposed price increase. Most experts believe that the more competition there is, the better off consumers and society will be through both higher quality products and lower prices.

Antimonopoly: Testing the "Monopoly" Monopoly

If someone told you there was a board game called "Antimonopoly," would you confuse it with "Monopoly," the popular game under trademark to General Mills' Parker Brothers division? It has taken several courts and dozens of lawyers to answer this question. And they haven't finished yet.[2]

When they do, General Mills may lose its "Monopoly" monopoly, its exclusive trademark to the word. And an independent game inventor, Ralph Anspach, may be able to finally pass Go and collect money on sales of his "Antimonopoly" game. (Before the court halted his sales, he had sold about a half million sets.)

Anspach, an economics professor at San Francisco State University, thought of designing his game when his youngest son, playing "Monopoly," asked his dad, "What's wrong with a monopoly?" Anspach decided to show him the benefits of competition. He ended up showing everyone how difficult and expensive it is to take on a company like General Mills.

But both little inventors and giant companies will end up ahead if the courts can figure out how carefully trademarks should be protected. After all, a trademark is awarded to whoever originates the product or name—and if someone tried to confuse customers by copying your trademark too closely, you'd be mad, too, even if you were a big corporation. (Trademarks will be discussed in more detail in Chapter 8.)

Productivity

Productivity is essential to the economy, whether it means designing faster microcomputers or better-tasting toothpaste. Increased productivity helps off-set inflation and keep prices down. **Productivity** is defined as real output (the value of the product independent of price changes) per working hour, and it is usually written as a percentage. So, if productivity increases 5 percent between 1982 and 1983, it means that the average employee has raised output by 5 percent each hour.

Productivity increases as a result of harder work, more efficient machinery, or both. Largely because of more sophisticated technology, U.S. productivity has, until recently, grown at a rate of about 3 percent a year since 1945. (This means that the average worker today produces about 80 percent more than in 1945.) But this is considerably less than the 9 percent annual increase in the major oil-exporting countries in recent years.

American productivity has failed to increase at an acceptable rate recently, and this is a source of concern for business and government leaders. During some years in the late 1970s, productivity actually declined. Inadequate productivity increases in the United States have been attributed to aging plants and equipment in some industries, occasionally to poor management, and to changes in life styles, which include a desire for more leisure time. To help this situation, many large U.S. businesses have launched "productivity improvement programs" designed to increase the output of both workers and managers.

How the Private Enterprise System Allocates Resources

To work successfully, the private enterprise system must allocate the nation's resources (or factors of production) effectively. Resources include land, labor, capital, and technology, all of which are *limited* at any given time. For example, food production in the United States is limited by the amount of land under cultivation, the number and work capacity of individual farmers, the amount of agricultural machinery available, and the state of knowledge about good farming methods.

On the other hand, society's demands for more goods and services are *unlimited*. So, even if every customer's need for necessities were met, there would still be a demand for more luxury goods. The tension between limited resources and unlimited human desires creates a need to allocate the available resources. Specifically, each society must answer four basic questions to determine how it will allocate its resources:

1. What products and services will be produced?
2. How will they be produced?
3. Who will receive them?
4. How much of society's resources will be saved each year for the future?

Private enterprise is efficient at allocating resources and raising living standards when (1) consumers rule and make wise buying decisions, (2) profits are high enough to encourage businesses to produce the goods and services consumers want, (3) competition rewards efficiency and punishes inefficiency, and (4) worker productivity is high. When all people and groups in our society—not just business—make informed decisions, private enterprise provides for our needs and sustains the quality of our lives.

BUSINESS ETHICS AND SOCIAL RESPONSIBILITY

Control Data Corporation's enormous computers churn out masses of information on everything from weather forecasts to paychecks. But under chief executive officer William Norris, Control Data emphasizes **social responsibility,** the idea that business should help society meet its social needs. Control Data does this in diverse ways. For example, it hires people who only want to work part time, like high-school students and mothers with school-age children, and accommodates them with split-shift schedules. And it trains disabled people who can't leave home to be computer programmers.

William Norris sums up Control Data's approach this way: "Social responsibility is not only the right thing to do but is good business."

"I'd like to invest in a nice, clean, wholesome company that makes obscene profits."

Business Ethics

"Ford Sued for Deliberately Building Unsafe Cars," "Oil Industry Attacked for Excessive Profits," "Women Sue AT&T for Job Bias." These headlines accompany stories about many of today's business practices. Increasing public awareness of these issues means today's business managers must answer hard questions from the public, the media, and influential groups representing consumers, employees, and environmentalists.

A business firm's traditional goal—to increase profits while obeying government laws and regulations—has partly given way to *external management.* This means cooperating with such outside groups as community leaders, government officials, and consumer and environmental organizations. As Figure 2–1 shows, today's manager must make decisions that weigh personal ethics and social responsibility, consumer and employee needs, and environmental factors.

Business ethics provide guidelines to what is right, good, or moral in commercial relationships. Should an older employee who is no longer fully productive be fired? Should a purchasing agent accept a Christmas present from a supplier? Should a magazine accept ads for products that may be harmful to users, such as cigarettes? In practice, answers to these and other ethical questions are usually based on moral or religious standards, on the situation, or on the perceived self-interest of the individual or firm.

Industrial Espionage: The Other Side of Business Ethics

"Business treason" is not a familiar term to TV audiences accustomed to Russian double agents and British spies "who come in from the cold." But Celanese Corporation found out how devastating it can be when a mild-mannered, middle-aged, middle-manager sold several million dollars' worth of trade secrets about his firm's plastic film products to Mitsubishi Plastics, a Japanese multinational.

"He sold it cheap, less than $100,000 over several years," said one of the prosecutors, quoted in *The Wall Street Journal.*[3] He added that industrial espionage—business spying—is very common but seldom reaches public courtrooms because embarrassed companies settle with the spy in private to avoid publicity. The Japanese, on the other hand, apparently consider it a patriotic duty to gather trade secrets any way they can; they even run one of the world's two major secret schools for industrial spies. (The Swiss allegedly run the other.)

Harold Farar, the guilty manager, apparently copied engineering drawings, manufacturing reports, test results, and research and development findings on 58 rolls of microfilm for his Japanese contacts. He also took them on secret after-hours tours of Celanese plants. They learned the Celanese process down to the finest detail.

But he's not taking any tours now. Farar was convicted of criminal conspiracy and racketeering, and he is now in federal prison.

FIGURE 2-1
A Manager's Dilemma: External Management.

Ethical Codes

Most businesses have developed their own **ethical codes**—statements describing the ethical considerations that should guide employees in their business dealings. Because it is difficult for one competitor to enforce ethical codes if other firms in an industry refuse to follow similar ethical guidelines, many businesses cooperate with one another to establish *industry-wide ethical codes* to which all participant businesses are expected to adhere. Various professions—notably lawyers, accountants, and doctors—have developed *professional codes of ethics*. Practitioners in these professions are expected to meet the highest standards set up by their professional organizations. Failure to do so may, in extreme cases, result in explusion from the profession.

Ethics and Management

The development of "ethical sensitivity" is a highly individual matter. Because today's ethical standards change so rapidly and because public opinion and the communication media focus so heavily on situations that are perceived as displaying unethical behavior, contemporary managers need to approach ethical issues with caution and sensitivity.

And people can have honest differences of opinion about business ethics. The questions that appear in the left-hand column of Figure 2–2 were asked of over 300 salespeople and later of 200 college students. Try it yourself. Then see the right-hand side of the figure for some surprises. The responses point out three important areas for consideration: (1) the differences (and similarities) that exist among people's ethical perceptions of a particular practice or situation; (2) the need for management guidelines where possible; and (3) the necessity for people to use their own good judgment when confronted with ethical decisions in "gray" areas.

Social Responsibility

What responsibility does a business have to society beyond obeying laws and following some type of ethical standards? Two opposite viewpoints—restrictive and expansive—exist. The **restrictive view** argues that business should provide jobs and earn profits for its owners and stockholders. In contrast, the **expansive view** extends businesses' business to include social responsibility. Those with this view argue that business should respond to efforts by government, consumers, environmentalists, minorities, neighborhood groups, and

Read each practice below and then answer the question. To compare your answers with those given by industrial salespeople and other students, see the right-hand side of the figure.

Question Do you believe this practice presents an ethical question for an industrial salesperson?*

PRACTICE	Definitely Yes	Probably Yes	Maybe Yes, Maybe No	Probably No	Definitely No	Percent answering "Definitely Yes" or "Probably Yes" to question: Do you believe this practice presents an ethical question for an industrial salesperson?
1. Exaggerating the seriousness of a buyer's problem to get a bigger order or other concessions.	☐	☐	☐	☐	☐	Salespeople 49 / Students 70
2. Giving preference to customers who are also good suppliers.	☐	☐	☐	☐	☐	Salespeople 36 / Students 31
3. Allowing personal feelings for a buyer to affect price or other terms of sale.	☐	☐	☐	☐	☐	Salespeople 52 / Students 66
4. Giving gifts, such as free sales-promotion prizes, to a buyer.	☐	☐	☐	☐	☐	Salespeople 39 / Students 24
5. Giving free luncheons, dinners, trips, or other entertainment to a buyer.	☐	☐	☐	☐	☐	Salespeople 34 / Students 33
6. Getting information about competitors by asking buyers to tell what they know.	☐	☐	☐	☐	☐	Salespeople 27 / Students 34

(Percent scale: 0%, 20%, 40%, 60%, 80%)

*An ethical question is one that arises when an individual feels pressure to take actions that are inconsistent with what he or she feels to be right.

Source: Alan J. Dubinsky and William Rudelius, "Ethical Beliefs: How Students Compare with Industrial Salespeople," *Proceedings of the 1980 AMA Marketing Educators' Conference* (Chicago: American Marketing Association, 1980).

FIGURE 2–2
Where Do You Stand on Ethical Judgments?

others to remedy social problems. And business should actively promote social welfare.

Who Manages Social Responsibility?

Whatever degree of social responsibility a business assumes, someone must manage it. As government regulations and voluntary corporate actions increase, businesses increasingly assign social responsibilities to their public affairs, personnel, or human resources departments. *Public affairs departments* in large businesses handle public relations, lobbying, and charitable contributions. Virtually unknown twenty years ago, these departments now are vital. *Personnel* or *human resources departments,* also growing in importance, usually ensure compliance with equal employment opportunity regulations and employee safety requirements.

Some Results of Social Responsibility

As more social responsibility is demanded of business—and more is volunteered, too—an impressive list of results has started to accumulate. These include telephone "hot lines" by appliance manufacturers to handle consumer complaints, "loaned executives" provided by businesses for community-action programs, and collective efforts of business firms to find jobs for the disadvantaged.

BUSINESS ACTIONS ON SOCIAL ISSUES

For a business, social responsiveness means recognizing and reacting to events in the external environment that may have a significant effect on the firm. A socially responsive business in the 1980s must be constantly aware of economic, technological, social, and political trends. It must also understand the rising influence of consumers, employees, and scarce resources—described below.

Business and Consumers

American business exists to serve the consumer. The production of goods and services is the means to an end: consumer consumption. American consumers spent more than $1.5 trillion in 1980 alone. And with that kind of money at stake, business listens!

Groups of consumers, led by activists like Ralph Nader, have worked to produce **consumer protection laws**—regulations affecting business behavior that promote consumers' interests. Such laws reflect the concept of **consumerism,** the view that government and business have a joint responsibility to inform and protect consumers. But while consumerism provides many benefits to us, it also has important costs.

The Case for Consumerism

The arguments in favor of consumerism are based on citizens' rights and on the complexity of products. Back in 1962, President John F. Kennedy argued for four inherent rights of consumers: the right to safety, the right to be informed, the right to choose, and the right to be heard. Consumerists say that government should guarantee these rights. And since there are now so many products on the market, and many of them are so complex, consumers need special help in evaluating them.

The old idea of *caveat emptor* or "let the buyer beware" is completely outmoded, consumerists say. Indeed, the Federal Trade Commission can now investigate the truth of ads and require firms to run *corrective advertising* if their claims prove false or misleading. Profile bread, for example, was ordered to correct its advertising to inform consumers that its claim for fewer calories per slice was true only because the bread was sliced thinner. Other regulations try to help consumers at the time they buy a product. *Open dating* requires telling the consumer the last day a food product should be purchased. *Unit prices* require figuring prices on a per-ounce or per-pound basis, to help consumers compare values. And *nutritional labeling* compares the nutritional value of the product with minimum daily adult needs (see Figure 2–3).

The Case Against Consumerism

Arguments against government regulations for consumers are three: (1) regulations are expensive; (2) they are not always useful; and (3) they restrict the freedom of consumers and businesses.

Food companies incur a big expense in complying with regulations to analyze all their products' ingredients by percentage. Each product must be retested and all packaging redesigned. And guess who the cost is passed on to!

Even so, such regulations are not always as useful as they are meant to be. In many cases nutritional labels can be understood only by well-educated people. And how many of us know the difference between grades of grapes, such as "fancy" and "U.S. No. 1"?

PURCHASE STAGE	CONSUMER PROBLEM	ACTION TAKEN TO PROTECT CONSUMER
Before the sale	Misleading advertising	The Federal Trade Commission (FTC) can ask advertisers to prove their claims; if claims are untrue, the FTC may require corrective advertising. The advertising industry now regulates itself through advertising guidelines and by reviewing questionable ads.
During the sale	Inadequate product information on package or product.	The 1965 Fair Packaging and Labeling Act ("truth in packaging") regulates the packaging and labeling of consumer goods. Food stores must provide unit pricing, open dating, and nutritional labeling on grocery products.
	Incomplete information on actual interest paid on installment loans and charge accounts.	The 1968 Consumer Credit Protecting Act ("truth in lending") requires the full disclosure of annual simple interest rates and other finance charges on consumer loans.
	High-pressure, door-to-door selling.	Many states require a cooling-off period of 3–5 days, during which consumers can change their purchase decisions.
	Advertised sales items that are "unavailable" in retail stores.	Advertised items must be stocked in reasonable quantities on sales days indicated, and consumers must receive a "rain check" to purchase the items later if the store runs out.
	Credit denial because of incorrect credit reports.	The 1970 Fair Credit Reporting Act gives consumers access to their own credit reports.
After the sale	Better quality and safer products.	Federal legislation on product quality and safety includes the National Traffic and Motor Vehicle Safety Act (1966), which requires manufacturers to recall defective cars, the Child Safety Act (1966), the National Commission of Product Safety Act (1967), and the Child Protection and Toy Safety Act (1969).
	Lack of effective business reaction to consumer complaints.	Manufacturers have installed toll-free "hot lines" to handle consumer complaints. Some trade associations review customer complaints. Consumers may take action on individual problems in small claims courts, where a lawyer is not required.

FIGURE 2-3
How Consumerism Has Helped.

Other regulations may seem to restrict our freedom both as consumers and as business people. Should ads directed at children, or for cigarettes or nitrate-preserved hot dogs, be completely forbidden? Or can we make our own decisions? Too many regulations may eventually hamper business enough to damage our private enterprise system.

Consumers: Who Is Responsible?

Consumers, working through government, have indeed helped business become more socially responsible, as can be seen from the information given in Figure 2–3. Regulations now cover problems before, during, and after the sale of a product. If they are reasonable—not ridiculous—they can be useful.

Responding to consumerism, many medium and large businesses have now established *consumer affairs departments*. These direct the firm's efforts to assist consumers and handle complaints. But ultimately consumers must decide for themselves what they want and need.

Business and Employees

Business—often with prodding from government—is working to improve employee satisfaction, employee safety, and equal opportunity for its employees.

Employee Satisfaction

Employees expect more from their jobs now than they used to. During the Great Depression, people were grateful to have a job at all. Today's affluent employees often demand work that provides some self-fulfillment, whether it is on the assembly line at Ford, in middle management at a multinational corporation, or in managing a fast-food franchise.

Business pays attention to these needs—and to the problems that can occur when they are not met. Poor productivity, high absenteeism, drug and alcohol problems, and sloppy workmanship are expensive by-products of worker dissatisfaction. So all sizes of businesses are making efforts to improve employee performance and satisfaction. Involving employees in key decisions, making jobs more interesting, and providing employee counseling are several of the ways in which they are doing it.

Employee Safety

Many jobs are physically dangerous. Equipment that is mishandled or in disrepair can kill or seriously injure an employee. And there are sometimes less obvious on-the-job dangers—excess asbestos can cause cancer, and years spent in a coal mine can cause "black lung" disease. In a typical year, work-related injuries kill more than 12,000 Americans and injure several hundred thousand more.

In 1970 Congress passed the Occupational Safety and Health Act to help protect employees. The act created the Occupational Safety and Health Administration (OSHA), which, in cooperation with state government agencies, sets safety standards, inspects plants, and requires that employers report all work-related injuries and deaths.

Equal Employment Opportunity

Since the 1960s, women and ethnic minorities—especially blacks, Chicanos, and American Indians—have sought equal employment opportunities. These include the desire for (1) equal pay for equal work; (2) jobs for women and minorities in high-pay, high-prestige occupations—in approximate proportion to their numbers in the general population; (3) a fair chance for women and minorities to be promoted to better jobs based on merit; and (4) recognition of the special problems women and minorities face.

Since World War II, the number of working women has grown eight times faster than the number of working men. Women now constitute 48 percent of the labor force. But they are concentrated in clerical and service jobs, where they earn about 20 percent less than men do for the same work—even when education and work experience are equal. Women also suffer from untrue stereotypes about absenteeism and emotional instability. And they sometimes have to do much better work than their male colleagues to be promoted.

Business can help create equal employment opportunity by providing women with "role models"—examples of productive and successful women—and by promoting them when they deserve it. Business can also offer flexible work schedules, day-care facilities, and leaves of absence for child-care when necessary.

Blacks, Chicanos, American Indians, and other ethnic minorities experience high unemployment rates, especially among teen-agers, and earn an average of about 70 percent of the incomes earned by whites. Jobs held by ethnic minorities are heavily concentrated in the operative, service, and labor categories. Past discrimination against minorities is also harmful, since they often lack business experience or live in areas far removed from business offices and plants.

Business can help minorities to achieve equal employment opportunities

Your Next Job
Future Trends by Industry

No once can forecast the future precisely. Yet, in making important career choices, it is helpful to know what past employment trends have been by industry (discussed here) and occupation (discussed in Chapter 3) and what they may be in the future.

Kinds of Industries

Industries produce either goods or services. The four main goods-producing industries are manufacturing, agriculture, construction, and mining. The five main classes of service-producing industries are wholesales and retail trade; government (local, state, and federal, including education); repair and maintenance services; transportation and public utilities; and finance, insurance, and real estate. In 1950, goods-producing and service-producing industries employed about 27 million Americans apiece. By 1978, jobs in service-producing industries more than doubled (to 60.5 million), but employment

Employment by Industry in 1978 and Projected Employment Change from 1978 to 1990.

	1978–1990 employment changes	
Goods-producing industries:	(in millions)	(percent)
Manufacturing	3.3	16
Agriculture	-0.4	-12
Contract construction	0.7	17
Mining	0.2	20
Service-producing industries:		
Retail and Wholesale Trade	5.4	28
Government	2.0	13
Services	8.4	53
Transportation, public utilities	0.5	10
Finance, insurance, real estate	1.6	34

0   5   10   15   20

1978 employment (in millions)

Source: U.S. Bureau of Labor Statistics.

in goods-producing industries remained almost unchanged. The figure shows the 1978 employment in nine different industries.

Goods–Producing Industries

In recent years, the number of available jobs in goods-producing industries has not grown perceptibly, mainly because automation and improved worker skills have led to large increases in output without corrresponding increases in employment. The total number of jobs in all goods-producing industries is expected to increase by about 3.8 million to 32.4 million between 1978 and 1990. Projected employment changes from 1978 to 1990 for each of the four types of goods-producing industries appear in the right-hand portion of the figure. The mining forecast illustrates the difficulty of estimating employment trends in some industries. Prior to the early 1970s, mining employment was declining. But with the continuing energy crisis, mining is expected to have continued growth.

Service–Producing Industries

The greatest employment growth is expected in the service-producing industries: about 17.9 million new jobs should be available between 1978 and 1990. But, as shown in the right-hand portion of the figure, each of the five types of service-producing industries will grow at a substantially different rate. Employment in service and miscellaneous industries is expected to increase dramatically (by about 8.4 million jobs); this industrial class includes a variety of services, such as restaurants, maintenance, repair, advertising, and health care. Government employment is expected to increase by more than 2.0 million during this period, virtually entirely at the state and local levels. From 1978 to 1990, jobs in wholesale and retail trade are expected to increase by more than 5.4 million. Employment in finance, transportation, and related areas is also expected to increase, but not as much in terms of total number of jobs as the other service-producing industries.

by actively seeking them as employees, by redesigning job requirements so as to rely more on skills and less on traditional backgrounds, by financially supporting minorities who want more education, and by placing minority employees in mainstream jobs where rapid promotion based on ability is customary. Many businesses are also helping minorities by buying some of their supplies from minority-owned small businesses.

The Civil Rights Act of 1964 created the Equal Employment Opportunity Commission (EEOC). This is a federal agency with power to prohibit discrimination based on an employee's sex, race, color, religion, or national origin. The EEOC and other federal enforcement agencies also can order businesses that deal with the federal government to actively seek women and minority employees and to establish percentage hiring targets in each job category based on the percentages of women and minorities working in the local community. Female employees at American Telephone and Telegraph were awarded millions of dollars in damages as a result of a lawsuit brought against AT&T for its failure to comply with equal employment opportunity legislation. So business is paying attention to EEOC regulations.

Helping Employees: Who Is Responsible?

Human resource departments or personnel departments are normally given formal responsibility for dealing with company-wide employee issues. But the day-to-day decisions that make up the quality of employees' working lives are made by managers at all levels in the business. Their sensitivity is a key to the firm's success. After all, a firm's greatest resource is its employees.

Business and the Environment

"Gas prices up another 7 cents a gallon." "Reserve Mining Company to keep tailings out of Lake Superior." Headlines like these slug us daily. The 1980s will see increased business efforts to address resource scarcities and environmental concerns.

Energy and Other Scarce Resources

Resources as thick as heavy crude oil and as light as water are running out. Ever since the Organization of Petroleum Exporting Countries (OPEC) quadrupled oil prices in 1973, oil prices have been oozing steadily upward. Those countries have the oil, we need it, and they know it. Americans, accustomed to

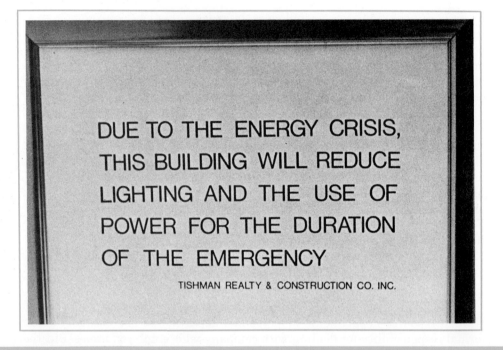

DUE TO THE ENERGY CRISIS, THIS BUILDING WILL REDUCE LIGHTING AND THE USE OF POWER FOR THE DURATION OF THE EMERGENCY

TISHMAN REALTY & CONSTRUCTION CO. INC.

Environmentalism: Successes . . .

- CUYAHOGA RIVER CLEANUP   A flaming river shocked Cleveland less than fifteen years ago. The Cuyahoga was so polluted with petrochemicals that it actually burst into flames. Everybody helped, and now fish swim safely in the river.

- GUNK   Every year, Americans throw away enough oil to fill fifteen super-tankers, *Time* magazine says. Now this "junk oil," most of it from oil changes for cars, trucks, and machinery, can be used. At least six U.S. companies are selling "junk oil heaters" to gas stations and factories that used to throw the oil away.

- NEW POLLUTION POLICIES   The old regulations required Armco in Middletown, Ohio, to clean up its air pollution from each smokestack individually. The cost: $15 million. The new method, called the "bubble plan," measures the total pollution from all the company's smokestacks. Under this plan, Armco will clean up six times as much pollution for a cost of $4 million.

. . . *and Failures*

- L.A. SMOG   The catalytic converter is one of the culprits in Los Angeles, where there has been no progress against air pollution for about six years. People tamper with the pollution-control devices in their cars, use leaded gasoline (which wrecks the engines), and don't maintain their cars properly. Weather, continued population growth, industrial pollution, and just plain sunshine are also partly responsible for this lack of progress.

- NUCLEAR AND TOXIC WASTES   No one yet knows where to put the wastes from nuclear power plants, and yet these wastes will be radioactive for thousands of years. Abandoned salt mines and ocean floors are imperfect solutions.

- ACID RAIN   Fish, forest land, and lakes are slowly turning to vinegar under acid rain clouds all over eastern North America. The main sources of the pollution are cars and coal-fired power plants. They add sulfur and nitrogen oxides to the air, which come down during rainfalls as sulfuric and nitric acids.

having 15 times more material possessions than all the citizens of under-developed countries put together, are having to adjust.

Our money supply and even our culture have been bent by the need for petroleum products. Why are so many businesses migrating to Sun Belt states? Partly because of lower energy costs in the South's warmer weather. The "energy-poor" population in our country is increasing too, putting pressure on our welfare system. And companies like Chrysler have been thrown into crisis partly because they underestimated the severity of our energy problems.

Oil is not the only scarce resource. Scarce and increasingly expensive are resources like platinum for microcomputers, zinc for car batteries, silver for camera film, and water—especially in the western United States. Copper is also scarce. If a "copper OPEC" formed among the Third World countries, the resulting price increases would further hurt American businesses and even dry up our supply of copper pennies.

The lowly copper penny may become extinct, just as the silver dime did in the 1960s.

The reasons: the price and scarcity of copper. In early 1980, the price of copper reached $1.30 a pound. When the price reaches $1.50 a pound—perhaps as you are reading this—there will be more than one cent worth of copper in a U.S. penny.

When that happens, watch copper pennies disappear from circulation.

Technology, which uses resources, contributes to resource scarcity but also to economic growth. Improved technology becomes more important as energy, resources, and labor become more costly. So business is investing more in *research and development departments,* where scientists and engineers seek ways to conserve energy and other resources by improving old products, designing new ones, and analyzing production techniques. General Electric, for instance, is now selling long-life consumer light bulbs. Although they cost more than standard light bulbs, they will burn four times as long on one-third the electricity.

Even without a formal federal energy policy, the Federal Department of Energy has designed useful programs to assist both businesses and consumers. These include giving subsidies and tax breaks to energy conservers, sponsoring research on nonpetroleum sources of energy, and providing incentives for domestic oil exploration.

Environmentalism

Will we choke from our car exhaust? Gag on our water? Sizzle under acid rain? Or will we learn to sell pollution-free electric cars, smokestack scrubbers, and chemical filters to purify water?

Since 1970 the Environmental Protection Agency (EPA), an arm of the federal government, has tried to protect the physical environment from various forms of pollution. The EPA has established standards for air, water, solid waste, pesticides, radiation, and noise emissions. It has the power to penalize violators by closing down their plants or imposing large fines. The EPA also frequently requires businesses to complete *environmental impact statements,* scientific studies analyzing the probable consequences to the local environment of a proposed plant or project.

Business generally supports the objectives of **environmentalism,** the view that the natural operation of ecological systems should often take precedence over economic and business goals. But many business leaders—who breathe the same air and drink the same water as the rest of us—question the judgment of environmentalists. They point out that too much environmental legislation raises business costs (which are passed on to consumers), delays or prevents new plants from opening, and reduces profits. Unrestrained pollution of the environment is no longer permissible. But neither is complete environmental cleanup. It costs too much in resources and lost jobs. Careful judgments about the benefits and costs of pollution control must be made by managers and government administrators.

Resources and Environment:
Who Is Responsible?

Economic, technological, political, and social pressures—as well as the need for modern business to consider the views of consumers, employees, and environmentalists—have caused business people to reconsider their role in society. In the spirit of social responsibility and private enterprise, they are trying to focus on solutions. Why not make profits out of energy shortages and environmental protection? Energy-conservation devices and antipollution equipment are already a multimillion dollar business throughout the world. If consumers want it, they will get it. That's how private enterprise works.

ALTERNATIVES TO PRIVATE ENTERPRISE

Many nations have economies different from the mixed private enterprise system of this country. And American businesses that sell or produce abroad must abide by their rules. So today's managers need to understand the two major alternatives to private enterprise—socialism and communism. (See Figure 2–4.)

FIGURE 2-4
Major Economic Systems.

ECONOMIC CHARACTERISTICS	PRIVATE ENTERPRISE SYSTEM	SOCIALISM	COMMUNISM
Goals	Individual consumers and businesses decide goals.	State modifies business goals.	Individual goals are subordinated to state goals.
Basic features	Private ownership of business; freedom of choice.	State owns basic industries; freedom of choice.	State owns and controls industry and agriculture.
Status of management	Independent; freedom to choose jobs.	State controls publicly owned enterprises.	State selects management.
Status of labor	Independent; few restrictions by state.	Restricted right to strike in public enterprises.	State controls unions and restricts occupational choice.
Status of consumers	Independent; freedom to purchase limited by consumer incomes.	Most accept prices established in public enterprises.	State sets prices of goods and income levels.
Economic role of government	To foster private enterprise.	To direct basic industries according to government plans.	To own and operate industries and agriculture.

Socialism

Socialism is a broad term that applies to two quite different economic approaches. Under *traditional socialism,* still popular in western Europe, the state owns the basic means of production: major raw materials (such as coal, iron, and oil), utilities, transportation, finance, communication, and other important industries. Recently, socialist nations in western Europe have tried to organize many of these industries as independent, publicly owned corporations.

Under *welfare-state-socialism,* government involvement is primarily in the areas of health, education, and welfare. In Sweden, for example, more than 90 percent of business, including most basic industry, is privately owned. However, Swedes enjoy a long list of such government-paid benefits as free medical care, inflation-protected pensions, and free university education. But for these benefits they pay the highest taxes in the world.

Communism

Communism as an economic system means that the government owns nearly all the nation's businesses and agriculture and plans the economy. *Central planning,* as practiced in the Soviet Union, meets the following specifications:

1. The Communist party sets basic economic goals. In the past, the party has stressed military power and manufacture of heavy materials like steel.
2. A government bureaucracy translates these basic policies into specific five-year production targets. It specifies the types, quantities, and prices of all goods and services to be produced, down to the number of shoes.
3. These production targets are then translated into goals for each plant. The local manager is given a target output—5,000 pairs of work shoes, for example—and the resources to be used in their production.

Managers who meet or beat their targets get bonuses and medals from the government. But some, in trying to reach the targets, may cut quality. And the planners themselves sometimes misjudge needs, sending too much steel to Siberia or too little coal to the Ukraine. The system distinctly lacks the flexibility of private enterprise.

Chapter Review & Applications

Key Points to Remember

1. The United States has a private enterprise system which includes elements of a mixed economy.
2. Private enterprise includes private ownership of property, freedom of choice, and limited government interference. Consumer sovereignty, reasonable profits, vigorous competition, and high productivity help make the private enterprise system work efficiently.
3. Ethical standards are ultimately set by the individual. Codes of ethics of individual firms and industries help guide actions.
4. Social responsibility is the idea that business should help society solve its problems.
5. Business prospers only if consumers are served. Consumerism is an organized movement to pressure business into informing and protecting the consumer.
6. Equal and satisfactory career opportunities and employee safety are vital aspects of effective management.
7. Environmental issues, such as resource scarcities and environmental protection, affect most businesses today.
8. Rapidly changing economic and social conditions require business managers to respond to the internal and external environment. Considering social issues is no longer optional.
9. Socialism and communism are the two major economic alternatives to the private enterprise system. In these systems government has a very powerful influence on people's lives.

Questions for Discussion

1. Define the following terms and explain their significance in the private enterprise system: (a) consumer sovereignty; (b) competition; (c) profits; (d) productivity.
2. There are only five automobile repair shops in a small town. All have agreed on a common price of $39.95 for a tune-up. Is this an example of pure competition? Explain your answer.
3. "High productivity is a very bad thing," a worker argued. "If we work hard and produce a lot, there will be fewer jobs and some of us will be unemployed." "Nonsense," a companion muttered angrily. "If everyone followed your suggestion, we would produce so few goods and services that our standard of living would decline." Which of these two views do you think is correct? Why?
4. Most people have their own views of the ethical standards of various occupations and professions.

   (a) In terms of ethics and honesty, rank the following occupations from highest to lowest:

automobile mechanics	columnists
business executives	physicians
clergy	politicians
college professors	T.V. repairers
judges	generals
union leaders	salespeople

   (b) How does your ranking compare with the rankings of other members of your class?

5. A steel plant manager is told to produce 100,000 tons of steel and to use 1,000 employees to do it. All profits are returned to the government, which also owns nearly all private property. Under what economic system is the manager working?

Short Case

There are two major airlines in Hawaii: Hawaiian and Aloha. Both fly similar routes among the islands, and both are financially strong enough to withstand a fairly long price war. Keeping in mind the amount of competition, would you recommend a fare cut to the top management of Aloha Airlines in order for that company to secure a larger share of the passenger market?

A Critical Business Decision

—made by Searle Lawson and Kermit Vandivier of B.F. Goodrich Company

The Situation

It is a spring day in June. The LTV Aerospace Corporation places an order with the B.F. Goodrich Company for 202 brake assemblies for a new Air Force fighter plane—the A7D. Unknown to either company, this order will trigger a series of events leading to one of the most bizarre Air Force procurements in history. At the Goodrich plant in Troy, Ohio, one of the company's most capable engineers is assigned to the project. His preliminary design for the brake calls for four disks and a total weight of only 106 pounds. Weight is a critical factor in aircraft design, since the lighter the aircraft part, the greater the plane's potential payload. When the preliminary design is completed, major subassemblies are ordered from Goodrich suppliers.

The Decision

In December, 26-year-old Searle Lawson, a newcomer to Goodrich, is assigned the task of converting the preliminary design into the final production design. But before the A7D brake can be produced in quantity, Lawson must subject it to quality-control tests specified by the Air Force.

Because time is crucial—LTV has scheduled flight tests for the A7D in only six months—Lawson decides to begin testing immediately. The brake housing and other parts have not yet been delivered by suppliers, but the brake disks have arrived. Using a brake housing and other parts similar to those proposed for the A7D brake design, Lawson builds a prototype and begins a series of lab tests by "landing" the wheel at the A7D's landing speed and braking it to a stop. The main purpose of these tests is to determine what temperatures will develop inside the four-disk brake and to evaluate proposed lining materials.

In a normal aircraft landing, the temperatures inside a brake can reach 1,000 degrees. To Lawson's astonishment, in the first simulated landing, the A7D brake glows a bright red and the temperature rises to 1,500 degrees. After several such stops, Lawson dismantles the brake and finds that the brake linings have almost disintegrated.

Lawson orders new brake-lining materials and tries again. The second and the third tests are carbon copies of the first. Inexperienced though he is, Lawson recognizes the seriousness of the problem. It is not defective parts or unsuitable lining materials that are at fault but a bad brake design. The brake is too small—there is simply not enough surface area on the disks to stop the A7D without burning up the brake linings. The solution is obvious: scrap the four-disk design and start from scratch on a new design using five disks—a long, costly process.

Lawson takes his results to both his boss and his boss's boss. Both refuse to recognize that a problem exists and order Lawson to find better brake-lining materials. In fact, LTV has already been told that the preliminary tests have been successful. During the formal Air Force qualification tests, the brake meets with fourteen successive failures.

Company managers order Lawson and Kermit Vandivier, a 42-year-old technical writer at Goodrich, to prepare the qualification report, fabricating whatever data are necessary to demonstrate that the brake has met all Air Force requirements. The two men are aware of the implications of their assignment: if the report is accepted and the brake is flight-tested, the test pilot will be exposed to possible injury or death.[4]

Questions

1. What courses of action are open to Lawson and Vandivier? Which do you recommend? Why?
2. This is one of the most dramatic cases of corporate irresponsibility in American business history. Why do you suppose B.F. Goodrich behaved as it did?

Business Ownership: You, Your Partners, Your Corporation

In this chapter you will learn . . .

- *about sole proprietorships, partnerships, and corporations.*
- *how to establish your own corporation.*
- *about the rights and responsibilities of the stockholders, boards of directors, and managers of corporations.*
- *what the difference is between profit and nonprofit organizations.*

he largest retail corporation in the United States began nearly a hundred years ago as a partnership. The two original partners started by selling only watches, then added cream separators and bicycles. Now, hundreds of their stores throughout the country sell everything from skis to contact lens to television sets. Whereas the partners once agonized before inviting two more partners into the firm, thousands of stockholders now buy and sell shares regularly on the stock market. Once, a Chicago warehouse full of "elevators, mechanical conveyors, endless chains, moving sidewalks, gravity chutes, conveyors, pneumatic tubes, and every mechanical device known to man" was the means of merchandise distribution. Today, orders are filled from all parts of the country with the aid of sophisticated computers.

One thing that didn't change was the firm's emphasis on high-quality, low-price products, and satisfied customers, as stressed in its first advertising copy: "Satisfaction guaranteed or your money back." The company is Sears, Roebuck. Sales of $745,000 in 1895 became $20 billion in 1980. When it grew beyond the business capabilities of a partnership, it incorporated, or became a corporation. What is a corporation, and why is it more capable than a sole proprietorship or partnership of handling very large businesses? Why and how firms choose one form of organization over another is the subject of this chapter.

THREE WAYS TO BE IN BUSINESS

Suppose you have saved enough money to realize your dream of starting your own sporting-goods business. But before you go out and rent store space and purchase an inventory of stock (covered in detail in Chapters 16 and 17), the law requires that you get a license to be in business. And even before you do this, you must decide what form of business ownership yours will be. You can do it by yourself. You can invite one or several people to do it with you. Or you can start your own corporation. The three most common types of business organizations in the United States are the *sole proprietorship*, the *partnership*, and the *corporation*. Their advantages and disadvantages are described in the following sections and outlined in Figure 3–1, below.

FIGURE 3–1
Three Ways to Be in Business: Forms of Ownership.

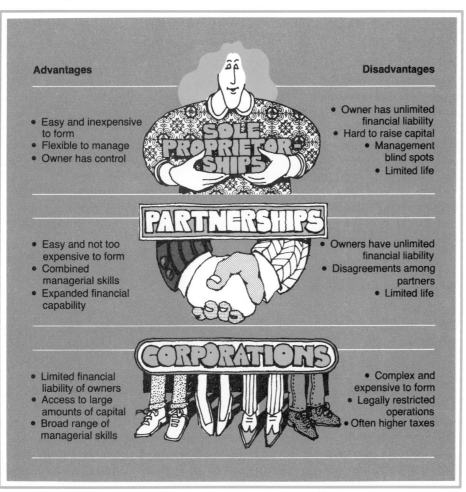

Advantages

• Easy and inexpensive to form
• Flexible to manage
• Owner has control

Disadvantages

• Owner has unlimited financial liability
• Hard to raise capital
• Management blind spots
• Limited life

SOLE PROPRIETORSHIPS

PARTNERSHIPS

• Easy and not too expensive to form
• Combined managerial skills
• Expanded financial capability

• Owners have unlimited financial liability
• Disagreements among partners
• Limited life

CORPORATIONS

• Limited financial liability of owners
• Access to large amounts of capital
• Broad range of managerial skills

• Complex and expensive to form
• Legally restricted operations
• Often higher taxes

Sole Proprietorships

Want to start your own restaurant? Or be a guide for wilderness canoe trips? Or set up your own law office? Each of these businesses would probably be set up as a **sole proprietorship**—a business owned and usually managed by a single person. These are generally small businesses, farming operations, or professional offices for doctors or lawyers. Sole proprietorships are by far the most common form of business organization in the United States. But while they comprise more than three of every four businesses, they account for less than one of every four dollars of profit earned by American firms.

Advantages

In a sole proprietorship, you set up the business and take in and pay out the money yourself. You pay only one set of taxes since your personal and business incomes are combined. Because you do not normally work for any other organization you are considered to be *self-employed*. Your business is easier to establish and dissolve than any other form of business ownership. Very few legal documents are required. There are no initial legal limits on the types of products or services you can sell. People open sole proprietorships to do everything from organizing one rock concert to starting a dental office for life. As with Freddie Laker (see box), many businesses begin this way and change their form of ownership as they grow. The Coca-Cola Company started as a sole proprietorship with an initial investment of only $2,300. (See color section at end of text.)

Problems

A sole proprietorship is not all gravy, though. Since your personal and business finances are pooled, you face **unlimited liability.** This means that if your business fails, your personal income must be made available to pay creditors. And, it is hard to raise initial capital. Very few people or institutions are willing to invest money directly in your business when they may face unlimited liability with you. Only when you, your family, or your friends have enough assets to use as collateral for a loan, will banks or other financial institutions normally lend money to your sole-proprietorship business.

Also, as a sole proprietor, you need to possess many diverse management skills. And you may not be equally good at all of them. You may be terrific at baking and marketing your specialty pies and cakes but flounder in the meringue when it comes to keeping proper financial records. Good employees may be hard to find and keep because salaries and promotion opportunities tend to be limited. And what if you are disabled? If the business depends on your skills or services, what will happen if you cannot work?

Partnerships

Want to open a record store? Or a solar-power home-outfitting company? Try a **partnership,** in which two or more persons act as co-owners of the business. Partnerships, the least common form of business ownership, are most often found in the fields of real estate and finance and among the professions (though the "professional association," a type of corporation, is becoming more common among doctors and lawyers).

    Limited partnerships, allowed in most states, have two kinds of partners. One or more *general partners* manage the business and usually collect a significant percentage of its profits. Like sole proprietors, general partners

Freddie Laker: Starting a Sole Proprietorship with a Few Jets

Freddie Laker has always liked to get things done by himself, whether it was his childhood model airplane collection, his charter airline company, or his own trans-Atlantic jet shuttle. He still likes the do-it-yourself approach, even though he has grown from a sole proprietorship to a corporation in the space of a few years. In the early 1970s Laker, a Britisher, made what everyone considered a rash proposal. His little airline would take on giant international airlines like Pan American and TWA by offering a $99, one-way, no-frills air passage from London to New York.

    Laker soon found his corner of the market invaded by Pan Am, TWA, Air France, Lufthansa, and others who began offering their own no-frills flights: no reservations, no free meals, no entertainment, and no elbow room. But Laker continues to offer the fewest frills and the lowest prices, and business is booming. The "backpack-and-guitar brigade," as he calls them, loves his own personal company, "little" Laker Airways. The major airlines, of course, do not.

face unlimited liability, meaning they are personally liable for any losses sustained by the business. *Limited partners,* on the other hand, invest in the business but are liable only for their initial investment. If the business fails, they lose only what they put into it. A limited partnership is quite common for real estate and other investment businesses.

Advantages

Do you know someone with an idea for a new kind of solar heat pump that you have the skills and materials to manufacture? Do you have an artistic friend

Sunrise, Ltd.: The Glamour Partnership That Really Wasn't

The best of all possible worlds! This is what customers believe Chris and Linda Kaiser have at Sunrise, Ltd.—their ski shop in Vail, Colorado. The shop is nestled in a village in the heart of the Rocky Mountains, and the Kaisers obviously enjoy what they do.

When they opened their ski shop seven years ago, they knew it would be a lot of work, but they expected to enjoy it. Linda says they felt "there was a need for a service-oriented store where we could take good care of customers, ski with them and give them an honest opinion of what they needed."

At first, the Kaisers sold only skis, boots, bindings, and poles. "It was really wild," Chris recalls. "It took us three months to balance the books the summer after our first year."

They learned a lot the hard way. For example, the only way for them to make a profit was to also sell ski clothing and accessories—like hats, gloves, and goggles. They found they had to make a one-shot order in March for the entire stock they would need for the four-month season the following December through March—a really tough forecasting job. And they overbought merchandise and had no money to buy the hiking gear they wanted to sell throughout the summer. Since they were short of cash, they took in three sets of partners at different times in Sunrise's history—all of whom insisted on some decisions the Kaisers knew were wrong because they'd made the same mistakes earlier. Finally, because the business is seasonable, there was high employee turnover—70 different employees in one year alone.

So where does that leave Sunrise, Ltd., and its glamour business? The Kaisers have decided to make their shop smaller, more manageable, and more profitable. This means making it more self-service oriented (to reduce the number of employees they need), lowering inventory (to plan to run out in February), and adding year-round items like hiking boots, T-shirts, and running shoes.

When they opened their business, the Kaisers expected a lot of free time for skiing. But they found they were always at the shop or solving cash problems. So they hope their new plans will give them more free time—to ski, to sail, to get away.

But no more partners![1]

who is interested in illustrating your stories for children? Combining skills can be a satisfying and profitable venture, and this is why most partnerships are formed. Another reason is that capital is easier to raise when more than one person shares responsibility at the bank.

Partnerships are quite easy to form. They require, basically, a *partnership agreement,* drawn up by a lawyer. The agreement legally binds the partners to some type of financial arrangement and usually provides a means for expanding or ending the partnership, with a provision for buying one another out. Many present corporations, such as Sears, Roebuck, mentioned at the beginning of the chapter, and the booming East Coast discount chain, Caldor, Inc., began as partnerships. Even the name Caldor—from Carl and Dorothy Bennett—bears testimony to the original partnership.

Problems

Partnerships can be risky. Since each general partner is financially liable for the actions and debts of the business, each can also be sued because of the misjudgment or malpractice of any of the other partners. Employees may develop divided loyalties to the partners. And even if problems do not reach this point, partners may disagree on how to run the business (see the box on Sunrise, Ltd.). In these situations, one partner may decide to buy the others out or find replacements. An example is Ray Kroc, an ex-salesman for Multi-Mixer, a machine that could churn out five milkshakes at once. When he found out that the McDonald brothers in California had bought eight Multi-Mixers for their hamburger stand and were doing a brisk business, he proposed a partnership. The result was McDonald's restaurants. But after six years of partnership, Kroc said, "I was out of tune with the McDonald brothers—I was one-stepping and they were waltzing." So he bought his partners out and went on from there.

Corporations

A **corporation** is the most influential form of business ownership, yet it is a difficult thing to describe. The nearest definition is that it is an association of persons that by law has authority to act and be financially liable apart from its individual owners.

The corporation has three key characteristics: many owners (from one up to several million stockholders); written rules (with many legal details); and **limited liability** (no one owner can normally lose more money than he or she puts in, even if the corporation goes bankrupt).

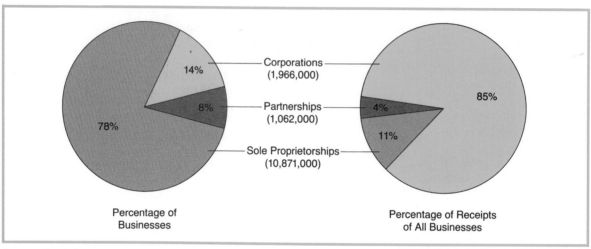

Corporations
(1,966,000)

Partnerships
(1,062,000)

Sole Proprietorships
(10,871,000)

14%

8%

78%

85%

4%

11%

Percentage of
Businesses

Percentage of Receipts
of All Businesses

Source: Statistical Abstract of U.S.

**FIGURE 3–2
U.S. Business
Ownership.**

Although corporations represent only 14 percent of U.S. enterprises, they earn 85 percent of all business income (see Figure 3–2). And they pack more clout every year.

Types of Corporations

Whether a proft-making corporation manufactures computers or sells crayons, it must be one of the following three types.

- A PUBLICLY HELD CORPORATION   These are owned by members of the public who have bought shares in the company. These **stockholders,** or **shareholders,** can buy and sell their shares conveniently on some stock exchange. The corporation must comply with many government regulations.
- A PRIVATELY HELD CORPORATION   These corporations do not regularly offer their stock to the public, so owners cannot buy and sell it conveniently. However, such businesses are subject to fewer government regulations than publicly held corporations; they can make long-range plans without having to worry about stockholder concerns over stock price or dividends; and they often are free to operate outside the public eye. For example, you probably have never heard of a grain and shipping company called Cargill, Incorporated. Yet its 1980 sales were more than $13 billion (see box on the opposite page).

- A CLOSELY HELD CORPORATION   A large proportion of the stock in these is usually owned by one or a few families. Often these companies are also privately held corporations, with stock ownership not available to the general public. For example, for many years the Ford Motor Company, one of the largest publicly held corporations in the United States, was controlled by the Ford family because of the volume of Ford stock it owned.

Corporations usually seek to grow. A few begin as sole proprietorships or partnerships and become corporations to handle their increased business. Some corporations grow internally by generating enough profit themselves to introduce new products and enter new markets. But they can also grow by **consolidation,** combining two or more corporations into one. Technically, there are two kinds of consolidations—a *merger* and an *amalgamation*. A **merger** (or **acquisition**) occurs when one corporation buys out one or more others; the purchasing corporation remains dominant and retains its original

Five Privately Held Corporations Nobody Knows

Five private companies dominate a $50 billion industry—and one that is at least as imporant as automobiles. These giants of international business are Andre Company, Bunge Corporation, Cargill Incorporated, Continental Grain Company, and the Dreyfus Company. Yet few people have ever heard of them. Fewer still are aware of the simplest business details that occupy the attention of these five companies.[2]

These are the "grain merchants to the world," dominating international trade in wheat, corn, soybeans, and other vital grains. Recently, the five privately held corporations drew attention by expanding their grain elevators and grain-milling operations. Although grain sales have long been a vital part of the international economy, it wasn't until 1972, when the Russians bought huge quantities of wheat by placing separate orders with each of the grain merchants, that the public became aware of their importance. The high domestic prices for grain-based foods and meats that resulted from this sale prompted the U.S. government to require grain merchants to notify it of all future major foreign orders before being permitted to fill them.

A major advantage of the privacy surrounding the grain merchants has been their ability to carry out confidential transactions without public involvement. An entire shipload of grain may change hands on the basis of a single phone call, and there will be no newspaper or magazine article reporting the deal and no public cry of outrage or approval. Among the grain merchants, a dealer's word is his or her bond. And the trust that these individual enterprises have built among themselves has enabled them to react to the ever-changing world food conditions with a rapidity unheard of in most other industries.

name. For example, when Campbell Soup Company merged with Pepperidge Farm (see box), the new firm retained the name Campbell Soup Company. An **amalgamation** occurs when two or more corporations unite to form a new one with a new name. The name General Motors, for instance, was established in 1917 when the Buick, Cadillac, Oldsmobile, and Pontiac Corporations were combined. In practice, however, the terms merger and acquisition often are used interchangeably today to mean amalgamation. About 2,000 to 4,000 corporate mergers and amalgamations occur in this country in a typical year.

Advantages

Corporations have access to large amounts of capital. Many investors, both individuals and banks, are willing to take a relatively small risk to participate in a large business, knowing they can buy and sell the stock easily. Shareholders have limited liability, meaning that their personal finances are not at risk, even if the corporation goes bankrupt. So the most that investors can lose is their initial investment. And the corporation itself enjoys certain tax benefits.

With their large size, corporations can offer good salaries, promotions, and job security. These benefits attract a wide variety of high-quality employees. Some corporations, like Digital Equipment Corporation, are even flexible

Homemade Bread Gets Merged

Margaret Rudkin's homemade bread, baked at first just for her allergic child, became the basis for a sole-proprietorship business when she started baking a few loaves at a time and selling them to the local grocery store. Her ingredients, especially the stone-ground wheat flour, attracted more and more customers. So she hired two employees, baked 100 loaves a week, and began to sell them in the nearby big city, too. Next came her first commercial bakery, then two more. Her company was soon baking more than a million loaves a week. A line of turnovers, strudels, and pastries was also added. The business was a huge success and became a corporation—Pepperidge Farm.

Nearly 25 years after Ms. Rudkin baked her first loaf, Campbell Soup Company came knocking on her door. They proposed a merger with her company. Margaret Rudkin said yes. She turned her company into a division of Campbell Soup and joined the corporate board of directors.

Ms. Rudkin baked her way into corporate success and a great deal of money.[3]

enough to keep the atmosphere of entrepreneurship that led to their success by encouraging a stream of new ideas from employees. Sole corporations seek a good mixture of management skills. And continuity of management is better assured.

Problems

Since corporations are *chartered* (given the right to operate) by state governments, they must comply with complex government regulations. Lawyers are required. Most state laws also require that the corporation's main businesses be designated, limiting flexibility.

Though tax structures offer corporations some advantages, corporate owners must pay taxes on business earnings *and* on the *dividends* paid to the stockholders. (Dividends will be discussed later in this chapter.) Only one kind of small corporation, called the **Subchapter S corporation,** avoids this problem. This special kind of corporation has ten stockholders or less (fifteen after five years) and is taxed the same way as a sole proprietorship or partnership to avoid corporate income taxes.

Since corporate managers are not sole owners, incentives such as **bonuses** (extra salary tied to higher business earnings) and **stock options** (opportunities to buy company stock at favorable rates) are often used to attract and keep them. This is considered necessary because the lives of these managers are filled with interruptions, uncertainty, and pressure (see box on page 71).

HOW TO START A CORPORATION

Because the corporation is the most powerful and complex form of business ownership, it is important to know how one is started. Several key steps in launching a corporation are described below. The advice of a competent attorney is necessary, though, before choosing a form of business ownership and certainly when forming a corporation.

Get a Corporate Charter

The first step of *incorporation* is to submit a formal application, usually to the secretary of state in the state in which you want to incorporate. This becomes the **corporate charter.** The document usually includes the name, address, and purpose of the business, a listing of the board of directors and the principal stockholders, the types of stock to be used by the company, and the mechanism to be used for amending the charter. Incorporation usually takes place when this corporate charter is approved by the state.

Distribute the Stock

After the charter is established, the second step is to distribute the **stock** (or **shares**), which are ownership rights in the company. Stock is sold to the public through a **stockbroker,** who creates a market for the stock by buying and selling it on behalf of investing customers and the company.

The corporation's founders must also arrange for a *transfer agent* for the stock. This is a bank or other financial institution that records who buys and sells the corporation's stock and that handles the mechanics of paying **dividends**—the portion of corporate profits the company decides to pay out to stockholders. The founders must also have **stock certificates** (legal documents showing ownership of stock) printed, listing the company's name, the owner's name, and the number of shares owned.

Owners of stock, the stockholders or shareholders, eventually may receive dividends according to how much they invest. The corporation's founders usually buy or receive some of the new stock in return for their initial services in organizing the company. The founders use part of the stock to pay expenses, such as legal fees. Stock, rather than money, is often used to pay initial expenses of the business because most young companies are short of cash. Then, if the electronic toy or frozen yogurt bar is really successful, the initial owners and investors can reap large financial benefits. For, of course, the more successful the business, the higher the value of the stock will be. An initial investment of, say, $3,000 (to buy 600 shares of stock) might well become $30,000 when the company's success increases the stock price from $5 to $50 per share.

Select the Board of Directors

Once the stock is distributed, the founders call a meeting of the stockholders to elect a **board of directors.** The board of directors is responsible for the overall welfare of the business, including the appointment of top management. Figure 3–3 shows how the board of directors relates to the shareholders, top management, and the corporation's remaining employees.

FIGURE 3-3
How a Corporation Is Structured.

In the United States, most boards of directors are composed of share-holders (who normally include the original founders), top managers, and some outside directors (persons with no formal connection to the company but who are chosen for their business ability). Most boards include about fifteen members.

The board must begin by approving the new company's *bylaws,* or internal rules. Bylaws usually include basic operating rules for such things as board of director responsibilities and vacancies, the naming of officers of the company, and procedures for issuing stock and selecting accounting methods.

The board also takes immediate charge of approving important corporate strategies and policies and monitoring major corporate activities to make sure they are legal and acceptable to stockholders. It is required to set up an audit committee, for example. This group reviews accounting standards, the issuance of company securities, and compliance with laws, such as the Foreign Corrupt Practices Act.

The typical board meets formally four or more times a year, doing much of its work in committees. Board members in large corporations are usually paid from about $5,000 to $15,000 or more a year, with $100 to $200 extra for each committee meeting they attend.

Hire Top Management

As shown in Figure 3–3, one of the board's key early responsibilities is to hire **top management** (the president or chief executive officer, the vice presidents, and the heads of major units within the company), which ultimately reports to the board. As we will discuss in Chapter 4, the top management team sets long-range strategy and policies but delegates day-to-day operations to lower-level managers and to other employees of the corporation.

Manage Stockholder Relations

When a corporation is launched, founders and managers soon find themselves working on relations with stockholders, who are often called "passive investors." The corporate charter and certain government demands set the stage for how these relations will be handled, and the annual meetings and annual reports are always part of the scene.

Providing Vital Information

Management and the board of directors are required promptly and consistently to disclose key information to stockholders and the general public. This includes information about the purchase or sale of stock by major stockholders or managers, major management changes, other events known to management that are likely to affect the business, and changes in the corporate charter. Otherwise, the *insiders* (those who are close to the company who could take advantage of their favorable position) could use their special information to buy and sell their stock on favorable terms.

Corporations not expert at stockholder relations can find themselves defendants in *stockholder suits,* claims filed in court by shareholders against the company. Some suits, for instance, have claimed that top management is incompetent and has lost stockholder money; others, that not enough information was provided on acquisitions and corporate investments.

What's it like at the top? Henry Mintzberg, a professor of management at Canada's McGill University, spent several months at the elbows of top U.S. executives and reported on the nitty-gritty of their working life styles.

- INTERRUPTIONS   Top managers, who may have fifty projects going on at the same time, live a life of interruptions. They juggle visitors and phone calls constantly, advise subordinates, and check on progress. They dispose of most problems within ten minutes.

- UNCERTAINTY   The simple or clear-cut issues are resolved by subordinates and never reach their desks. Instead, top managers draw the ambiguous, complex problems.

- SOFT-SOLVING   Once all possible "hard" information is in, top managers have to rely on gossip, hearsay, and speculation to reach decisions. So they skim through business reports and periodicals to improve their hunches and intuition.

- EFFECTIVE COMMUNICATION   Since top managers spend more than half their time dealing with persons outside the business—peers in the business community, important customers, community leaders, and government officials—they have to be especially good communicators.

If calculated chaos, pressure, difficult decision making, and interpersonal demands are your element, you might want to join them.

Life at the Top

Your Next Job
Future Trends by Occupation

Occupations can be divided into four groups: white-collar jobs; blue-collar jobs; service jobs; and farm jobs. Job prospects from 1978–1990 will be, from best to worst, white-collar (clerical), service, blue-collar, and farm occupations.

White-Collar Occupations

Professional and **technical workers** numbered over 13 million in 1978. They include teachers, doctors, engineers, accountants, and clergy. Professional occupations are expected to grow by 19 percent from 1978 to 1990.

Managers and **administrators** numbered about 10.7 million in 1978, and these jobs are expected to increase by about 21 percent over the 1978–1990 period. The demand for managers is likely to continue to increase as firms depend more and more on trained management specialists, especially in highly technical fields.

Clerical workers were the largest occupational group in the United States in 1978, totaling 16.9 million. It is also the fastest-growing group. Clerical workers keep records, take dictation, type, and operate computers and office machines. The need for such workers is expected to increase by about 28 percent from 1978 to 1990, largely because of needs in electronic data-processing and personnel work.

Salesworkers sell goods and services for retail, wholesale, insurance, real-estate, and door-to-door businesses. More than 6 million salesworkers were employed in 1978. Since sales go up with increases in population and in new-product development, these occupations will continue to grow.

Service Occupations

Service workers maintain law and order, assist hospital professionals, cut hair and give beauty treatments, serve food, and clean and care for homes. Employment in this diverse occupational group totaled about 12 million in 1978; it is expected to increase 35 percent between 1978 and 1990.

Blue-Collar Occupations

Craftworkers accounted for about 12.4 million workers in 1978. These include carpenters, tool and die makers, instrument makers, general machinists, electricians, and typesetters. Their number is also expected to increase by about one-fifth by 1990. **Operatives** (sometimes called **semiskilled workers**) may assemble goods or operate machines in factories or may drive vehicles like trucks, buses, and taxis. Over 10 million operatives were employed in 1978, and the number of jobs in this occupational area is expected to increase by about 15 percent by 1990. **Laborers** (excluding miners and farmers) totaled about 4 million in 1978 but will grow only slightly in the future (about 9 percent).

Farm Occupations

Farm workers, including farmers and farm managers, laborers, and supervisors, totaled about 2.8 million in 1978. By 1990, continued advancements in farm mechanization are expected to cause this number to decline by about 14 percent.

Thus, in general, the more education or occupational training men and women have, the brighter their employment outlooks will be.

The Annual Meeting and Annual Report

From the first annual meeting on, stockholders vote to select members of the board of directors, hear about new company developments, and address questions to top management. All stockholders are legally entitled to attend the annual meeting and are supplied by mail with **proxies,** documents authorizing others to vote for them in their absence, if they choose not to attend. Stockholders are allowed one vote per share owned. Figure 3–4 shows what typical proxies look like.

The issues that are considered at annual meetings are usually routine—the choice of an accounting firm to audit the company's financial statements, for example. Management recommends a position on each issue that comes before the annual meeting and is usually supported by the stockholders.

Occasionally, though, a controversy develops over something like top-management bonuses or overseas investments. But the small groups of stockholders raising issues like these are usually voted down by the others.

In fact, corporations usually try to liven up their annual meetings with free lunches or free samples of company products. The 3M Company, for example, opens a "company store" at the meeting place, where stockholders flock to buy baskets full of Scotch tape and other 3M consumer products at reduced rates.

Another responsibility of the corporation is to produce an annual report to stockholders. This details company accomplishments and highlights the financial performance of the past year, explaining reasons for good or bad performance of the corporation's various operations. (See box on page 284.)

NONPROFIT ORGANIZATIONS

Many organizations in our society do not seek profits as a primary goal. These include government agencies, many hospitals, research and educational institutions, and foundations. Although profits are not sought, these organizations often—or, at least, should—apply good business principles in order to operate efficiently.

Two types of nonprofit organizations are cooperatives and government-owned organizations.

Cooperatives

A **cooperative** is a business chartered under state laws that seeks to better its members economically. It is owned by its members, who elect a board of

CITIES SERVICE COMPANY
Box 300, Tulsa, Oklahoma 74102
THIS PROXY IS SOLICITED ON BEHALF OF THE BOARD OF DIRECTORS

The undersigned hereby authorizes and directs R. V. Sellers, C. J. Waidelich and George O. Nolley and each of them, with full power of substitution, to vote the stock of the undersigned at the Annual Meeting of Stockholders of CITIES SERVICE COMPANY on April 29, 1980 or any adjournments thereof as hereinafter specified and, in their discretion, to vote according to their best judgment upon such other matters as may properly come before the meeting or any adjournments thereof.

DATE:_____, 1980

_____
Signature

_____
Signature if owned jointly

Please sign exactly as name or names appear to the left. When signing as a Trustee, Executor, Administrator, or Officer of a corporation, give title as such.

P R O X Y

COMMON STOCK

Please vote. You must <u>sign, date</u> and <u>return</u> your proxy for it to be voted.   (over)

Pfizer
PFIZER INC.
235 East 42nd Street, New York, New York 10017

Proxy

This Proxy is Solicited on Behalf of the Board of Directors
The undersigned hereby appoints Edmund T. Pratt, Jr., Gerald D. Laubach, and John J. Powers, Jr., and each of them, as Proxies, each with full power of substitution, and hereby authorizes them to represent and to vote, as designated below, all the shares of common stock of Pfizer Inc. held of record by the undersigned on February 25, 1980, at the annual meeting of shareholders to be held on April 24, 1980 or any adjournment thereof.

A vote FOR is recommended by the Board of Directors:
1. ELECTION OF DIRECTORS   FOR all nominees listed below (except as marked to the contrary below) ☐   WITHHOLD AUTHORITY to vote for all nominees listed below ☐

Barry M. Bloom, Grace J. Fippinger, Joseph B. Flavin, Sheldon G. Gilgore, William J. Kennedy III, Gerald D. Laubach, Donald C. Lum, James T. Lynn, Paul A. Marks, John R. Opel, John J. Powers, Jr., Edmund T. Pratt, Jr., Felix G. Rohatyn, Henry L. Ross, Jr., Robert D. Royer, J. William Stuart and Jean-Paul Vallès.

(INSTRUCTION: To withhold authority to vote for any individual nominee write that nominee's name in the space provided below.)

A vote FOR is recommended by the Board of Directors:
2. PROPOSAL TO APPROVE THE APPOINTMENT OF MAIN HURDMAN & CRANSTOUN   ☐ FOR ☐ AGAINST ☐ ABSTAIN
3. PROPOSAL RELATING TO INCREASE IN AUTHORIZED COMMON STOCK   ☐ FOR ☐ AGAINST ☐ ABSTAIN
4. PROPOSAL RELATING TO AMENDMENTS TO STOCK AND INCENTIVE PLAN   ☐ FOR ☐ AGAINST ☐ ABSTAIN

A vote AGAINST is recommended by the Board of Directors:
5. SHAREHOLDER PROPOSAL RELATING TO CUMULATIVE VOTING   ☐ FOR ☐ AGAINST ☐ ABSTAIN

Sources: Cities Service Company and Pfizer Inc.

FIGURE 3-4
Two Examples of Proxies on Behalf of Boards of Directors.

directors. The most common "co-ops," as they are often called, are agricultural co-ops (see box), credit unions, and consumer co-ops (such as natural-food stores). Each member of a cooperative has a single vote, may purchase a limited number of shares (based either on the amount of his or her investment or the frequency of use of cooperative-supplied services), and is eligible to receive some of the co-op's profits (based on the proportion of shares held).

Government-Owned Organizations

A **government-owned organization** is a business established by government to achieve goals felt to be in the public good. Profits are put into future operations or are returned to the U.S. Treasury. An example is Amtrak, now responsible for most U.S. passenger rail service. All shares in these organizations are owned by the government.

The Land O' Lakes Story, or Look What a Professor Did!

Professor Theophilus Levi Hacker, an outspoken teacher of agriculture for more than 30 years, tirelessly delivered the same message: farmers would never successfully market their butter until they acted as a group.

Finally, in 1922, under the aggressive leadership of a young Litchfield, Minnesota, farmer named John Brandt, 310 creameries formed a cooperative. Commercial creameries publicly attacked the farmers' "new and absurd ideas." And the Blue Valley Creamery Company of Chicago tried to stop the cooperative by threatening to open competing creameries throughout Minnesota. But the embattled farmers stood firm.

The goal of the young co-op was to market as well as produce butter. So the imaginative farmers ran a statewide contest with a $500 prize, in gold, to select the best name. The winner: "Land O' Lakes." (Surprisingly, there were two winning entrants who split the prize.)

Today, Land O' Lakes is a giant among American cooperatives, with nearly 900 local affiliates in seven midwestern states and more than 150,000 individual members. In addition to butter, Land O' Lakes markets ice cream, dry milk, meats, cheese, turkeys, soybean oil, soybean meal, and dozens of other food items. It provides its members with feed, fertilizer, seed, chemicals, petroleum products, and dozens of other items for their farms. In 1980 its sales reached nearly $2.5 billion.

Land O' Lakes is only one of a dozen or so producer cooperatives that have edged into the marketing of food products. Well-run (they like to hire business students with farm backgrounds), retaining some of the idealism of their founders, and enjoying their nontaxable status, the cooperatives are formidable competitors. Giants of the food industries, beware![4]

Chapter Review & Applications

Key Points
to Remember

1. A sole proprietorship is owned and usually managed by one person. Advantages are that it is easy to form, flexible, and under the owner's control. Disadvantages are that the owner is personally liable for debts, may have trouble raising capital, and must have a full range of management skills.

2. A partnership is jointly owned by two or more people who are equally responsible for the business's success or failure. Advantages are that it is fairly easy to form, brings together a combination of skills and resources, and has a better chance to raise capital. Disadvantages are that owners are still personally liable and are subject to disagreements that could dissolve the partnership.

3. A corporation is owned by its shareholders, who elect a board of directors and select top management. Advantages are that it can raise money easily, attract a wide range of skilled employees, and allow the owners (shareholders) to be free of personal liability for business debts. Disadvantages are that it is quite expensive to form and maintain and is subject to many legal restrictions and high taxes.

4. Launching a corporation involves forming a charter, distributing stock, selecting a board of directors, hiring top management, and managing stockholder relations.

5. Cooperatives and government-owned organizations operate on a nonprofit basis. In cooperatives, members have one vote each, may purchase a limited number of shares, and receive a portion of whatever profits are made on a per share basis. In government-owned organizations, the government owns all shares, and any profits that are made are returned to the organization or put into the U.S. Treasury.

Questions for Discussion

1. What is a sole proprietorship? A partnership? A corporation? What are their principal advantages and disadvantages?

2. Define limited and unlimited liability. Why are they important to the individual investor?

3. What steps must you take to incorporate and operate a business?

4. What is a board of directors? What responsibilities does it have?

5. Who "owns" a corporation? What responsibilities do these owners have?

6. Government-owned organizations are designed to serve important public needs. Name as many of these organizations as you can and identify the ways in which each helps society.

Short Case

You are the manager of a small business that incorporated five years ago. Since then the company has grown by more than 300 percent. Your title is president and you have two vice presidents, one for marketing and one for production. Profits are excellent, but you feel harried and overcommitted. As you spend more time dealing with day-to-day problems, your company begins to lose its lead over its competitors.

What is your problem? What can you do about it? Why do you suppose many presidents of growing corporations fail to take effective action in this situation?

A Critical Business Decision

—made by Berry Gordy, Jr.
of Motown Industries

The Situation

"I never really wanted to establish my own business—to be an entrepreneur," observes Berry Gordy, Jr., president of Motown Industries, Inc., the large, Detroit-based recording company. When asked what makes an entrepreneur, Gordy responds, "You have to be a gambler capable of facing failure and coming back again."

Writing in *The New York Times*,[5] Gordy gives some insights into failures he encountered before Motown's success. "My first love was writing, creating songs as a hobby," he explains. But he couldn't try that right away. So in 1953, after an Army stint, Gordy opened a record store in Detroit, using his personal savings and a loan from his father. Gordy featured jazz records, but consumer taste at that time was leaning toward the newly arrived rhythm-and-blues recording style. His business went bankrupt in two years, and Gordy worked for his father as a plasterer.

Unhappy at that, Gordy went back to his first love and tried his hand at songwriting. The Beatles recorded his song "Money." A few of his other tunes were produced by major recording companies, but their renditions often weren't really what Gordy had in mind.

So Gordy decided to start a company for young songwriters—against the advice of his lawyer, who said he would need a lot of money to start it. Gordy was determined to prove him wrong. With $700 borrowed from his family, Gordy began a company for creative writers. Motown was born.

In 1960, Gordy joined forces with songwriter William "Smokey" Robinson to write "Shop Around." When that song was recorded in 1961, Motown was on its way to its first million-record seller. The ultimate result: Motown Record Corporation and its "Motown Sound."

By the 1970s, Motown had become a multimillion-dollar corporation. In 1975, Gordy and Motown signed Stevie Wonder to a seven-year contract for $13 million—a light-year's distance from the $700 of borrowed funds Motown started with. Besides Stevie Wonder, the names of many of its recording artists—Diana Ross, Smokey Robinson and the Miracles, the Supremes, the Temptations, and the Jackson 5, among them—were internationally known. The company was also producing television specials and films like *Lady Sings the Blues*, for which Diana Ross won an Academy Award nomination for best actress.

The Decision

Black Enterprise magazine[6] notes that "these feats were largely accomplished through Gordy's firm business sense and his almost clairvoyant ability to spot talent in Detroit's inner city and to develop it." Being able to recognize which songs and which artists are likely to succeed is critical in the recording business. This is especially true for Motown, since, although extremely successful, it still must compete in a record industry dominated by two giants: RCA Victor and Columbia. Yet Motown has always been at or near the top of the industry in terms of the percentage of its releases that have become strong sellers. For example, during one year, three-fourths of Motown's 75 singles and two-thirds of its 46 albums reached the national charts and were considered hits.

A key decision illustrates Gordy's and Motown's good business judgment. The recording business thrives on album sales, which represent 78 percent of total industry sales. Yet Motown enjoys the unique position of selling a greater number of single records than any other company—even its giant competitors. Motown's goal is to maintain its leadership position in single-record sales while increasing its album sales.

Question

If you were Berry Gordy, Jr., what strategy would you try to use Motown's strength in single-record sales in order to sell more albums?

SUCCESS

2 Management

and Production

Planning and Decision Making

In this chapter you will learn . . .

- that management is both a group of people and a process for achieving organizational goals.
- how managers set objectives, assess the future, and design and carry out programs.
- how managers use information to make effective decisions.

4

 o organization, whether it is the U.S. Department of Energy, the RCA Corporation, or a corner newsstand, is without problems. And someone—or whole teams of people—must anticipate, recognize, and resolve these problems. This requires people to make timely, accurate decisions.

Managers are these decision makers. They are found in all kinds of public and private organizations, at all levels, and have in common the responsibility of helping their organizations meet their objectives. Who are they, and what sort of problems do they face? A quick glimpse provides a few examples:

PROBLEM	DECISION MAKERS
An effective energy program for the country	The president, Congress, Department of Energy, the voters
A plan to boost your college's enrollment	The college president, board of trustees, department chairmen
Declining sales in a nation-wide retailing firm	The chairman of the board, board of directors, top managers, regional managers
Finding the best way to reward a high-performance employee	First- or middle-level manager

How managers achieve organizational goals is the subject of this and the two following chapters. This chapter describes how managers plan for the future and make decisions to carry out those plans.

WHAT IS MANAGEMENT?

The term **management** is often used in a very vague way, and yet everyone always seems to understand what it means. You may have heard something like, "The reason W.T. Grant failed in the retailing business was bad management." Or, "Boeing's success in commercial jet airliners is due to innovative management." What—or who—is management? Actually, it is both a what *and* a who.

Management as a Process

"Management is the act of getting things done through people." This popular definition is fine as far as it goes. But what things are getting done through which people—and how does it happen? A more complete definition is that *management is the process of planning, organizing, leading, and controlling an organization's people and resources to achieve its stated goals.*[1]

Suppose, for example, you are the manager of a local rock band (in this case, the band is considered to be the organization). Its *goal* is to sign a contract with a big record company and become famous; its *resources* are talent and enthusiasm; and its *people* are, of course, the individual musicians. They have hired you to help them meet their goal. What do you do? Your four key functions could be defined in the following way. (Keep in mind that these same functions could just as easily apply to a manager of Safeway or IBM or any other organization.)[2]

1. PLANNING   Setting objectives (auditions with record company executives); assessing the future (what types of music are becoming popular); and designing an action program (club dates, benefit concerts, demo tapes). (The planning area of management will be covered in detail later in this chapter.)
2. ORGANIZING   Structuring jobs (equipment handling, promotion) and placing qualified people in them. (Organizing will be discussed in Chapter 5.)
3. LEADING   Guiding the activities of subordinates toward objectives. (Leadership will be covered in Chapter 6.)
4. CONTROLLING   Comparing results with plans and taking appropriate corrective action. (The controlling aspect of management will be discussed in Chapter 6.)

You can see that a manager's job covers a wide range of responsibilities, and that without someone to perform these duties the organization could not survive. To succeed and grow, an organization calls on five key resources, often referred to as the **5 M's.** These are *management, men and women, materials, machinery,* and *money.* Management is the unifying resource that welds the other four together. Figure 4–1 shows how the 5 M's fit together with the four key managerial functions to achieve organizational goals. The figure also shows that decision making is a part of the entire management process.

We will come back to the planning and decision-making functions of managers later, but first we need to find out who these people are.

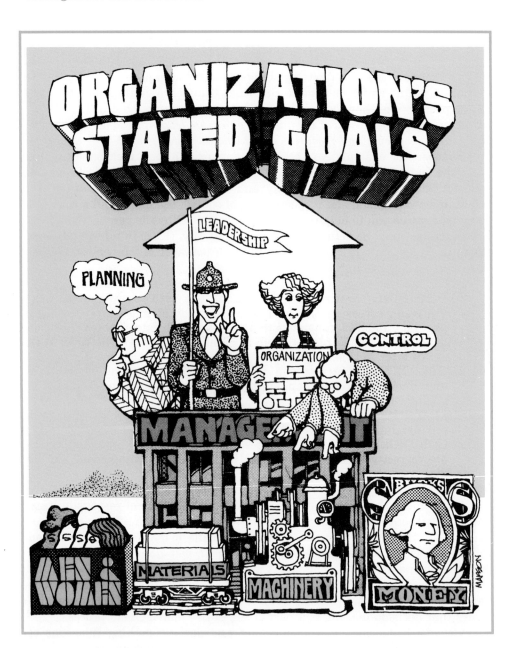

FIGURE 4–1
The 5 M's.

Management as People

In the example of the rock band above, management is *you*. For the corner newsstand, management is probably the owner, who is also the personnel and, in a sense, the whole organization. But in large businesses (which are the primary focus of this book) there are many managers with many different types of responsibilities. In these organizations managers can be classified in two ways: (1) by their level—top, middle, first-line—and (2) by their responsibilities—functional and general.

Management Levels

Top management, at the top of the pyramid in Figure 4–2, is responsible for overseeing the whole organizational structure. These few managers establish broad, long-range objectives and set policies for the organization. Typically, their titles are chief executive officer, president, executive vice president, and group vice president. Among their duties are meeting with government and consumer groups, deciding on which new products or services to introduce, acquiring or selling subsidiary companies, and hiring key high-level personnel. For a profile of chief executive officers, see Figure 4–3 and the accompanying box.

    Middle management, the next level of managers shown in the pyramid in Figure 4–2, is responsible for specific operations. The duties of these man-

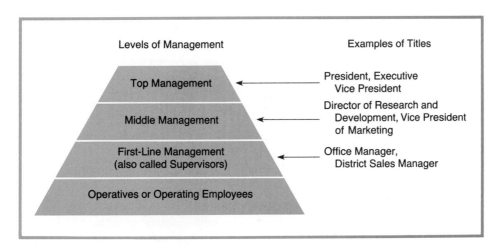

FIGURE 4-2 *Levels of Management.*

agers—usually called by such titles as director of finance and budgeting, national sales manager, or division head—include things like long- and short-range planning, establishing specific goals, overseeing lower-level managers, and organizing and implementing procedures to carry out the broad objectives set by top management.

First-line or **first-level management** is the lowest level in an organization that involves directing the efforts of others. First-line managers direct operatives or operating employees only, not the work of other managers. Typical titles of first-line managers might be shop supervisor, office manager, district sales manager, or personnel director. Their duties include short-range planning, hiring and training employees in their own area of supervision, and solving immediate problems.

Functional and General Managers

Whatever their level in the organization, managers can also be classified as *functional* or *general* managers, depending on the type of activities they manage. A **functional manager** oversees the activities of a single department or part of a firm, such as manufacturing or marketing or accounting or finance. A **general manager** is responsible for an entire unit, such as an operating division of a company, a whole company, a government agency, or a college. He

Chief Executives: What Are They Like?

The background of 800 key chief executive officers, surveyed by *Fortune* magazine, turned up some surprises. The results can be seen in Figure 4–3. Unlike a generation ago—when many business leaders came from wealthy families—these executives come from the middle-class and lower-middle-class. Most are at least 50 years old and lead the country's largest manufacturing, publishing, banking, life insurance, finance, retailing, transportation, and utility businesses. All but one (Katherine Graham of *The Washington Post*) are men. They are well-educated (86 percent graduated from college), and all concentrated on marketing and distribution, finance, or production during their climb to the top. Their median income (in 1980 dollars) is $314,000 a year, which they earn by working an average of 55 hours or more each week with short yearly vacations. Although not shown in Figure 4–3, *Fortune* also reported that almost half studied business at the graduate level and about one-third as undergraduates. And loyalty counts: more than 60 percent of the executives have not switched companies more than once.

FIGURE 4-3
A Profile: Chief Executive Officers in America's Largest Businesses.

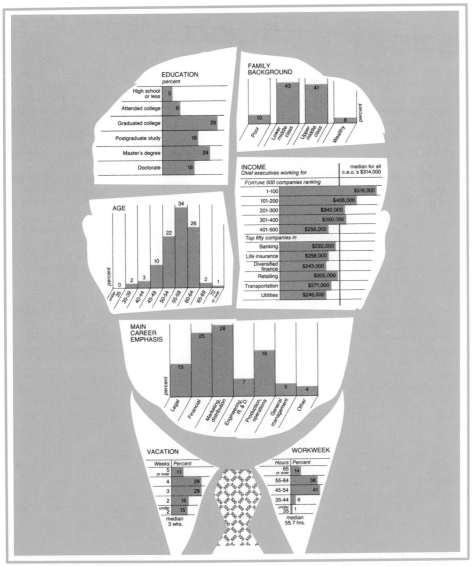

Source: Charles G. Burck, "A Group Profile of the Fortune 500 Chief Executive," *Fortune* (May 1976), p. 173. Income data have been adjusted for inflation to reflect estimated income for 1980.

Your Next Job
Positions in Management and Planning

Managerial and Administrative Careers

Hotel managers coordinate and supervise accounting, housekeeping, kitchen, personnel, and maintenance functions, and make decisions on room rates and credit policy. In large establishments, they have a staff of **hotel assistants** (often management trainees) who head various departments. Managers are usually recruited on the basis of experience, although a bachelor's degree or a community-college degree in hotel and restaurant administration is becoming increasingly important. Yearly salaries generally start at $12,000 for hotel-manager trainees who are graduates of specialized college programs and can grow to $55,000 for experienced managers at top hotels. In some hotels, managers may earn bonuses of 10 to 20 percent of their basic salary. (*Additional information:* The Educational Institute of the American Hotel and Motel Association, 888 7th Avenue, New York NY 10019.)

Health services administrators coordinate and supervise departmental activities, determine personnel and equipment needs, plan future facilities, prepare the budget, and raise funds. Positions are generally filled by experienced assistant administrators. A master's degree in health and hospital administration qualifies an applicant for a hospital's highest executive position. Middle-management jobs require a bachelor's or an associate degree. Hospital administrator's salaries range from $36,000 to over $55,000. Additional employment opportunities should be available for applicants with graduate degrees. (*Additional information:* American College of Hospital Administrators, 840 North Lake Shore Drive, Chicago, Illinois 60611.)

Professional Planning Careers

Economists study the production, distribution, and consumption of goods, analyze supply and demand factors, and formulate policies to utilize scarce resources efficiently. Many work for business organizations, providing planning information essential to resource allocation, marketing, and pricing decisions. Others work for government agencies or colleges. They need a thorough understanding of statistical techniques and good communications skills. College teaching positions generally require a doctoral degree. Most business and government positions require a bachelor's degree. Annual salaries range from $12,000 to $33,000. While employment is expected to grow in the 1980s, competition for jobs will increase as the number of qualified college applicants continues to exceed available positions. (*Additional information:* American Economic Association, 1313 21st Avenue South, Nashville, Tennessee 37212.)

Geographers analyze the relationship of physical variables (such as climate and terrain) to human population characteristics. Economic geographers analyze the geographical distribution of manufacturing, farming, mining, and communication activities. Urban geographers investigate human activities in city environments. Many geographers teach, but a growing number are filling planning jobs in business firms where their skills are useful in analyzing new locations. Businesses require a bachelor's degree. Teaching and governmental research positions require one or more graduate degrees. Annual income ranges from $10,700 to $23,000. Employment opportunities for geographers with graduate degrees are expected to increase due to the growing emphasis on ecological issues. However, geographers without advanced degrees will face stiff job competition. (*Additional information:* Association of American Geographers, 1710 16th Street, N.W., Washington, D.C. 20009.)

or she is responsible for all the activities of that organization, such as manufacturing, marketing, accounting, and finance.

A small company like a local sporting goods store probably has one general manager—its president. But a large company has several. General Mills, for example, hires a general manager for each division. That manager is in charge of all operations necessary to produce and sell either grocery products or games or apparel. General managers in charge of such large-scale operations ordinarily are vice presidents of the company.

Both types of managers need three kinds of skills: (1) *technical skills,* the ability to use the tools, procedures, and techniques of a specialized field; (2) *human skills,* the ability to understand, work with, and motivate others; and (3) *conceptual skills,* the mental ability to see the organization as a whole and integrate its interests and activities.

Each level of management uses a different combination of these skills, as can be seen in Figure 4–4. First-line managers need more technical skills than

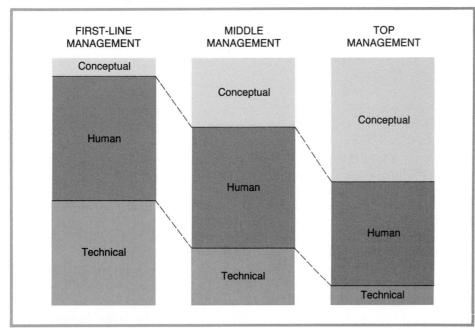

FIGURE 4-4
Mix of Skills Needed at Three Levels of Management.

Source: Based on Robert L. Katz, "Skills of an Effective Administrator," *Harvard Business Review* (Sept.–Oct. 1974), pp. 90–102.

do top managers. For example, a foreman in a machine shop of Zenith TV needs to know the capability of lathes and drill presses in his department so he can help his operators with their machining problems. He also probably needs more human skills than any other level of managers because he spends so much time working directly with his subordinates.

But the higher the level of management, the more important conceptual skills become. At Zenith, for instance, top- and middle-level managers must be able to spot trends in consumer demand and technology to determine what products to manufacture.

HOW MANAGERS PLAN

We are now ready to discuss the first major management function—planning—in depth. As we saw earlier, **planning** involves setting objectives, assessing the future, and designing an action program. Decision making, a part of management that applies to all the other managerial functions, will be discussed separately at the end of this chapter.

Setting Objectives

Without goals, aims, or aspirations people would flounder—nothing would be accomplished because there would be nothing to work toward. The same, of course, is true for organizations. The things that people and organizations strive for are **objectives.** At this moment, for example, your goal is to read and learn something from this chapter. That is a specific, short-range objective. But you also have long-range objectives—perhaps an "A" in the course, or a college degree, or a career in business. You also have many other short- and long-range objectives, all of which you are working for more or less at the same time. You are your own manager. You are setting your objectives, assessing your future, designing plans to accomplish your goals, and making decisions along the way. This is no easy task, as you no doubt have found out. Just imagine, then, how much more complicated this job would be if you had to do the same thing for a huge organization and hundreds or thousands of people. Of course no one person could do all that, which is why large organizations have many different managers.

To set objectives in the most effective way possible, managers must understand, first of all, the difference and the interrelationship between organizational objectives and the personal objectives of the people they direct.

Even in a very small organization, such as the rock band, organizational and personal objectives may conflict if, for instance, one or two of the members are unwilling to write or play "commercial" hits at the expense of music they admire. In big organizations, employees' personal goals are often at odds with organizational goals. And in very large organizations, some employees may not even know what the organizational objectives are. It is the job of managers to iron out the differences, make sure that at least the specific organizational objectives are known, and evaluate employee performance in terms of how well the stated objectives are being met.

Organizational Objectives

Organizational objectives are designed to direct the efforts of all the people in the organization. They must include general and long-range goals for the top of the organization and more specific and short-range goals at the lower levels. Managers must set these goals and make sure they are consistent.

If you are in top management at Eastman Kodak, your principal corporate goal may be maximizing profit. Your subordinate goals might include corporate responsibility, personnel development, and a profit increase on new product lines. But this last goal may conflict with the principal goal. If the new products begin to crowd out the photo-finishing business, the managers of the separate departments may have to appeal to the president to decide on priorities.

Reconciling Personal and Organizational Objectives

Generally, employees work hardest when they see that their organization's goals are consistent with their personal goals. Employees who want higher incomes will be motivated to produce more if their company rewards greater productivity with bonuses or institutes a profit-sharing program.

But sometimes a manager cannot reconcile an employee's personal goals with the firm's goals. A salesman with a large sales territory may want to spend more time at home. He may choose to leave the company rather than accept a promotion to a job that demands even more travel. In this case, even a good manager may not prevent the firm from losing a valuable employee.

Assessing the Future

Until the stock market crash of 1929, economic conditions were fairly stable, so long-range planning—even in giant corporations—was rare. Today, economic, technological, and political trends change so rapidly that future planning is vital to any business, large or small. The importance of accurate, timely decisions has created the need for **business forecasting**—assessing and projecting the future to improve business decisions. IBM, for example, risked more than $3 billion on its "360" line of computers, which depended on technology that was not yet available when the decision to produce and market the product was made. In this case, the future was assessed correctly and the decision was fantastically successful. But forecasting does not always guarantee success. The Edsel, a Ford disaster, was one of the most carefully researched new products in the history of American business.

How do managers assess the future to minimize mistakes?

Typical forecasting techniques used by managers include (1) indicators of economic activity: (2) judgmental methods, such as "lost-horse forecasting"; (3) statistical methods, such as extrapolation; and (4) surveys of experts, salespersons, purchasing agents, consumers, and others, such as the Delphi method. Each of these is discussed below.

Indicators of Economic Activity

Conventional barometers of general economic activity include such things as the length of the average work week, the percentage of companies reporting slower deliveries, the volume of newspapers' classified advertising, and the unemployment rate.

These measures are used by business firms to get a general picture of where the nation is headed—into a recession or into boom times. For example, sales of Whirlpool home freezers is tied to whether consumers have jobs and money to spend. So Whirlpool follows barometers like length of the average work week and the unemployment rate very carefully.

Judgmental Methods

Judgmental forecasts rely on the forecaster's subjective interpretation of the future. Usually these forecasts are based on a combination of past experience, hunches, "inside" information, and educated guesses. A somewhat more formal method is *lost-horse forecasting*. This technique is based on a common-sense procedure for finding a lost horse. To find the horse, you would go to the last place it was seen. Then you would assess the factors determining where it went next (hunger might have driven it to the hayfield; thirst might have driven it to the river; and so on). Finally you would proceed in that direction to find it.

How would this work for a business firm? Suppose that a manager in a firm that manufactures tennis rackets wants to forecast sales for 1982. He would first go to the last known sales figures—those for 1981. Next he would identify the factors determining 1982 sales and their probable effects (increased cost of living will tend to decrease racket sales; the longer life of metal rackets will decrease replacement sales; and so on). And then he would forecast 1982 sales by estimating the net dollar effect of these changes on the 1981 sales figures.

Economic Indicators: Smokestacks, Turtles, Brooms, and Waiters

Steelmaker Andrew Carnegie had his own method of forecasting steel orders. He would stand on a hill overlooking Pittsburgh and count the number of smokestacks belching smoke.[3]

If you think this technique was a bit unconventional, consider some of these modern economic indicators:

- THE SUPER BOWL   If the NFL wins, the stock market will go up the following December; if the AFL wins, stocks will go down.
- ARKANSAS TURTLES   If the turtles crossing the roads walk *away* from the creeks, a wet, prosperous growing season will follow. If they move *toward* the creeks, the state is headed for drought.
- MOPS AND BROOMS   People buy them when they have money and postpone them when they don't.
- GREETING CARDS   These sales move opposite to the state of the economy. When times are good, people send a gift and a cheap card. When times are tough, they send no gift but a more lavish, $1 to $5 card.
- WAITERS   When times are bad, waiters are on their best behavior. When times are good, they're ruder.

Polish Your Crystal Ball

Large corporations need to know when major technological breakthroughs are likely, so that they can use the new technology. Compare your ability to forecast technological breakthroughs with that of the experts in Delphi surveys, as defined in the text. Note the year you think each of the following events will occur:

1. Reliable weather forecasts.
2. Production of 20 percent of the world's food by ocean farming.
3. Growth of new organs and limbs through biochemical stimulation.
4. Use of telepathy and ESP in communications.

The estimates of a previous panel of experts can be found in Figure 4–5 on page 96. (Daggers indicate the estimates that are to be compared to your own.) The experts were polled in 1963, and their forecasts were imperfect. For examples of these missed forecasts, see the text.

Extrapolation: Predicting More People

Extrapolation extends past trends into the future. Suppose you had wanted in early 1978 to forecast the U.S. population for 1978 and 1979. You might have used data from 1968 to 1977. Fit a straight line to the past data by eye (although more elaborate statistical methods are available), as shown on the right. Then extend the line to 1978 and 1979, marking the two points with black dots. In this case, the forecasting procedure would have worked quite well—the circled X's mark the actual population.

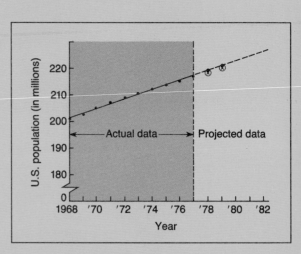

Statistical Methods

Most statistical forecasting techniques are based on extending past trends into the future. One such technique, *extrapolation,* can be very direct. Assume, for example, you know that sales for your company rose about $8 million a year for every year from 1961 to 1981. You might conclude, therefore, that 1982 sales will be $8 million higher than they were in 1981. Extrapolation usually involves fitting a straight line to past data and extending the line into the future (see box at bottom of opposite page).

Surveys

Do you want to know what people think of your new haircut? Ask them. This is just what political candidates, consumer groups, and businesses do whenever they want to find out how the public will react to such diverse things as reinstatement of the draft, a new stoplight on a residential corner, or blue toothpaste.

The *Delphi method,* now regularly used by more than 100 large corporations, is a forecasting technique that asks experts what they think. It gets its name from the ancient Greek oracle at Delphi who was supposed to see into the future. Here is how it works:

1. A panel of experts from inside and outside the organization is assembled. Each person is asked to prepare an anonymous estimate (often by mail) of the probable date or value of a future event. For example, the McDonnel-Douglas Corporation asked for estimates of when air cargo revenues would equal airline passenger revenues.
2. Each panelist is given a summary of the panel's views. Then he or she is asked to make a second, still anonymous, estimate based on the information and reasons given in the summary.
3. After the process in step 2 is repeated one or more times, a final summary is made. By this time, bias is compensated for and extreme estimates are removed. In the McDonnel-Douglas case, for example, aerospace experts were found to forecast earlier dates than the company's own executives.

A major advantage of this type of survey is the anonymity. The expert does not have to defend his or her own views or feel obligated to agree with a supervisor's estimate. Figure 4–5 gives some examples of the type of future events experts are asked to predict, the estimates they come up with, and their accuracy. This figure shows that the Delphi forecasters missed the mark on

FIGURE 4-5
Delphi Survey of Scientific Breakthroughs.

BREAKTHROUGH	PROJECTED YEAR		
	Opinion of one-quarter of panel*	Opinion of half of panel*	Opinion of three-quarters of panel*
Economical desalting of sea water	1964	1970	1980
Automated language translators	1968	1972	1976
Reliable weather forecasts†	1972	1975	1988
Economical ocean-floor mining (other than offshore drilling)	1980	1989	2000
Limited weather control	1987	1990	2000
Production of 20 percent of the world's food by ocean farming†	2000	2000	2017
Growth of new organs and limbs through biochemical stimulation†	1995	2007	2040
Use of drugs to raise intelligence levels	1984	2012	2050
Use of telepathy and ESP in communications†	2040	3000+	3000+

* Projecting the most rapid breakthrough in this area.
† The breakthroughs you were asked to estimate in the box "Polish Your Crystal Ball."
Source: Adapted from *Business Week* by special permission. © 1970 by McGraw-Hill, Inc.

two events that should have occurred by now: while technical breakthroughs have been made, the economic large-scale desalting of sea water and effective automated language translators probably aren't due until at least the mid-1980s. And perhaps your estimate as to when we will have reliable weather forecasts or use telepathy and ESP in communications is as good as the experts'.

Controlled experiments indicate that results obtained by the Delphi method are useful, though certainly not perfect. But no attempt to forecast the future is perfect. Even futurist Alvin Toffler, in his 1970 best-seller *Future Shock*, completely overlooked the energy crisis, for example.

Designing an Action Program

Once objectives have been set and the future assessed, the final step in the planning process is to design a program of action.

At Fotomat Corporation the future looked pretty bleak, and management concluded that it needed to come up with something besides film processing to sell from its yellow-roofed kiosks. But what? They had already tried—and failed with—shoe repair, key cutting, and instant printing services. The new gamble: videotape. Fotomat managers developed a three-part action program based on their faith in the future of videotape: (1) provide a service for transferring home slides and movies onto videotape; (2) sell discount-priced blank videotapes; and (3) rent and sell prerecorded videotapes of movies, golf and tennis lessons, and other kinds of programming.

Figure 4–6 is a graph showing Fotomat's past, present, and future situation. Will the Fotomat plan prove successful? In 1980, Fotomat started its action program by running newspaper ads and radio commercials promoting the new service; you should be able to see the results for yourself by 1983.

Action programs are not arrived at casually. They result from carefully designed procedures, such as strategic and tactical planning and implementation through scientific management and Gantt charts. These are discussed in the following sections.

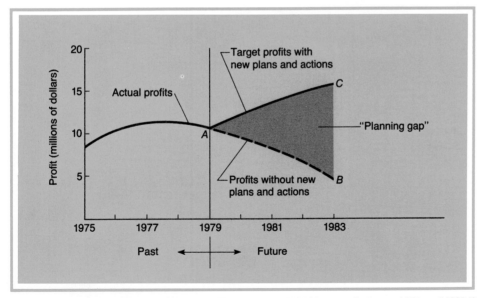

FIGURE 4–6
The Situation Facing Fotomat in 1979.

The "planning gap" shows the difference between what would happen between 1979 and 1983 if trends continued and Fotomat took no action (dotted line AB) versus Fotomat's planned target (solid line AC) by using new plans and actions.

Superman lands at Fotomat!

"© D. C. Comics, Inc."

Great Caesar's Ghost!

Superman, disguised as Clark Kent, mild-mannered reporter for a great metropolitan newspaper, makes a spectacular new addition to our Fotomat Drive-Thru Movie videocassette collection. Along with seven other terrific new motion picture titles, including *Grease* and *Foul Play.*

And this is just one more step in our shameless quest to make Fotomat the best, most complete, most affordable, most convenient source for all your video entertainment.

Just check out all these great titles:

SUPERMAN
One of the most spectacular movies ever made, starring Marlon Brando as Jor-El and introducing Christopher Reeve as the Man of Steel. After seeing this extraordinary film epic, you really will believe that a man can fly...as well as rescue speeding trains, hold up the San Andreas fault and defeat the archvillain of Metropolis, Lex Luthor. Jack Kroll, Newsweek, called *Superman* "...A mass entertainment of high class and energy ...a major feat in filmmaking."
Beta #B0295 VHS #V0295   For purchase only — $6995

GREASE
Travolta's back and Fotomat's got him! This film version of the international smash hit play has all the pegged pants, poodle skirts, chopped Chevies and ramalama-ding-dongs a '50's fanatic could ask for. A rousing and revealing look at a simpler decade... the age of rock 'n' roll.
Beta #B0005 VHS #V0005   Rent — $1395 Purchase — $6995

FOUL PLAY
Goldie Hawn teams with movie industry newcomer Chevy Chase in a zany comedy that'll have you cheering the villain and booing the hero...or is it the other

way around? Charles Champlin, L.A. Times, called it "A celebration of the movies the way they used to make them...a vividly adventurous romantic comedy."
Beta #B0009 VHS #V0009   Rent — $1395 Purchase — $6995

THE IN-LAWS
Peter Falk and Alan Arkin are both very funny fellows. Put them together in the same movie, with at least 27 bizarre plot twists, and you have what Gene Shalit of NBC TV hailed as "one of the funniest films in years."
Beta #B0291 VHS #V0291   For purchase only — $5995

OLIVER'S STORY
A sensitive and moving continuation of the phenomenally successful *Love Story.* Director John Korty guides the tenuous romance between the bereaved Oliver Barrett IV (Ryan O'Neal) and the shy, recently-divorced Marcie Bonwit (Candice Bergen) with a gentle and optimistic hand.
Beta #B0229 VHS #V0229   Rent — $995 Purchase — $5995

KING OF THE GYPSIES
"A remarkable introduction to...probably the most exotic surviving subculture within the American diversity." So said Charles Champlin of this film which, much like its cinematic predecessor, *The Godfather,* deals with three generations of a violent family. A gypsy family.
Beta #B0227 VHS #V0227   Rent — $995 Purchase — $5995

THE BUGS BUNNY/ ROAD RUNNER MOVIE
A real collector's anthology of classic Warner Bros. cartoons, starring the likes of Bugs Bunny, Wile E. Coyote, the Road Runner, Daffy Duck, Porky Pig, Elmer Fudd, Pepe Le Pew. And that's not all, folks! There's even some all-new animation never before seen!
Beta #B0293 VHS #V0293   For purchase only — $4995

WATERSHIP DOWN
Watership Down, named Time Magazine's Family Movie of the Year for 1978, is an exciting and moving animated allegory of hope, courage and the search for personal freedom. "A touching, sophisticated and ultimately powerful piece of adult film making."—Rex Reed
Beta #B0311 VHS #V0311   Rent — $995 Purchase — $4995

Pick a Flick.
You can order one of our new movies right from this ad by calling our toll-free video line: **800-325-1111**. (In Missouri, call 800-392-1717.) Order the title you want from the Fotomat operator. Then just pick it up (usually the very next day) at your convenient Fotomat Store. You can pay with Visa, Master Charge, or, if you prefer, cash. And you can keep your movie for five days.

When you order, be sure to ask the operator to send you our free Fotomat Drive-Thru Movie Guide. It has all our other title listings and a complete explanation of our service. Or pick up a Guide at the convenient Drive-Thru Movie box office: your Fotomat Store.

Also appearing at Fotomat.
In addition to Drive-Thru Movies, we're proud to present the best of the brand-name blank videocassettes. In both VHS and Beta formats. At low Fotomat prices.

And our state-of-the-art Videocassette Transfer Service can transfer your home movies and slides to convenient, compact, easy-to-handle, easy-to-watch videocassettes.

For a free Videocassette Transfer Kit, with complete details and ordering instructions, call our toll-free 800 number. Or pick up a kit at the best place yet devised to meet your video needs.

The Fotomat Store.

Fotomat Drive-Thru Movies.™

Strategic and Tactical Planning

Strategic planning means formulating plans to achieve a combination of organizational goals over a long-range period of time—at least two years. A strategic plan by Exxon in the 1960s resulted in one of that corporation's most significant decisions.[4] Here's how it happened:

1. SETTING OBJECTIVES   In 1960, Exxon set a key company objective: to maintain a continuous supply of crude oil, from which gasoline and other petroleum products could be refined.

Fotomat: Planning for the Future

Fotomat Corporation had real troubles. By the late 1970s its 3,800 yellow-roofed photo-finishing kiosks scattered across the country were facing rising costs and reduced sales volume. Profits were falling. Fotomat executives had an answer: squeeze a second business into the tiny huts. But which business? They tried everything from selling pantyhose to key cutting without success. In 1979 Fotomat put a new plan into operation that focused on videotape (see text). But this plan presented both great opportunities and dangers for Fotomat.

The Opportunities

Selling discount-priced videotapes and transferring home movies and slides to videotape were a minor part of the plan. The high-volume, high-profit goal was to rent and sell prerecorded tapes of movies and of golf or tennis lessons. The price for renting a movie for 48 hours was set at $10 to $12; for buying it, $50 to $70. In 1980 Americans owned more than one million videotape recorders, and Fotomat figured that each owner would spend $100 or more annually on tapes, $75 of it on prerecorded ones. That means an annual tape market of over $100 million, of which Fotomat hopes to capture 20 percent—$20 million its first full year.

The Dangers

But of course this new venture is not without risks. Although the choice kiosk locations have been taken, Fotomat plans to open about 300 new huts per year. And photo-finishing sales per kiosk have been falling for several years. To boost sales, Fotomat increased its advertising budget by 55 percent, got $12.5 million in financing from a Japanese filmmaker, and sought new outlets in store-front locations.

Will the energy crisis cause sales of videotape recorders to grow dramatically as people save gas by relying on home entertainment? Or might a recession cut demand for videotapes? The drawback is the requirement that consumers must order prerecorded tapes from a catalog and pick them up on a specified day.

"I'm leery of anything that asks consumers to do forward thinking," one financial analyst told *Business Week* magazine.[5]

Still, Fotomat believes its picture of the future has helped it find the right "second business" for the ailing kiosks.

2. ASSESSING THE FUTURE   At that time, the company faced what seemed to be a minor problem, too much oil on the market. However, Exxon saw major trouble in the future: with the demand for oil outrunning new oil discoveries, oil would become scarce, enabling oil-producing countries in the Middle East to be able to restrict the oil supply and raise consumer prices.

3. DESIGNING AN ACTION PROGRAM   Exxon's top management developed a logical but tremendously expensive program of action: an immediate $700 million search for oil outside the Middle East. This strategic plan was well worth its cost: new sources were found that today provide Exxon with a continuing supply of oil.

Tactical planning means making plans to achieve organizational sub-goals over a shorter period of time, usually less than two years. Examples include weekly or monthly plans for an entire company, for specific departments or plants, or for particular projects. Tactical plans must dovetail with strategic plans. For example, the success of a strategic plan to open a new shopping center depends on the success of each of a number of tactical plans, such as making financial arrangements, choosing a site, selecting an architect and builder, and selling space to store owners.

Management develops *guidelines* to help people in the organization achieve their plans more quickly, easily, and consistently. These guidelines are called policies, practices, procedures, or rules, depending on their importance and on the strictness with which they are to be followed. Policies generally are unwritten understandings about "the way things are done here," whereas rules are precise statements about specific situations. Practices and procedures fall between these two extremes.

Implementation Through Scientific Management

Scientific management is a systematic approach for implementing plans. It seeks to increase productivity through careful planning and execution. The four key principles of scientific management, developed by Frank Gilbreth to increase the output of bricklayers, are listed below. The box, "How to Increase a Bricklayer's Output," describes how he applied these principles.

1. *Develop the best method.* Analyze each job to find the best way to do it. Then set a pay standard for average performance and a pay incentive for work beyond the average. For instance, if an average bricklayer can lay 150 bricks an hour, the pay might be set at $15 an hour (based on a

rate of 10 cents a brick). Thus, workers who lay 200 bricks an hour would receive $20.

2. *Select workers well.* Managers should find the right workers. Bricklayers might be screened for manual dexterity and strength, for example.

3. *Train workers to use the best method.* Workers must specialize and collaborate. Under Gilbreth's plan, some were trained to lay bricks, others to carry and stack them properly. Cooperation was encouraged by tying brickcarriers' pay to the number of bricks laid by the bricklayers they served.

4. *Separate planning and preparation from the execution of the task.* To promote efficiency, managers do the planning and workers carry out the plans.

Scientific management was devised to reduce wasted effort, develop standards of performance, train workers more efficiently, achieve specialization, and provide for someone other than the worker to do the planning. Scientific management has been responsible for dramatic productivity improvement—and for some worker dissatisfaction.

How to Increase a Bricklayer's Output

While working as a bricklayer's apprentice, Frank Gilbreth noticed that experienced bricklayers laid bricks in many different ways. He reasoned that since bricklaying dated back to biblical times, trial and error should have produced a "best method" for laying bricks. But there seemed to be no best method—yet. So Gilbreth first analyzed each phase of the bricklaying process: the bricklayer, the tools, the physical positions of the bricklayer and the bricks to be laid, how the worker selected the bricks to be used, and the mortar. Then he developed his own system using the best elements. For example, he designed a scaffold that placed the bricklayer, the bricks, and the mortar at three different levels for the greatest efficiency. He also assigned a separate worker to carry the bricks to the bricklayers and place each brick with its best face up, saving the time usually spent on this job by the bricklayer.

As a result of Gilbreth's changes, the number of movements made by a bricklayer decreased from 18 to 5, and individual output increased from 120 to 250 bricks per hour. Gilbreth's scientific approach accomplished in several weeks what the trial-and-error method had failed to achieve in some 2,000 years.[6]

Implementation Through Gantt Charts

Implementing a program of action involves (1) identifying the main tasks and the time required to complete them and (2) arranging the activities to meet the deadline.

Suppose, for example, that three college students are asked to do a term project on the problem "How can the college increase attendance at home football games?" And suppose further that the instructor limits the project in the following ways:

1. The project must involve a mail survey of the attitudes of a sample of students.
2. It must be submitted by the end of the 11-week quarter.

To begin the assignment the students first need to identify all the tasks they need to perform. Then they must estimate the time they can reasonably allot to each one. As shown in Figure 4–7 it would take the students 15 weeks to complete the project if they did all the tasks one by one. So, to complete it in 11 weeks, the students must work on different parts at the same time, and some activities must be independent enough to overlap. This requires specialization and cooperation. Suppose that of the three students (A, B, and C), only student C can type. Then, student A might assume the task of constructing questionnaires and selecting samples, and student B might tabulate the

FIGURE 4–7
Term Project Tasks.

TASK	TIME (in weeks)
1. Construct and test a rough-draft questionnaire for clarity (in person, not by mail) on friends.	2
2. Type and mimeograph a final questionnaire.	2
3. Randomly select the names of 200 students from the school directory.	1
4. Address and stamp envelopes; mail questionnaires.	1
5. Collect returned questionnaires.	3
6. Tabulate data from returned questionnaires.	2
7. Write final report.	3
8. Type and submit final report.	1
Total time necessary to complete all activities:	15

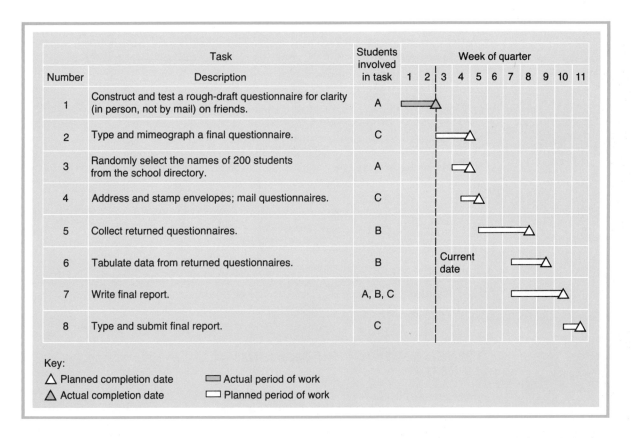

Task		Students involved in task	Week of quarter
Number	Description		1 2 3 4 5 6 7 8 9 10 11
1	Construct and test a rough-draft questionnaire for clarity (in person, not by mail) on friends.	A	
2	Type and mimeograph a final questionnaire.	C	
3	Randomly select the names of 200 students from the school directory.	A	
4	Address and stamp envelopes; mail questionnaires.	C	
5	Collect returned questionnaires.	B	
6	Tabulate data from returned questionnaires.	B	Current date
7	Write final report.	A, B, C	
8	Type and submit final report.	C	

Key:
△ Planned completion date   ⬜ Actual period of work
△ Actual completion date   ⬜ Planned period of work

FIGURE 4–8
Gantt Chart
for Term Project.

data. This division of labor allows each student to concentrate on and become expert in one area. But they should also cooperate. Student C might help A and B in the beginning and A and B might help C later on. Sharing tasks is a good way to learn new skills.

The students must also figure out which activities can be done concurrently to save time. Referring back to Figure 4–7, you can see that task 2 must be completed before task 4. However, task 3 might easily be done before, at the same time as, or after task 2. So, task 3 is independent of task 2, and both could be done at the same time by different students.

Scheduling management and production activities—from a term project to a manned space launch—can be done efficiently with **Gantt charts.** Figure 4–8, a Gantt chart for the class project, shows how the concurrent work on several tasks enables the project to be finished on time. Developed by Henry L. Gantt, this method for scheduling work is the basis for most scheduling techniques used today, including elaborate computerized methods. Scheduling a program of action—perhaps with the help of a Gantt chart—does three things: (1) it translates plans into specific, understandable, tasks; (2) it forces planners to distinguish sequential from concurrent tasks, aiding efficiency; and (3) it forces people to allot their time as needed to specific tasks (otherwise, people tend to concentrate on the tasks they prefer and neglect the others).

HOW MANAGERS DECIDE

Decision making is the most important of all managerial activities. From first-line supervisors to the chairman of the board, decisions are made constantly about all aspects of the organization's life. **Decision making** is the act of consciously choosing from among alternatives. But making good decisions is not a simple thing. How do managers go about the task of making decisions to solve problems?

Steps to Effective Decisions: DECIDE

No magic formula exists that assures a good solution to all problems all the time. But managers often can improve their ability to make decisions by using a formal, systematic series of steps. Those who do not use a system—and there are many who do not—often make poor decisions. One such system is based on the word DECIDE, which is used as an acronym, where each letter represents a different step of the decision-making process. Figure 4–9 shows what each letter stands for, and each is described more fully below using our earlier example of Fotomat.

D—Define the Problem Precisely
Identify the objectives to be achieved, the constraints placed on solving the problem (for example, its priority and the time and money available), and the measure by which its success can be judged. This measure is then used in choosing the best alternative and, later, for evaluating the choice.

Fotomat managers defined their problem as the need to choose a new item or items to increase profits. Constraints included limited space in the 3,800 kiosks, the need for speed, and limited money to spend. The measure of success is the profit targets for 1980–1983, as shown in Figure 4–6.

E—Enumerate Two Groups of Decision Factors
First, identify all the realistic alternatives that you can control. (For Fotomat, these are the products that might realistically be sold in a kiosk: pantyhose, instant printing services, videotapes, and so forth.) Second, note the important factors that are beyond your control. (In Fotomat's case, the amount of competition and consumers' willingness and ability to purchase videotape machines are surely crucial and relatively uncontrollable factors.)

C—Collect Relevant Information
Sometimes relevant information may be found quickly and easily, for instance by making a telephone call or examining existing reports. At other times, obtaining such information may be expensive and time-consuming—surveying hundreds of consumers about their reactions to a product, for example. (Fotomat has done and is doing extensive research on consumer reactions to their video items.)

I—Identify the Best Alternative
First, summarize and condense the collected information. Then find the *solution,* the alternative that best meets the measure of success. (Fotomat's early research indicated that pantyhose took up too much space and instant printing wasn't strongly desired by consumers. Their later research indicated that videotape was the best bet.)

D—Develop and Implement a Detailed Plan
This may involve obtaining approval for the plan. And when the plan is complex, management controls must be set up to ensure that it is fully implemented. (The details of Fotomat's plan is known only to its key managers.)

E—Evaluate the Decision
Match objectives to the measure of success determined in step 1. (Fotomat's success or failure will not be known with certainty until its 1983 profits are in.)

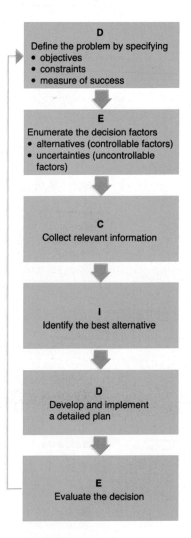

FIGURE 4-9
The DECIDE Process: Six Steps to More Effective Decisions.

Chapter Review & Applications

Key Points to Remember

1. Management may be viewed both as a group of people and as a process.
2. Four functions of management are planning, organizing, leading, and controlling.
3. Planning involves three key steps: setting objectives, assessing the future, and designing a program of action.
4. In setting objectives, management must help employees realize that they can achieve personal goals by working toward organizational goals.
5. Making business decisions has become more and more expensive. Therefore, more emphasis is now placed on assessing the future. Examples of business forecasting techniques are lost-horse forecasting, extrapolation, and the Delphi method.
6. Management can make plans more successful and meaningful to subordinates by translating them into a program of action with scientific management and by using a Gantt chart.
7. Strategic planning normally involves planning to achieve organizational goals over two years or more. Tactical planning involves low-level objectives and a shorter time period.
8. Decision making is more effective if a systematic approach, such as DECIDE, is used.

Questions for Discussion

1. List four or five personal goals that you have set for yourself. Which goals would be most consistent with and most in conflict with (a) one another; (b) the organizational goals of a large corporation you might work for; and (c) being in business for yourself?
2. "Clear statements of policy make it easier to delegate decisions to lower levels in the organization." Explain this statement and discuss why it is desirable to delegate responsibility for some decisions.

3. It was mentioned in the chapter that scientific management, although responsible for dramatic improvements in efficiency and productivity, also causes some worker dissatisfaction. What do you think is the reason for this dissatisfaction? How would you, as a manager, improve the problem?
4. In Figure 4–8, it was shown that writing the final report of the class project is begun in the middle of the seventh week. If the schedule is to be completed as planned, what parts of the report should be written this early and what parts must wait?

Short Cases

1. Suppose that from 1970 to 1980 car sales by one manufacturer rose by an average of 20,000 units per year. In 1980, total domestic sales were 800,000 units.
   (a) Using extrapolation, estimate car sales for 1990. What difficulties do you find in this estimation method?
   (b) What other estimation methods might be considered?
2. Frank Gilbreth studied the discrete movements of individual workers. From these observations he designed more efficient work methods and increased worker productivity. Lillian Gilbreth extended these concepts to activities in the home, such as washing dishes, mowing grass, and making home repairs. Suppose you have written a term paper and your task now is to cite your sources in an appendix. You have already assembled all the appropriate magazines and books on your subject.
   (a) Diagram the best way to lay out the materials (references, writing paper, and so on) on your desk so as to economize your motions and to reduce the problem of misplacing reference books and papers.
   (b) What adjustments could you make in your planning and work layout to reduce the possibility of having to make repeated trips to the library to collect additional information?

A Critical Business Decision

—made by Bill Blanck and Grant Evanson of Jostens, Inc.

The Situation

Jostens, the nation's leading manufacturer of year-books and class rings for high schools and colleges, knows how Mark Twain must have felt. For returning home one day, he found the town mourning his death by drowning. (Whereupon Twain observed: "The reports of my death are greatly exaggerated.")

For almost a decade, financial analysts outside Jostens have been predicting near-drowning for the company because demographic trends seemed to be against its success. High-school enrollments started leveling off in the early 1970s, peaked at about 15 million in 1978, and will decline by about 2.8 percent a year during the first half of the 1980s.

So what has happened? Did Jostens' sales and profits "drown" with the declining enrollments? No way. Since 1974 both its sales and profits have spurted ahead by more than 15 percent a year. In fact, Jostens is one of only eleven companies traded on the New York Stock Exchange that have had twenty-two consecutive years of increases in sales and profits. *Business Week*[7] observes that "Jostens has been a textbook example of how a business can cope with fundamental demographic changes." One of Jostens' secrets: precise planning and scheduling.

The Decision

It is now early 1980. Plans are needed by the year-book product area of Jostens' yearbook division. Bill Blanck, product manager, and Grant Evanson, operations manager, are developing plans for this area's main product—high-school and college yearbooks. Their problem: to try to reach all possible students who might want to buy a school's yearbook and then to get it printed and into the students' hands when wanted.

This is critical. Their product area has a professional sales force—many of them former teachers—of 300 people. They call on most grade schools, junior and senior high schools, colleges, and vocational-technical schools in the nation at least once a year. But most sales come from high schools and colleges.

Even when a school signs a contract with Jostens, the planning problems are only starting. Bill Blanck's concern is how the school's yearbook staff can sell the yearbook to each student. From one year to the next there is almost a complete turnover among yearbook staff members. So selling experience gained by the previous year's staff is largely gone. Clearly, the staff needs an effective, straight-forward program to sell yearbooks to the students.

Grant Evanson knows that his problems start where Blanck's end: with the signed student order for a yearbook. As operations manager, Evanson is charged with seeing that the yearbooks get printed correctly and delivered when the students want them. Because this is usually the month right before graduation, Evanson's scheduling tasks are critical to Jostens' success. To print more than five million yearbooks annually, he utilizes printing plants at four regional locations: Topeka, Kansas (the only location that also prints covers); Visalia, California; Clarksville, Tennessee; and State College, Pennsylvania.

Jostens' experience has shown that all of the typesetting and art work going into a school's year-book can't be dropped on its plants simultaneously. So Evanson concludes that he, too, should develop a system to help new yearbook staffs do the planning, scheduling, and delivery of yearbook copy that will enable Jostens' printing plants to meet their deadlines.

Questions

1. What can Bill Blanck do to help a yearbook staff reach and sell its yearbooks to the school's students?
2. What kind of system can Grant Evanson develop to help a yearbook staff plan and schedule the delivery of its copy so Jostens can meet its printing deadlines for five million yearbooks a year?

Organizing and Staffing

In this chapter you will learn . . .

- **how managers structure the jobs in an organization through organization charts, delegation, and line and staff positions.**
- **about the importance of informal communication in an organization.**
- **some principles of organizing that managers use.**
- **how a firm's human resources (or personnel) department works with managers to select, train, promote, and retire employees.**
- **how to write an effective resume and what steps are involved in getting a new job.**

5

enry Ford started with nothing in 1905. By 1920 he had built the world's largest manufacturing firm. He was a genius at invention and manufacturing. Yet by 1927 his business empire was a shambles. The reason: Ford felt business did not need a structured organization, or even managers. He believed that all a business needed was an owner and some "helpers." He actually fired "helpers" who dared to act as "managers."

Down the road in Michigan, in the early 1920s, Alfred P. Sloan, Jr., realized that the automobile business had become too complex to depend on one person's orders. So he bought a group of small car companies, up for sale because they couldn't compete with Ford, and devised an organization. Each company became a division in his new organization, but each kept authority over its own day-to-day operations. A strong central staff developed forecasts against which the performance of each division was measured. Within five years, Sloan's firm became the world's leading automobile manufacturer, a position it still holds today. The firm is General Motors.[1]

Sloan and General Motors pioneered many of the organization concepts now used throughout industry. These will be discussed in the first half of this chapter. The last half will deal with the related concepts of staffing and personnel—or human resource—management.

HOW TO ORGANIZE A BUSINESS

Organizations, as their name implies, must be organized. This is true of the local pizza place, your college, General Motors, or the federal government. But no organization organizes itself. Managers must do it. So the **organizing** function of management involves *structuring the jobs and placing qualified people in them*. This enables organizations to make plans and achieve their objectives. As an organization grows and hires more people, it becomes more complex. And jobs must generally be more formally structured.

Letting you face typical organizational problems in your own business will show the concepts of structure, delegation, line and staff positions, and formal and informal organizations.

Structure It

Suppose you decide to open a bookstore near your college to sell used textbooks. Since you have to go to class as well, you hire two college friends, Joan and Stan, to clerk when you're not there. You are clearly the boss since you have taken the financial risk, and you pay your two friends an hourly wage. Your organizational structure at this point is shown in Figure 5–1(a).

After a couple of years you and your friends are ready to graduate. Fortunately, your store is wildly successful. You have added new textbooks to your stock as well as popular paperbacks and hardcover books (trade books). You've expanded your store space and hired six new clerks. Four of these employees report to Joan (because textbook sales are growing faster than

FIGURE 5–1
A Simple (a) and More Complex (b)
Organizational Structure for a Growing College Bookstore.

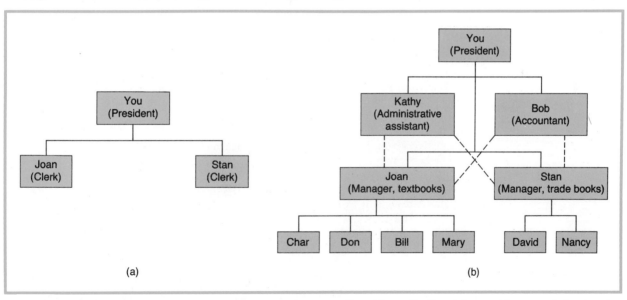

The solid lines indicate line positions; the dotted lines show staff positions. (Staff and line positions are defined and discussed on page 115.)

trade-book sales) and two report to Stan. You've also hired an administrative assistant, Kathy, and a part-time accountant, Bob. Your new organizational structure is shown in Figure 5–1(b).

Delegate

The first few months in business you found it easy to supervise four or five employees reporting directly to you. But you found this wouldn't work for ten subordinates. You were spending so much time giving directions that you didn't have enough time for your other management duties. So you assigned part of your activities to your two managers, your accountant, and your administrative assistant. Assigning duties to subordinates in this way is **delegation.**

Ten Terrific Companies to Work For . . . and Why

The ten best U.S. companies to work for, according to *Money* magazine's survey of executive recruiting firms,[2] are:

1. IBM
2. Procter and Gamble
3. Eastman Kodak
4. Xerox
5. 3M

6. General Electric
7. Weyerhaeuser
8. Cummins Engine
9. DuPont
10. J.C. Penney

Why? Recruiting firms, who find key executives for companies, gave reasons like these: The best companies have room for different kinds of people with different skills and working styles. They have a commitment to excellence—in their products, research, marketing, management, and people. IBM, for example, wants to be best at everything it does, and Procter and Gamble people believe their products are better than others. And they are sensitive to human problems—employees are given real responsibility and real work. 3M, for example, promotes from within so much that it's been decades since an outsider got a high-level job there.

How can you identify firms that are especially bad to work for? Recruiters say beware of companies with a high turnover rate; a management that is rigid, unsure of itself, or many-layered; and companies that are family-owned or run by an autocrat.

Joan, your textbook manager, now has the responsibility for running the textbook department. **Responsibility** is the obligation to perform delegated duties. For your delegation to work, Joan's responsibility must be enhanced by giving her **authority,** the right and power to issue orders. For example, Joan cannot be held responsible for the textbook department's performance unless she is given the authority to make decisions and give orders to her four subordinates. The proper blend of responsibility and authority makes a person **accountable,** answerable for results.

There is a management saying that "a manager can delegate the authority but not the ultimate responsibility and accountability for results." The president of the United States may delegate the authority for the country's military preparedness to the secretary of defense, but the nation ultimately holds the president responsible and accountable. Harry Truman understood this. When he was president, he had a sign on his desk that read, "The buck stops here."

In large companies, delegation is complicated, as you can see from the organization chart shown in Figure 5–2. This one is for The Toro Company, which manufactures lawn mowers, snow throwers, and irrigation systems both for consumers and for golf courses and parks. The company includes the chart in the employee handbook, with the name, mailing address, and phone number of everyone listed so that employees can figure out who to talk to to get a job done. As complete as Toro's organization chart may appear, it has been considerably simplified here. It is complete at the level of the president and above, but only the subordinate units reporting to the "Group Vice President, Outdoor Power Equipment Group" and the "Vice President, Marketing and Sales" are shown in detail.

At Toro, the chairman of the board is also the chief executive officer. He sets the long-range goals. Reporting to him in a line position (explained below) is the president and chief operating officer (who is responsible for day-to-day operations), two key staff senior vice presidents, and one director. Also reporting to him are three group vice presidents, with line responsibility for their product groups, and one vice president for customer relations, a staff position (also explained below). This entire group can be considered top management because each of the group vice presidents has the responsibility of a president in a smaller firm.

Key middle-management positions in the outdoor power equipment group are also shown in Figure 5–2. Although the international group and the irrigation group are not shown, they have similar structures.

First-line sales management, also shown in Figure 5–2, includes six sales managers, each responsible for a specific geographic district. Sales representatives report to each of them. (The Coca-Cola bottling industry is another example of delegating responsibilities on a geographic basis. See the color insert at the end of the text for details.)

FIGURE 5–2
Organization Chart of The Toro Company.

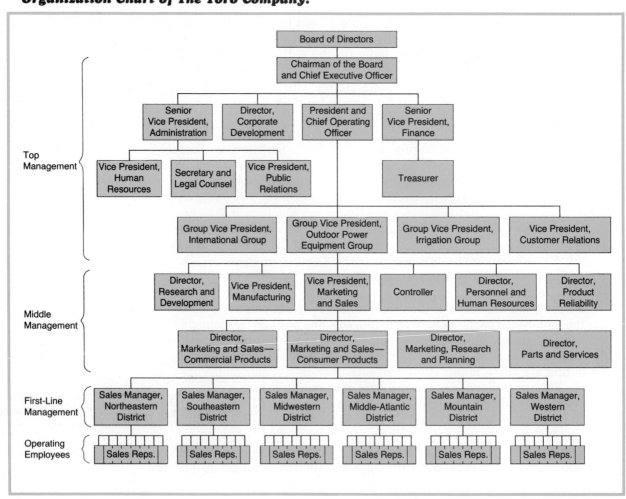

Include Both Line and Staff Positions

The terms *line* and *staff,* mentioned above, refer to organization structures and also to positions in an organization.

The simplest type of formal business organization used by managers is **line organization.** This means that each position has direct authority over the position below it, indicated on an organization chart by boxes connected with solid lines. Widely used in small businesses, this organizational structure is rarely found in medium-sized or large companies. Your bookstore in Figure 5–1(a) is a line organization.

Line organization has three advantages: simplicity, clear-cut division of authority, and quick decision-making ability. However, it has two major disadvantages: there are no advisory specialists and there is too much reliance on high-level managers. As the bookstore owner in Figure 5–1(a), you were buyer, accountant, advertising specialist, and so on. If you become ill, your bookstore could quickly fail.

Line-and-staff organization was devised to overcome these disadvantages. It supplements the line positions with *staff positions,* which provide advice and special services. Your bookstore accountant in Figure 5–1(b), for example, is in a staff position, connected by a dotted line to the two managers he advises. The dotted line shows an advisory staff relationship, rather than a line one. Bob may warn them that their book inventories seem too large or the wages of their clerks too high, but he does not give direct orders. Your administrative assistant, responsible for advertising, is also in a staff position.

No dotted lines are shown on the Toro organization chart in Figure 5–2, because it would be too complex. So it is hard to distinguish line and staff positions for this organization. (Question 1 at the end of the chapter asks you to try to do so.)

Line and staff differ in their authority and are equally important to managers. **Line authority** is the right to issue orders to lower units. **Staff authority** is advisory to the line structure, with no specific power to issue orders. However, staff members may sometimes be powerful enough to override line authority. When this happens, the resulting conflict between line and staff can cause problems for the firm (see box on next page).

Line functions contribute directly to the organization's primary objective—like buying and selling paperbacks in a bookstore or building microcomputers in an electronics manufacturing firm. Staff functions provide secondary, supportive objectives, such as legal advice to top management or drug counseling to employees. When line functions are performed poorly, the firm's revenue is quickly affected. Poor performance of staff functions ordinarily does not show up until later.

It is often difficult to neatly classify every position into the line or staff category. Where, for example, would you place accounting, finance, and production control? But in terms of achieving organizational goals, categorizing positions is less important than recognizing line versus staff *authority*.

Recognize Both Formal and Informal Organization

Organizations with definite, orderly arrangements of line and staff positions are called **formal organizations.** Even when your bookstore had only two

Conflict Between Line and Staff:

October 3, 1968, was an auspicious occasion for General Motors: at the opening of its gleaming, white, 50-story General Motors Building in midtown Manhattan, board chairman James M. Roche announced that in two years GM would introduce a new subcompact car. This minicar was designed for American tastes and was intended to take the market away from foreign cars. Roche went even further: he predicted that the subcompact—code-named the XP-887—would be priced at the level of the Volkswagen Beetle and have about the same weight.

American consumers were elated. Led by GM, American car makers were finally going to flex their industrial muscle and compete with the foreign imports in the small-car market, according to the account in *On a Clear Day You Can See General Motors.*[3]

Everyone expected GM's Chevrolet division—with its powerful existing line organization anxious to build and sell the new car—to be assigned the XP-887. Not so. General Motors' corporate central staff in its Detroit headquarters building took on the project. It was being developed by people one step removed from the marketplace! Only after development would it be assigned to the Chevrolet line organization to produce and sell.

Troubles arose quickly. The first prototype ran 8 miles on the test track when the front end broke off. So the front end had to be beefed up structurally—which added 20

THE CHAMP
VW's Beetle.

employees and you as boss, it was a formal organization, because the lines of authority were well-defined. In larger organizations, with many employees, it is usually essential to diagram authority relationships in a formal **organization chart** like the one in Figure 5–2.

Besides the formal relationships shown in the organization chart, every organization has a network of personal relationships, known as the **informal organization.** This network is at least as important as the formal organization. In Figure 5–2, for example, all the group vice presidents appear equal. But they probably are not. Although they are equal in *rank,* if one happens to be a golfing partner of the president (the informal organization), he will have more *power* and *authority* than the other vice presidents. Thus, a key decision may be reached on the golf course—long before it ever comes up at a managers' meeting in the office.

GM's XP-887 Subcompact

pounds of weight. Despite advice that overheating problems would occur, the corporate staff insisted an aluminum cylinder block be used.

The car was finally assigned to the Chevrolet line organization, which tried to salvage the now overweight, overpriced prototype by adding bigger tires and new styling features to give the car a luxury motif but adding only $12 to $15 to its cost. The corporate staff vetoed the idea.

At this time, the manned space flights were in progress and marketing research showed that consumers overwhelmingly preferred the name Gemini for the new car. Chevrolet line management recommended this, but corporate staff killed the name and selected a name at the bottom of the "acceptable list"—Vega.

When the Vega got to market in September 1970, it failed by a wide margin to meet chairman Roche's two-year-old promises: it now weighed 382 pounds more than a VW standard Beetle and its price was $311 more. The Vega was literally priced out of its market!

Defective carburetors and burned-out aluminum engines caused later problems for the Vega. It never lived up to GM sales expectations, and it was phased out of production at the end of the 1977 model year—a silent monument to organization problems and line-staff conflict.

THE CHALLENGER
GM's XP-887 (Vega).

ORGANIZATIONAL TIPS FOR MANAGERS

Most successful managers structure jobs systematically. Although there are exceptions, the six principles described below are good organizational tips for managers.[4]

Observe the Unity of Command

The idea of **unity of command** is simple: it means one person, one boss. No member of an organization should report to more than one superior. This avoids the problem of conflicting orders. If you refer back to Figure 5–2, you can see that unity of command is represented by the solid vertical lines. The person in each box reports only to the person in the box above him that he is connected to.

Polaroid: Organizing Without an Organization Chart

"Seldom, if ever, has a large American company so faithfully reflected one man as does Polaroid Corporation," says *Business Week* magazine.[5] The "man": Dr. Edwin H. Land, Polaroid's founder, past board chairman, presently the consulting director of basic research, and 15-percent owner.

Land thrives on informality, so the company has no organization chart. Land is extremely secretive. So is Polaroid. Land works prodigious hours. So do key employees, who are resigned to receiving phone calls from Land at all hours.

When he tackles a project, Land assumes that none of the conventional rules apply—for example, he refused to believe that an inch-thick SX-70 camera could not be built. His leadership style for new projects is "crisis management": concentrating on what he sees as the most critical problem, attending to the most minute details until the problem is solved, then going on to the next problem. This management style works at Polaroid probably because Land sets very high goals, hires talented people whom he pays well, gives them all the authority and responsibility they can handle, and holds them accountable.

Check for Span of Control

The number of people reporting to any one manager represents that manager's **span of control.** A manager should not have too many subordinates. An acceptable span of control is often set at four to eight people. But more people can be supervised effectively if their jobs are routine ones. Look again at Figure 5–2. The director of marketing and sales for consumer products has six sales managers under his span of control. Each sales manager, in turn, has eight sales representatives in his span of control.

Use the Exception Principle

Only unusual, exceptional, nonroutine problems should be referred to high-level managers. Problems should be successively "filtered": the most important problems are handled by the president of the firm, the next most important by the vice presidents, and so on down the organization. That is the **exception principle.** In your bookstore, for example, your two managers schedule the hours of the sales clerks and handle sales problems. Your time is thus freed to think about such long-range plans as financing and expansion.

Apply the Scalar Principle

Known in the military as "chain of command," the **scalar principle** says that authority and responsibility should flow in a continuous line from the highest person in the organization to the lowest person. The scalar principle ensures that each manager's control over his or her area remains intact. If, for example, the controller of the outdoor power equipment group (shown in Figure 5–2) reported directly to the senior vice president of finance, the authority and responsibility of her group vice president would be undermined.

Group into Departments

Departments are formed in an organization when people and activities have similar functions, the same objectives, or a need to be coordinated. They are often organized on the basis of geography, product, function, or customer, or on a combination of these bases. Salespeople in a nationwide computer company, for example, can be grouped by the region they serve (geography), the kinds of computers they sell (product), or the type of firms they sell to, such as retailing or manufacturing (customer). The Toro Company's sales force in Figure 5–2 is grouped by geography; the group vice presidents are organized by function. Your two bookstore managers are grouped by product—textbooks and trade books.

Decentralize

Decentralization means helping lower organizational units set goals and then giving them the responsibility and authority to meet these goals. De-

The Need for Personal Chemistry: Going Beyond Organization Charts

Billy Martin and Reggie Jackson don't have it. Anwar Sadat and Menachem Begin do. The "personal chemistry" between two people can be amazingly important. When Henry Ford II fired Lee Iacocca as the president of Ford Motor Company, he said there'd been "poor body chemistry between us for many years," says *Fortune* magazine.[6]

This personal chemistry is a kind of gut reaction, the way one person feels about another. With participatory management at its height in business now, a lack of "chemistry," especially in top management, can curdle working relationships quickly. People must work well together and feel that their ability and creativity are being recognized.

To encourage good "chemistry," most management experts believe that the chief executive officer of a firm should look for a "C-type," a complementary deputy for his or her own shortcomings. Edgar Bronfman, Seagram's chairman, for example, sees himself mainly as a production man. To fill a professional void in his company, he hired Philip Beckman, a marketing expert from Colgate-Palmolive, to be Seagram's president. Irving Shapiro, DuPont's chief executive officer, is one who invites constructive dissent in personal management relations. "Whoever sits in my chair is fallible," he says. "When mistakes happen, it's because people who knew better didn't speak up."

Formal relationships are what show on organization charts. But it is often the good chemistry—obtained through informal relationships and personal trust—that actually moves organizations forward.

centralizing your bookstore, for example, could mean giving each of your two managers profit goals for their own departments and then allowing them to make the necessary decisions to reach those goals.

In the 1950s, Ralph Cordiner, president of General Electric, decentralized his company into about 100 departments (small steam turbines, major appliances, and so on). Then he measured the success of each department by its profit contribution to the entire company. Cordiner was simply extending the ideas that Alfred Sloan had used to organize General Motors (the example that opened this chapter).

Implementing these six principles cannot guarantee a successful organization. And several of them can sometimes conflict with one another. But they are sound advice for any manager—regardless of the nature of his business.

STAFFING AND HUMAN RESOURCE MANAGEMENT

Andrew Carnegie, a young radical, stepped onto U.S. soil for the first time in 1848. He had a revolutionary faith in "the improvement of mankind." He began working in a cotton mill for $1.20 a week. Later, earning $25 million a year as president of the Carnegie Steel Company, he led the steel industry into its period of greatest expansion.[7]

Carnegie recognized that his most important resource was people. The proof is the epitaph he wrote for himself: "Here lies the man who was able to surround himself with men far cleverer than himself."

Without competent and committed people, brilliant ideas like heart pacemakers and microwave ovens would not become reality. Planning, recruiting, and training new personnel—a company's **human resources**—are the first steps in building a successful company. People are so important that large firms like Toro, for example, have a corporate vice president of human resources responsible for overall personnel planning, and a director of human resources for each of the separate operating groups (see Figure 5–2). These directors are responsible for employment and training, wage and salary administration, benefits, and employee counseling. The managerial task of staffing—including preemployment and postemployment activities—is the subject of the remainder of this chapter.

Your Next Job
Positions in Personnel, Clerical, and Library Science Work

Careers in Personnel Work

Personnel workers fill open positions with competent people. They counsel employees, classify jobs, and develop pay scales—responsibilities that require a general business background and interview skills. Both private industry and government employ personnel workers, but often for different applications. In private business firms, personnel people usually interview and screen job applicants and try to place them in positions where their interests and their skills will be most useful. In government, they often devote more time to classifying jobs and to scoring competitive examinations. A bachelor's degree in business or in personnel administration is preferred, though many personnel workers have been promoted from lower-level jobs. Experienced personnel workers earn about $22,000 a year. With the increasing emphasis on worker needs, the demand for personnel workers is expected to expand rapidly. (*Additional information:* American Society for Personnel Administration, 30 Park Drive, Berea, Ohio 44017.)

Careers in Clerical Work

Secretaries are responsible for the efficient transmission of business information. They answer customer letters, write reports, and do statistical research, as well as type and refer telephone calls. Most employers require a high-school diploma and occasionally some college work. An adequate knowledge of grammar and vocabulary is necessary. Yearly income averages $10,000 for secretaries. Opportunities are expected to increase rapidly despite a greater use of automatic office equipment. **Executive secretaries** work closely with top executives to relieve them of administrative work and assist in routine office procedures. Salaries of executive secretaries range from $12,000 to $25,000 a year. **Office managers** supervise the clerical staff and devise ways to improve office operations, receiving annual salaries from $14,000 to $28,000. (*Addi-tional information:* National Secretaries Assoc., 2440 Pershing Road, Suite G10, Kansas City, Missouri 64108; and State Supervisor of Office Occupations Education, State Department of Education, your state capital.)

Careers in Library Science

Although an assortment of library occupations exist, private industry provides three primary career alternatives: *special librarian, information-science specialist*, and *library technical assistant*. **Special librarians** are often employed by advertising agencies and research laboratories to accumulate and to arrange an organization's information resources. Special librarians also find information or compile bibliographies upon request. **Information-science specialists** perform many of the same functions as special librarians and an additional number of more responsible jobs, including summarizing technical data, preparing computer-programming techniques, and improving microfilm technology. **Library technical assistants** are instructed by professional librarians to operate data-processing and audio-visual equipment and purchase and catalog new books. Special librarians and information-science specialists generally have graduate degrees in library science. Library technical assistants are either high-school graduates who have acquired necessary on-the-job training or community-college graduates who have Associate of Arts degrees in library technology. Yearly incomes varies: professional librarians earn from $10,000 to over $20,000 annually; library technical assistants, about $8,000 to $10,000. The employment outlook for librarians is expected to remain very competitive through the 1980s. Opportunities will be best for those with scientific and technical backgrounds. (*Additional Information:* American Library Association, 50 East Huron Street, Chicago, Illinois 60611; and American Society for Information Science, 1110 16th Street, N.W., Washington, D.C. 20036.)

Staffing—Preemployment

Staffing is the process of selecting, training, promoting, and retiring people. It is done both by the human resources (or personnel) department and by the employee's immediate manager. Its steps, shown in Figure 5–3, include activities both before and after hiring. In the preemployment phase, managers requisition, recruit, and select the employees.

Requisition

To *requisition* personnel means that managers analyze and specify their current and future needs. Toro's top management, for example, might identify a favorable business outlook for next year and conclude that ten new salespeople are needed to staff the field sales offices. Or maybe one of Toro's field sales managers has an opening as a result of a retirement, transfer, promotion, or resignation.

The human resources department and the manager of the future employee then do a *job analysis* and an explicit *job description*. In these they first study what the job involves and then list the tasks the person holding the job should perform. The human resources department and manager may also write a *job specification,* which describes the skills, work experience, and education

FIGURE 5-3
Sequence of Staffing Activities.

needed to perform the job effectively. An example of a combined job description and specifications for a sales representative at Toro appears in Figure 5–4.

Recruit

The human resources department takes the requisition information and begins *recruiting*—a systematic search to fill the firm's personnel requirements. Toro, for example, could fill a job with someone from inside or outside the company. When feasible, management "promotes from within," meaning that a current employee is transferred or promoted into the open position. Toro might fill five of its openings by promoting equipment-service personnel who have an ability to deal well with customers. A policy of promoting from within tends to motivate employees and improve morale.

For the remaining five sales positions, Toro managers decide to recruit from outside the company—from colleges and universities, state and private employment services, and technical institutes. They may also place ads in newspapers and review unsolicited job applications.

The managers' recruiting efforts uncover quite a few applicants, including Chris Davis, a college senior. Chris has just polished his resume, which is shown in Figure 5–5. It includes his personal history, educational background, job experience, and employment goals. On the advice of Henry A. Brown, manager of recruiting and placement at the Pillsbury Company, Chris has also included a section on "potential." He has also analyzed his accomplishments in terms of the job he's applying for. Because he is seeking a career in sales and management, he wants to show that he (1) enjoys people and can lead them; (2) is flexible with changing job requirements; and (3) is highly motivated. If Chris were applying for a computer-programming job, he would have emphasized his electronics experience more.

Select

A generation ago, hiring decisions for many jobs were often based on scant information. Frequently, the data were not even as complete as the descriptions given for the three job applicants in the box "Would You Hire These People?" on page 129. How these "losers" eventually turned out (see the box "Who They Are" on page 130) shows why such brief descriptions are of little use in predicting the job performance of applicants.

Systematic screening of candidates is common today. Poor hiring decisions can be quite expensive: time and money spent training employees are lost if

TORO The Toro Company

APPROVED:

RDM Date 4/20/80
Originator

JNK Date 4/25/80
Human Resources
Department

MLC Date 4/27/80
Group or Corporate
Vice President

JOB DESCRIPTION AND SPECIFICATIONS

POSITION TITLE: SALES REPRESENTATIVE -- CONSUMER PRODUCTS · JOB CODE 14

GROUP OR CORPORATE DEPARTMENT _____ OUTDOOR POWER EQUIPMENT GROUP _____

REPORTS TO: District Sales Manager

SUPERVISES:

MAJOR FUNCTION:

Manage the implementation of company marketing and merchandising programs through the distribution system within his assigned district. To interpret company policies and to assist in assurance of their compliance.

LIST OF RESPONSIBILITIES:

1. Responsible for the attainment of all district performance objectives and controls district expenses within established budgets.

2. Responsible for the implementation of company performance programs through independent distributors and company branches.

3. Develops forecasts and budgets for review and approval by the District Sales Manager.

4. Develops, in concert with the distributor, an annual plan that encompasses marketing by product line, dealer development, distributor salesmen territories, local promotional activity and budgeted advertising expenditures.

5. Evaluates the quantitative performance to plan for each distributor in his district and reviews the performance at regularly scheduled intervals.

6. Evaluates the qualitative performance of each distributor in his district including designated areas of evaluation, e.g. effectiveness of employees, training, supervision, local promotions, service levels, and etc.

7. Assist distributor in training distributor and dealer personnel how to effectively merchandise TORO Consumer Products.

8. Assures that each distributor in his district supplies timely reports required by TORO.

9. Communicates in a comprehensive and accurate manner all matters relating to the promotion of TORO products including competitive intelligence.

H/R#421 (11/78)   (OVER)

LIST OF RESPONSIBILITIES:

10. Advises and assists in
to effectively and pro

11. Assists in the organiza
including training mee

12. Carries out all specia

13. Advises and makes inno
product improvement, m
improvement programs.

14. Responsible for the ev
in distributorship sho
This recommendation wo
marginal performance,
alternatives for consi

JOB SPECIFICATIONS:

BS or BA Degree in business preferred. 1 to 3 years experience in selling consumer durables to retail trade is desirable. Experience in working with distributors or wholesalers would also be desirable.

DATE: 4/27/80

H/R 421 (11/78)

FIGURE 5-4
**Combined Job Description and Specifications
for a Sales Representative at Toro.**

RESUME

Chris Davis   Born September 2, 1958
5713 State Street   Single, 5 feet, 10 inches
Gainesville, Florida 32601   165 pounds

904-370-2870

Career Objectives

My immediate goal: selling office or technical equipment to retail, commercial,
or industrial accounts. My long-range goal: sales or marketing management in a
manufacturing firm.

Potential

Three positions in the past six years have given me an opportunity to supervise
others and to improve job procedures:

  • As the buyer for a new food cooperative while in college, I
    planned, ordered, and set up inventory procedures.

  • I supervised four men in repairing electronic equipment in
    the Army.

  • I drew up the weekly work schedule and managed the counter
    at Burger Queen.

Business Experience

September 1978 to present. Worked as a buyer approximately 20 hours a week in
          cooperation with C. M. Spreigl, co-op president, Chateau Co-op,
          1321 University Avenue, Gainesville, Florida.

September 1976 to July 1978. Worked as Specialist 5 supervising electronics
          equipment repair reporting to Lieutenant M. M. Leary, U.S. Army,
          Fourth Military Service Unit, Fort Jackson, South Carolina.

June 1974 to August 1976. Worked as counter manager reporting to Peg L.
          Tonneson, restaurant owner, Peg's Burger Queen, 5119 Highway 280,
          Gainesville, Florida.

Education

B.S. degree expected from the University of Florida, June 1982. Major in
marketing (B average) and minor in journalism (B average). Course work
emphasized marketing (21 credits) and journalism (15 credits).

References

Professor John Faricy   Professor Joyce Hegstrom
Department of Marketing   Department of Journalism
College of Business Administration College of Liberal Arts
University of Florida   University of Florida
Gainesville, Florida 32601   Gainesville, Florida 32601
(Adviser)   (Independent study supervisor)

          Eric Walton, Director
          University Student Services
          University of Florida
          Gainesville, Florida 32601
          (Co-op adviser)

Annotations (right margin):

→ Personal Data

→ "Career Objectives" that are specific without unduly limiting possible jobs

→ "Potential" demonstrates unique capabilities that help provide an advantage compared to other applicants

→ "Business Experience" & "Education" information pertinent to job sought

→ "References" from both educational and work situations

FIGURE 5-5
A Concise, Effective Personal Resume.

they quit or are fired right away, and inefficient workers who are kept on may cost the company more than they are worth. Some of the most common methods used to screen job applicants are discussed below.

Application Blank   An application blank provides a clear and concise format for collecting information about prospective employees. It also shows whether the applicant can follow directions. If there are no immediate job openings, the application may be filed and referred to later. If the candidate is hired, the application is put into the permananent personnel record.

Interview by Human Resources Department   Interviewers usually want to find out whether an applicant talks well and answers questions directly, especially for a position that requires talking to people outside the company—like suppliers or customers. Interviews help both the firm and the applicant study each other to see whether there is a good fit.

Assessment Centers: A Way to Spot Managers?

"I never really thought of myself as a manager," says Jean Underside, a section head in the films packaging division of Union Carbide. She had worked as a secretary for 22 years when her boss suggested she take some tests at an assessment center. She did so well that she was offered a management position, according to *The New York Times*.[8]

Assessment centers use management exercises to simulate the work an employee would do in a higher-level job. (The exercises are modeled on those used to select spies during World War II.) They try to test for seven key managerial qualities: problem analysis, judgment, decisiveness, leadership, interpersonal sensitivity, initiative, and organizational planning.

The exercises typically use "in-basket" problems and leaderless group discussions. In one "in-basket" exercise, the participant acts as a supervisor in a soft-drink factory. He or she has three hours to sort out an ill supervisor's overflowing "in-basket." The point is to select the most important problems, write memos, and issue orders to straighten things out. In one type of leaderless group discussion, each participant is given a one-page resume on a candidate for promotion. Each has to make a five-minute oral report on behalf of the candidate and discuss competing candidates. "Assessors" then evaluate how well participants have done.

Are assessment centers the wave of the future? It is too soon to know. But the American Telephone and Telegraph Company has already assessed more than 200,000 employees at 70 centers across the United States. Many metropolitan newspapers send reporters to them, as do dozens of other firms and government agencies.

Psychological Tests   Many firms ask applicants to take aptitude, achievement, mental ability, or personality tests. These are interpreted by a trained psychologist in the company's human resources department, and the results are used to supplement—not replace—the other information on the applicant.

Interview by Prospective Manager   Once applicants have passed the screening by the human resources department, they are interviewed by their prospective boss or department manager. Normally, it is this person—not a member of the human resources department—who decides whether to extend a job offer.

Reference Checks   The references cited in an applicant's resume and application blank are checked by mail or telephone to make sure that he or she has not exaggerated or misrepresented qualifications.

At any point in this process, negotiations can be terminated by either side. If, for example, the applicant finds out during the first interview that the job requires too much travel for him, he should stop the process immediately, saving both parties time and effort.

Staffing—Postemployment

The staffing function of management is not confined only to hiring new employees. Postemployment activities are an equally important concern of human resources managers. These activities include training, appraisal, compensation, laying-off, firing, and other services.

Would You Hire These People?

The three personal sketches below contain more information than is often available when a hiring decision is to be made. Decide whether or not you would hire each of these three people. Their names are given in the box on the next page.[9]

Applicant A: He dreamed of being an inventor, had only three months of formal schooling, and was expelled because the schoolmaster considered him "retarded." In early life, his biggest joy was playing pranks to anger his father, who once beat the boy in public in the village square. He was fired from his first job for accidentally starting a fire. In his 30s, he paid little attention to his family, neglected his clothes, chewed tobacco, was rejected by "polite society," and was ridiculed by theoretical scientists as an "anti-intellectual." He was egotistical and, to fellow workers, both a tyrant and their most entertaining companion.

Applicant B: At the age of 21, he was of medium height and thin. He wore glasses, had an unpleasant toothy grin, and wore flashy clothes. He spoke indistinctly, stumbled, hesitated, appearing to have almost a speech impediment. His companions thought he was queer and eccentric, and his seniors were irritated by him. He was a particular nuisance in class—a cocky know-it-all. He was earnest, outspoken, and tactless. His hot temper, nervousness, and childish manner made an unfavorable impression. But he was a good student and made Phi Beta Kappa in his senior year in college. Nevertheless, after graduation he was unable to decide on a job.

Applicant C: He was red-haired, sturdy, and not handsome. He had a distinct speech impediment, a combination of a stammer and lisp. He was uncommonly self-assured, obstinate, and arrogant. He was foolhardy, often taking unnecessary chances with his life. He hated school; he refused to study anything that didn't interest him. When students were ranked scholastically, he was always at the bottom. In the army, he was a wild and careless soldier, but he did receive several decorations for bravery. He was thrown out of politics shortly after trying it as a career.

Who They Are

Some firms rely so rigidly on tradition that they hire carbon copies of existing employees. For example, a creative genius who deviates from traditional company hiring standards may be rejected, even though his or her potential contributions may exceed those of people hired. The information given in the brief sketches of the three applicants on the preceding page would probably eliminate them from consideration as job candidates. It is even more unlikely that inventor Thomas Edison, U.S. President Theodore Roosevelt, or British Prime Minister Winston Churchill—applicants A, B, and C, respectively—would have gotten much further in the screening process.

Edison's resume would be hopeless: he had no formal education, having quit school at the age of seven. Reference checks with his only school teacher and first employer would have been disastrous. The teacher had expelled him, calling him "retarded." The employer had fired him for accidentally starting a fire with some chemicals in the baggage car of a train. Yet, Edison's 1,093 patents make him one of the outstanding technical geniuses in history.

The brashness of both Theodore Roosevelt and Winston Churchill might not have caused them to flunk a prospective employer's personality test; yet this behavior would certainly have screened them out during their personal interviews. Each of these men, however, altered the course of history.

(top) Thomas Edison; (middle) Theodore Roosevelt; (bottom) Winston Churchill

Training

Training—providing employees with the skills and knowledge they need to do their jobs well—happens both on the job and off the job. *On-the-job training* is given in the course of day-to-day work. A new salesperson who sells General Electric stoves and refrigerators to stores might spend the first two to six months making sales calls with an experienced G.E. salesperson. At first, the new employee would just watch and do no selling herself. Then, in the second half of the training period, she would make most of the sales presentations and answer questions herself. The experienced salesperson would answer only special questions and offer constructive suggestions in private.

Off-the-job training involves attending courses, seminars, or workshops run by the firm, an outside organization, or a college. General Electric sales management, for example, would probably offer an initial five-to-fifteen week program run by company personnel. In it, they would teach new salespeople all about the company's stoves and refrigerators. After that, week-long sessions might be held annually to inform salespeople of additions to the line. The G.E. human resources department might also offer workshops on effective speaking or writing, designed for employees from several departments.

Appraisal

Managers at the top of an organization, such as Charles Schwab, a former president of Bethlehem Steel, often evaluate their own performance. (At the time, Schwab was earning $1 million a year and was probably doing a very good job.) Schwab asked management consultant Ivy Lee how to accomplish more work each day and avoid getting bogged down in details. Lee handed him a blank sheet of paper and said: "Before you leave work tonight, list the six most important things you have to do tomorrow. Tomorrow morning start on item one. Work on it until it's finished. Then go on to the second item, and do the same." When Schwab asked Lee what his fee was, Lee answered: "Try it and pay me what you think it's worth." Schwab was so pleased with the results that he sent Lee a check for $25,000. Schwab had applied two key lessons used by many successful managers: recognizing room for improvement and asking for constructive appraisal from another person.

All employees in an organization—including the president—usually receive a written evaluation once a year. The purpose is to provide counseling to increase their effectiveness, perhaps by suggesting training programs. And it also is tied to their compensation (see below). In some firms, appraisal and compensation done by the employee's immediate superior are tied closely together. In other companies, great pains are taken to separate these two activities so that continuing constructive feedback can be given to employees without their having to worry about whether it affects their paychecks.

Compensation

Compensation not only includes money but also such fringe benefits as vacations, holidays, paid sick leave, disability, and retirement allowances. Human resources managers develop a compensation plan to attract and to retain qualified, productive employees. They typically use the following factors to decide on the money compensation of their plan: How important is the job to the company? What are the wages and salaries in comparable firms? What are the federal and state laws governing compensation (minimum wage, no wage discrimination)? And what (if any) is the union collective-bargaining position (to be discussed in Chapter 19)?

These factors are used to establish the *basic element*—"wages" for blue-collar or hourly workers and "salary" for white-collar workers. Most wages are hourly and paid only for the time worked. A machinist earning $10 an hour

The Peter Principle,
Or Are We All One Level Too High?

Professor Lawrence J. Peter of the University of Southern California examined many organizations and humorously concluded that good people are seldom in the right jobs.[10]

Peter cites many people whose outstanding performance on one job earned them promotions to positions for which they were unqualified: brilliant automobile mechanics who became inept garage repair supervisors; outstanding salespeople who became ineffectual sales managers; and spellbinding teachers who proved to be incompetent academic administrators. Unfortunately, we can be happy knowing this pattern of ineptness has held true throughout history. Some evidence: examining the roster of officers assigned him for his Portugal campaign, the Duke of Wellington observed: "I only hope that when the enemy reads the list of their names, he trembles as I do."

Peter concludes that most people in an organization eventually achieve a position one level higher than where they belong. To describe this phenomenon, he formulated the Peter principle: "In a hierarchy, every employee tends to rise to his level of incompetence."

who works 40 hours a week is paid $400 for the week. Salaried personnel are paid on a weekly, monthly, or annual basis. An office clerk might receive a weekly salary of $200; a junior accountant might earn an annual salary of $18,000, paid in monthly installments of $1,500.

A compensation plan may also include an *incentive element,* that is, extra money paid to employees who produce above standard. To determine the amount of extra compensation, management must establish a standard of performance and an easily measured work output (for example, the bricklayer on page 101 in Chapter 4). Business firms use a variety of incentives, such as profit sharing, bonuses, and commissions. Compensation will be discussed further in Chapter 19.

Another form of employee compensation is *promotion,* rewarding good performance with a more responsible, higher-paying job. This policy benefits both the employee through improved morale and motivation and the company through increased productivity and less turnover.

Laying-off and Firing

Sometimes employees must be dismissed because of lack of work in the company or because they are performing poorly. Human resources managers try to avoid laying off employees for reasons of lack of work because it is not good for the morale of those who remain. Thus, Xerox chairman of the board, C. Peter McColough, is so concerned that he reserves the right to veto the dismissal of any employee with eight years or more experience at Xerox. And in IBM's entire 35-year history no worker has ever been laid off because of a business slowdown. Instead, they are retained and transferred to different departments—even though this may involve as many as 1,700 workers a year.

Yet IBM does fire and demote people for disciplinary and other causes. "We're not running a home for unproductive people," says IBM chairman Frank T. Carey. It is not easy to demote people in a way that preserves morale, but managers must learn how to do it.

Providing Other Services

The human resources department also provides services designed to improve employee welfare and satisfaction. These can include a company credit union (which pays interest on savings and extends low-interest loans), group insurance programs, and pension plans. Increasingly, human resources managers also offer recreational programs, legal aid, company-subsidized cafeterias, and personal counseling.

Chapter Review & Applications

Key Points to Remember

1. The management function of organizing is structuring jobs and placing qualified people in them.
2. Two common organizational structures are (1) the line organization and (2) the line-and-staff organization.
3. Formal organization charts clarify authority and reporting relationships for employees, but they do not show another important relationship: the informal communication network.
4. Management experts have developed some principles of organization that are useful in designing effective organizations: unity of command, span of control, the exception principle, the scalar principle, grouping by departments, and decentralization.
5. Both the human resouces (or personnel) department and individual managers share the responsibility for staffing, which includes selecting, training, promoting, and retiring subordinates.
6. Preemployment aspects of staffing include identifying personnel needs, requisitioning, recruiting, and selecting employees.
7. Candidates applying for jobs must "sell" themselves—demonstrate their unique abilities in competition. A concise, effective personal resume helps to do this.
8. To select new employees systematically, employers use a sequence of steps including application blanks, interviews, tests, and reference checks.
9. Postemployment activities include training, appraisal, compensation, laying-off and firing, and additional services.

Questions

1. The dotted lines in Figure 5–1(b) show that the secretary and accountant are really staff positions in your bookstore. But most real organization charts, like Toro's in Figure 5–2, don't show dotted lines. Which of the boxes in Toro's organization are staff positions?
2. Often, distinctly different kinds of people are attracted to line positions and staff positions. (a) What would you see as the appeals and frustrations of each kind of position? (b) What kind of personality would each position appeal to?
3. The text cited four factors (importance of job, pay in comparable firms, laws, and collective bargaining) as influencing an employee's pay. In what ways does each factor affect pay? What else affects pay for specific jobs?
4. Cite the advantages and disadvantages of following a company policy of promotion from within.
5. How might the normal screening process used by a firm eliminate potentially talented employees?

Short Cases

1. Suppose you are a college recruiter for The Toro Company and Chris Davis's resume (Figure 5–5) is one of several in a stack on your desk. Chris is scheduled for an interview in ten minutes.

   (a) What information in the resume especially interests you?
   (b) What important information does not appear that you would want to hear more about?
   (c) How would you obtain the information in (b) during the interview?

2. In 1979 The Toro Company acquired a lawn-care business. How would you fit this new business into its organization chart in Figure 5–2?

A Critical
Business Decision

—made by Robert F. Six
of Continental Airlines

The Situation

By 1975, Robert F. Six had been president of Continental Airlines for 37 years. Six's flamboyant personality has left its mark on Continental. From the first, he envisioned the little mail-plane company battling big impersonal competitors, such as United Airlines, which is five times as large. The result is a remarkable, cohesive company spirit among Continental employees. Many know and most see Six personally. He insists that company officers rub elbows with pilots, secretaries, and mechanics in the employee cafeteria. And Six has an instinct for what customers want: Continental was the first airline to offer hot meals and wide seats on coach flights. The company has realized a profit in 36 of the 37 years Six has been its president.

The Decision

Six is a hard act to follow. And no one knows it better than Six himself, who, by 1975, had spent eight years seeking his own replacement. The search was thoughtful, deep, and deliberate. Earlier, with the aid of a management consultant, Six searched for qualified candidates within Continental who could run the airline. The search indentified four men, each of whom was described in a separate bound report that covered his backgound, character, education, management experience, personal aspirations, and private life. In 1975, *Fortune* magazine summarized the records of Bob Six's four potential successors:[11]

- Richard M. Adams, 56, senior vice president, operating and technical services. He is a quiet engineer who enjoys good music and photography. He moved over from Pan American Airways in 1962 to head Continental's maintenance division and soon was put in charge of flight operations as well. Under him, Continental has achieved the best record in the industry for aircraft utilization and jet safety.

- Charles A. Bucks, 47, senior vice president, marketing. Showing natural selling ability, he rapidly moved up through the marketing division until, at 34, he became the air-transport industry's youngest vice president. Bucks is second only to Six in popularity among Continental's rank and file.

- G. Edward Cotter, 57, senior vice president, legal and diversification, and the company secretary. Cotter has an extraordinary conceptual grasp of such broad issues as the airline's needs for long-term growth. Most employees are unaware of his achievements, but everyone is aware that his sister, actress Audrey Meadows, is Six's wife.

- Alexander Damm, 59, senior vice president and general manager. Continental's money-man, Damm installed tight budget controls and a monthly head count that allows Six to veto the most minute addition to the payroll. He is not well liked by employees, but his rigid control system has kept Continental profitable.

In 1975, Six organized a selection committee—three members of the board of directors and himself—to choose his replacement. They were also concerned that in choosing Six's successor, Continental might lose the other three men, valuable employees who would be equally valuable to competitors.

Questions

1. If you were Bob Six, on what criteria would you base your selection of a new president?
2. Which of these men would you select? Or would you select someone from outside Continental? Why?
3. What action would you take to keep from losing the men who were not chosen to succeed you as president of Continental?

Leading and Controlling

In this chapter you will learn . . .

- *how managers lead organizations by motivating and communicating effectively with their employees.*
- *which leadership styles are best in which situations.*
- *what the three essentials of managerial control are and how these techniques can be applied to your own career in business.*

6

138

As for the best leaders, the people do not notice their existence. The next best, the people honor and praise. The next, the people fear; and the next, the people hate. When the best leaders' work is done, the people say, "We did it ourselves!"

LAO-TZU, AS QUOTED BY ROBERT TOWNSEND,
RETIRED PRESIDENT, AVIS RENT A CAR

ow do you lead and control an organization? "I think you do it by kidding people along. I don't believe in confrontation—not for myself, anyway. The greatest thing is example," says Catherine Cleary, president and chief executive officer of First Wisconsin Trust. William M. Agee, when he was chief executive officer of Bendix Corporation, believed in "participatory management." He included a wider than normal range of people in top decision-making groups, encouraged free-wheeling discussion on corporate goals, and scrapped the pecking order in the company parking lot. At the other extreme, "creative tension" was the management style of Wilfred J. Corrigan, president and chief executive of Fairchild Camera and Instrument Corporation. A no-nonsense manager, he fired a division vice president at 9:15 one morning and gave him until noon to get out. As one of his other vice presidents said, "Corrigan makes sure people don't get comfortable in their jobs."

There are as many management styles as there are managers. But whatever the style, a good manager will understand—and use—the basic techniques of leading and controlling employees. This chapter introduces you to those critical aspects of management.

LEADING AND MOTIVATING EMPLOYEES

Leading means guiding the activities of subordinates toward organizational goals. To lead effectively, managers must motivate employees and communicate with them in ways that produce the desired results. These activities, plus the manager's personal style, add up to his or her *leadership ability*.

How to Motivate Employees

What would happen to an organization if assembly-line workers called in sick regularly, supervisors left after a year or two, middle-managers wrote sloppy marketing reports, and design engineers helped themselves to the platinum used in building computers? These sorts of things can happen when workers are unmotivated and unhappy in their jobs. And the result would be disaster for the company. So supplying **motivation**—anything that creates, directs, and sustains people's behavior—is an essential task for managers.

What Motivates Workers?

Although theories conflict, three different families of motivating characteristics have been identified by Lyman W. Porter and Raymond E. Miles (details appear in Figure 6–1):

1. JOB CHARACTERISTICS   The degree of responsibility in the job, the variety of tasks, and the opportunity for satisfaction all affect employee motivation. The more the better, usually.
2. INDIVIDUAL CHARACTERISTICS   The interests, attitudes, and needs a person brings to a job are important too. Some people are more

FIGURE 6–1
What Affects Worker Motivation?

JOB CHARACTERISTICS	INDIVIDUAL CHARACTERISTICS	WORK–SITUATION CHARACTERISTICS

1. Types of rewards
2. Degree of freedom
3. Amount of feedback
4. Amount of variety
	1. Interests
	2. Attitudes
	  (a) Toward self
	  (b) Toward job
	  (c) Toward aspects of the work
	      situation
	3. Needs
	  (a) Security
	  (b) Social
	  (c) Achievement
		1. Immediate work environment
		  (a) Peers
		  (b) Supervisor(s)
		2. Organizational actions
		  (a) Reward practices
		    (1) Systemwide rewards
		    (2) Individual rewards
		  (b) Organizational climate

Source: Adapted from Lyman W. Porter and Raymond E. Miles, "Motivation and Management," in Joseph W. McGuire, ed., *Contemporary Management: Issues and Viewpoints* (Englewood Cliffs, N.J.: Prentice-Hall, 1974), p. 547. Adapted by permission of Prentice-Hall, Inc.

motivated by prestige—a fancy title and a sumptuous office; others, more exclusively by money.

3. WORK–SITUATION CHARACTERISTICS The atmosphere of the organization is an important factor. Do colleagues encourage quality work or discourage it? Do supervisors reward high performance or ignore it? Does the organization genuinely care about its employees?

For each of these sets of characteristics, management theories and applications have been developed, as discussed below.

Job Characteristics and the Hawthorne Studies

The job itself became a focus for motivation when Frederick Taylor devised his theory of scientific management. This attention to work methods led to some curious results—and eventually to a new idea.

Back in 1927, managers at the Hawthorne plant of Western Electric in Chicago wanted to find out whether changes in the work environment and in salary could improve worker productivity. Hawthorne researchers experimented with different lighting, temperature, humidity, layout, work groups, rest time, and pay scales. They interviewed and checked the productivity of thousands of workers over a five-year period before they could believe the results.[1]

Improving Morale Can Be Tricky

The Case of the Empty Briefcase

At one Bell Telephone district office, one-year sales goals were not met. So management ordered marketing employees to stay one hour longer at work every day. After a while, one of the vice presidents got an anonymous letter, which read:

> Production has *decreased*. . . . Many individuals are actively seeking other employment. . . . Employees who used to put in long hours and take work home now leave with empty briefcases. . . . Does anyone really believe that . . . by shortening the time [employees] have with their families, breaking up car pools, eliminating the use of mass transportation for many . . . would result in anything other than a feeling of humiliation, anger, and defeat?[2]

The extra-hour rule was soon dropped.

In their first experiment, factory lighting was brightened. Production increased. But it also increased almost equally in another group whose lighting had not been changed. Next, lighting was reduced. Surprisingly, worker output rose again. It continued to rise until the light level fell to the equivalent of ordinary moonlight. Experiments in the other Hawthorne studies showed similarly bewildering increases in worker productivity.

For a long time, the researchers had difficulty interpreting the results. But finally, after many more experiments, it became clear that it was not lighting or any other specific condition that was responsible for increased productivity—it was that workers knew they were being observed, even those in the control groups. So simply paying attention to people motivates them to achieve, often more than working conditions or additional pay does. This phenomenon is now known as the **Hawthorne effect.**

These studies led management to focus for a while on morale instead of efficiency. Since then, however, managers have learned to consider both. One outcome is that many organizations have developed robot-like machines for efficient performance of basic assembly tasks. Then they have enriched and enlarged the jobs of workers, allowing them more decisions. So recognizing good performance—with methods as simple as offering an honest compliment or tokens for a job well done (see the accompanying box)—raises employee morale.

The Case of Tokens at the Amusement Park

When they opened a giant new amusement park, managers realized that employee treatment of customers would be a key to success. A consultant was brought in to motivate the young work force. He presented the job this way:

> This job will teach you about yourselves as you work with a wide variety of people. . . . People will ask a lot of questions. Here are some techniques for handling them. . . . And customers will be given tokens to award to especially helpful employees. You may wear them on your work clothes.[3]

Employees wore their tokens proudly as they ran the roller coasters and manned the hot dog stands. And as many as 82 percent said they wanted to return to work there next summer.

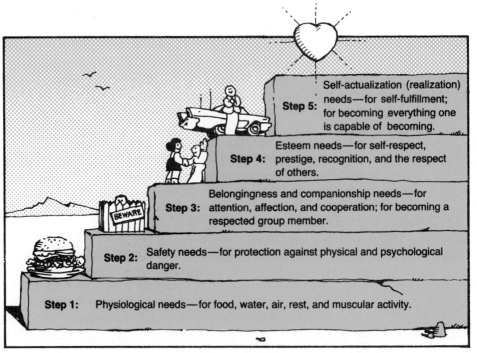

**FIGURE 6-2
Maslow's
Hierarchy
of Human
Needs.**

Source: A.H. Maslow, *Motivation and Personality,* 2nd ed. (New York: Harper & Row, 1954), Chapters 4 and 5.

Individual Characteristics and Maslow's Hierarchy of Needs

After the Hawthorne studies, psychologists began to analyze human motivation in greater depth. One, psychologist Abraham Maslow, developed a theory of motivation that classifies human needs into five groups (see Figure 6–2). These sets of needs exist in a hierarchy, which means that as one set is largely satisfied, the person becomes motivated by the set on the next highest level. For example, the need for prestige and recognition (step 4) cannot motivate you if you are still seeking to satisfy your need for affection (step 3).

Good managers attempt to recognize the different need levels of their subordinates and provide a job environment and reward system that satisfies them. Company reorganizations are often necessary but can be especially stressful to employees affected by them. So some companies like AT&T (see box on page 144) make special efforts during difficult transition periods.

Work-Situation Characteristics and Theory X and Theory Y

Would you work if no one was looking? **Theory X** is the traditional, and pessimistic, view that workers must be closely supervised and regularly prodded if they are to accomplish work goals. **Theory Y,** the counterpoint to Theory X, argues that workers are self-motivated when job conditions permit opportunities for achievement and a sense of accomplishment. This controversial and much-discussed theory, first presented in 1960 by psychologist Douglas McGregor, is detailed in Figure 6–3.

FIGURE 6–3
Theory X and Theory Y.

ASSUMPTIONS UNDERLYING THEORY X	ASSUMPTIONS UNDERLYING THEORY Y
1. People usually dislike work and try to avoid it.	1. People usually don't dislike work. Work can be satisfying or punishing depending on the conditions that surround the job.
2. Employees must be forced to work toward an organization's goals by threat of punishment.	2. People needn't be punished to work toward organizational goals. They will control themselves to attain the objectives to which they are committed.
3. People usually want direction, no responsibility, and a great deal of security.	3. Commitment to objectives depends on the rewards associated with their achievement, the most significant of which is self-actualization.
	4. Under the right conditions, people usually learn to seek responsibility. Avoiding it is generally the consequence of negative experience; it is not an innate characteristic.
	5. The ability to creatively solve organizational problems is widely, not narrowly, spread among the general population.
	6. In modern industry, the intellectual potential of the average person is only partially utilized.

Source: From *The Human Side of Enterprise* by Douglas McGregor, pp. 33–35 and 45–49. Copyright © 1960. Used with permission of McGraw-Hill Book Company.

Communicating

Direct communication with employees uses up 55 to 80 percent of a manager's time. Countless more hours are spent reading and writing memos, letters, and reports. Without effective communication, managers could not carry out their four key functions: planning, organizing, leading, and controlling. Something this important should be done well, but usually it isn't.

Bases of Effective Communication

Communication in an organization can take any number of forms. It may be formal organizational communication or informal communication by way of the grapevine. If formal, it may be written or verbal. In face-to-face communication, nonverbal facial expressions, gestures, and body movements are an important part of the message and often conflict with what is said. The manager who says to a harried employee "Yes, tell me about your problem" while continuing to open and read the morning mail is guilty of transmitting conflicting messages. The employee is probably correct in weighing the indifference of the manager's nonverbal behavior more heavily than the manager's spoken message. When communications conflict, nonverbal behavior is usually more believable than verbal behavior.[4]

Handling Anxiety at AT&T

No matter how high your employees are on Maslow's hierarchy, a drastic corporate reorganization can plunge most people back down to the anxieties of step 2 for a while. When the organizational structure at American Telephone and Telegraph (AT&T) was completely revised, managers had to take action to relieve the anxiety felt by 250,000 employees who were dealt new job titles, duties, superiors, and work methods, according to *Business Week* magazine.[5]

So AT&T launched a series of seminars to help people handle their stress. In these sessions people were helped to draw and discuss their "life charts," which included points of transition in both their family and work lives. Employees, usually in groups of three, then discussed their reactions to these changes. The point was to shown them that they were not alone in their feelings, that everyone experiences stress and anxiety while trying to adjust to new situations. It worked. Employees paid more attention to their jobs, so AT&T could concentrate on getting its messages through.

Assuming that a communication is timely and relevant, it can have real value only if it is (1) received (heard or seen), (2) understood, (3) accepted, and (4) acted on. So managers who wish to determine whether they have communicated effectively with an employee must ask: Did the employee hear the message? Does that employee really know what it means? Has he accepted the responsibility? And has he taken the desired action?

For a communication to achieve these four goals, the communicator must verify the action through feedback, by either watching or listening. In one study, college and business people were asked to summarize one or two key points from a short, simple spoken message. Results: the typical listener understood less than half the message content. This poor result occurs because few people are trained as well in listening as they are in reading, writing, and speaking. Recognizing this problem, many firms have employees attend courses on effective listening.

Barriers to Effective Communication

There are a variety of barriers to effective communication between people in an organization. Some arise from personal differences. Others relate to the methods of transmitting messages. These barriers, and several ways to overcome them, are described below.[6]

Different Frames of Reference Because of different backgrounds and experiences, each person has a personal *frame of reference* or a unique way of looking at things that determines how that person interprets what is seen and heard. In general, an employee who has had good relationships with previous supervisors will accept requests without question; an employee who in the past was deceived by supervisors will react to even simple, straightforward requests with suspicion. One way for managers to make employees feel less threatened and defensive is to talk to them in their own work places instead of in the manager's office.

Status Differences Managers are not always free to communicate everything to a subordinate because of conflicting responsibilities to other subordinates and to superiors. The result is that downward communication in an organization declines. Only about 20 percent of the information moving down through management channels reaches the worker. This downward communication loss, sometimes called *dilution,* can be reduced when managers work at

Careers in Communications

Public relations writers and **producers** are responsible for communicating written, spoken, and visual material about their organization to the public. They usually do it through newspapers and magazines, radio, and TV by working with reporters and editors. A bachelor's degree and some media-related experience is required. Salaries range from $12,000 to $20,000 or more. (*Additional information:* The Public Relations Society of America, 845 Third Avenue, New York, New York 10022.)

Publications editors prepare everything from employee newsletters to the glossy annual report for their organizations. They need oral skills to gather information, and writing and graphics skills to present it most effectively. Salaries range from $12,000 to $18,000 and a bachelor's degree is required. (*Additional information:* The Public Relations Society of America, 845 Third Avenue, New York, New York 10022.)

Special events coordinators launch events from product introductions to retirement ceremonies. They also work with outside media producers when, for example, they are arranging special programs to advertise the company's products. With a bachelor's degree, they earn from $12,000 to $18,000. (*Additional information:* The Public Relations Society of America, 845 Third Avenue, New York, New York 10022.)

Technical writers communicate scientific developments and new product information to professional and consumer audiences. They write publicity releases and instructions for the use of new products. Along with writing skills, they must have up-to-date knowledge of the technological developments in their field. Most have bachelor's degrees, often in technical journalism. Technical writers start at about $12,000 and average about $19,500 annually. Employment opportunities are expected to expand moderately, based on management's need for understandable information about complex scientific and technical products. (*Additional information:* Society for Technical Communications, Inc., Suite 506, 815 15th Street, N.W., Washington, D.C. 20005.)

Careers in Information Collection

Medical-record administrators are employed by health-care facilities to organize and to maintain files on patients and the hospital treatments they receive. Qualified applicants have a bachelor's degree in medical-record administration, with a solid background in medical science and terminology, health law, and statistics. Experienced medical-record administrators may advance to higher-level, hospital-management positions. Starting salary is about $14,500. Employment opportunities are expected to increase rapidly given the growing number of health-care facilities and health-insurance programs. (*Additional Information:* The American Medical Record Association, Suite 1850, John Hancock Center, 875 North Michigan Avenue, Chicago, Illinois 60611.)

providing subordinates with enough information to obtain effective, enthusiastic work from them.

Incomplete information also flows upward. No one likes to admit mistakes, especially to a boss. So upward communications from worker to boss are frequently *filtered*—intentionally sifted of information in order to place the sender and the message in a more favorable light. Managers may unwittingly encourage this. Remedies for filtering are (1) developing a well-designed control system so that realistic assessments reach higher management, and (2) establishing trust, confidence, and rapport with subordinates so that they can discuss their problems with their supervisors.

Unclear Messages   Confusion haunts many written and verbal messages. One common source of confusion is the use of *gobbledygook,* a mishmash of unnecessarily long words and overly complicated sentences. Like presents, the best messages often come in small packages. Lincoln's Gettysburg Address, for example, used 266 words, while one government order on cabbages used 26,911. Writing expert Robert Gunning's obvious—but hard-to-apply—solution for the gobbledygook problem: shorter words and shorter sentences. (See Figure 6–4 on page 148.)

Poor Listening   The biggest barrier to communication is poor listening. This bad habit can cost people and their companies money. A listening seminar held recently at Sperry Corporation caused 24 engineers to realize that their combined listening failures had cost their firm more than $122,000. Because listening is basically a passive activity, people sometimes use the time to daydream or plan their answers instead of paying attention to what is being said. Or, more serious, they receive the wrong message because they hear only what they want to hear. You can practice active listening by keeping an open mind, taking notes, asking questions, and—most important—repeating the gist of the message to yourself.

Leadership

Leadership, like leading, means guiding activities of subordinates toward organizational goals. This includes everything from actual demonstration of work tasks to an attitude that is conveyed through the leader's own style and personality.

Keep It Simple

Strike three.
Get your hand off my knee.
You're overdrawn.
Your horse won.
Yes.
No.
You have the account.
Walk.
Don't walk.
Mother's dead.
Basic events
require simple language.
Idiosyncratically euphuistic
eccentricities are the
promulgators of
triturable obfuscation.
What did you do last night?
Enter into a meaningful
romantic involvement
or
fall in love?
What did you have for
breakfast this morning?
The upper part of a hog's
hind leg with two oval
bodies encased in a shell
laid by a female bird
or
ham and eggs?
David Belasco, the great
American theatrical producer,
once said, "If you can't
write your idea on the
back of my calling
card,
you don't have a clear idea."

FIGURE 6-4
*Simple,
Direct
Messages
Are Very
Effective.*

Source: United Technologies.

Choosing a Leadership Style

Finding the right style of leadership is a tough job, and styles vary dramatically among different people. As battalion commander in France during World War I, Winston Churchill greeted his officers with: "Gentlemen, I am your new commanding officer. Those who support me, I will look after. Those who are against me, I will break. Good afternoon, gentlemen."[7] Churchill did not appear to be encouraging group participation or minority opinions. In 1770, Ben Franklin offered the following low-key approach:

> The way to convince another is to state your case moderately and accurately. Then scratch your head and say, "at least that's what it seems to me, but of course I may be wrong." This causes your listener to receive what you have to say, and, like as not, come about and try to convince you of it, since you are in doubt. But if you go to him in a tone of positiveness or arrogance, you only make an opponent of him.[8]

Although this is slightly manipulative, at least Franklin gave his listener the opportunity to be heard. Figure 6–5 (on page 150) shows a range of leadership styles, from boss-centered to subordinate-centered. Where do you think Churchill and Franklin fit on this scale?

Machiavellianism: A Boss-Centered Leadership Style

For some leaders, anything goes. The end justifies the means—deceit and manipulation included. This leadership style is known as **Machiavellianism,**

DOONESBURY   by Garry Trudeau

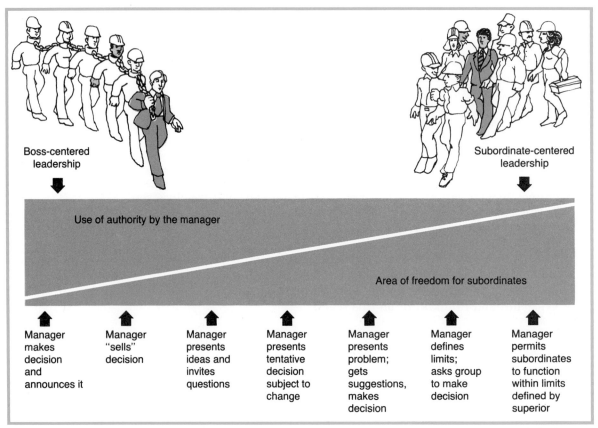

Boss-centered
leadership

Subordinate-centered
leadership

Use of authority by the manager

Area of freedom for subordinates

| Manager makes decision and announces it | Manager "sells" decision | Manager presents ideas and invites questions | Manager presents tentative decision subject to change | Manager presents problem; gets suggestions, makes decision | Manager defines limits; asks group to make decision | Manager permits subordinates to function within limits defined by superior |

Source: Robert Tannenbaum and Warren H. Schmidt, "How to Choose a Leadership Pattern," *Harvard Business Review* (March–April 1958), p. 96.

**FIGURE 6–5
Range
of a
Manager's
Leadership
Style.**

after Niccolo Machiavelli, who set it out in 1532 in his book *The Prince*. He argued that a leader is justified in using any technique, no matter how deceitful, to manipulate and to control people and to strike down enemies. Researchers have devised various tests to determine the degree to which individuals are "High Machs" (manipulators of other people) or "Low Machs" (not manipulators of other people). The short test in Figure 6–6 should give you some insight into your own managerial style.

High Machs are coolly aloof. They appraise a situation and other people in a logical and detached fashion rather than emotionally. Apparently this insensitivity permits them to manipulate others while pursuing their own goals.

Instructions: For each statement, circle the number that most closely resembles your attitude.

STATEMENT	DISAGREE			AGREE	
	A lot	A little	Neutral	A little	A lot
1. The best way to handle people is to tell them what they want to hear.	1	2	3	4	5
2. When you ask someone to do something for you, it is best to give the real reasons for wanting it done rather than the reasons which might carry more weight.	1	2	3	4	5
3. Anyone who completely trusts anyone else is asking for trouble.	1	2	3	4	5
4. It is hard to get ahead without cutting corners here and there.	1	2	3	4	5
5. It is safest to assume that all people have a vicious streak and that it will come out when given a chance.	1	2	3	4	5
6. One should take action only when sure it is morally right.	1	2	3	4	5
7. Most people are basically good and kind.	1	2	3	4	5
8. There is no excuse for lying to someone else.	1	2	3	4	5
9. Most people forget more easily the death of their father than the loss of their property.	1	2	3	4	5
10. Generally speaking, people won't work hard unless they're forced to do so.	1	2	3	4	5

Source: Adapted from *Studies in Machiavellianism* by Richard Christie and Florence Geis, Copyright © 1970 by Academic Press. Reprinted by permission of the publisher.

Results: To find your "Mach score," add up the numbers you circled on questions 1, 3, 4, 5, 9, and 10. For the other four questions reverse the numbers you circled (5 becomes 1, 4 is 2, and so on). Your Mach score is the total of the ten numbers. Many people average 25 on this test. The higher you score above 25, the greater your tendency to be a High Mach—a manipulator. (If you score above 40 points, you should probably conceal it!)

FIGURE 6-6
A Test: Do You Manipulate People?

The Low Mach, the typical "nice guy" who likes and trusts people, is not detached enough to exploit others.

Participative Management: A Subordinate-Centered Leadership Style

A manager can choose a style of **participative management** and encourage subordinates to contribute ideas and actually make decisions within the limits the manager establishes. The amount of participation a leader or manager allows subordinates in the decision-making process depends on trade-offs between three key factors present in a given situation:

1. *Quality of the decision.* Consider the likelihood and the need for the "right" decision and who is in the best position to make it.
2. *Acceptance of the decision by the group.* In general, a group is more likely to accept and to execute decisions that it has helped to make.
3. *Timeliness.* If speed is crucial, the leader can usually make a quicker decision than the group.

Often some aspects of one factor must be sacrificed to gain advantages offered by the other two factors. The specific situation may affect the amount of participation in decision making that a manager allows subordinates, as shown in the Short Cases at the end of the chapter.

The Middle Ground: Flexible Leadership

Successful managers usually do not use a single leadership pattern for all circumstances. Not only have they learned that different situations call for different approaches, but they know that three other sets of factors must be assessed: (1) their own strengths and limitations; (2) the company and the social environment; and (3) their employees, both as individuals and as members of work groups. So effective managers often use the entire range of leadership styles shown earlier in Figure 6–5. When managers face imminent deadlines, particularly with new employees, they manage subordinates through direct orders. When they need new ideas, greater involvement, and face no time pressure, they use participative management.

To support the idea that the same style does not work for everyone, management expert Robert Townsend draws this conclusion on leadership:

How do you spot a leader? They come in all ages, shapes, sizes, and conditions. Some are poor administrators, some are not overly bright. One clue: . . . the true leader can be recognized because, somehow or other, his people consistently turn in superior performances.[9]

CONTROLLING TO ACHIEVE BUSINESS OBJECTIVES

Controlling is the managerial function of comparing plans with actual results and taking appropriate corrective action when necessary. How management control works, an actual management control method, and ways in which you can control your own career are described below.

Essentials of Control

Effective control requires three things: (1) a measurable goal, set in advance; (2) a measure of actual performance to compare with the goal; and (3) feedback for corrective action. For example, suppose that the manager of a factory producing RCA television sets establishes a target for the coming year of building 10,000 sets a month (the measurable goal). On February 1, his production-control specialist reviews the daily manufacturing reports for January to see how many sets actually were produced (the measure of actual performance). When the plant manager is told only 9,500 sets were produced, he identifies the cause—say, a shortage of tuner parts—corrects it, and orders 10,500 sets produced in February (feedback for corrective action).

Lack of control can result in more employees but less output. In his book *Parkinson's Law*, British author and historian C. Northcote Parkinson said: "Work expands so as to fill the time available for its completion." His wisdom is startling and can even be seen in your own college library. A student with two weeks to complete a term project works on it or worries about it for two weeks, then stays up all night before the day it is due to finish it. The same student, with four weeks to complete the project, works on it or worries about it for four weeks, then still stays up all night before the day it is due to finish it!

For organizations, Parkinson is a true prophet. In 1914, the British navy—then the most powerful in the world—needed 4,366 officials to stay afloat. By 1967, when Parkinson judged the British navy "practically powerless," more than 33,000 civil servants were barely sufficient to manage it.[10]

What a Way to Run a Navy: Parkinson's Law

Company goals are most likely to be achieved by motivated employees who participate in making them, who receive sincere supervisory help, and who find their own goals consistent with the organization's goals.

Management by Objectives

FIGURE 6–7 MBO.

Many managers are now using a technique called **management by objectives (MBO)** to control their organizations. Specific objectives are set—by managers *and* their subordinates—for each unit, subunit, and individual in the organization, using specific criteria. For example, a production manager and his or her supervisor might set the specific goal of reducing costs by 10 percent. The hard part is to set objectives so that results can be measured—and to focus on *what* and *when,* not *why* and *how.* For an example of how supervisors and employees work together in MBO, see Figure 6–7.

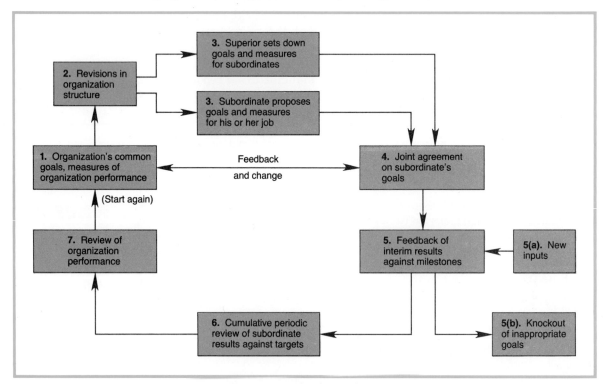

Source: Adapted from *MBO II: A System of Managerial Leadership for the 80's* by George S. Odiorne. Copyright © 1979 by Pitman Learning, Inc., Belmont, California.

Controlling: Your Own Career

Why bounce from job to job or fester in a dead-end position when you could be planning your career? See Figure 6–8 (on page 157) for Alan N. Schoonmaker's ten-step approach to career planning. His ideas, combined with the Your Next Job sections in each chapter of this book, may suggest practical job opportunities you hadn't considered before. Schoonmaker recommends some powerful medicine for people with career-planning problems.

Set Goals

You are the person most interested in your career. So, you—not your parents, spouse, or friends—should set the broad goals stated in the first box of Figure 6–8. How much do you value recognition, money, power, service, and independence? Are you too shy to go into sales but greatly talented as an organizer or a "computer jock"? What job can you realistically start with, according to job ads and the advice of knowledgeable people? A mentor, or trusted adviser, at work can often be extremely valuable (see the box at the top of page 156).

Plan and Act

Jot down a plan. If it calls for asking for a raise or a transfer, or finding a new job, or turning down a job offer, don't just ponder it—do it!

Learn the Rules

All games have rules, including your game of "career monopoly." What's good for your organization may be in conflict with what's good for you. If this can't be resolved, consider leaving.

Accept, too, that your superior may be indifferent to your career ambitions once they go beyond the objectives at hand. Don't feel too guilty about looking out for your own interests, including asking for a raise or leaving the job. Also, you must do more than work well in silence. Office politics are important, deadly important. It doesn't do you any good to write brilliant research reports if your boss takes credit for them in meetings with the president. Figure out a clever way to let the president know it's your work—without antagonizing your boss. Also, realize that "the rules" that successful younger top executives are observing now are different than they used to be (see the box at the bottom of the next page).

Needed: Mentors for Mark and Mary

Many women are much better at their job tasks than they are at "politicking" at work, according to Paula L. Gottschalk, Director of Corporate Relations for CBS. The reason: men have traditionally had older executives, "mentors," to show them the ropes in the organization. Women haven't, says *Business Week* magazine.[11]

But women at CBS, Olin Corporation, Honeywell, and other firms now do. Margaret Kennedy, Director of Personnel Services and Management Staffing at Olin, is mentor to two women. She meets with each woman once a month formally to discuss how things are going and how she can help. Both new managers have received promotions.

At Honeywell Information Systems, Irma Wyman, a 25-year corporate veteran, advises new women managers on their career goals. And at CBS, 14 female executives have volunteered to be "career advisers" to other women.

What kinds of advice do they give? One mentor helped a woman manager choose between two promotions by telling her that one of her prospective bosses could easily lose his job, leaving subordinates in a mess. Generally, though, the mentors encourage the women to temper their idealism with political and diplomatic skills and to realize that subject-matter skills don't count for everything. And they help them face, as one said, "everyday problems that give you a sinking feeling—like being the only woman in a group of 50 men."

At the Top and under 40

Under 40 and a chief executive officer? A generation ago, people would have been aghast at the idea. Now, *Business Week* magazine says,[12] there are more and more opportunities to climb to the head of an organization, or near there, before your hair turns gray. But these younger top executives play by slightly different rules than their older colleagues.

Combining the roles of entrepreneur and organization man, these executives have four key characteristics: a flexible management style (they share decision making with subordinates and delegate a lot of responsibility); worries about the breadth of their knowledge (they're trying to learn more to make up for their inexperience); extraordinary work commitment (hobbies are few, spouses and kids seldom seen); and a big drive for money (for a Mercedes and for independence in the future).

Do these rules appeal to *you*?

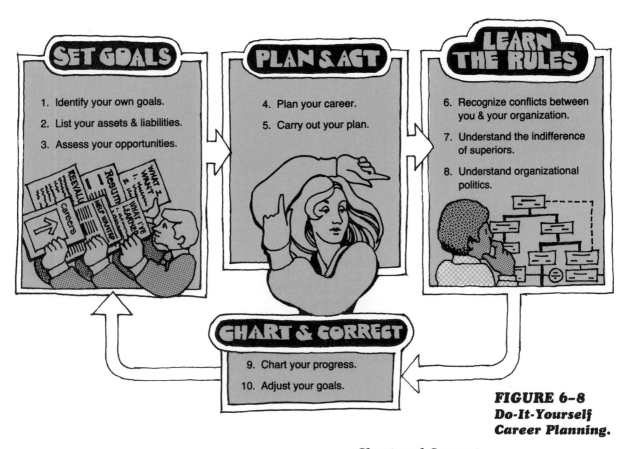

FIGURE 6-8
Do-It-Yourself
Career Planning.

Chart and Correct

Your plans may be thrown out of kilter when your firm is sold to another company. Or a new "star" in the department may eclipse you. Your own values and interests may change too. Some salespeople come to prefer the personal contacts and lose interest in being promoted to sales management where paperwork can be mountainous. Control means measuring progress and taking action.

Planning your own career involves the same decision-making steps as in the DECIDE process of Chapter 4. It also uses the same management skills—planning, organizing, leading, and controlling—needed to direct an organization. Careful planning and good control of your career is like a parachute—it can ensure you a happy landing.

Chapter Review & Applications

Key Points to Remember

1. Leading is guiding the activities of subordinates toward organizational goals. This requires a manager to motivate subordinates and communicate with them effectively.
2. Motivation is anything that causes, directs, and sustains a person's behavior.
3. Employees receive motivation from their job (the type of work and amount of satisfaction it affords), from their individual characteristics (need for prestige, money, and so on), and from their work situation (colleagues, supervisor).
4. Managers can apply concepts from the Hawthorne studies, from Maslow's hierarchy of needs, and from McGregor's Theory X and Theory Y as guidelines for motivating employees.
5. A communication must be received, understood, accepted, and acted on. Good managers watch and listen to verify that the message is received.
6. Good managers are not rigid in their styles—they often use different leadership patterns in different situations.
7. Controlling is the process of comparing results with plans and taking any necessary corrective action. It requires a measurable goal, a measure of actual performance to compare with the goal, and feedback for corrective action.
8. Management by objectives helps employees set personal goals that fit the firm's goals.

Questions for Discussion

1. What factors affect motivation in terms of the (a) job, (b) individual, and (c) work situation?
2. What do you think experimenters in the Hawthorne studies expected to find? What did they actually find?
3. How could differences in people's frames of reference and status lead to poor communication?
4. What three key factors affect the amount of participation a manager might allow subordinates in a specific situation?
5. In what ways does management by objectives relate more closely to McGregor's Theory Y than to his Theory X?

Short Cases

You are a manager of a small group of people. You must decide how much the group should be allowed to participate in decision making. You have three alternatives: (1) make the decision yourself without the group; (2) obtain the group's opinions and then make the decision; or (3) let the group make the decision. For each of the cases below, select the best alternative and justify it.

Case A: As office manager, six clerks report to you. Every day, you close the office from noon to 1:00 P.M. while everyone goes out to lunch. However, the president has just announced that effective next week at least one person must remain in every office throughout the lunch hour to answer incoming telephone calls. How do you implement this?

Case B: You are a highway department supervisor in Montana. A blizzard has been raging for eight hours, and your four snowplow crews—all with widely different levels of experience—have just completed an exhausting day and are ready to go home. A call arrives that a snowplow must be sent to free a school bus snowbound on a treacherous mountain road. How do you decide which crew to send?

Case C: As supervisor of an engineering design unit, you must select one of two design concepts for a complex new piece of equipment. The design incorporates mechanical, electrical, and hydraulic features. Your group consists of two mechanical engineers, three electrical engineers, and one hydraulics engineer. How do you choose the design you will use?

A Critical
Business Decision

—made by James S. Campbell
of Xerox Corporation

The Situation

It is 1980. The Xerox Corporation is a far different organization from the one that converted Chester Carlson's xerography process into the first workable office copier two decades earlier (see page 16). The near-monopoly that Xerox had on plain-paper copiers in its early years is gone. Competitors like Savin, Canon, IBM, and 3M have taken over major parts of the copier market—especially for low-priced, limited-volume copiers. In 1975, Xerox wrote off the large-scale computer market and $84 million in losses. But in 1980, Exxon, with eight times the assets of Xerox, decided to enter the office machine business and Xerox needed to retaliate.

So Xerox sought new stategies. It introduced less-expensive copiers to serve the needs of smaller offices, and even got into the retail business and designed "a supermarket for office supplies." The Xerox goal: to open one hundred U.S. retail stores and fifty European outlets by the start of 1982. By offering everything from small copiers and calculators to personal computers and electric typewriters in these stores, Xerox hopes to reach four million small businesses and six million offices in the home that its sales force hasn't reached in the past.

The Decision

James S. Campbell, president of Xerox Business Systems, a major division of the Xerox Corporation, now faces a key business decision: to develop a strategy for selling customers "the office of the future."

Back in 1964, IBM had revolutionized office equipment with its magnetic-tape Selectric typewriter. Basically, this Selectric was an electric typewriter wired to a tape recorder, which permitted a typist to make corrections directly on a tape without retyping an entire document. When the typist pressed a button, the machine produced a perfect final copy. IBM coined the phrase "word processing" to describe this revolutionary technique.

To promote word processing—and the eventual linking of many key office machines—IBM recommends the complete reorganization of the standard office. The traditional secretarial job is abolished and divided into two parts. The typing is now handled by "correspondence secretaries" in a centralized word-processing center. Managers dictate messages by phone to the center and receive typed letters and reports in return. The much-reduced secretarial staff—without typewriters—deals with the administrative aspects of the job, each staff member handling a group of managers.

By 1980, Campbell's Xerox has its own word-processing system. Campbell now startles competitors with Xerox's view of the office of the future: its Ethernet communications network. This will enable office equipment (made by either Xerox or competitors) in separate offices to "talk" back and forth. It will combine elements of both word processing and data processing. Eventually, Campbell announces, distant offices will be linked by satellite.

For the 1980s, Xerox is clearly in the communications business.

Questions

1. If you were James S. Campbell, what advantages could you cite to prospective users as to how Ethernet might improve both office communications and productivity?
2. If you were a prospective user, what disadvantages might there be in using IBM's approach to reorganizing traditional office procedures? Do you see personal communications problems? Explain.

Production

In this chapter you will learn . . .

- the steps involved in designing new products.
- what purchasing managers and their departments do.
- how manufacturing departments work.
- how mass production and automation have revolutionized manufacturing.
- what transportation managers do.

7

162

*If a man . . . make a better mousetrap . . .
the world will beat a path to his door.*

RALPH WALDO EMERSON

ade in Texas" may replace "Made in Japan" by the end of the 1980s. The reason? Consumer electronics by Texas Instruments, Inc., whose headquarters are in Lubbock, Texas.

Since 1976, Texas Instruments (TI) has been taking on Japan in two key consumer products—watches and calculators. Out of hundreds of companies entering these competitive markets a decade ago, only a few remain. TI's innovation and production efficiency have made it successful in these markets. Innovation reduced the number of parts in its lowest-priced calculator from 119 to 22. And the simpler design produced on automated assembly lines reduced the calculator's retail price from $45 to $10 in only two years.[1]

Robots are a key to TI's automated assembly lines (see box), and they are also helping out on production lines across the U.S., especially in auto plants, which were their first major employers. By early 1980 Ford had installed 236 robots, General Motors 160, and Chrysler 80. The robots can also work where people can't—at high temperatures or in noxious gases. They are an exciting part of **production**, the topic of this chapter.

Robot Arms
. . . on the Automated Assembly Line
for Calculators

Texas Instruments produces 75 percent of its hand calculators using continuous assembly lines like those shown on the left.

Business Week describes this process: "The continuous lines . . . employ several robot arms that do 'pick and place' tasks. At one work station, for example, a television camera locates the calculator on the conveyor for a robot, which picks it up and loads it into a carousel that applies foot pads and the date code. A second robot off-loads the calculator. Farther down the line, a similar setup loads a completed calculator into a test system that pushes the keys with bursts of air while a camera-equipped minicomputer 'reads' the calculator display in a check for errors."

STAGES IN PRODUCING A PRODUCT

A **production manager,** whether at Texas Instruments or at a frisbee-manu-facturing plant, has three tasks: designing the product, buying what materials go into it, and making and getting it to the consumer. The first stage is *product development.* Here, employees develop the designs, models, and prototypes (working models) of the items to be produced. In the second stage, *purchasing,* buyers procure the right amount of raw materials and parts at the right price and see that they arrive on time for manufacturing. In the third stage, *manufacturing,* the materials are made into products and transported to customers.

How the Three Stages Are Managed

Each of these stages—product development, purchasing, and manufacturing—is supervised by a manager or vice president who reports directly to the president. Figure 7–1 shows this reporting relationship for a medium-sized firm. It also shows how each department is divided into subsections.

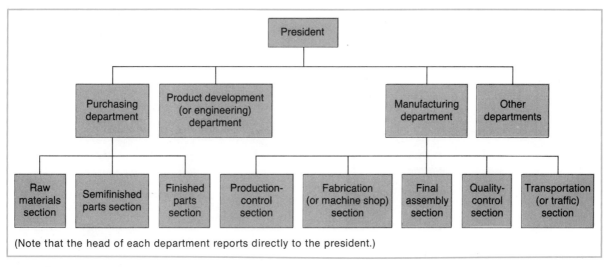

(Note that the head of each department reports directly to the president.)

FIGURE 7–1
Organization Chart for a Medium-Sized Manufacturing Firm.

The product development (or engineering) department is usually managed by an engineer or a physical scientist. Department members are responsible for detailed designs of the products.

The purchasing department is headed by a purchasing manager, or agent, who supervises the buyers. Each buyer is responsible for a particular group of items—such as raw materials, semifinished parts, and finished parts—as shown in Figure 7–1.

The manufacturing department, headed by a manufacturing manager, is often divided into sections, such as production control, fabrication, final assembly, quality control, and transportation (again, see Figure 7–1). Sometimes, these sections are also divided into specialized groups. The transportation (or traffic) section, for example, is responsible for moving purchased items in and final products out to customers.

How Production Activities Work Together

FIGURE 7-2
Production Path.

The path a product follows through the company is shown in Figure 7–2. For illustration purposes, we have chosen jeans, but the process would be just the same for any product—from airplanes to a new hamburger cooker. Once the

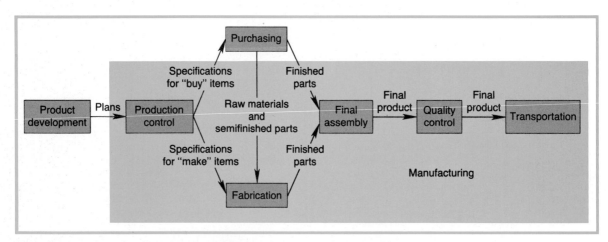

(Note that manufacturing department activities are shown in the most detail.)

decision has been made to produce a new line of jeans, the idea is turned over to the product development department, which comes up with designs for the finished product. These designs are then sent to the manufacturing department, where the production-control section schedules each step necessary to produce the product. The schedule includes everything from cutting the fabric to attaching the embroidery. This involves consulting with other departments on the critical *make-buy decision*—that is, which parts or pieces will be purchased from outside vendors and which will be made by the firm itself. The production-control section also develops the necessary *specifications*—detailed descriptions of materials, dimensions, and performance requirements—for all the parts of the finished product. For example, the type of denim, corduroy, or suedecloth; the particular shades of blue, brown, or red; and the measurements for each size must be exactly specified. The production-control managers then route the job through the various fabrication steps, scheduling each step in with the firm's other work.

Next, specifications for the items to be bought are sent to the purchasing department. It buys the raw materials, semifinished parts, and finished parts that are requested. This would include such things as the fabric, thread, buttons, and embroidered appliqués. When the ordered materials arrive, they are sent to the fabrication section, which makes the finished parts (leg panels and pockets, for instance) according to specifications. Finished parts from both the purchasing department (buttons, appliqués) and the fabrication section (leg panels, pockets) are then sent to the final assembly section.

After coming off the final assembly line, each pair of jeans is inspected by the quality-control section. It must meet the company's specifications, as did the incoming purchased pieces and materials this section tested earlier. Unsatisfactory products are returned for reworking.

Finally, the inspected products move to the transportation section, where they will be shipped to the stores and shops that have ordered the jeans.

PRODUCT DEVELOPMENT

The objective of **product development** is to generate profitable new products and improve existing ones. This may sound easy, but product development people who worked on the Edsel or on Corfam (the "breathable" synthetic leather) know better. The spectacular failure of the Edsel in the early 1960s cost Ford about $250 million. And in the 1970s DuPont had to withdraw

Corfam from the market after the company lost about $100 million in eight years. Thousands of other lesser-known products quietly fail every year.

Steps in New-Product Development

To minimize the chances of failure, product development managers carefully evaluate their new product at each stage of a six-step development process. At each stage, decisions are often made to drop or redesign the product based on new information that is obtained. Only about one in 58 product ideas ever becomes a commercial success. The six steps to rags or riches—idea generation, screening, business analysis, product development, test marketing, and commercialization—are described in the following pages and illustrated in Figure 7–3.

Generate Ideas

The person who first thought of the paper clip or the minicomputer had a good idea. Most often, the sources of new product ideas are creative people. If you

**FIGURE 7-3
Steps in the
Development
of a New
Product.**

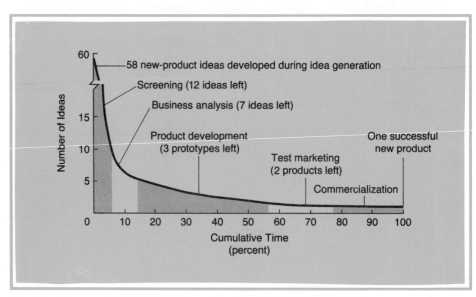

Source: From *Management of New Products* (Chicago: Booz, Allen, & Hamilton, Inc., 1968), p. 9.

were put in a room for two hours with a few friends or co-workers, could you come up with 75 to 100 ideas for new products? One food company does this regularly, with its chemists, food technologists, and marketing people. Other companies collect ideas from their customers, scientists, engineers, top managers, salespeople, and competitors.

Ideas also come from a sudden inspiration. Edwin Land's young daughter asked him one day why she had to wait so long to see the pictures he took with his camera. The result: the instant Polaroid Land Camera. Another dreamer was ice-fishing in Labrador. The temperature was 20° below zero, and when Clarence Birdseye placed his catch down next to the hole, the fish instantly froze solid. Later, he dropped the frozen fish into a pail of water. To his shock, it began to swim again. Birdseye thought about this for a while. The result: the beginning of the frozen-food industry.

Many of today's creative ideas deal with services rather than products. Gelco is 100 times its size of ten years ago (see box) because its managers encourage innovative thinking.

Everything Bud Grossman's company does could be done by his clients. But they couldn't do it for themselves as cheaply. He and his General Leasing Company, called Gelco, must be onto something. *Time Magazine* recently called him the "Minnesota Money Machine."

What Grossman does is lease or manage almost anything that moves. He began with autos, trucks, trailers, forklifts, and refrigerated vans, leasing the vehicles to companies. But he also offered to manage their upkeep schedules and trade-in times, all by computer. Companies could, of course, keep track of their own vehicles, but it was cheaper to use Gelco's large-scale computerized program than to do it themselves. As a result, Gelco now manages a larger fleet than the U.S. Postal Service—at least 275,000 vehicles for thousands of firms that own them. For moving packages, Grossman bought a courier service in 1979. It is now moving toward $95 million in business.

Gelco also contracts to provide huge freight-shipping containers anywhere on earth, a business involving an elaborate computer system. Grossman's plans for the future include handling all of a firm's expense accounts, airline tickets, and hotel reservations. For example, Gelco might contract for 10,000 tickets from United Airlines and get a price discount for this volume, resell them to business firms in smaller quantities, and split the price savings with them.

The result is a company that moved from $6.5 million in revenues in 1969 to more than $445 million by the end of 1979, to close to $650 million at present. All on operations seemingly anyone could do. As Grossman tells *Time* magazine, "Ideas are really all we have."[2]

"Ideas Are All We Have"

Screen Them

Many ideas, though good, are not right for a particular business. So new-product ideas must be screened according to company objectives and available resources. If they are judged unsuitable or inappropriate, they are discarded at this stage. Other ideas graduate to the next step of the product development process.

Do a Business Analysis

In the business analysis stage, managers make a detailed estimate of the profitability of manufacturing and marketing the proposed products. They consider market size, production and distribution costs, and financial requirements. Up to this point, each product is still only an idea, a blueprint, or a rough, nonworking model. Products that are not expected to be profitable enough are dropped.

A New Wrench, a Little Guy, and Justice

A tool or production method doesn't have to look like something from Mars to be a significant innovation. Sears sold millions of a new kind of quick-release socket wrench piling up huge profits, thanks to the invention of Peter Roberts. Now the owner of a delicatessen in Chattanooga, Tennessee, Roberts invented the wrench almost twenty years ago, when he was 18. He patented it, then sold the rights to Sears for $10,000.

It was the last step that was his least inventive. Lawyers are now trying, with some success, to get the contract for this sale overturned, on the theory that Sears deceived Roberts about the profit potential of his invention when it bought the rights. In 1980 the U.S. Court of Appeals agreed to award Roberts $1 million and to reassign the patent to him, according to an Associated Press story.

Roberts' reaction: "It shows how a small man can receive justice even against an enormous corporation if right is on his side. Right is the strongest weapon a person can have."[3]

Develop the Product

If a product idea has passed the first three stages, the next step toward its eventual development is to produce a limited number of **prototypes,** or working models. The object here is to see whether it works and, if so, whether it can be produced at a reasonable cost.

Many potential products do not survive this stage. One was a candy that could be blown into bubbles—sort of a bubble gum that could also be eaten. The problem was that the edible foaming agents didn't make good bubbles, and when kids blew bad bubbles, the sticky stuff dribbled down their chins. Their faces were scraped and the idea was scrapped.

But if a product does pass the financial and workability tests, it is given a name, its packaging is planned, and it is made ready to be introduced to consumers.

Test-Market It

Products are introduced first only to a limited number of customers so that their responses can be carefully watched. Products that receive completely unfavorable reactions are dropped immediately. Those that seem likely to sell well after certain changes are made are returned to the development department with specific improvement instructions. Xerox is probably here today because of such changes and "serendipity"—accidentally discovering one thing while looking for another. The firm (when it was Haloid) had asked four customers to test its first copier. Their universal answer: its twelve manual operations needed to produce a finished copy made it too hard to operate. But one user happened to mention it was perfect for making paper printing plates for offset duplicating. This provided critically needed sales revenue that allowed the firm—and its xerography process—to survive.

Another example of a new product with room for improvement was a catsup with the natural flavor of tomatoes, the result of millions of dollars of product development. Consumer reactions in supermarkets were immediate: they avoided it like the red plague because they missed the overcooked, scorched flavor they associated with the taste of a high-quality catsup. So the firm adjusted its equipment to overcook and scorch. Sales of the "improved" catsup soared.

Pricing is another important factor in product acceptance. For example, in its first test market, Procter and Gamble's disposable diaper, Pampers, bombed

out because the price was too high. So P & G simplified the package, speeded up assembly lines, and cut other costs. Pampers became a hit in its fourth test market, and today it is a booming success.

Commercialize the Product

Once a product has "passed" its test market, it is offered for sale nationally. This involves carefully selecting the channels of distribution (such as choosing between department or specialty stores, or newsstands or subscriptions) and arranging for advertising and promotion campaigns. But even at this stage, there is no guarantee of success. Products that do not generate adequate profits—and many do not—are withdrawn from the market. The accompanying box describes things you may be ready for in the 1980s, and also some you may survive without.

Test Carefully for Quality

Product quality testing has become increasingly important for two reasons: (1) managers want products that are clearly better than those of competitors, and (2) they want to protect their company from rumors, damage claims, and legal action by federal agencies.

New Products off the Drawing Boards for the 1980s

The products listed in the left-hand column are those that, according to experts, American consumers are ready and waiting for. In the right-hand column are new-product ideas that might be acceptable but that we probably can survive without.

- *Interferon*
A wonder drug that might fight everything from cancer to the common cold when its current price—$22 billion a pound—is reduced.

- *Hand-Held Translators*
Travelers in foreign countries would carry them to display—even speak—everyday words and phrases.

- *The "Microcar"*
An electric car, recharged by plugging into your house outlet, that costs $2,000, weighs 300 pounds, seats 2, and has a 35-mile range at up to 20 miles per hour.

- *Wide-Screen Home TV Sets*

- *"Intelligent Copiers"*
They not only copy but also make charts and graphs.

- *Quench Sport Gum*
A low-calorie lemon-flavored chewing gum. It's designed to solve the jogger's thirst problem.

- *Waldo, Gronk, and Rodney*
These home-built robots will be the latest household pets.

- *A Battery-Powered Egg Scrambler*
It scrambles the egg while it's still in the shell.

- *Pop Wheels*
These shoes are instant roller skates, with retractable wheels.

- *Polyester Soft-Drink Bottles*
Drink the pop, then recycle the bottle to be woven into fabric.

For example, advertising claims must be justified. One firm went to a lot of trouble to prove that the flavor of its chewing gum really lasted longer. It hired a panel of gum chewers, who were required to standardize their chewing speeds by chewing in unison to the beat of a musician's metronome.

But even elaborate testing cannot completely protect a product against rumors, especially for children's products. Life Savers, for instance, had to buy $100,000 worth of ads to offset tales that Bubble Yum, its bubble-gum product, was crammed with spider eggs or caused cancer. Still, the rumor persisted in the New York City area and caused sales to drop. Similarly, McDonald's had to convince consumers that its hamburgers didn't contain ground worms.

Pop Rocks—a candy that "explodes" on the tongue—caused General Foods a real stomachache. The rumor: "A little kid across town (or sometimes a TV celebrity) ate three bags of Pop Rocks and drank a soda pop. His stomach exploded and he died." Merely denying this untrue rumor wasn't enough. General Foods Corporation took full-page newspaper ads to finally squelch the horror stories.

A company must also protect itself against problems with federal agencies. For example, some 77,000 injuries a year are caused by power lawn mowers. The Consumer Product Safety Commission decided to act. It issued a regulation requiring mowers to be equipped with a device to shut off the blades within three seconds after the user releases the handle. This device should prevent 60,000 injuries a year. But it will add $36 to $50 to the price of a power mower. Other federal regulations are more complex. Standards for wood, metal, and plastic ladders now run to eighty pages—an uphill struggle for a business to interpret.

PURCHASING

To make a product—whether it is nail polish or tractors—someone must purchase the necessary raw materials and parts. This is the job of **purchasing** managers. It is also their responsibility to see that these parts and materials arrive at the right time and place, for the right price.

Typically, there are six steps a purchasing department follows when buying raw materials, semifinished parts, and finished parts.[4] These are described in the following sections and shown in Figure 7–4 on the next page.

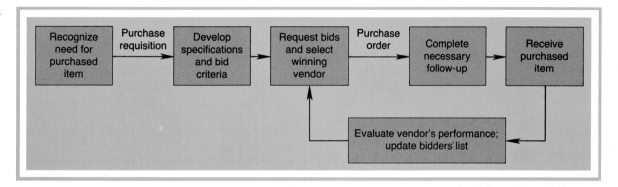

FIGURE 7-4
Steps in the Purchasing Process.

Recognize Needs

When materials are needed for the first time (as for new products), the product development department usually contacts purchasing. For example, an appliance manufacturer might need a new motor and other parts for its new line of clothes dryers. After make-buy decisions have been made for these parts, the production-control section sends purchasing the specifications for items to be bought from outside sources. The *purchase requisition* authorizes purchasing to begin contacting vendors (suppliers) for bids.

When there is a need to restock existing materials, the order generally arises from the group that is in charge of maintaining an inventory. Again, a purchase requisition that describes the materials, quantity, and date needed is sent to the purchasing department.

Develop Specifications

Purchasing managers often can cut costs with a careful look at the specifications and a *value analysis*. This is a systematic appraisal of the design, quality, and performance requirements of an item. For instance, the product development engineers for the clothes dryer manufacturer may have specified at least a 3/16 horsepower motor. But the purchasing department's value analysis might recommend that they buy a 1/4 horsepower motor, available as a standard item, which may involve vendors, rather than a 3/16 horsepower motor, which must be made-to-order at a higher cost.

The purchasing department also tries to find more than one vendor to bid on a contract and to generate genuine competition among them. To do this, purchasing managers must set their priorities carefully to enable them to evaluate bids. Four typical bid criteria are price, quality, delivery, and service. Frequently, a trade-off is required. One company's low price must be weighed against the quality of its supplementary services, such as design-improvement ideas. For standard items, though, price is generally the key factor. Only for more technical products, such as computers, is price much less important.

Request Bids and Select a Vendor

Once selection criteria are set, the next step is to solicit bids from potential suppliers. Vendors names are selected from a *bidders' list,* those qualified to supply the item. Each vendor receives a quotation request form, describing the desired quantity, delivery date, and specifications of the product. To ensure competition, many firms require at least three bids for purchases over a specified dollar amount.

Next, purchasing managers evaluate the bids submitted. On large or important orders, they may divide the final contract between two or more bidders. This guarantees a supply in case of a strike or an extended shutdown at one supplier's plant. The awarded contract is in the form of a *purchase order*—an authorization for the vendor to provide the items and to receive a specified payment for them.

Follow-up with the Vendor

Vendor follow-up is essential when the item is expensive, in short supply, or crucially important to the firm. If an item must be redesigned, the purchasing manager must also see that the required changes are made. This many involve negotiating new terms of sale or making sure that the order arrives on time. For example, the first Polaris nuclear submarines had to be cut in half to insert new missile silos. This change required considerable contract renegotiation.

Receive the Order

The purchasing department's clerks and inspectors must check the items against the purchase order. Quantities and specifications must be correct. If the order is unsatisfactory, the purchasing department must negotiate with the supplier for a correction or arrange for an entirely new shipment.

Evaluate the Vendor

Purchasing managers then note evaluations on a vendor rating sheet and use these to update their bidders' lists. Suppliers who show poor performance on several contracts are usually dropped from the list. As names of new, qualified vendors are uncovered, their names are added to the bidders' lists to ensure competition for future purchases.

In their buying decisions, purchasing managers must also consider the conflicts among their six major goals: low prices, high quality, no out-of-stock problems, a small investment in inventory, continuing sources of supplies, and good vendor relations. Out-of-stock problems can be minimized, for example, by keeping more of the item on hand, but this will mean a large investment in inventory. Buying in large volume lowers price but creates higher inventory costs. Conflicts like these can cause unavoidable managerial headaches.

MANUFACTURING AND TRANSPORTATION

The **manufacturing** department converts purchased items into finished products and then supplies these products to customers. To see how these objectives are accomplished, we shall look at some key characteristics of modern manufacturing, classifications of manufacturing operations, and transportation modes used.

The Characteristics of Modern Manufacturing

Modern manufacturing, which relies on *mass production* and *automation,* has changed our society as surely as did the cars and televisions it made possible. The standardized quality and enormous quantity of today's products are the result of these two manufacturing techniques.

Mass Production

A method of organizing manufacturing to multiply the output of standardized articles, **mass production** began with Eli Whitney's concept of interchangeable parts. But it was brought to efficiency by Henry Ford, who implemented four key principles:

1. STANDARDIZATION OF PARTS Each part in the final product must be the same as all other parts of its type. A solid-state circuit for a given TV model, for example, must fit into any set of that model.
2. SPECIALIZATION OF PEOPLE AND MACHINES Each part is produced by trained workers who operate machines that perform specific operations. Thus, an expert drill-press operator may drill all the holes on the chassis of a television set. Specialization has greatly expanded worker output and reduced production costs because skilled workers operating highly efficient machines are faster, more accurate, and less expensive than twice as many unskilled workers. Time-and-motion studies speed up operations not only in conventional factories but also in hamburger chains like Burger King (see box).

3. GROUPING OF PARTS INTO SUBASSEMBLIES   Items produced by specialized labor and machines are grouped into *subassemblies*. These are collections of parts that can be put together and stocked until they are ready to be combined on the final assembly line.
4. USE OF MOVABLE ASSEMBLY LINES   Components of the final product pass by people and machines on a carefully planned and timed movable assembly line. This stage utilizes and combines each of the three preceding principles.

Burger King: A Small Food Factory?

Burger King's executives like to point out that their company is run by 50,000 teen-agers. And they go on to say that their labor costs are increasing at an even faster rate than beef prices. So it is essential that each Burger King restaurant be as efficient and productive as possible.

As noted in Chapter 1, most experts believe that increases in productivity are hard to achieve in service industries, such as fast food, where quality is important. Burger King disagrees. At its bright, sunny corporate headquarters in Miami, each step in its restaurant operations is measured. These measurements are analyzed by computer to find the most efficient method.

In this process Burger King looks at each of its restaurants as a small food factory. But there is one big difference between a fast-food factory and other assembly lines: an increase in production translates immediately into extra sales rather than into inventory. "The demand at the peak hours is so great that if we can produce more we can sell more," says Donna Nicol, Burger King's communications director. "We have to do it within a very tight time frame," she says. "Nobody cares how many hamburgers we can make between 11:00 P.M. and 6:00 A.M.," she explains to *Fortune* magazine.[5]

Burger King applies the classic time-and-motion-study methods to analyze every movement of each employee in a prototype restaurant. For example, one study recommended moving the bell hose—which triggers a loud ring when cars drive over it—at its drive-in windows back by ten feet. This meant eleven extra seconds of time, enough to alert the order taker to be ready when the car arrives at the window. With this and some other small changes, Burger King drive-in windows can now handle an extra thirty cars per hour. To handle the extra cars, Burger King is now installing computerized french-fry machines. It foresees machines that will mix, pour, and cap soft drinks automatically.

These and other ideas are tested on a computer model of a typical Burger King restaurant. Ideas that survive are tested further at one of its five research-and-development restaurants in the Miami area. Many of the ideas come from Burger King restaurant managers, who receive cash rewards for good ideas. The ideas are fed to teams that study them, like the Drive-Through Task Force and the Whopper Hotness Program.

. . . The Whopper Hotness Program???

178 *Management and Production*

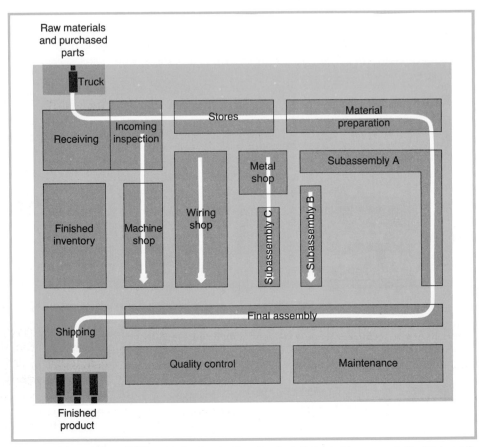

**FIGURE 7-5
Plant Layout
Used in
Appliance
Production.**

Source: Adapted from William Voris, *Production Control,* 3rd ed. (Homewood, Ill.: Richard D. Irwin, 1966), p. 41.

Mass production is most sophisticated in the manufacture of cars, appliances, and electronic products. A typical continuous, high-volume production line for home appliances is shown in Figure 7–5.

Automation
Automation is production by self-regulating machines. It is also the process of making machines automatic. A self-regulating machine has continuous *feedback* (or *feedback control*), meaning that information about its output is trans-

mitted back by an automatic control device. Feedback is necessary for spotting and correcting performance problems.

Levi-Strauss's Servo-Server is an example of the impact of automation. The Servo-Server is a computer-controlled pocket maker that helps with some of the 37 different steps in making a pair of Levis. It pushes the two parts of the pocket together under the sewing needle. They are then sewn together; the thread is cut; and the finished denim pocket is dumped into a collection basket—all in less than one second. This automation doubles the machine operator's output, cuts production costs, and improves product quality.

Classifications of Manufacturing Operations

Texas Instruments' calculators and Ford's Mustangs, quite different products, are produced by remarkably similar manufacturing operations. In fact, all manufacturing methods are based on a combination of the three classifications discussed on page 181.

Movable Production Lines . . . for Lettuce and Spinach

Movable production lines aren't all fast and noisy. And they don't all crank out cars and appliances. Some are slow and quiet, and gradually turn lettuce and spinach seedlings into salad greens, ready to be bagged and trucked to nearby groceries and restaurants.

General Mills' new movable production-line method of growing vegetables is called *hydroponics*. This means that the vegetables are grown in water, with nutrients and artificial light, and a computer to monitor them. Since everything's inside, no herbicides or pesticides are necessary. The vegetable starts as a seed or seedling at one end of the production line and comes out full-grown at the other end. And the production line runs year around. How long it takes to produce an individual plant is a trade secret.

With this system, General Mills hopes to garner a good share of the salad greens market in groceries and in restaurant salad bars. They are also glad to grow your salad near where you live and hope to open other vegetable factories near other metropolitan areas if their pilot plant in DeKalb, Illinois, works out well. General Mills believes that as energy costs rise, these vegetable factories will compete effectively with California growers who ship their produce all over the country, according to a story in the *Minneapolis Tribune*.[6]

Your Next Job
Positions in Product Development, Purchasing, Manufacturing, and Transportation

Careers in Product Development

Drafters prepare detailed drawings of manufactured goods and calculate the strength, quality, quantity, and cost of the materials required. Technical training is mandatory and may be acquired in technical institutes, community colleges, or on-the-job training programs. Yearly income averages $12,000. Future job opportunities are promising due to the increased production of technically complex items. (*Additional information:* American Institute for Design and Drafting, 3119 Price Road, Bartlesville, Oklahoma 74003.)

Industrial designers use their artistic talents to develop attractive, functional products and symbols that appeal to prospective buyers. Large firms generally require a bachelor's degree in industrial design or fine arts. Annual salary ranges from $10,000 to more than $25,000. Employment opportunities are expected to expand gradually because of increasing consumer population and emphasis on ecology and product safety. (*Additional information:* Industrial Designers Society of America, 1717 N Street, N.W., Washington, D.C. 20036.)

Careers in Purchasing

Purchasing agents buy the machinery, raw materials, and component parts required by the firm. Purchasing agents also negotiate price, quality, delivery dates, and other terms of sale with their suppliers. An ability to analyze numbers and technical data is essential. Large firms often require a bachelor's degree in business administration or liberal arts. Annual salary ranges from $12,900 to over $50,000 for corporate purchasing directors. The demand for purchasing agents knowledgeable in specific areas is expected to increase as business functions and products become more specialized. (*Additional information:* National Association of Purchasing Management, 11 Park Place, New York, New York 10007.)

Careers in Manufacturing

Manufacturing inspectors decide whether raw materials, parts, and finished products conform to specifications. They are trained on the job, then assume limited responsibilities under close supervision, and later advance to the level of skilled inspectors or quality-control technicians. An aptitude for numbers and measurement is indispensable. Annual earnings vary from $8,000 to $18,500. Employment opportunities are expected to increase moderately as population and income grow, and manufactured products become more complex. (*Additional information:* American Society for Quality Control, 161 W. Wisconsin Ave., Milwaukee, Wis. 53203.)

Department supervisors communicate company policies to blue-collar workers. They train new workers, schedule work assignments, and maintain production and employee records. Most have been promoted through the ranks of blue-collar workers. A college education is not mandatory but increases the likelihood of advancement to higher management positions. Annual income is approximately $15,000. Employment opportunities are expected to increase moderately. (*Additional information:* American Management Association, 135 West 50th Street, New York, New York 10020.)

Careers in Transportation

Traffic managers oversee the movement of materials and finished goods. They select the most efficient mode of transportation and the specific routes and carriers. They must keep informed of changing transportation technology and government transportation regulations. College graduates comprise a growing proportion of the nation's 20,000 traffic managers. Yearly salary ranges from $11,000 to more than $50,000. Employment opportunities are expected to increase moderately due to widening distribution markets. (*Additional information:* American Society of Traffic and Transportation, Inc. 547 W. Jackson Blvd., Chicago, Ill. 60606.)

Standard Versus Custom Manufacture

A firm that produces items according to its own specifications performs *standard manufacture*. A firm that produces items to a customer's specifications is doing *custom manufacture*. Standard manufacture is more common and includes almost all consumer products from breakfast cereals to cars. Examples of custom-manufactured items are specialized machine tools, some vans, and made-to-order clothing.

Continuous Versus Batch Process

In a *continuous process*, the manufacturing is unchanged for months or years. Steel, petroleum, and automobiles are produced this way. This method is highly efficient, but an unforeseen shutdown or other significant change can be extremely costly. In a *batch* (or an *intermittent*) *process*, the manufacturing time is shorter. Tasks, people, and machines are changed often to meet the manufacturing requirements of different products. A print shop uses the batch process to handle the many small orders of different customers.

Analytic Versus Synthetic Process

In an *analytic process*, the final product is manufactured by breaking something down into its components. In meat packing, for example, a side of beef is disassembled to produce the various cuts—from T-bone steaks to pot roasts to soup bones—found in the meat department of the grocery stores. In a *synthetic process*, final products are built or assembled from basic parts. Appliances and chemical items like nylon and rayon are made by synthetic processes.

Texas Instruments' calculators and Ford's Mustangs are both produced by standard manufacture using continuous, synthetic processes (see the boxed insert on page 162).

Transportation

Transportation (or traffic) managers in the manufacturing department arrange for the inbound delivery of raw materials and parts, and for the outbound shipment of the final manufactured products. They are responsible for selecting the best *mode of transportation* so that products reach customers on time in good condition and with minimum cost.

Select the Best Mode

The transportation manager must choose one or more of the following transportation modes: highway, rail, air, water, and pipeline. Cost must sometimes be balanced against other factors in the decision. For instance, perishable foods or flowers, or turbine generators needed to keep a power plant in operation, are usually moved by air, even though other modes are cheaper.

Besides cost, five major *operating characteristics* weigh in the manager's decision: speed, frequency, dependability, capability, and availability. Figure 7–6 shows how these factors are measured and ranked. If speed is most

College Term Papers Pay: The "Absolutely, Positively Overnight" Express Company

Frederick W. Smith *did not* build a better mousetrap and wait for the world to beat a path to his door. Instead, using the ideas he developed in a college term paper, he set out to show the world that with his simple new invention *he* could beat a path to *everybody else's* door, says *Fortune* magazine.[7]

He gave the name Federal Express to his door-to-door, flying parcel service. And he advertised "absolutely, positively overnight" delivery for his overnight small-parcel service—limited to seventy pounds, the weight one person could carry. "I figured we had to be enormously reliable," says Smith, "since our service is frequently used for expensive spare parts, live organs, or other emergency shipments."

But Federal Express isn't your typical fly-by-night outfit. After all Smith *did* write his term paper at Yale. And he *did* use a family trust of $4 million to get started. And Federal Express *did* lose $29 million in its first twenty-six months of operation.

What Smith had, though, was a good idea, good execution, and the tenacity (in addition to the resources) to stick with it. First, Smith reasoned, he had to own his own jet aircraft so he would not have to depend on commercial flights. Second, *all* parcels had to be picked up early in the evening, flown to a single sorting center (Memphis), and rerouted to their final destination before dawn. Even a Los Angeles-San Francisco shipment made the Memphis detour. Finally, in spite of heavy early losses, some key loans and a lot of hustle turned the business around.

Today, Federal Express has 6,700 employees and flies 65,000 packages a night to 89 cities in 52 garish orange, white, and purple jets. All the traffic still funnels through the Memphis sorting center. But then that's part of Fred Smith's KISS ("Keep it simple, stupid") principle.

And the Yale term paper? It barely got a passing grade, but its idea is now worth about $260 million in annual sales revenue.

FIGURE 7-6
Comparison of Operating Characteristics
of the Five Modes of Transportation.

OPERATING CHARACTERISTIC	HOW CHARACTERISTIC IS MEASURED	RANKING (BEST TO WORST)				
		1	2	3	4	5
Speed	Time from origin to destination.	Air	Highway	Rail	Water	Pipeline
Frequency	Movements in a given time period.	Pipeline	Highway	Air	Rail	Water
Dependability	Performance according to schedule.	Pipeline	Highway	Rail	Water	Air
Capability	Flexibility in moving a variety of goods.	Water	Rail	Highway	Air	Pipeline
Availability	Number of end points served by the mode.	Highway	Rail	Air	Water	Pipeline

Source: Adapted from J. L. Heskett, Robert J. Ivie, and Nicholas A. Glaskowsky, Jr., *Business Logistics,* pp. 70–71. Copyright © 1964 by The Ronald Press Company. Reprinted by permission of John Wiley & Sons, Inc.

important, air transportation is best, followed by highway, rail, water, and pipeline. Pipeline transportation is frequent and dependable, but it is also slow, inflexible, and relatively unavailable.

A third set of decision factors includes product, location of customer, urgency, and changes in the relative cost of different modes. Heavy products, such as iron ore and grain, are moved by water whenever possible. But an equally heavy machine replacement for a stalled production line is moved by air if urgency is a factor.

Combine Modes and Use Containers

Intermodal transportation, combining two or more modes, is often most efficient. The best-known combination is *piggyback,* highway trailers loaded onto railroad flat cars.

One way of simplifying intermodal transportation is by using standard containers. *Containerization*—packing goods in boxes—eliminates the expense of handling individual items during shipment. Normally containers are fitted with fixtures that allow them to be easily transferred from one mode to another. These containers can then be moved from rail to plane to truck, for example, with ease.

Chapter Review & Applications

Key Points to Remember

1. Production is the use of people and machines to convert materials into finished products and supply these products to customers. Production includes three key stages: product development, purchasing, and manufacturing.

2. The development of a new product involves six steps: idea generation, screening, business analysis, product development, test marketing, and commercialization. Roughly one in 58 new-product ideas becomes a commercial success.

3. When the product development department designs a new product, a make-buy decision determines which components will be bought from outside suppliers and which will be made by the firm itself.

4. The six steps in purchasing raw materials and semifinished and finished parts are (1) recognizing what is needed, (2) developing specifications, (3) requesting bids and selecting a vendor, (4) following up with the vendor, (5) receiving the order, and (6) evaluating the vendor.

5. Mass production and automation have revolutionized manufacturing methods and have made higher quality, standardized products available at lower prices.

6. The three classifications of manufacturing operations are standard versus custom manufacture, continuous versus batch process, and analytic versus synthetic process.

7. Once final products are assembled, the transportation section must ship them to customers on time and in good condition. The managers here use one or more of the five modes of transportation: highway, rail, air, water, and pipeline. Developments such as piggyback service and containerization allow a business to use two or more transportation modes to move one shipment over long distances.

Questions for Discussion

1. How does each of the six steps in the development of a new product help a firm maximize its chances for a commercial success?

2. What factors might help a firm decide which components of a final product to buy and which to make?

3. Describe how the following pairs of purchasing objectives might conflict and how the conflict might be resolved: (a) low inventory investment, few out-of-stock problems; (b) good vendor relations, low purchase prices; (c) low inventory investment, low purchase prices.

4. How does the movable assembly line use each of the following mass production principles: (a) standardization; (b) specialization; and (c) grouping of parts into subassemblies?

5. Explain how the manufacturing functions of production control, fabrication, assembly (or disassembly), and quality control differ in (a) the production of made-to-order kitchen cabinets and (b) meat packing.

6. What factors should a firm consider in selecting a mode of transportation for moving its finished products? Describe your choice of transportation mode(s) for the following products: (a) coal; (b) petroleum; (c) computers; (d) urgently needed machine parts.

Short Case

Texas instruments has been very successful in manufacturing consumer electronic products like watches and calculators. It uses highly automated assembly lines, which have both advantages and disadvantages over competitors using less automation and more human labor.

(a) What are the advantages of automated assembly lines?
(b) What are the disadvantages?

A Critical
Business Decision

—made by Sherry Lansing
of Twentieth Century Fox Films

The Situation

It was a series of downs and ups in the 1970s for Twentieth Century Fox Film Corporation, a glamour company in a glamorous business. First it lost $77 million on "Hello, Dolly!," "Star," and "Tora! Tora! Tora!," three high-budget movies that failed at the box office. Next, under Dennis Stanfill, a financial executive with no previous experience in the film business, two films—"The Poseidon Adventure" and "The Towering Inferno"—turned out to be huge successes. The other early 1970s films were conservative, low-budget ventures that didn't lose much or win much.

In 1976 Stanfill, looking for new leadership for Fox, chose Alan Ladd, Jr., (son of the late actor) as president of the company's movie division. As a vice president Ladd had signed Mel Brooks, then a relative unknown, whose "Young Frankenstein" cost $3 million and brought in $45 million. Encouraged by this success, Ladd began his presidency with another unknown, despite advice to the contrary. The producer wanted to do a sort of space western, with spaceships, bad guys, good guys, and lots of special effects. Ladd agreed to put up $10 million. The result: "Star Wars," a film that grossed more than $230 million in 1977 and 1978.

But when Ladd's next planned blockbuster, "Alien," didn't quite live up to expectations, profits fell again. Ladd quietly resigned in 1979, clearing the way for a successor who would be under considerable pressure.

The Decision

Enter Sherry Lansing. In 1980, at age 35, she was named Fox's new president. Lansing has sound credentials for the job, including experience as Columbia Studio's vice president, where she was responsible for massively popular films like "China Syndrome" and "Kramer vs. Kramer."

Lansing knows that her new job is a high-risk position—that most movie studio presidents last five years, maximum. But her attitude is realistic: "I know there are pressures . . . but I am not afraid of failure. Failure is inevitable, and if you fear it then you are really going to fail." And, on her managerial style, "When I make a decision, I make it fast and I like to see it executed quickly," she explained to journalist David Lewin.[8]

Sherry Lansing has some immediate and important decisions to make. She has an annual budget of up to $125 million for producing twelve to fifteen films. And she has ideas in an "orderly mind": "I know what I want in stories. I want characters which audiences can care about," she says.

Questions

1. If you were Sherry Lansing, how would you develop ideas and characters for new movies? How would you "test market" the audience appeal of proposed films before risking millions of dollars on them?
2. What criteria should Lansing use to find new films that will (a) generate substantial box-office revenues, (b) have "reasonable" production costs, and (c) succeed against competitive films?

PICK THE WINNER

1 2 3 4 5

PLACE BETS →

3

Marketing

Consumers and Products

In this chapter you will learn . . .

- how to develop a successful marketing program.
- which market factors can be controlled to best reach customers.
- what a marketing executive needs to know about American consumers.
- how to identify target markets and use market-segmentation strategies.
- how the life cycle of a product runs, from its development to its disappearance.

s a child, John DeLorean dreamed about cars. And in the 1950s, as a design engineer for General Motors, he made his dreams come true by earning nearly 200 patents. He also showed a rare flair for marketing and became the youngest head ever of GM's giant Chevrolet Division. In 1973 he was a candidate for the GM presidency.

Then abruptly he quit.

Too confining, too many meetings, and not enough freedom to pursue personal goals were the reasons he gave. "He's the only man ever to fire General Motors," observed one admiring auto executive in the *Wall Street Journal*.[1]

John DeLorean decided to start his own firm—DeLorean Motor Company—to produce cars and compete with General Motors and the other auto giants. He immediately needed the answers to several important marketing questions:

1. What key product features will his cars need to satisfy buyers? The design he plans is a low-slung, high-performance, two-seat, Italian-style sports car. Early models had an unusual plastic inner body, covered with a stainless-steel, rust-proof skin. Air bags were installed to protect passengers in 80-mile-per-hour crashes, an important feature since the car went from zero to 55 in half the time of most Detroit cars. But are these the features that buyers really want?

2. What outlets can be found to sell and service the DeLorean cars so that consumers can see and buy them? Are the 400 outlets he plans to franchise across the country enough?

3. What price will buyers be willing to pay? At about $15,000, the car is between two potential competitors—Chevrolet Corvette at a base sticker price of $14,000 and Porsche 924 at $15,600. Is this the right price?

4. How should it be advertised? If DeLorean uses television commercials, TV star Johnny Carson has already been promised first chance as public spokesman. Is Carson the right image to project?

By the time you read this, John DeLorean's new dream car may be cruising—or it may have crashed. His marketing decisions, brilliant or disastrous, are what will set the course. His four decision areas outlined above—product, place, price, and promotion—are the same as those for any product, and they are the subjects of this and the two following chapters.

MARKETING PRODUCTS

Marketing means directing goods and services from the producer to the customer to satisfy consumers and achieve company objectives. This area of business has become steadily more important since the 1950s, and executives have learned that their decisions here are crucial to the success or failure of their products.

Until the 1850s the United States was a land of scarcity. Businesses could stress the production of goods, since consumers would buy virtually everything that was produced. It was the *production-oriented period* in American business history (see Figure 8–1).

But as our productive capacity began to provide a vast array of new products, it became necessary for firms to convince consumers to buy their goods. This was the *sales-oriented period* and *caveat emptor* ("let the buyer beware") was good advice. This tough, sales-oriented approach often produced goods that reflected the manufacturing and selling talents of the company—not the needs of the consumer. Surpluses developed. To counter them, some firms adopted the hard-sell approach. Techniques ranged from high-pressure personal selling to misleading advertisements.

Then, starting in the 1950s, many firms began to think in terms of the *marketing concept*. They shaped products to meet consumer needs instead of trying to mold consumer needs to fit their products. In this *consumer-oriented period* of American business, many tests and new product surveys were performed to discover what consumers really wanted. This trend is still in progress and will probably continue through the 1980s. Business, in its own enlightened self-interest, will be more responsive to consumers than ever before.

Thus, developing a successful marketing program has become much more important than it was in the days of selling canisters of tea to pioneers, patent medicines to nineteenth-century housewives, or pogo sticks to your parents.

FIGURE 8–1
Three
Different
Buyer
Orientations
in American
Business History.

Production-oriented period
1750 – 1850

Sales-oriented period
1850 – 1950

Consumer-oriented period
1950 – 1980

The Steps of Successful Marketing

To manage a successful marketing program, marketing managers must (1) identify the **target market,** the specific groups of customers for its products or services, and (2) reach the market with satisfying products, through a blend of marketing activities.

Identify Target Market Buyers

Not all consumers are equally likely to buy all products. Stereo equipment, surfboards, trombones, baby food, Rolls Royces, and chain saws appeal to different people. So, although a firm must consider all prospective buyers, it must focus its efforts on its target market—the specific group of buyers it intends to reach. Those not in the target market are less likely prospects, and so efforts to reach them are generally not worth the expense.

The target markets discussed in this chapter are composed of **ultimate consumers**—the individuals, households, or families who buy for their personal needs. In contrast, buyers in purchasing departments (discussed in Chapter 7) represent other target markets—organizations like business firms, government agencies, and educational institutions. These groups are often called **organizational buyers.**

Reach Buyers with Satisfying Products

Once the target market is identified, a strategy must be developed to reach it. This strategy should focus on the four elements of marketing that can be controlled. Professor E. Jerome McCarthy has called these the **4 P's** of the marketing mix:[2]

- PRODUCT The right product (or service) must be developed for the target market.
- PLACE The right channels of distribution, including retailing and wholesaling institutions, must be found to ensure that the product reaches the right target market at the right time and place.
- PRICE The right price must be set for the product—good value to the consumer and adequate revenue to the producer.
- PROMOTION The right combination of personal selling and advertising must be used to tell the consumer about the product.

The marketing executive's job is to decide how to emphasize and balance these factors (see Figure 8–2). This decision is especially important because it is a way to counteract the other factors that are not controllable. These include (1) the entire firm's objectives and resources, (2) the actions of the competitors, and (3) environmental conditions such as energy shortages, inflation, and legal restrictions.

FIGURE 8-2
Steps in a Successful Marketing Program.

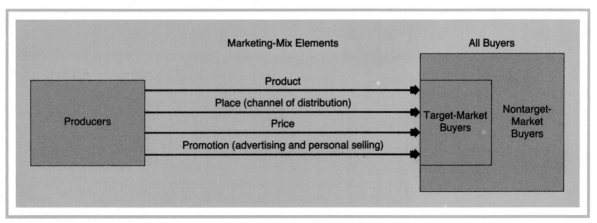

The first step is identifying the target-market buyers, and the second is reaching them with satisfying products, through the right blend of marketing activities. This blend involves four key marketing-mix elements—product, place (or channels of distribution), price, and promotion (mainly advertising and personal selling).

Since American consumers constitute the group most U.S. business firms try to reach, a brief discussion of this important target market follows. After that, we will return to the first element in the marketing mix: the product.

UNDERSTANDING CONSUMERS

Consumers make up a **market:** (1) people, (2) with income, and (3) a desire to buy. An understanding of some of the recent changes that have affected American consumers can make the difference between a successful and a disastrous marketing program.

The Consumer Population

On April 1, 1980, the U.S. Bureau of the Census estimated the population at 222 million—about 18 million more people than in 1970. This growth means more consumers for goods and services and more workers for job openings, now and in the decades to come.

What Do You Design for a One- or Two-Person Household?

"We were the first in our industry to recognize a fundamental change in American society," crows Melvin S. Cohen, board chairman of National Presto Industries, an appliance maker. "It's simple," he said. "The Census Bureau says 51 percent of all U.S. households now consist of singles and doubles, not the traditional family group. They have informal, casual lifestyles and money to spend. Yet everybody designs appliances for that old, 5.8-member family," Cohen tells *Forbes* magazine.[3]

Cohen came up with products that were obvious—and brilliant. (He needed to, because National Presto's other major product line, 105 mm howitzer shells, fizzled out when the Vietnam War stopped.) What appliances do you suppose Cohen and National Presto conjured up? For the answer, see the text.

Size of Households

More than half of all American households now contain only one or two people, a big change from the large households of the 1950s. Grocery-product manu-facturers were among the first to see the marketing implications of this change. Campbell Soup's "Soup for One" and Green Giant's single-serving casseroles are only two examples. National Presto Industries, Inc., has achieved spectacular success designing for "singles and doubles" (see box on opposite page). Its products include the single hamburger cooker, the double hamburger cooker, the "Hot Dogger," and the "Fry Baby" (a miniature, easy-to-clean deep-fat fryer). Car manufacturers are also discovering the power of the small household. Although single people buy only one-fourth of all cars, they have bought half of all Ford Mustangs sold.

Age Range

An analysis of the population by age groups from 1947 to 2000 appears in Figure 8–3. A quick glance shows that average age is increasing. In 1970, the median age was 28, but by 2000, the median age will be 35. The "youth culture" should recede a little as America grays. People in the "65 and over" age group have grown steadily and are still increasing. During the 1980s, specifically, the most spectacular growth will be among the 25- to 44-year-olds.

Trends like these provide the basics for marketing decisions. As the number of 15- to 24-year-olds falls, publishers of high school and college text-books will need to look for new markets. But as the 25- to 44-year-olds become more numerous, housing, appliances, and furniture will be more in demand. As more people enter the retirement age groups, new sports products should appear on the market. The Wilson Sporting Goods Company has already introduced its "Squire" line of golf clubs to enable the mature golfer to improve on accuracy and distance. This group will also provide a bigger market for health products and services. You will be asked to look for other marketing opportunities and dangers, based on Figure 8–3, in Short Case 1 at the end of the chapter.

Geographic Differences

Since 1950 two dramatic geographic "migrations" of Americans have occurred. One is the movement from the Frost Belt to the Sun Belt. Millions have forsaken northeastern and midwest winters for the sunshine (and summer heat) of Florida, Georgia, Texas, Arizona, and California. This population shift

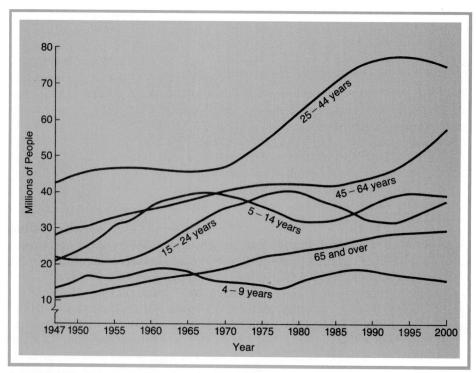

Source: "Americans Change," *Business Week* (February 20, 1979), pp. 64–65.

FIGURE 8-3
Number of Americans in Various Age Groups, 1947-2000.

has carried with it tremendous marketing opportunities in the sunshine states for such things as home construction, restaurants, and cars.

A second migration has been from central cities to suburbs. Retailers who followed consumers to the suburbs, especially to suburban shopping centers, have benefited. But many downtown stores have suffered.

Both these population movements, however, have slowed in recent years. Population experts explain it this way: young adults in their early twenties are the ones most likely to move, and as the size of this age group declines, so does the geographic movement. Sun Belt states may, however, continue to appeal to retired people.

Consumer Income

People alone do not make a consumer market. They must also have income—the purchasing power to buy the products and services they want. Two aspects of consumer income are especially important to marketing people: (1) how much income a typical American household has, and (2) how the total national income is divided among these households. The typical American household has more than doubled its income in the 1970s and increased its purchasing power in spite of inflation. Also, by 1980, although not all Americans were rich, national income was distributed more evenly than ever before in history. More households, then, could afford color TV sets, vacation trips, and theater tickets—though often because families were living on two incomes instead of one.

Yet in the early 1980s the combination of double-digit inflation, soaring energy and home-mortgage costs, and increasing unemployment has caused many households to have less money to spend on nonessentials. Still, the 25- to 44-year-old age group is expected to boost its income especially fast. For ten years ending in 1985, the real purchasing power among this group will have risen by 80 percent and will account for half of all consumer spending in the United States.

Consumer Tastes and Attitudes

Even people with income don't make a market. They must also want to spend that income on products and services. Their personal tastes and attitudes, shaped by cultural and social values, determine how they spend it. Some current values with implications for marketing are discussed below:

1. *Accent on youth and vitality.* Sales of sports cars, youthful clothes, and health-club memberships are among those that have zoomed, and for all age groups, as a result of this trend. In fact, Coca-Cola has found that although teen-agers consume the most soft drinks, Americans in their forties now drink more of these beverages than when they were younger. As the generation that came of age in the sixties becomes the middle-aged generation of the eighties, "youth products" are no longer marketed only for the young. Blue jeans, for example, are now being designed for all age groups.

2. *The women's movement.* More women are employed now than ever before, and they are earning better salaries. The result is that women now make 60 percent of all vacation-destination decisions, half of color-TV brand selections, and 30 percent of new-car purchases. Another side effect of women's liberation is an increase in the sales of time-saving products, from Polaroid cameras to frozen gourmet dinners.

3. *Changing attitudes toward debt.* For decades, Americans were hesitant about installment buying because of the Puritan taboo against debt. Then came the age of the credit card, urged upon consumers by banks, gas companies, and department stores. Americans' values quickly adjusted to the new ethic of "buy now, pay later." But unfortunately, the price has been more than we bargained for. The massive debt owed by American consumers was a contributing factor to the spiraling inflation that began in the late 1970s. So the trend now is a decrease in credit buying—a trend that may cause problems for auto and appliance producers, among others.

4. *A more relaxed way of living, with a shift in consumers' spending priorities.* When lower-income people move into middle-income levels, they buy traditional goods and services such as living-room furniture sets. But many young, well-educated, middle-income consumers put their dollars into travel and education—even when it means a furnitureless home. This decreased concern for material goods and for conforming to old social norms has been dubbed "Keeping down with the Joneses."
5. *Impatience with low-quality products and with the lack of product information.* This is consumerism. It is reflected in federal laws, prompted by public pressure, to provide better and safer cars, toys, and food products. Consumerism also seeks better information—on products, interest charges on credit, and the status of credit ratings.

As *Business Week* magazine puts it, "the consumer is harder and harder to pigeonhole."[4] Yet, marketers must be aware of the array of trends so that they can link consumers with satisfying products and services.

IDENTIFYING THE TARGET MARKET

Why Segment Markets?

Marketing executives must "psych out" the consumer market. This means identifying prospective customers (the target market), shaping a product to their needs, and then bringing customers (demand) and products (supply) together.

But since all customers are not the same, it is necessary to divide them into *market segments,* meaningful buyer groups for a specific product or service.

Market segmentation, the process by which a firm attempts to identify a target market, involves three steps: (1) finding relevant characteristics that divide both a market into smaller segments (buyer groups) and what it might buy into smaller categories (product groups); (2) noting all significant market segments and relating them systematically to the products each segment might buy; and (3) selecting the target market, the collection of market segments most consistent with the firm's objectives and capabilities.

How to Do It: An Example

You see the need for a fast-food restaurant near a metropolitan-area college campus. Your first task is to identify the target market—the specific customers you want to reach. Begin by asking yourself questions like these:

1. Who would patronize the restaurant? Just college students? What about the dormitory residents who have meal contracts? What about students who commute? Would neighborhood people and college faculty and employees be likely to eat there too?
2. Would most people want to eat breakfast, lunch, or dinner at the restaurant? Should between-meal snacks be served? What about late-evening meals after campus events or when the library closes?
3. Is there any relationship between the types of people likely to eat at the restaurant and the meals these people would want?

When trying to determine who your prospective customers will be, you might first divide the market into students and nonstudents. For the students, you will need subcategories of dormitory residents, apartment residents, and commuter students. For the nonstudents, your subcategories might consist of college faculty and clerical staff, area residents, and area workers. All these categories constitute your market characteristics. You then need to determine your product characteristics. To do this, you divide the meals you will offer into breakfast, lunch, between-meal snacks, dinner, and late-evening meals.

To organize all this information, you need a **market-product grid,** the kind of checkerboard seen in Figure 8–4. The grid relates the characteristics of potential consumers to the products they want. In this grid, two important market dimensions are emphasized: the type of meal served and the groups of people who might buy it.

The X in each rectangle shows the potential market for a particular meal. For example, dormitory students who hold meal contracts with the college would probably patronize the restaurant only for late-evening meals and between-meal snacks; commuting students would only eat lunch and between-meal snacks there. The size of the X is a rough measure of the dollar volume of each potential market.

The next step is to select the target market—those market segments you will try especially to attract.

The large segment shaded in Figure 8–4 represents the best target market on the basis of your estimate of sales revenue from each group listed.

MARKET CHARACTERISTICS	PRODUCT CHARACTERISTICS				
	Breakfast	Lunch	Between-meal snacks	Dinner	Late-evening meals
College students: residents in contract dorms			X		X
College students: apartment residents	X	X	X	X	X
College students: commuters		X	X		
College faculty and clerical staff		X			
Noncollege area residents				X	X
Noncollege area workers		X			

Target market is shaded.

FIGURE 8-4
Market-Product Grid of Potential Customers for a Restaurant near a College Campus.

Since the breakfast market is so small, you may choose not to open the restaurant until 11:00 A.M., placing breakfast eaters outside the target market. You may also decide to neglect area residents and workers who have no connection with the college, since they, too, fall outside the target-market area. So your marketing effort will concentrate on college students and faculty and staff members. In this case, the best way to reach potential customers is through ads in the college newspaper, mailings to dorm residents, and ads inside area commuter buses and on campus bulletin boards.

Criteria for Segmenting Markets

A major key to success is finding the best ways to classify potential customers for the particular products in your market-product grid. Two common methods are (1) using various demographic descriptions of the purchasers (such as sex, age, income, and occupation), and (2) using geographic location of the purchasers (for example, region of the country and urban or rural). In the restaurant example, the market was segmented by combining occupation (college student, clerical staff, faculty) with place of residence (dormitory, on-campus apartment, off-campus residence). If you were marketing bubble gum or retire-

How Should Toothpaste Producers Segment Their Market?

During the past twenty years, toothpaste producers have done extensive market research to determine what consumers want in a toothpaste. The researchers found that conventional demographic and economic characteristics were of little use in segmenting the market. Instead they divided consumers into three main groups, based on what they expected from a toothpaste.

Study the three ads below. What benefit does each ad promise you in return for using that toothpaste? For the answers, see the text and the market-product grid shown in the box at the right.

CREST

ULTRA BRITE

CLOSE-UP

ment homes, age would be a primary consideration in your market segmentation. For surfboards or snowblowers, geography would be a critical factor.

But the benefits derived from the product are also important as a basis for market segmentation. Toothpaste preferences, for example, do not seem to depend much on one's age, sex, or income (demographic characteristics) or even on factors like region of the country or city or farm residence (geographic characteristics). Instead, customers can be segmented based on their interest in decay prevention; cleaner, prettier teeth; and fresher breath and a cleaner mouth. For how three toothpaste manufacturers have used this market-segmentation strategy, see the boxes below.

How Toothpaste Producers Actually Segment Their Market

Toothpaste users often look for one of three specific benefits from their toothpaste:

- DECAY PREVENTION People who want a toothpaste that will reduce cavities.
- CLEANER, PRETTIER TEETH People who want a toothpaste that will make their teeth whiter.
- FRESHER BREATH AND A CLEANER MOUTH People who want a toothpaste that will rinse their mouth and help fight "bad breath."

From this knowledge, competing firms created three types of toothpaste, one aimed at each of these three market segments. The market-product grid is shown below.

The three leading brands are products of three different companies: Crest is produced by Procter & Gamble, Ultra Brite by Colgate-Palmolive, and Close-up by Lever Brothers. Since these toothpastes were first introduced, at least one of the brands has been "repositioned" slightly. Close-up now seeks to benefit consumers in two ways—by whitening teeth and freshening breath.

MARKET CHARACTERISTIC	PRODUCT CHARACTERISTIC		
	Cavity fighter	Tooth whitener	Breath freshener
Decay prevention	√ Crest		
Cleaner, prettier teeth		√ Ultra Brite	
Fresher breath, cleaner mouth			√ Close-up

Your Next Job
Positions in Marketing Research and Product Management

Careers in Marketing Research

Marketing research workers analyze data, design questionnaires, and conduct interviews to determine what features a new product should have and what its profitability is likely to be. Most have bachelor's degrees. Graduate degrees are usually essential for high-level research jobs. Applicants with solid backgrounds in statistics, psychology, and economics begin as research trainees and may advance to supervisory or to management positions. Annual salaries range from $14,000 to $35,000. The demand for market research workers—especially those with graduate degrees—will increase rapidly as business firms continue to base more of their marketing policies on sophisticated research data. (*Additional information:* American Marketing Association, 222 South Riverside Plaza, Chicago, Illinois 60606.)

Home economists are employed by educational institutions, private businesses, and government agencies to study and to improve products and services for home consumption. Home economists communicate product information to consumers and assist in developing products to meet consumer needs. Entry positions require a bachelor's degree in home economics. Teaching, supervisory, and research jobs often require graduate degrees. Annual salaries range from $9,000 to $25,000. Job competition is keen for home economists with bachelor's degrees; there are considerably more job opportunities for home economists with graduate degrees. (*Additional information:* American Home Economics Association, 2010 Massachusetts Avenue, N.W., Washington, D.C. 20036.)

Careers in Product Management

Product management personnel are responsible for developing programs to market one brand or one product line effectively. They work for both consumer-goods firms like Procter & Gamble and the Pillsbury Company and industrial-goods firms like the 3M Company and Xerox. For example, product management (sometimes called *brand management*) personnel working for the Pillsbury Company might be responsible for that firm's line of cake mixes. In this capacity, they would decide how to reach consumers most effectively in the four marketing-mix areas—product, price, place, and promotion. Product management personnel utilize marketing research information developed by marketing research workers and home economists.

Although the job titles vary from firm to firm, careers in product management usually involve a sequence of three related jobs: *marketing* (or *brand*) *assistant; assistant product* (or *brand*) *manager;* and *product* (or *brand*) *manager.* The entry-level job is **marketing assistant,** for which a master's degree in business administration is normally required. The marketing assistant usually analyzes past sales trends, projects these trends into the future, and then devises possible pricing or advertising strategies. Annual starting salary is approximately $20,000 to $24,000. Length of work as a marketing assistant is about one year.

Men and women who demonstrate their capabilities as marketing assistants are promoted to the position of **assistant product manager.** There they may be responsible for one or two present or future items within the firm's product line. Length of work as an assistant product manager is one to three years; annual salary range is $25,000 to $29,000.

Successful assistant product managers are promoted to the position of **product manager.** Then they are responsible for marketing decisions that concern the entire product line. Product managers can expect to earn over $30,000 annually. In many firms, successful product managers can attain positions of increased responsibility and may become marketing manager (supervising several product managers), vice president of marketing, and perhaps eventually president of the company. (*Additional information:* contact the marketing departments of specific employers.)

Strategies for Identifying the Target Market

Once the market-product segments (potential consumers) have been identified, the firm must plan a strategy to attract them to its product. Three different strategies can be followed: *undifferentiated marketing, differentiated marketing,* or *concentrated marketing.*[5]

In **undifferentiated marketing,** the firm manufactures a single product and tries to attract all buyers with one marketing program. As Henry Ford said about colors for the Model T: "They can have any color they want as long as it's black." And until the 1970s, Volkswagen offered only a single, basic design—its "Beetle." Such a single-minded approach is less expensive because the product does not have to be produced and inventoried in many varieties.

In **differentiated marketing,** separate products and marketing programs are designed for each market segment. This is the strategy that most car manufacturers now follow. Among the bewildering variety of sedans, compacts, station wagons, vans, and sports cars, available in an array of colors and at varying prices, one is bound to appeal to every potential consumer. Differentiated marketing is effective, but it is always a more expensive way to go.

A compromise strategy is **concentrated marketing.** This means that the firm concentrates on one or a few profitable market segments. For example, the Checker Cab Manufacturing Company makes one basic automobile to be used solely as taxi cabs. By offering a single product to only a single market segment, it avoids competing with General Motors, Ford, and Chrysler, all of whom have many designs for all market segments. Economics Laboratory makes only special washing compounds for dishwashers. It thereby can afford to ignore soap and detergent giants like Procter & Gamble and Lever Brothers.

Marketing strategy decisions are made by people in marketing-research and product-management positions, such as those detailed in the Your Next Job section.

UNDERSTANDING PRODUCTS

In a marketing sense, **products** are any physical items or services that satisfy customers' needs. So "the product" can be a candy bar, computer, or cleaning service. Dividing products into two basic categories—*consumer goods* and *industrial goods*—is important because each requires quite different marketing strategies. **Consumer goods** are used by ultimate consumers (individuals

FIGURE 8-5
Kinds of Consumer Goods Marketed.

KIND OF GOOD	EXPLANATION	EXAMPLES
Convenience goods	Goods that the customer characteristically purchases frequently, immediately, and with a minimum of comparison shopping.	Cigarettes, soap, newspapers, chewing gum, many food products.
Shopping goods	Goods that the customer, in the process of selection and purchase, characteristically compares on such bases as suitability, quality, price, and style.	Millinery, furniture, dress goods, ready-to-wear clothing, shoes. (These goods are frequently unbranded or, if branded, the names are not very important to the consumer.)
Specialty goods	Goods with unique characteristics and/or brand identification for which a significant group of buyers is habitually willing to make a special purchasing effort.	Specific types and brands of fancy goods, stereo components, photographic equipment, custom-made suits. (Such goods are generally branded, and the brands are important to the consumer making a buying decision.)

Source: AMA Committee on Definitions, Ralph S. Alexander, Chairman, *Marketing Definitions: A Glossary of Marketing Terms* (Chicago: American Marketing Association, 1960), pp. 289–293.

or households) and need no commerical processing. **Industrial goods** are sold to firms that use them to produce other goods, or to incorporate into a final product, or to help administer their operations. Often, the lines between these two classes blur. Candy bars are always consumer goods and iron ore is always an industrial good. But automobile tires can be a consumer good—if purchased by a car owner to replace worn tires—or an industrial good—if sold to an auto manufacturer to be used on a new car. Consumer and industrial goods may themselves be divided into several classes, as shown in Figures 8–5 and 8–6.

The reason for different marketing strategies for consumer and industrial

FIGURE 8-6
Kinds of Industrial Goods Marketed.

KIND OF GOOD	EXPLANATION	EXAMPLES
Foundation goods	Items of fixed plant and equipment purchased by the organizational buyer.	Machine tools, printing presses, electric generators, typewriters.
Entering goods	Raw materials and parts the buying organization incorporates in the final products ultimately destined to be consumer or industrial goods.	Wheat, iron, ore, sheet steel, radios installed in new cars on the production line.
Facilitating goods	Maintenance, repair, and operating supplies that help the plant, equipment, and people perform their function in the buying organization.	Lubricants, paint, cleaning materials, stationery, paper clips.

Source: Adapted from Theodore N. Beckman, William R. Davidson, and W. Wayne Talarzyk, *Marketing,* 9th Edition (New York: Ronald Press, 1973), pp. 154–155. Copyright © 1973 the Ronald Press Co., New York.

goods is that the buyers of each type of good have different buying motives and skills, and they also view prices quite differently. For example, when a firm sells 50,000 ballpoint pens (industrial "facilitating goods" in Figure 8–6) to a large company, it will use a quite different marketing plan from when it sells three dozen pens (consumer "convenience goods" in Figure 8–5) to a suburban gift shop. Even within the consumer-goods category, marketing strategies differ dramatically. Bic may sell its inexpensive ballpoint to college students through vending machines as a convenience item, while Cross may sell its twelve-carat gold-filled pen as a specialty item for $150 through jewelry stores.

The Life Cycle of New Products

Periodically, a unique product (the first color TV, the first liquid laundry soap) appears on the market. Any new product generally goes through a life cycle, consisting of four different stages, that affects the product's sales revenues and profits. These stages are described below and illustrated in Figures 8–7 and 8–8 on the next page.

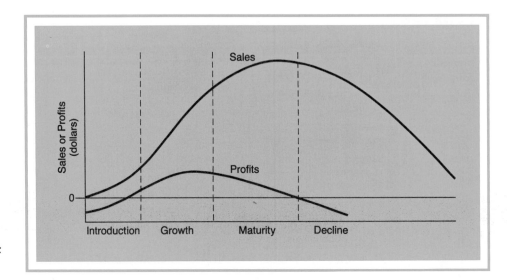

FIGURE 8-7
Stages
in the Product
Life Cycle.

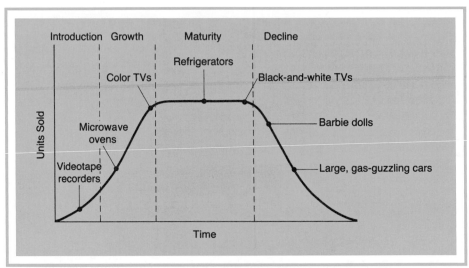

FIGURE 8-8
Stages
in the Product
Life Cycle of
Various Home
Appliances.

Source: Adapted from John E. Smallwood, ''The Product Life Cycle: A Key to Strategic Marketing Planning,'' *MSU Business Topics* (Winter 1973), p. 30. Reprinted by permission of the publisher, Division of Research, Graduate School of Business Administration, Michigan State University.

1. INTRODUCTION   The product is placed on the market. Sales rise as consumers start to purchase it. Losses become profits as the costs of product development are gradually recovered. No competition exists.
2. GROWTH   Extremely rapid sales occur because of initial product promotion and word-of-mouth advertising from satisfied customers. Profits reach a maximum—even though sales continue to rise rapidly—because the firm reduces its prices when the first competitive products appear.
3. MATURITY   Sales grow more slowly and then hit a peak as most customers purchase the product only as a replacement. Similar products introduced by competitors vie for consumer dollars. Price competition is severe, and profits fall.
4. DECLINE   Both sales and profits decline as the product is edged out by improved substitutes.

Marketing executives need to assess carefully the position of their products on the life-cycle curve in order to keep their marketing strategies current and effective. Fad items, such as the hula hoop, may last only ninety days while certain TV models last for decades. What causes problems for executives is the fact that one stage of the product life cycle often overlaps the next. For example, marketing managers for television manufacturers are now in the position of trying to sell color TV sets as the household's main set while simultaneously selling smaller and portable black-and-white sets as its second and third sets.

A further complication is that the life cycles of new products seem to be getting shorter. DuPont was the only source of nylon for fifteen years. But its Delrin—a synthetic fiber that the company considered potentially as important as nylon—faced competition from a similar fiber within two years of its introduction. And within two years after General Electric introduced its automatic toothbrush, fifty-two competitors were producing close substitutes.

The life-cycle phenomenon applies to services, too. Introduced in 1925, a new kind of life-insurance policy took thirty years to be adopted by 88 percent of the firms in the industry. But a new policy introduced in 1957 was as fully adopted in less than two years.

Although most products have a limited useful life—they are born, grow to some extent, and then disappear—their life cycles can sometimes be lengthened by modifying them. In 1974, National Presto brought out an electric hamburger cooker that cooked a single, round meat patty in one to three minutes. Consumers gobbled it up. Then competitors introduced their own versions. So National Presto tried to extend the hamburger cooker's life by introducing, one year later, a square version (it also grilled toasted cheese sandwiches). Still later, it introduced its "double burger cookers." National Presto's strategy proved successful for a while. Now, though, the firm is looking for newer products with high consumer appeal.

Why Products Fail

Thousands of products fail every year, at a cost to American businesses of billions of dollars. The cause of a product's failure usually can be traced to one or more of the following reasons: (1) the target market is too small; (2) there is no important difference between it and existing products; (3) product quality is poor; and (4) execution of one or more of the marketing-mix elements is poor. For examples, consider the products listed below:

- *Revlon's Super-Natural Hair Spray.* Revlon lost millions of dollars on this product in the 1960s. Why? Mainly because customers were con-

Polaroid: From Spectacular Success . . .

No one doubts that Edwin Land is a technical genius. He personally holds 524 U.S. patents, second only to Thomas Edison's 1,093. He dropped out of college to develop filters to cut down the glare of car headlights, and later used this technology to found the Polaroid Corporation at age 28. He started by manufacturing nonglare sunglasses and goggles.

Land and Polaroid have achieved spectacular new-product successes. Two examples are the Polaroid Land camera in 1948, which started the instant photography business, and the SX-70 camera in 1972, whose color pictures appeared in front of the viewer's eyes. Polaroid considered marketing research a "waste of money" and said that not one dollar went into it for either product.

Then came Polavision, Polaroid's instant-movie-camera system, in 1978. A year later, Polaroid wrote off $68.5 million in losses on the system. Polavision's problems illustrate all of the four key problems often cited for new-product failures (see text):

1. *Target market too small.* In 1978 only 560,000 8-millimeter movie cameras were sold, about half the annual sales of six years earlier. Clearly, consumers were cooling off on home movies, and the trend was down.
2. *No important difference from substitutes.* Videotape cameras were becoming popular because they used tape that could be run on the family TV set. While Polavision's price was about $700 compared with $1,800 for a videotape camera and recorder, the videotape was more flexible and could be reused.

fused by the meaning of "Super-Natural." "Super" implied more holding power and "Natural" suggested less holding power. Since consumers didn't know what to expect, even those few that bought it were disappointed. Selecting a better name (a function that falls under the product element) might have avoided this expensive fizzle.

- *Pillsbury's Gorilla Milk.* The target market was high-school and college-age consumers—notorious breakfast skippers. But Carnation was already marketing its Instant Breakfast, and buyers didn't feel that Pillsbury's new product was significantly better. Also, target-market customers thought the name "Gorilla Milk" sounded too childish. The product failed in the test-market stage, before it even reached full national distribution.
- *Menley and James' Duractin.* The target market for this eight-hour pain-relief capsule was simply too small and the point of difference between it and other products already on the market was not great enough. In addition, the long-term relief promised by the product was not as important to customers as immediate pain relief. If you have a headache, what do you want? The answer: immediate pain relief like you might get from two aspirin! If the headache comes back four hours

. . . *to Devastating Failure*

And the instantaneous pictures were not nearly as important a benefit to consumers for movies as for snapshots.

3. *Poor product quality.* Initially Polavision required a bright light that annoyed small children. Also, the developed movie film gave grainy pictures, could be seen only on a 12-inch screen when you stood directly in front of it, ran for only two-and-one-half minutes, and lacked sound. Polaroid underestimated the devastating effect on sales of this combination of problems.

4. *Poor execution of marketing mix elements.* Polaroid tried to distribute Polavision through all possible outlets—like drug stores —and then wait for sales, a strategy that worked spectacularly for the SX-70. But for Polavision this marketing strategy was a failure, because consumers needed much more education on how to use it than they needed for the SX-70, and sales clerks were unable to help them.

And what of Polavision's future? As a consumer product, it's probably dead except for a few die-hard home-movie buffs. But Polaroid is working to salvage some of its losses through industrial applications of time-and-motion studies, sports training, and medicine, according to *Fortune* magazine.[6]

But effective early marketing research to discover what consumers wanted could have saved Polaroid millions of dollars.

later, you merely take two more aspirin. Duractin caused the company real pain: several million dollars' worth.

- *General Foods' Post Cereals with Freeze-Dried Fruit.* Many consumers eat dry breakfast cereal with fruit on top. They are probably a large target market. But the problem was poor product quality. By the time the fruit reconstituted, the cereal was soggy. General Foods lost about $5 million on this almost-good idea.
- *Del Monte's Barbecue Ketchup with Finely Chopped Onions.* Here the target market was not large enough and the product's point of difference actually worked against sales in an important target segment. The primary users of catsup are children, but most children dislike onions. The product failed in the test market, so the company changed its approach. A variation of the product is now reentering the market, this time as a gourmet sauce for meat cooked on outdoor grills.

Brand-Name Products

Out of 38,000 brand-name products available to grocery stores alone, a typical supermarket stocks 6,500 brands and sizes, from Cheer detergent to Sealtest ice cream. Brands are everywhere. The name, symbol, trademark, or design identifies the product, distinguishes it from the competition, reassures the customer, and saves people time when shopping.

A well-known brand name is extremely valuable. And a company will spend lavishly to advertise it, control the quality of the product, and protect the name. For example, the Coca-Cola Company spends about $2 million a

A Coke by Any Other Name Is Not the Same

A new customer sat down in Rosie O'Grady's bar and restaurant in Pensacola, Florida, and ordered a Coke. A while later Robert Snow, Rosie O'Grady's owner, found himself in court mixing it up with the Coca-Cola Company.

The charge against Mr. Snow: serving customers Pepsi when they asked for Coke.

And Coca-Cola doesn't just take on the little guys. In 1974, it took the Howard Johnson chain, about 900 restaurants, to court for passing off another cola as "The Real Thing." And it won.[7]

Why does Coca-Cola spend $2 million a year protecting the names Coke and Coca-Cola? See the text.

year in trademark protection. It sends investigators into restaurants and bars across the country to order "Coke" and "Coca-Cola." These "customers" send what they are served back to corporate headquarters in Atlanta for chemical analysis. If lab analysis reveals a cola other than Coke, the offending restaurant or chain is hauled into court. Coca-Cola Company wants to prevent the names Coke and Coca-Cola from becoming generic terms, merely names for any cola soft drink. If that happened, trademark laws would no longer protect the names Coke and Coca-Cola, with the result that other companies could use the names and Coca-Cola Company would lose a unique asset. (For more on the Supreme Court decision that upheld the trademarks "Coke" and "Coca-Cola," see the color insert at the end of the text.)

The manufacturers of Kleenex, Scotch tape, Xerox, and Frigidaire also take great pains to prevent this from happening to them. Kimberly-Clark Corporation, the manufacturer of Kleenex, expects druggists to hand customers its brand alone when they ask for Kleenex at the counter. They don't want to go the way of Sterling Drug, Inc., which lost "aspirin" as a U.S. trademark in 1921, and the Otis Elevator Company, which lost "escalator" as a trademark in 1950.

Chapter Review

Key Points to Remember

1. Marketing means directing the flow of goods and services from producer to customer to satisfy buyers and to achieve company objectives.

2. In recent years, because of the vast array of available products, the marketing concept has become consumer-oriented rather than sales-oriented.

3. A target market is the specific group of buyers a firm is trying to reach. Successful marketing involves two key steps: identifying the target market and reaching it effectively using the 4 P's.

4. The 4 P's are the controllable elements of the marketing mix. These are product, place, price, and promotion.

5. The uncontrollable elements of marketing are (1) the entire firm's objectives and resources, (2) actions of competitors, and (3) environmental conditions.

6. A market refers to (1) people, (2) with income, and (3) a desire to buy.

7. Market segmentation is the process of dividing potential customers into meaningful groups (or market segments) for a specific product or service.

8. The market-product grid provides a particularly useful framework for identifying customers in the target market. It relates the characteristics of potential consumers to the products they want.

9. Three strategies for attracting potential consumers are differentiated, undifferentiated, and concentrated marketing.

10. In the marketing mix, the product is the physical item or service that satisfies certain customers' needs. Products are classified as consumer goods or industrial goods, depending on who buys them.

11. New products introduced into the market often go through different stages that affect the product's sales revenue and profit. This is called the product life cycle.

12. Four key factors often account for the failure of a new product: (a) an insubstantial target market; (b) an insignificant difference when compared with existing products; (c) inadequate quality; and (d) poor management execution in one or more of the marketing-mix elements.

13. Brand names are extremely valuable assets to manufacturers. They identify the product, distinguish it from competitors, reassure the consumer, and save people time when shopping.

Questions for Discussion

1. If marketing means effectively shaping products and services to consumer needs, manufacturers and retailers should be seeking feedback from consumers. In what ways do you think you, your family, or your friends have been surveyed to obtain such information? If you were marketing a unique new product—say a battery-operated coffee maker—what type of information would you seek from prospective customers?

& Applications

2. In each of the following pairs, the products and/or services are related but offer a different form of satisfaction to customers. What are these satisfactions or benefits?
   (a) A brand-name suit purchased at a department store versus an "all sales final" suit purchased at a discount store.
   (b) Dinner at the best restaurant in town versus a hamburger and shake at the local fast-food place.
   (c) A rental rug shampooer versus a carpet-cleaning service.

3. Give several examples of products whose market demand would be affected by changes in the following population factors: (a) size of household; (b) age range; (c) regional location; (d) income; (e) cultural attitudes and values.

4. The market-product grid in Figure 8–4 in the text is a simplification of the facts. In reality, one would need more information than appears there. Refer to the grid on page 201 and answer the following questions.
   (a) Is each box in the grid an equally important part of the total market? Why or why not?
   (b) Could the grid dimensions be presented in even greater detail? If so, how would you break them down?
   (c) What other dimensions might be added?
   (d) What other factors, besides those that can be shown on a grid, should you consider when making the final decision about opening the restaurant?

Short Cases

1. Jostens, Inc., produces and sells class rings and yearbooks for high schools and colleges (see the Critical Business Decision on page 107). How might the changes in U.S. population, income, and consumer attitudes and values discussed in this chapter affect Jostens future sales? (*Hint:* First, check the age distribution of the U.S. population, shown in Figure 8–3 on page 196.)

2. The market-product grid is a method used to analyze a specific business problem—in this case, identifying the target market for a new product. As the marketing manager of a firm that manufactures jeans, analyze your market segments.
   (a) What characteristics of potential purchasers might you use to segment the market?
   (b) Develop a market-product grid using the most useful characteristics for the jean market at the present time.

3. You have decided to go into business for yourself. You are trying to decide whether to open (a) a sporting goods store, (b) a grocery store, (c) a drug store, or (d) a radio-television-stereo store. What effects might the changes in population, income, and consumers' tastes and values cited in this chapter have on your decision?

A Critical

—made by Steven M. Rothschild
of Yoplait USA

The Situation

"We're new to the dairy business," observes Steven M. Rothschild, "and it's a dramatic new business for General Mills." Rothschild is president of Yoplait USA, a subsidiary of General Mills, Inc., whose experience is in more traditional grocery products like breakfast cereals and cake mixes.[8]

But Yoplait's business is far removed from General Mills' regular product lines. Yoplait's sole product is yogurt.

In 1977 Rothschild investigated yogurt as a new business opportunity for General Mills. He discovered that yogurt, a cultured milk product, had been around for centuries. It is widely consumed in the Middle East and parts of Europe, where it enables people to store a nutritious milk product for several days when they don't own a refrigerator. Yogurt first came to the United States in the 1930s but didn't have much consumer appeal until the 1960s. Then, in the late 1970s, yogurt became one of the fastest-growing food products in the country, with more than $500 million in annual sales.

Upon investigating the market, Rothschild discovered that about 95 percent of the yogurt consumed in the United States is mixed with fruit or flavoring and about 5 percent is plain. About 95 percent is consumed in eight-ounce cups. He also found there are four basic types of yogurt:

- Sundae style—fruit on bottom of cup
- Swiss style—fruit blended throughout using "stabilizers" to keep the fruit from settling
- Western style—fruit on bottom and flavored syrup on top
- Frozen style—ice-cream or soft-custard form.

Other research showed that yogurt is available in twenty different flavors and a wide range of textures. When refrigerated, it has a shelf life of twenty-one to sixty days, depending on whether preservatives are added.

The U.S. annual per capita consumption of yogurt is low (four cups per person) compared with consumption in European countries (twenty-seven cups per person a year in France). Research data showed that 25 percent of U.S. households had eaten yogurt in the past month; 30 percent had eaten it, but less frequently; and 45 percent had never bought or eaten it.

Business Decision

The Decision

In October 1977 General Mills bought the U.S. marketing rights to Yoplait yogurt from Sodima, a large cooperative in France. At that time Yoplait was the best-selling yogurt in France and was already being distributed in about one-sixth of the United States. General Mills established Yoplait USA and named Rothschild its president.

Steven Rothschild assesses Yoplait's key consumer benefits: (1) 100 percent natural yogurt without artificial sweeteners or preservatives, (2) Swiss style, with real fruit mixed throughout, and (3) outstanding taste with a creamy texture. Because of competition, he knows he must move quickly to gain acceptance for Yoplait among American consumers.

Questions

1. Where is yogurt in its product life cycle in France? In the United States? How might this affect Rothschild's marketing strategy for Yoplait?
2. Why do you think Americans eat yogurt? What do you see as the demographic characteristics of the key target market segments on which Rothschild should focus Yoplait's marketing effort?

One feature that helps differentiate Yoplait from its competitors is its distinctive package. There are many brands of natural yogurt on the American market, but only Yoplait comes in a cone-shaped container with an aluminum foil cover.

SMiLES MARY'S

OPEN TILL 11:00

FANTASTIC SANDWICHES

UNDER *NEW* MANAGEMENT!

6 PAK /s $1.59 +TAX

LOWENBRAU BEER LIGHT or DARK 12-oz. BTL. 6/s $2.29 +TAX

HEINEKEN BEER LIGHT or DARK 12-oz. BTL. 6/s $3.69 +TAX

MICHELOB BEER 12-oz. BTL. 6 PAK /s $1.99 +TAX

PENTAGON WI
SALT PACT IN

PENTAGON WI
SALT PACT IN

Distribution and Pricing

In this chapter you will learn . . .

- *how to move products from manufacturers to consumers (the place element in the marketing mix).*
- *what middlemen do.*
- *about the beginnings of retail stores.*
- *how supply, demand, costs, and competition affect the price of a product.*
- *what three methods managers use to set prices (the price element in the marketing mix).*

ack in 1963 Kay and Bob Holker were barely making it. They were living in a house trailer. Kay was earning $1.35 an hour at the local department store, and Bob was in college.

Today things are different. The Holkers are earning more than $400,000 a year and enjoying life in their $600,000 home. The reason for their good fortune? Shaklee.

The Holkers worked their way up to become the top distributors for the Shaklee Corporation, a company that manufactures and distributes—on a door-to-door basis—food supplements, cosmetics, and household items. Shaklee sells the products and the right to distribute them to other people, including the Holkers.

The company's methods are controversial. The U.S. Food and Drug Administration has pressured Shaklee into curbing some of its overenthusiastic claims, about cures for diabetes and cancer, for example. But its success, and the Holkers', is not in doubt. Shaklee has become a master of the direct approach to selling and distributing products, says *Forbes* magazine.[1]

The right pricing decisions are also responsible for this success. A recent Shaklee price of $5.35 for 100 vitamin C tablets is well above the $2.80 listed in a typical vitamin catalog. But apparently the convenience to consumers of being able to buy the Shaklee products at home more than makes up for this higher price.

Shaklee's unique approach to marketing is but one example of the ways firms place (or channel) and price their products. These two elements of the marketing mix are the subjects of this chapter.

THE PLACE ELEMENT IN THE MARKETING MIX

Packages of chewing gum must somehow end up in vending machines and flowers must be moved from where they are grown to the florists' shops. Seeing that products are delivered to consumers when and where they want them is the responsibility of marketing managers. This is the **place** element in the marketing mix. Manufacturers, wholesalers, and retailers are the main forces in the strategy of place. Wholesalers and retailers who distribute the finished products are called the **middlemen.**

In Praise of Middlemen

It is a principle of marketing that "you can do away with the middleman but not his functions." Some institution or person must do the work, but performing these functions costs money—money that must eventually be paid by the

Where the Money Goes: The Costs of Producing and Marketing a $7.98 Record

Do excessive marketing costs drive up prices? Are wholesalers and retailers the villains? Here is where the money goes when a consumer pays $7.98 for a record from an independent record company:

Vinyl and pressing	$ .39		
Record jacket	.77		
American Federation of Musicians	.07		
Songwriter's royalties	.19		
Recording artist's royalties	.65		
Freight to wholesaler	.05		
Independent's advertising and selling expenses	.55		
Independent's administrative expenses	.53		
Independent's cost	$3.20		
Independent's profit	.40		
Independent's price to wholesaler		$3.60	
Freight to retailer		.04	
Wholesaler's advertising, selling, and administrative expense		.21	
Wholesaler's cost		$3.85	
Wholesaler's profit		.45	
Wholesaler's price to retailer			$4.30
Retailer's advertising, selling, and administrative expense			.98
Retailer's profit			2.70
Retailer's price to consumer			$7.98

Do the profits of the wholesaler and the retailer seem too large? Perhaps. But hundreds of record retailers go out of business every year because selling prices don't cover costs. In fact, many retailers who sell their records at "discount prices" make less than $1.00 profit per record. For example, low-overhead stores may buy directly from the manufacturer, add a slight markup, and sell a record with a list price of $7.98 for less than $5.00. At such a low price and profit level, a few bad decisions—for example, about which records to stock—can cause a retailer to fail.

buyer. For example, only about $2.07 of a $7.98 record goes to producing the record and jacket and paying royalties to the songwriter, recording artist, and music union. The balance goes to firms in the distribution channel that ship, advertise, handle, and sell the record (see box on the preceding page). So managers use middlemen when they are the cheapest way to get the job done—even though some control over the product is lost.

Without middlemen, each manufacturer would have to hire a larger sales force or operate its own warehouses and retail outlets. Let's look at what these middlemen do.

Wholesalers

Wholesalers sell to retailers, to other wholesalers, to industrial users, and to virtually anyone but the consumer. They exist because they perform services for suppliers or customers more efficiently than the manufacturers themselves can. For suppliers, they find customers, store inventories, and furnish market information. For customers, they forecast needs, regroup goods into required quantities, carry stock, transport goods, grant temporary credit, and provide specialized sales information.

Retailers

Retailers purchase only consumer goods from manufacturers or wholesalers and sell them only to consumers. They do not sell industrial goods or sell to other marketing institutions. Retailers work on a level that is closer to the consumer than to the manufacturer. Their job includes forecasting customer needs (choosing the right products for the shelf), dividing large purchases into smaller groups, delivering goods to consumers' homes, granting credit, and providing specialized sales information.

Career opportunities in both retailing and wholesaling are discussed in the Your Next Job section of this chapter on page 226.

Marketing Channels

A product moves from manufacturer to customers through **channels of distribution** or **marketing channels.** These are critically important because the product must be where the buyers are. How many smokers—no matter how much they like the brand—would really "walk a mile for a Camel," as the old advertising slogan claimed? If a low-priced convenience product is easy to get, it is more likely to be bought. Magazines strategically placed next to supermarket check-out counters are good examples.

Who Owns It and Who Gets It

Marketing managers plan their channels of distribution according to (1) who should take title to (actually own) the goods and (2) who should take physical possession of them. Most institutions in a channel do both, but this is not always the case. A wholesaler may arrange for a manufacturer's order to be shipped directly to a retailer. The wholesaler, then, takes title to the goods and bills the retailer, but the wholesaler never actually has possession of the product. L'eggs panty hose managers decided on the opposite strategy: supermarkets should take possession of their product but not own it. This allows L'eggs delivery people to keep the display cases in markets well-stocked and neatly arranged, and also saves the supermarket the trouble (see box).

One example of an outstanding marketing success is L'eggs, the panty hose from Hanes Corporation.

Hanes wanted to sell quality panty hose through supermarkets. But they didn't want their product confused with the inferior brands of panty hose already on sale there. So Hanes' managers and advertising agency came up with a four-step marketing strategy described by *Marketing News:*[2]

1. Find the key consumer benefit. (It turned out that what women wanted was a good fit.)
2. Design a name, package, and display to set the product apart from inferior substitutes. (The answer was L'eggs, the unusual egg-shaped package, and the unique L'eggs boutique display.)
3. Develop an advertising and promotion plan to build sales quickly in order to persuade skeptical retailers to devote space to L'eggs. (The theme stressed: "Our L'eggs fit your legs.")
4. Find a distribution technique to solve supermarkets' housekeeping problems. (Hanes' managers decided to retain ownership of the inventory and stock the display itself. So they hired a staff and bought their own delivery trucks.)

The 70,000 outlets, complete with customers, are well-satisfied.

How Hanes Corporation Drove Its L'eggs Off to Sell Panty Hose

Who Moves It

In determining the best way to move their products, marketers usually choose from among the four common marketing channels shown in Figure 9–1. The first, the *manufacturer-consumer channel,* is also called *direct marketing.* Specialized industrial goods, such as large electric generators, are usually sold this way, since there are few customers. Shaklee and Avon also market their products directly to consumers, through door-to-door sales representatives.

The *manufacturer-retailer channel* is chosen most often when large retailers purchase a big volume of goods directly from the manufacturers. Large department stores, discount houses, and supermarket chains often order through this channel.

When orders are small and the number of separate retail outlets large, the *manufacturer-wholesaler-retailer channel* is often used. This allows the manufacturer to use a wholesaler instead of having to maintain its own sales force to call on thousands of different retailers for just a few products. Patent drugs, hardware, and convenience foods with a low-profit margin move through this channel.

Sometimes more than one wholesaler enters the picture, creating the *manufacturer-multiple wholesaler-retailer channel.* In the meat packing industry, for example, large wholesalers often find it convenient to sell to smaller wholesalers who in turn serve individual supermarkets or food chains. In fact, the average meat product goes through more than ten middlemen.

Retailing: A Brief History

Although general stores stocked with barrels of licorice and wedges of cheese are fashionable now, they once were the only place to shop in town. Today, we have a multitude of choices, from highly specialized stores—that sell only one brand of tennis shoes, for example—to huge combination department stores/supermarkets—like Fed-Mart, where you can find everything from TVs to house paint to peanut butter. Retailing is—and always was—the process of staying one step ahead of society's changing needs. A look at Figure 9–2 on page 227 shows how the evolution of retailing has paralleled the evolution of our wants and needs.

General stores (or trading posts) were the pre-Civil War version of today's food co-ops, but they stocked more products. They carried everything from

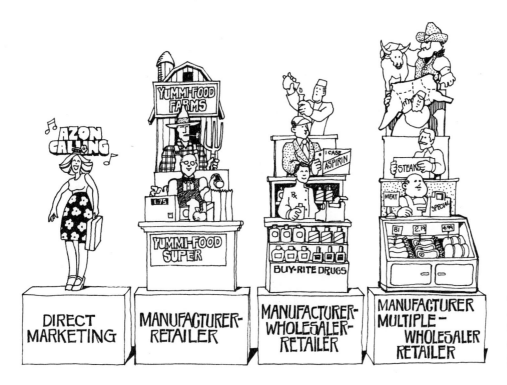

FIGURE 9–1
*Four
Common Channels
of Distribution
for Consumer Goods.*

flour, sugar, and cloth to animal feed, nails, and farm implements. Their selection was diverse enough to accommodate people's needs, but at that time needs were primarily centered around food, clothing, and shelter.

After the Civil War, the economy became more complicated. Cities grew, transportation improved, trade expanded, and family income increased. As a result, department stores came into being. Separate lines of the same items— from clothes to furniture to toys to cosmetics—were sold under one large roof. Stores like Macy's and Marshall Field began early. And department stores are still evolving. Lately, they have been responding to competition from smaller stores by slicing their large spaces into specialty shops.

A short while later, mail-order houses rode in on the improved rail and postal services. The two best-known—Montgomery Ward and Sears, Roe-buck—began in 1872 and 1886, respectively. Today these firms operate large

Your Next Job
Positions in Retailing and Wholesaling

Careers in Retail Sales and Display

Retail trade salesworkers sell customers everything from records to farm machinery, dresses to used cars. They must be able to communicate clearly and persuasively. Employers generally hire high-school graduates or people with some college and provide them with on-the-job training. Promotional opportunities are excellent: many salesworkers advance to jobs as buyers, advertising or personnel administrators, or general managers. Annual salaries average about $9,000. The job market is expected to increase moderately due to an increase in consumer income. (*Additional information:* The National Retail Merchants Association, 100 West 31st Street, New York, New York 10001.)

Displayers design and install exhibits in retail stores. Applicants are usually high-school or college graduates with creative ability and mechanical aptitude. Most employers provide on-the-job training in woodworking, merchandising, and window dressing. An experienced displayer may be promoted to display director or even to general manager. Annual salaries vary from $6,500 to over $25,000. (*Additional information:* contact large local retailers.)

Careers in Wholesaling

Manufacturers employ **wholesale trade salesworkers** to distribute their products to retailers. They check customer inventories, advise them of pricing and advertising strategies, and provide technical assistance with complex products. They are generally either high-school or college graduates who have sold for several years. Opportunities for advancement to supervisory or management positions are good. Annual salaries range from $11,000 to over $20,000. The job market for wholesale trade salesworkers is expected to expand moderately due to increases in population and in consumer income. (*Additional information:* Sales and Marketing Executives International, Career Education Division, 380 Lexington Avenue, N.Y., N.Y. 10017.)

Careers in Retail Buying

Challenging careers in department-store buying move through four positions: (1) management trainee; (2) suburban sales manager; (3) assistant buyer; and (4) buyer.

Department stores normally recruit college graduates as **management trainees.** They often have a degree in business administration (with a major in marketing or retailing), but students with backgrounds in liberal arts, home economics, and fashion merchandising are also considered. Management trainees earn about $13,500 annually and work in a variety of departments within the store until they are familiar with all aspects of the retail business. They work as salespeople, learn merchandise display, and perform essential inventory and record-keeping duties.

After six to twelve months of training in a large metropolitan department store, a management trainee is promoted to **suburban sales manager.** In this position, the employee is responsible for promoting and selling—but *not* buying—the merchandise to be carried in a group of related departments in a large suburban store. He or she learns which styles and fashions sell well and which do not. Annual salary ranges from $14,000 to $19,000.

After 12 to 18 months as a suburban sales manager, the employee is promoted to the position of **assistant buyer.** The assistant buyer helps the **buyer** to select and order merchandise that is expected to sell well in a department-store chain. They also negotiate prices and quantities with the manufacturers' salespeople and work with department-store salespeople in planning special sales and promotions. An assistant buyer earns $14,000 to $19,000 annually, and a buyer $15,000 to $32,000 (depending on experience and the sales volume of the department a particular buyer serves).

Job opportunities in department-store buying are expected to increase moderately and to be closely related to the growth in both population and disposable consumer income. (*Additional information:* contact the personnel manager of a large, local department store.)

department stores in addition to a modern version of their old popular catalogs, *catalog stores*. Customers have the choice of shopping in the department stores or ordering catalog items and picking them up in a few hours or days.

Mail-order retailers are growing in popularity. In the 1980s, catalog sales by mail will add up to more than $25 billion per year—a figure that surpasses every other retail sector. Perhaps one reason for this enormous success is the range of items available. For instance, recent Christmas catalogs from Neiman-Marcus have included "his" and "her" volcanic craters imported from Greece, a $30,000 solid-gold omelette pan, and a $300 mink sling for a lady with a broken arm. Nor are these simply page decorations: all of them were sold.

In the 1920s *chain stores* emerged. In an urban society, they were an economical way to buy, warehouse, advertise, and deliver products. *Supermarkets* are one example. They opened their doors in the 1930 Depression years, operating on a self-service, cash-and-carry basis to reduce personnel costs, increase volume, and offer lower prices. *Planned shopping centers* were the next step, opening in the 1940s. They were a response to the many families who were moving to the suburbs. These centers are often enclosed to protect shoppers from the weather.

Discount houses arrived in the 1950s as an answer to increasingly higher prices at department stores. The latter were offering charge accounts, free delivery, and a wide variety of products, all of which made their operations

FIGURE 9–2
The Evolution of American Retail Institutions.

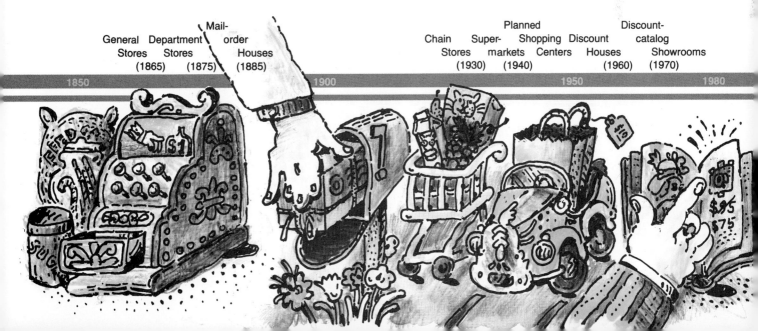

| General Stores (1865) | Department Stores (1875) | Mail-order Houses (1885) | Chain Stores (1930) | Super-markets (1940) | Planned Shopping Centers | Discount Houses (1960) | Discount-catalog Showrooms (1970) |

1850   1900   1950   1980

more expensive. Discount stores were able to keep their prices down by avoiding charge accounts, by increasing volume, and often by offering a narrower selection of products in a less elaborate setting.

Automatic merchandising—vending machines—became prominent during the late 1950s and 1960s, especially after the invention of coin and bill changers. Colleges and large industrial plants now rely on vending machines for much of their food and drink sales.

Franchise establishments began to boom in the 1960s. A **franchise** is a contract between a manufacturer and a local retailer that gives the retailer the exclusive right to sell the manufacturer's products in a given territory. The best-known franchises are the fast-food restaurants, like McDonald's and Kentucky Fried Chicken. But they are also now a major form of business in virtually every area of consumer goods and services, including bowling alleys, miniature golf courses, motels, dry cleaners, and pre-schools. (Franchises will be discussed in more detail in Chapter 16.)

The *discount-catalog showroom* was the fastest-growing retail trend of the 1970s. It is a combination of (1) mail-order and catalog stores, (2) department stores with elaborate merchandise showrooms, and (3) discount stores. A showroom like Modern Merchandising, LaBelle's, or Best Products mails out thousands of catalogs to prospective customers. They often list two prices—a "regular" retail price and the showroom price. About 95 percent of the items on the showroom floor can be bought on the spot and carried home.

The 1980s will see even more intense retail development, with cable television likely to be used to show a greater variety of products directly to consumers sitting in their own homes. And the Big Three of American retailers—Sears, K-Mart, and Penney's—are embarking on new strategies to increase their appeal to consumers (see box).

THE PRICE ELEMENT IN THE MARKETING MIX

Pricing, the third element in the marketing mix, means establishing a monetary value for a product or service. From the manager's perspective, pricing must include allowances, discounts, and servicing. Thus the $12,000 "price" paid for a new sports car is not its actual price if a $3,500 allowance is paid for the customer's trade-in or if the "price" also buys a service warranty on defective parts.

Factors That Affect Price

The price of everything—from bubble gum to a space shuttle—is determined by some combination of *demand and supply* as analyzed by managers. **Demand factors** are the things that determine the strength of consumers' desire and ability to pay for goods and services. **Supply factors** are the things that determine the amount of goods and services producers place on the market. Figured in supply are the costs of producing and marketing a product and the number of competing producers. So when pricing, managers must consider (1) demand, (2) production and marketing costs, and (3) competition.

The Three Largest U.S. Retailers Plan for the 1980s

Americans' shopping habits are changing rapidly. The consumer-rights movement, inflation, slower population growth, and price cutting by discounters are all taking their effect.

So 1980s retailers are developing marketing strategies to attract and keep consumers. Below is a list of some of the things that the three largest U.S. retailers—Sears (#1), K-Mart (#2), and Penney's (#3)—are doing.[3]

- SEARS, ROEBUCK AND COMPANY.   For decades, Sears worked hard on its reputation for quality merchandise. Now it is launching a major campaign to show that it offers low prices too. Before, its separate catalog-sales departments often went unnoticed in its stores. Now, sales from them have become a major responsibility of the store managers.
- K-MART CORPORATION.   In the 1970s, K-Mart converted many of its old Kresge variety stores into low-overhead discount stores for nationally known brands of hardgoods. This strategy was a smashing success. Now K-Mart is trying to market more items carrying its own K-Mart brand.
- J.C. PENNEY COMPANY.   For seventy-five years Penney's has been a retailer to small-town America, selling its private-brand softgoods in a bargain-basement atmosphere. Now it is transforming itself into a chain of moderate-price department stores, with an emphasis on higher-price fashion—in hardgoods, housewares, and especially apparel.

With more intense competition in selling products, virtually all retailing chains are trying to sell new services too. Montgomery Ward is offering dental and pharmacy services and diet instruction. Other chains offer income-tax help, day-care facilities, automotive service, driving lessons, carpet cleaning, and self-improvement lessons ranging from belly dancing and yoga to backgammon and golf.

Demand for the Product

Would you pay $1,000 for a digital watch, even the best model imaginable? Probably not. Would you pay $10 for a satisfactory model? Probably. And so would millions of other people. It is a fundamental principle of economics that as the price of an item falls, the number of the item purchased normally rises.

The **demand curve** (shown in Figure 9–3) illustrates this principle. It shows the maximum number of products that customers will buy at each price. Managers in the digital-watch industry might collect the following information on the maximum demand for digital watches at six different prices. Notice that as the price falls, people buy more.

POINT ON DEMAND CURVE (FIGURE 9–3)	IF THE PRICE CHARGED PER WATCH IS . . .	THE NUMBER OF WATCHES SOLD PER YEAR WILL BE . . .
A	$25	200,000
B	20	300,000
C	15	600,000
X	10	1,000,000
D	7	1,500,000
E	5	2,000,000

But price is not the whole story. Other factors that affect demand are (1) consumer taste; (2) the price and availability of other products, especially close substitutes; and (3) consumer income. The first two factors influence what consumers *want* to buy and the third affects what they *can* buy.

Taste is hard to predict. Who would have thought that roller skates would be so popular in the early 1980s? Consumer taste reflects a combination of physical needs (like hunger) and psychological needs (like status and acceptance). Its analysis requires detailed marketing research.

Related products shape demand too. The price and availability of *close substitutes* are especially important. Steel and aluminum, for example, are substitutes used in many goods, from beverage cans to car bumpers. If both meet the technical requirements, beverage and auto manufacturers will purchase one or the other depending on which offers the best price and greatest availability.

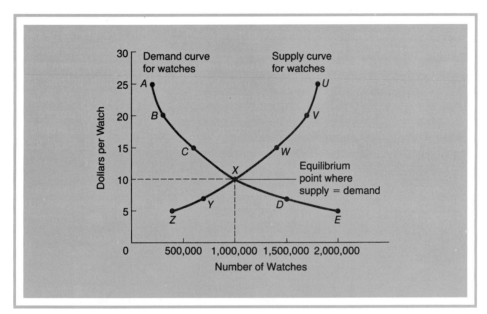

FIGURE 9-3
Supply and
Demand Curves.

The equilibrium point for watches is the market price at which the number of watches demanded by consumers is exactly equal to the number of watches offered for sale by the manufacturers. Here the point is at a market price of $10 per watch and a quantity of 1,000,000 watches.

Consumer income also determines demand. If you can't afford to see the new film playing in a nearby theater, you will probably settle for a rerun on television.

Production and Marketing Costs

In setting the price, a manager must also consider the costs of producing and marketing the good. These costs put a floor under a selling price, below which it cannot fall, except temporarily. If a price is set below the cost of producing and marketing each unit of a good, the business will lose money and fail.

Production and marketing costs partly determine how many businesses will try to sell a given product. In the digital-watch industry, for example, a few manufacturers may be very efficient. They can cover all their costs and still make a profit even if their watches are priced at $5. More firms, though, will step into the field if digital watches can be sold for $10 or $15 or $20. At those prices, even the less-efficient companies will be able to cover their costs and make a profit.

Suppose that all companies who could make digital watches were asked how many they would be willing to produce at various selling prices. This hypothetical description of the maximum number of units offered for sale at various prices by all firms in the industry is expressed in a **supply curve.** An example of six prices and the corresponding volume of watches that would be produced at each of these prices appears below and in Figure 9–3 (page 231).

POINT ON SUPPLY CURVE (FIGURE 9–3)	IF THE PRICE CHARGED PER WATCH IS . . .	THE ANNUAL NUMBER OF WATCHES PRODUCED WILL BE . . .
U	$25	1,800,000
V	20	1,700,000
W	15	1,400,000
X	10	1,000,000
Y	7	700,000
Z	5	400,000

Why "Demand" Isn't Quite a Law

A basic economic principle states that as the price of an item falls, the number of them purchased by customers normally rises. But exceptions do occur. Consider the following:

- In the 1970s, the Whirlpool Corporation manufactured 18,000 too many vacuum cleaners on one of their production runs.
- K-Mart bought a few of these vacuum cleaners and test-marketed them in two stores at $29 apiece. Consumers wouldn't buy them.
- Western Auto Stores bought all the vacuum cleaners they could from Whirlpool. They priced them at $49 each and sold them all.

Why? Consumers thought that the low $29 price at K-Mart meant poor quality. When Western Auto Stores raised the price to a reasonable—but bargain—level, customers bought them. So sometimes the number sold increases as the price increases.

Supply and demand work together. Figure 9–3 shows that lower prices bring a greater demand for the product from consumers. But lower prices also lead to a lower supply from manufacturers.

The point where the demand and supply curves intersect is an important one for managers. It is where the market is said to be in **equilibrium.** This means that the market price at which a good is demanded by consumers is exactly equal to the quantity of the good supplied by manufacturers. In Figure 9–3 this point is at a market size of 1,000,000 watches and a price of $10. Here all this applies to the entire watch industry. But similar demand and supply curves could be drawn for each manufacturer in the industry.

Managers in an individual company have several ways to cover their costs and make a profit. Usually, when costs increase they simply raise the selling price. But there are often other means available. For example, Mars, Inc.— manufacturer of Snickers and M & M's—keeps the same selling price when sugar and cocoa prices rise but reduces the weight of its candy (see box on page 235).

Competition

Another factor that affects price is competition: the number of firms in the same industry that produce basically the same product, including the prices they set. A digital-watch producer might like to set a price of $15. But if several competitors set their price at $8, most consumers would buy that product instead. So price must be adjusted according to competitors' prices.

How to Set a Price

The three factors affecting price—demand, costs, and competition—are summarized in Figure 9–4. Marketing managers try to take all these into account in setting the price. But since this is not always feasible, they usually work with one of the following methods: (1) demand-oriented pricing; (2) cost-oriented pricing; or (3) competition-oriented pricing.

Price by Demand

Managers of new products often use **demand-oriented pricing** because the initial price influences the demand for the product. It can determine how fast the target market is penetrated. For example, a high price slows demand for a new product and a low one can attract extra customers or those with lower

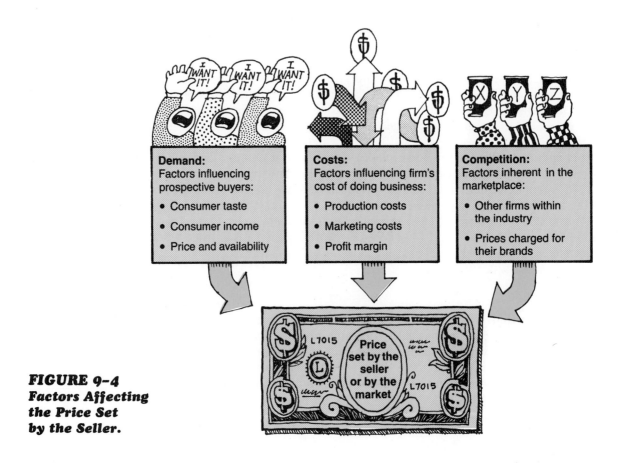

FIGURE 9–4
Factors Affecting the Price Set by the Seller.

incomes or those whose desires for the product are weaker. Both high and low prices have different advantages. *Skim-the-cream pricing* and *penetration pricing* are two opposite ways for managers of new products to find these advantages.

Skim-the-cream pricing is setting a high initial price to get high profits quickly. This strategy relies on the fact that some buyers are willing to pay a much higher price than others. The reasons range from status-seeking to product quality. Later, the initial price may be reduced gradually. Digital watches selling for $400 in 1972 are an example; by 1980 several brands were priced at less than $10.

Penetration pricing is setting a low initial price to attract as many buyers as possible. Home trash compactors are an example. The first manufacturers set prices low enough to discourage early competition from other manufacturers.

Odd pricing is setting a price of $395 instead of $400. Consumers supposedly focus on the first digit. This strategy was originally used for low-priced items, to force retail clerks to ring up the sale on the cash register to make change. This prevented them from pocketing the money themselves when waiting on customers who were in a hurry, paid the exact amount, and did not bother to wait for their sales receipt.

Price by Cost

Marketing managers who deal with a large number of products find that estimating the demand for each item separately is too expensive and time consuming. So instead, they use the **cost-oriented pricing** method. This can involve either *standard-markup pricing* or *cost-plus-percentage-of-cost pricing*.

Standard-markup pricing, used by most retail managers, means adding a fixed percentage to the cost of all items in the same product class. The

---

How to Price a Candy Bar

What candy manufacturer produces five of the six best-selling chocolate candy bars? Hershey? Wrong! It's Mars, Inc., with Snickers (#1), M & M's Peanut (#3), M & M's Plain (#4), 3 Musketeers (#5), and Milky Way (#6). Only Hershey's Reese Cup—ranked #2—has a taste of the top six, according to *Business Week* magazine.[4]

Mars' sweet strength comes from its product quality and marketing magic with retailers. The company won't produce red M & M's because it is dissatisfied with the substitute red colors developed after the ban on red dye number 2. And it helps retailers by taking back dated candy after four months on the shelf.

But Mars' managers get stomachaches from setting prices. Sugar and cocoa prices are never stable. So they've developed a delectable pricing "recipe" in which the size of the bar follows the cost of the sugar and cocoa, its main ingredients. This can mean changing the size as often as every two or three weeks, even though the retail price stays the same. Mars' managers think consumers prefer a smaller candy bar with the same recipe to a lower quality, larger bar, the option chosen by some other manufacturers.

And they have five of the six top brands to prove it!

percentage varies depending on the type of retail store (furniture, clothing, or grocery) and on the type of product. High-volume products usually have smaller markups than low-volume products. For example, a supermarket might have a standard markup of 10 percent on the cost of dairy products, which are fast-moving items. Thus, if it paid its supplier $1.00 per dozen eggs, the supermarket's selling price would be $1.10 ($1.00 for cost *plus* 10 percent of $1.00, or 10 cents, for markup). On spices, a slow-moving item, the markup might be 20 percent or more. The markups must cover overhead costs (store rent, manager's salary, and so on) and profit. (Markups based on both cost and selling price are discussed in Chapter 17.)

Cost-plus-percentage-of-cost pricing is often used for one- or few-of-a-kind items. For example, an architect may charge a fee of 13 percent of the

What's the Price for Green Beans?

If Green Giant prices its national brand of French-style green beans at 39 cents in a supermarket chain, what price will the supermarket set for its private brand (Cherry Valley)? What about the price of a "generic" can? For the answer, see the text discussion on the next page.

construction costs of a house. Thus, whether the house costs $80,000 or $280,000, the architect's fee remains a fixed 13 percent.

Price by Competition

Sometimes managers set prices based on what all competitors (the market) or one or a few competitors charge. Farmers selling wheat and investors selling IBM stock deal with market, or **competition-oriented pricing.** Going-rate, below-market, above-market, loss-leader and sealed-bid pricing are examples.

Soap and detergent manufacturers often match their competitors' prices, following a policy of **going-rate pricing.** Discount stores and grocery chains usually use **below-market pricing** for their private brands to make them more competitive with nationally known brands. In the box "What's the Price for Green Beans?" the grocery-chain managers might choose 29 cents for their "house brand." And a generically packaged can of beans might be priced at 23 cents.

Boutiques and specialty stores often choose **above-market pricing.** They can get premium prices because of the special attention and services they provide (free alterations, for example). Even the H.J. Heinz Company uses above-market pricing. H.J. Heinz himself once asserted, "Unless you charge a grocer a fair price for quality, he will not appreciate the goods." This advice seems to work. When Gerber raised its baby-food price by 20 cents per case in the 1970s, Heinz managers responded with a 23-cent per case increase. And the price held.

Loss-leader pricing, another strategy used by some retail stores, is a policy of advertising well-known goods at prices below the going rate. These few advertised goods are intended to attract customers in the hope that once they are in the store they will buy not only the loss leaders but the more conventionally priced goods as well. Supermarket "meat specials" or "milk specials" are examples.

Sealed-bid pricing, widely used in government purchases, requires administrators to prepare a precise, written specification of what they want and then ask interested manufacturers to submit sealed bids. These bids are opened and read aloud, and the contract is awarded to the company with the lowest bid. This method is designed to ensure fair and open competition. The winning bidder must deliver the contracted items at the bid price— even if the contract price does not cover costs.

Chapter Review & Applications

Key Points to Remember

1. The place element in the marketing mix refers to all the institutions and activities responsible for delivering products to consumers.

2. Wholesalers and retailers, called middlemen, are the two major institutions through which goods are distributed to consumers.

3. Marketing channels are the paths products take from manufacturers to customers (either business firms or ultimate consumers). Four common channels are (1) manufacturer–consumer; (2) manufacturer–retailer–consumer; (3) manufacturer–wholesaler–retailer–consumer; and (4) manufacturer–multiple–wholesaler–retailer–consumer.

4. The United States has a mixture of retail institutions. Just since 1950, discount houses, vending machines (automatic merchandising), franchises, and discount-catalog showrooms have arrived on the retailing scene.

5. The price element in the marketing mix establishes a monetary value for a good or service.

6. The price of everything is determined by demand and supply factors. Factors influencing the demand for a product are (1) its price; (2) consumer taste; (3) the price and the availability of other products, particularly close substitutes; and (4) consumer income. Supply factors include (1) production and marketing costs, and (2) competition.

7. As the price of an item falls, the number of those items purchased by consumers normally rises. This economic relationship is generally expressed as a demand curve, which shows the maximum number of products that customers will buy at each price.

8. Production and marketing costs put a floor under a selling price, below which it cannot fall, except temporarily. A hypothetical description of the maximum number of units offered for sale at various prices by all firms in an industry is expressed in a supply curve.

9. The equilibrium point on the supply and demand curves is the market price at which the quantity of a good demanded by consumers is exactly equal to the quantity of the good supplied by manufacturers.

10. Managers usually follow one of three price-setting strategies: (1) demand-oriented, (2) cost-oriented, or (3) competition-oriented.

Questions for Discussion

1. Not all retailers perform all functions for all customers on all purchases. List the functions that *are* and *are not* performed by the retailer in each of the following transactions:

   (a) The purchase at a hardware store of something (the customer isn't sure exactly what) to fasten a wood lath to a concrete wall.
   (b) The purchase at a supermarket of a box of Wheaties, your favorite cereal.
   (c) The purchase of a brand-name refrigerator at a department store.

2. Look at Figure 9–3 and suppose that people suddenly began to buy more digital watches. What would be the impact on the demand curve? On the market price?

3. Suppose a major invention permitted digital-watch manufacturers to reduce their production costs dramatically. What would be the impact on the supply curve in Figure 9–3? On price?

Short Case

You are president of a small lumber company that presently sells to independent lumber retailers who, in turn, sell to consumers. You are considering opening a chain of retail outlets to sell your lumber directly to do-it-yourself consumers.

1. In terms of Figure 9–1, describe the present and proposed marketing channels available.

2. List the advantages and the disadvantages of (a) the present method of selling to independent lumber retailers, and (b) the proposed method of opening your own chain of retail outlets.

A Critical
Business Decision

—made by Shri Kumar Poddar
of Educational Subscription Service, Inc.

The Situation

Shri Kumar Poddar, while an engineering student at Michigan State University, concluded that he needed more money to finish college. So he decided to start his own business selling magazine subscriptions. But no sooner had he launched his new business than Poddar had to leave MSU's engineering school—only eleven credits short of a degree. He had failed a course in which he had a personality conflict with the instructor. Determined to keep up his studies, Poddar transferred to business administration and continued his education in philosophy, politics, economics, as well as business.

The son of a Shell Oil distributor in Calcutta, India, Poddar began his business by writing major magazine publishers and asking to be their sales agent. *Time, Newsweek, McCall's, Reader's Digest,* and *Mademoiselle* responded favorably. His first sales were to MSU students, to whom he personally sold subscriptions. But he quickly realized that the number of people he could reach personally was rather limited and that college students everywhere might be potential buyers. What he needed was a low-cost method of reaching college students across the country.

The Decision

Poddar designed a special subscription card offering "courtesy rates" to students and educators, and he called his new business Educational Subscription Service, Inc. But he couldn't decide how to distribute the cards to his target market—college students and faculty—inexpensively. Finally he made his decision, a three-point approach he described in an interview with a *New York Times* reporter.[5] First, he notes, "In my business, there is no personal contact with the customer whatsoever. I am totally opposed to the forced sale of subscriptions." Second, "The magazine-subscription business is not known for its honesty, so the recipe is to be honest." Finally, Poddar says, "We guarantee the subscriber the lowest price—or a refund."

Apparently Poddar's straightforward marketing decision—a low-key sales presentation, honesty, and low prices—makes sense. Five years after he started, Poddar's business generated annual sales of more than $1 million. And he opened a 5,000-square-foot office to house his ten employees in a business plaza in Lansing, Michigan, about four miles from the MSU campus.

Questions

1. What are some of the methods Poddar might have used to distribute his subscription cards to hundreds of thousands of college students and faculty across the United States?
2. Select the method that you would have used and justify your choice.

Advertising and Personal Selling

In this chapter you will learn . . .

- how promotion works to increase sales, profits, and buyers' awareness.
- how to develop an advertising campaign.
- what jobs and skills are involved in personal selling and in managing a sales force.

10

ou may have seen an ad like that on the left in your campus newspaper. It's not a put-on. Beetleboards of America, Inc., is coming to town, whether your town is in the United States, Canada, or Puerto Rico.

Formed by Charles Bird, a Los Angeles advertising consultant who specializes in reaching the "youth market," Beetleboards is an answer to this problem: how should a company promote a product to an age group with no stable reading, viewing, or listening habits? Bird got the idea in 1971 while walking across a campus parking lot crawling with Volkswagen Beetles. He thought, why not pay students to decorate their VWs with national ads? Today about 10,000 cars have been decorated, courtesy of Beetleboards.

In case you or a friend drives a VW, here are some details. Student drivers are interviewed and chosen for their personality, poise, and "product interest." You have "product interest" if you cheerfully agree to continue to answer questions about your VW from astonished passersby. Similar ads have sought college men who like pipe tobacco and want their VWs customized with Sir Walter Raleigh ads. And Clairol wants college women with nice hair to drive around its Herbal Essence ads.

Student VW drivers get a new paint job, the decals, and $20 a month. They also get the chance to earn $25 a day by driving their bugs in parades or renting them out for shopping-center displays. At the end of the campaign they receive $70 to $100 for decal removal. Advertisers pay an average of $140 a month for use of a moving bug.

Beetleboards is a creative example of *promotion,* the fourth element in the marketing mix. The two main kinds of promotion, to be explored in this chapter, are advertising and personal selling.

WHAT IS PROMOTION?

Promotion is communication between sellers and buyers intended to inform, persuade, or remind people about a product. *Informing* is the main objective when promoting a new product. *Persuading* is the focus when a product faces

competition from close substitutes. And *reminding* is the key later, when more substitutes have appeared in the marketplace and customers need to be encouraged to continue using (or to return to) the product. This life cycle of promotion is shown in Figure 10–1 on the next page.

The two most important forms of promotion are *advertising* (mass selling) and *personal selling*. Other promotional activities, not discussed here, include free samples, trading stamps, sweepstakes, cents-off coupons, and trade-show exhibitions.

Candy, gum, cigarettes, and other convenience goods are sold mostly through advertising. There is very little personal selling. Industrial goods and Avon and Shaklee products, on the other hand, are bought because of personal selling. There are relatively few ads for these goods. Each product on the market uses a slightly different blend of these two promotional activities. The blend may also vary according to the product's place in its own life cycle. Because of this, a company's promotional "recipe" sometimes has to change.

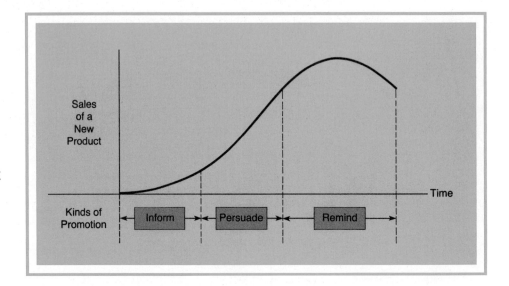

**FIGURE 10–1
How the Kind
of Promotion
Relates to a
Particular
Product's Life
Cycle.**

Hershey Chocolate Corporation did without ads for sixty-six years. Its sales force simply sweet-talked Hershey bars into the country's retail outlets. But then other candy companies melted Hershey's monopoly on popular taste, and Hershey decided to run its first ad in 1970.

ADVERTISING

Advertising is any nonpersonal communication between seller and buyer conducted through paid media under clear sponsorship. Because it is not personal, it is unlike personal selling. Because it is paid and clearly sponsored, it is unlike publicity—a minor part of most promotional budgeting—which is free and without an identified sponsor.

Kinds of Advertising

Advertising works either quickly or slowly. The former is called *direct-action* and the latter *delayed-action advertising*.

Direct-action advertising, the most common form used by retailers, seeks a fast purchase. Examples: a newspaper ad announces a special department-store sale to start at 9:30 A.M. Wednesday morning; a direct-mail ad offers low subscription prices on magazines; a radio ad proclaims a "last chance" to buy your car today at $100 over cost. These ads are not designed to have significant impact once a few hours or days have passed.

Delayed-action advertising, most commonly used by manufacturers, seeks longer-range effects. Its goals are to improve brand awareness, increase product preference, and present a more favorable company image. These ads are designed to gradually influence potential buyers to become brand-loyal, repeat customers. Such advertising is necessary to counteract the influence of competitive products and short memories. Beer ads during TV football games and car ads in magazines are designed to have this kind of delayed effect. The consumer is not expected to run to the store within the hour.

Running an Ad Campaign

If you direct one or more ads at a target market, you are launching an advertising campaign. Whether you operate a small shoe store or run the advertising campaign for Camaro at General Motors, you will sell more products if you follow a systematic plan, as shown in Figure 10–2 and described in the following sections.

Set the Goals and Budget

This is the first step and must be done as precisely as possible. The goals guide the campaign and even help measure its effectiveness at the end. The budget is a careful ceiling on the money to be spent.

What are precisely defined goals? Sell 100 more pairs of shoes or 10,000 more Camaros. As a shoe-store owner, you might aim to sell 100 more pairs of shoes in a given week. At General Motors, you might launch a delayed-action campaign to gradually shape consumer awareness. If, for example, only 40 percent of American adults from 18 through 49 (your target market) know about the sporty small Camaro, your goal might be to raise this awareness to 60 percent by the end of one year.

The budget for an individual ad campaign must fit into a firm's annual advertising budget. There are two common methods for arriving at ad budgets:

- OBJECTIVE-AND-TASK METHOD Set specific advertising goals; define the tasks required to achieve them; and estimate the cost of performing these tasks. This cost is then the estimated advertising budget.

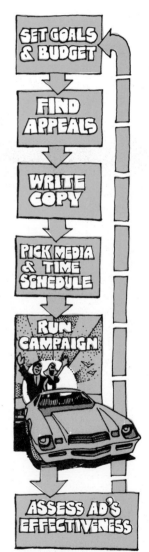

FIGURE 10–2
Steps in Developing an Advertising Campaign.

- PERCENTAGE-OF-SALES METHOD The budget is a specific percentage of sales revenue for a particular period. It might be based on last year or last month, or estimated for the coming year or month.

As a shoe-store owner, you might use the objective-and-task method. To sell 100 extra pairs of shoes, you find that you need to spend $100 for advertising. The budget is then $100. The percentage-of-sales method is a bit more elaborate. You can see how it is arrived at by referring to Figure 10–3. Notice that some firms—especially the ad-conscious food and soap companies—have advertising expenditures exceeding 5 percent of their sales. Suppose the average selling price for a Camaro is $7,000 and expected annual sales are 100,000 cars. Figure 10–3 shows that GM spends 0.2 percent of its annual sales on advertising. GM's projected national advertising budget for the Camaro would then be $1.4 million annually ($7,000 per car × 100,000 cars × .002). An individual ad campaign budget is provided from some share of this total annual budget.

FIGURE 10–3
National Media Advertisers—
The Ten Leading U.S. Companies for 1979

RANK	FIRM	1979 ADVERTISING EXPENDITURES ($1,000,000)	1979 SALES ($1,000,000)	ADVERTISING EXPENDITURES AS % OF SALES
1	Procter and Gamble Co.	$463	$9,329	5.0%
2	General Foods Corp.	291	5,472	5.3
3	American Home Products	165	3,401	4.9
4	General Motors Corp.	147	66,311	0.2
5	General Mills Inc.	142	3,745	3.8
6	Bristol-Meyers Co.	141	2,753	5.1
7	McDonald's Corp.	138	1,958	7.1
8	Ford Motor Co.	128	43,514	0.3
9	Pepsi Co. Inc.	119	5,091	2.3
10	Lever Brothers Co.	112	952	11.8

Sources: 1979 advertising expenditures from Bill Abrams, "Firms Fret Over Rising Costs of TV Spots; Some Raise Budgets and Shun Prime Time," *The Wall Street Journal* (April 4, 1980); and 1979 sales from "The Fortune Directory of the 500 Largest U.S. Industrial Corporations," *Fortune* (May 5, 1980), pp. 274–295.

Find the Appeals

A major part of an advertising campaign is to find the right sort of appeal. An *advertising appeal* is a theme that arouses interest. It is designed to trigger buying decisions or project a better company image among the target market. Some campaign appeals are directed to consumers' intellects (emphasizing higher quality at a competitive price, for example). Others are directed at consumers' emotions (offering greater popularity or improved social status). Still others rely on a straightforward economic appeal (promising great savings during special sale periods).

Automobile companies like General Motors have stressed virtually every appeal at one time or another. Examples are appeals to economy, such as the Volkswagen series of "Think Small" ads, and appeals to a better life (the disastrous Edsel campaign pointed toward "the young executive on the way up"). Sometimes car ads do not look like ads at all, since they provide useful general information to car owners instead of promoting a particular brand. Nevertheless, they are intended to project an image of the company that is trustworthy, reliable, and genuinely concerned with people's welfare. (Wouldn't you rather buy a car from someone—like General Motors in the ad in the margin—who really cares about protecting your car's paint?)

Write the Copy

The next step in developing an ad campaign is to translate the selected appeal into *advertising copy*. This is what the prospective buyer will actually see or hear through such media as billboards, TV, radio, magazines, or newspapers.

As an appliance-repair-shop owner, your copy might be a simple, straightforward ad written by you or by a copywriter at the local newspaper. But as a Camaro manager, your copy development is far more complex. It involves advertising that will be seen by tens of millions of people and will probably be handled by an advertising agency, hired by GM. The agency's copywriters might conclude that they need a clear and simple message. After much brainstorming, they create copy emphasizing "hug a road," and develop the ad shown in the margin.

What makes good advertising copy? Many advertising copywriters suggest the following criteria: an ad should be attention-getting, easy to read and to understand, believable, informative, and memorable. Copywriters have developed creative slogans, trademarks, and catchy animated figures that have boosted sales and even become part of our popular culture. (See the color insert at the end of the text.)

Read the box below to check their skill (and your memory) before looking at these answers.

1. Wheaties breakfast cereal
2. Kellogg's Frosted Flakes cereal
3. United Airlines
4. Memorex recording tape
5. Starkist tuna
6. Pillsbury
7. Hallmark greeting cards
8. Marlboro
9. 9 Lives cat food
10. Pepsi

Because many people remember ads like these, the firms, products, and brands have benefited dramatically.

In developing and assessing ad copy, copywriters must come up with answers to the following questions:

1. Would a testimonial by a well-known person or by a testing agency present the appeal best?
2. Should the copy identify the company's name or just the product's name?

Name It

The American consumer is pelted with hundreds of advertisements every day. The punchy slogans sing out from radio and TV, and the eye-catching pictures peer out of magazines, newspapers, and billboards. A successful ad is one that is remembered. It will also be associated in the consumer's mind with the brand or product that is being promoted. This attention-getting association can be created with ads, trademarks, slogans, and catchy animated figures.

How well have they succeeded? Try to identify the brand name or firm behind each of the following slogans.

1. "Breakfast of Champions"
2. Tony the Tiger
3. "Fly the Friendly Skies of _____"
4. Singer Ella Fitzgerald sang a high note to shatter a glass for _____
5. Charlie the Tuna
6. The _____ Doughboy
7. "When You Care Enough to Send the Very Best"
8. The rugged cowboy smokes _____ cigarettes
9. Morris the Cat
10. "The _____ Generation"

For the answers, see the text above.

3. Should the copy stress pictures rather than words?

4. What specific pictures and words should be used?

5. What layout is most aesthetically pleasing?

6. Is the message clear and understandable to the target audience?

7. Will the copy accomplish the goals set for it?

Well-known personalities are often used in ads to promote products. Although it is expensive, this technique often grabs attention for an ad. O. J. Simpson has chased a lot of business through airports for Hertz Rent-A-Car. But the personality must have credibility for a particular product. Actor Karl Malden, famous as detective Mike Stone in "Streets of San Francisco," did wonders for American Express Traveler's Checks because TV viewers believed he knew how to help them protect their money. But the late actor Peter Sellers was a flop for Trans World Airlines. He not only had no built-in association with the product, but his slapstick comedy roles actually clashed with the image the airline wanted to project.

Sometimes personalities can be held financially liable for their claims in ads. The Federal Trade Commission ordered singer Pat Boone to stop claiming that Acne-Statin would cure or eliminate the cause of acne. And he was told to help pay any damages the manufacturer may be liable for. Another drawback

Loretta Swit, O. J. Simpson, and Tracy Austin: Among the many celebrities selling for fees.

is that when ads are built around well-known personalities, like quarterback Joe Namath, for example, million-dollar promotional campaigns often must be scrapped if they lose their jobs or become unpopular with the public.

Pick the Media and the Time Schedule

The next task is to select the media for the advertisements and to plan their timing.

Advertising media are all the vehicles for communicating an ad to the target market. They include magazines, newspapers, radio, television, billboards, novelties (calendars, key chains), direct mail (brochures, letters), bus and train posters, and catalogs.

For a small-business owner with a $100 budget, media choices are limited. If the store is in a small town, handbills could be delivered directly to homes in the store's trading area. Or an ad could be taken in the local daily newspaper. If the store is in a suburb of a major metropolitan area, the owner might run an ad in the weekly suburban newspaper. Since most metropolitan newspapers publish separate editions for different geographic areas, the store owner could also place ads in one or two metro-area regional editions. Depending upon cost, one or more of these media might be selected.

The selection of media by the Camaro campaign managers is more complex. Potential buyers are all over the country, and much money is involved. The General Motors executives must first choose which media they will use—television, radio, magazines, and so on. Then, within each medium, they must select the specific vehicles (*Time, TV Guide,* or *Reader's Digest* among the magazines, for example).

In making these decisions, the executives must consider which medium presents a particular message best and which medium delivers the greatest target-market audience for the least cost. Here, the appeal of the campaign counts. If new colors and new styling are to be stressed, a four-color magazine ad would certainly be preferable to a radio ad and probably even to a television ad. But, if the road-hugging feature is to be emphasized, a television ad would probably show it best. Of course, both magazines and television could be used.

Cost is generally measured in terms of the number of consumers reached. Some network television programs and high-circulation magazines are quite expensive, as can be seen in Figure 10–4. And special situations can prompt even higher advertising costs: one minute on the Superbowl Game costs more than $200,000. But even this can be "cheap" when weighed against the fact that the ad is seen by almost 100 million people in this country alone.

The measures for these media extravaganzas are cost per thousand households watching a TV program and cost per thousand households buying a magazine. An index like this also allows a manager to compare TV and magazines for a particular target market.

Here is how it works. Suppose there is one member of Ford's target market (adults from 18 to 49) watching each television set or reading each magazine. On the basis of the information given in the right-hand column in Figure 10–4, GM's best television buy would be "Sports Spectacular" (at $2.42 per thousand television households reached). The best magazine buy would be a full-page black-and-white ad in *TV Guide* (at $3.09 per thousand circulation).

To refine their media choices further, executives at major companies and their ad agencies use detailed demographic information. Magazines and TV programs profile their readers and viewers by sex, age, income level, and other factors. Figure 10–5 shows the Nielsen ratings of the top ten 1980 TV programs watched by 18- to 49-year-old adults, compared with the programs most

FIGURE 10–4
Typical Advertising Costs, 1980.

ADVERTISING MEDIUM		ADVERTISING VEHICLE	COST PER 30 SECONDS OR PER ISSUE	NUMBER OF VIEWING HOUSE-HOLDS OR TOTAL CIRCULATION	COST PER THOUSAND HOUSEHOLDS OR PER THOUSAND CIRCULATION
Network television	Sports	"NFL Football," Monday evening, (ABC)	$ 90,000	14,880,000	$ 6.04
		"Sports Spectacular," Sunday afternoon, (CBS)	16,500	6,790,000	2.42
		"NFL Football," Sunday afternoon, (NBC) Game 1	36,300	10,150,000	3.57
		Game 2	72,500	13,960,000	5.19
	Regular programs	"Dallas," Friday evening, (CBS)	63,800	19,760,000	3.22
		"Alice," Sunday evening, (CBS)	81,300	20,220,000	4.02
		"Three's Company," Tuesday evening, (ABC)	119,000	20,830,000	5.71
General magazines	Full-page four color, one time	*Reader's Digest*	82,200	17,889,000	4.60
		TV Guide	69,500	19,043,000	3.65
		Time	70,285	4,273,000	16.45
	Full-page black and white, one time	*Reader's Digest*	68,400	17,890,000	3.82
		TV Guide	58,800	19,043,000	3.09
		Time	45,055	4,273,000	10.54

Sources: A.C. Nielsen Company Television Index and Standard Rate and Data Service, May 27, 1980.

FIGURE 10–5
The 10 Most Popular Television Shows
for Two Different Age Groups in 1980.

ADULTS 18–49 YEARS OLD	ADULTS 55 YEARS AND OVER
1. That's Incredible (ABC) 19.9%	1. 60 Minutes (CBS) 38.1%
2. Chips (NBC) 19.6	2. Alice (CBS) 36.2
3. M*A*S*H (CBS) 18.6	3. Archie Bunker's Place (CBS) . . . 32.5
4. Dallas (CBS) 18.3	4. One Day at a Time (CBS) 31.9
5. 60 Minutes (CBS) 18.0	5. Jeffersons (CBS) 31.7
6. Jeffersons (CBS) 17.6	6. Waltons (CBS) 27.4
7. Alice (CBS) 17.1	7. M*A*S*H (CBS) 26.4
8. Sunday Night Movie (ABC) 17.1	8. Little House on
9. Movie of the Week (NBC) 16.8	the Prairie (NBC) 26.2
10. Big Event (NBC) 16.5	9. Trapper John, M.D. (CBS) 24.0
	10. Dallas (CBS) 23.2

Note: The numbers represent the Nielsen TV ratings. They show the percentage of people in this age group with TV sets tuned to a specific program. To see how this information is used in selecting advertising media, see the text.

Source: Adapted from A.C. Nielsen Company Index (February 25–March 9, 1980).

watched by adults over 55. Note that half the programs appear on both lists. But GM would try to reach the target market for its Camaro by buying ads at the top of the left-hand column in Figure 10–5—"That's Incredible," "Chips," "M*A*S*H," and "Dallas"—if their Nielsen ratings hold up and their cost per thousand is low.

In its actual 1980 Camaro campaign, GM hedged its bets. Its executives purchased network time on the three sports shows and in all three of the magazines listed in Figure 10–4.

Once the media are selected, the advertiser must decide how often to run a specific ad. Some television ads are run hundreds of times. Magazine ads are occasionally run in later issues of the same magazine but more often appear at the same time in different magazines. This repetition is designed to reinforce consumer desire to buy the product or boost awareness and image of the product or sponsor. (See, also, color insert at end of text.)

Run the Campaign

Now the campaign is on. But events may cause changes. If, for instance, a small-business owner planned to run a direct-action ad in three successive issues of the local newspaper but sales did not increase significantly after the first two ads, he may decide to cancel the third. On the other hand, a successful response might cause him to extend the ad campaign.

Bank of America Tackles Its Image Problem

Charles R. Stuart, Jr., Bank of America's vice president of marketing services, discovered the hard way that his bank had an image problem. In the past, Bank of America had used a number of trademarks or logos that it thought represented the ideas of equity and stability. But when Bank of America surveyed consumers to see what they saw in the logo of a nineteenth-century sailing ship with Old English script, the bank discovered that most people thought it was the trademark for *Encyclopaedia Britannica*. People had really seen the logo as a sign of a stodgy, stagnating bank. "So much for our equity," Stuart told *PSA Magazine*.[1]

So Bank of America called in Walter Landor, chairman of his own San Francisco design firm. Landor and his associates do elaborate market surveys to help a company improve its logo, trademark, or package; change its name; or rework its image. For Bank of America, Landor developed a flowing monogram logo (shown above). Landor's description of this: "To symbolize the biggest bank in the world, an early tie-line accompanies a monogram we devel-

oped to suggest that the bank is run *by* individuals *for* individuals."

Some of Landor's other eye-catching design strategies for logos and packages:

- SPRITE AND TAB "Redesigning well-established brands like Sprite and Tab requires sensitivity of how to attract new consumers without alienating existing ones."
- AGREE SHAMPOO "The shape of a container can be a powerful tool in establishing a unique brand image for a new product."
- LITE BEER "Making history in the hotly competitive beer market, the strong design of Lite's label communicates the opposite of low-calorie beer—a beer drinker's beer."
- COTTON "Cotton's natural answer to the wool mark has helped bring it back into fashion's favor."

Assess the Ad's Effectiveness

The last step in a well-organized ad campaign is to measure its effectiveness. As the feedback loop in Figure 10–2 indicates, this step helps the advertiser to assess the campaign's value, eliminate wasted effort, and apply the experience to future campaigns.

Actual results of the ads are compared with intended goals. In the case of the shoe-store owner, whose goal was to sell 100 additional pairs of shoes, the campaign is a success if he actually sells 120 more pairs.

In this direct-action campaign, the owner may carry the analysis further. He knows that the actual advertising cost was $100. Suppose that he usually sells 40 pairs of shoes a week at an average profit of $5 per pair, but the average profit on each pair of shoes sold in the sale week is only $3 (because of the $2 price reduction he offered). To determine the profit margin, the owner multiplies 120 pairs of shoes by $3, then subtracts the $100 advertising cost and $80 of lost profits on the 40 pairs of shoes (which would normally have been sold during the week with no $2 price reduction). Conclusion: the advertising campaign created a $180 profit.

Evaluating the success of GM's delayed-action campaign is harder, since a clear measure like sales or profits is not available. Instead, GM managers conduct a consumer survey. They find that consumer awareness of the Camaro in the target market has increased by 25 percent. Since the goal was an increase of at least 20 percent, the campaign is judged a success.

PERSONAL SELLING

Personal selling is a person-to-person sales presentation made to a prospective buyer. A sales representative of United Airlines or a travel agent representing the airline may sell a customer a flight ticket, either at the airport counter or in the agency. Both people are engaged in personal selling.

Kinds of Sales Jobs

Sales jobs may be divided into four main categories, each of which is described in the following paragraphs.

Manufacturer's Sales Representatives

These salespeople represent producers of both industrial and consumer goods. Some are technical sales representatives, such as engineers employed by industrial-goods manufacturers to call on other manufacturers and help them solve technical problems. Others are salespeople employed by consumer-goods manufacturers to call on wholesalers and retailers.

Wholesaler's Sales Representatives

These salespeople work for wholesalers who stock many items from different manufacturers. They sell to retailers and to other customers who find it more convenient to place one large order for many kinds of items than to send separate small orders to each manufacturer. There are about 800,000 wholesaler's sales representatives in the United States today.

Retail Sales Representatives

This category comprises the largest portion of sales occupations. It includes all salespeople who sell consumer goods in retail stores—currently about 2.7 million people.

Direct Sales Representatives

These salespeople usually sell a single product or product line directly to consumers, either in person or by phone. Examples are insurance salespeople, stock and bond brokers, and door-to-door sales representatives, like those employed by Shaklee, Inc., and Avon Products, Inc.

From these job descriptions, it can be seen that sales representatives perform marketing and communications functions at every stage of a channel of distribution. Several selling occupations will be described in more detail in the Your Next Job section of this chapter.

The Professional Salesperson

For many people, personal selling has a negative connotation. Yet professional salespeople are crucial to American business because they are customers' problem solvers.

Professional Objectives

Through hard work and integrity, many salespeople at all levels have attained a professional reputation. They generally follow these guidelines:

1. Focus on the customer's needs.

Your Next Job
Positions in Advertising, Public Relations, and Manufacturer's Sales

Careers in Advertising

Advertising account executives plan and direct advertising programs for their agencies' clients. They plan according to client objectives and budgets, develop the advertising copy, and select the proper media and timing. A college degree and 5 to 15 years of agency experience in copy layout, media buying, or campaign planning are normally required. Annual salary varies from $20,000 to $80,000.

Advertising copywriters consult with account executives and clients to gather information about the products or services to be advertised. They develop original written material for newspaper and magazine advertising and scripts for radio and television commercials. Some college is desirable; creativity is essential. Annual salaries range from $10,000 to $50,000.

Job opportunities for both advertising account executives and copywriters are expected to expand moderately as the U.S. economy expands. (*Additional information:* contact local advertising agencies.)

Careers in Public Relations

The public image of a business is maintained and enhanced by **public relations workers.** They promote the firm's business projects and accomplishments in newspapers and magazines and through personal contact with the public. Applicants must be socially and psychologically adept. Employers generally require a bachelor's degree in public relations, journalism or English. Journalism or advertising experience is helpful. Seasoned public-relations workers may advance to supervisory jobs and eventually to top-management positions. Annual salaries can range from $10,000 to $50,000, depending on the level of responsibility and the size of the business. Job opportunities are expected to increase moderately and will be best for highly qualified applicants with sound academic preparation. (*Additional information:* Service Department, *Public Relations News,* 127 East 80th Street, New York, New York 10021.)

Careers in Manufacturer's Sales

Manufacturer's salesworkers sell products for virtually all manufacturers—from computers to cake mixes. They sell to business firms and to institutions such as schools and hospitals, visiting prospective customers in their work places. They must be completely familiar with their products and able to answer customer questions, transact sales, and handle paperwork. Although high-school graduates can be successful salespeople, many manufacturers are now hiring sales trainees with some college background—even applicants with engineering degrees for technical sales positions. Most salesworkers receive formal training programs, especially to sell complex technical products. An ability to get along well with diverse customers is necessary. Most manufacturer's salesworkers are paid on a salary-plus-commission basis. Beginning salesworkers now earn from $15,400 to over $24,000 annually. Experienced sales personnel earn from $19,200 to more than $38,000 annually. Sales opportunities are expected to expand and contract in the future, depending on manufacturing output.

Manufacturer's agents also sell. But unlike manufacturer's salesworkers, these agents are not employees of producing firms. Instead, they act as the firm's sales representatives. Manufacturer's agents usually sell lines of complementary, noncompeting products for several manufacturers (for example, springs for one firm, nuts and bolts for a second firm, and small bearings for a third). Agents receive a straight commission and can earn $50,000 to $100,000 annually. The average, though is $20,000.

Sales managers supervise sales personnel at the firm's district, regional, or national level. Salesworkers with good sales records and managerial ability are often promoted to sales-management positions. Sales managers may earn $20,000 to $60,000 annually.

Future job opportunities in personal selling and in sales management for manufacturing firms will vary depending on the industry involved. (*Additional information:* contact your local chapter of the Professional Sales Executives, a national organization for salespeople.)

2. Provide personal service.
3. Solve the customer's product or economic problems.
4. Sell only items that you feel are *good* for the customer.
5. Recommend a competitor's product if you believe it will satisfy the customer's needs better than your own product.
6. Establish a long-term relationship with the customer that will result in repeat business.

The Salesperson's Important Role

In addition to their role as problem solvers for customers, salespeople serve in another key capacity: they are for most customers, "the company"—the only contact customers have with the firm whose goods or services they are buying. In this sense, salespeople hold the marketing channel together. For instance, a technical salesperson demonstrates how a product can solve a customer's problems and also transmits the customer's suggestions for new products back to the firm. Some salespeople also transport goods, check on delayed orders, and find lenders to finance a purchase.

The Steps of Selling

There are four basic steps to selling: prospecting, presale preparation, sales presentation, and postsale follow-up. These steps are discussed in the following sections and shown in Figure 10–6 on the next page.

Prospecting

Salespeople must specifically identify their target market for each sales presentation. This *prospecting*—whose paydirt is a list of names, addresses, and telephone numbers—is not as easy as it sounds. Insurance salespeople must do research to find out who needs additional insurance. Computer salespeople must develop lists of organizations that could use their equipment. Prospecting sources include library reference books, published corporate data, lists of old customers in company files, referrals from satisfied customers, and advertising inquiries.

One especially good prospector is Benjamin Feldman, an Ohioan who has been featured in *Fortune* magazine as "the greatest life insurance salesman in history." He prospects only in one specific target market: principal owners of private businesses (see box on page 259).

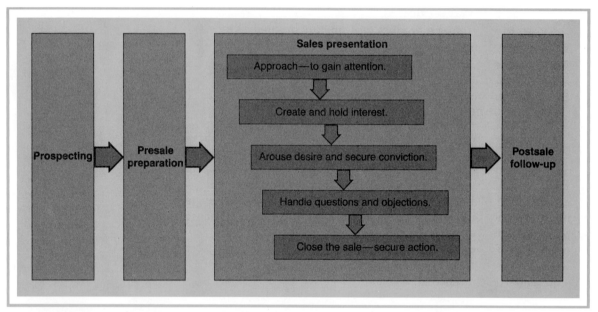

Source: Adapted from Allan J. Reid, *Modern Applied Salesmanship*, pp. 159–213. Copyright © 1970 by Goodyear Publishing Co.

FIGURE 10-6
Steps in the
Selling Process.

Presale Preparation

Salespeople seldom find prospective customers sitting around waiting to be called on so that they can buy a product. This is why *presale preparation* is an important part of selling. It involves finding out everything possible about the prospect's needs for the products and how the products can satisfy these needs. It also entails arranging an interview, either with or without a prior appointment.

Sales Presentation

The *sales presentation* is a direct communication between salesperson and prospective customer that is intended to complete the sale. Allan L. Reid, a professional salesman, divides the presentation into five steps (also summarized in Figure 10–6):

1. APPROACH Gain the prospect's attention by encouraging him to provide information about needs, wants, and problems. Then emphasize ways in which the product can benefit him.

2. CREATE AND HOLD INTEREST Retain the prospect's interest by clarifying his needs, wants, and problems. The prospect must admit to

having problems and remain willing to consider the salesperson's solution to them.

3. AROUSE DESIRE AND SECURE CONVICTION Develop a desire in the prospect for the product's benefits. Assure the prospect that these benefits fulfill real needs and wants.

4. HANDLE QUESTIONS AND OBJECTIONS Present the advantages and disadvantages of each product. Answer the prospect's questions and objections. To help him make the best choice, demonstrate the product. If a customer is indecisive, describe the merits of the various alternatives and help the decision along.

5. CLOSE THE SALE Don't hesitate to ask for the order. Inexperienced salespeople often fail to "close the sale." This may occur because they are afraid to ask for the order or because they ask at the wrong time in the sales presentation. A salesman may be so busy making the sales presentation that he doesn't realize when the customer is ready to buy. If given too much time to reconsider, the prospect may decide not to buy. This can be tricky. Joan Thomas, a successful New York real-estate agent, is a good listener. She is also quick to spot the signals of serious interest in a house. "When customers start finding fault with a house, that's when you know they're ready to buy," Thomas says. "When they say a house is 'so nice,' that means they aren't interested."

Prospecting for Millions

Benjamin Feldman is an agent for the New York Life Insurance Company. He lives in East Liverpool, a city of 20,000 in southeastern Ohio. *Fortune* magazine describes him as "a stocky, amiable man, with a deceptively sleepy appearance" who "by almost everybody's reckoning, . . . is the greatest life insurance salesman in history."[2] In thirty-two years, Feldman has personally sold more life insurance than most of the country's insurance firms have on their books! In recent years, he has been averaging $50 million in annual sales; his best year was in 1971 when he sold $65,000,000.

Feldman left a $10 a week delivery job in 1939 to take an insurance firm's aptitude test. He flunked! And then proceeded to demonstrate his selling abilities by convincing the firm to hire him anyway.

One secret to Feldman's success is his approach to prospecting: he focuses almost exclusively on a very specific target market—the principal owners of private businesses. His reasons: because these owners have personal businesses representing substantial assets that cannot be easily converted to cash, they have the greatest need for large amounts of life insurance. Feldman explains that an executor for a deceased person who owned an uninsured business might have to sell the business to pay estate taxes; with insurance the business can be passed on to heirs.

Even with these five steps, each sale is unique and a sales career is quite a challenge. A successful salesperson must be highly motivated to overcome the frustration of a "No, thank you—I'm not interested." A typical industrial salesperson has to call on a prospect six times before making a sale (at an average cost of $97 per call). But astute salespeople also know when to stop calling on a prospect who does not want or need their product. The effective salesperson must be able to distinguish the "no-need-ever" prospects from the "may-need-in-six months" ones—and work hard at selling (see box).

Postsale Follow-up

The salesperson's job does not end with the sale. *Postsale follow-up* is necessary to ensure the customer's future business and to attract new customers through word-of-mouth advertising. Retail and industrial salespeople may suggest related purchases such as a shirt and a tie to go with a new suit, or a set of carbide-tipped drills for a new drill press. After big sales, a good salesperson calls in several weeks to make sure that the customer is satisfied.

Sales Secrets of the "Most Improbable" Salesman

Mehdi Fakharzadeh, a Middle Easterner, works in New York City selling life insurance for the giant Metropolitan Life Insurance Company. He has been the company's top salesman and is often called on to give speeches revealing his selling secrets. They are deceptively simple:

"*Number One:* You have to be honest.

"*Number Two:* When making a proposal to somebody, put yourself in the shoes of that person.

"*Number Three:* You've got to know your business. Constantly increase your knowledge.

"*Number Four:* You must work. If you have all the knowledge in the world and are the most honest man, if you're going to stay home, can you make any business?

"*Number Five:* Never, ever get discouraged and disappointed. No matter what business you're in will have ups and downs. Don't think this is the end of the world."

As *Fortune* magazine puts it, "Of all the big-time insurance salesmen, Mehdi must surely qualify as the most improbable. For although he has lived half his life in the U. S., he still struggles with the English language."[3] Yet Mehdi has achieved fantastic success—because of his honesty and his extraordinary instinct for serving clients personally.

Managing a Sales Force

Sales managers are responsible for selecting and training salespeople and for paying and motivating them.

Select and Train the Sales Force

A sales manager usually selects his or her sales force through personal interviews, personality tests, and aptitude tests. Training begins then, but it never truly ends. Salespeople must be continually trained and retrained in response to changes in company policy (such as new policies about returned goods), changes in products sold (the addition of new products or modifications of old ones), and changes in selling techniques (stressing an entire computer system rather than a single piece of computer equipment).

Pay and Motivate Them

Sales managers must answer two related questions about compensation and motivation: "What is appropriate pay?" and "What is the best method of payment?"

To decide the amount of pay, sales managers use two standards: (1) the pay of salespeople in similar jobs in other companies, and (2) the pay scale of other employees within their own firm. Salespeople who must seek out customers work harder and receive better pay than those who only take orders from customers. Some experienced insurance salespeople, who must prospect intensively, can earn more than $150,000 a year in commissions. But many retail salespeople earn only minimum wage.

Payment strategies are straight salary, straight commission, and salary plus commission. *Straight salary,* a fixed dollar amount, does not vary according to the sales made. It provides maximum security for salespeople and maximum control for management. *Straight commission* is a fixed percentage (say, 7 percent) of the sales volume. It provides maximum incentive for salespeople but sometimes too little control for management. (A salesperson may focus only on immediate sales and not on developing new accounts, for example.) To provide a balance between security and incentive, many firms offer *salary plus commission,* a combination plan.

Compensation plans should be flexible enough to adapt to changing conditions or different territories. They should also be simple enough for salespeople and management to understand them.

Chapter Review & Applications

Key Points to Remember

1. Promotion, the fourth element in the marketing mix, is communication between seller and buyer, intended to inform, persuade, or remind people about a product. Its two most important components are advertising and personal selling.

2. Advertising is any nonpersonal communication between seller and buyer conducted through paid media under clear sponsorship. It can be divided into direct-action and delayed-action advertising.

3. Regardless of the size of the firm, an effective advertising campaign involves the same six steps: (1) set the goals and budget; (2) find the appeals; (3) write the copy; (4) pick the media and the time schedules; (5) run the campaign; and (6) assess the campaign's effectiveness.

4. Personal selling is a person-to-person sales presentation made to a prospective buyer.

5. There are four main categories of sales job: manufacturer's sales representatives, wholesaler's sales representatives, retail sales representatives, and direct sales representatives.

6. The salesperson's two key roles are to act as the customer's problem solver and to represent the firm whose products are being sold.

7. The four main steps in the selling process are prospecting, presale preparation, sales presentation, and postsale follow-up.

8. Sales management involves selecting and training salespeople and paying and motivating them.

Question for Discussion

1. Effective advertising copy must be attention-getting, easy to read and understand, believable, informative, and memorable. Using a five-point scale (1 = very poor; 2 = moderately poor; 3 = average; 4 = moderately good; 5 = very good),

evaluate the two GM ads that appear in the margin on page 247 on each of these five criteria. Total the points for each ad. Which ad is better? How do these results compare with your initial response to the ads when you first came across them in the chapter?

2. Is the appeal of each of the two GM ads mainly rational or emotional? Describe the appeal using terms such as price, quality, status, and vanity.

3. What are the problems in selecting which advertising media to use?

4. What was your feeling about personal selling as a vocation before reading the chapter? How do you feel about it now? If there is a difference, describe what caused you to change your mind.

5. Which of the sales steps shown in Figure 10–6 are most important in selling (a) women's clothing in a store near a college campus; (b) computers used for data processing by large business firms; (c) encyclopedias?

6. What type of compensation would you provide for salespeople handling (a) Avon cosmetics; (b) life insurance; (c) office equipment; (d) men's suits; (e) groceries; and (f) advertisements for a college paper? Give your reasons for each choice.

7. Some marketing experts stress a four-step approach to promotion that applies to both advertising and personal selling. The approach is called AIDA: *attention, interest, desire,* and *action.* Explain how the steps of AIDA apply to advertising and personal selling.

Short Case

You own a bicycle store near a college campus and have an annual advertising budget of $500. Using Figure 10–2 as a guide, select the goals, appeals, media, and timing for your advertising. How would you measure the effectiveness of your campaign?

A Critical
Business Decision

—made by Ed Tashjian and Tom Tipton
of Hanes Hosiery and Vanguard Advertising

The Situation

It is early 1980, and Ed Tashjian, assistant product manager at Hanes Hosiery, is asked to reevaluate the company's strategy to market hosiery and pantyhose to black consumers. Hanes, located in Winston-Salem, North Carolina, markets a complete line of hosiery and pantyhose in department stores throughout the United States.

Tashjian knows that the Hanes brand competes nationally with several other brands. Some are even produced by other divisions within Hanes: L'eggs, sold through supermarkets and mass merchandisers; and Underalls and Slenderalls sold through department stores. Other companies also have strong brands, such as Round-the-Clock, Givenchy, and Modern Heir.

Digging into the available research data, Tashjian reaches some key conclusions: (1) awareness of the Hanes brand and its advertising is extremely high among black consumers, though not quite as high as awareness of L'eggs, with its much higher ad budget; (2) Hanes has the highest market share of any brand among black consumers, who buy about 15 percent of all hosiery sold in the United States; and (3) interviews with black consumers show that they are very satisfied with Hanes' sheerness and colors and with Hanes ads. Tashjian concludes that he needs more help and hires Vanguard, a black-owned advertising agency, for ideas.[4]

The Decision

Tom Tipton, Vanguard's president, and Tashjian analyze other research data. They conclude that color and sheerness are more important to black consumers, and fit less important. They also learn that black women buy about 30 percent more pairs of hosiery than white women, most frequently in department stores, and that they resent stereotyped models or artificial settings in ads directed at them. Also, black women who buy hosiery are younger and more likely to hold jobs than their white counterparts.

Tipton and Tashjian conclude—against marketing's "conventional wisdom"—that they should *not* have a completely different creative ad strategy (appeals and copy) for black consumers. Instead, they will use the same creative strategy for both groups, but the ads targeted at black consumers will feature black models and appear in media directed especially to black audiences.

With an increased advertising budget for 1981, Hanes wants to buy ads on national television and local radio stations across the country and will collect more information on their costs. They already have information on recent ad costs for magazines targeted at black consumers:

BASIS OF COMPARISON		Ebony	Essence	Flair
Price of one 4-color ad		18,087	7,398	975
Total Women	Reached[a]	7,047,000	4,410,000	1,783,000
	CPM[b]	2.57	1.68	0.55
Working Women	Reached	4,228,000	2,690,000	1,033,000
	CPM	4.28	2.75	0.94
Women Buyers	Reached	2,185,000	1,764,000	676,000
	CPM	8.28	4.19	1.44

[a] reached by the magazine
[b] cost per thousand; see page 251

Questions

1. Tom Tipton and Ed Tashjian must choose media for the Hanes ads. What do you see as the advantages and disadvantages of running Hanes ads in magazines? On TV? On radio?

2. Which measure of a magazine's effectiveness in reaching an audience seems most important here—total women, working women, or women buyers? Why?

3. Suppose Tipton and Tashjian budget $200,000 for ads in the three magazines. If they try to buy an equal number of insertions from each magazine, how will they allocate their advertising budget? What are the advantages and disadvantages of allocating the advertising budget this way?

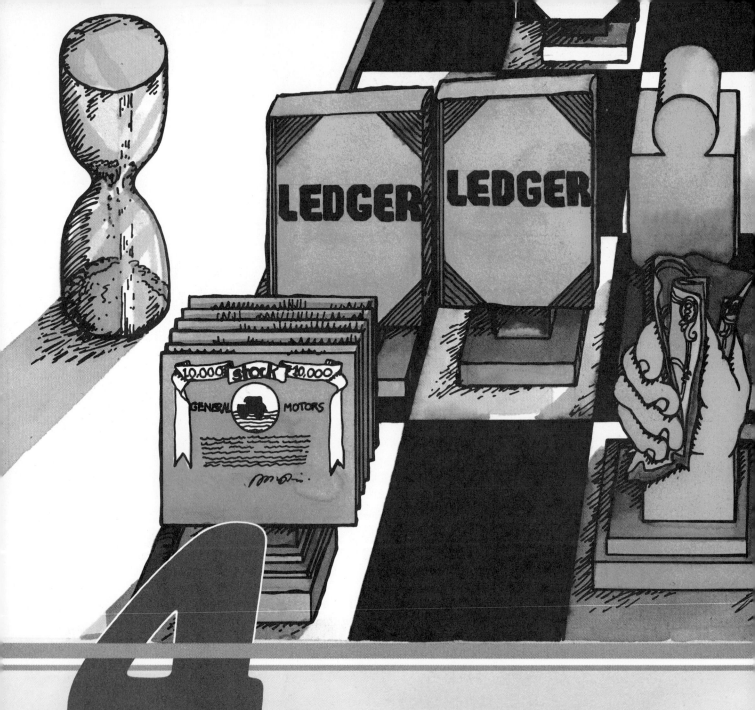

4 Accounting, Finance,

and Management Information

Accounting and Budgeting

11

Never ask of money spent
Where the spender thinks it went
Nobody was ever meant
To remember or invent
What he did with every cent.

ROBERT FROST

homas Edison, a genius at invention and manufacturing, nearly went bankrupt because of his poor bookkeeping. His "accounting method" was quite simple. He put the bills he owed in one book and the accounts due in another, but somehow his records kept getting lost.

Eventually, he hired an accountant to unravel his tangled finances. Two weeks later, the accountant reported that the business had made a $3,000 profit. Edison gave a party for his employees to celebrate his success. But several days later, the downcast accountant approached Edison with the news that he had found some more bills in a pigeonhole, and the $3,000 profit suddenly turned into a $500 loss. The famous inventor was appalled. The accountant kept looking. Finally, he approached Edison with a smile and said, "I think I have found the last of your missing records, and I find you have been operating at a profit of $7,000."[1]

This incident illustrates the importance of accurate record-keeping in business. How can a firm operate profitably if its managers do not know exactly how money is being earned and spent? In fact, it can't. So in this chapter—the first of five dealing with accounting, finance, and management information—we will explore the accounting process.

WHAT IS ACCOUNTING?

Accounting is the collection, organization, analysis, and presentation of financial information. Because financial information is used to make nearly all important business decisions, accounting data must be reliable, understandable, relevant, and timely. Such a system is just as important for a neighborhood gift shop as it is for the Standard Oil Company.

Who Needs It?

A firm's accounting data are needed and used by people both inside and outside the company. Managers make extensive use of accounting data to determine the financial status of the business and to aid in decision making. It also helps them in their planning, controlling, and personnel decisions. Boards of directors, partners, and owners use accounting statements to check management performance. Investors and their stockbrokers examine accounting statements before deciding whether to invest in a company. Creditors rely on financial information to determine whether to lend money to the firm. Federal, state, and local government agencies use accounting statements to check on a business' social security contributions, wage and hour standards, and tax payments. And the general public needs accounting information to evaluate wage demands, prices, and the financial status of local businesses.

The Role of Accounting in Business

If accountants ever were little men with green visors sitting on high stools adding up long lists of numbers, they certainly aren't now. These days, they have comfortable chairs in well-appointed offices and use sophisticated computers. They work in industry, in government, in tax practice, and in public accounting firms. For a glimpse of what goes on at one "small" tax accounting firm, see the box on the next page.

Besides being responsible for computerizing many functions, accountants, especially at the Big Eight firms, are expanding into tax services, actuarial services, and even management consulting, executive recruiting, and marketing analysis—subject to scrutiny by the Securities and Exchange Commission (SEC). Even in relatively small firms, accountants are no longer just looking backward and reporting on what the firm did financially. Today they also perform *managerial accounting* functions—looking forward and providing managers with financial projections from which they can plan for the future. To do this, they use traditional accounting data as a base, then interpret it to answer such questions as, "In which operations are costs too high compared with production and distribution costs in the past?" or "In forecasting output and cost, is it better to buy a new machine or to keep the old one?"

RECORDING AND CLASSIFYING TRANSACTIONS

A basic objective of accounting is to present all of a firm's relevant financial information in a form that can easily be understood by potential users. The first step toward achieving this goal is to record **accounting transactions.** These are activities that have an immediate and measurable monetary impact on a firm. They are the basic units of accounting, and include such activities as wages paid to employees, issuance of corporate stock, and the sale or purchase of a product or service. A listing of all accounting transactions of a particular type (like company sales) is called the **register** or *ledger*. And the **account** is the name given to a specific register or ledger.

Recording Accounting Transactions

Transactions can be recorded by hand or by computer. Some small businesses still use *journals* or *ledgers,* large books containing multicolumned sheets of

H & R Who?

Richard Bloch

Henry Bloch

They started as Henry and Richard Bloch, brothers and founders of a small accounting firm in Kansas City, Missouri, in 1955. They called themselves H & R Block to ensure the correct pronunciation of their name.

Soon, they noticed that tax laws and tax forms were becoming more complicated. Would the public, confused by all the rules and procedures, pay professional tax accountants to do their federal income tax returns? They decided to rent more offices from December to mid-April, hire extra employees only for that period, and find out.

Now they hire close to 50,000 people and prepare about 10 million tax returns. The brothers own 30 percent of the company's 3.3 million shares and have made a (taxable) fortune.[2]

They're trying to out-distance competitors now by offering tax-preparation courses, opening centers at Sears stores, investigating foreign offices, and opening several special centers to do executives' tax returns on an appointment-only, year-round basis.

But their main competitor is you and your pencil. So their TV ads keep reminding you of "the 17 reasons" why you should let H & R Block prepare your tax return.

paper. However, even small operations are now taking advantage of computerized record-keeping services offered by public accounting firms, banks, and computer-service firms.

A fully computerized department store, for example, works like this: when the customer buys a pair of shoes, the sales clerk records the transaction on a computer terminal. The clerk types in numbers for the date of the sale, department, dollar value, specific item sold (the style and size of shoes), and whether payment is made by cash or credit. The computer terminal prints a sales check and a receipt. At the same time, all the information is transferred to the master computer, which maintains a continuous record of day-to-day sales and inventory.

But even with fully computerized accounting systems, accountants must rely on their own judgment when recording certain transactions. Suppose, for instance, that a company buys a new photocopier. In recording such a transaction, accountants must consider such questions as, "How fast will this machine wear out?" and "What will it be worth when the company wants to sell it?" Answers to these and other questions will have an effect on the financial statements of the firm and on the taxes it pays.

Often, there is more than one acceptable way to record a transaction. Thus, to avoid confusion, accountants and managers must agree upon a consistent method. Overall, the entire system of Generally Accepted Accounting Principles, GAAP, is determined by the Financial Accounting Standards Board. Sponsored by industry and accounting firms, the board issues rules based on research, public hearings, and on political pressure from government (especially from the Securities and Exchange Commission), the accounting industry, bankers, stockbrokers, and other groups (see box on page 273).

Classifying Accounting Transactions

Accountants organize financial data by classifying every accounting transaction into an appropriate category (or account) and recording it in the firm's register. For example, a department-store customer's payment of $150 on his charge account is recorded by Bloomingdale's as a $150 decrease in the store's receivables account and as a $150 increase in its cash account. A key principle here is **double-entry bookkeeping,** in which each dollar amount is recorded at least twice. The double-entry system sharply reduces the number of errors that can be made when recording and classifying transactions. Accountants must master the principles to place each transaction in its appropriate account.

Your Next Job
Positions in Accounting and Credit

Careers in Accounting and Bookkeeping

Important managerial decisions are based on financial reports prepared and analyzed by accountants. **Industrial accountants** draw up financial statements for their employers. Most large companies have accounting departments headed by a controller, vice president, or chief accountant. Since accounting practices vary in different industries, most high-level industrial accountants have some prior experience in their firm's industry. **Government accountants** construct financial statements and audit data from firms regulated by government agencies. **Tax accountants** specialize in helping businesses and individuals find tax deductions. Most of these three types of accountants have a bachelor's degree in accounting; some firms require a master's degree.

Certified public accountants, CPAs, constitute about 20 percent of all accountants. They are considered the top professionals in their field. Usually college graduates with at least two years of accounting experience, they have passed a tough examination to earn their CPA. (Requirements vary from state to state.) CPAs usually work in public accounting firms where they verify the procedures and data in client firms' accounts, certify the accuracy of the client's accounts in terms of conformance to "generally accepted accounting principles," and perform other financial services for these clients.

Annual salaries range from $15,000 to $45,000; for partners in large CPA firms, salaries can go higher than $100,000 a year. In industry, qualified accountants are often promoted to higher-level management and supervisory positions. Because of the growth of businesses and their constant need for sound financial data, the job market for accountants should remain excellent. (*Additional information:* National Association of Accountants, 919 Third Avenue, New York, New York 10022.)

Bookkeepers record a firm's financial transactions, calculate the payroll, and prepare customer invoices. In large firms, bookkeepers may perform specialized duties, such as preparing daily sales records or operating reports. Most are high-school graduates with backgrounds in arithmetic and bookkeeping. However, some employers only hire applicants from business schools or community colleges. Competent bookkeepers may be promoted to supervisory positions and, with the completion of college accounting courses, may advance to accounting positions. Annual salary averages $9,600. Employment opportunities are expected to expand slowly due to increasing computerization. (*Additional information:* State Supervisor of Office Occupations Education, State Department of Education, your state capital.)

Careers in Credit

Credit officials accept or reject customer credit applications. Developing a credit policy that increases sales and reduces risks requires sound decision-making skills and the ability to carefully interpret financial statements. A college degree in liberal arts or in business administration is becoming increasingly important, although many employers provide on-the-job training for high-school and community-college graduates. Credit officials begin in a trainee capacity and may advance to credit manager or to other top management positions. Annual salaries range from $11,000 to more than $40,000. Increased use of telecommunication networks and bank credit cards is expected to slow growth of occupational opportunities. (*Additional information:* The National Consumer Finance Association, 1000 16th Street, N.W., Washington, D.C. 20036.)

Credit managers evaluate customers' credit worthiness and deal with delinquent accounts. A bachelor's or master's degree in accounting or finance is becoming essential. Salaries range from $15,000 to upward of $40,000. Positions as assistant to a credit manager are frequently entry-level jobs in the corporate finance area. (*Additional information:* The National Consumer Finance Association, 1000 16th Street, N.W., Washington, D.C. 20036.)

CONSTRUCTING ACCOUNTING STATEMENTS

Raw financial data are of little value unless they are summarized in an organized form and presented in **accounting statements.** The most important accounting statements are the *income statement,* which shows the revenues, costs, and profits for a selected period, and the *balance sheet,* which shows the financial position of a firm as of a given date. These are described below and illustrated in Figures 11–1 and 11–2, using the 1979 statements of Simplicity Pattern Co., Inc. Simplicity is a publicly held corporation and is listed on the New York Stock Exchange. It manufactures paper patterns for home sewing, which are sold through 24,000 retailers in the U.S. and abroad.

The financial statements for Simplicity shown in Figures 11–1 and 11–2 are taken from the firm's annual report, which covers one fiscal (or accounting) year of activity. As shown in Figure 11–1, Simplicity's 1979 fiscal year ends on January 31, 1980—thereby covering the period February 1, 1979, through January 31, 1980. In the United States, firms are permitted to select their own fiscal years, which need not correspond to the calendar year. Since the preparation of annual reports is time consuming, a firm usually picks a period of slack activity as the close of its fiscal year.

Accounting by the Rules

The Financial Accounting Standards Board (FASB) is a private group, composed of leading accounting and financial experts who issue accounting standards for the profession. For example, the FASB requires that accountants report the foreign operations of their clients' income statements and balance sheets in certain specified ways. The FASB replaced the Accounting Principles Board (APB), which issued similar statements regarding standards, some of which are still in effect. To provide the general public with accurate financial information on a firm, the Securities and Exchange Commission (SEC), a government agency, issues accounting regulations that most businesses must follow. For example, the SEC recently ordered businesses to report accounting data by line of business. As a result, if you look through the annual reports of most companies, you will find that revenues, costs, and profits are shown for each major product line sold by the company.

If you take advanced courses in accounting, you are likely to study FASB standards and SEC accounting regulations in detail. Managers also need to be aware of FASB and SEC actions, since significant changes in their accounting guidelines can dramatically influence the financial data on which key decisions are based.

Besides annual reports, management frequently has its accountants prepare monthly or quarterly financial reports for internal use. And accountants also develop *supplemental accounting statements*—special statements that include financial data other than that shown on income statements and balance sheets. The most important of these is the *statement of changes in financial position,* which shows how a company acquired and used funds during a given period (usually one year).

The Income Statement

The **income statement** shows the profits or losses sustained by a business during a given period of time, usually a month, quarter, or year. Income statements for management are often prepared monthly so that potential financial difficulties and trends can be spotted. (Managers also frequently request separate income statements for each of the firm's products.) Quarterly income statements are also prepared, and are often sent to stockholders. And yearly statements—the most comprehensive of all financial reports—are made available to all those, both inside and outside the company, who need to be aware of the firm's financial data.

The income statement of Simplicity, shown in Figure 11–1, is a series of line items added and subtracted to produce a business's **net income,** or profit after expenses. In this case, a profit of $11,766,000 after taxes was earned in 1979. A firm's **revenues** (monies earned) minus its **expenses** (costs incurred) equals its **profit** or **loss.** If revenues exceed expenses, the business earns a profit. If expenses exceed revenues, the business suffers a loss. A business that suffers continuing losses will eventually be forced into bankruptcy.

The income statement is divided into three basic categories: revenues, expenses, and net income. (The retained earnings part of the net income section will be discussed later in the chapter.)

Revenues
Revenues are the monies obtained from all the firm's commercial activities. For most businesses, sales to customers are the major source of revenues. **Gross sales** is the total value of all sales, including those not yet collected. But the firm doesn't take in all this money. First, adjustments must be made for *discounts and allowances*. These include price reductions offered for prompt payment or for buying in large quantities. Then there are further adjustments

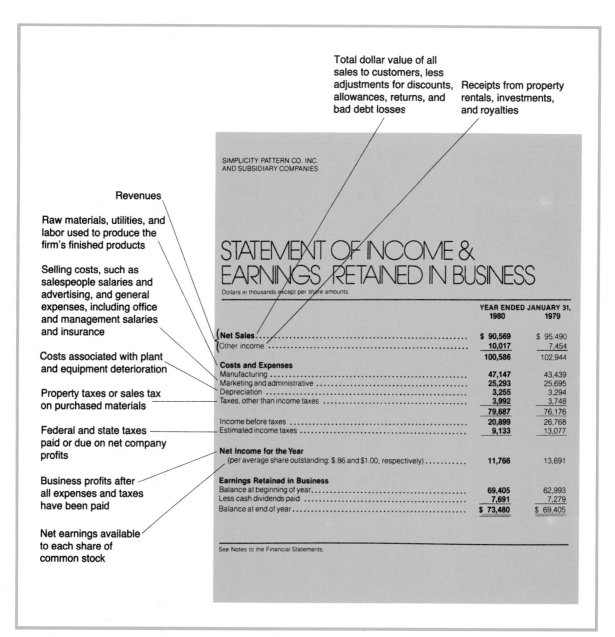

Total dollar value of all sales to customers, less adjustments for discounts, allowances, returns, and bad debt losses

Receipts from property rentals, investments, and royalties

Revenues

Raw materials, utilities, and labor used to produce the firm's finished products

Selling costs, such as salespeople salaries and advertising, and general expenses, including office and management salaries and insurance

Costs associated with plant and equipment deterioration

Property taxes or sales tax on purchased materials

Federal and state taxes paid or due on net company profits

Business profits after all expenses and taxes have been paid

Net earnings available to each share of common stock

SIMPLICITY PATTERN CO. INC.
AND SUBSIDIARY COMPANIES

STATEMENT OF INCOME & EARNINGS RETAINED IN BUSINESS

Dollars in thousands except per share amounts

| | YEAR ENDED JANUARY 31, | |
	1980	1979
Net Sales	$ 90,569	$ 95,490
Other income	10,017	7,454
	100,586	102,944
Costs and Expenses		
Manufacturing	47,147	43,439
Marketing and administrative	25,293	25,695
Depreciation	3,255	3,294
Taxes, other than income taxes	3,992	3,748
	79,687	76,176
Income before taxes	20,899	26,768
Estimated income taxes	9,133	13,077
Net Income for the Year		
(per average share outstanding: $.86 and $1.00, respectively)	11,766	13,691
Earnings Retained in Business		
Balance at beginning of year	69,405	62,993
Less cash dividends paid	7,691	7,279
Balance at end of year	$ 73,480	$ 69,405

See Notes to the Financial Statements.

FIGURE 11-1
Income Statement for Simplicity Pattern Co., Inc., and Its Subsidiaries for the Year Ending January 31, 1980.

for *returned merchandise* (refunds to customers for unsatisfactory goods) and for *bad debts* (uncollected money from charge-account customers). Once these "minuses" are figured, the result is **net sales.** For Simplicity this amount was $90,569,000 for fiscal year 1979 (the year that ended January 31, 1980).

Expenses

Expenses are the costs that a firm incurs. These can be divided into various categories: costs of goods sold, operating expenses, and nonoperating expenses. *Cost of goods sold* includes materials purchased and inventory used, direct labor costs, and depreciation (costs associated with the deterioration or age of plant and equipment). *Operating expenses* include all salaries, advertising costs, office supplies and equipment, and the like. *Nonoperating expenses* relate primarily to financial items, such as interest and income taxes.

Simplicity's total expenses during fiscal year 1979 were $79,687,000. Some firms present more detailed data than Simplicity or use different formats. The exact choice of income-statement presentation varies by business type (wholesale, retail, manufacturing, or service), industry conventions, company tradition, and the preferences of the firm preparing the statements.

Net Income

Net income, or net profits, is the final result after all expenses have been subtracted from total revenues. In the case of Simplicity, the net income was $11,766,000 in fiscal year 1979.

Net income is one of the most closely watched figures in U.S. businesses. Management, creditors, investors, labor unions, and the general public frequently make decisions about a firm solely or mainly on the "bottom-line" figure, which shows the business' profit performance.

The Balance Sheet

Whereas the income statement shows the flow of revenues, expenses, and profits for a specified point of time, the **balance sheet** summarizes the firm's finances as of the last day of the accounting period. To make up a balance sheet, accountants use a fundamental tool of accounting called the **accounting equation,** the relationship between assets, liabilities, and owner equity. **Assets** are the resources available to a business that it uses to earn a profit. To acquire assets, businesses typically obtain funds from owners and creditors.

The financial obligations thus incurred are called **liabilities.** The part of the assets owned outright by a firm is called **owner equity.**

The accounting equation expresses the relationship between assets, liabilities, and owner equity:

$$\text{Assets} = \text{Liabilities} + \text{Owner Equity}$$

This equation always holds, because the total assets of a business must be paid for either by its creditors or by its owners. Referring to Figure 11–2, the balance sheet for Simplicity Pattern Co., Inc., you can see how the equation is expressed in dollar amounts:

$$\text{Assets} = \text{Liabilities} + \text{Owner Equity}$$
$$\$146{,}346{,}000 = \$13{,}681{,}000 + \$132{,}665{,}000$$

For Simplicity, the owner equity of $132,665,000 is actually composed of two items, a reserve for pattern discards plus shareholders' equity. Simplicity's balance sheet is fairly typical, except for its lack of long-term debt.

How to Organize a Balance Sheet

Accountants usually group similar assets and liabilities into a few basic categories or accounts. Assets usually are grouped into the following general categories:

- CURRENT ASSETS   Cash or highly liquid assets converted into cash within one accounting period.
- LONG-TERM INVESTMENTS   Assets held exclusively for investment (not resale) longer than one accounting period.
- FIXED ASSETS   Property, buildings, and equipment—the tools of the business.
- INTANGIBLES   Assets that derive their value from the rights they accord the holder, such as patents, copyrights, trademarks, and franchises.

Liabilities are organized as follows:

- CURRENT LIABILITIES   Obligations that must be met within one accounting period.

Cash, bank deposits, money orders, and drafts

Obligations owed the firms, usually from sales

Goods purchased or produced for sales and supplies bought for use in production

Goods and services already paid for, to be used in future business operations

Land, buildings, machinery, and equipment used in the business

Debts owed to creditors for goods and services

An appropriation earmarked for a special purpose (possible merchandise returns)

Funds contributed by stockholders according to the preset par value of each share of common stock

Funds contributed by stockholders over and above par value

Corporate profits less all dividends paid to stockholders in the past

SIMPLICITY PATTERN CO. INC.
AND SUBSIDIARY COMPANIES

BALANCE SHEET
Dollars in thousands

	JANUARY 31,	
ASSETS	**1980**	**1979**
Current Assets		
Cash	$ 1,621	$ 1,734
Short term investments, at cost (approximate market value)	76,559	74,372
Accounts receivable, less allowance for doubtful accounts—		
$2,603 and $3,038, respectively	16,021	18,896
Inventories	16,077	14,650
Prepaid expenses	1,552	1,476
	111,830	111,128
Property, Plant & Equipment, at cost, less accumulated depreciation	28,545	30,442
Long Term Investments	1,603	1,719
Prepaid Income Taxes	4,368	3,758
	$146,346	$147,047
LIABILITIES		
Current Liabilities		
Accounts payable and accrued expenses	$ 6,241	$ 6,721
Estimated income taxes	4,488	5,805
Other current liabilities	2,952	3,205
	13,681	15,731
Reserve for Pattern Discards	10,013	12,739
SHAREHOLDERS' EQUITY		
Common stock, 8⅓¢ par value		
Authorized—20,000,000 shares		
Issued—13,733,229 shares	1,144	1,144
Capital in excess of par value	48,028	48,028
Earnings retained in business	73,480	69,405
	122,652	118,577
	$146,346	$147,047

See Notes to the Financial Statements.

Salaries, taxes, insurance premiums, and other costs incurred but not yet paid

FIGURE 11-2
Balance Sheet for Simplicity Pattern Co., Inc., and Its Subsidiaries on January 31, 1980.

- LONG-TERM LIABILITIES   Obligations that need not be satisfied in a single accounting period.

Owner (shareholder) equity accounts for a corporation are typically related to:

- CAPITAL STOCK   Financial contributions made directly by each category of stockholder (common or preferred, for instance).
- RETAINED EARNINGS   Profits not otherwise distributed.

Because sole proprietorships and partnerships do not issue public stock, the equity accounts of those organizations are somewhat different.

By examining these general asset and liability categories, an accountant can quickly assess the general financial health of a business, for a business that shows a profit on its income statement can still be unhealthy. One wants to know its current liabilities to see whether they exceed its current assets, since if creditors demand payment, the business could fail. Other danger signs are unusually high inventories, which are hard to sell fast, and a high level of accounts receivable, bills that customers may never pay. Even excess cash may be a sign of trouble—it could indicate that money isn't being invested efficiently in bonds, new equipment, or other income-producing assets.

But the balance sheet is only as reliable as the accuracy and judgment of the accountants who prepare it. For this reason, it usually includes explanatory notes describing the accounting principles used in its development.

The Relationship Between Income Statement and Balance Sheet

A firm's income statement and its balance sheet are closely related. When a firm earns a profit, shown on the income statement, owner equity increases on the balance sheet. Similarly, a loss decreases owner equity.

This is displayed for Simplicity Patterns in the Earnings Retained in Business section on its income statement (Figure 11–1). Notice that the last dollar amount, $73,480,000, is carried over to the Earnings Retained in Business line on its balance sheet (Figure 11–2).

Verifying Accounting Statements

As mentioned earlier, in addition to preparing accounting statements, accountants also audit companies. **Auditing** is the process of verifying that an organization has properly recorded and reported its financial data. This can involve examining the assets and liabilities of the business, physically counting the reported cash or inventories, contacting its debtors, checking individual accounting transactions, and testing the accounting procedures and judgments used.

If everything looks satisfactory, the result is a "clean," or unqualified, standard opinion, like the one from Simplicity's annual report, shown in Figure 11–3. But auditors are careful not to say too much, for if it happens that a business becomes financially troubled, they could be sued by shareholders who relied on the accountant's glowing reports when deciding to invest in the company. "Qualified opinions" are more common in recessions or if a company is in difficulty, although firms that receive qualified opinions sometimes change accountants. A "disclaimed opinion" shows severe doubt about a firm's financial health and can cause the stock exchange to suspend trading of the company's stock.

REPORT OF INDEPENDENT ACCOUNTANTS

Price Waterhouse & Co. 153 EAST·53rd STREET NEW YORK, N Y 10022

TO THE BOARD OF DIRECTORS
AND SHAREHOLDERS OF
SIMPLICITY PATTERN CO. INC. March 24, 1980

In our opinion, the accompanying consolidated financial statements appearing on pages 14 through 19 of this report present fairly the financial position of Simplicity Pattern Co. Inc. and its subsidiaries at January 31, 1980 and 1979, the results of their operations and the changes in their financial position for the years then ended, in conformity with generally accepted accounting principles consistently applied. Our examinations of these statements were made in accordance with generally accepted auditing standards and accordingly included such tests of the accounting records and such other auditing procedures as we considered necessary in the circumstances.

Price Waterhouse & Co.

FIGURE 11–3
A "Clean" Opinion.

Large- and moderate-sized businesses often open their accounts to an *outside audit,* usually made by a public accounting firm. And the Internal Revenue Service may conduct a *tax audit* to see if a business has computed its taxes properly. Banks, government contractors, and a few other businesses are legally required to undergo governmental audits.

Organizations can order a *complete audit* (or a *special audit*) if management suspects employee theft or fraud, or if it cannot solve its own accounting errors. Most large businesses also do unannounced *internal audits.* Internal audits are conducted by company accountants who are *not* responsible for those accounts, in order to obtain an independent assessment of their accuracy.

EVALUATING ACCOUNTING DATA WITH FINANCIAL RATIOS

Like doctors tapping knees and peering into ears, accountants and other financial experts have special diagnostic tricks for determining the financial health of a business. These are key **financial** (or accounting) **ratios**—mathematical comparisons of selected items from a firm's accounting statements. They are used to compare (1) this year's results with those of previous years; (2) this year's results with the results of other firms in the same industry or in the industry as a whole (found in publicly available reports); and (3) this year's results with acceptable target (budget) ratios. Four common ratios are discussed in the following sections.

Current Ratio

The **current ratio,** an expression of the relationship between current assets and current liabilities, shows how well a firm can meet its short-term obligations. Current assets are highly liquid, meaning they can be converted into cash within one year. So it is from these that managers expect to obtain the funds needed to meet their current, or short-term, liabilities.

Simplicity Pattern's current ratio for January 31, 1980, is:

$$\frac{\text{Current assets}}{\text{Current liabilities}} = \frac{\$111,830,000}{\$\ 13,681,000} = 8.17$$

This means that Simplicity could cover each dollar of short-term obligations with $8.17 of current assets. Although accountants discourage using a single

How Touche Ross & Company Spots Fraud

Here's what one of the country's largest public accounting firms looks for to uncover fraud or financial mismanagement among the organizations it audits, according to a story in *Business Week:*[3]

- Accounting transactions that involve more than 5 percent of the income of a division or a business.
- Major accounting transactions that are bunched at the end of a quarter or at the end of a fiscal (accounting) year.
- Key financial figures and ratios that differ from trends over the past five years.
- Insufficient working capital or credit.
- The urgent need for high profits to support the firm's stock price.
- Dependence on a few products or customers.
- A declining industry with a history of many business failures.
- A great number of lawsuits, especially stockholder lawsuits.
- Rapid expansion or numerous acquisitions in the past few years.
- Difficulty collecting fees from key customers.
- A management dominated by a few key persons.
- Inadequate internal auditing staff and controls; separate accounting divisions using different systems; a large number of separate auditors for each accounting division; rapid turnovers of key financial personnel.

Usually it is financial mismanagement they find, if anything. Touche Ross estimates that fraud occurs in only 1 percent of its cases. But even 1 percent can have a big impact on the financial world.

standard, it is generally agreed that a current ratio of 2.0 or more is desirable for the "average" company in the "average" industry.

Return on Investment

Return on investment is a percentage figure comparing the after-tax profits of a firm with the assets used in its operations. It can be calculated for a firm's total assets or for the portion of total assets represented by owner equity. Using equity as the investment base, Simplicity's return on investment is:

$$\frac{\text{Net income after taxes}}{\text{Equity (including reserve)}} = \frac{\$\ 11{,}766{,}000}{\$132{,}665{,}000} = 8.87 \text{ percent}$$

Return on investment (or equity) in American business has averaged 12 percent annually since World War II. Investors are particularly interested in this figure since it is a means of determining whether their money would earn more for them elsewhere—say, in a savings account paying an interest rate of 7 or 8 percent.

Return on Sales

Return on sales is a percentage expressing the relationship between a business' net income and its revenues. For Simplicity, return on sales for the year ending January 31, 1980, is:

$$\frac{\text{Net income}}{\text{Sales}} = \frac{\$\ 11{,}766{,}000}{\$100{,}586{,}000} = 11.7$$

This figure is widely used to evaluate the performance of a firm's various product lines or to compare the whole business with other firms in the industry. Return-on-sales figures average about 4 percent for American business as a whole, but percentages differ widely among industries. Figures below the industry average may indicate excess costs and inefficiency.

Earnings per Share

Earnings, or income, per share—shown in Figure 11–1 as net income per average share—is a statement of the amount of profit a firm earns for each share of common stock outstanding. Income taxes, interest paid to bondholders, and dividends distributed to preferred stockholders are deducted from total corporate profits before earnings-per-common share calculations are made. (The difference between common and preferred stock will be explained in Chapter 13.) Simplicity's earnings per share for the fiscal year ending January 31, 1980, are:

$$\frac{\text{Net income after taxes}}{\text{Number of shares outstanding}} = \frac{\$11,766,000}{13,733,229} = \$0.86 \text{ per share}$$

Earnings per share is the most closely watched financial ratio in business. Persistent lack of growth in earnings per share usually indicates a declining business—an unsound investment for shareholders and creditors.

To see one way in which these ratios and other accounting information are presented, see the box on the next page.

BUDGETING

Budgeting is a form of planning expressed in financial terms. Because budgets specify future dollar targets for all areas of a business, they help management plan, control, and evaluate activities.

The **master budget** shows projected revenues and expenses for the entire firm. **Specialized budgets** provide individual department guidelines. For a large corporation like General Motors, budgets might include the following:

1. Projected receipts and disbursements by division (Chevrolet, Buick, Frigidaire, and so on) and by administrative unit within a division (Chevrolet's sales department).
2. Projected receipts and disbursements by activity (Chevrolet's advertising budget, for example, which is a combination of projected advertising expenditures for several departments).
3. Projected levels of assets, liabilities, cash inflows, cash outflows, investments, purchases, inventories, and personnel for the business as a whole or for individual divisions.

A budget committee helps the president prepare a detailed budget. In large corporations, this committee may include several vice presidents, the heads of various operating departments, and the controller. Since it is so important, the president of a firm usually has final authority to modify the complete budget before submitting it to the owners or the board of directors.

The Budget Cycle

Budgeting is a cyclical process with three distinct phases: (a) preparation and approval; (2) execution; and (3) accounting and auditing of the results. The completion of one phase of the cycle automatically initiates the next phase.

Budget Preparation

The budget committee begins preparing the budget by requesting estimates from the operating departments. Managers and their assistants work within committee-established guidelines to estimate the funds they will need for their activities. Eventually, the department head combines all these estimates into a departmental budget, which is sent to the budget committee. The committee then prepares a consistent and realistic master budget for the entire firm. This is a balancing act requiring attention to company goals and resources, past financial performance, and company politics. The preparation phase is concluded when the budget is approved by the president and the board of directors.

Company Slick

It's full of financial data . . . and executive pronouncements, four-color graphs, orations by the board chairman, photos of top managers hard at work, and general company fanfare. It goes to stockholders and to employees, suppliers, customers, Wall Street analysts, government agencies, and journalists. It's the company's annual report and it may cost millions to produce and distribute.

Now required of all companies with publicly traded stock, the report is an annual smorgasbord of audited financial statements, quarterly stock prices and dividends for the past two years, a five-year summary of operations, lists of the board of directors, data on the effect of inflation, and other business information. Even more is contained in the company's SEC 10-K report, usually requested by only a few stockholders.

Budget Execution

Budget execution—carrying it out—begins on the first day of the new fiscal year. In many large businesses, the controller is formally responsible for budget execution and reports any serious deviations to top management.

Accounting and Auditing

The controller uses accounting information and internal auditing procedures to determine whether units are within their guidelines and to revise the budget when necessary. It is also the responsibility of the controller to prepare interim progress reports for management.

Uses of Budgets

Budgets are used by every major business and by most nonprofit organizations. Their widespread adoption by management is a good measure of their importance and of the many functions they serve.

- PLANNING   Budgets express financial plans in concrete, quantitative terms. They help management allocate resources and reassess priorities.
- CONTROLLING   As a budget is implemented, actual performance can be compared with projections. Since management controls the allocation of funds, departments and divisions cannot use more than their budgeted amounts without management's knowledge and approval. By comparing actual with budgeted performance, management can spot potential trouble and take remedial action. For example, if actual sales do not keep pace with projected sales revenues, a firm may expand its advertising or cut production costs.
- EVALUATING PERFORMANCE Carefully developed budgets also permit management to set reasonable goals for individual employees or divisions and to measure their performances accordingly. In this way, employees know exactly what management expects and what resources are available.

But rigidly applied budgets can be straitjackets. A budget may become obsolete with a decline in consumer demand, high prices, a strike, new competitive tactics, or other changes. Managers need to maintain an attitude of flexibility toward budgets and to view them only as very good guidelines.

Chapter Review & Applications

Key Points to Remember

1. Accounting is the collection, organization, analysis, and presentation of financial information concerning a business.
2. The basic unit of accounting is the accounting transaction—any activity that has a measurable monetary impact on a business.
3. A firm's accounting transactions are recorded in registers (or ledgers), by hand or by computer. They are summarized in income statements and balance sheets in a manner that is consistent with Generally Accepted Accounting Principles.
4. The basic objective of an income statement is to show the net income of a business for a given accounting period (usually one year).
5. The primary objectives of a balance sheet are to show the financial position of a business at a given point in time and to indicate the basic categories in which its assets, liabilities, and owner equity are held.
6. Auditing is the process of verifying that a firm has properly recorded and reported its financial data. Audits are also used to uncover fraud or mismanagement and to verify taxable income.
7. The main financial ratios used to assess a company's financial health are the current ratio, return on investment, return on sales, and earnings per share. These ratios are generally reported in the firm's annual report.
8. Budgets specify future dollar targets in all areas of a business. As such, they help management plan, control, and evaluate the firm's activities.

Questions for Discussion

1. Describe the ways in which a firm's accounting information is used by management, investors, government, and the general public.
2. Give an example of an accounting transaction and describe how it would be recorded.
3. What is the income statement of a business? What items appear on it? How are income statements useful?
4. What items appear on the balance sheet? What are their uses?
5. Describe the major financial ratios and indicate how they can be used.
6. Describe the phases in the budget cycle and discuss the ways that managers use budgets in running an organization.

Short Cases

1. Construct an income statement and a balance sheet based on the following year-end totals in the accounts of Century Cycle, Inc., a small bicycle shop.

Cash	$12,000
Cost of goods sold	60,000
Accounts receivable	30,000
Telephone expenses	6,000
Utilities expenses	5,000
Accounts payable	20,000
Furniture and fixtures	8,000
Common stock	
(10,000 shares outstanding)	12,500
Sales salaries	40,000
Store supplies	10,000
Cycle inventory	25,000
Notes payable	35,000
Depreciation (store and equipment)	5,000
Mortgages payable	50,000
Sales	200,000
Building	40,000
Advertising expenses	20,000
Land	10,000
Parts inventory	17,000
Insurance expenses	5,000
Income taxes	14,000
Retained earnings	24,500
Interest expenses	8,000

2. From the information given above, calculate the following financial ratios: (a) current ratio; (b) return on investment; (c) return on sales; and (d) earnings per share.

A Critical Business Decision

—Made by Charles F. Knight
of Emerson Electric Company

The Situation

It is early 1980 and the chiefs have gathered in St. Louis. The heads of Emerson Electric Company's forty far-flung divisions have come to hear and act upon top corporate judgment. "The recession will be tough," they are told. "Your financial plans are too optimistic. Cut budgets to assure success."

Budget-cutting is not new to the highly successful electric motor producer, according to a story in *The New York Times*.[4] It became a way of life under the company's long-time leader, W.R. Persons. "Limiting phone calls and picking up paperclips help keep costs in line," Persons once explained. "But the real dollars and cents are saved on manufacturing products." A typical Emerson procedure: assign a group of engineers a cost-reduction target on a product under a specific deadline. "If you watch what you eat, you don't have to diet," one executive explained. "If you watch your costs, you don't have to institute crash cost-reduction programs overnight."

Budgets are used as planning tools at Emerson. Its ABC budgeting process is a finely honed system based on economic models. The "ABC" consists of three plans—an optimum track, then two fallback tracks if the economy is weaker than expected.

Emerson's budget leaves little room for maneuvering by operating executives. Every month, division managers and key subordinates are scrutinized at corporate headquarters. Chief among the chiefs is Charles F. Knight. "There is nobody here wondering about what he should be doing next year," Knight asserts. "We set tough targets."

The Decision

So far, so good. For twenty-two years Emerson's sales and earnings have topped the previous year's. The tight controls system has also enabled Emerson to develop new products quickly. Its profitable Weed-

Eater, a power lawn trimmer, took only four years to move from design to full-scale production.

Emerson's philosophy on plant location is simple. Its ninety plants are small, with an average investment of only $5 million each, and are located in towns and rural areas. "Each is administered completely independently of the others. This makes us very flexible, able to respond to changes in our markets," Knight comments.

But the company is growing. It now has forty divisions, churning out more than two hundred products—ranging from electrical engines to laboratory instruments, and from ceiling fans to chain saws—produced in thirty-three countries. Sales in 1980 are expected to reach $3 billion. And Knight wants to double sales and profits by 1985. As Knight reviews Emerson's diverse operations, he wonders whether the company can combine rapid growth with its traditional approach to budgeting.

Questions

1. What principles of accounting and budgeting does Emerson Electric Company illustrate? Will these principles continue to be appropriate if the company meets Knight's growth targets?
2. What type of accountants would you hire if you were a plant manager at Emerson? Why?

Obtaining Financial Resources

In this chapter you will learn . . .

- about the role that finance plays in business.
- how a firm's financial structure is developed.
- the sources of short-, intermediate-, and long-term financing.
- the difference between internal and external financing and equity and debt financing.
- how a firm raises money by selling stocks and bonds.

12

ames J. Ling started his career by selling surplus government equipment to the construction industry, financing his new business with a $2,000 mortgage on his house. Seven years later, Ling Electronics was so successful that Ling sold nearly half the company to the public for $800,000, issuing the stock himself from a booth at the Texas State Fair for $2.25 a share.

Soon he hired managers to run the business so that he could devote all his attention to building a financial empire. During the next thirteen years, Ling bought dozens of companies, from Braniff Airways to Jones and Laughlin Steel. He financed these acquisitions with a bewildering array of common stock issues, loans from banks and insurance companies, and corporate bonds. By 1968, his LTV Corporation, as Ling Electronics was eventually renamed, became the country's fourteenth largest business with annual sales of $3.75 billion. Because of his genius for **finance,** the functional area of business that deals with the acquisition and disbursement of funds, Ling has enjoyed one of the most spectacular business careers in American history.

But even James Ling makes mistakes. Ironically, in the 1970s the LTV Corporation suffered financial hardships, and Ling was forced to retire because of his financial mismanagement.

WHY FINANCE IS IMPORTANT

The survival of a business, even one as extraordinary as the LTV Corporation, depends on sound financial management. For this reason, managers in charge of a company's finances hold high positions with titles like financial vice president, treasurer, controller, secretary-treasurer, or treasurer-controller. These are the people who, along with the president and owners, decide whether the firm should build a new plant or how it should raise $10 million to acquire a new company. Their assistants deal with the day-to-day financial matters, such as handling cash receipts and disbursements, making loans, and formulating budgets.

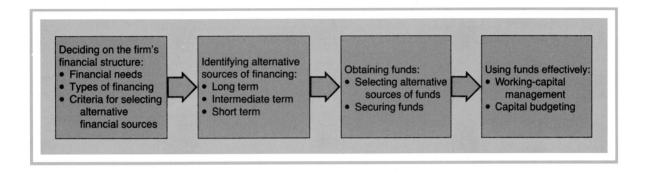

Nearly every business decision—from hiring a new employee to acquiring a new subsidiary—has a financial effect on the firm. So good financial management is good business. But it is more than that. A firm that is financially well-managed uses its funds to buy and use resources effectively in order to produce goods and services that consumers will buy.

Financial management is an expanding and challenging area of business. Over the past several decades, the role of financial managers has grown from helping a firm acquire financial resources to helping it allocate these resources. And in time of high interest rates and "credit crunches" when money is expensive to borrow—perhaps over 15 percent annual interest for a bank loan—and nearly impossible to find, careful financial management can save the business.

The principles of modern finance provide guidelines for obtaining funds (discussed in this chapter) and for effectively using them (described in Chapter 13). To get funds, the financial manager must (1) establish an appropriate financial structure for the business; (2) identify alternative sources of funds; (3) obtain the necessary funding; and (4) use the funds effectively. This process is illustrated in Figure 12–1 and discussed in both this and the next chapter.

FIGURE 12–1 The Four Steps of the Financial Management Process.

A FIRM'S FINANCIAL STRUCTURE

A firm's **financial structure** is built around the finance manager's assessment of the company's financial needs, the types of financing available, and the firm's stated criteria for choosing financial sources. These elements are shown in the first box of Figure 12–1.

Assessing Financial Needs

Although every firm operates differently because of its needs and situation, certain general rules apply to establishing a firm's financial structure. Usually, the financial manager begins by considering the business's (a) future investment opportunities (for which funds are necessary); (2) basic objectives (the profit goals and the amount of risk it is willing to assume, for example); and (3) the funds available from within the company (such as retained earnings). Based on these findings, the financial manager can then estimate what additional funds he or she needs to raise.

Types of Financing

Money can come from inside or outside the firm and can be raised through equity (selling of stock, for example) or debt financing (such as loans).

Internal and External Financing

Internal financing means acquiring money from inside the firm. The two main sources of internal funds come from depreciation and earnings retained in the business after taxes and dividends are paid. These generate about 60 percent of total corporate financing. **External financing,** funds obtained from outside the firm, comes from present or new owners or from borrowing, and provides the remaining 40 percent of total corporate financing. Figure 12–2 shows what portion of each dollar of financing is obtained from these two sources and their subdivisions.

Equity and Debt Financing

External financing may be raised through *equity* or *debt*. **Equity financing** pertains to all financial resources supplied by a firm's owners. It includes ownership interests in sole proprietorships and partnerships, proceeds from the sale of corporate stock to stockholder "owners," and past retained earnings. Equity owners receive a return on their investment, with the amount of their return depending on the amount of their investment, on the firm's profits, and on how much of these profits it disburses (as opposed to using them internally). Besides retained earnings, most equity financing comes from a sale of new stock.

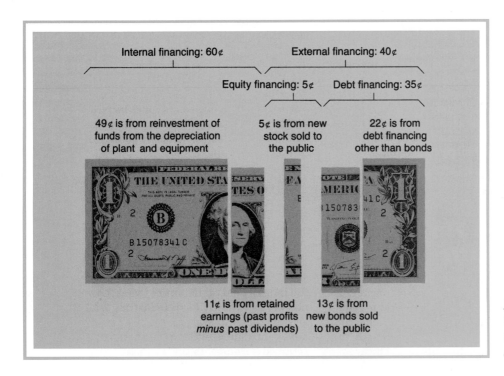

Internal financing: 60¢   External financing: 40¢

Equity financing: 5¢   Debt financing: 35¢

49¢ is from reinvestment of funds from the depreciation of plant and equipment

5¢ is from new stock sold to the public

22¢ is from debt financing other than bonds

11¢ is from retained earnings (past profits *minus* past dividends)

13¢ is from new bonds sold to the public

FIGURE 12-2
Where Business Gets Each Dollar of Funds.

Debt financing comes from any legally binding obligation to pay back a fixed amount of principal or interest. Sources of debt financing include bonds, notes, mortgages, drafts, and trade acceptances. The biggest difference between equity and debt financing is that debt holders are promised a fixed return whereas the return to equity owners depends on the business's profits.

Maturity of Debts

Different lenders offer different maturities or "due dates" for loans to borrowers. Three major categories into which debts are classified are **long-term loans,** which mature in ten years or more; **intermediate-term loans,** which mature in one to ten years; and **short-term loans,** which must be repaid in a year or less. The differences are very important, because the borrowing firm must plan in advance to have the cash on hand when its debts are due. Timing can be critical to a private investor, too, as can be seen in the boxed insert at the top of the next page.

Hold onto Gold, Antiques, and Acreage?

Dabbling in collectibles has become a very popular money-making activity among private investors. People are amassing gold, silver, and jewels; antique ceramics, furniture, and oriental rugs; fine art; and real estate. Even fads in Victorian paper weights have swept investment circles. Although none of these items pays back a return on a regular basis, the way stock or even a savings account does, the collector is betting on a chance for a bigger return when inflation and demand cause prices to soar.

Timing is the key to this type of investment. Collectors must be willing to have their money tied up for many years. One rarely makes a "quick killing." But for those who can afford it, and who are careful and knowledgeable about quality and brokers' commissions, the return can be well worth the wait.

Two Approaches to Financing: Skydiver Versus Little Old Lady

One top manager says, "I love to borrow money. I love to owe money. I think the whole world is committed to inflation and borrowed money is cheap." He calls himself a "skydiver" for his approach to borrowing. But he calls his chief financial officer an "old lady" when he resists borrowing. The approach has paid off: the company is Dow Chemical.

One rags-to-riches entrepreneur takes the opposite tack. The owner of a private conglomerate, with a personal wealth of more than $200 million, Jack Simplot owes no one a cent. He hasn't even a single stockholder to worry about. As he told *Fortune* magazine,[1] "What I own, I built. It's mine. Nobody ever had to put a penny at risk. I make the decisions and, believe me, I enjoy it." It has worked for him.

Approaches somewhere between these extremes often depend on one's attitude toward risk. If the economic future makes you a bit apprehensive, repaying fixed debt may alarm you. In prosperous times, selling additional shares of stock may look like a chance for stockholders to make a huge profit.

Even entire industries vary in the amount of debt they incur, as shown in the table on the right. The numbers are "leverage ratios," a comparison of the industry's total liabilities (what it owes) with its net worth (what it has). Industries with leverages greater than 1.0 owe more than what their owners have contributed, either as original investment or as retained earnings, to the business.

INDUSTRY	TOTAL LIABILITIES/ NET WORTH RATIO
Radios, television, and communications equipment	1.8
Farm machinery	1.7
Motor vehicles and equipment	1.7
Coating and engraving metal products	1.4
Grain mill products	1.1
Office and computing machines	1.1
Bottled soft drinks	0.8
Drugs	0.8
Tobacco products	0.7
Newspaper printing and publishing	0.6
Photographic equipment and supplies	0.5

Source: *Almanac of Business & Industrial Financial Ratios,* 1979.

Criteria for Selecting Sources of Funds

Once a business has developed a satisfactory financial structure, the financial manager must evaluate each potential source of funds in terms of specific criteria, such as the following:

1. The costs of obtaining funds.
2. The timing of principal and interest payments.
3. Future constraints, especially the possibility that borrowing funds now may restrict future borrowing from the same source.
4. Whether control of the business may be affected. For example, a company that obtains new funds by selling a large block of stock to a single private investor may find that outsider taking over management decisions.
5. The risks involved, especially the possibility that a financial contributor may someday try to withdraw an investment or extract a higher interest rate.

Costs are usually the main considerations.

ALTERNATIVE SOURCES OF FUNDS

The discussion above pointed out that three major loan categories are short term, intermediate term, and long term. Within each of these categories, various options are available.

Long-Term Financing

Corporations that need funds for the long term—ten years or more—typically raise money by offering common and preferred stock (equity financing) and bonds (debt financing).

Common Stock

Nearly all corporations raise funds by selling **common stock** to owners or investors. Any new offering must be made through a *prospectus*–a brochure that describes the company, its financial condition, and the terms of the stock

FIGURE 12-3
Example of a Prospectus Offering a New Stock Issue.

issue. (Figure 12–3 shows a page from a prospectus for Pacific Power and Light Company, offering a new issue of common stock.) The corporate charter specifies the maximum number of shares of stock the company can issue. The number of authorized shares can be increased by amending the charter. Newly issued corporate stock is sometimes given to managers as bonuses or to stockholders in lieu of dividends. The stock actually outstanding, which is normally less than the amount of authorized shares, is called *issued stock* (see Figure 12–4).

Warrants and *options* allow stockholders to purchase newly issued stock on favorable terms. A **warrant** might permit a stockholder to purchase one share of American Telephone and Telegraph at a price of $60 until January 1, 1984. The market value of the warrant depends on the $60 *striking price* (the permitted purchase price), on the current price of the stock, and on investor expectations about the future price of the stock. An **option** is a purchase of a right to buy a certain number of shares at a specified price during a specific period of time.

Investors buy stock to get *cash or stock dividends* and to realize *capital gains.* **Cash dividends** are based on the firm's profits and are paid quarterly or yearly. **Stock dividends** are issued on a percentage basis. For example, a 5-percent stock dividend gives the stockholder five additional shares for each hundred shares owned. Dividends increase with a company's earnings. So does the price of the stock, which the shareholder may decide to sell. Buying at a low price and selling when the price is high creates a **capital gain**—income that is taxed at a favorable rate. Studies show that capital gains earn the investor more income than dividends do.

But there are risks to owning stock. If a firm is unprofitable, shareholders receive no dividends and may be forced to sell at a **capital loss**—a price lower than the original cost of the stock. For example, stock for Minnie Pearl Fried Chicken (now Performance Systems, Inc.) sold at a high of $23 per share but fell to 12½ cents per share a few years later. So investors who bought one hundred shares at the peak price and held on saw their investment fall from $2,300 to $12.50! Also, if a firm goes bankrupt, common stockholders are entitled to receive back their investment from remaining company assets only after all other creditors have been paid.

Preferred Stock

Another source of long-term equity financing for corporations is the sale of **preferred stock.** Holders receive a fixed dollar dividend for each share they

FIGURE 12-4
Example of a Stock Certificate.

own, and they also enjoy priority over common stockholders in claiming corporate assets if the firm dissolves. This type of investment is bought mainly by conservative investors and nontaxable institutions, such as universities, that prefer the relative safety of a fixed return. Holders of a company's 6-percent $20 preferred stock, for example, would receive $1.20 per share on dividends each year. If the firm is unprofitable, though, the board of directors may omit these dividends.

Owners of **convertible preferred stock** can exchange their preferred shares for common stock on specified terms. The 6-percent $20 preferred issue, for example, might include a conversion privilege allowing holders to exchange one preferred share for two common shares. Owners of the preferred issue may find it profitable to convert when the market value of the common stock rises above $10.

Preferred stock is cumulative or noncumulative; participating or nonparticipating; voting or nonvoting; par or nonpar; and callable or noncallable. (Definitions are in the glossary.)

Bonds

The most important source of long-term debt financing for business is the sale of **bonds**—certificates representing a fixed obligation on the part of the issuer. (See Figure 12–5.) In addition to the specified sum, called the *principal,* the issuer agrees to pay the bondholder interest. Thus, if the Tampa Electric Company issues a 9-percent $5,000 bond on January 1, 1980, due January 1, 1995, it must pay the bondholder $450 in annual interest from 1980 through 1994 and return the $5,000 principal on January 1, 1995. The terms of the bond issue are described in a document called an *indenture.* A variety of bonds—including debentures, subordinated debentures, and income, mortgage, and municipal bonds—are defined in the glossary.

The differences between stocks and bonds are summarized in Figure 12–6. Unlike holders of common and preferred stock, bondholders do not enjoy voting rights and do not participate in the firm's profit beyond the stipulated interest payments and return of principal. In fact, when the general price level in the economy rises, the purchasing power of the money repaid to bondholders falls.

FIGURE 12–5
Example of a Corporate Bond.

FIGURE 12-6
A Comparison of Stocks and Bonds.

CHARACTERISTIC	STOCKS	BONDS
Type of financial instrument	Equity	Debt
Order of claim	Dividends can be issued only after interest on all debts (including bonds) is fully paid.	Interest must be paid before any dividends on stock are issued.
Legal obligations to holders	Dividends may be varied or omitted by the board of directors; no principal or maturity dates are involved.	Interest must be paid regularly to avoid insolvency; principal must be repaid at stated maturity date.
Rights of holders	Voting stockholders can influence management by electing members of the board of directors.	Bondholders have no voice in management as long as they receive interest payments.
Tax status for the issuing firm	Dividends are not tax-deductible.	Interest, as an expense of doing business, is tax-deductible.

But bondholders are creditors of the business and have priority over stockholders if the firm dissolves. Bondholders' rights are represented by a *trustee* (usually a bank or financial institution) that serves as a liaison between bondholders and the business and defends bondholder interests.

Bonds are safe, so they attract investors with fixed incomes who prefer a specified return. In recent years, their yields have also been 3 to 5 percent higher than dividends on common stocks. Pension funds and insurance companies, which must meet fixed claims, are the largest bond buyers.

The market price of a bond often differs from its *face value* (or *nominal value)*—the amount indicated on the bond certificate. But bond prices don't fluctuate as much as stock prices do. After an investor buys the 9-percent, $5,000 Tampa Electric issue, a shortage of investment funds might arise and other companies may have to start offering 10 percent interest (instead of 9 percent) to attract investors. If the Tampa holder wants to sell, he or she will have to sell at a *discount,* a price below the initial $5,000 paid, since potential

buyers will prefer the 10-percent yields on new bond issues. But if general interest rates fall, the Tampa Electric bondholder will realize a *premium* on the $5,000 bond, and it will sell for more than $5,000.

A bond's yield also depends on the financial soundness of the issuing firm. If a firm is a bad risk, it must offer higher interest rates to attract investors. Bond-rating services, such as Standard and Poor's, Moody's, and Fitch's, impartially rate the quality of most corporate bonds.

When Long-Term Financing Is Used

Businesses normally use long-term financing to buy long-lived assets like land, buildings, and machinery. It is a very costly method of financing, because people who invest their savings in a firm's stocks or bonds for ten years or more expect a high return. But past long-term financing can be used to meet financial crises, because the funds are already in hand. It also permits businesses to negotiate for intermediate- and short-term funds from a sound financial base.

Intermediate-Term Financing

The major sources of intermediate-term financing are term loans and government loans from the Small Business Administration (SBA). These are a form of debt financing and may occasionally be used for long- or short-term financing.

Term Loans

A **term loan** is an extension of credit by a bank or insurance company for more than one year. A business typically pays ¼ to ½ percent more for a term loan than it does for a loan with a shorter maturity from the same source. The exact terms of interest rates, maturity, and so on are negotiated and incorporated into a *loan agreement*. An alternative to a term loan is a financial or operating lease. To see the advantages of leasing, read the box, opposite.

Government Loans

Loans from the U.S. Small Business Administration are a major source of finance for small businesses. Government-licensed small business investment companies (SBICs) offer both equity and debt capital. Special arrangements are sometimes also made for businesses that agree to operate in specific regions in the state or for minority-owned businesses. To obtain these loans, you generally must prove that you have exhausted all other likely funding sources.

When Intermediate-Term Financing Is Used

Businesses normally use intermediate-term financing to purchase assets with intermediate lives—that is, one to ten years. Examples are cars and trucks and rapidly depreciating machinery and tools. Intermediate-term borrowing avoids long-term or permanent financial commitments. It is also cheaper than continuously renewing short-term loans or issuing long-term bonds or stock certificates to finance each major asset. And it does not affect a firm's short-term financial position. Too much short-term borrowing makes current liabilities rise relative to current assets. This can lead to financial crisis or to loss of investor confidence in the firm.

Short-Term Financing

Three major sources of short-term funds are available: trade credit, commercial paper, and short-term loans. Each is an important financial resource for small businesses.

Lease a Xerox Machine, Building, or Cow

You can lease almost anything, most easily for an intermediate period. And it may be as good or better than borrowing money to buy it. That depends on how your accountant classifies it for tax purposes.

It is quite common now to lease airplanes, oil tankers, copy machines, buildings, computers, generators, cars and trucks, and even dairy cows (with the payments based on the cow's milk-production record). The deals come from banks, finance companies, and specialized leasing companies.

Leases come in two main forms: financial leases and operating leases. Financial leases are long-term and cannot be cancelled. You pay by the month and maintain the item yourself. This usually costs about the same as buying the item with long-term debt. But it may pay, in a given situation, because buildings and equipment leased this way can be recorded as assets and liabilities on the balance sheet.

Operating leases are shorter term, cancellable, and the owner services the item. Cars, trucks, and office equipment are often leased this way. Nothing appears on the balance sheet as an asset.

When you make your decision, remember: It's all in the way you keep the accounts!

Trade Credit

When a business buys goods or services, it must pay the supplier. Because they want to sell products, most suppliers are willing to extend **trade credit**—an arrangement by which a supplier allows customers several weeks or months to make payment. Several variations of trade arrangements—with and without extension of credit—are described in Figure 12–7 on the next page.

Open-account credit is the most common form of trade credit. The buyer sends the supplier a *purchase order,* describing the types of goods desired. When the supplier ships the goods, it sends an *invoice* detailing the items shipped, their destination, and the previously negotiated selling price. Usually, there is both a grace period and a cash discount for prompt payment. For example, "2/10 net 30" means that the purchaser must pay the total price within thirty days after the invoice is received but will be granted a 2-percent discount if payment is made within ten days. Businesses can use the ten-day grace period as a kind of free loan. But waiting thirty days and losing the discount is not a good idea. An interest rate of 2 percent for twenty days is equivalent to an annual interest rate of 36.5 percent, so it's better to borrow from a bank than from a supplier.

Commercial Paper

Commercial paper is a short-term promissory note issued by a business, usually in multiples of $100,000. Interest rates on commercial paper are generally 1 to 2 percent lower than those charged by bankers for short-term business loans. Commercial paper, however, is *unsecured*—issued without a pledge of specific collateral by the borrower—so only financially strong, well-established businesses can issue it.

About 40 percent of all commercial paper is sold to dealers. They charge a fixed commission, usually 1¼ percent of the note's face value for the service of selling the note for the business. Most issuing firms place their commercial paper directly with bankers and other businesses that have temporary cash surpluses.

Short-Term Loans

Short-term loans, available from banks and other financial institutions, account for less than 10 percent of financing among U.S. businesses. *Unsecured short-term loans* involve no pledge of collateral, and they are generally issued only to businesses with high credit ratings. *Secured short-term loans,* on the

FIGURE 12-7
A Comparison of Various Trade Arrangements.

TYPE OF TRADE ARRANGEMENT	DESCRIPTION	TRADE CREDIT EXTENDED TO CUSTOMER?
Progress payments	The purchaser pays the supplier while the goods are being manufactured; progress payments are often made in installments, with each payment becoming due as the supplier completes a given stage of manufacture.	No
Cash before delivery (CBD)	The supplier asks for payment before delivery of the goods; this arrangement is often used when the financial status of the purchaser is unknown or questionable.	No
Cash on delivery (COD)	The supplier asks for payment when the goods are delivered; COD is used in the same circumstances as CBD, except that the supplier takes the risk that the purchaser may not accept delivery.	No
Open-account credit	The purchaser pays the supplier according to the terms indicated on the invoice, which usually allow the purchaser a grace period during which it can owe suppliers money without paying interest.	Yes
Notes payable	The purchaser signs a promissory note agreeing to pay the supplier on a specified date after the goods are delivered; under this arrangement, the supplier can sell the promissory note to a bank.	Yes
Trade acceptance	The supplier sends the goods to the purchaser with a draft—a promissory note payable to the supplier. The transporting agency is instructed to give up physical possession of the goods only when the purchaser signs the draft and designates at what bank the draft will be paid. When the draft is accepted and signed by the purchaser, it becomes a trade acceptance.	Yes

Your Next Job
Positions In Finance

Accounting and finance specialists may be found in the same occupational categories, though titles vary widely from business to business. The careers discussed here are in industrial or service businesses. Jobs in insurance, real estate, banking, and security markets are often held by finance specialists and will be described in the Your Next Job sections of Chapters 13 and 14. For additional information, contact the financial manager of a business in your area.

Finance Specialists

Cash budget analysts maintain records of cash inflows and outflows and may also be responsible for a firm's short-term investments. Some accounting training is essential, and a bachelor's degree in accounting or in finance is becoming a common prerequisite. Salaries range from $15,000 to $20,000.

Inventory control specialists try to balance the costs of inventory maintenance against the benefits of a large inventory that appeals to customers. They may also maintain records of inventory levels and locations. Training in production or finance, often at the bachelor's or the master's level, is becoming a common requirement. A knowledge of quantitative methods and statistics is especially helpful. Salaries normally range from $18,000 to $25,000.

Project analysts (also known as **financial analysts, capital budget analysts, capital expenditure analysts,** and **capital project analysts**) help decide the major investments a firm will make in new products, expensive plant and machinery purchases, and other long-term financial commitments. A keen analytical ability is vital, and main-taining effective working relationships with accounting, marketing, production, and management specialists is essential. The project analyst projects revenues and costs for alternative investments. A bachelor's degree in finance or accounting is minimal. More advanced training at the MBA level or beyond is becoming increasingly common. Salaries range from $20,000 to $35,000. Opportunities are expected to grow rapidly, because many firms are trying to develop standard methods of analyzing financial information and to get financial expertise at the divisional as well as the corporate level.

Top-Management Careers in Finance

Financial vice presidents and **treasurers** are the chief financial officers of a business. They supervise accounting and financial personnel, communicate with top management, maintain relationships with investment bankers, and communicate financial matters to stockholders and the public. Financial vice presidents also participate in most key business decisions, helping to decide how much of the firm's profits will be returned to the owners and how much will be retained in the business. A keen analytical ability, a thorough knowledge of accounting and finance, a capacity for effective administration, and public relations skills are desirable. Financial vice presidents normally have received training in either accounting or finance, increasingly at the MBA level or beyond. Salaries range from $30,000 to $500,000, depending on the size of the business and the responsibilities of the job. Considerable work experience in accounting or finance is usually essential. Financial vice presidents are often promoted to president or to chief executive officer of the business.

other hand, require the pledge of some asset (such as inventories) to guarantee repayment of the debt, and most require a *security agreement* (or *security-type device)* detailing the terms filed with the state. In case of default, the lender may seize the asset. The major types of unsecured and secured short-term loans are described in Figure 12–8. For another type of short-term loan, also open to individuals, see the box "How Long Is Your Line of Credit?"

When Short-Term Financing Is Used

Businesses normally use short-term credit to meet seasonal or unexpected demands for funds caused by sales fluctuations. The cost is usually low, especially when commercial paper is issued, and the arrangements are quite flexible.

FIGURE 12–8
Types of Short-Term Loans.

TERMS	TYPE OF LOAN	DESCRIPTION
Unsecured (no collateral)	Transaction	A firm borrows funds for a particular transaction and repays the loan when it is over. A developer may draw unsecured short-term funds to pay subcontractors for their assistance in constructing an office building.
	Line of credit	The firm establishes a line of credit—the maximum amount it can borrow on a short-term basis—with a bank. Although bankers are not legally obligated to provide the designated funds, they almost always do. The maximum amount is renegotiated each year.
	Revolving credit	Revolving credit resembles a line of credit, except that the banker is legally obligated to lend the money.
Secured (specific assets pledged as collateral)	Accounts receivable	Accounts receivable from a firm's customers are used as collateral. In a nonnotification arrangement, the firm's customers are not involved in settling the loan. In a notification arrangement, customers send their checks for purchased items directly to the borrower's bank.
	Inventory	The borrower's inventories serve as security. If a mortgage on the borrower's inventories is obtained by the lender, inventories are identified specifically and cannot be sold without the lender's permission.
	Other assets	Stocks and bonds held by a firm, the cash value of a firm's paid-up life insurance, and other assets are often used as collateral.

OBTAINING FUNDS

Once a firm's financial objectives are set and its available sources of funding identified, the financial manager must actually get the funds. This involves (1) selecting preferred sources of funds and (2) arranging the terms of financing.

Selecting Preferred Sources of Funds

Financial managers select funding sources on the basis of the interest rates, maturities, and other conditions quoted by potential investors or lenders, so a business will deviate from its desired financial structure when funds suddenly become available at favorable terms. When stock prices rise very high, for example, many firms issue new stock. Others may need more intermediate financing when they add a product and need machinery and equipment.

So sensible financial managers watch developments in security markets. Some may also seek financial advice from bankers or from **underwriters,** firms specializing in the sale of new securities to the public. Rapidly growing businesses are always looking for external funding sources willing to invest in the firm on reasonable terms.

Arranging Financing

Once the preferred source of funds has been selected, the business manager must decide on the best way to acquire them. Should discussions be initiated

How Long Is Your Line of Credit?

Both businesses and individuals can have lines of credit at the bank. A small flour mill may have a $500,000 credit line at the Bank of America. Yours may be $2,000. Once your credit is checked, the agreement allows you to borrow that amount of money over a certain time period. This is usually cheaper than paying a fee when your bank balance drops below a certain level, paying for bounced checks, or paying interest on overdue charge-account or installment-loan bills. Businesses must pay a little—½ to ¾ of 1 percent of the line—even if they don't use theirs. You don't have to.

with several competing financial organizations? Or should negotiations be made directly with a single lender or underwriter on the theory that a good relationship may lead to good treatment later when money gets tight?

If the business decides to obtain financing by selling stocks and bonds, it may sell them to existing owners of the firm *(preemptive placement),* to the public *(public offerings),* or to a few selected investors *(private placement).*

Preemptive Placement

When new stock is issued through **preemptive placement,** the stockholders are sent a *stock right.* This entitles them to subscribe to the new issue, usually one stock right for each share of common stock held. The market value of the right is roughly equal to the current selling price of the common stock *minus* the discount price of the new issue. Stockholders either exercise or sell their rights, usually within thirty days (or they lose money). A company whose common stock is selling for $20 may offer owners the opportunity to buy a new share for $12 plus four rights. In this case, the rights to purchase each new share are worth about $8 to owners, $2 apiece.

Public Offering

In a **public offering,** a firm's stock is sold to the public rather than to just its present owners. Occasionally, a small business operating in one state will sell its stock directly to the public. Usually, though, a firm hires an investment banker or underwriter to place its stock or bond issues. When the issue is large, several investment banking firms may form an underwriting syndicate—then they share the responsibility and the commission.

The underwriter markets a new issue to individual investors or to financial institutions. They agree on the prices quoted by the underwriter, creating a market for the securities. Usually the investment banker agrees to buy any unsold part of the issue, though in some cases new issues are handled on a "best-efforts" basis (unsold securities are returned).

Private Placement

Private placement (also called *direct placement*) is selling securities to a single investor or to a small group of investors. Terms are negotiated by the issuing firm and the potential investors, often with the advice of an investment banker. This is popular with small- or medium-sized businesses that are not well known enough to make a successful public offering. It is expensive, because private investors can demand attractive terms for taking a risk on the business.

Chapter Review & Applications

Key Points to Remember

1. Finance is the functional area of business that deals with acquiring and disbursing funds. This involves four key steps: deciding on the firm's financial structure, identifying alternative sources of funding, obtaining the funds, and using the funds effectively.

2. The financial structure of a business is built around the firm's financial needs, the types of financing available, and the company's criteria for choosing financial resources.

3. Long-, intermediate-, and short-term financing typically support purchases of assets with useful lives of ten or more years, one to ten years, and less than one year, respectively.

4. Common stock is a form of long-term equity financing in which stock is sold to existing or new owners. Stockholders receive dividends—payments determined by profits and made at the discretion of the board of directors. Preferred stock is equity financing with fixed dividends.

5. Bonds are a form of long-term debt financing in which the firm must pay back fixed interest and principal on designated dates.

6. The major sources of intermediate-term financing are term loans and government loans. These are a form of debt financing. The main sources of short-term financing are trade credit, commercial paper, and short-term loans.

7. Preemptive placement is selling securities to existing stockholders. A public offering is selling securities to the general public. And private placement involves selling securities to a private individual or a group of private investors.

Questions for Discussion

1. As financial manager for a local newspaper, what factors should you consider in establishing a desirable financial structure for the company?

2. What are the primary sources of funds for most U.S. corporations?

3. Distinguish between internal and external financing and equity and debt financing.

4. What are the advantages and disadvantages of investing in common stocks? In preferred stocks? In corporate bonds?

5. What is a term loan? A government loan? Trade credit? Commercial paper? A short-term loan?

6. Discuss the advantages and disadvantages of long-, intermediate- and short-term financing.

7. Differentiate between preemptive placement, public offering, and private placement of stock.

Short Cases

1. Two students are arguing. Martha comments, "If I were in business, I would insist on cash on delivery. There are too many untrustworthy people who don't pay their bills." "No," Linda says, "I think most companies are reasonably honest, and a business should extend open-account credit." As a business manager, what are the advantages and disadvantages of insisting on cash on delivery? Of extending open credit?

2. Spare-a-Part Auto Stores owes $10,000 to a supplier on terms 2/10 net 30. Spare-a-Part can borrow money at its bank at an interest rate of 10 percent. How much money would it save by borrowing at the bank and taking advantage of the trade discount?

3. The Hasselrig Corporation plans to buy two $200,000 machines, each with an expected life of eight years. Each should save the firm $100,000 a year (after taxes) in labor and other costs. What types of loans should Hasselrig consider? What factors should it consider in evaluating alternative sources of funds? If money can be borrowed at an interest rate of 10 percent and if the machines have no salvage value at the end of eight years, how much money would Hasselrig make each year if it bought the machines and borrowed the $400,000 to pay for them?

A Critical
Business Decision

—made by Mary Hudson
of Hudson Oil

The Situation

Mary Hudson's strategies in gasoline retailing reflect the national standard for independent operators. She runs a lean operation, cutting costs to the bone. Each station contains only a small house, just large enough for the cash box and restrooms. There are no service bays or grease racks, only gas pumps. Customers serve themselves, and attendants are needed only to collect the money. There are more than three hundred of these gas stations in thirty-six states, employing about 1,300 people. Together they make up the oldest and one of the largest independent gasoline marketing companies in the United States.

The company is Hudson Oil. Mary Hudson is its president and chief executive officer.

A widow at twenty-one, she began her empire by borrowing $200 to buy a closed-down service station in Kansas City to support herself and her infant daughter. Within six years she had bought thirty-nine more stations in Kansas, Missouri, and Nebraska. After joining her brothers in a series of partnerships, she went her own way in 1968. Since then, she has competed with them nose-to-nose.

Hudson's company is a no-frills and no-nonsense operation tightly within her control. Her unannounced visits to her stations are legendary. Greasy pumps or dirty restrooms draw stern "shape-up" lectures for station managers. She also pressures regional supervisors to hire more women managers. In the late 1970s women ran over forty of the stations. Her good business sense shows in other ways, too. Large technicolor signs push the low prices. And penny-pinching policies keep costs to a minimum: cash only, no credit cards, little advertising, and no more than two attendants on duty. The results speak for themselves: each Hudson station sells its gasoline for about one to two cents per gallon less than major oil company stations. And each station pumps nearly five times as much gasoline as a major station per month: 150,000 gallons versus about 30,000 gallons at a major station.

The Decision

Mary Hudson is thinking about buying a petroleum refinery. It would mean more control over her business in one way, but perhaps less control in another. The Oklahoma refinery she is considering—with a price tag of $20 million—would produce half the gasoline her stations need each day, 450,000 gallons. This would be excellent insurance in another oil crisis. (In the 1973 crisis she had to temporarily close half her stations when she couldn't get enough refined gasoline.) And it would allow her to proceed to modernize her stations with more confidence. Canopies over the pumps, more efficient equipment, and a computer system to provide instant information to corporate headquarters on each station's sales and profits are some of her ideas, according to *Fortune* magazine.[2]

"All my life I've been a gambler," she says. But she has no experience in refining. And she is accustomed to financial control. (She and her daughter own 90 percent of the stock in the consolidated company that owns the ten Hudson corporations.)

Questions

1. If you were Mary Hudson, what would you see as the advantages and disadvantages of buying and running your own refinery? Would you buy it? Why?

2. What are the advantages and disadvantages of Mary Hudson's approach to financing Hudson Oil by obtaining financial resources without selling corporate stock to the public?

Using Financial Resources and Managing Risk

13

ick Schaak was about to receive Stanford University's "Entrepreneur of the Year" award when trouble hit. To his surprise, Schaak discovered that his firm, Schaak Electronics, had lost almost a million dollars during the previous year, couldn't pay its suppliers, and shareholder equity had fallen by one-third.

As president of the firm, Schaak knew that he was good at marketing but bad at finance. There was no question that Schaak's "financial management" system had some rather unusual features. Consider the following:

- Checking accounts were balanced only every six to nine months.
- Little effort was made to collect on accounts receivable.
- Inventory was counted only once a year.
- Suppliers were paid late, thereby forfeiting cash discounts available for prompt payment.

When the trouble was discovered, Schaak called in a professional financial manager who designed a new system for the electronics firm. The result: a daily survey of checking-account and cash balances, credit given only to buyers holding major credit cards (whose companies absorb any losses), a quarterly check on inventories, and a policy of paying suppliers within the discount period.[1]

Today, Dick Schaak has thirty-nine radio-stereo-electronics retail stores located in five states. And he is enjoying annual sales of $40 million. He is also proud of the financial system that made his success possible. It is the system of **asset management,** which we will examine in this chapter. Asset management deals with two kinds of assets. **Working capital management** refers to decisions about current assets and short-term debts—anything like accounts receivable or inventories that can be converted to cash within a year. The other area of asset management is **capital budgeting,** which is the use of financial resources to buy assets like land and buildings and to subsidize research and development and new products—anything that will pay off in more than a year.

These two asset-management activities and the related areas of risk management and insurance are the subjects of this chapter.

WORKING CAPITAL MANAGEMENT

The three basic categories of working capital are cash and near cash, accounts receivable, and inventories. The financial manager must make decisions about each of these types of company assets.

Managing Cash and Near Cash

Cash and **near cash** (interest-bearing assets easily converted to cash) are needed to conduct day-to-day business operations like paying employees and meeting emergencies. How much of these assets managers need depends on how well they have done their financial planning, how many other current assets the firm holds, and the range of normal business fluctuations.

Cash itself pays no interest. So the financial manager must be careful to: (1) speed up collection of monies due; (2) conserve funds; and (3) place idle cash in interest-bearing assets (near cash) until it is needed.

Speeding Up Collections

A company needs to offer credit to remain competitive. But since "time is money," collection of monies due is a major concern of financial managers.

So Much Loose Change

At the end of the 1970s, IBM was sitting on $5.4 billion, twelve other big companies on $1 billion or so apiece, and 175 more on at least $100 million each. They were up to their ears in cash.

Why? Companies had been piling up profits because of inflation. They wanted a cash cushion, because they had been hit hard by a recent credit crunch and the approaching recession made them reluctant to invest in new plant, equipment, and research and development. The resulting cash on hand created great opportunities (and challenges) for cash managers.

Three ways they can speed up the collection process are:

1. *Use regional collection centers,* instead of the main office, to send invoices directly to local customers who, in turn, mail their payments to the collection centers. This saves a day or so in mailing time both going out and returning.
2. *Rent a local post office box* and authorize a regional banker to pick up customer mail payments several times a day. The receipts can be deposited immediately, short-cutting even the collection center.
3. *Use express mail, special delivery, or messenger services* to collect large payments.

Conserving Funds

On the other side of the coin, financial managers must pay out money in ways that best conserve funds—for instance, by paying suppliers on the last day before the discount is lost. This requires carefully organized and efficient bill-paying procedures. Also, by anticipating cash inflows from accounts receivable, managers can offset cash outflows needed to pay bills. This way, the company doesn't need to keep a lot of money on hand. Finally, the firm's bank accounts should be monitored, so that if excessive cash accumulates in one account, it can be transferred to another account with a low cash balance.

Converting Cash to Near Cash

Since cash brings in no interest, it should be efficiently converted to interest-bearing investments. The basic financial instruments used for this purpose are described in Figure 13–1. Intermediate- and long-term securities that are about to mature may also serve as near cash.

Managing Accounts Receivable

Since most firms extend credit to their customers, managers must develop sound procedures for handling accounts receivable. This involves determining a credit policy and establishing a credit-management program.

The **credit policy** is the company's rule for extending credit on its accounts receivable. The open-account system discussed in Chapter 12 has, for example, many variants. Usually, credit terms are uniform within an industry. But individual businesses occasionally compete for new customers by offering more favorable credit terms.

FIGURE 13–1
Examples of Traditional Financial Instruments Used by Financial Managers as Investment Opportunities.

FINANCIAL INSTRUMENT	DESCRIPTION	MATURITY
Treasury bill	Obligation of the U.S. government; weekly auctions determine yield.	91-day maturity 182-day maturity
Federal agency issue	Obligation of a federal agency, such as the National Mortgage Association.	6-month maturity (Federal Home Loan Bank)
Banker's acceptance	Business agreement to pay a given sum at a future date, guaranteed by a bank.	Highest quality, 1- to 180-day maturity.
Certificate of deposit (CD)	Bank deposit on which a specified interest rate is paid. Most CDs can be resold to third parties in advance of indicated maturities.	90- to 149-day maturity (in $100,000 units or larger)
Commercial paper	Unsecured note issued by a firm.	Highest quality, 30- to 270-day maturity
Tax-exempt note	Short-term obligation of a local or state government	Various maturities

Nevertheless, in establishing its credit policy, the firm must comply with certain federal regulations for corporate customers and for ultimate consumers. For example, the Equal Credit Opportunity Act prohibits discrimination in lending to individual consumers on the basis of sex, marital status, race, color, religion, national origin, public assistance, exercise of federal consumer rights, and age. Credit seekers must be notified within thirty days and, if denied credit, must be told the reason. The Fair Credit Reporting Act gives the consumer additional rights, e.g., to review and correct his or her own credit file at any commercial credit bureau. And the Truth in Lending Act requires creditors to tell consumers about all finance charges and methods of computing interest.

In large firms there is normally a credit manager in addition to the financial manager. The **credit manager** investigates credit applicants, decides how much, if any, credit to extend to each, and establishes collection

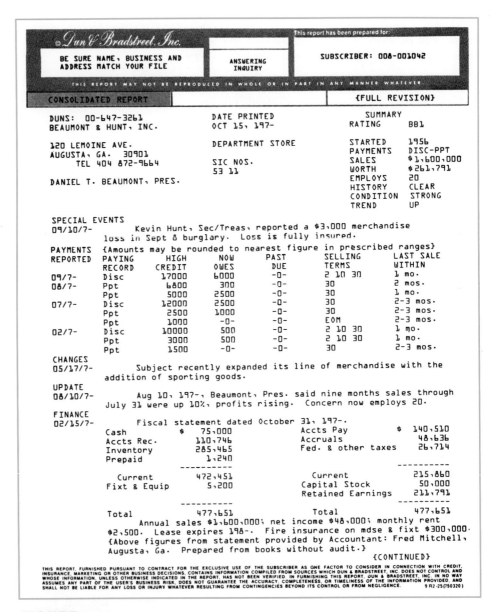

FIGURE 13-2
A Typical Dun and Bradstreet Credit Report.

policies. To do this, credit managers rely on past experience with a customer or on accounting statements supplied by a new customer. Standards of credit-worthiness for specific customers are usually based on the following factors:

1. *The profitability involved.* If a firm generally earns profits of, say, 1 percent of sales, failure to collect 1 percent of accounts receivable will cancel all profits. Such a firm extends credit cautiously.
2. *The influence of credit on sales.* If customers are not greatly influenced by credit, a firm can be restrictive without reducing sales substantially.
3. *The probability of default.* If many credit customers are expected to default or to delay payment, a restrictive policy is necessary.
4. *The risk preferences of management.* A management that wishes to avoid risk is careful about extending credit.

Credit managers also may contact the credit departments of commercial banks, organizations like the National Association of Credit Management, or commercial credit-rating services. A typical credit report prepared on a corporate customer by Dun & Bradstreet, perhaps the best-known and most comprehensive credit-rating service, is shown in Figure 13–2.

Once credit-worthiness has been checked, the next step is to make a **line-of-credit arrangement.** This is the fixed maximum amount of credit that will be extended. The amount is based on the customer's short-term liquidity, payment record, quality of management, and other factors. Financial ratios (discussed in Chapter 11) also are frequently used. Even corporations sometimes have trouble paying their bills and must be nudged by bill collectors (see accompanying box).

Corporate Deadbeats

They use excuses like, "My money isn't turning over for me" or "I'm already borrowed up to the hilt." And they don't pay their bills. Some of the country's largest corporations have acted like "deadbeats" at one time or another. And these are customers that most suppliers don't want to annoy by rude bill collecting.[2]

Nevertheless, financial managers increasingly are willing to send out commercial collection agencies to corporations that are more than 120 days overdue. There are now about 180 U.S. firms that collect from corporations for other corporations. Their services aren't cheap: the fee is usually 25 percent of the first $2,000 recovered and 20 percent of the rest. But even at these rates, and even when it doesn't work, companies find it cheaper than hiring their own collection staff. Only about 35 percent of the agencies collect more than half of what they are asked to collect.

Managing Inventories

Financial managers also have to balance **inventories,** stockpiles of raw materials and partly or completely finished goods on hand. The main factors in deciding how large an inventory to keep are listed in Figure 13–3. In large businesses, the manufacturing department estimates how much inventory is on hand and decides when it should be replenished by using the marketing department's sales forecasts. Large inventories may tie up capital, but they do provide protection against costly out-of-stock problems.

Goals of Working Capital Management

Managing **working capital** cash and near cash, accounts receivable, and inventories—is like walking a tightrope between risk and return. The risk comes from not having enough funds on hand to support long-term investment and to pay bills if short-term credit dries up. And the return comes from what you can earn if you invest the money instead of holding onto it. Financial managers want to borrow just enough in short-term loans and invest just enough near cash to keep the tightrope tipped toward the side of return—or profit. This is not an easy balancing act. Firms occasionally misjudge working capital needs, or discover that the credit market has changed. So some excess working capital is usually held for safety.

FIGURE 13–3
The Pros and Cons of Keeping Large Inventories.

Inventories Provide Benefits, Because They Allow Businesses to . . .	Inventories Cause Problems, Because They Require Businesses to . . .
• meet sudden spurts in customer demand.	• tie up scarce and costly financial resources that could be used elsewhere.
• provide adequate service from stocks of spare parts.	• cost money to count, control, protect, insure, and maintain.
• keep the production line moving during strikes or shortages of raw materials.	• depreciate in value if the prices of materials or of finished products decline.
• increase profits if suppliers raise their prices later.	• become obsolete and possibly worthless if models, styles, or fashions change quickly.

CAPITAL BUDGETING:
ANALYZING MAJOR INVESTMENTS

Although working capital management is more time consuming, capital budgeting is more important. It requires decisions on long-range projects such as building a new plant, closing a division, extending a product line, replacing worn-out machinery, changing research and development expenditures, and figuring out how much money to raise for working capital. These financial commitments are for one year or more and involve three steps: (1) determining return on investment; (2) using financial leverage; and (3) assessing risk.

Determining Return on Investment

Return on investment (ROI) is a measure of how well funds are used. Expressed as a percentage, it is figured by dividing the estimated profits of a project by the assets used in it. The higher the ROI, the better. Say, for example, you are considering the alternatives of opening a shoe store or buying an apartment building. Each requires an investment of $50,000. If you project profits at $20,000 for the shoe store and $15,000 for the apartment building, returns on investment are:

$$\text{ROI (shoe store)} = \frac{\text{Estimated annual profit}}{\text{Total assets used}} = \frac{\$20,000}{\$50,000} = 40\%$$

$$\text{ROI (apartment building)} = \frac{\text{Estimated annual profit}}{\text{Total assets used}} = \frac{\$15,000}{\$50,000} = 30\%$$

The shoe store is the better bet.

The desire for a high return on investment applies to every business activity, from a new product whose failure could bankrupt the company to the purchase of a new typewriter. (The typewriter should boost worker output enough to yield an acceptable return on its investment cost.)

Using Financial Leverage

Instead of choosing between the shoe store and the apartment building, you might want to borrow enough to buy both. If you already have $50,000 and a local banker will loan you $25,000 for each project at 10 percent interest, you could calculate the possibility of buying both in the following way:

Project	Total Investment Required	Total Investment after Borrowing $25,000 on Each Project	Estimated Annual Profit	Interest Paid to Bank (25,000 × 10%)	Profit after Interest Payment
Shoe store	$50,000	$25,000	$20,000	$2,500	$17,500
Apartment building	50,000	25,000	15,000	2,500	12,500

You can see that your total profit from both projects will be $30,000 ($17,500 from the shoe store and $12,500 from the apartment building), which is a much better return than the $20,000 from the shoe store alone.

The principle behind this calculation is **financial leverage,** or the value of a firm's debt expressed as a percentage of its total investment. Financial leverage can be applied to an entire firm or to specific activities within the firm. Using the shoe store and the new apartment building as an example, your combined financial leverage can be computed using the following formula:

$$\text{Combined financial leverage} = \frac{\text{Dollars of debt}}{\text{Dollars of total investment in the businesses}}$$

$$= \frac{\text{Owner's debt}}{\text{Owner's debt} + \text{investment}}$$

$$= \frac{\$50,000}{\$50,000 + \$50,000} = 50\%$$

The financial leverage shown in this example is clearly profitable. The ROI on the shoe store is 40 percent, and the ROI on the apartment building is 30 percent. Borrowing $50,000 at 10 percent interest to buy both is a good decision on your part. It yields a 40 percent return on the apartment—10 percent goes toward the interest, but the "extra" 30 percent is pocketed by you as profit. And it yields a 30 percent return on the shoe store—10 percent toward the interest and 20 percent as additional profit.

Leverage is a basic principle of finance. It states that as long as funds can be borrowed reasonably, borrow as much as possible to increase financial leverage. In fact, even a low return-on-investment rate on a project may be attractive if lots of money can be borrowed for it.

If a firm's rate of return on investment is more than the interest rate it must pay, it is said to enjoy *favorable financial leverage*. Banks do this by paying depositors 7 percent on their savings and lending these dollars to borrowers at 10 or 12 percent. *Unfavorable financial leverage* occurs when a firm's rate of return on investment drops below the interest rate it must pay.

Assessing Risk

Risk may be defined as variations in expected outcomes of decisions. And it is always present. Estimates of potential returns on investments may be wrong; earthquakes or floods may occur; or a recession or a new zoning ordinance may wreak havoc with investments. If a firm has extensive financial leverage, an unexpected, unpleasant occurrence can mean catastrophe.

So most businesses try to minimize risk by making safe investments, such as in U.S. government bonds and corporate bonds from stable companies, even though low-risk investments offer a lower return than high-risk ventures. This principle of finance is called the **risk-return relationship.** The greater the risk, the higher the anticipated return on investment.

Every business owner—from oil wildcatter to real-estate developer to conservative banker—makes two key decisions about risk, based on his or her attitudes toward risk and on the firm's financial strength:

1. In view of the dangers of leverage, how much debt am I willing to assume to try to increase profits?
2. How much risk will I accept to increase my expected return on individual projects and activities?

In deciding whether to invest in a particular project, the financial manager typically lists all the alternative projects, rating them from highest to lowest based on their projected rates of return. The cut-off point between investing and not investing then depends on the funds available and on the cost of acquiring them. This decision to invest or not invest is the final step in capital budgeting—allocating funds to major investments.

To summarize, sound financial management involves three main steps: (1) obtaining funds on the most favorable terms possible (Chapter 12); (2) providing the appropriate level of working capital for day-to-day operations (Chapter 13); and (3) using capital budgeting to allocate funds wisely to major investments (Chapter 13).

RISK MANAGEMENT

Risk is everywhere in business. Economic fluctuations, changes in consumer taste, actions of competitors, strikes, inflation, shortages of raw materials and energy, fires, wars, and new laws and regulations disrupt the most carefully managed businesses and can throw off even excellent ROI estimates. So financial managers must reduce risk to the lowest possible level while maintaining the firm's desired rates of return. Specialists called *risk managers* often draw this job. In broad terms, risk managers reduce risk through sound management, reduction or avoidance of physical hazards, self-insurance, and transference of risk to other individuals or organizations through hedging, business insurance, and employee insurance. Each of these applications of risk management is discussed in the following sections.

"And so, extrapolating from the best figures available, we see that current trends, unless dramatically reversed, will inevitably lead to a situation in which the sky will fall."

Drawing by Lorenz;
© 1972, The New Yorker Magazine, Inc.

Sound Management

Normal business risks can be reduced through sound management. Good planning can help the financial manager adjust to economic fluctuations or changes in consumer taste. An aggressive research and development program can help offset vigorous competition. Well-conceived personnel programs may reduce strikes. And good working capital management and capital budgeting surely help.

Reduction or Avoidance of Physical Hazards

Risk managers and *safety engineers* control physical hazards within the firm by:

1. Designing and buying buildings and machinery that reduce the chances for fire and accidents to occur.
2. Protecting property by hiring plant guards, screening employees, and improving burglar alarms, locks, and safes.
3. Introducing safety-education programs and inspecting and repairing safety devices.

The role of safety engineers has become especially important since the passage of the Occupational Safety and Health Act (OSHA). The Occupational Safety and Health Administration, a federal agency created by law, sets federal job-safety and health standards and makes periodic on-the-site inspections.

Self-Insurance

Firms may want to provide their own coverage for losses through **self-insurance,** paying for them with a special contingency fund or absorbing the losses directly. This is a good idea when the value of the insured assets is small, the danger to them low, or the chances of replacing them high. A small manufacturer, for instance, would not carry fire insurance on a small rented office. Nor would an international oil company with several hundred tankers carry such insurance, since it would be cheaper to lose even one tanker a year (very unlikely) than to pay the insurance premiums. In both these instances the companies would opt for self-insurance.

Hedging

Businesses that earn profits mainly by processing major raw materials (like grain, coffee, or copper) can **hedge** their risks, or transfer them to another party. This is done through commodity markets, such as the Chicago Board of Trade and the New York Mercantile Exchange. For example, in late September 1981, the Chicago market might quote a price of $5 a bushel for wheat to be delivered in September 1982. A baking company could hedge against crop failures or huge foreign sales by buying a September 1982 **futures contract** in wheat. In this way, it would be sure to get the wheat at $5 a bushel. Farmers can do the same thing. They can be sure of a fixed price for their wheat by *selling* a futures contract, agreeing to deliver it to the buyer at a certain price on a certain date. Therefore, through such hedging, bakeries and farmers transfer the risk of price fluctuations in wheat to others, in order to concentrate on what they do best—baking and raising crops.

Like stock prices, the prices specified in futures contracts fluctuate, depending on the supply and demand for future deliveries of the product. Thus, a futures contract bought in December 1981 may specify $7 a bushel for the September 1982 wheat, because the demand has increased during the past three months. This fluctuation is what encourages speculation on the commodities markets. Futures prices are quoted in most major newspapers and are watched closely by businesses and investors.

Businesses may also hedge against price fluctuations by negotiating **requirements contracts.** These are long-term agreements on prices and quantities between buyers and suppliers. Both parties benefit. A twenty-year requirements contract between an electric utility and a coal producer, for example, ensures enough coal for the utility and a market for the coal producer.

INSURANCE

The most common way to transfer risk is to buy **insurance.** The underlying concept is simple: for a fee (an *insurance premium*), one party (the *insurer*) agrees to pay another party (the *insured*) a sum of money specified in advance if the second party sustains a loss covered by the contract (*insurance policy*). The premiums are based on statistical probabilities recorded in **actuarial tables.** These come from the insurer's past experience. A simplified actuarial table is shown in Figure 13–4.

FIGURE 13-4
Life Expectancies for Americans:
A Simplified Actuarial Table.

Age	Probability of Survival to Age 65	Average Remaining Lifetime (Years)	Average Remaining Lifetime Beyond Age 65 (Years)
0	.72	70.7	5.7
10	.74	62.6	7.6
20	.74	53.0	8.0
30	.75	43.7	8.7
35	.76	39.1	9.1
40	.77	34.5	9.5
45	.79	30.1	10.1
50	.81	25.9	10.9
55	.85	22.0	12.0
60	.90	18.3	13.3

Source: U.S. Department of Health, Education, and Welfare, Public Health Service, National Center for Health Statistics *United States Life Tables: 1969–71* (1973), I, p. 1, as cited in *Risk Management,* 4th ed., by C. Arthur Williams and Richard M. Heins, p. 158. Copyright 1981 by McGraw-Hill Book Company. Used with permission of McGraw-Hill Book Company.

An insurance policy benefits both the insured and the insurer. For an annual premium of $1,000, a business might insure itself for $200,000 against the death or disability of a top executive. The probability of the executive dying or becoming seriously disabled is low, but if he does, the company gets the $200,000. The insurer benefits by setting premiums high enough to make money on the law of averages. In other words, if 300 firms buy the $200,000 policy and pay annual premiums of $1,000, the insurance company receives $300,000 ($1,000 × 300) a year. If, according to the tables, one of those insured executives can be expected to die or become disabled each year, the insurance company will pay out $200,000 in benefits. So its profit, before deducting other expenses, is $100,000. And insurers can invest all the premium money in the meantime.

Insurable and Uninsurable Risks

Many risks—like changes in demand and competitors' actions—are not insurable. To be insurable, a risk must be:

1. *Predictable and measurable.* If an insurance company cannot figure out the probability of a loss or measure its dollar value, it will refuse to provide insurance.
2. *Geographically confined.* No insurance company would be willing to insure an entire town against hurricane damage, for example, unless the company was able to reinsure (sell individual policies at a discount to other insurance firms).
3. *Recoverable.* The potential loss cannot be so large as to wipe out the insurance company if the insurer collects. So utility companies, for example, are able to insure against explosions in nuclear power plants only with the federal government.

Most risks, though, *are* insurable. Lloyd's of London, the world's largest insurance underwriter, will even insure against such events as injury to a concert pianist's hands or rain at a college football game. But even Lloyd's makes occasional bad decisions and bets on poor risks—such as computer leasing (see box).

The Role of the Risk Manager

Risk managers decide what their companies need to insure, how much coverage to buy from whom, and how to collect benefits. Their jobs—and salaries—have grown in recent years. They now must assess risks in product liability (protection against consumer lawsuits over products), large property management, operations in unstable and perhaps anti-American political climates, and the kidnapping of key executives.

Evaluating the coverage and costs of potential insurance policies is called *contract analysis.* This has become an important job for risk managers, for they must be able to tell whether it is cheaper to buy a *comprehensive* (or *package*) *policy* from one company—if it includes the right kinds of coverage—or to buy separate policies from several different insurers. And just the ability to understand what a policy offers is no small accomplishment (see box on page 330).

Business Insurance

Basic business insurance includes fire, automobile, marine, worker compensation, liability, burglary or theft, fidelity and surety, business interruption, and business life insurance policies. Each is explained in the following sections.

Fire Insurance

Fire (or property) *insurance* protects a business against fire damage. Usually a *rider* (an extra agreement with a higher premium) is attached to protect the business against other natural disasters such as wind damage, earthquakes, and hailstorms. Separate coverage can be bought for protection against plant explosions, electric power loss, and so on.

Most policies include a *coinsurance clause*. This typically states that the insurance company will pay for losses only up to the proportion that the insurance purchased is 80 percent of the market value of the property being

Lloyd's of London: The "Simultaneous-Sinking" Problem

The most famous insurance dealer in the world, Lloyd's of London, got its start back in 1688 with one bright idea: insure ocean-going ships. The reasoning was that the premiums paid by all the insured ships would more than pay for losses on the few that sank. A key assumption was that there was practically no chance that many ships would sink at the same time.

It was the "simultaneous-sinking-ship" assumption that got Lloyd's into trouble in 1979 and 1980. Among the 279 ships that sank in 1979, some caused Lloyd's special concern—such as a $45 million tanker that went down with a $40 million cargo of naphthalene. In January 1980 another tanker sank off Africa, and its owner filed a $56.3 million claim for the oil on board. Lloyd's investigators now believe the ship was intentionally sunk *after* its oil was unloaded in South Africa.[3]

Lloyd's, which has a reputation for insuring almost anything (for the right price), paid out millions for an insured communications satellite that got lost in space in 1980 and was also liable for $75 million when the United States pulled out of the 1980 Moscow summer Olympics.

But Lloyd's biggest problem is now computers. Starting in 1974, it wrote insurance to protect computer-leasing companies against the possibility that customers would cancel before their seven-year leases ran out. Lloyd's was betting against the chance that a breakthrough in computer technology would make many computer users cancel their leases at the same time—the "simultaneous-sinking-ship" assumption. Normally, it's a pretty safe bet. But in 1977 and again in 1979, IBM announced new lines of computers that caused a flood of lease cancellations. And by 1980, almost $600 million in computer leasing claims was filed against Lloyd's.

Large claims are nothing new to Lloyd's, which paid $130 million in losses for Hurricane Betsy in 1965. But insurance experts say the fiasco is especially astounding, because Lloyd's broke its own three-century tradition: insuring against the possibility of simultaneously occurring losses rather than against a one-time natural disaster.

Your Next Job
Positions in Insurance

Underwriting and Actuarial Careers

Insurance companies employ **underwriters** to evaluate the risk of extending insurance coverage to new clients. They draw up preliminary insurance contracts and suggest appropriate premium rates. This requires sound judgment and mathematical aptitude. Applicants generally have a bachelor's degree in liberal arts or business administration. Qualified underwriters may advance to **chief underwriter** or to **underwriting manager.** Yearly salaries for underwriters range from $14,000 to $23,000. (Additional information: Insurance Information Institute; 110 William Street; New York, New York 10038.)

Actuaries compile and analyze statistics to determine profitable, yet competitive, insurance premium rates. They assemble actuarial tables on the expected losses for all types of insurance risks. The minimum requirement is a bachelor's degree in mathematics, statistics, or a related field. Professional actuaries must also have passed standardized examinations. (These may take up to ten years to complete, but many actuaries have passed one or two of them before college graduation.) Advancement potential is good; many actuaries move into administrative and supervisory positions. Annual salaries range from $11,000 to $47,000. Employment opportunities are expected to expand rapidly with the growing demand for insurance coverage. (Additional information: Society of Actuaries; 208 South LaSalle Street; Chicago, Illinois 60604.)

Careers in Sales and Claims

Businesses and individuals buy insurance from **insurance agents** and **brokers.** They develop programs to fit clients' needs, help with claim settlements, and interview insurance prospects. Good communications skills are essential. Brokers are not employed by a particular company, whereas agents usually represent one or more insurance companies. A bachelor's degree in liberal arts or business administration is helpful, but most employers also recruit high-school and community-college graduates who have had some practical experience. Licensing exam preparation is generally provided on-the-job. A competent agent can be promoted to sales manager or another top-management position. Annual salaries range from $12,000 to over $30,000. Some highly successful agents and brokers earn more than $100,000 a year. The increase in insurance sales is expected to create a moderately expanding job market. (Additional information: American Council of Life Insurance; 1850 K Street N.W.; Washington, D.C. 20006.)

Insurance companies employ **claim adjusters** to investigate and negotiate claims filed by policyholders. They assess losses and authorize payments to policyholders. Sound judgment is necessary. A bachelor's degree in business administration is becoming increasingly important, although many claim adjusters are hired on the basis of specialized experience and receive on-the-job training. (For example, automobile repairers are often recruited as auto adjusters.) Most states require adjusters to pass an examination before obtaining a license. Experienced adjusters can be promoted to supervisory or to managerial positions. Annual incomes average from $14,700 to $20,000. The demand for adjusters is expected to continue to grow moderately as the number of insurance claims continues to increase. (Additional information: National Association of Public Adjusters; 1613 Munsey Building; Baltimore, Maryland 21202.)

Claim examiners verify claim applications, authorize payments for insured losses, and supervise the adjusters. A bachelor's degree in business administration is a definite advantage, although many insurance companies hire and train high-school and community-college graduates who have communications and clerical skills. Annual salaries average from $13,300 to $17,300. Jobs are expected to expand moderately. (Additional information: Insurance Information Institute; 110 William Street; New York, New York 10038.)

insured. If that explanation sounds like the insurance jargon we're trying to avoid, an example should help. Say a business owner buys $60,000 of insurance on a $100,000 building. He is insured for only three-fourths of any losses to the building ($60,000 ÷ $80,000 = ¾), since 80 percent of $100,000 is $80,000. Therefore, if a fire causes $40,000 in damages to the building, the insurance company will pay for only $30,000 of the losses (¾ × $40,000). Through coinsurance clauses, full insurance protection up to the face value of an insurance policy can be obtained only by insuring property at 80 percent or more of its market value.

Automobile Insurance

Comprehensive fire and theft coverage insures vehicles up to their current market value against fire, theft, and damage from flying objects. *Collision coverage* reimburses the owner of a vehicle for damage incurred from colliding with another vehicle or a stationary object. Nondeductible collision coverage reimburses the entire loss. Deductible collision coverage, cheaper and more common, requires the owner to pay the first part of any loss (usually $50 to $200). *Liability coverage* protects a vehicle owner against damage inflicted on other persons or property. For example, a $50,000/$100,000/$20,000 liability coverage policy provides a maximum protection of $50,000 if one person is hurt in an accident, $100,000 if more than one person is hurt, and $20,000 for property damage. Payments are made to the people injured. Many states now require motorists to carry a specified minimum amount of insurance to cover damage caused to others. This is especially important, since the driver or owner of a vehicle responsible for an accident could otherwise be sued for millions of dollars by the victims. For these and other kinds of car insurance, businesses and consumers should "shop around." Safe driving records, higher deductibles, "good student" discounts, or a different company can mean much lower rates.

No-fault automobile insurance, which is becoming increasingly popular, means that everyone collects from his or her own insurance company, no matter whose fault the accident is. Payments are made according to a schedule that depends on the seriousness of the injury and is specified in advance by state law. The idea is to lower premiums by avoiding long and costly lawsuits.

Marine Insurance

Ocean marine insurance covers the shipment of goods across the seas. *Inland marine insurance* covers land shipments by truck, train, barge, or airplane.

Worker Compensation

Worker compensation protects employees from job-related accidents or ill health. Benefits are established by state law and vary from state to state. The premiums are normally paid by collecting a percentage of an employer's payroll. This percentage depends on the level of benefits required in the firm's state and on the jobs covered (clerical workers cost less to insure than coal miners, for example). It also depends on the employer's *experience rating*—its past record of accidents. So an unsafe plant costs the employer more money.

Liability Insurance

Public liability insurance protects businesses and people from damages resulting from negligence. These "umbrella policies" can cover everything but vehicles. A customer may slip on a freshly waxed floor, another may be hurt by an unsafe toy. These are potential lawsuits to insure against.

Burglary Insurance

Business and people can safeguard themselves from most or all of the cost of illegal property seizure by buying *burglary insurance*. This insures against losses for break-ins that leave visible marks of entry. Unfortunately, it does not cover employee theft and shoplifting, which account for billions of dollars of loss annually.

Fidelity and Surety Bonds

Fidelity bonds, issued by bonding companies, protect a business against employee dishonesty and theft—whether a department-store employee steals a

Jargoned to Death?

In one Woody Allen movie, the prisoner is sentenced to spend thirty days in solitary confinement with a life insurance salesman. As Allen trudges into the subterranean pit, the dapper salesman is rattling off phrases like "convertible," "renewable," "decreasing term," "endowment," and "graduated variable life plans."

Insurance jargon has become so thick—because of legal necessities and government regulations—that consumer groups have pushed some insurance companies to adopt "easy-to-understand" policies. Still other companies have kept the policies in their own lingo but issue pamphlets explaining them in ordinary language. That way, lawyers and insurance professionals can keep their careful language, and the rest of us can tell whether we've just insured our car or our house.

suit or a bank clerk embezzles funds. The amount of the policy is based on the value of the money or goods to which the employees have access. *Surety bonds* protect a business against nonperformance of a contract. For example, a business might purchase a surety bond on the construction of a new building. If the contractor fails to finish it on time, the bonding company must pay.

Business Interruption Insurance

Business interruption insurance protects a firm against disruption from natural disasters, like fires and storms, and from strikes. The amount of coverage is based on the profits that would have been made without the interruption.

Business Life Insurance

Business life insurance (also called key executive insurance) protects a firm against the loss of an executive vital to its operations. Benefits are paid to the business. This type of insurance is also widely used in sole proprietorships to protect the heirs from being forced to sell the firm in order to pay estate taxes. Partnerships often purchase key executive insurance that provides benefits to the deceased partner's heirs. By agreement, if one partner dies, the ownership of the business usually reverts to the remaining partners.

Employee Insurance

Businesses also buy insurance for their employees as part of a key benefits program or because of government requirements. They often buy health or accident coverage as *employee insurance* on a group basis, under a single *master agreement* or a general insurance policy. This *group insurance* is cheaper than buying individual policies. Some insurance and retirement programs are contributory, with employer and employee sharing premium expenses. Others are paid completely by the employer.

Health and Accident Insurance

Health and accident insurance protects people against the high medical costs of illness and accidents. It generally covers all or part of hospital, medical, and surgical expenses. The most popular plans are those offered by Blue Cross, for hospital benefits, and Blue Shield, for doctor fees. Both are private, nonprofit organizations. In addition, some companies have their own medical insurance programs or enroll their employees in a Health Maintenance Organization (HMO).

Health and accident insurance usually includes sick pay (wages for up to twenty-six weeks), disability pay (a percentage of wages as long as an employee is physically unable to work), and benefits for dismemberment (loss of an eye, hand, or foot) or death. Many companies also offer employees *major medical insurance* to cover the costs (above a stated minimum) of extended illnesses.

Life Insurance

Life insurance provides financial protection for heirs upon the death of a family member. Life insurance is the most widely used form of insurance, with some $2.5 trillion of it in force today. Premiums are based on the age, sex, and health of the insured, and the type of insurance purchased. Since older and sicker people have a shorter life expectancy (refer back to Figure 13–4), their premiums are higher.

Pizazz and the Solid Basics of Insurance

Gary Fink has pizazz. This Minneapolis life insurance salesman does more than $20 million worth of business each year, earning for himself more than $150,000. Out of Prudential Insurance Company of America's more than 25,000 agents, he has ranked first for three years out of ten, according to a story in *The Wall Street Journal*.[4]

He does it with a zany style, in a T-shirt or pink safari suit. All of it decorates an impressive work ethic. Fink was once introduced as "the original low-profile guy" to the Million Dollar Roundtable. He was to speak to this exclusive group of agents, each of whom had sold at least $1.25 million in life insurance in a year. Mr. Fink appeared on the platform accompanied by a crescendo of the "Theme from 2001." On the screen behind him, his face slowly rose over the horizon.

After the speech, the audience gave him a standing, five-minute ovation for his style and his message.

Fink typically gets a client's attention with a gimmick: a mildly offensive birthday card or an ad that shows his picture over the caption, "Would you let this man into your home?" His office is decorated with rock-music posters and garish furniture.

He believes that such antics create trust in customers who are put off by the entire idea of insurance. Once trust is established, he relies on his four ingredients for success: (1) gain an unassailable reputation for being open to new ideas, (2) develop a team of specialists to use according to a client's needs, (3) work hard, and (4) always add pizazz.

There are two main kinds of life insurance: *term* and *whole-life*. Term insurance is cheaper but offers protection only if the insured dies within a certain period of time, or term. Whole-life policies, more expensive, offer some protection for the holder's entire life. They also include a kind of savings plan. The buyer can cancel his insurance at any time and receive the "cash value" that has thus far accumulated. He can also borrow against the whole-life policy. Term insurance does not include the savings-plan element present in whole-life.

Consumer advocates generally recommend term insurance for young people just starting families. Whole-life insurance policies are often oversold by agents. For some whole-life policies, you may actually need to live ninety-five years to get all your money back. And you could take the extra money required to buy whole-life and invest it yourself for greater earnings. Whole-life is preferable only if you are in a high tax bracket or have extreme trouble saving money.

Many businesses now offer customers a form of life insurance called the *credit-life policy*. Under it, decreasing term insurance is available for credit customers. For example, bankers often require homeowners with mortgages to purchase it. As monthly mortgage payments are made, the face value of the insurance decreases. But if the homeowner dies before the mortgage is completely paid, the insurance company pays the balance and the mortgage is canceled.

Pension Plans

Technically, pension plans are not insurance, but many businesses elect to sponsor them for their employees' retirement. In *trustee pension plans,* a bank or a trust company administers the pension payments. Labor unions also administer pension plans. And in *profit-sharing pension plans,* a percentage of the firm's profits is placed in the retirement fund each year, and employees may also contribute. Federal guidelines for the administration of private pension plans are designed to protect employees' rights.

Social Security

The *social security system* provides disability income to employees unable to work; health and old-age income for retired persons; and a variety of other benefits. Social security funds are administered by the federal government, with both employers and employees contributing to the program.

Chapter Review & Applications

Key Points to Remember

1. Asset management includes working capital management and capital budgeting.

2. Working capital—assets normally converted into cash within a year—consists of cash and near cash, accounts receivable, and inventories.

3. The central goals of working capital management are to invest the minimum amount consistent with prudent levels of risk, to promptly collect money owed the business, and to place as much cash or near cash as possible into interest-bearing securities.

4. Capital budgeting involves committing funds—for more than one year—to major projects such as building new plants, expanding existing capacity, purchasing new machines, or introducing new products.

5. Capital-budgeting decisions determine the amount of return a business expects from its investments.

6. Return on investment (ROI), expressed as a percentage figure, is a measure of how well funds are used. The higher the ROI, the better.

7. To obtain financial leverage, a business borrows funds. This allows a firm to undertake more projects than its current available capital allows. Favorable financial leverage—when the ROI exceeds the cost of borrowing—increases earnings. Unfavorable financial leverage decreases earnings.

8. Business investments normally include an element of risk, since uncontrollable economic and market factors may make initial ROI estimates inaccurate.

9. Successful risk management usually consists of sound management, the reduction or avoidance of physical hazards, self-insurance, hedging, and insurance.

10. Major forms of business insurance include fire, automobile, marine, worker compensation, liability, burglary, fidelity and surety, business interruption, and business life insurance. A firm also purchases insurance for its employees.

Questions for Discussion

1. Referring to Figure 13-2, would you, as credit manager of a furniture manufacturer, extend $30,000 credit to Beaumont and Hunt, Inc. to purchase a new line of living room furniture?

2. After taxes, the net profit of a large grocery-store chain is 1 cent on each dollar of sales. Therefore, the supermarket chain has a low return on investment. Do you agree with this statement? Why or why not?

3. You have $1,000 in savings and can borrow $9,000 at 7 percent interest. You are trying to decide whether to invest in a vacant lot that costs $10,000, and that is expected to increase in value by 10 percent a year, or to buy fifty shares of a nonmarginable common stock (a stock on which money cannot be borrowed), at $20 a share, that you expect to increase in value by 15 percent a year. Which purchase will earn you a greater return on investment?

Short Cases

1. Suppose you are the risk manager in a firm with assets of $1.5 million and no debts. Your firm has six plants, each worth $150,000 if sold on the open market. Because inflammable chemicals are used in your plants, you estimate that there is a 5 percent chance of a plant fire and that the entire plant will be destroyed if a fire occurs. The insurance company sets a premium at $10,000 per plant. What are the advantages of buying this insurance? Of self-insuring? What type of insurance would you choose? Why?

2. Suppose that you purchased only $100,000 of insurance on each plant in Problem 1 and that the policy included the standard coinsurance clause. How much insurance would you collect if fire completely destroyed one of your plants? If the fire caused only $10,000 of actual damage?

A Critical
Business Decision

—made by Frank Borman
of Eastern Airlines

The Situation

Frank Borman, called "The Colonel" from his days
as an astronaut, is the boss at Eastern Airlines.
Rules at the Miami headquarters are strict: dress
(white shirts and dark suits) is formal, loyalty is
mandatory, and there is no drinking at lunch. In
1975, when Borman took over as president, Eastern
was a bit sloppy financially. The debt to equity ratio
was 3.0 with $100 million in debt due at the end of
the year. Oil prices had recently tripled and morale
among the 35,000 employees was low.[5]

Borman took action. He sold all of Eastern's
fuel-inefficient 727-QCs to Federal Express and returned nine DC-9-10s (also for reasons of fuel economy) to McDonnell Douglas. As replacements, he
ordered twenty-three fuel-efficient, European-built
airbuses and twenty-one Boeing 757s. Financiers
Felix G. Rohatyn and Laurance S. Rockefeller
agreed to serve on the Board of Directors. Borman
also showed political savvy. When an Eastern stew-
ardess publicly labeled Elizabeth Bailey, a member
of the Civil Aeronautics Board (the government body
that regulates the airlines) a "witch" for insisting on
a nonsmoking section, Borman personally called
Bailey to apologize.

Results were soon favorable. Eastern became
profitable. By 1979 it had $1.1 billion in debt, but its
equity capital amounted to $477 million. Although
an improvement, the 2.5 debt-equity ratio was still
high, even by airline standards. "The situation is
much improved since 1975," Borman said. "I would
never have dreamed that we would make such progress."

The Decision

But Eastern is not out of the woods yet. In 1979,
OPEC forced the price of aviation fuel to more than
double. And actions by the CAB to deregulate the
airlines made it difficult to raise passenger fares.
Deregulation also means that Eastern faces new
competition on its most profitable routes, East Coast
cities to Miami.

Questions

1. In the face of higher fuel costs, lower fares, and
   probably less passenger traffic, is Eastern in an
   especially vulnerable position as a result of its
   2.5 debt-to-equity ratio? Why or why not?

2. If you were Frank Borman, how would you deal
   with lower profit margins and less passenger
   traffic?

Understanding Financial Markets

In this chapter you will learn . . .

- *how the U.S. financial system is organized.*
- *how banks are regulated to protect depositors.*
- *about the Federal Reserve System and how and why it controls the amount of money in circulation.*
- *how to buy and sell stocks and bonds.*

14

he business looked impressive. Its offices were on Park Avenue in New York City, on Wilshire Boulevard in Los Angeles, and elsewhere around the country. Its investors included the president of First National City Bank, the former chairman of the board of directors of both General Electric and Pepsico, the presidents of Time Incorporated and American Express, and such well-known entertainers as Alan Alda, Mia Farrow, Liza Minelli, Barbra Streisand, Barbara Walters, and Andy Williams. Some 2,000 of the elite in entertainment, sports, and business had invested more than $100 million in it.

The firm: the Home-Stake Production Company. The promoter: a smooth-talking Oklahoma lawyer named Robert S. Trippet. The scheme was simple: Home-Stake would use the investors' money to drill oil wells. If the oil wells were successful, the company would pay fabulous investment returns. If they were unsuccessful, investors could deduct their losses on their federal income tax returns.

But there was no "black gold" at the end of this rainbow. Instead of using the invested funds to drill for oil, Trippet and his colleagues paid themselves handsome salaries. They also sold their personal property investments to Home-Stake at inflated prices. Very little money was returned to the original investors, just enough to make them think the company was making progress. And the money that was returned came from new investors attracted by Home-Stake's glamour.

Home-Stake's marketing strategy was extraordinarily effective. Trippet would approach a potential investor, casually dropping the names of celebrity investors. As one rueful client observed, "When investors like the top executives at First National City Bank have a piece of the action, there is a tremendous psychological effect." To make the hoax even more convincing, Home-Stake "drilled" five "oil wells" on a California vegetable farm. Actually, they were the farmer's irrigation pipes, painted orange and coded with oil-field markings. Potential investors were impressed by the apparent "oil-field" in full operation.

The Home-Stake fraud, later exposed,[1] stands as a warning to anyone still dreaming of "easy money." Money rarely comes easily, but it is not difficult to see why so many people wish it did. For individuals and businesses alike, money is an essential ingredient of day-to-day life within our society. Where it comes from, how it is channeled through banks and other financial institutions, and how it is bought, sold, and regulated are the subjects of this chapter.

FINANCIAL INSTITUTIONS

Financial institutions and security markets make up the U.S. financial system. **Financial institutions** are organizations that receive and lend money. They include commercial banks, the Federal Reserve System, investment banks, savings banks, savings and loan associations, credit unions, and insurance companies. Each is discussed in the sections that follow.

Commercial Banks

Commercial banks accept deposits, make loans, and traditionally differ from savings and loan associations in that they handle checks. They issue more than one-third of the credit in this country, with the ten largest holding more than $450 million in assets (see Figure 14–1).

FIGURE 14–1
The Ten Largest Commercial Bank Holding Companies
(Assets as of December 31, 1979).

RANK	BANK	ASSETS (Millions of Dollars)
1	BankAmerica Corp. (San Francisco)	$108.4
2	Citicorp (New York City)	106.4
3	Chase Manhattan Corp. (New York City)	64.7
4	Manufacturers Hanover Corp. (New York City)	47.7
5	J.P. Morgan & Co. (New York City)	43.5
6	Chemical New York Corp. (New York City)	39.4
7	Continental Illinois Corp. (Chicago)	35.8
8	Bankers Trust New York Corp. (New York City)	31.0
9	First Chicago Corp. (Chicago)	30.2
10	Western Bancorp. (Los Angeles)	29.7

Source: ''The 50 Largest Commercial Banking Companies (July 14, 1980). Reprinted by permission from *Fortune* magazine, © 1980, Time Inc.

Although commercial banks are private businesses run for their owners' profit, they are regulated by state and federal laws to protect depositors:

1. *Charters.* To organize a bank, one must secure a **bank charter,** a legal document issued by the federal or a state government. To obtain the charter, potential bank owners must prove that their community needs and can support a bank, and that they can contribute sufficient capital and managerial talent to make the bank financially sound.
2. *Examinations. National banks* are examined by officials from the U.S. Department of the Treasury. *State banks* are examined by employees of state regulatory agencies. Examiners check the banks' accounting records and make sure the banks have adequate capital on hand.
3. *Deposit insurance.* **The Federal Deposit Insurance Corporation (FDIC)** was established in 1933 to protect depositors against bank failure. Each account in an FDIC-member bank is insured for up to $40,000. For this service, the bank pays an annual fee equal to 1/12 of 1 percent of its total deposits.

Among the many valuable services that banks offer are **checking accounts.** These provide a convenient and safe way to exchange money for goods or services, and they afford the user a permanent record of his or her transactions. To open a business checking account, the firm's board of directors (or owners) must authorize it and specify who can write company checks or borrow money from the account.

In addition to checks written against checking accounts, there are also *cashier's checks* and *certified checks.* A **cashier's check** is drawn on the bank itself, so default occurs only if the bank fails. They are widely used in commercial transactions (see Figure 14–2).

A **certified check** (shown in Figure 14–3) is an ordinary check, except that it is guaranteed (or certified) by the bank, indicating to the recipient that the payer's account contains sufficient funds to cover the check.

Other bank services are *savings accounts, time certificates,* and *negotiable certificates of deposit.* **Savings accounts** pay better interest than checking accounts but they cannot be used to cover checks, unless the bank offers special transfer provisions. **Time certificates** are savings that pay more interest than savings accounts, with the condition that funds cannot be transferred or withdrawn before the end of a specified time period without penalty. **Negotiable certificates of deposit,** called CDs, are issued for commercial bank deposits of large amounts ($100,000 or more). These certificates typically are

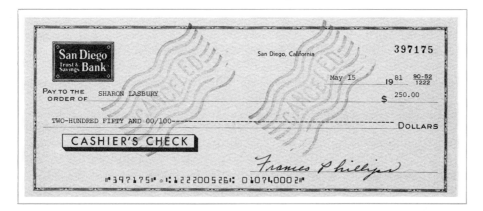

FIGURE 14-2
A Cashier's Check.

bought by large organizations that want to earn high interest on their idle short-term funds. They may be resold to third parties when the firm needs cash again, since whoever holds the certificate receives the interest.

Commercial banks also make *commercial loans* and *installment loans*. **Commercial loans** are made to large and small businesses. And **installment loans** are extended to consumers for expensive items, such as cars and home improvements. Commercial banks loan money to the construction industry by purchasing mortgages and other financial instruments issued by builders and

FIGURE 14-3
A Certified Check.

property owners. And they invest funds, too, typically in U.S. government securities and in high-quality municipal bonds.

Other commercial bank services include safety-deposit boxes, traveler's checks, credit cards, financial services to businesses, foreign currency, bond buying for consumers and businesses, trust services for estates and preferred stockholders, and pension plans. And many banks now offer automated teller machines for the convenience of their customers.

From these services, banks earn profits in two ways. They must collect more from interest on loans and investments than they pay out in interest to depositors and CD holders. They must also charge enough interest on loans to make up for some losses on bad loans and to pay for operating expenses. Banks also earn profits by charging fees for their services, from safety-deposit box rentals on up.

The Federal Reserve System

The **Federal Reserve System,** an agency of the U.S. government responsible for regulating the amount of money in circulation, can dramatically affect the nation's economy. If banks have a lot of money to lend, consumers can borrow easily and have more to spend. If banks have only a little money to lend, consumers have less to spend, there is a decreased demand for goods and services, and the economy tends to slow down.

The "Fed" is run by a seven-member Board of Governors, appointed by the president with the advice and consent of the Senate. The Board supervises the more than 5,600 commercial bank members of the System, which is organized into twelve districts, each with a headquarters and some also with branch banks (see Figure 14–4).

How the Federal Reserve System Molds the Money Supply

The Fed has three tools with which to influence the amount of money commercial banks have available to lend their customers and thus to affect the economy:

1. *Changing reserve requirements.* A bank's **reserves** represent the cash or cashlike funds it has on hand to cover possible withdrawals. It is the Federal Reserve System that decides the amount of reserves banks are required to have. Thus it can tighten the money supply by requiring a larger reserve, which means there is that much less money for loans, or it can increase the money supply by requiring a smaller reserve. The

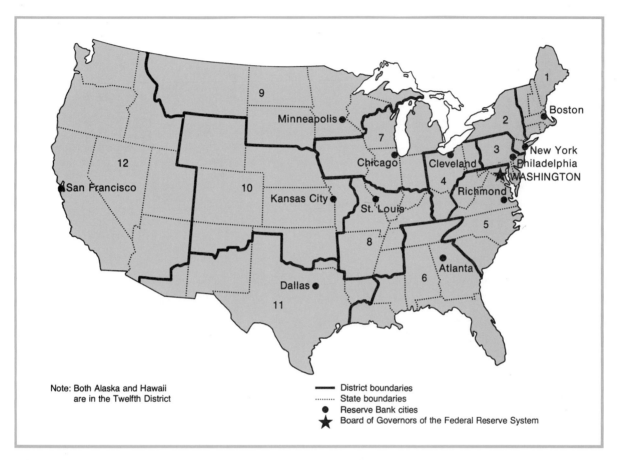

FIGURE 14-4
The Federal Reserve System.

Fed changes these requirements periodically in an effort to help the economy. Thus, in a period of inflation, reserve requirements will be increased in order to discourage more spending. The process is reversed during a recession.

2. *Regulating the discount rate.* Banks may get cash by selling their assets (U.S. government bonds or other high-quality instruments) to the Federal Reserve Bank. The Fed charges banks a **discount rate** similar to interest for this service. By raising or lowering the discount

Your Next Job
Positions in Banking, Real Estate, and Financial Securities

Careers in Banking

Banks are managed by bank officers, who may specialize in a variety of areas. **Tellers** process bank transactions and may handle a particular service, such as savings, foreign exchange, or securities; **trust officers** evaluate investment risks; **operations officers** coordinate work schedules and keep the organization efficient; **loan officers** evaluate loan applicants; and, in larger banks, **investment officers** oversee the bank's own investments in treasury securities, commercial paper, corporate bonds, and the like.

Salaries range from $7,000 for tellers, to $11,000 for management trainees (with an undergraduate degree), to $16,200 for MBAs, to several times this for high-level bank officers.

Careers in Real Estate

Property owners who wish to sell or rent their homes, other buildings, or land contact **real-estate agents** or **brokers.** They show property to potential buyers and make the necessary financial arrangements for property purchases. Brokers are self-employed and hire salesworkers to help them sell real estate, compile listings, and manage rental properties. Employers usually hire high-school and college graduates who have some knowledge of selling, psychology, and finance. On-the-job training programs are often provided. A bachelor's or associate degree in real estate is a competitive advantage. Both brokers and agents must pass a comprehensive, standardized examination to obtain a license. Qualified salesworkers may advance to the position of sales manager or general manager. Commissions represent the largest part of annual salaries; full-time agents average $15,000, brokers $30,000, and experienced agents and brokers can earn $40,000 a year and up. (*Additional information:* National Association of Realtors, 430 N. Michigan Avenue, Chicago, Illinois 60611.)

Careers in Financial Securities

Securities salesworkers, often called **stockbrokers** or **registered representatives,** represent investors who buy or sell stocks, bonds, or mutual-fund shares. They relay buy or sell decisions to security exchanges and provide clients with investment advice. They are employed by brokerage firms, investment banks, insurance companies, and mutual funds. Successful job applicants are generally high-school or college graduates who are motivated, outgoing, personable, and honest. Large firms often require college degrees in business administration or finance. Short-term, on-the-job training programs prepare them for the standardized examination they must pass to obtain licenses. Salesworkers may advance to the position of office manager. Annual salaries are primarily based on commissions. Experienced salesworkers average $29,000 a year; some earn more than $50,000. Job opportunities are expected to expand moderately. (*Additional information:* contact the personnel department of a local securities firm.)

Security analysts are employed by brokerage firms, banks, mutual funds, or pension funds to evaluate individual common stocks. A bachelor's degree in business administration, with specialization in finance or economics, is usually required. An MBA or a master's degree in economics is desirable. Security analysts must have high-level analytical abilities and be able to present their recommendations understandably. Annual salaries range from $15,000 to $25,000 and up. Job opportunities are expected to increase moderately. (*Additional information:* Contact the personnel department of a local securities firm.)

rate, extra cash is made less or more expensive. Banks then pass on these savings or expenditures to their customers in the form of lower or higher interest rates on loans and savings accounts.

3. *Changing open-market operations.* The Fed can sell or buy government bonds under the direction of its Open Market Operations Committee. When the System *sells* government bonds directly to banks, the banks have less money to lend their customers. The reverse is true when the Federal Reserve System *purchases* bonds.

Changes in reserve requirements, in the discount rate, and in open-market operations are known collectively as **monetary policy.** The Fed's monetary policy for any given time is established by government economists. Their objective in establishing policy is to keep economic growth high and inflation and unemployment at a minimum. So when inflation is high, the Fed's monetary policy is "tight" (less money and credit in circulation); and when economic growth is slow, an "easy" monetary policy is established (that is, more money and credit are made available).

How Do Banks Feel about the Federal Reserve System?

Although the Fed stabilizes the money supply and tries to mold the economy to benefit us all, some individual banks are less than enchanted with their membership in the Federal Reserve System. Membership is voluntary, and, in the past, banker dropouts threatened to limit the effectiveness of the Fed's monetary policy. But the 1980 Financial Institutions Deregulation and Monetary Control Act reversed this trend by increasing the powers of the Federal Reserve System. Major provisions of the Act include:

1. Permitting financial institutions, like savings and loan associations and credit unions, to offer checking accounts.
2. Requiring all major financial institutions that offer checking account-like services to keep reserves with the Fed in order to ensure the Fed's control of the money supply. Financial institutions are not required to become formal members of the Federal Reserve System.
3. Directing the Federal Reserve System to "unbundle" by pricing its services separately so financial institutions can compare Fed services with those provided by the private sector.

4. Gradually eliminating government ceilings on the interest rates that financial institutions can pay on checking and savings accounts.

The provisions of this new law promise to revolutionize business practices among financial institutions.

Blipping out on Wall Street

The tall glass and concrete building at 111 Wall Street is a money factory. Inside, forty-foot-long sorting machines roar and hiss. Robot forklift trucks ferry money from station to storage bin and back again.

Each day the factory handles three million checks worth $20 billion. Its 6,500 employees debit and credit accounts and send checks to clearing houses and to endorsers. The factory is part of the First National City Bank System, and check processing costs are low because of its efficient operations.

Life in the Branch Channel of Checking Operations is the most hectic. Each evening, bags containing one and a half million checks from First National's 215 branch offices in the New York City area are dumped into the sorting room. On the right-hand bottom corner of each check, an encoder uses magnetic ink to translate the check amount into a series of squarish numbers that can be read by computers. Encoders are paid on an incentive basis. Their goal: to encode as many checks as possible. To date the record is 2,400 checks per hour. "You really don't see a check," an encoder who earns about $18,000 a year observes. "You sense it. It doesn't really go through your brain. Your fingers feel it."

The encoded checks are then placed on trays and fed, at forty miles per hour, into a climate-controlled computer. Each check is recorded on tape, photographed on microfilm, and stamped with a code number by the computer. Rejects are sent to the "reject repair" room for recoding. Each check must be accurately sorted and marked for delivery to the proper bank before it can be sent to the Federal Reserve Bank. They must work fast: every $1-million worth of checks that does not make the 11:30 P.M. delivery truck to the Fed costs First National City $167 in lost interest.

Slang and computer talk are rampant. A "rock" is a tough problem; and to "blip" is to fall short of one's assigned goal.

Blipping is serious. Each job has a specific set of duties, an annual target developed by management, and a required improvement factor. No excuses or rationalizations are accepted. "You sort of expect to meet the forecast or else," one young manager commented ruefully to *The Wall Street Journal*.[2]

Investment Banks

Investment banks are financial "middlemen." They market securities—bonds, notes, and preferred and common stocks—for businesses. For these marketing services, investment bankers charge a commission, perhaps 10 percent of the stated price of a new common stock issue, for example. Many commercial banks and brokerage firms have investment-banking sections. Investment bankers must be thoroughly grounded in economics and must relish large and complicated financial transactions.

Savings Banks

Savings banks, located mostly in the northeastern part of the United States, hold savings accounts for depositors but do not provide checking accounts. They make investments in bonds, mortgages, real estate, and, where law permits, in corporate stock. They earn a profit if investment income exceeds their operating expenses and the interest paid to depositors.

Savings and Loan Associations

With combined assets in 1980 of more than $500 billion, savings and loan associations are America's second most important financial institution (after commercial banks). Because of their aggressive advertising and promotional activities and their generally favorable suburban locations, the assets of the approximately 4,800 savings and loan associations have grown more rapidly than those of commercial banks.

"S and L's" invest more than 95 percent of their deposits in home mortgages, especially single-family dwellings (banks tend to invest in commercial real estate). Because of deregulation, S and L's are expected to make more non-real-estate loans in the future.

Credit Unions

A credit union is a lending institution formed and owned by a group of people, usually employees in a large company. There are about 23,000 in the country, with assets in 1980 of about $53 billion. The "shareholders' " ownership in the union is in proportion to the savings they deposit. Credit unions make small loans at interest rates lower than banks. They also offer share drafts, which work much like checks.

Insurance Companies

Insurance companies, with combined assets of more than $500 billion in 1980, are our third most important type of financial institution. They receive premiums from policyholders and invest them to earn interest until policyholders' claims are paid. Businesses frequently sell most or all of a new debt or equity issue to large insurance firms that invest policyholders' premiums in them. This may be done directly or through an investment banker.

FIGURE 14-5
Other Financial Intermediaries.

FINANCIAL INSTITUTION	HOW IT WORKS
Commercial-paper dealers	Commercial-paper dealers buy *commercial paper*—the unsecured notes of businesses with good credit ratings—and, after adding a fixed fee, resell it.
Factors	Factoring companies purchase a firm's accounts receivable. The *factor* typically makes a cash payment which is less than the value of the accounts receivable and then tries to collect the amount due.
Finance companies	*Consumer finance companies,* such as Household Finance, make small loans to consumers. *Sales finance companies,* such as General Motors Acceptance Corporation, loan consumers money to purchase automobiles.
Mutual funds	*Mutual funds* take the combined savings of many investors and buy bonds, equities, and other assets. Returns, from which a fee is often deducted, are paid directly to investors or are credited to their mutual-fund accounts for future use.
Pension funds	*Pension* or *retirement funds,* often administered by a bank or a business firm, are invested in bonds, stocks, and other financial assets to provide additional income upon retirement.

The Role of Financial Intermediaries

Commercial banks, investment banks, savings banks, savings and loan associations, credit unions, insurance companies, and the other financial institutions listed in Figure 14–5 are often described as **financial intermediaries.** They earn profits by placing themselves between savers and borrowers. They protect investor deposits, hold depositors' money in convenient form, and spare savers the detailed and complex task of analyzing investment opportunities. For an example of a relatively new vehicle for convenient investment, see the box "Money Market Mutual Funds: May We Help You?"

SECURITY MARKETS

Financial institutions and individuals buy stocks and bonds in **security markets**—central areas, such as the New York Stock Exchange and the New York Bond Exchange, where financial assets are traded.

Money Market Mutual Funds: May We Help You?

Money market mutual funds are one way to invest in good-paying securities for a short time without having to buy the whole issue yourself (for $10,000 to $100,000).

Mutual funds, in general, help relatively small investors share good financial opportunities. This particular kind of mutual fund invests only in "short-term debt securities," offerings that pay off in less than a year and are called "near money." The securities may be U.S. government bonds, negotiable certificates of deposit, or commercial paper.

These funds are almost as safe and convenient as a savings account, though the money is not insured by the government. You put in $1,000 or more, the fund manages your money in a pool with the other investors, and sends you a monthly statement. You may withdraw your money at any time. When the prime interest rate is high, so is the popularity of these funds, because the interest they pay is sometimes far higher than that available to bank or savings-and-loan depositors.

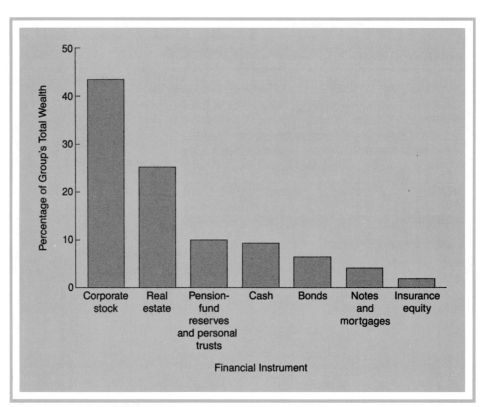

Source: Internal Revenue Service.

FIGURE 14-6
Where the
Wealthiest
1 Percent Invests.

Managers watch their own company's stock prices to monitor stockholders' and the general investment community's confidence in their firm. A rapid fall in the price of a company's stock is a warning of future discontent among stockholders and potential trouble for management. The purchase of a large percentage of a company's stock by a small number of people may indicate a company "takeover." Since new owners often replace existing managers with their own people, most companies carefully watch for changes in their stockholder lists. Also, a firm's ability to attract new employees, issue new stocks or bonds, and raise money from other sources is affected by its stock price.

Security markets are also vitally important to this country's nearly 35 million individual stockholders. Wealthy Americans are especially attracted to stock and bond investments, as can be seen in Figure 14-6. Contrary to popular belief, the market is a good hedge against inflation, providing in the late 1970s a return considerably greater than the rate of inflation.

Stock and Bond Markets

The major security markets in the United States—the New York Stock Exchange, the American Stock Exchange, and over-the-counter markets—are giant auction floors where only members may participate. Everyone else must work through a member, paying a commission for the privilege. The New York Stock Exchange, for example, has about 1,400 members who have been found financially sound and who have bought "seats." The price of a seat rises and falls with the value of stock in general, because members can earn bigger commissions when stock prices are high. In 1929, before the crash, a seat cost $635,000; in 1978, the price was down to between $50,000 and $75,000. In other years, it has varied between these amounts. Trading on a security exchange is like an auction in which members, as agents for investors, bargain over the prices of securities. An exchange member is obligated to purchase security for a buyer at the lowest possible price. A member who represents a seller must get the highest possible price. A sale is made only when two members can agree on the price, which is why stock prices fluctuate daily even when there is no major change in the company or in its markets.

Listed securities are traded on established exchanges like the New York Stock Exchange and the American Stock Exchange. To have its securities listed, a firm must be approved by that exchange's board of governors. And it must meet minimum financial qualifications. This is so there will be sufficient investor interest in the securities.

Unlisted securities are traded in over-the-counter markets. These operate the same way as security markets, except that auctions are negotiated by telephone rather than on a floor. Trading in unlisted securities is done by brokerage firms or dealers who are self-regulated. A brokerage firm markets a security by announcing its willingness to buy shares at a given price—the **bid price**—and to sell these shares at a slightly higher price—the **asked price.**

When several brokerage firms handle the same security, each firm uses competing bid and asked prices as guides in setting its own price. This tends to establish a fair and orderly market for the issue. The *spread* (or difference) between bid and asked prices, available instantly via computers to all dealer members, is a good profit opportunity for the dealers. Dealers often take advantage of the spread by purchasing stock at the lower bid price from

Computer Monitor Showing Bid and Asked Prices.

security owners who are anxious to sell. In turn, the dealers may be able to sell the securities to interested buyers at the higher asked price.

Eventually, all national, regional, and over-the-counter markets could be linked by computer, the way they are in Great Britain. Since the computer could be programmed to set market prices, the big stock exchanges would then have much less influence.

How to Read Stock and Bond Quotations

The results of each day's securities trading are reported in detail in the financial pages of most newspapers. Samples are shown in Figures 14–7 and 14–8, including explanations of how to interpret stock and bond quotations.

Newspapers also print stock-market averages, or indexes, that summarize daily trading activities. The best-known listings are the Dow Jones average, Standard and Poor's average of 500 stocks, and the New York Stock Exchange Index. These averages try to show, through a sampling of stocks, the general direction of prices on the exchange that day.

How to Buy Securities

For individual investors and businesses, buying securities is done in a series of steps, described below:

1. *Open an account with a brokerage firm.* An investor must sign a few simple papers and, depending on his or her credit rating, may have to make a small deposit.
2. *Select an account executive.* The investor is assigned or chooses an account executive (broker). This person gives advice, prepares information, and supervises the account.
3. *Order the security.* The investor places an order with the broker to buy or sell a security. In most cases, this is a **market order.** This means that the transaction will be carried out on the most favorable terms available when the order is received at the stock exchange or, for over-the-counter stocks, at the brokerage house dealing with that security. Or, the investor can place a special **buy order** or **sell order.** This instructs the broker to buy or sell when the security reaches a specified price.

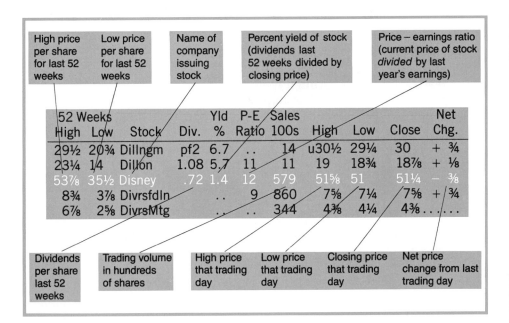

FIGURE 14-7
Reading Newspaper Stock Quotations.

High price per share for last 52 weeks

Low price per share for last 52 weeks

Name of company issuing stock

Percent yield of stock (dividends last 52 weeks divided by closing price)

Price – earnings ratio (current price of stock *divided* by last year's earnings)

52 Weeks High	52 Weeks Low	Stock	Div.	Yld %	P-E Ratio	Sales 100s	High	Low	Close	Net Chg.
29½	20¾	Dillngm	pf2	6.7	..	14	u30½	29¼	30	+ ¾
23¼	14	Dillon	1.08	5.7	11	11	19	18¾	18⅞	+ ⅛
53⅞	35½	Disney	.72	1.4	12	579	51⅝	51	51¼	– ⅜
8¾	3⅞	DivrsfdIn		..	9	860	7⅝	7¼	7⅝	+ ¾
6⅞	2⅝	DivrsMtg		..	..	344	4⅜	4¼	4⅜	......

Dividends per share last 52 weeks

Trading volume in hundreds of shares

High price that trading day

Low price that trading day

Closing price that trading day

Net price change from last trading day

FIGURE 14-8
Reading Newspaper Bond Quotations.

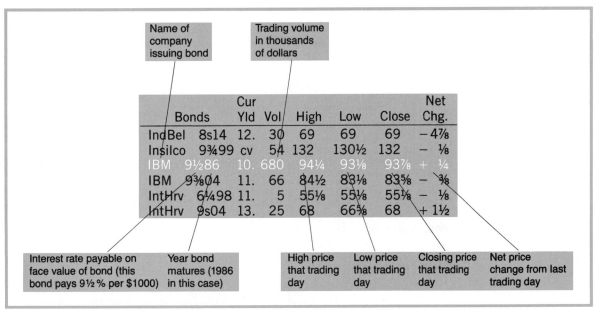

Name of company issuing bond

Trading volume in thousands of dollars

Bonds		Cur Yld	Vol	High	Low	Close	Net Chg.
IndBel	8s14	12.	30	69	69	69	– 4⅞
Insilco	9¾99	cv	54	132	130½	132	– ⅛
IBM	9½86	10.	680	94¼	93⅛	93⅞	+ ¼
IBM	9⅜04	11.	66	84½	83⅛	83⅝	– ⅜
IntHrv	6¼98	11.	5	55⅛	55⅛	55⅛	– ⅛
IntHrv	9s04	13.	25	68	66⅝	68	+ 1½

Interest rate payable on face value of bond (this bond pays 9½ % per $1000)

Year bond matures (1986 in this case)

High price that trading day

Low price that trading day

Closing price that trading day

Net price change from last trading day

Source: *The Wall Street Journal*, July 18, 1980.

4. *Pay for the security.* Securities are usually paid for within five trading days after the order is placed. Receipts from sales of securities normally reach an investor within a week of sale.

5. *Pay the commission.* For its services, the brokerage firm charges a commission, usually 1 to 2 percent of the total value of the stock transaction, with some variation among firms. The lower the value of the transaction, the higher the percentage of commission charged. You must pay when you buy and also when you sell.

Selecting Securities

Besides knowing how to buy, an investor needs to know what to buy. Many rely on "hot tips"—information from friends or acquaintances. These are not necessarily reliable. Neither is unverified advice from a broker, whose livelihood depends on promoting securities.

The careful investor (1) checks investment objectives, (2) obtains reliable information about securities, and (3) uses sensible investment strategies.

Investment Objectives

Investors normally seek a reasonable rate of return on their assets consistent with a moderate degree of risk. They look for stable profits and hold stocks for a year or more. **Speculators** seek a high rate of return on their investments and take high risks for quick profits. They buy and sell stock within a single day or a week, basing their decisions on the anticipated psychological reactions of buyers and sellers of the security rather than on its underlying value.

There are two main categories of investors. *Income-oriented investors* look for safe, stable investments with good dividends. They tend to buy bonds or preferred stock rather than common stock. *Growth-oriented investors* emphasize capital gains, which are received when the stock price goes up. They tend to buy common stock in companies with good growth in sales and earnings. Dividends are not really important to them, as you can see from the example in the box, opposite.

Getting Information

Information on stock-market performance as a whole can be found in stock-market averages. The most widely known, the *Dow Jones average,* is a composite of thirty industrial stocks, twenty transportation stocks, and fifteen public-utility stocks. If the Dow Jones average rises from 800 to 810 on a given day, that does not mean that the price of a single share has risen by $10. It means that the sixty-five stocks in the Dow Jones average have risen by 10/800, or 1.25 percent. So a typical stock that day, selling for $100, went up 1.25 percent, to $101.25. The New York Stock Exchange (NYSE) Index is different from the Dow Jones. It includes all of the securities traded on the New York Stock Exchange. And it also features a weighted average: changes in the stock prices of big corporations like General Motors and American Telephone and Telegraph are weighed more heavily in the index than changes in the stock prices of smaller companies. Stock-market averages are also available for the American Stock Exchange and for over-the-counter markets.

Stock-market averages are important for timing your purchases and sales. When market averages indicate that the stock market has reached a peak, the prices of most securities are high. When stock-market averages are low, many individual securities are available at bargain prices.

Investors also need information on individual companies. This can come from reports, available in libraries and brokerage houses, such as: Moody's Investment Service, Standard and Poor's, Babson's, United Business Service, Value Line Investment Service, and reports of security analysts employed at brokerage firms. But, remember, even top experts can be wrong.

When deciding whether to buy stock in a company, investors typically consider such factors as the firm's price–earnings ratio, its past achievements, the future prospects of the industry or industries in which the firm is located, the firm's growth record in profits and sales, new products that may become available to the firm, and the return the firm normally earns on its equity investments. A major but intangible factor is the quality of the firm's management. Does it aggressively and imaginatively take advantage of new oppor-

Pinball Machines: A Good Investment?

When Bally Manufacturing offered a new stock issue in the early 1970s, some investors weren't interested. The company was the country's largest maker of slot machines and pinball games, outlawed in most states. Rumors of organized crime and grand jury indictments were in the air.

But other, growth-oriented investors were quite interested. Bally's profits were way up. And seventeen states were considering legalized gambling.

Was Bally a good investment? Well, once gambling became legal and popular in Atlantic City, New Jersey, Bally common stock more than doubled in price. The end of the 70s saw many Bally investors smiling, glad they took a chance on a pinball machine and cashed in at the slot.

tunities? Is it more efficient than its major competitors? Does it utilize talented employees? For an example of blatantly fraudulent investment management, see the box "Ponzi Never Dies."

Investment Strategies

Price trends in security markets can be unpredictable, so smart investors consider several strategies. One of these is **dollar averaging,** meaning that a fixed amount, say $500, is invested in a stock or a group of stocks on a regular basis—every six months, for example. Thus, $500 will purchase ten shares when the price of the stock is $50, but only five shares when the price goes up to $100. The point is that, over a period of time, the investor ends up buying at a favorable *average* price. This strategy works well, unless the price of the stock remains low for a long time.

Another strategy is **diversification,** which involves buying a large number of different securities, preferably from firms in widely varied industries. In this way the investor avoids risking everything on one venture. This strategy may be expanded to buying different types of financial assets, such as stocks, bonds, land, buildings, mortgages, and so on.

Ponzi Never Dies

Ponzi schemes, named after the well-known chiseler, Charles Ponzi, include the Home-Stake swindle described at the beginning of this chapter as well as other scams, like chain letters. Ponzi schemes are con games in which the first investors are paid with funds from later investors. It works well, for a while.

Ponzi became famous during the 1920s with his slogan, "40 percent in ninety days." What it meant was that he'd invest people's money in coupons from the Universal Postal Union's international bureau. The coupons, which were indeed available at the time, were redeemable for postage of foreign countries. And, according to Ponzi, if the foreign currency went up, the coupons for the stamps could become much more valuable—40 percent more valuable within ninety days.

There were only two hitches. One, because coupon prices were actually fixed by international agreement, they could not really be used for speculation. And two, Ponzi never bought any coupons with the investors' money. He kept it.

In the first month, fifteen investors paid him $870. By the fourth month, he had $24,724 from 110 investors. By the sixth—and last—month, 20,000 people had given him nearly $10 million. By then, the jig was up.

Ponzi is not around anymore, but his idea is always being born again—and there are always people ready to believe in the dream.

Many securities investors pool their resources in mutual funds. This strategy offers several benefits:

1. Mutual funds employ professional security analysts to direct investments. Their expertise minimizes risk to the investor.
2. Investors get diversification with very limited initial cash outlay. Since a mutual fund pools the savings of thousands of investors, it normally buys dozens of different types of securities. Investing $500 or less in a mutual fund can get you more worthwhile diversification than investing $500 directly on a securities market.
3. Broker's fees are lower. Because a mutual fund buys and sells thousands of shares in a single transaction, the commissions it pays per share are lower than commissions on individual investor transactions.

Mutual funds are quoted in most daily metropolitan newspapers.

Government Regulation of Security Markets

During the Great Depression of the 1930s, the Securities and Exchange Commission (SEC) was established. Still the most effective supervisor of the securities industry, it has vast watchdog responsibilities:

1. Most publicly traded companies in interstate commerce must submit registration statements and periodic reports to the SEC to fully disclose their financial status. Their accounting standards are subject to examination, and they must also present investors with a prospectus, a summary of relevant financial information, when issuing new securities.
2. Brokerage firms, mutual funds, and security exchanges are required to file periodic reports with the SEC.
3. Account executives dealing in listed and over-the-counter securities must pass an SEC-approved examination.
4. Since 1975, the SEC has had the authority to spur development of truly national security markets through an electronic trading system.

Government regulation also includes the Securities Investor Protection Act of 1970. It insures investor accounts up to $500,000 against losses resulting from the failure of a brokerage firm.

Chapter Review & Applications

Key Points to Remember

1. Financial institutions include commercial banks, the Federal Reserve System, investment banks, savings banks, savings and loan associations, credit unions, and insurance companies.

2. Commercial banks accept deposits, make loans, and handle checking accounts. They are run for profit and are regulated by state and federal laws.

3. The Federal Reserve System is a government agency responsible for regulating the amount of money in circulation. It does this by establishing a monetary policy—based on the current state of the economy—that either restricts or expands the amount of money commercial banks may lend.

4. Investment banks are financial "middlemen" that market securities for businesses. Savings banks hold depositors' savings and make investments; they do not provide checking accounts. Savings and loan associations invest most of their deposits in home mortgages. Credit unions are owned by depositors in proportion to the savings they put in them. Insurance companies invest policyholders' premiums to earn interest.

5. The major U.S. security markets are the New York Stock Exchange and the American Stock Exchange. Only members who have bought seats may buy and sell in these exchanges.

6. Listed securities are traded on established exchanges; unlisted securities are traded in over-the-counter markets by telephone.

7. Individual investors buy or sell securities by setting up accounts at brokerage firms, selecting account executives, placing market orders, paying for the security, and paying the commission.

8. To decide which securities to buy, individual investors consider their investment objectives, collect and analyze information on the securities of individual companies, and investigate systematic investment strategies, like dollar averaging, diversification, and mutual funds.

Questions for Discussion

1. Why is a good understanding of financial institutions important to businesses and individuals?

2. How do businesses and individuals benefit from knowing how security markets operate?

3. How are commercial-bank depositors protected by federal and state government regulations?

4. How is the Federal Reserve System organized? Describe the process by which it regulates the amount of money in circulation.

5. As a member of the Board of Governors of the Federal Reserve System, what policies would you advocate during a recession? During inflation?

6. You want to invest some of your savings in stock. Describe the possibilities that are available to you and the steps you will need to take.

Short Case

1. You are a manager considering the purchase of a $10,000 van. You check three financial institutions, which offer you the following terms:
   (a) A bank loan at 10 percent simple interest for one year.
   (b) A bank loan at a discounted 9 percent interest rate. In effect, you would borrow $9,100 (the $10,000 note *minus* the $900 in interest) initially; at the end of the year, you would pay the entire $10,000 back.
   (c) A sales finance company offers to lend you $10,000 at 8 percent interest; the $10,800 (principal and interest) loan would be payable in twelve monthly installments of $900 each.

Since simple-interest, discount, and installment credit are all common business practices, you will have to make this kind of choice often. If your only concern is obtaining the funds at the lowest cost, which form of credit would you choose?

A Critical Business Decision

—made by Howard J. Ruff
of Ruff Enterprises

The Situation

He has been called "middle America's foremost financial adviser" although his formal training in economics is limited to a minor in college. His television show, "Ruffhouse," is watched by millions. His newsletter, *Ruff Times,* has more than 150,000 subscribers, each paying $125 per year. His book, *How to Prosper During the Coming Bad Years,* sold more than 3.5 million copies in hardcover and paperback editions. His fee for delivering a single lecture ranges up to $15,000. He is Howard J. Ruff and his San Ramon, California, enterprises gross as much as $20 million a year.

Ruff's success is no accident. He learned about financial prudence and hard work from his Mormon heritage in California and developed his communications abilities from performances in hundreds of Gilbert and Sullivan plays. His first business venture, as owner of an Evelyn Wood speed-reading franchise, ended in failure. But subsequent ventures in food supplements and real-estate education were successful. They had to be sold only because of possible conflicts of interest with *Ruff Times.*

At the *Ruff Times* newsletter, nothing is left to chance. An IBM Systems 3 computer sends out and tracks one million pieces of mail a month. The computer is so accurate, according to Ruff, that "we can tell everything, including the best days of the week to mail."

Why do people pay to hear the views of someone who admittedly has little academic training in economics and finance? Part of the reason is that Ruff is willing to take unpopular and unconventional positions. And one observer remarks in the *New York Times,* "Ruff takes the 'con' out of economics."[3]

The Decision

It is early 1980. Ruff has consistently told his subscribers to buy gold rather than stocks or bonds.

Many of Ruff's customers are "gold bugs," people who fervently believe that gold is the best possible investment. But gold has reached the unprecedented price of $600 an ounce. Ruff must decide whether to recommend against it, his most agonizing decision in the four-year life of *Ruff Times.* He comes to the conclusion that gold, which used to be reasonably related to such fundamentals as inflation, war, and a falling dollar, has become "the captive of wild-eyed, get-rich-quick amateur speculators." "I haven't rejected gold by any means," he says. "I've rejected the markets as they are behaving now."

Questions

1. Should the already controversial Ruff clearly state his feelings about gold in his newsletter, knowing that this may lose him thousands of his gold-bug subscribers? How might he recoup the losses?

2. Assuming that the speculation in gold dies down, what do you see as the advantages and disadvantages of holding gold as compared with common stocks and bonds?

Computers and Their Use in Business

362

If the auto industry had done what the computer industry has done in the last thirty years, a Rolls Royce would cost $2.50 and get 2,000,000 miles a gallon.

FORTUNE (1978)

e doesn't fit the stereotype of a bureaucratic paper-pusher. In fact, U.S. Assistant Secretary of Transportation Edward W. Scott is part of an elaborate experiment—to train managers and clerical help to push buttons instead of paper.

Scott pushes a button on his desk-top computer keyboard and his day's calendar pops up on a television screen. If he wants to set up a meeting with subordinates, he doesn't have to call ten people and juggle their schedules. Instead, he calls up their calendars on the screen, and can see immediately when a meeting would fit their schedules. Everything from an old memo to a sample expense-account voucher is in the memory bank for him and his 900 subordinates. When on a trip, Scott can obtain computer printouts on his portable system that is linked by telephone to a minicomputer back in Washington.

Managers need access to information quickly. And electronic digital computers are giving it to them. Also a part of the computer revolution are stock-market traders, typists, insurance company clerks, medical diagnosticians, and newspaper reporters, to name just a few. Hundreds of computer-equipment firms are racing to turn out products for the "automated office" of today and tomorrow—merging telephones, keyboards, computers, screens, and people in imaginative ways to move information between and around offices.

There can be problems, though, in this electronic Eden. An American Telephone and Telegraph vice president had an electronic "tickler" built into his calendar to tell him when his subordinates' reports were overdue. It gave him a perfect memory. "The pressure was unbelievable," the vice president says. "No follow-up was ever missed." His people finally told him it was driving them nuts. The electronic reminders were removed, according to a story in *The Wall Street Journal*.[1]

This chapter is about computers—how they are used and misused; how they collect, analyze, and provide information; and how they are useful to today's business managers. The chapter also describes the kinds of information managers use to make decisions.

USES AND MISUSES OF COMPUTERS

A well-managed computer system can improve management decisions by quickly and accurately processing masses of raw data. Many industries are already totally dependent on computers. Without them, banks would close within the hour; and a simple telephone call would quickly become impossible.

But poorly designed systems can cause more problems than well-designed systems can solve. So managers need to understand how to use computers effectively.

How Businesses Use Computers

Computers can be programmed to process data for many purposes or for one particular purpose. **General-purpose computers,** sometimes called *data computers,* perform diverse jobs for clerical and professional personnel, such as handling scientific problems or figuring payrolls. **Special-purpose computers,** sometimes called *process computers,* do jobs for manufacturing-shop personnel, such as measuring changes in a work process and then correcting for them. An auto manufacturer, for example, uses a computer-controlled system to adjust a boring tool, when necessary, to compensate for the effects of heat and wear. And a computer controls the steel-rolling process in a steel mill—along with an operator who must override it for about eighteen minutes during every eight-hour shift.

All this help can be expensive. Large computers, such as Control Data Corporation's Cyber 174 model, rent for more than $100,000 per month and sell for anywhere from $5 to $10 million (depending upon the "extras"). **Minicomputers** are far less expensive (selling for $15,000 to $100,000) and are versatile, suitable for both general-purpose and specific applications. They are small enough to fit on a desk top, and all kinds of business firms are finding new uses for them every day. **Microcomputers**—smaller, less expensive versions of minicomputers—have lately gained widespread use (see box on the bottom of next page). The rapid advances in computer technology have already caused the distinctions between large computers, minicomputers, and microcomputers to blur.

Batch and *on-line processing* are the two most common computer data-processing uses. With **batch processing,** work is accumulated and then processed by the computer all at once. This type of processing is used for clerical

and accounting jobs, such as payroll and customer billing. With **on-line processing,** the data are processed immediately. When an on-line query is sent to the computer, it is responded to instantly, based on the information stored in the computer at that time. Meanwhile, routine batch operations are processed concurrently with on-line work. On-line processing is used for specialized applications requiring immediate information, such as making airline and motel reservations, finding the latest stock prices, taking inventory, selling concert tickets, dispatching trucks, and investigating credit.

An increasingly popular way to accomplish on-line processing is **time sharing.** This procedure links many remote terminals (usually teletypewriters or video-display units) to a large central computer. The links are ordinary telephone lines, so users may be miles away from the main computer. The

The Little Apple

It can keep track of your diet program, operate an oil rig off California, display data graphically, and synthesize rock music. It is the Apple, a microcomputer, or "personal computer," manufactured by the Apple

Computer Company in Cupertino, California. Introduced in 1977 as the first programmable personal computer that could be bought fully assembled, Apples are becoming more popular every year (100,000 were sold in 1979). The little Apples look like typewriter keyboards, take orders from thin disks, display their information in color, weigh eleven pounds, and plug into any TV set. Designed mainly for small businesses, schools and colleges, and professionals—such as stockbrokers—a "starter system" costs about $1,200 and a business manager's system about $5,000.

Apple I was the 1976 brainchild of two college dropouts—Steven Jobs and Stephen Wozniak, aged twenty and twenty-three at the time. They built it from scrounged parts in Jobs' garage. Apple II, a major improvement, was launched in 1977. From $100,000 in sales in 1976, Apple Computer made over $150 million in sales in 1980.

Because of the computer's low price and multiple uses, Jobs and Wozniak are trying to come up with new software packages that users need. They know they'd better, because a flock of domestic and Japanese firms are hot on their trail. But Jobs and Wozniak haven't been ignoring the hardware side of their business: Apple III arrived in 1980.[2]

computer is programmed for on-line operation, with everybody's programs stored in it. Users identify the programs they need, enter the data at their terminals, and receive their output after a fractional-second time delay. Since many people can use the computer simultaneously, they all share the cost. Many colleges and universities use time-sharing systems. And business executives can use them to get answers to "what if" questions about proposed price changes or new-product ideas.

How Businesses Misuse Computers

Businesses can misuse computers by ignoring them or by collecting too much information from them. Another common misuse, and one that is increasing, is computer crime. Armed bank robberies now average about $10,000 per take, according to the FBI, but a "respectable" computer crime can net a thief $1 million. Nationwide, computer thefts now run close to $300 million per year. And with sales up on mini- and microcomputers, things could get much worse.

The strategies used to outwit computers are illegal, but fascinating. One involved a young New Yorker who knew something about computers and got a twelve-month installment loan from his bank with a book of twelve computer-coded coupons for his payments. Right away, he tore out the *last* coupon, not the first, and sent it to the bank, along with a monthly payment. He quickly received a computer-generated letter from the bank. It thanked him for paying off his *entire* loan so promptly . . . and assured him of his excellent credit standing.

More exotically complex is the famous fraud at Equity Funding Corporation of America. In the early 1970s Equity Funding, an insurance company, was the hottest stock on the market. But by 1973 the company was racked by scandal. One-quarter of the firm's $737 million in assets were computer-generated fakes. So were 64,000 of the 97,000 insurance policies. Customer losses approached $2 billion. See the box on page 369 for some other examples.

Business firms and government agencies worry about computer penetration, for money *or* information. A U.S. Department of Agriculture computer system, for example, was penetrated more than 6,400 times in one year by unauthorized people. Some violations were comparatively harmless—an employee's children played computer games from his terminal—but other penetrators could have issued themselves fraudulent government checks, seen confidential Census Bureau information, or stolen commercial trade secrets. Government defense agencies were especially concerned when two security consultants penetrated a U.S. Air Force system in two hours, using a keyboard connection to their home telephone. It was only a test, but anyone with a home telephone and a bit of computer knowledge could have done the same thing.

HOW COMPUTERS WORK

Because computers play an increasingly important role in day-to-day business operations, managers need a basic understanding of how they work. The electronic computer is a data-processor, like the abacus, slide rule, typewriter, adding machine, and calculator. It is a powerful and complex descendant of these devices, invented to fill a need for fast, cheap and accurate information.

Kinds of Computers

Two types of computers are in use today: *digital* and *analog*.

A **digital computer** manipulates separate bits of data according to a sequence of instructions stored inside. Since digital computers are the most widely used for business problems, they are simply called "computers" in this chapter. An **analog computer** translates continuous physical variables (like temperature or speed) into electrical quantities for the purpose of solving problems. They are used for scientific and engineering problems and can do things like project pictures of buildings from architectural drawings.

The difference between the two kinds of computers can be illustrated with clocks. A digital clock is like a digital computer. It displays its output in separated values of hours, minutes, and seconds. On the other hand, a standard clock face is like an analog computer. Its hands move continuously. The observer must interpret the distances to tell the time.

Computer Parts

The electronic digital computer has five basic components:

> INPUT DEVICE   Brings data into the computer for processing.
> STORAGE (or MEMORY) UNIT   Stores and recalls the data. Large computers also include *secondary storage (or memory) units*.
> ARITHMETIC-LOGIC UNIT   Adds, subtracts, multiplies, divides, compares two values, and senses positive and negative values.

CONTROL UNIT   Directs the sequence of operations, interprets coded instructions, and commands the computer circuits.

OUTPUT DEVICE   Translates electrical impulses into a usable form, such as printed copy or punched cards.

All these components are part of the computer's **hardware**, which refers to all the physical equipment in a computer system. Hardware is divided into two categories: the *central processing unit* and *peripheral equipment*.

The **central processing unit** (often called the CPU or "main frame") includes the memory or storage unit, the arithmetic-logic unit, and the control unit, along with the operating console for the programmer. (The console looks like an electronic switch panel attached to an electric typewriter and desk.) **Peripheral equipment** includes all the equipment not part of the main frame, such as the input and output devices and the secondary storage or memory units (see Figures 15–1 and 15–2).

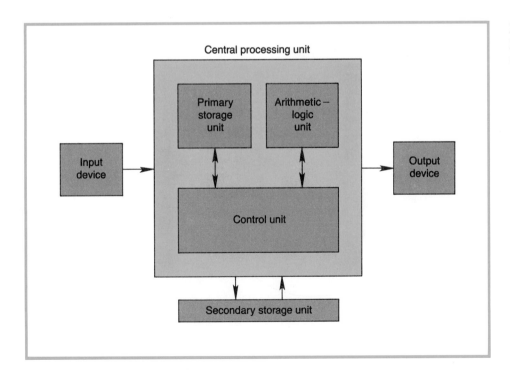

FIGURE 15–1
Parts of a
Computer.

FIGURE 15-2
Components of a Modern Computer.

Input Devices

A computer cannot use data unless they are in a form that it can understand. Such data are called *machine-readable media*. These media include punched cards, punched paper tape, magnetic tape and disks, magnetic ink characters (on checks, for example), mark-sensed cards, video-display terminals (a TV screen combined with a typewriter keyboard), and an electronic stylus. The computer input device then translates information from these media into electronic impulses that the computer can understand. Examples are shown in Figure 15–3 on the next page.

Output Devices

Output devices translate the results of the computer's efforts back to the users. The devices take the electrical impulses from the computer's storage unit and translate them into other electrical impulses. These are then stored on mag-

Computer Crime: Very Creative—and Terribly Illegal

- The head teller of a New York bank skimmed off more than $1.5 million in customer accounts by ordering the computer to divert them. He was betting up to $30,000 on horse racing—on an annual salary of $11,000. The bank didn't catch him, but a raid on his bookmaker's did.

- A programmer at a mail-order sales firm had the computer round down odd cents on every one of the firm's many accounts. Instead of $886.676, for example, he had it pay $886.67 —and channeled the extra money into a dummy account for himself. The pennies added up very quickly.

- An electronics expert tapped into a large telephone company's computerized inventory system and stole almost $1 million worth of equipment, much of which he resold back to the company. After being caught and spending forty days in jail, he was hired by the phone company to improve its computer security, a common fate for expert computer criminals.

People like these "beat the program," which is not extremely difficult for someone on the inside. For those who are unhappy at work and want to "get even" with their company, there are other ways. One programmer, before he was fired, instructed the firm's computer to destroy its listing of all accounts receivable. The firm went bankrupt.

Most computer criminals are male amateurs, aged eighteen to thirty. Although most are eventually discovered, they are rarely given long jail sentences. Judges and juries seem to be fascinated with the nonviolent conquest of an impersonal machine. Many are not even prosecuted, because the company fears ridicule from the publicity.[3]

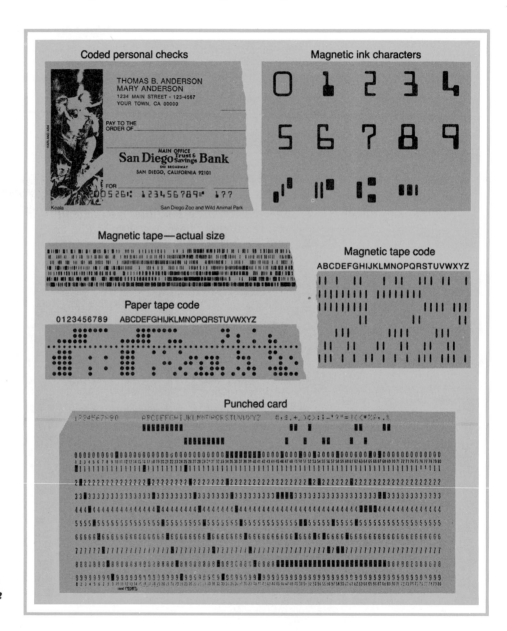

netic tapes, disks, and drums, or displayed on video-display terminals or remote teletype terminals.

Other output devices translate the electrical impulse into mechanical action. These include the printer, which prints data results on paper (called hard-copy printouts), and the card punch, which punches the information on cards. Then computer outputs can be read by people or used by other machines.

Programming: Talking to a Computer

You have to talk to a computer with a program. A **computer program** is a sequence of instructions used by the computer to solve a problem. These

How Computers Count

In 1946, mathematical genius John Von Neumann had a revolutionary idea for computer designers: use the binary numbering system for a computer's calculations. His idea was subsequently incorporated into all computer designs.

The decimal system we use for arithmetic contains ten digits from 0 through 9 (the Latin prefix "deci-" means "ten"). In contrast, the binary numbering system contains only two digits, 0 and 1 (the Latin prefix "bi-" means "two"). This system enables designers to program computers to count and perform arithmetic operations. With binary arithmetic, programmers can say to their computers, "Let an on switch be 1 and an off switch be 0."

In decimal arithmetic the right-hand column contains units, the column to the left contains "tens," the next column to the left contains "hundreds," and so on. For example, the number "725" contains 5 units *plus* 2 tens *plus* 7 hundreds, which *equals* 725.

In binary arithmetic, reading from the right, the columns have the following values that are powers of 2:

Column	5	4	3	2	1
Actual Value	16	8	4	2	1
Powers of 2	2^4	2^3	2^2	2^1	2^0

(Remember that 2^0 is equal to 1.)

But each column can have only a "0" or a "1" in it, indicating whether the value in that column is to be included and summed to obtain the entire number. Thus, some simple decimal numbers in binary arithmetic are:

Decimal Number	Binary Number	Calculation
1	00001	$0+0+0+0+1=1$
4	00100	$0+0+4+0+0=4$
5	00101	$0+0+4+0+1=5$
29	11101	$16+8+4+0+1=29$

As in decimal arithmetic, larger numbers are obtained by using columns which would be to the left of those shown in the first table.

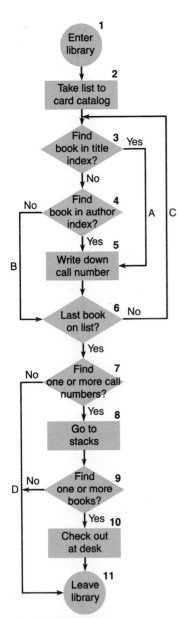

FIGURE 15–4
A Flow Diagram.

programs are the computer's **software. Computer programming,** which is the actual writing out of these instructions, is done by a trained computer programmer, who knows one or more programming "languages."

When computers were first invented, each computer used a different language. A programmer familiar with one machine couldn't write instructions for another.

To overcome this Tower-of-Babel problem, researchers developed multipurpose programming languages. Three of the most common are FORTRAN (*FOR*mula *TRAN*slating System), COBOL (*CO*mmon *B*usiness *O*riented *L*anguage), and BASIC (*B*eginners' *A*ll-purpose *S*ymbolic *I*nstruction *C*ode). Although originally designed for engineers and scientists, FORTRAN is now used in business, too. And COBOL and BASIC are widely used to process administrative and accounting information.

For the computer to solve a problem, the programmer must write a precise sequence of instructions for it to follow. This involves analyzing the elements of the problem, then outlining the steps required for its solution. The programmer writes a flow diagram and chooses a computer language. The program is transcribed onto a machine-readable medium, such as punched cards, by a trained operator.

Next, the program must be "debugged"—all potential errors or problems must be found and corrected. This is where programmers really earn their pay, since very few new programs are flawless. When "bugs" are discovered on a test run, the program must be revised. Programmers may spend as much time debugging programs as they spend writing them.

About 99 percent of all computer errors are the result of incorrect programming (the rest are hardware errors), and some have been quite dramatic. For example, several years ago a rocket was launched from Cape Kennedy to fly past Venus. It wandered off course and finally had to be blown up by ground control. Why? A computer programmer had accidentally left out a hyphen, a symbol that in this program represented an entire formula—an $18.5 million omission. Gimbel's department-store chain also encountered a major programming error. Many of its charge customers were not billed for two years or more. By the time the error was discovered, some debts were so old they were uncollectable. Computer operators occasionally have their frustrations, too. Recently, one even shot his computer with a handgun (it died).

Programmed instructions typically are in the form of **flow diagrams,** graphic representations of the steps required to solve a problem by computer. Figure 15–4 shows a flow diagram for solving a basic library research program.

Suppose you have a rough list of the titles and authors of several reference books that you need to check out of the library. Circles show the beginning or the end of the program. Rectangles, or *operation boxes,* show actions to be taken. Diamond-shaped *decision boxes* illustrate the logic the programmer must apply to instruct the computer. Note that each decision box in Figure 15–4 (numbers 3,4,6,7, and 9) asks a yes or no question, because computers work on an *on-off (two choices) principle* using *binary arithmetic.* The sequence varies with the answer. In Figure 15–4, note the two different paths, called *branching,* leading out of each of these boxes. *Looping* is when one of the paths returns the flow to an earlier step; Path C is an example.

The power and flexibility of the computer lie in its ability to perform these two operations: (1) selecting different paths through branching, and (2) repeating a sequence as many times as necessary through looping. Programming, then, is just a matter of translating flow-diagram questions and yes/no answers into an electronic circuit. The result: instant information for managers.

MANAGEMENT INFORMATION AND BUSINESS DATA

Management information comes from many sources—a conversation with the sales manager down the hall, an analysis of manufacturing costs, a glance at the personnel files. It is defined as the facts and figures decision makers use to identify and solve problems.

In a well-run and complex business organization, decisions can rarely be made "off the cuff." Large masses of information must be analyzed. To do this, a **management information system (MIS)** is often used. MIS is an organized method of providing relevant data for decisions in accounting, finance, production, marketing, or any other functional area of the business. Because of the massive amount of data involved, an MIS is usually computerized.

To develop or use an MIS, managers need to know the features of useful management information, the two main kinds of management information, and how to analyze data.

Features of Useful Management Information

Information is useful to managers if it is: (1) accurate, (2) timely, (3) complete, (4) concise, (5) relevant, and (6) not too costly. Since these criteria often

Your Next Job
Positions in Data Processing and Statistical Analysis

Careers in Computer Operations

Jobs in data processing include **console operators,** who feed the coded data into the computer, run the computer, and watch for programming errors or mechanical problems; and **auxiliary equipment operators,** who translate computer output into intelligible words and numbers. These electronic computer operating personnel are usually high-school graduates who receive on-the-job training. Auxiliary equipment operators become console operators and console operators can assume some supervisory duties. Annual salaries average $7,500 for auxiliary equipment operators and $9,400 for console operators. With the rapid increase in computer installations, employment opportunities for console and auxiliary equipment operators are expected to be favorable. (*Additional information:* American Federation of Information Processing Societies; 1815 North Lynn Street; Arlington, Virginia 22209.)

Careers in Programming and Systems Analysis

If computers appear to think, it is only because of **programmers.** They figure out the logical sequence of problem-solving steps in a flow diagram and develop detailed instructions for both the computer and the computer operator. Programmers also "debug" instructions by running sample programs through the computer to correct errors. Educational requirements vary. An engineering or a scientific programmer must have a college education. A business data programmer must usually have a high-school or a two-year college education and subsequent training. Annual salaries range from $12,700 to $24,000. Positions in the programming field are expected to increase rapidly. (*Additional information:* American Federation of Information Processing Societies; 1815 North Lynn Street; Arlington, Virginia 22209.)

Systems analysts plan and assign data processing activities. Analysts identify the information needed and how to process it. They use sophisticated techniques like cost accounting and mathematical model building. They also supervise programmers. Most systems analysts have either a bachelor's degree or a graduate degree. But some positions are filled by promoting experienced programmers or computer operators. Annual income ranges from $19,000 to $25,000. Employment opportunities for systems analysts are expected to increase rapidly. (*Additional information:* Association for Systems Management, 24587 Bagley Road; Cleveland, Ohio 44138.)

Careers in Statistical Analysis

Statistical clerks compile numerical reports on which management decisions are based. Their tasks include recording transactions, as well as compiling, coding and tabulating data. Diverse jobs exist. For example, *actuary clerks* tabulate numerical data for insurance studies, and *demurrage clerks* are employed by railroads to analyze data for transportation reports. Most of the nation's 300,000 statistical clerks are high-school graduates and many also have college or vocational training in business mathematics. With experience, they may advance to the ranks of statistician or supervisor. Yearly salaries average $7,500. Since many statistical jobs cannot be computerized, employment should expand moderately. (*Additional information:* State Supervisor of Office Occupations Education; State Department of Education; your state capital.)

Statisticians collect, analyze, and interpret numerical data. This requires expertise in statistical techniques and knowledge of the subject matter under investigation. So *market-research statisticians* have educational backgrounds in probability as well as in marketing and business administration. A bachelor's degree either in statistics or in business administration with a minor in statistics is often required for a job in private industry. Advancement to upper-level management positions is possible. Annual income for beginning statisticians is about $10,000. Jobs are expected to expand moderately. (*Additional information:* American Statistical Association; 806 15th Street, N.W.; Washington, D.C. 20005.)

conflict, they must be balanced against each other. Information may be so complete that it overwhelms the user. This "information overload" can waste time and money and encourage poor management decisions.

Kinds of Management Information

There are two main types of management information: *secondary data* and *primary data*. **Secondary data** are previously published facts and figures; **primary data** are facts and figures collected for the first time to solve a current problem. Either may or may not be computerized.

Secondary Data

Secondary data include internal data and external data. **Internal secondary data** are found within the organization, an important source of information for managers. Examples are accounting records, customer-service complaints, quality-control reports, sales reports, and personnel files.

External secondary data are facts and figures obtained from outside the firm. The main sources are U.S. government census reports, which cover many topics of direct interest to the business. Three of the most relevant reports are:

1. *Census of Population and Housing* Numbers and characteristics of the population and its housing.
2. *Census of Business* Number of establishments; employment figures; and amount of sales for retail, wholesale, and service trades.
3. *Census of Manufacturers* Number of establishments; employment figures; and value of manufacturers' shipments.

Census reports are compiled and updated periodically and appear in a variety of government publications, such as the annual *Statistical Abstract of the United States*.

Most federal reports are for public use and are available free or for a small fee. The same is true for data published by state and local governments and by many colleges and universities. Trade associations, organizations made up of firms in the same industry, also provide useful data to their members.

Secondary data are easily obtainable, cheap, and, in the case of federal census data, unique. But they have certain disadvantages. They may not be

Electronic scanners can be hooked up to an on-line computer to operate inventory control and remember prices. The key to this type of management information is the Universal Product Code— that little square with lines—which has been appearing on more and more grocery products.

timely—1980 census data aren't much good in 1989—and they are not always specific enough for the problem at hand. This is why managers also need primary data.

Primary Data

These can be collected in three ways: by observation, by survey, and by experiment. All may eventually be computerized.

Observational data are collected either by mechanically recording or personally observing behavior. An example of the former is the Nielsen Television Rating Index, which works by an "audimeter" connected to the TV sets of 1,200 families scattered throughout the United States. This device mechanically records the exact times the set is turned on and off and what channel it is tuned to. Figure 15–5 shows the results of these recordings in the form of the ten most watched TV programs for a two-week period in early 1980. The Nielsen Index is not foolproof, though. One congressional investigation revealed that the ratings for one week included a couple who left their television set on all day to entertain their dog while they were at work! Another example of mechanically collected observational data used as part of an MIS is the electronic scanner at supermarket checkouts (see photo).

FIGURE 15–5
Nielsen Ratings of the Top Ten National Television Programs, January 28–February 10, 1980.

RANK	NETWORK PROGRAM	RATING (IN PERCENT)
1	*Dallas* (CBS)	29.9
2	*Dukes of Hazzard* (CBS)	29.1
3	*60 Minutes* (CBS)	28.3
4	*Three's Company* (ABC)	28.3
5	*Little House on the Prairie* (NBC)	27.9
6	*M*A*S*H* (CBS)	26.0
7	*Alice* (CBS)	25.5
8	*Eight is Enough* (ABC)	25.4
9	*Ten Speed and Brown Shoe* (ABC)	25.2
10	*Real People* (NBC)	25.0
Source: A. C. Nielsen Company Television Index		

Personal observations can also be used to solve problems—perhaps a parking problem at your college. If you don't have a mechanical device to count the cars entering the lots, you could simply count them. And, if preference is to be given to car pools, you might count the number of people in each car.

Survey data are obtained by asking people questions, either in person or by telephone or via questionnaires. The most common is the mail survey, used by firms, colleges, and government agencies to collect information. You can discover for yourself the problems with this method by answering the questions from one survey by a state legislator shown in Figure 15–6.

FIGURE 15–6
How Would You Answer These Questions from Your Legislator?

QUESTION	YES	NO
Consumer Protection: 1. Would you favor a further infringement upon free enterprise by permitting the law to require all retail products to be priced per unit (that is, by the pound, ounce, quart, etc.) instead of by the package or as preferred by the packer?	____	____
2. Should we leave the free market system to the free enterpriser and let the best and the thriftiest come out on top, as was intended by our Constitution?	____	____
Environment: 3. Do you think that our state should enact Gestapo-type laws that would reward citizens for spying on and reporting on other citizens for such offenses as air or water pollution?	____	____
University Autonomy: 4. Would you agree that administrators of state-supported educational institutions should be discharged for pampering revolutionaries?	____	____
Drug Abuse: 5. Recent research indicates marijuana may be more harmful than many medical authorities previously believed. Considering these facts, do you think the selling of marijuana should be regarded as a crime, and punishment administered accordingly?	____	____
(To find out what the legislator wanted to hear, see the text.)		

Survey methods, especially personal and telephone interviews, are more flexible than observations. They also allow the participants to explain themselves in greater depth. But they have limitations, too. If questions are confusing, trivial, too personal, or too controversial, people may not give useful answers. A family who typically consumes four cases of beer a week may be unwilling to admit it in a consumer survey. And questions must be written and interpreted carefully. All five of the questions in Figure 15–6 are "leading questions," biased by the legislator to obtain the following answers: no, yes, no, yes, yes.

Experimental data are often used when business problems require particularly careful analysis. In experimental studies you see exactly how people react to what you're considering. One firm does these studies for TV broadcasters. Unlike Nielsen, which figures ratings *after* the fact, Audience Studies Incorporated (ASI) uses a computer to measure the chances of a show's success *before* it is aired. They "diagnosed" a pilot version of *Angie* for ABC when executives were concerned about two key factors: (1) Does the husband in the pilot lack audience appeal? and (2) Is a marriage between a rich, "blue-blooded" Philadelphian and a hash-slinging waitress believable?

Participants sat in a 400-seat theater with a black plastic oval case attached to each seat. The dial on the face read "very dull," "fair," "good," and "very good." The recruited audience rated the pilot by turning the dial throughout the viewing time. A computer captured their feelings instantly. The ASI test showed that the executives were right about the characters. As a result, the script and actors were changed, and, when it was finally aired, *Angie* made Nielsen's top-ten shows during some rating periods, according to *The New York Times.*

Experiments may use observation or survey methods, but often a more rigorous approach is desirable. Here, the experimenter uses two groups—an *experimental group,* which is exposed to the condition being studied, and a *control group,* which is in an identical situation but not exposed to the condition. Since the only difference between the two groups is exposure to the condition, the researchers can tell what effects it produces. Fisher-Price uses such experiments to improve its toy designs (see box).

How to Analyze Data

For many business problems, armies of numbers must be summarized before a manager has enough information to take action. A convenient way to summarize many numbers, by hand or by computer, is to use a **measure of central value**—a figure that condenses a whole set of numbers into a single value. Three measures of central value are the **mean, median,** and **mode:**

Mean   This is the "average" or "arithmetic" center. It is found by dividing the sum of all the numbers by the number of items being measured.
Median   This is the exact middle of the numbers when written from lowest to highest. The median is the most typical number—half the numbers lie above it and half below.
Mode   This is the number that occurs most often in the set.

To see how these measures work, look at the scores for one of the most bizarre sporting events of this century—the 1960 World Series between the New York Yankees and the Pittsburgh Pirates. The number of runs scored by each team in each of the seven games, written from lowest to highest, appears on the following page.

Research by Three- and Four-Year-Olds

How would you decide which toys will be popular with preschoolers? Fisher-Price, the largest toy maker for little kids, uses experiments with preschoolers to find out.[4]

The company sets out a sumptuous array of toys in two different rooms. The sets are the same, with one exception. Room 1 has the new toy, and Room 2 has an older version of it. In rush two groups of three- and four-year-olds.

While they play, Fisher-Price measures the minutes of playtime spent with the new toy compared with the old toy. The design with the most minutes is produced.

RUNS SCORED BY NEW YORK YANKEES	RUNS SCORED BY PITTSBURGH PIRATES
2	0
2	0
4	3
9	3
10	5
12	6
16	10
Total 55	27

The three measures of central value for each team are as follows:

	NEW YORK YANKEES	PITTSBURGH PIRATES
Mean	7.9	3.9
Median	9	3
Mode	2	0,3

The median is the middle number in each set of numbers, 9 for the Yankees and 3 for the Pirates. The mode is the number that occurs most often, 2 for the Yankees and 0 and 3 for the Pirates, who scored each of these numbers twice and all other numbers once. It looks like the Yankees won.

But statistics can be tricky. Look at the scores below for each of the seven games:

GAME	RUNS SCORED BY NEW YORK YANKEES	RUNS SCORED BY PITTSBURGH PIRATES
1	4	6
2	16	3
3	10	0
4	2	3
5	2	5
6	12	0
7	9	10

The Pirates actually won the series, even though the Yankees scored more than twice as many runs! And the lesson should be clear. Although measures of central value are extremely useful, one must be careful to consider all the relevant facts surrounding the figures.

THE FUTURE OF COMPUTERS

Tomorrow in your home, touch one button and your telephone will dial numbers, your stereo will play concert-hall-quality music, your sprinklers will automatically turn on, and your TV set will flash better pictures; your children will play electronic spelling games, check their homework, and compose poetry on their computers; and sensors will direct heat and light only to rooms where they are needed. When you take the last package of hamburger from the freezer, say it aloud. Voice-recognition equipment will "hear" the message and add hamburger to your shopping list. And a computer in your car's engine will automatically minimize pollution and maximize fuel economy.

At the office, most of your management paperwork and files will be replaced by a video-display terminal. Some of your business trips will be replaced by video conferences—on a wall-size TV screen. Your mail will be transmitted electronically by facsimile systems. You will dictate a letter aloud and voice-recognition equipment will type it—excluding, of course, your stammers and interjections.

At the hospital, a computer will help diagnose your illness, test your blood sample, and remind nurses when to give you which pills. At the garage, a computer will diagnose your car's problems and spot potential trouble.

Science fiction? Not at all. Many of these computer conveniences are already in use. And it will not be long before home computers are as common as TV sets.

This chapter opened with a quotation saying that if the auto industry's technology had grown at the same rate as the computer industry's during the past thirty years, a Rolls Royce would cost $2.50 and get two million miles to a gallon. However, by 1985, according to C. Lester Hogan, vice-chairman of Fairchild Camera and Instrument Corporation, we will have a pocket computer more powerful than and nearly as fast as the nine-million-dollar Cray-1, which, in 1979, was the world's mightiest computer. A comparable achievement in the auto industry would have the price of a 1985 Rolls Royce down to less than a penny and it would go more than two *billion* miles on one gallon!

Chapter Review
& Applications

Key Points to Remember

1. General-purpose computers process data for many purposes, such as handling scientific problems or figuring a payroll. Special-purpose computers process data for a particular task, such as adjusting machinery.

2. Batch processing means accumulating data for processing at one time. On-line processing means that a user has immediate computer access, time sharing being a common form.

3. The digital computer has five main components: input device, memory or storage unit, arithmetic-logic unit, control unit, and output device.

4. A computer's ability to process data depends on its hardware (its physical components) and on its software (the programs that supply problem-solving instructions to the computer).

5. Computer programming is the task of writing a sequence of instructions for the computer to use in solving a problem. A flow diagram shows the sequence of instructions. Computers calculate using a binary—or on-off—system.

6. A management information system (MIS) is an organized method of providing relevant data for decisions and is usually computerized.

7. The two main kinds of management information are secondary data (previously published facts and figures) and primary data (facts and figures collected for the first time).

8. Primary data can be collected by observation, surveys, or experiments.

9. A measure of central value is a figure that condenses a whole set of numbers. Three common measures are the mean, median, and mode.

Questions for Discussion

1. Assume that you own a clothing store and are looking for ways to improve your operations. How might you use observation, survey, and experimental methods to decide what to do?

2. Looking back at Figure 15–6, how would you restate the questions to avoid biased responses?

3. What is the difference between computer hardware and computer software?

4. Referring to Figure 15–4, describe the complete sequence of steps you would follow in each of these situations:
   (a) You have one book on your list and do not find it in the card catalog.
   (b) You have three books on your list, find only the second and third books in the author index, and find only the third book in the stacks.
   (c) You have four books on your list, find all the call numbers by the most direct route possible, and find all the books in the stacks.

Short Case

1. Assume that a restaurant owner must decide how many pounds of hamburger to order for July, August, and September, a total of thirteen weeks. Her records show that in the same period a year ago she used the following amounts per week:

JULY	AUGUST	SEPTEMBER
100	90	100
90	100	110
120	100	80
90	80	100
110		

She receives hamburger from her supplier once a week. Her business is about the same this year as it was last year.
   (a) Calculate the mean, median, and mode for hamburger usage last summer.
   (b) What problems may the owner encounter if she orders the mean usage from last summer each week during the coming three months?
   (c) What problems may arise if she orders 120 pounds (the highest weekly usage rate during the same period last year) each week during the coming three months?

A Critical
Business Decision

—made by Steven Jobs and Stephen Wozniak of Apple Computer

The Situation

Californians Steven Jobs and Stephen Wozniak started their Apple Computer Company in 1976 with $1,500 they raised by selling a van and a calculator.[5] When they built their first Apple I personal computer in Jobs' garage, their success wasn't sheer luck (see the boxed insert on page 364). Although in their early twenties, the two college dropouts had impressive experience to draw on—Jobs as a designer of video games for Atari and Wozniak as an integrated circuit designer for Hewlett-Packard.

They soon discovered the $1,500 of initial capital wasn't quite enough to get into the computer business seriously. Fortunately, the improvements in their new Apple II programmable, memory-equipped computer caught the eye of some key financial backers who put $3 million into the firm.

A personal computer is a general-purpose computer inexpensive enough and simple enough to be owned and operated by an individual or a small business. Jobs and Wozniak got into the personal computer business, because friends wanted a computer like the one they had built to amuse themselves. So the first market for Apples was computer hobbyists who simply wanted their own computers to play around with. But that group wasn't large enough by itself.

Besides schools and colleges, Jobs and Wozniak found that much of the initial demand for the Apple II came from people in small businesses or professions whose office work was speeded up by the computer's flexibility. For small businesses, the company designs an accounting system to handle accounts payable, accounts receivable, and other financial information. Among the professions, stockbrokers can use the Apple to maintain records on stocks and bonds and to analyze their performance.

The Decision

Jobs and Wozniak feel that the household market offers a special marketing opportunity. So they have added a number of features to the basic unit, like special computer commands for color displays of data and even for sound—for example, in their STAR WARS game a player can actually hear the phasers fire through a built-in speaker.

Although Apple Computer has an early lead in some parts of the personal computer market, it already has fifty competitors and more are ready to jump in. Besides Apple, the two major American manufacturers of personal computers are Commodore Business Machines (with its PET computer) and Tandy Corporation (whose TRS-80 computer is sold through its 8,000 Radio Shack retail outlets). Texas Instruments introduced a new model in 1979, and now, in 1980, Jobs and Wozniak know that giant IBM is eyeing the personal computer market. Five Japanese brands are also coming to American shores— Hitachi, Matsushita, Nippon Electric, Oki Electric, and Sharp.

Jobs and Wozniak know that they must penetrate the American household market even more effectively than they have done in the past. To do this, they believe they must put more development dollars into new software packages and expansion hardware that will make their Apple III even more useful in American homes.

Questions

1. If you were Jobs and Wozniak, what "personal" applications would you look for to increase the appeal of Apple III among household buyers?
2. What kind of retail outlets would you try to use to reach these buyers?

5 Small
Business and

Franchising

Small Business: Your Own Franchise

In this chapter you will learn . . .

- what small business is.
- about the attractions and drawbacks of being in business for yourself.
- ways to evaluate whether a small business is right for you.
- what a franchise is and the steps involved in starting and operating one.

16

everal years ago, McDonald's opened a new restaurant in Chicago. Normally, this would not be a big event; after all, there are thousands of them. But this one was really new. Its "golden arches" graced the fifth floor of elegant Water Tower Place, a seventy-five-story complex of lavish condominiums, a Ritz-Carlton Hotel, and elite shops like the Halston Boutique.

Some of the wealthy shoppers had apparently never been in a McDonald's before. They sat in booths in their fur coats waiting to be served, only to be informed they had to step up to the counter. But they came. And they ate. And after only nine months, the McDonald's was so popular that it had to be doubled in size, according to a story in *Business Week* magazine.[1]

This McDonald's turned into a spectacularly successful small business. But it doesn't always work out that way. There are great risks involved. For one thing, the small-business owner has to be a jack-of-all-trades, doing the marketing, finance, management, and so on without a back-up army of specialists. But for those who enjoy challenges and seek independence, the rewards far exceed the risks.

While studying this chapter and the next one, consider yourself as a potential small-business owner. Explore the challenges and pitfalls. In this chapter the focus will be on franchises, and in Chapter 17 we will discuss how to start your own business from scratch.

WHAT IS A SMALL BUSINESS?

About 95 percent of businesses in this country are small. There are about 5½ million of them, and they produce about 37 percent of the gross national product and employ 55 percent of all American workers. For many, they represent the realization of the American dream: success through innovation and competition.

So what's small about small business? A **small business** is (1) small in sales dollars and employees; (2) run on capital from one or a few people; and (3) under the management of a sole proprietor, a partnership, or a family-owned corporation that is responsible only to itself, not to a board of directors or a corporate office.

The U.S. Small Business Administration (SBA), which is a federal agency created by Congress to help small businesses, defines them in these categories:

1. RETAIL OR SERVICE FIRMS   Annual sales or receipts of up to $1–$5 million, depending on the industry.
2. WHOLESALE FIRMS   Annual sales of up to $5–$15 million, depending on the industry.
3. CONSTRUCTION FIRMS   Annual sales or receipts of not more than $5 million, averaged over a three-year period.
4. MANUFACTURING FIRMS   Up to 250–1,500 employees, depending on the industry.

Firms classified this way are eligible for loans and management assistance from the SBA. Assistance includes workshops, conferences, and management counseling through volunteer programs like the Service Corps of Retired Executives (SCORE) and the Active Corps of Executives (ACE).

A HARD LOOK AT SMALL BUSINESS

To honestly evaluate your interest in owning your own business, consider the attractions and the drawbacks.

Attractions of Small Business

Small businesses offer:[2]

1. *Sense of independence.* You are in charge. You report to no one and cannot be fired.
2. *Immediate chance for higher income.* You can collect a salary and earn a profit or a return on your investment. Profit-sharing is generally not possible if you work for someone else.
3. *Long-run pride in and benefits from ownership.* You can build an investment in your firm that may be marketable if you decide to sell it later.
4. *Opportunity to be a jack-of-all-trades.* You are not pigeon-holed as a salesperson or accountant. If you choose, you can wear many hats—manager, personnel specialist, salesperson, accountant, and so on.

5. *Operating advantages compared with large competitors.* You can react quickly to change and can adapt to local conditions. This flexibility is quite important. Large corporations are rarely as agile in the marketplace.

Drawbacks of Small Business

The drawbacks include:

1. *Less independence than you think.* The independence is partly illusory. After all, you must satisfy your employees, customers, and creditors, as well as government tax and wage laws. And your competitors largely dictate your prices and your hours. Sometimes you may have to share the stage with family members (see box). And, at least at first, you will work long hours with few vacations.

A Common Small Business Lament: The Plight of the Nation's Bosses' Kids

I love my dad. He's a terrific guy. But the business wasn't big enough for both of us. . .So about a year ago, I sent him on a vacation to Europe. While he was there, I called him up on the phone and told him he was fired, that he was out of a job. Wham! That was it. There wasn't much he could do about it.[3]

Richard Pocker is an SOB. That means Son of Boss. The *Wall Street Journal* observes that Pocker is "an accomplished SOB and wears the title with pride." He seized power with his sister Robin, now a full partner in the business. And their father accepted it better than most bosses. In 1954, he had fired his own father, the founder.

An "SOB" used to qualify as a member of Sons of Bosses International if he was an heir who had taken over or was likely to take over control of a family business. Daughters of bosses (DOBs) and sons-in-law of bosses (SLOBs) also qualified for membership in the organization. The bad vibes from the group's name caused problems. It is now called the "National Family Business Council."

Meetings of the council are held throughout the United States. Common problems include how much authority a relative is willing to yield to a younger family member. If the answer is "none," one must leave and management turnover is essential.

2. *Sole responsibility for the business.* Your bad judgment can lose you employees, customers, and creditors. Even if you are a capable manager, uncontrollable business factors (recession, more efficient competitors, a highway relocation, and so on) can force you into bankruptcy. Generally, you must face these alone.

3. *Continual need to meet financial obligations.* You must meet your financial obligations to employees and creditors, to a landlord (if you rent) or to a bank (if you have a mortgage), and to tax collectors.

4. *Lack of expertise.* You may be an excellent salesperson but a poor accountant, or vice versa. Either may bring about your downfall. Many highly skilled carpenters, for example, start their own businesses after working years for other people. But they spend so much time trying to sell, bid on new jobs, and schedule work crews that they have no chance to build. And their businesses fail.

5. *Operating disadvantages compared with large competitors.* Large competitors have specialists in all business areas and vast financial resources to weather emergencies. They also can attract better employees with higher wages and opportunities for advancement. And the savings they enjoy from large-scale production may enable them to set prices you cannot compete with.

After weighing these attractions and drawbacks, Americans establish almost 400,000 new businesses every year (most of them small). But about 350,000 businesses stop operations each year (voluntarily or involuntarily). About 10,000 of these go bankrupt or cannot meet creditor demands—failures that are caused by some common problems described below.

Why Small Businesses Fail

Immediate causes of failure include inadequate sales (cited by 49 percent of the failing firms studied), competition (23 percent), and heavy operating expenses (16 percent). In addition, manufacturers and wholesalers cite difficulty in collecting accounts receivable as a primary reason. And retailers feel poor location and inventory difficulties are also important. But by far the main underlying cause for failure is managerial inexperience or ineptitude, as you can see by looking at Figure 16–1 on the next page.

So merely having some experience in business is not enough. The small-business owner must be familiar with the specialized areas of sales, finance,

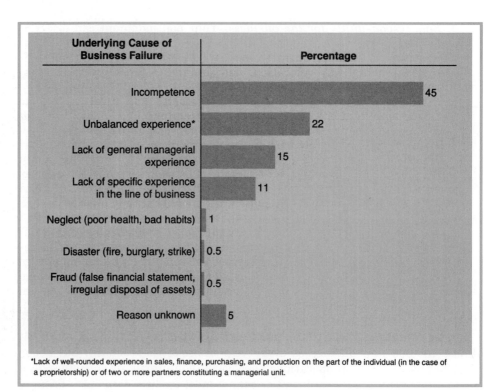

Underlying Cause of Business Failure | **Percentage**

Incompetence — 45
Unbalanced experience* — 22
Lack of general managerial experience — 15
Lack of specific experience in the line of business — 11
Neglect (poor health, bad habits) — 1
Disaster (fire, burglary, strike) — 0.5
Fraud (false financial statement, irregular disposal of assets) — 0.5
Reason unknown — 5

*Lack of well-rounded experience in sales, finance, purchasing, and production on the part of the individual (in the case of a proprietorship) or of two or more partners constituting a managerial unit.

**FIGURE 16–1
Why
Businesses
Fail.**

Source: *The Business Failure Record: 1977* (New York: Dun & Bradstreet, Inc., 1978), pp. 12–13.

purchasing, and production. "Typically, the person starting the business is a salesman who doesn't know much about production or an engineer who doesn't know much about sales," says Rowena Wyatt, a vice president of Dun & Bradstreet, Inc. Or the owner may have little actual experience in the firm's specific line of operations.

IS SMALL BUSINESS FOR YOU?

To decide if you and a small business are meant for each other, evaluate yourself, consider the types of business that appeal to you, and take a look at the franchise route. The following sections describe this process in detail.

Evaluate Yourself

Assess your strong and weak points truthfully and objectively. After all, you are "interviewing" your most valuable future employee.

Your Personal Characteristics

Look at the checklist in Figure 16–2, developed by the U.S. Small Business Administration to help people see if they are suited to the small-business lifestyle. (The figure is on the next page.)

Rate yourself. And consider having a friend ask several people who know you well to rate you anonymously. Although it is no guarantee, this evaluation gives you a general idea of your *potential* for success or failure.

Move from left to right and assign values of 4, 3, 2, and 1, respectively, to each of the four choices in each line. Total your score. A rough interpretation of your potential: 25–28 is excellent, 21–24 is very good, 17–20 is good, 13–16 is fair, and 12 or less is poor.

You can compensate for some weaknesses by finding partners or employees strong in your weaker areas. But too many marks on the right side of Figure 16–2 may indicate that small-business ownership is not for you.

Your Background and Experience

To match what you like to do with what you can do well, reflect on your past education, part-time and full-time jobs, and hobbies.

If your work experience has included a part-time job in a fast-food restaurant, waiting on tables and doing odd jobs at a resort, and waiting on customers and stocking inventory in a small shoe store, write down the things you were good at. Did you work up to helping keep the record of inventory at the shoe store? Did the owner ask your advice on what shoe styles to buy? Did you have a knack for meeting people and recognizing what customers wanted? If you felt competent in ways like these, small business might be for you.

Finding the Right Small Business

If your checklist and background indicate some talent and interest in small business, what business should you choose? Important facts to consider are: (1) customer needs and competition and (2) financial risks and rewards for you.

INITIATIVE	☐ Seeks additional tasks; highly ingenious.	☑ Resourceful; alert to opportunities.	☐ Performs regular work without direction.	☐ Routine worker; awaits direction.
ATTITUDE TOWARD OTHERS	☐ Positive; friendly interest in people.	☑ Pleasant, polite.	☐ Sometimes difficult to work with.	☐ Can be quarrelsome or uncooperative.
LEADERSHIP	☐ Forceful; inspires confidence and loyalty.	☐ Order giver.	☐ Driver.	☐ Follower.
RESPONSIBILITY	☑ Welcomes responsibility.	☐ Accepts without protest.	☐ Unwilling to assume without protest.	☐ Avoids whenever possible.
ORGANIZING ABILITY	☐ Highly capable of logical approach to organizing.	☑ Able organizer.	☐ Fairly capable of organizing.	☐ Poor organizer.
DECISIVENESS	☐ Quick and accurate.	☑ Good and careful.	☐ Quick, but often unsound.	☐ Hesitant and fearful.
PERSEVERANCE	☑ Highly steadfast in purpose; not easily discouraged.	☐ Maintains steady effort.	☐ Average determination and persistence.	☐ Little or no persistence.

Check a box in each line; then refer back to text discussion on page 393.

FIGURE 16–2
Are You a Potential Small-Business Owner?

Customer Needs and Competition

Would you like a business with customers flocking to your door and almost no competition? Businesses like that are hard to find, whether you're running a bookstore or a pie-throwing service. So consider questions like these:

1. What do consumers currently want?
2. What are they likely to want in the future, when economic conditions change?
3. Which industries are not overrun by a few large or many small businesses?
4. Will competition get tougher or easier?

Studies of small businesses give useful hints about your chances.[4] First, survival rates vary by industry. Wholesale firms have the best survival rate, followed by real estate, finance, construction, and manufacturing firms. Service trades (appliance repair, dry-cleaning, travel agencies, and the like) have a below-average survival record. And retailers have the worst record of all. Of course, many people are attracted to service and retail businesses, because they have experience in them and can afford the start-up costs. Opening your own picture-framing shop is much cheaper than launching a TV manufacturing firm.

Also, failure rates vary, even within a specific industry. The number of failures per every 10,000 businesses in each of ten retail and service industries is shown in Figure 16–3. Sporting goods stores have the worst record: for every 10,000 in operation in 1978, 46 failed. Small motels and inns, one-sixth as likely to fail, had the lowest rate—only 7 for every 10,000.

Chances for success do improve with time. About half of all businesses are sold or liquidated within the first two years of operation. And about 90 percent of small businesses stop operation before their tenth year. So buying a well-established business has an advantage over starting your own business.

Financial Risks and Rewards

Starting a small business is not cheap. Look again at Figure 16–3, which shows estimates of the necessary cash investment and annual return for ten different businesses. You may be in for some surprises. To start a small motel you will most likely need from $10,000 to $150,000. Even a hardware store costs $50,000 to $100,000 to start. And the returns are not always as high as you might expect. Although business services and bookstores average more than 10 percent return on investment—a good reward for the effort—for many of the others you would do just as well to put your money in the bank, and save yourself a lot of effort and worry. Nevertheless, for many people the rewards of being their own boss far outweigh all the risks involved.

Your Next Job:
Positions in Franchising

Collecting Information

Your first step toward owning your own franchise is to learn about the franchising business. Two pamphlets of special interest are available by writing the Superintendent of Documents, U.S. Government Printing Office, Washington, D.C., 20402: *Franchise Opportunities Handbook*, published by the U.S. Department of Commerce ($5.50 per copy). *Franchise Index/Profile*, published by the U.S. Small Business Administration ($2 per copy). Also, you may call your local office of the Better Business Bureau to obtain a free copy of *Facts on Selecting a Franchise*.

The International Franchise Association (IFA), founded in 1960, seeks to set standards of business practice and provide data about franchising. The IFA also publishes two pamphlets of interest to prospective franchisees that may be obtained by writing them at International Franchise Association, 1025 Connecticut Avenue, NW, Suite 1005, Washington, D.C., 20036: Jerome L. Fels and Lewis G. Rudnick,

Investigate before Investing: Guidance for Prospective Franchisees, 1978 ($5 per copy). *International Franchise Association Membership Directory*, 1979 ($1.50 per copy). In addition, your library probably has a number of reference books on franchising, such as: Charles L. Vaughn, *Franchising*, (Lexington, Massachusetts: D.C. Heath and Company, 1979).

Some Typical Franchisors

Everyone knows common names among the fast-food franchises, such as those used as examples in this chapter. But few people realize there are franchises available in such diverse industries as automotive products and services, beverages, florist shops, and sewing/fabric centers. The *IFA Membership Directory* lists the following names and addresses for some of these diverse franchises that may interest you, including several of the well-known, fast-food franchises:

AUTOMOTIVE
Transmission Service Centers
AAMCO Transmissions, Inc.
408 East Fourth Street
Bridgeport, PA 19405

Automotive Exhaust Systems
Midas-International Corp.
222 South Riverside Plaza
Chicago, IL 60606

Hard Line Retail Stores
Western Auto Supply Co.
2107 Grand Avenue
Kansas City, MO 64108

BEVERAGES
The Coca-Cola Co.
P.O. Drawer 1734
Atlanta, GA 30301

Dad's Root Beer Co.
2800 North Talman Avenue
Chicago, IL 60618

BICYCLE SHOPS
Schwinn Bicycle Co.
1856 North Kostner Avenue
Chicago, IL 60639

BOOKSTORES
Little Professor Book Centers, Inc.
33200 Capitol Avenue
Livonia, MI 48150

ELECTRONIC STORES
Radio Shack
1600 One Tandy Ctr.
Forth Worth, TX 76102

EMPLOYMENT SERVICES
Temporary Personnel
Temporaries, Inc. (A)
1015 18th Street NW
Washington, D.C. 20036

FLORIST SHOPS
Flowerama of America, Inc.
3165 W. Airline Hwy.
Waterloo, IA 50701

Flower World of America, Inc.
1655 Imperial Hwy.
Mid-Atlantic Park
West Deptford, NJ 08086

REAL ESTATE SALES
Century 21 Real Estate Corp.
18872 McArthur Blvd.
Irvine, CA 92707

RESTAURANTS
Burger King Corp.
P.O. Box 520783
Biscayne Annex
Miami, FL 33152

KFC Corp.
Kentucky Fried Chicken
P.O. Box 32070
1441 Gardiner Ln.
Louisville, KY 40232

McDonald's Corp.
1 McDonald's Plaza
Oak Brook, IL 60521

Wendy's International, Inc.
P.O. Box 256
Dublin, OH 43017

SEWING/FABRIC CENTERS
Knit Fabric Specialty Stores
Stretch & Sew, Inc.
P.O. Box 185
Eugene, OR 97402

FIGURE 16-3
The Risks and Rewards
in Ten Popular Small Lines of Business.

INDUSTRY	SPECIFIC BUSINESS	1978 FAILURES PER 10,000 BUSINESSES	ESTIMATED CASH INVEST-MENT* (IN $ THOUSANDS)	ESTIMATED RETURN† (PERCENT)
Retailing	Sporting goods	46	40–60	6–8
	Books, stationery	38	25–35	10–14
	Cameras, photo supply	36	40–60	5–8
	Gifts	25	20–30	7–10
	Toys, hobby crafts	20	20–30	4–6
	Hardware	16	50–100	5–7
	Eating and drinking establishments (small)	14	25–50	5–7
Services	Business services (consulting, steno-graphy, etc.)	21	10–15	15–20
	Travel agencies	19	30–50	8–10
	Motels, inns (small)	7	100–150	6–8

* Investment is cash needed, assuming maximum borrowing.
† Return is after all costs, including taxes and reasonable salaries.

Source: "How to Start a Sideline Business," *Business Week*, August 6, 1979, p. 97. Reprinted by permission of McGraw Hill, Inc.

Franchise or Not?

One important form of small business in this country is the *franchise*. A **franchise** is a contract between two parties in which one grants the other the right to sell goods or services using a prescribed marketing plan, trademark, and advertising. The party granting the rights is the **franchisor;** the one receiving them is the **franchisee.** For the benefits provided by the franchisor, the franchisee pays a monthly or annual fee.

If you buy a franchise, you get an established name and method of operation. But you pay a relatively high cost for those benefits and must abide by the rules of your franchisor.

One important key to a successful franchise business is knowing your franchisor thoroughly. Kentucky Fried Chicken franchisees who opened in the early 1970s learned this the hard way. In 1971, KFC was sold to Heublein, Inc., which sells products like Smirnoff Vodka and A-1 Steak Sauce. According to recent admissions by Heublein executives, the company's blunders almost drove KFC into the ground by 1977. The stores became run-down and dirty; managers got surly; and the quality of the food was unreliable. So, during the following year, about 1,500 franchisees and store managers were trooped back to KFC's school in Louisville for refresher courses.

But problems remain for KFC franchisees. Because KFC has stressed take-out business, many of its small shops have been unable to compete with McDonald's and Wendy's, which have space for sit-down customers. Also, KFC is now spending $50 million to tear down its garish red cupola roofs and remodel its buildings in a style more compatible with today's subtler tastes. A further problem for KFC and McDonald's, both of which use frozen meat to hold prices down, is that they are having trouble competing with chains like Wendy's and Chuck's Fried Chicken, which use fresh meat in their products.

If you're considering a franchised fast-food restaurant and have no partner, the International Franchise Association, a trade organization, offers a

Is That Franchise a Gold Mine or a Dry Well?

Think about these things before you buy into a franchise:

1. ABOUT THE FRANCHISOR AND INDUSTRY Who is the franchisor? What are the products or services sold? Are there trademarks, patents, or copyrights to protect what is sold? Is the company legitimate? Is it involved in any lawsuits? Is its management qualified?
2. LOCATION, TERRITORY, and OPERATING FACILITY Is your proposed franchise for a specific location in a particular territory? Just that one location? Who finds the site and selects the plans for your facility? Are other franchisees allowed in your area? How near?
3. EXPENSE AND PROFIT PROJECTIONS Are there initial fees? Monthly fees? Other kinds of fees? Are profit projections provided? Are they realistic?
4. TRAINING, START-UP, AND OPERATIONS Is training provided? What kind? How much? Will there be start-up assistance? What kind of advertising and other assistance is provided once you start?
5. TERM, RENEWALS, TERMINATION How long is the franchise agreement in effect? What are the bases for renewal and termination? Can the franchise be sold?

helpful booklet. And the box (lower left) provides examples of the types of questions for which you will need good answers. (Starting a new business without a franchise will be described in Chapter 17.)[5]

GOING THE FRANCHISE ROUTE

Let's assume you've decided to use the franchise route to owning your own small business. Four key steps in starting and operating your own franchise are: (1) finding the right location, (2) obtaining the financing, (3) running the business, and (4) assessing your performance. These steps will be discussed in detail throughout the remainder of this chapter, using three of the largest fast-food franchise restaurant chains as examples—McDonald's, Kentucky Fried Chicken (KFC), and Wendy's International, Inc. So let's also assume that you've provided the information on the qualification report (an example of which is shown in Figure 16–4) and that you've been accepted as a franchisee.

Finding the Right Location

To be a successful fast-food restauranteur, you need a location that will attract customers and generate sales revenue. Your franchisor will give you tips or perhaps a site survey kit. Important factors include traffic past your door, future highway or zoning changes, nearness of present and future competition, and the number of potential customers in area homes and businesses. KFC is one franchisor which also sends a field manager out to personally check your site. If the company approves the site, you may buy or lease it. And the franchisor provides building and site plans.

Obtaining the Financing

How much money do you need? Where will it come from? You need very careful answers to the first question before you can begin work on the second. A bank or the U.S. Small Business Administration (SBA) may give you technical advice but will not loan money without seeing a sound, formalized financial estimate.

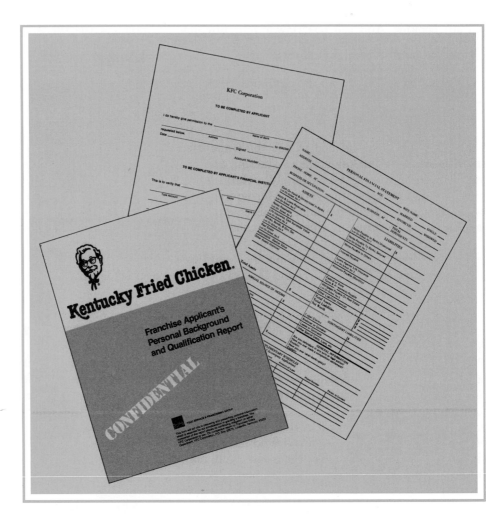

FIGURE 16-4
*Franchise
Application
Form for
Kentucky
Fried Chicken.*

Franchisors provide special financial planning assistance. Wendy's, for example, provides an income statement of what a "typical" restaurant operation looks like at three different levels of sales (see Figure 16–5). Notice that expenses for each level of sales are also expressed as a percentage of sales revenue. This is a big help in developing your financial plans and in measuring

FIGURE 16-5
How It Goes at a "Typical" Wendy's.

Income statement for one year of operations at three different levels of annual sales: $300,000; $400,000; and $500,000.

FINANCIAL ITEMS	AMOUNT	PERCENT	AMOUNT	PERCENT	AMOUNT	PERCENT
Sales	$300,000	100.00	$400,000	100.00	$500,000	100.00
Cost of Goods Sold:						
Manager or Owner	$ 13,000	4.33	$ 13,000	3.25	$ 13,000	2.60
Co-Manager	10,500	3.50	10,500	2.62	10,500	2.10
Crew	27,750	9.25	37,000	9.25	42,500	8.50
Total Labor	$ 51,250	17.08	60,500	15.12	66,000	13.20
Food (1)	111,000	37.00	148,000	37.00	185,000	37.00
Paper	12,000	4.00	16,000	4.00	20,000	4.00
Laundry	1,050	.35	1,400	.35	1,750	.35
Total Cost of Goods Sold	$175,300	58.43	$225,900	56.47	$272,750	54.55
Gross Profit	124,700	41.57	174,100	43.53	227,250	45.45
Operating Expenses:						
Rent (2)	$ 25,800	8.60	$ 25,800	6.45	$ 25,800	5.16
Royalty	12,000	4.00	16,000	4.00	20,000	4.00
Insurance	2,100	.70	2,100	.53	2,100	.42
Taxes—Payroll	3,450	1.15	4,200	1.05	5,000	1.00
Taxes—Real Estate	2,000	.67	2,000	.50	2,000	.40
Taxes—Other	1,000	.33	1,000	.25	1,000	.20
Supplies	3,750	1.25	5,000	1.25	6,250	1.25
Utilities	10,250	3.42	10,750	2.69	11,250	2.25
Repair & Maintenance	4,500	1.50	5,000	1.25	5,000	1.00
Telephone	500	.17	500	.13	500	.10
Trash Removal	1,500	.50	1,500	.37	1,500	.30
Advertising & Promotion	12,000	4.00	16,000	4.00	20,000	4.00
Office Expenses	1,200	.40	1,200	.30	1,200	.24
Miscellaneous	250	.08	250	.06	250	.05
Total Operating Expenses	$ 80,300	26.77	$ 91,300	22.83	$101,850	20.37
Cash Flow	$ 44,400	14.80	$ 82,800	20.70	$125,400	25.08
Depreciation (3)	$ 6,000	2.00	$ 6,000	1.50	6,000	1.20
Pre-tax Profit ($)	$ 38,400		$ 76,800		$119,400	
Pre-tax Profits (% of sales)		12.80		19.20		23.88

Source: From D. Daryl Wyckoff and William L. Berry, "Wendy's Old-Fashioned Hamburgers," 6-677-122, Harvard Business School, p. 22. Copyright © 1976 by the President and Fellows of Harvard College. Reproduced by permission.

your restaurant's performance once it is in operation. (Examples of financial projections are given in Chapter 17.)

Franchises are not cheap. The "shoestring" investment you might be thinking of may turn out to look more like a bootstrap. At Wendy's, for example, the total initial investment can be as much as $455,000. Exact amounts vary from $287,000 to $455,000, depending on location, design, and seating capacity of the restaurant. The franchise fee to Wendy's is $15,000 for the technical assistance; the rest goes to various suppliers. McDonald's estimates are about the same. Costs are less for a Kentucky Fried Chicken franchise, because it stresses take-out business, with less seating capacity, smaller buildings, and less land.

Sources of Financing

Wendy's, McDonald's, and KFC all require the franchisee to raise the necessary money. It can come from (1) the future owners; (2) loans from private financial institutions, such as banks and insurance companies; and (3) loans from federal agencies, especially the SBA. The owners, they say, should contribute substantial cash, because it represents personal commitment and will lead to extra effort—and because it provides protection for prospective lenders. (The business could be liquidated—converted to cash—to pay creditors and lenders if it failed.)

Commercial banks are especially important here. Except for trade credit, they are the major source of short-term funds. And though they are usually not very eager to finance a beginning business, they provide more than 80 percent of the intermediate- and long-term funds for small-business expansion. They should be approached first, because, by federal law, the SBA may not loan a small business funds that it can obtain from a bank or elsewhere.

The SBA, though, may make loans directly or jointly with banks to assist small firms to finance construction, conversion, or expansion; to purchase equipment, facilities, machinery, supplies or materials; and to acquire working capital. So the SBA is a very important source of financial assistance.

Qualifying for a Loan

Collect from anywhere you can about one-fourth of the cash you require. Then go to a bank to get the intermediate- and short-term funds you need for the balance. Loan decisions are usually made on the "three Cs" of credit:

CHARACTER The borrower must be reliable and must conserve business assets to ensure the loan's repayment.

CAPACITY The inherent soundness of the business and the expertise of its owner must indicate that the firm is likely to succeed.

COLLATERAL The owner of the business must have substantial assets in an existing firm or must be willing to back up his or her credit standing with personal collateral, such as a privately owned home, life-insurance policies with cash-surrender values, or marketable securities.

If the bank agrees to lend you the cash, based on your character and financial information and business projections, you are ready to go.

Running the Business

Large franchisors like McDonald's, Wendy's, and Kentucky Fried Chicken have excellent training facilities for new franchise owners. A new McDonald's franchisee spends 300 hours in one of the chain's restaurants, progresses to a two-week Business Operations Course at another restaurant, and then spends two more weeks at the company's Hamburger University outside Chicago (see box on the bottom of next page).

Wendy's and KFC also help their franchisees by finding them qualified suppliers, giving them advice from field consultants, offering "refresher" courses when needed, and distributing detailed operations manuals, bulletins, and brochures. And, of course, they all design national and local advertising campaigns and other promotional material for use by their franchisees.

These services are valuable and not free. The franchisee pays an initial fee of $12,500 to $15,000 and a fixed monthly percentage of gross sales. McDonald's charges 11½ percent of gross sales; Wendy's, 4 percent. Both companies also require the franchisee to spend an additional 4 percent of monthly gross sales on advertising.

All three franchisors discourage absentee ownership. They want their franchisees to run the business on a full-time basis in order to spot problems as they arise. Usually, the problems concern staffing. Scheduling forty to eighty part-time teen-age employees to handle peak and off-peak demand can pose tremendous difficulties. For one thing, the average teen-age employee quits after only four months. Because teen-age employees are the backbone of the fast-food industry, most chains now give their managers—usually in their early 20's—special training to develop skills in dealing with young employees.

The franchisors are continually looking for ways to build sales for themselves and their franchisees. McDonald's, which used to open at 11 A.M., wanted to crack the breakfast market. After four years of test marketing, it developed the "Egg McMuffin," and began service at 7 A.M. Breakfast now accounts for 10 percent of sales.

Assessing Your Performance

How well will your franchise do? It's hard to know for sure, but estimates are available. Look again at Figure 16–5, which shows predicted profits for a "typical" Wendy's at three levels of annual sales. After being in business for one year, a franchisee can compare his or her profits against charts such as this one. A quick glance can show you if any of your expenses are out of line.

Hamburger University

While many students from Stanford and Harvard receive degrees in journalism or engineering, each year nearly 2,000 graduates of H.U. receive bachelor's degrees in Hamburgerology.

H.U. is Hamburger University, the international management training center for McDonald's Corporation licensees (franchisees) and managers.

Since 1961, over 17,000 men and women have studied in the hallowed halls of Hamburger University. Their curriculum includes actual work experience in a McDonald's restaurant as well as an intensive classroom program. Subjects, which are taught by H.U. professors, range from the day-to-day management of a McDonald's to courses in business management, accounting, marketing, personnel management, and community relations. Heading the school is a dean chosen from the professional ranks.

The first classes of H.U. were held in the basement of a suburban Chicago McDonald's. But in 1968, the company built a modern training center in Elk Grove Village, Illinois, which was doubled in size in 1973.

Hamburger U. offers lectures in real classrooms, has a complete research library on restaurant management and the food industry, a closed-circuit television studio, sophisticated film-processing equipment, and a United Nations-type simultaneous translation system for non-English-speaking students. Hamburger University also hosts graduate seminars for alumni and prepares audio-visual training programs for management and crews, both in the United States and in McDonald's twenty-six international markets. And in 1972, a "branch campus" of H.U. opened in Tokyo, Japan.[6]

Also check your pre-tax profits as a percentage of annual sales. The "typical" Wendy's restaurant earns 12.8 percent, 19.2 percent, and 23.9 percent on annual sales of $300,000, $400,000, and $500,000, respectively. So, if you had to invest $400,000 to start your Wendy's, at these three annual sales volumes you would respectively receive 9.6 percent, 19.2 percent, and 29.8 percent annual pre-tax return on your initial investment. These returns are much better than what you would have earned had you put the money in a local bank. And Figure 16–5 assumes that you also pay yourself $13,000 annually as salary for your work as owner-manager.

Low pay, distasteful working conditions, and autocratic bosses are common fare for the millions of teen-agers who work part-time in the country's fast-food restaurants. Large chains are usually covered by federal minimum wage laws ($3.35 per hour as of January 1, 1981, with some exceptions for teen-agers) and overtime pay provisions. Yet some employees have had to go to court to get it. And most teen-agers don't know that they must be paid for "waiting time" spent in the back room until things get busy and they are allowed to punch in, says The Wall Street Journal.[7]

Four out of five teen-agers quit after only four months on the job in a fast-food restaurant.

But even these numbers don't tell the whole story about your performance and the chances for long-term success. We just saw in Figure 16–5 that a typical Wendy's restaurant with annual sales in the range of $300,000 to $500,000 earns pre-tax profits of from 12.8 to 23.9 percent of annual sales. These profits are far higher than the typical 5 to 7 percent profits earned from a much smaller, *unfranchised* restaurant (Figure 16–3). And other sources estimate pre-tax profits on sales for restaurants—even as large as the Wendy's—at only 2 to 4 percent. So if you achieve the profits shown in Figure 16–5, you have done far better than the typical restaurant and can pat yourself on the back.

If a franchise sounds like it may not be for you, perhaps you would prefer to start your own small business from scratch. Chapter 17 describes how to do it.

Chapter Review & Applications

Key Points to Remember

1. The term "small business" generally means that: (a) the business is relatively small in sales dollars and employees; (b) its capital is provided by only one or a few people; and (c) its owner-managers are independent of a "corporate office."

2. The most common reason for failure of small businesses is managerial inexperience or ineptitude.

3. To find the right small business, you should consider (a) customer needs and competition, and (b) the potential financial risks and rewards.

4. A franchise is a contract between two parties in which the franchisor grants the franchisee the right to sell goods or services using a prescribed marketing plan, trademark, and advertising.

5. Four steps for starting and operating a franchise are (a) finding the right location; (b) obtaining the financing; (c) running the business; and (d) assessing your performance.

6. Starting a franchise can cost as much as a half-million dollars, and banks generally require one-quarter of the amount in cash before they make a decision on loaning the balance.

7. Large franchisors offer their franchisees valuable assistance, such as training programs; help finding suppliers; advice from field consultants; refresher courses when needed; operations manuals, bulletins, and brochures; and advertising and promotional materials.

8. For these services, franchisees pay an initial fee of $12,000–$15,000 and a fixed monthly percentage of gross sales.

Questions for Discussion

1. Each year about 350,000 businesses in the United States cease operations, either voluntarily or involuntarily.
   (a) What are some of the reasons for business failures?
   (b) How can prospective business owners reduce their chances of failure before they begin?

2. Review the example of job background and experience on page 393. If this were you, what education and job experience would you want your partner to have?

3. What are the potential disadvantages of buying an existing retail business? The potential advantages?

4. Most people are familiar with franchise fast-food restaurants. What other businesses are franchised?

5. If other restaurants in your franchise chain are slipping on quality and cleanliness, how could it affect you?

Short Case

Figure 16–5 shows a typical income statement for one year of operations of a Wendy's Old-Fashioned Hamburgers restaurant at three different levels of sales revenue.

(a) What expenses change with the volume of sales? Explain each change.

(b) In the 1980s, the costs of meat, energy, and labor are expected to increase dramatically. Which of your expense items will be most affected? If you owned a Wendy's, how would you try to neutralize these increases?

A Critical
Business Decision

—made by Brad Hubbart
of McDonald's

The Situation

The scene is McDonald's "Hamburger U," in Elk Grove, Illinois, where you can earn a two-week "Bachelor of Hamburgerology, with a minor in french fries." Each course at old H.U. is divided into two parts: basic operations (for all new owner-operators) and advanced operations (a refresher course).

Let's join a *New York Times* reporter in the back row as Basic Operations 120 begins.[8] The instructor is Jerry Gorman, a genial and informal man, who speaks firmly to his audience of new owners: "All classes require your attendance. Keep your manuals and notebooks with you at all times."

One of the first topics is production control. Gorman explains that McDonald's is dedicated to speed —to turning out a hamburger, a shake, and french fries in fifty seconds. Since the company also stresses freshness, any cooked hamburger not sold in seven minutes must be thrown away. The burger is a machine-stamped, 1.6-ounce patty 3.875 inches wide and 0.221 inches thick before cooking, garnished with a quarter-ounce of onion, a pickle slice, mustard, and ketchup, resting on a 4.25-inch-diameter bun.

Gorman points out that the major problem is to regulate production. Customers shouldn't have to wait more than a minute to be served, and no hamburger should be thrown away. This job is handled by the production control manager, operating near the middle of the counter yelling instructions to grillers, shakers, and fryers.

"Our basic run of burgers is twelve," Gorman explains. "But the production man must add enough for doubles. If he thinks he'll need six doubles, he yells, 'twelve and six.' The griller lays eighteen burgers down, and so on. The griller yells, 'Cheese on six and six?' This means, 'Of the six doubles and six regulars I've got, how many do you want cheesed?'

"Now if the production control manager wants two cheeseburgers and two double cheese burgers, he'll yell back, 'two and two.' This tells the griller what he needs to know, unless you get some 'grills'— orders for burgers without some of the normal ingredients. The grills come in on slips from the counter, and the griller has to deduct the grills from the other total. Got that?," asks Gorman.

He surveys his class skeptically. Only one student in the front row seems to understand.

"O.K.," Gorman says. "Let's see. If he calls, twelve and four, cheese on four and eight, two and two, and you get two 'ketchup only' grills, what do you make?"

Most of the students still seem at a loss. But the big man in the front row calmly answers: "Two double cheeseburgers, two double hamburgers, two regular cheeseburgers, four regular hamburgers, and two hamburgers with ketchup only."

Gorman nods, "You got it."

The Decision

After class, someone asks Gorman who the big guy is. "Oh," he replies, "that's Brad Hubbart. He used to play fullback for the San Diego Chargers."

Later, the reporter wrote: "Suddenly it all fell into place. I realized what McDonald's operation reminded me of—pro football. All those signals. . . the mathematical precision. The sheer technology of it all. . . . No wonder Brad Hubbart understood."

Hubbart is already back at work studying his McDonald's manuals. He's decided to be a franchisee instead of an independent restaurant owner, an important decision.

Question

Considering Brad Hubbart's experience, what are some of the advantages and the disadvantages of joining a franchise rather than being an independent restaurant owner?

Small Business: On Your Own

In this chapter you will learn . . .

- how to plan for your own retail business without a franchisor's help.
- how to find your market and to estimate your prospective annual sales revenue.
- how to develop financial plans and where to get the money to start your business.
- some of the key factors in day-to-day business operations.
- how to assess your business' performance.

17

hen Rory Fuerst graduated from college in 1974, his plan was to go into the fast-food business. While hanging around a lot of fast-food places, he noticed people's sneakers, says *Fortune* magazine.[1] The tops looked okay, but the soles were mostly worn out. So—fast—he bought pliers, glue, and some rubber soles for a total of $37 and asked tennis players at a nearby court if they wanted new soles. In his parents' oven, he heated the shoes to 375°. Off came the old soles, and on went the new ones.

After a month of the warm smell of old sneakers cooking, his mother kicked him out of the kitchen. So Fuerst got a bank loan and took out an expensive, full-page ad in *Sports Illustrated*. The result: 900 pairs of sneakers were dropped at his door to be resoled at $8.95 each. Fuerst was in business. He's now resoling 700 pairs of sneakers every day, at $13.95 plus postage. And his three plants manufacture 100,000 pairs of his new "Tred 2" shoes a month, accounting for about 90 percent of his $10 million annual revenue.

Rory Fuerst went into small business for himself—without the help of a well-established franchisor—and became very successful. At least for this chapter, see what it's like to go into the shoe business. You'll be selling shoes to the whole family—from sneakers to dress shoes to baby shoes. Remember, in boom times or bust, people always buy shoes. Since you know more about buying and selling than about accounting and finance, you decide to form a corporation with an accountant friend. He will work part-time in return for a share of the profits. The two of you each put in $25,000 to start The Shoe Place, Inc.

After reading this chapter, you should have some idea of whether you might like to try your hand at starting a small business from scratch, without a franchisor's help.

Having decided to make the plunge into a business of your own, you'll need to know four basic steps of starting a small business: (1) finding your market, (2) obtaining your financing, (3) running your business, and (4) assessing your performance. You'll notice that these are very similar to the steps outlined in the last chapter; but without the help of a franchisor, you will have to do all the work on your own.

FINDING YOUR MARKET

Finding the market for your business means choosing a location for your store, determining the size of the trading area, and estimating the store's annual sales revenue.

Choosing a Good Location

The right location can mean the difference between success and failure for a retailer. Do enough people live or work in the area to support your store? Can they afford your product? What is happening to the area's population and income? Will the customers like what you're selling?

One small restaurant, Greco's, offered Italian foods to a solid, middle-income neighborhood. But the residents, mostly Swedish-American, stopped eating at Greco's once the novelty wore off. They preferred their own style of cooking—and Greco's went bankrupt in ten months. Yet Jeno Palucci, a small manufacturer, started selling Chinese food all across the country and became a millionaire. He is now working on his next million offering Italian pizza in pubs around Great Britain.

Competition is also critical. How close are your competitors? How successful are they? Will more competitors come in? One small-grocery-store owner learned the significance of competition the hard way. He opened one and a half blocks from two established stores, one a medium-sized grocery and the other a supermarket. His store failed within six weeks.[2]

Also consider the physical site. Does the street or highway provide adequate access? Are highways likely to be relocated, affecting access? Do barriers like freeways, lakes, or rivers limit your geographic market area? Could changes in zoning laws alter the area significantly?

Small-business owners who are not bound to a particular area of a large city may systematically select the community, then the area within it, and finally the specific business site. Those who are committed to a particular location must assess the profitability of that specific site.

Judging the Size of the Trading Area

The *trading area* of a retail store or shopping center is the geographic region that provides most of the store's customers and sales revenue. This varies with

(1) the size of the store or center and (2) the kinds of goods sold. A regional shopping center with one hundred stores, for example, may attract customers from twenty-five miles in all directions. But a neighborhood grocery will probably draw from a three-block radius.

Related to these are the issues of barriers to customer travel—lakes, rivers, limited-access highways, railroad tracks, parks—and customer mobility. Is travel mostly in private cars or on public transportation? In lower-income areas or in times of serious gas shortages, mobility is more restricted and the trading area is smaller. The location and quality of competitors also help determine the size of a trading area.

Suppose you are seriously considering a neighborhood shopping center for The Shoe Place. The center's ten to fifteen stores would typically draw customers from about a mile away. Figure 17–1 shows the situation. The numbers are U.S. census tracts, each an area of thirty to sixty city blocks (six to eight blocks on each side). The black line shows the probable boundaries of your trading area:

- To the west, there is a park and golf course, a physical boundary.
- To the north is Broadway Street, halfway between your shopping center and a similar one with a shoe store.
- To the east, one mile away, is the main downtown area.
- To the south is Olson Memorial Freeway, another physical boundary.

Estimating your trading area takes some judgment. For example, it seems clear that your store cannot attract more business from the west because of the park and golf course there. But it might be possible to get customers from the other three directions, so your trading area might extend in those directions. (Question 3 at the end of the chapter asks you to consider what factors might extend your trading area to the north, east, and south.)

Estimating Sales Revenue

Consumer demand depends on (1) people, (2) income, and (3) a desire to buy (see Chapter 8). To translate this into estimates of annual sales revenue, we need to consider the following four factors (also shown in Figure 17–2). Three of these factors are based on secondary data and one is based on primary data:

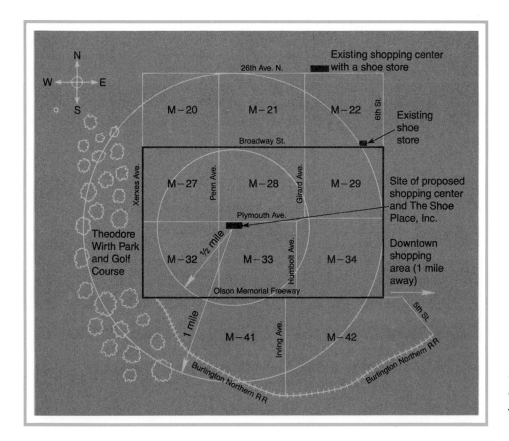

FIGURE 17-1
Estimated Trading Area of The Shoe Place (outlined in black).

FACTOR A   The number of households in a census tract in your retail trading area. (Secondary data from the U.S. Census of Population and Housing.)

FACTOR B   The median annual income of these households. (Secondary data from the U.S. Census of Population and Housing.)

FACTOR C   The proportion of each household's annual income spent on the kind of products you sell. (Secondary data from sources such as the U.S. Bureau of Labor Statistics.)

FACTOR D   The proportion of Factor C that will be spent in your store. (Primary data from personal interviews with area residents, in which you can also investigate their shoe preferences and needs.)

To get an estimate of the annual sales revenue for your store in that retail trading area, multiply the four factors together, as shown in the lower portion of Figure 17–2. Now refer to Figure 17–3 to see how these factors are translated into estimates for The Shoe Place, Inc. Using available secondary data, gathering primary data, and completing the calculations gives an estimated annual sales revenue of $420,000.

Is this enough to make a profit? For that, you need to know your operating costs, discussed in the following section.[3]

OBTAINING YOUR FINANCING

Begin by examining the performance of firms your size in your business. The type of information you need is found in firms' standard income statements and balance sheets and related financial ratios, which are published by various trade associations and organizations like Dun & Bradstreet. (Refer back to

FIGURE 17-2
Factors a Retail Store Can Use to Estimate Annual Sales Revenue from a Specific Census Tract.

FACTOR	A		B		C		D		
METHOD	Number of households in a census tract in the retail trading area	×	Median annual income of the households in the census tract	×	Proportion of a household's annual income spent on items sold by the kind of store being studied	×	Proportion of money spent on those items that will be spent in the store	=	Annual revenue (sales) obtained from all households in the census tract served by the store
Example: a proposed shoe store	1,000 households	×	$15,000 per year	×	0.013*	×	0.50†	=	$97,500 per year

*The proportion of 0.013 means that 1.3 percent of the typical household's annual income of $15,000 per year is spent on shoes.

†The proportion of 0.50 means that 50 percent of the shoes purchased by all the households living in this census tract are estimated to be from the proposed shoe store.

(1) Census tract in the trading area (factor A)	(2) Number of households in the census tract (factor B)	(3) Typical (median) annual household income	(4) Total personal income (column 2 X column 3)	(5) Proportion of households annual income spent in shoe stores (factor C)	(6) Personal consumption expenditures in shoe stores (column 4 X column 5)	(7) Proportion of Column 6 captured by proposed shoe store (factor D)	(8) Estimated annual sales revenue of proposed shoe store (column 6 X column 7)
M-27	1,088	$16,700	$18,169,600	0.013	$236,205	0.35	$82,671
M-28	916	$15,100	$13,831,600	0.013	$179,811	0.40	$71,924
M-29	1,026	$13,400	$13,748,400	0.013	$178,729	0.30	$53,619
M-32	780	$17,450	$13,611,000	0.013	$176,943	0.45	$79,624
M-33	960	$14,550	$13,968,000	0.013	$181,548	0.45	$81,713
M-34	755	$12,850	$9,701,750	0.013	$126,123	0.40	$50,449
Total	5,525	—	$83,030,350	—	$1,079,395	—	$420,000

FIGURE 17–3
Worksheet for Estimating Annual Sales Revenue for The Shoe Place.

Figures 11–1 and 11–2 on pages 275 and 278, respectively.) Figures for the performance of small shoe stores in 1979 are shown in Figure 17–4. These figures vary a great deal, depending on the state of the economy. For example, the typical profits of shoe stores in 1979 were about two to three times what they were five years earlier.

The Budgeted Income Statement

The **budgeted** or **projected income statement** shows the profitability of a business, or its ability to continue operating. To develop your budgeted income statement, first estimate The Shoe Place's total revenue for the first two years of operation. From the worksheet shown in Figure 17–3, you know that your estimated annual revenue is $420,000, or about $35,000 a month. However, this revenue builds gradually, as shown in Figure 17–5. So you can probably expect sales of only $18,500 the first month, with regular monthly increases of $1,500 during the first year, as you begin to attract loyal customers. Only by the last month of the year will sales reach a plateau of $35,000 per month. So your total sales will be only $321,000 in the first year and will not climb to $420,000 until the second year.

The budgeted income statement for these first two years is shown in Figure 17–6. The expense estimates shown on your statement will come from two sources: a reference book on financial ratios and from your's or your partner's own calculations of expenses for the six items listed below, which are keyed to the letters in the right-hand column of Figure 17–6.

FIGURE 17–4
Financial Ratios for Small Shoe Stores.

DESCRIPTION	FINANCIAL RATIO*		
	Bottom One-Fourth of Firms	Most Typical Firms	Top One-Fourth of Firms
Current Ratio: Current assets *divided by* current debt.	2.18	3.80	7.50
Net Profits on Net Sales: Net earnings after taxes *divided by* net sales (sales *less* returns, allowances, and cash discounts).	2.51%	5.61%	10.10%
Net Profits on Tangible Net worth:† Net profits *divided by* tangible net worth (total assets, after deducting intangibles, *less* total liabilities).	7.36%	16.36%	28.76%

* Ratios come from the financial statements of a sample of shoe stores, arrayed from lowest to highest. The "most typical" is the median value, in the middle of the array. The lower one-fourth is halfway between the median and the lowest value. The upper one-fourth is halfway between the median and highest value.

† A value of at least 10 percent is often necessary to provide dividends and funds for future growth.

Source: *1979 Key Business Ratios: Retailing* (New York: Dun & Bradstreet, 1979).

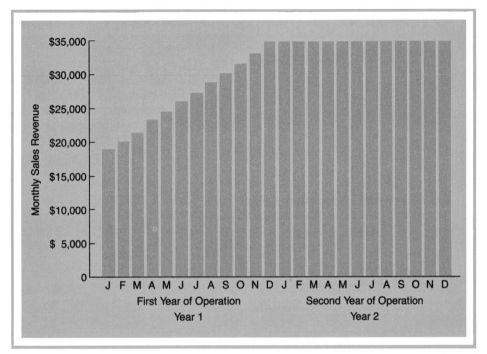

FIGURE 17–5
Estimated Monthly Sales Progress for The Shoe Place.

(a) RENT   Your research indicates a need for about 2,000 square feet of floor space. At $10.90 per square foot per year—a typical rental price—the yearly rent is $21,800.

(b) DEPRECIATION   Standard ratios suggest that $15,000 worth of furniture and fixtures are required to maintain an annual sales volume of $420,000. Assuming equal depreciation each year, a life of ten years, and no salvage value at the end of ten years, your yearly depreciation expense will be:

$$\frac{\$15,000 - 0}{10} = \$1,500$$

(c) INSURANCE   You estimate that during the first two years of operations the insurance premium will be $4,000 annually, payable in semi-annual installments of $2,000.

(d) INTEREST   After completing your projected balance sheet, you find that you will need a five-year bank loan of $55,000 (probably to be guaranteed by the SBA). Your interest will be 14 percent. The bank requires payments in equal annual installments of $16,021, which covers both interest and principal. Of course, as you pay off the principal, the annual amount of interest decreases each year. So your interest payments will be $7,700 the first year and $6,535 the second year, as shown in Figure 17–6.

(e) UTILITIES   You estimate that charges for light, heat, telephone service, and so on will be $200 per month, or $2,400 annually.

(f) INCOME TAX   Because your store is incorporated, you must pay 20 percent of your first $25,000 of profits in annual income taxes, of which 17 percent is federal corporate tax and 3 percent is state tax.

Note that some of the expense items above, such as depreciation and interest,

FIGURE 17–6
The Shoe Place's Budgeted Income Statement (First Two Years).

Income Statement Item	Year 1	Year 2	Basis of Estimate Percentage of Sales	Other
Annual Sales	$321,000	$420,000	100.0	
Less: Cost of Goods Sold	193,909	253,700	60.4	
Gross Profit	$127,100	$166,300	39.6	
Less: Operating Expenses				
Owner's salary	$17,300	$22,700	5.4	
Employee Wages	31,800	41,600	9.9	
Rent	21,800	21,800		(a)
Depreciation	1,500	1,500		(b)
Advertising	8,000	8,000	1.9	
Insurance	4,000	4,000		(c)
Interest	7,700	6,535		(d)
Utilities	2,400	2,400		(e)
Miscellaneous	24,956	39,489		
Total Expenses	$119,456	$148,024		
Net Profit (Loss) before Income Taxes	$7,644	$18,276	3.5	
Less: Income Taxes (20%)	1,529	3,655		(f)
Net Profit (Loss)	$6,115	$14,621		

cannot be filled in until the budgeted balance sheet (Figure 17–7) is completed. So you must prepare the two statements simultaneously.

The Budgeted Balance Sheet

The **budgeted** or **projected balance sheet,** shown in Figure 17–7, estimates how much of the various assets will be needed to open and operate the business. With this information you can subtract your personal investment and the store's earnings to see how much you need to borrow the first year.

To reach this point, you must make specific estimates of your assets (like cash, accounts receivable, inventory, and equipment), your liabilities, and owners' equity. As Figure 17–7 shows, the contribution of you and your partner to start the business amounts to $50,000 (owners' equity). You also have first-year profits or retained earnings of $6,115, which can be reinvested in the business. So you have $56,115 to work with the first year. Your total assets required for that year are $118,386. The difference of $62,271 must be borrowed to acquire the assets. Loans are generally made in round numbers, so you might ask your bank for an initial intermediate loan of $55,000. Other short-term financing must be arranged with your suppliers or other lenders to make up the difference.

The Cash Budget

The **cash budget** shows your store's ability to meet its cash needs on time, no matter what the sales revenue turns out to be. Your cash needs include employee salaries, interest costs and repayment of principal, suppliers' fees, and taxes. Substantial default on any one of these can lead to bankruptcy.

A profitable budgeted income statement does not guarantee that a firm will be solvent (have sufficient cash to meet its short-term obligations) at all points during the accounting period. So you need to reassess the cash budget monthly or quarterly to pinpoint cash inflows and outflows and anticipate extreme cash deficits or surpluses. Then you can get a short-term loan or arrange a short-term investment, if necessary. While the cash budget is too detailed to present here, it is essential for good financial planning. Let's assume your partner does the cash budget for the shoe store and concludes you need short-term financing of $15,592—to be arranged with your suppliers or other lenders—in the first year (Figure 17–7).

Balance Sheet Item	End of Year 1		End of Year 2	
Assets				
Current Assets				
Cash	$ 8,010		$ 10,480	
Accounts Receivable	8,747		11,444	
Inventory	88,129		115,309	
Total Current Assets		$ 104,886		$ 137,233
Fixed Assets				
Equipment (furniture and fixtures)	$ 15,000		$ 15,000	
Less: Accumulated Depreciation	(1,500)		(3,000)	
Total Fixed Assets		13,500		12,000
Total Assets		$ 118,386		$ 149,233
Liabilities and Owners' Equity				
Liabilities				
Short-term Financing	$ 15,592		$ 41,304	
Intermediate-term Loan (14%)	46,679		37,193	
Total Liabilities		$ 62,271		$ 78,497
Owners' Equity				
Capital	$ 50,000		$ 50,000	
Retained Earnings	6,115		20,736	
Total Owners' Equity		56,115		70,736
Total Liabilities and Owners' Equity		$ 118,386		$ 149,233

FIGURE 17-7
The Shoe Place's Budgeted Balance Sheet (First Two Years).

Talking to the Bank

To obtain the intermediate-term loan of $55,000 you and your partner need, you both must take your financial projections and records of your personal net worth to a local bank. Suppose the loan officer there is satisfied with your character but not with your capacity and collateral (the three C's of Chapter 16). So your loan is refused.

But the loan officer is impressed with the details of your budgeted income statement, budgeted balance sheet, and cash budget. So he or she agrees to go with you to the local SBA office. The SBA agrees to guarantee the bank loan to you at 14 percent interest for five years. This means the SBA will repay 90 percent of the loan to the bank if your business fails. The other 10 percent, the bank risk, is acceptable to the loan officer. The bank also agrees to provide you with short-term loans to meet your cash needs during the first two years.

So far, so good: your detailed financial plans for what appears to be a viable small business have enabled you to get the intermediate- and short-term loans to open The Shoe Place, Inc.

RUNNING YOUR BUSINESS

Now that you are ready to begin your business, you will need to learn some basic aspects of its operation. The key areas of running a business are buying and pricing products, and advertising and selling products. Each of these will be examined below.[4]

Buying and Pricing Products

Many small businesses fail because their owners lack the experience and judgment to buy the right products and to price them properly.

A retailer must first find out what type, brand, quality, color, size, and style of a product will sell best. There are more kinds of shoes to choose from than there are feet. So pay close attention to customers, salespersons, trade journals, and catalogs to identify trends. You must also select suppliers who can provide the kind and quality of goods you want. And repeated decisions must be made on the quantity of shoes to buy—you will need an inventory large enough to ensure quantity discounts and prevent stock-outs, but small enough to avoid getting stuck with obsolete, hard-to-sell styles and colors.

To set prices, you must first consider general pricing factors related to cost, demand, and competitors' prices (discussed in Chapter 9). To avoid under-pricing (a common early error), you should examine standard operating ratios for similar businesses. These ratios include estimates of the average percentage of gross profit that must come from each dollar of sales if operating expenses and net profit margins are to be met.

Your Next Job
Occupations Leading to Small-Business Ownership

Thousands of men and women who now run their own small businesses started with various levels of education, obtained experience working for others, and then went off on their own. Here is a small sample of some typical small-business positions.

Positions in Service and Repair

Appliance servicers repair and occasionally install consumer appliances. They often specialize in one category of household appliances, such as washers and dryers or refrigerators and freezers. Most servicers have a background in electronics, often receiving specialized further training in the use of tools and testing devices from technical schools or community colleges. Employers generally hire trainees, who must complete several years of on-the-job training before they are considered fully qualified servicers. Experienced repairers frequently open their own service shops. Annual income ranges from $10,400 for trainees to $21,000 for experienced servicers. Job opportunities for appliance servicers and repairers are expected to increase as the production of technically complex consumer goods increases. (*Additional information:* Association of Home Appliance Manufacturers; 20 North Wacker Drive; Chicago, Illinois 60606.)

Television and radio service technicians, often self-employed, repair many types of electronic equipment, including televisions, radios, tape recorders, and stereos. Employers generally hire people who have backgrounds in electronics, mathematics, and physics; technical-school training is a competitive advantage. Technicians begin as trainees and gradually acquire a sufficient knowledge of electronic components and circuits to be considered fully qualified to repair complex electrical equipment. Annual income ranges from $10,000 to $18,500. Job opportunities are expected to expand moderately as consumer demand for highly technical products increases. (*Additional information:*

National Alliance of Television and Electronic Service Associations; 5908 South Troy Street; Chicago, Illinois 60629.)

Positions in Other Small Businesses

In their capacity as drug experts, pharmacists in retail drugstores dispense prescription and nonprescription medicines. Pharmacists also advise customers as to the proper selection and use of drugs. Self-employed pharmacists need a basic business knowledge, since many of their responsibilities like accounting and staffing are not directly related to their pharmaceutical training. The minimum educational requirement is a bachelor's degree in pharmacy. Pharmacists must also pass a state board examination to obtain a license. Annual salaries vary from $14,000 to $21,000. The employment outlook is promising due to both the growing number of pharmaceutical products and a rising consumer demand for them. (*Additional information:* American Pharmaceutical Association; 2215 Constitution Avenue, N.W.; Washington, D.C. 20037.)

Jewelers make and repair precious jewelry, which requires both dexterity and patience. Jewelers often specialize in one particular type of jewelry or in a specific skill, such as jewelry design, polishing, or stone setting. Private industries provide apprenticeship programs for applicants who have a high-school or a technical-school background in chemistry, mechanical drawing, or art. Training programs in small jewelry shops are also available and may be preferred by apprentice jewelers who want to supplement their specialized skills with a knowledge of general business. Industrial salaries average $13,500. Self-employed jewelers have a much greater earning potential. Employment of jewelers is expected to grow as fast as the average for all occupations. (*Additional information:* Retail Jewelers of America, Inc.; Time-Life Building; 1271 Avenue of the Americas; Suite 650; New York, New York 10020.)

To understand what this means, look first at the figures below (suppose they come from The Shoe Place's income statement):

ITEM	AMOUNT	PERCENTAGE OF SALES
Annual Sales	$500,000	100%
Less: Cost of Goods Sold	350,000	70
Gross Profit	$150,000	30%
Less: Operating Expenses	100,000	20
Net Profit Before Taxes	$ 50,000	10%

The item termed *gross profit* (also called *gross margin* or **markup**) refers to the amount available to cover operating expenses and net profit. As long as these terms are expressed in dollar amounts, their meaning is clear. But when they are expressed as a percentage (as the term *markup* often is), confusion arises over whether one means percentage of selling price or of cost.

Suppose that the $500,000 of annual sales shown above was from selling 10,000 units at $50 apiece. The cost of goods sold was $35 per item, which indicates a markup of $15. So markup as a *percentage of cost* would be $15 divided by $35, or 42.9 percent. But markup as a *percentage of selling price* would be $15 divided by $50, or 30 percent. The latter is more common.

To set prices accurately, a retailer must often convert from one markup to the other. Many suppliers provide retailers with conversion tables. If not, use the following formulas:

$$\% \text{ markup on selling price} = \frac{\% \text{ markup on cost}}{100 + \% \text{ markup on cost}} \times 100$$

$$\% \text{ markup on cost} = \frac{\% \text{ markup on selling price}}{100 - \% \text{ markup on selling price}} \times 100$$

If all 10,000 units above were actually sold at $50 apiece, the markup percentage on each item would be equal to the gross-profit or gross-margin percentage taken from the income statement. But it is not so simple, since retail stores generally use different markup percentages for different items. Also, not all retail items are actually sold at the original selling price, because of markdowns and shrinkage. **Markdowns** are reductions in price due to overstocking, sudden style changes, damaged goods, and leftover sizes. **Shrinkage** means losses due to theft, spoilage, or breaking. The final markup percentages must be high enough to cover these.

After negotiating with several shoe suppliers, you have bought the brands and styles you think your customers will like. Now you must price them. If the average pair of shoes costs you $25, and your budgeted income statement (Figure 17–6) shows that your cost of goods sold is 60.4 percent of annual sales, you have a gross profit of 39.6 percent. To allow for markdowns and shrinkage, you increase your gross-profit figure to 44 percent. So your markup is:

$$\% \text{ markup on cost} = \frac{\% \text{ markup on selling price}}{100 - \% \text{ markup on selling price}} \times 100$$

$$= \frac{44}{100 - 44} \times 100 = \frac{44}{56} \times 100 = 78.6\%$$

So the retail selling price for an average pair of shoes at The Shoe Place is:

$$\begin{aligned} \text{Retail selling price} &= \text{cost} + \text{markup on cost} \\ &= \$25 + 78.6\% \text{ of } \$25 \\ &= \$25 + (0.786 \times \$25) \\ &= \$25 + \$19.65 = \$44.65 \end{aligned}$$

Now suppose you decide to further revise your price by **odd pricing**—pricing a few pennies below an exact dollar value. So your retail price becomes $44.95 for an average pair of shoes. This markup on cost of 78.6 percent may seem excessive, but it is necessary. It means that you can earn an average gross profit of 39.6 percent (with a higher markup on dress shoes, lower on sports shoes) to meet your operating expenses and to earn some profit.

Advertising and Selling Products

Advertising can be an effective way to build retail sales, especially direct-action advertising (explained in Chapter 10). The media available include newspapers, trade papers, the Yellow Pages, radio, television, handbills, and direct mail. If you are part of a shopping center, you are also expected to participate in cooperative advertising and promotions. When possible, you should try to measure the effectiveness of your ads, using the method outlined in Chapter 10.

In a retail store, selling involves personal selling and merchandise display. Personal, committed selling can create loyal customers and repeat sales. Refer back to the steps presented in Chapter 10. They apply to you and your sales personnel.

ASSESSING YOUR PERFORMANCE

To measure how well The Shoe Place, Inc. is doing, you need adequate accounting records (see Chapter 11). Various SBA reports, such as *Financial Recordkeeping for Small Stores* and *Management Audit for Small Retailers* provide checklists for planning, budgeting, buying, pricing, and insurance.

After two years you may wish to make a detailed analysis of your business. From your records, you should be able to develop an income statement and a balance sheet to compare your store's performance with your original projections and with other shoe stores of similar size. Figure 17–8 contains the information you need to help you do this (see the Short Case at the end of this chapter).

Income Statement
End of Year 2

Annual Sales	$425,000	
Less: Cost of Goods Sold	267,750	
Gross Profit		$157,250
Less: Operating Expenses:		
Owners' Salaries	$ 23,000	
Employee Wages	46,750	
Rent	21,800	
Depreciation	1,500	
Advertising	6,800	
Insurance	4,000	
Interest	6,535	
Utilities	2,400	
Miscellaneous	34,722	
Total Expenses		$147,507
Net Profit (Loss) before Income Taxes		$ 9,743
Less: Income Taxes (20%)		1,949
Net Profit (Loss) after Income Taxes		$ 7,794

Balance Sheet
For Year 2

Assets		
Current Assets:		
Cash	$5,300	
Accounts Receivable	8,200	
Inventory	121,300	
Total Current Assets		$134,800
Fixed Assets:		
Equipment (Furniture and Fixtures)	$ 15,000	
Less: Accumulated Depreciation	(3,000)	
Total Fixed Assets		12,000
Total Assets		$146,800
Liabilities and Owners' Equity		
Liabilities:		
Short-term Financing	$ 46,813	
Intermediate-term Loan (14%)	37,193	
Total Liabilities		$ 84,006
Owners' Equity:		
Capital	$ 50,000	
Retained Earnings	12,794	
Total Owners' Equity		62,794
Total Liabilities and Owners' Equity		$146,800

FIGURE 17–8 The Shoe Place's Income Statement and Balance Sheet for the Second Year.

Chapter Review & Applications

Key Points to Remember

1. Starting your own business from scratch—without a franchisor's help—requires you to assume more responsibility for planning and operations.

2. Finding the right market for a new retail store means choosing a location, determining the size of the trading area, and estimating annual sales revenue.

3. To determine how much financing is required, you need to prepare a budgeted income statement and a budgeted balance sheet.

4. The cash budget is another important tool in business financing, since many small businesses project sizable profits in their budgeted income statements but go bankrupt, because they are unable to meet day-to-day cash obligations.

5. Three important aspects of business operation are (a) buying and pricing products, (b) advertising and selling products, and (c) selecting and training personnel.

6. New small-business owners often underprice their merchandise. The price generally must include a high enough markup to cover all operating expenses and to produce some profit.

7. Adequate financial records must be maintained to assess business performance and to see when corrective action must be taken.

Questions for Discussion

1. What are the advantages and disadvantages of locating The Shoe Place, Inc. (a) in a shopping center or (b) by itself?

2. In what months might The Shoe Place, Inc. have especially good sales? Especially poor sales?

3. Study Figure 17–1 again and the discussion that accompanies it. What factors might cause the trading area for The Shoe Place to extend further to the north, east, and south? As the owner of the store, how would this affect your marketing activities?

4. Assume that revenue and expenses shown in the budgeted income statement (Figure 17–6) turn out as projected.
   (a) What are the net profits on tangible net worth (defined in Figure 17–4) for each of the first two years of operation?
   (b) If you and your partner each spend an average of forty hours a week operating your store and keeping business records during its first two years, what would your average hourly pay rates be?
   (c) Would it be more profitable to work for someone else? Why or why not?

5. A retailer must be careful to note whether markup percentages are based on selling price or on cost.
   (a) Convert the following markups on cost to markups on selling price: 10 percent; 40 percent.
   (b) Assume that the markups in part (a) are based on selling price and convert them to markups on cost.

Short Case

Suppose that The Shoe Place, Inc. actually operates for two years. The results are shown in Figure 17–8.
(a) Using the ratios of expenses to sales revenue (in Figure 17–6) and the financial ratios for shoe stores (shown in Figure 17–4), identify the apparent problems your store has.
(b) What do you recommend?
(c) In general, the higher the financial ratios shown in Figure 17–4, the better the financial condition of the firm. But there are exceptions. Can you think of any reason why a high current ratio might be *undesirable*?

A Critical
Business Decision

—made by Michael Croslin
of Medtek

The Situation

His life would make a rags-to-riches movie, except for one thing—no one would believe it. *Black Enterprise* magazine calls him a "biomedical businessman" and points out that his mere survival depended on his inventiveness.[6] Born on the island of St. Croix, he was abandoned as an infant. He was given the name Miguel Britto by the family who raised him. Seeing his job opportunities after grammar school limited to being a waiter or a beach bum, he borrowed money at age twelve for a plane ride to the United States.

School was vital to him. He graduated from high school at fourteen and from the University of Wisconsin with a B.S. in biology at seventeen. About that time he was adopted and was named Michael Croslin. Later, he received B.S. and M.S. degrees in mechanical and electrical engineering. In 1968, he received a Ph.D. in biomedical engineering, one of less than 200 such scientists in the U.S. and the only one who is black.

Croslin holds patents on forty-two inventions, most of them in the medical field. Probably his best-known invention replaces the traditional device used for taking blood pressure—the sphygmomanometer, which involves watching a falling column of mercury and listening for the pulse with a stethoscope. Croslin's "Medtek 410" does away with all that. Still using the air pad around the upper arm, the doctor can now take the blood pressure and pulse rate directly from a black box slightly larger than a hand calculator—the Medtek 410. Croslin began work on the device in 1958, and today it is the only electronic device for measuring blood pressure that has been approved by the Food and Drug Administration and Underwriters Laboratory; it was also tested by the U.S. Army for more than eight years.

The Decision

In 1961, Croslin began International Applied Science Laboratory, Inc., to design and develop instruments for medical uses. Croslin, recognizing his lack of business knowledge, sought and found a knowledgeable partner to help. The company prospered, reaching $2.5 million in annual sales, and began to sell stock to the public. But disaster struck in 1971 when Croslin's partner skipped town with $840,000 of the company's money.

Croslin now offers this advice to anyone thinking about going into business for himself: "No matter what background you have or what situation you intend to get into, attend a business school of some type. This ... enables you to speak intelligently about profit and loss statements, cash flow, and so on." Croslin paid off his business debts and then took his own advice: he earned a master's degree in business administration, and then tried again.

He established Medtek Corporation, retained 62 percent of its stock himself, and began producing medical diagnostic devices. He built the first eighteen Medtek 410 instruments by hand himself. Croslin does some painful agonizing and tells *Black Enterprise:* "When I started, I wanted to be head guy. I had the ownership crisis. I was holding the titles of chief engineer, production manager, and vice president of operations—which was crazy. I was getting no work done. It got to the point where I could not work in the hustle and bustle environment of getting orders shipped out. It was stopping me from designing the things I have yet to build."

Croslin concludes that he can't do everything—personally handling all the inventing, producing, marketing, and financing decisions for Medtek.

Questions

1. Which business activities should Michael Croslin perform himself? Why?
2. Which ones should he delegate to others? Why?

6 The Environment

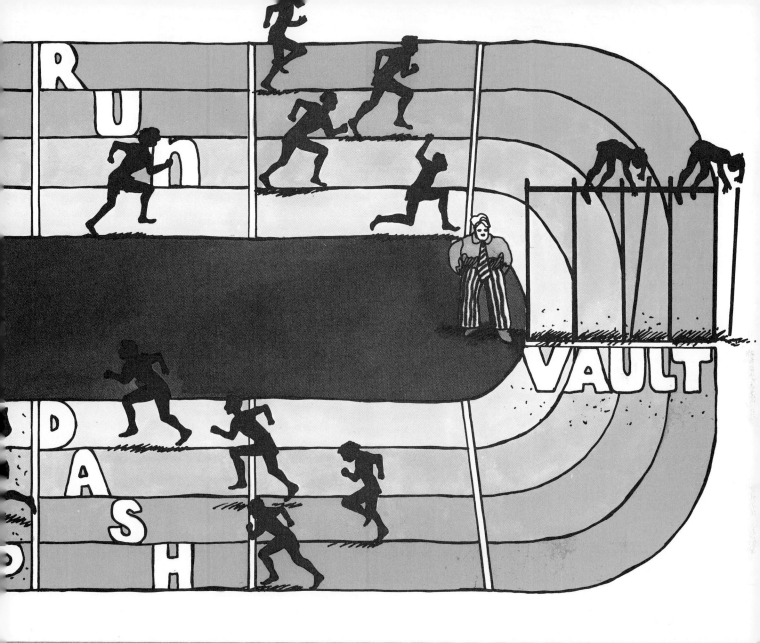

of Business

Government and Business Law

18

dward Richard, chief executive officer of Magnetics International, Inc., often spends more time down at City Hall in Cleveland than he does in his corporate office. He's part of a volunteer task force that worked for three months to develop 800 recommendations that would make Cleveland a more efficiently run city.

Joel Goldberg of Rich's retail stores, a division of Federated Department Stores in Atlanta, is lobbying for better crime legislation. He began to do it full-time after a mail clerk at Rich's was killed at mid-day in downtown Atlanta, according to a story in *The Wall Street Journal*.[1]

Nearly three-fourths of all big-company chief executive officers fly to Washington at least twice a month, according to one recent survey.

Involvement with government—on the federal, state, and local levels—is an increasing part of business activities, especially for chief executive officers. They may testify one day before a Senate committee in Washington, help the next day on a local savings bond drive, and appear the following afternoon at a campaign luncheon in the state capital. Many corporations are now hiring executives to deal specifically with these public affairs functions, or they are making government liaison work part of "the office of the chairman," to be shared by several top executives. In this chapter, we will look at the reasons why businesses are devoting so much time and energy to interactions with government.

THE ROLE OF GOVERNMENT IN BUSINESS

At one large auto company, managers must fill out 40,000 government forms each year. In every company, personnel managers must understand and comply with the regulations of the Equal Employment Opportunity Commission concerning hiring of minority and female job applicants. In companies that produce waste products, managers need to be aware of pollution standards and penalty procedures as set forth by the Environmental Protection Agency. And

all of us feel the effect of government on business when tax reductions are stiffened or an entire industry (such as airlines) is deregulated.

"Government should do those things that people cannot do as well for themselves," Abraham Lincoln once said. But exactly what those things are is not always clear. Some people believe in an *activist government,* one that steps in quickly to prevent widespread hardship, such as would occur if public employees went on strike, or to punish those who abuse the environment with excessive pollutants, illegal strip mining, or killing of endangered species. Others think government should play a much more *limited role.* In fact, government limits are built into the U.S. Constitution and follow three key principles:

1. DIVISION OF FUNCTIONS   The American government is organized into three separate levels—federal, state, and local. Powers not specifically assigned to the federal government are delegated to the states. And the states delegate some of their powers to local governments.
2. SEPARATION OF POWERS   The federal government is divided into executive, legislative, and judicial branches. Each has its powers and cannot exceed them.
3. RESTRICTIONS ON GOVERNMENT   The Constitution and the Bill of Rights restrict government's activities in the private sector. Government may not, for example, abridge such basic individual rights as free speech, free assembly, and access to due process of law.

Figure 18–1 summarizes the major ways in which government affects business generally. Throughout the rest of the chapter we will concentrate on the more specific areas of government and business interaction, such as business and antitrust laws, government regulation of business, taxation, the effect of business on government, and the future of government–business relations.

THREE KEY AREAS OF BUSINESS LAW

Business law, or commercial law, establishes "the rules of the game" for business transactions. It is based upon *statutory law,* the statutes or laws passed by the people or their elected representatives. An example is the Occupational Safety and Health Act (OSHA), which sets standards for safety in workplaces. Business law also comes from *common law,* the patchwork of

What Government Does		How This Affects Business
Establishes basic laws for conducting business. Administer justice, protect property, develop money for exchange, and establish a system of business law.		Business must follow the rules established by law. For example, a written contract with a supplier will usually be in a form that is enforceable in court.
Tries to stabilize the economy. Maintain employment, control inflation, and promote economic growth.		Business pays close attention to these efforts, since levels of economic activity, inflation, and changes in interest rates affect business decisions.
Regulates the economy. Assure fair competition, regulate business where monopoly is inevitable, and require businesses to report accurate information.		Most businesses seek to avoid prohibited practices.
Regulates the social policies of business. Issue regulations to protect consumers, ensure equal employment opportunity, protect the environment, and meet other social goals.	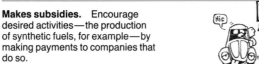	Most businesses seek to avoid these prohibited practices.
Procures supplies. Purchase goods and services. (The government is now the largest buyer in the U.S. economy.)		Many businesses sell directly to the government and follow government *procurement policies,* the rules and regulations government units establish to make their purchases.
Makes subsidies. Encourage desired activities—the production of synthetic fuels, for example—by making payments to companies that do so.		Business can benefit from direct subsidies, such as federal support of highway construction or indirect subsidies like tariff protection.
Taxes business. Tax businesses to raise revenues for government and to encourage or discourage selected types of business activity.		Businesses pay taxes, which strongly influence their activities. For example, tax specialists are employed to help reduce company taxes.

FIGURE 18-1
Seven Ways Government Influences Business.

past court decisions in this country and in Great Britain. For example, someone who sells a business cannot, under common law, be required by a buyer to stay out of that industry forever. And it also derives from *administrative law,* the rules developed by governmental regulatory agencies. The Environmental Protection Agency's specifications on particulate emissions from diesel engines is an example here.

Requirements and decisions from these three sources of law can be appealed in court. The judicial system is composed of three levels of courts. First are the *trial courts,* where cases are originally heard by judges and juries. Trial courts exist on both the state and federal levels (federal trial courts are called U.S. District Courts). Next come the *appellate courts.* These include the U.S. Court of Appeals (at the federal level), as well as specialized courts like the U.S. Tax Court. There the court affirms, reverses, or modifies trial court decisions. At the top federal level, the U.S. Supreme Court hears final appeals involving important legal issues (for an example, see the color insert that follows Chapter 20).

Business law is also strongly influenced by the Uniform Commercial Code (UCC), a comprehensive statute covering everything from bank checks to broken contracts to bankruptcy. The UCC has been adopted by all states except Louisiana, so that many business laws are the same across the country. Three key areas of business law influenced by the UCC—the law of contracts, the law of agency, and the law of bankruptcy—are discussed in the following sections.

A Modern Time Bomb from the Old Common Law: Product Liability

Product liability is based on old common-law ideas of civil wrongs, negligence, safety, and responsibility. Product liability suits have major implications for modern products and for consumers who don't know how they work.

One customer decided that she wanted a perfumed candle. So she poured some Faberge perfume onto a lighted candle. Burned by the resulting explosion, she sued the producer for damages. She won.

The court ruled that Faberge should have labeled the perfume "flammable." Another customer decided that if a power mower was useful for cutting grass, why not tip it vertically and cut his hedges with it? He was hurt. He sued and won.

Product liability is a time bomb in our midst, according to many business managers. It involves millions of dollars in claims by injured customers against businesses. And it is almost impossible to foresee how some customers might use products or to always use the best available technology. Certainly the law should protect consumers from dangerous products, but perfume might be stretching that category a bit too far.

The Law of Contracts

A **contract** is an agreement between a buyer and a seller that is enforceable in court. Every time you use a credit card at a gas station, buy a ticket to a concert, or pay to ride the bus, you are involved in a contract. Contracts do not have to be signed or even written to be enforceable, though certain kinds must be. These include contracts for the sale of land and contracts for the sale of personal property over some specified amount (usually $500).

But, written or unwritten, a legal contract must meet these conditions:

1. There must be an offer.
2. There must be an acceptance.
3. There must be consideration.
4. The parties must be competent.
5. The contract must have a lawful purpose.

An Offer

An **offer** is a proposal by one party (the offeror) to enter into a contract with a second party (the offeree). It must be made in definite terms and with the specific intention of creating a contract. For example, the courts have ruled that advertisements and store window displays are not offers, because they do not necessarily propose a contract with potential customers.

An Acceptance

An **acceptance** is an acknowledgment by the offeree that the terms are satisfactory and that the offeree is willing to be bound to these terms.

Offers and acceptances can be spoken, written, or in the form of an action. For example, the presence of a bus on a city street is an offer. And the action of getting on the bus and putting money in the coin box is an acceptance of the bus company's offer. Offers and acceptances must be voluntary; a contract signed at gunpoint, as in the movies, would never hold up in court. The agreement of both parties must also be based on an understanding of the facts. If one party signs under a mistaken impression, the contract may not be valid.

Consideration

For a contract to be enforceable, each party must give **consideration**—something of value in exchange for the agreement of the other party to the contract.

Consideration may be in the form of money, goods, an action, or an agreement to refrain from an action.

Competent Parties

A person is considered **competent,** or legally fit, unless he or she is (1) a minor (in most states, anyone under eighteen years of age), (2) emotionally unbalanced, or (3) intoxicated.

Lawful Purpose

A contract is not enforceable if the parties have agreed to something that is illegal or that is not in the best interests of society. In states where gambling is against the law, for example, contracts involving gambling debts are not enforceable.

The Law of Agency

Agency is a legal relationship in which one party (the agent) is authorized to act on behalf of another (the principal) in dealings with a third party. Virtually all types of transactions, except voting or making a will, can be negotiated by an agent. Insurance representatives who make policy agreements with clients are agents of their company. Manufacturers' representatives are agents of their clients. So are real-estate brokers. The law of agency involves two key aspects:

1. *The principal's obligations to the agent.* The principal gives the agent the authority to make, modify, or terminate contracts with a third party on behalf of the principal. For this, the agent is usually paid. If the agent suffers a loss or is sued for unintentionally injuring a third party while following the principal's instructions, the principal must reimburse the agent.
2. *The agent's obligations to the principal.* The agent must be loyal to the principal and cannot use agency powers to further his or her own interest at the principal's expense. The agent is expected to follow the principal's instructions and manage the principal's money carefully and cautiously or reimburse the principal for any losses suffered. The agent must also keep the principal informed of relevant facts.

The Law of Bankruptcy

Bankruptcy—insolvency to the point where a person or business is legally declared unable to pay its debts—involves a set of legal rules for distributing what is left of the debtor's assets. In a normal year, more than 250,000 bankruptcies occur, involving accumulated debts of about $50 billion.

ANTITRUST LAWS

Over forty years ago in *The Modern Corporation and Private Property,* Professors A.P. Berle and Gardner C. Means noted that many key American industries were dominated by a few giant corporations. Based on the relative growth rates in large and small businesses, Berle and Means projected that in 360 years the American economy would be dominated by a single giant business whose life expectancy would rival that of the Roman Empire!

The problem of *economic concentration*–the control of an industry by one or a few businesses–first appeared in the United States after the Civil War. A public outcry soon arose over the high prices and the dubious commercial tactics of some monopolists and oligopolists (see Chapter 2). Popular dissatisfaction led to the passage of **antitrust laws** designed to prevent economic concentration.

You Be the Judge

Jim has a rich and doting uncle named Horace. While visiting one day, Horace says, "Jim, I think you smoke too much. If you stop smoking for six months, I'll give you $60,000." James agrees to the offer. Is this a legally binding contract?

The Alvarez family has a lovely old house overlooking a lake. But they have been transferred and must sell it. The real-estate agent values the house at $100,000, but finds a purchaser who pays $110,000. Without informing the Alvarezes, the real-estate agent closes the sale and pockets the $10,000 difference as a "finder's fee." Later, the Alvarezes discover what happened. Can they recover the $10,000 from the real-estate agent? _____

ANSWERS: If Jim and Horace are both over eighteen years of age, mentally competent, not intoxicated at the time of the agreement, and Jim can prove that the conversation took place, then it is a legally binding contract.

Agents must be loyal to their principals and cannot benefit at their expense. So the Alvarezes can legally recover the $10,000.

The Sherman Antitrust Act

In 1890, the **Sherman Antitrust Act** was passed to curb the growth of conspiracies and monopolies. The Sherman Act prohibits conspiracies in restraint of interstate commerce. Examples of illegal conspiracies include:

1. PRICE FIXING   Bookstores near a college campus agree to price used books in good condition at 75 percent of the retail price of new books.
2. MARKET DIVISION   Soft-drink bottlers divide up the market for their products. Each competitor agrees to sell to retailers only within an assigned area.

To prosecute firms for alleged conspiracy, the government must prove by direct or by circumstantial evidence that some formal or informal meeting has taken place among competitors.

The Sherman Act also makes the monopolization of an industry illegal. **Monopolization** occurs when a firm attempts to gain control over the price of a product or to exclude new competitors from the market it dominates.

The Clayton Act

The **Clayton Act** of 1914 was passed to strengthen Section 2 of the Sherman Antitrust Act by preventing the formation of monopolies rather than by directly attacking well-entrenched monopolists. Section 2 of the Clayton Act, which was supplemented in 1936 by an amendment known as the Robinson–Patman Act, prohibits price discriminations that lessen competition or that tend to create a monopoly. **Price discrimination** occurs when a business charges customers different prices for products "of like grade and quality." Under the terms of Section 2 of the act, businesses are allowed to reduce prices to favored customers only if the discounts are intended to meet competition or are based on the costs of servicing the customers.

Section 3 of the Clayton Act condemns **tying contracts,** which force customers to purchase a firm's products only in combination. For example, Eastman Kodak originally sold its color film only with processing included in the retail price. As a result of a federal antitrust investigation in 1954, Kodak was forced to make its color film available separately as well as at a higher price that included processing.

The key provision of the Clayton Act is Section 7, which was strengthened in 1950 by an amendment known as the **Celler-Kefauver Act.** Section 7 prohibits a firm from acquiring the assets or stock of competitors "where in any line of commerce in any section of the country the effect of such acquisition may be to substantially lessen competition or to tend to create a monopoly." One of the most common business practices covered by this provision is the **merger**—a combining of one or more businesses into a single firm. A **horizontal merger** occurs when firms acquire competing businesses. The acquisition of the Chevrolet Motor Company by General Motors in 1919 is an example of a horizontal merger. A **vertical merger** involves a firm's acquisition of one of its suppliers or customers—for example, the purchase of the Fisher Body Corporation by General Motors in 1919. A **conglomerate merger** unites firms that produce dissimilar products. The acquisition of Philco, an important producer of radio and television sets, by the Ford Company in 1961 is an example of a conglomerate merger.

The Federal Trade Commission Act

The **Federal Trade Commission Act** was passed in 1914 to deal with unfair methods of competition not covered by the Clayton Act. The 1914 act provides for the establishment of the five-member Federal Trade Commission (FTC), which has the power to enforce the act. In 1938, an amendment, the Wheeler–Lea Act, considerably strengthened the FTC's authority. The core of the Federal Trade Commission Act provides that "unfair methods of competition in commerce, and unfair or deceptive acts in commerce, are hereby declared unlawful." Typical unfair or deceptive practices prosecuted by the FTC are shown in Figure 18–2.

The Federal Trade Commission is empowered to take action against any business practices that are deemed harmful either to competing firms or to consumers. Consumers and business owners who believe they have been harmed by unfair or deceptive practices may complain to the FTC, which carefully investigates such allegations. If the FTC believes that a violation has occurred, it issues a formal complaint, which must be answered by the alleged violator within thirty days. If, after additional investigation, the FTC is dissatisfied with the response to its complaint, it can issue a *cease-and-desist order* requiring that the offending act be discontinued. The business owner who is charged with a violation has three available options: to discontinue the

FIGURE 18-2
What Does the FTC Consider Unfair?

FALSE ADVERTISING	MISLEADING ADVERTISING
• All verbal claims must be truthful and supportable by evidence. EXAMPLE: Manufacturers of a brand-name aspirin product cannot claim that it will relieve pain and fever faster than another brand unless they can prove that it actually does. • All demonstrations must be exactly what they appear to be and supportable by evidence. EXAMPLE: Makers of a TV ad showing how well a detergent gets stains out of a shirt cannot substitute a clean shirt for the one shown going into the washing machine.	• Advertisers cannot create an overall impression that leads people to believe a false conclusion. EXAMPLE: An actor or model cannot appear in a doctor's or dentist's white jacket while recommending a particular remedy or toothpaste. EXAMPLE: A printing company that does only simulated engraving cannot use the word "engraving" in its corporate name.

practice as requested by the FTC; to appeal the case through the federal courts; or to continue the violation and risk a substantial fine.

Antitrust Enforcement

State and federal government agencies charged with enforcing antitrust laws often run into enormous time and money problems. The cases can take years to prosecute and cost so much that they are not even worth initiating. And penalties are often smaller than the profits the companies would gain by continuing the violation (see Figure 18–3). Furthermore, some important industries—most public utilities and some transportation companies, for example—are not covered by antitrust laws. **Natural monopolies** such as these, where competition is impractical or unworkable, are allowed to exist, but only under careful government regulation. Thus, if a local gas and electric company wants to increase its rates, it must usually obtain approval from its regulatory agency, the Federal Energy Regulatory Commission, or, more typically, its corresponding state agency.

FIGURE 18-3
Penalties for Antitrust Violations.

TYPE OF PENALTY	WHO PAYS	WHAT HAPPENS
Imprisonment and fine	Business executives	Executives who participate in antitrust violations can be jailed for a maximum of three years or fined up to $100,000 for each violation, or both.
Fines	Business firms	Firms can be assessed a maximum fine of $1,000,000 for each violation.
Injunctions	Business firms	Businesses can be ordered by the courts to cease any practice that violates the law.
Dissolution	Business firms	The courts can order that a violating firm be divided into smaller units, so the firm will not be powerful enough to reinstitute the violation.
Treble damages	Business firms	Private businesses as well as state and local governments harmed by an antitrust violation can recover three times the amount of their damages.

GOVERNMENT REGULATION OF BUSINESS

The regulatory commissions that govern natural monopolies are composed of members appointed by the president with the advice of the U.S. Senate. Major industries in the American economy that are subject to regulations issued by federal and state governments are:

- TRANSPORTATION   Railroads, airlines, water carriers, and trucking. Regulatory agency: Interstate Commerce Commission (ICC) and Civil Aeronautics Board (CAB).
- FINANCIAL INSTITUTIONS   Banks, savings and loan associations, securities markets, insurance companies, and other financial organizations. Regulatory agency: Securities and Exchange Commission (SEC) and the Federal Reserve System.
- PUBLIC UTILITIES   Electrical utilities and natural gas utilities and pipelines. Regulatory agency: Federal Energy Regulatory Commission (FERC).

   ● COMMUNICATIONS MEDIA   Telephone and telegraph companies
     and the radio and television industries. Regulatory agency: Federal
     Communications Commission (FCC).

   Traditional regulation normally involves governmental approval of (1)
prices the regulated industry can charge; (2) who is allowed to stay in the
industry; and (3) what persons and geographic areas each business must serve.
About 11 percent of the private sector in the United States is subject to direct
governmental regulation.
   There are five basic reasons for regulating the activities of natural monopolies: (1) to prevent excessive profits; (2) to provide service at relatively low
rates to hard-to-serve customers (for example, telephones and utilities to those
who live in isolated areas); (3) to prevent self-destructive competition; (4) to
fairly allocate public facilities of limited capacity (such as airwaves); and (5) to
protect consumers from being cheated and endangered.
   In addition to the agencies that watch over the monopolies, there are the
socially oriented regulatory agencies.
   Social regulation is primarily directed toward achieving noneconomic
objectives, like equal employment opportunities for all Americans. Social
regulation also differs from direct regulation in that all industries (not just
monopolies) are affected. Some of the major social regulatory agencies and
their responsibilities are listed below:

   1. *Consumer Product Safety Commission (CPSC)*. Deals with product
      safety.
   2. *Food and Drug Administration (FDA)*. Regulates health, safety, label-
      ing, and branding of foods, drugs, health products, and cosmetics.
   3. *Equal Employment Opportunity Commission (EEOC)* and *Office of
      Federal Contract Compliance (OFCC)*. Establish regulations designed
      to prohibit hiring and on-the-job discrimination based on sex, race,
      nationality, age, or religion.
   4. *Occupational Safety and Health Administration (OSHA)*. Regulates
      on-the-job safety and health conditions.
   5. *Environmental Protection Agency (EPA)*. Establishes permitted levels
      of air, water, land, and noise pollution.
   6. *Nuclear Regulatory Commission (NRC)* and *Energy Resources and
      Development Agency (ERDA)*. Regulate energy use and development.

(The activities of several of these regulatory agencies have been dealt with in
some detail elsewhere in this book. See especially Chapters 1 and 2.)

Problems of Regulation

As with the antitrust enforcement agencies, regulatory agencies also suffer from limited resources and from long delays between violation and prosecution. They have other problems, too.

Since the agencies must authorize price increases for products such as natural gas and telephone service, regulated businesses deal closely with them and often manage to partly control them. Consumers may not notice a few cents' increase in their bills, but for an industry it can add up to millions when it comes from hundreds of thousands of customers. Thus, regulated industries have a strong interest in fighting for favorable regulations, while consumers often remain silent.

In direct regulation, profits are determined according to the *fair rate of return*. This is defined as the profit that could reasonably be expected in comparable unregulated businesses. But allowing regulated industries a fair rate of return provides them with no incentive to be efficient, since they are normally permitted to raise their prices to cover any cost increases.

Trends Toward Deregulation

It began with a lot of gripes from business people, Congress, and even consumers. Regulations were for the birds, they said. So the Civil Aeronautics Board dropped them for airlines. The result: less regulation of fares and routes. Fares fell, planes and airports became crowded, and airline profits soared.

Deregulation, the reduction or elimination of direct government regulations on whole industries, may help to restore competition to many American industries, but its effects may not be all good. Will smaller cities be dropped from air routes, for example? What will happen to airline profits—and air fares—as oil prices increase?

The results of deregulation are not yet all in, though the practice is still spreading. Congress and the ICC, for example, are phasing out some regulations of railroads and trucking companies, so that business and consumers will get a chance to see how much government we really need or even want.

GOVERNMENT TAXATION OF BUSINESS

With possibly 20,000 returns to fill out each year and 42 percent of net profits on average going to pay federal income taxes, a large corporation can never forget that business and government interact through taxes.

A **tax** is a sum levied by government on an activity to raise revenue to support public expenditures. The four-cent federal tax on every gallon of gasoline sold is a typical tax. The amount of money collected depends on both the *tax base* and the *tax rate*. The **tax base** is the volume of economic activity taxed—all the gasoline sold, for example. The **tax rate** is the tax per unit of the product—for example, four cents per gallon. Sometimes, a tax rate can be high enough to reduce consumption. Then the tax base shrinks. This seems to have happened with high taxes on hard liquor.

Taxes should perform six functions:

1. Raise enough revenue.
2. Cause minimum distortions. Excessive taxes may reduce the incentive to work and cause prohibitively high prices.
3. Be fair. Under the **benefit principle,** you should pay for the services you get. Motorists pay the tax that pays for roads, for example. But under the **ability-to-pay principle,** people and businesses with more money should pay more.
4. Be inexpensive to collect.
5. Be direct. Hidden taxes can mislead people about the cost of government services.
6. Have a purpose. Besides raising money, taxes are often used by the government to mold our behavior. High taxes on gambling and tax exemptions for churches are examples.

Types of Taxes

There are five main types of taxes: income taxes, sales taxes, property taxes, payroll taxes, and estate taxes.

Income Taxes

These are paid by businesses and by all people above a federally set income level. Corporate income taxes are levied by the federal government, most states, and many local governments. Individuals must also fill out a *tax return,* listing income and certain expenditures. The *withholding system* ensures that all wage earners will be able to pay, because the employer must deduct part of the wages from each paycheck and send the money to the government.

Your Next Job
Positions in Government

There are nearly twenty million employees at the federal, state, and local levels of government, and the jobs they fill are of nearly every description and salary range. At the federal level, pay scales for lower- and middle-level employees equal or, if job stability and fringe benefits are taken into consideration, exceed equivalent standards in the private sector. More than 95 percent of federal employees belong to the Civil Service System. At higher managerial levels, pay is decidedly lower than in the private sector, and top-level managerial employees are often political appointees. Further information regarding federal jobs can be obtained from the Civil Service Commission in Washington, D.C., or, frequently, from your local post office. The positions described below are just a few of the thousands available.

Careers as Government Inspectors

Health inspectors enforce government regulations to protect the public welfare. **Food and drug inspectors,** the largest subcategory of health inspectors, ensure that products are wholesome, safe, and honestly labeled; **meat and poultry inspectors** enforce proper sanitation practices and check the accuracy of product labeling; **foreign quarantine inspectors** guarantee that both immigrants and imported cargoes are free from contagious disease. The educational requirements for health inspectors vary: food and drug inspectors must have a bachelor of science degree; meat and poultry inspectors and quarantine inspectors are often high-school graduates who have had several years of work experience in a related field. All health inspectors begin as trainees and, after learning the specialized inspection procedures in their particular field, may advance to the position of **supervisory inspector.** Inspectors must also score satisfactorily on a civil service examination. Annual income averages $16,000. (*Additional information:* Interagency Board of U.S. Civil Service Examiners for Washington, D.C., 1900 E Street, N.W., Washington, D.C. 20415.)

Like health inspectors, **regulatory inspectors** enforce government regulations to safeguard and protect the general public. An assortment of specialized positions exists: **customs inspectors** ensure that imported and exported goods meet legal and health standards and that travelers comply with immigration laws; **aviation safety officers** inspect both aircraft equipment and aircraft personnel to see that they meet safety and quality regulations; **mine inspectors** enforce safe and healthy mining practices; **wage–hour compliance officers** verify that minimum-wage, overtime, and equal-employment procedures comply with federal law. Most regulatory inspectors must have three to five years previous experience in a related field; applicants with some education at the college level can qualify with less actual work experience. Only wage–hour compliance officers must have a bachelor's degree, usually in accounting, business administration, or economics. All regulatory inspectors must pass a civil service examination. (*Additional information:* Interagency Board of U.S. Civil Service Examiners for Washington, D.C., 1900 E Street, N.W., Washington, D.C. 20415.)

Careers in Urban Planning

Urban planners develop proposals to improve the quality of city life. Some of the specific urban planning problems that require an imaginative decision-making ability are the restoration of blighted residential and industrial districts, the development of recreation and transportation facilities, and the reduction of air and noise pollution. A bachelor's degree in city planning, architecture, or engineering is essential. Advancement is limited, although exceptional planners may be promoted to **planning director.** Annual salaries range from $10,000 to $30,000. The trend toward urbanization is expected to moderately expand the job market for urban planners in the immediate future. (*Additional information:* American Institute of Planners, 917 15th Street, N.W., Washington, D.C. 20005.)

Sales Taxes

A *general sales tax* is a tax on all commodities (with the exception of food and other basic necessities). It is a percentage of the selling price, usually 3–5 percent, and must be collected by businesses and sent to the government. *Excise taxes* are sales taxes on specific commodities; cigarettes, for example.

Property Taxes

Local governments make *assessed valuations* of homes and business plants, usually at much less than the market value. The tax assessor then multiplies this amount by the set tax rate. If the property tax rate on your home is $50 per $1,000 of assessed valuation and your home is assessed at $80,000, your property tax would be $4,000 per year.

Payroll Taxes

These are the taxes withheld from paychecks by employers and sent to various government agencies. Major ones are social security taxes, workers' compensation taxes, and local payroll taxes.

Estate Taxes

These are taxes on the value of all your assets above a certain level, to be paid out of your estate when you die. Related to them are *inheritance taxes,* paid by your heirs on what they receive. Small-business people who don't want their businesses sold in order to pay these taxes often set up *trust funds,* which are managed by financial institutions, as a legal way of reducing these taxes.

How Taxes Mold Business Behavior

Many business decisions are made according to their tax consequences. For example, an international grain company may decide to process cereal in one state or country over another, because the tax rates on the plant are more favorable there. A computer manufacturer may borrow money instead of issuing stock, because the interest payments on the loan are tax-deductible. A top executive may choose attractive fringe benefits over a salary raise, because many benefits are not taxable. And, of course, businesses must hire many accountants, lawyers, and clerks just to plan for and keep track of taxes.

HOW BUSINESS INFLUENCES GOVERNMENT

Lobbyists, public affairs managers, tax accountants and lawyers, and public relations executives are all a response by business to the growing power of government. They carry the business point of view to the executive, legislative, and judicial branches of government.

At the executive branch, lobbyists may argue the business side on deregulation of trucking to regulatory agency officials. Or the chief executive officer may appeal to the president's staff to change a plant safety regulatory order. In many cases, the people hired to present businesses' views have worked in government themselves.

Work at the legislative branch, which is composed of Congress and its many committees, may include testifying before congressional hearings or *lobbying,* appealing to individual committee members. Most trade associations maintain representatives in Washington to monitor legislative activities affecting their members. And sometimes even Washington employees do some lobbying (see below).

Ernest Fitzgerald, a cost analyst at the Pentagon, blew the whistle on his own employer. He told a congressional committee that a giant transport plane project would end up costing $2 billion more of the taxpayers' money than had previously been announced. The Department of Defense tried to fire him.

John Moffatt, employed by the IRS, revealed that his agency planned to spend hundreds of thousands of dollars on unnecessary office equipment. He took his whistle to the press and to high Washington officials, causing his superiors considerable unhappiness.

Work within the judicial branch involves managing cost cases and their appeals, usually by the firm's legal department. But businesses often hire additional lawyers, *outside counsel,* familiar with the local courts in an area where an appeal is necessary.

GOVERNMENT AND BUSINESS RELATIONS IN THE FUTURE

Will the suspicions, complaints, and endless regulation between business and government continue forever? Or will our country become more like the "partnership" of Japan, Inc. (the nickname for Japan's brand of cooperation between government and business)? The relations of government and business have not been positive in the last few decades, but there are signs that things may be getting better. One reason may be that government is now adopting many of the same business principles that guide private enterprises. For example:

- BENEFIT–COST ANALYSIS Many government programs must now submit to this statistical technique. It systematically compares the advantages and the costs associated with each program.
- MORE BUDGET AUTHORITY A single congressional committee now may place a limit on government spending unless the entire Congress votes against it.
- CAMPAIGN SPENDING LAW REFORMS Public financing of some campaigns is setting limits on how much one person or group may contribute to a candidate. So business, labor, and large individual contributors no longer have as much influence.
- ZERO-BASE BUDGETING (ZBB) Government agencies must now justify all programs as though they were beginning from point zero.
- SUNSET LAWS Now in effect in several states, these make the sun set (and the money stop) for government programs every few years, unless officials can show that they are working well.
- PUBLIC SERVICE OPTIONS A new choice for public services, such as garbage collection or school-lunch programs, this policy allows private firms to compete with one another for the chance to perform government services, instead of having a government agency do them.

The idea is to reduce government power, direct it into areas where it is most valuable, and improve the efficiency of government's "delivery system."

We may even decide to follow the example of "Japan, Inc.," where the government develops long-term policies to help business in areas such as innovation and tariffs, while business provides experts to government and faithfully carries out government policies. The system seems to work.

Chapter Review & Applications

Key Points to Remember

1. Government affects business in the following ways: it establishes basic laws for conducting business; it tries to stabilize and regulate the economy; it regulates the social policies of business; it purchases goods and services from the private sector; and it makes subsidies and collects taxes.

2. Business law establishes "the rules of the game" as far as many commercial transactions are concerned. Like other laws, business laws are based on statutory law, common law, and administrative law (regulations from government agencies).

3. Three important aspects of business law are the law of contracts, the law of agency, and bankruptcy law.

4. Federal antitrust legislation seeks to promote competition and to prevent economic concentration. Antitrust laws prohibit price fixing and monopolies and regulate mergers.

5. Government regulation of business extends throughout much of the transportation, public utility, and financial industries. Rates, services, and profits are the main areas regulated by commissions, whose members are appointed by government officials.

6. To finance their activities, federal, state, and local governments rely on taxes collected from consumers and businesses.

7. An effective tax raises revenue, causes minimum economic distortions, is fair, inexpensive to collect, direct, and serves some purpose.

8. There are five major types of taxes: income taxes, sales taxes, property taxes, payroll taxes, and estate taxes.

Questions for Discussion

1. Imagine yourself in a top business position in a particular industry. How do federal and local governments affect you in your work?

2. Government has been viewed as a mediator—and as an active economic and social force. Define and contrast these roles. Which role or roles do you believe government should play?

3. "The antitrust laws are designed to promote competition among businesses and to direct competition into economically desirable channels." In what specific ways do the antitrust laws attempt to accomplish the objectives outlined in this statement?

4. How do regulatory agencies try to limit and control monopolies? Do they confine themselves to this function? Explain your answer.

5. Can tax rates be set too high? Explain.

Short Cases

1. Evaluate the following business practices in terms of (1) their probable effect on the business proposing them; (2) their impact on competition in the industry; and (3) their legality. Which are in the public interest?
   (a) Slope Ski Co. sells skis and ski boots only in combination, charging $89.95 for both.
   (b) Gasoline stations in your area raise prices by 25 cents a gallon.
   (c) Baking companies charge 75 cents per loaf of bread in Nebraska and 90 cents or more per loaf elsewhere.
   (d) Slimline bread is advertised as containing fewer calories per slice. The claim is accurate only because Slimline bread slices are thinner than other brands.

2. Assume that you are an executive in charge of transformers. Because of tough competition, prices have been lowered below production costs. Your boss informs you that there will be a major shakeup in the company unless the transformer division's profits rise. You know that price-fixing is successfully restoring profits in other company divisions. With your job on the line, you are invited to meet with competitors at an isolated Canadian lodge. What is your response?

A Critical
Business Decision

—Made by Alice H. Rivlin
of the Congressional Budget Office

The Situation

Although largely unknown to the public, she may be the most influential woman in the United States. Her career followed a classic pattern. With an undergraduate degree from Bryn Mawr and graduate degree in economics from Radcliffe, she then became a fellow at the Brookings Institution, an influential Washington, D.C., "think tank" organization that, among other things, investigates government programs and recommends changes in government policies. In 1966, she became an Assistant Secretary for Programs Coordination of the giant Department of Health, Education, and Welfare. And in 1975 she was appointed as director of the newly established Congressional Budget Office. Her name is Alice H. Rivlin.

Popular dissatisfaction with the large budget deficits of the federal government and soaring inflation of the late 1970s led to changes in the congressional budget-making process. Formerly, the House of Representatives and the Senate agreed on appropriations bills on a piecemeal basis. The only fiscal discipline Congress faced was from the president, who proposed an overall budget. But temptation proved irresistible to most congressional representatives—to please their constituents they tacked on a little more spending to each appropriation. The result when all the "extra" appropriations were added up: billions of dollars of red ink in the federal budget.

Today, the congressional budget-making process is different. A joint Senate–House committee proposes a federal spending limit. Spending targets for each area of the federal budget are based in large part on projected revenues and whatever deficit or surplus Congress can agree on. Once the budget ceiling is approved by Congress, total spending is not allowed to exceed that amount. Appropriations bills exceeding the general spending targets established for each area of the budget are disallowed unless Congress overturns the expenditure limits established earlier. The people largely responsible for recommending spending limits and for projecting revenue to Congress: Alice H. Rivlin and the Congressional Budget Office.

The Decision

It is 1980, an election year. Candidates from both political parties are proposing large tax cuts. At the same time, groups representing many poor people are unhappy with what the lower federal spending limits imply. "Dismantle the programs I've been working for as an old liberal?" questions Thomas (Tip) P. O'Neill, Jr. (D—Mass.), Speaker of the U.S. House of Representatives. "I haven't changed my philosophy," he asserts.

Nor are the "right" economic policies clear. The United States has just experienced five years of unprecedented inflation, and tax cuts combined with possible election-year increases in federal spending could cause U.S. prices to soar. On the other hand, the United States is entering a deep recession, with unemployment expected to reach 9 or 10 percent. Lower taxes and larger budget deficits could possibly save thousands of jobs.

Questions

1. What are the political and economic pressures placed on Alice Rivlin? How would you handle them if you were in her position?

2. Assuming that her proposals are carried out, how would her recommendations affect a typical business? A typical consumer?

Unions and the American Worker

In this chapter you will learn . . .

- *how labor unions are organized.*
- *about the sources of labor-management conflict.*
- *how labor and management settle their differences.*
- *about the legislative acts that laid the ground rules for today's labor-management relations.*

 he union hall was crowded. Douglas Fraser, head of the United Automobile Workers (UAW), was about to make a revolutionary and unprecedented proposal. The union would help Chrysler Corporation.

Chrysler was having dire financial problems, and the UAW was prepared to do four things to help. It would accept lower wages from Chrysler than from General Motors and Ford. It would invest part of its pension funds in the ailing company. It would help Chrysler seek government-guaranteed loans. And Douglas Fraser would sit on the auto company's board of directors.

Why was the union offering help to big business, its traditional foe? Because if Chrysler went under, more than 200,000 union members would lose their jobs.

No one had expected to see this day. After all, labor–management relations are based on conflict (see Figure 19–1). The UAW had been born in the sit-ins and violent riots of the late 1930s. The large car companies had been forced to recognize the union only under extreme pressure.

But time has brought change. And union–management relations, although still antagonistic at contract time, are no longer the good guys against the bad guys. Things are more complicated now. The two groups now approach Congress together for protection from foreign imports. They band together against government regulations. And they work jointly to preserve jobs when bankruptcy threatens. Today, cooperation is as characteristic of labor–management relations as is confrontation.

BIG LABOR

Labor today is big and powerful, and no manager can afford to be ignorant of its structure and its sources of influence. Labor includes the traditional craft unions, like the Brotherhood of Machinists, representing workers in a single profession, and the industrial unions, like the United Auto Workers, representing all workers in a particular industry, regardless of their occupation. Labor has also come to include, by some definitions, the professional associa-

FIGURE 19–1
Milestones in the History of Labor.

YEAR	EVENT	SIGNIFICANCE
1636	Fishermen employed by Robert Trelawney of Richmond Island, Maine, mutiny when their wages are withheld.	First recorded American labor dispute.
1794	The Federal Society of Journeymen Cordwainers (shoemakers) is formed in Philadelphia.	First permanent continuing labor union.
1827	The Mechanics Union of Trade Associations is founded in Philadelphia.	First association of unions on a city-wide basis.
1886	Samuel Gompers organizes the American Federation of Labor (AFL) around four principles: (1) internal independence of each affiliated union; (2) nonencroachment of affiliates on other members' jurisdictions; (3) assistance to friends, regardless of political party; and (4) achievement of wage increases and other employee benefits by direct negotiation rather than by legislation.	First strong national federation of craft unions.
1938	John L. Lewis organizes the Congress of Industrial Organizations (CIO), an association of industrial unions, after splitting with the AFL in 1935.	Independent organization of industrial unions.
1955	The American Federation of Labor and the Congress of Industrial Organizations merge to form the AFL-CIO, which represents about three-fourths of all unionized workers.	First merger of national labor organizations.
1960	Government employees gradually win, state-by-state, the right to bargain collectively and, in such states, the right to strike.	Encourages organization of government employees by organized labor.

tions, like those of teachers, nurses, and others. The ten largest unions are listed in Figure 19–2. How are these huge memberships structured?

How Unions Are Organized

Labor unions operate at the local, regional, and national levels.

The Local Level
The basic unit of a union is the **local** (or the *local union*). Each member has a vote and must pay dues, which support meetings and the salaries of union

FIGURE 19-2
The Ten Largest Unions.

RANK	UNION	MEMBERSHIP
1	Teamsters, Chauffeurs, Warehousers, and Helpers	1,899,000
2	Automotive, Aircraft, and Agricultural Implement Workers	1,358,000
3	Steelworkers	1,300,000
4	Electrical Workers	924,000
5	Machinists	917,000
6	Carpenters and Joiners	820,000
7	State and County Employees	750,000
8	Retail Clerks	690,000
9	Laborers	627,000
10	Service Employees	575,000

* Excludes professional groups like the American Medical Association and the National Education Association.

Source: *Statistical Abstract of the United States,* 1980.

officials. At the meetings, members select representatives for regional and national conventions.

The most important local union official is the *shop steward* (or the business agent). This is an elected position, and the person who holds it is responsible for collecting union dues, handling worker grievances, and representing the local's members before the union as a whole.

The Regional Level

At the state or regional level, unions have district officers, regional councils, and joint boards. They coordinate the activities of locals and represent the union before appropriate public bodies.

The National Level

National (or international) unions, composed of elected representatives of the locals, hold meetings at least once every five years. The most important labor negotiations take place at this level. And the national leaders represent union members before Congress and the executive branch. They also can discipline corrupt or overly militant locals.

Lane Kirkland, who replaced George Meany as the national leader of the powerful AFL-CIO, represents a new breed of labor leader. Unlike Meany, Kirkland rose through the ranks of the union organization without a blue-collar background.

Representing labor to Congress and the president, Kirkland takes a different approach from the blunt and blustering Meany. His background (he studied for the diplomatic service at Georgetown University) may have something to do with it—he's much more diplomatic. Rather than confrontation, he uses conciliation. He tries to bring warring factions of organized labor together, to present a united national front for labor's interests.

Will Women Help Unions Grow?

Lane Kirkland, president of the AFL-CIO, said in 1980 that the federation—with its 13.6 million members—is "sensitive to, and conscious of, the increasing role of women in the work force and the trade union movement." While male union membership was stagnating, union membership among women grew by more than 10 percent annually between 1976 and 1980. The AFL-CIO is mounting major organizing drives to unionize industries and occupations with large numbers of women. The prize: the eleven million women who are expected to join the work force by 1990.

Relations between organized labor and women have not always been comfortable. The seniority system, favored by unions, has made it hard for women to get blue-collar jobs. And it has meant that women are often the first employees to be laid off in hard economic times. Groups like the Coalition of Labor Union Women and the Committee of Concerned Women Steelworkers are pressuring organized labor for equal employment opportunities for women in blue-collar occupations, according to a story in *The Christian Science Monitor*. The AFL-CIO has a long way to go. But it is taking some unprecedented steps forward. In 1980, its Executive Committee held a conference on ways women could be given an expanded role in organized labor—including a possible seat for a woman on the Committee's all-male board.[1]

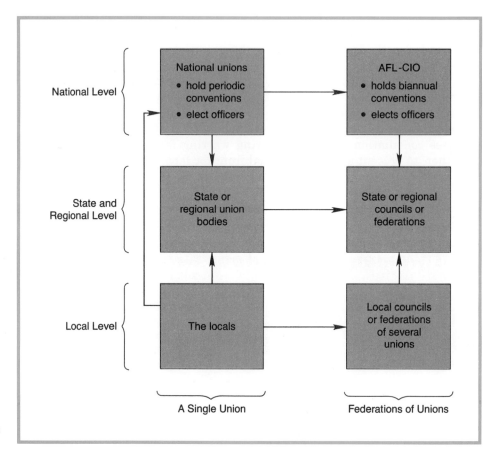

FIGURE 19-3 Union Organization in the United States.
(Arrows indicate how each level of the organization normally elects or appoints representatives to the appropriate union.)

Federations of Unions

It is not uncommon for different unions to cooperate with one another at the city, state, and certainly at the national level. Among other things, they often coordinate political activities and respect one another's picket lines. The ultimate expression of such cooperation was the formation of **federations** (or mergers) of unions, such as the AFL and the CIO, which themselves then merged in 1955 to form the powerful AFL-CIO. Refer back to Figure 19–1 for a historical account of this important event and look at Figure 19–3 for a hierarchical perspective of the relationship between unions.

The Challenges Unions Face

Despite consolidation and improved relations with management, unions face a number of problems and challenges. Among these are problems of membership, conflicts between younger and older workers, and political difficulties.

Membership in the 1980s

The number of union members has been decreasing in proportion to the total civilian (or private) labor force since membership reached its peak in 1943 (see Figure 19–4). Aging leaders, less energy and commitment to membership drives, more service workers (who are harder to organize), and more automation in factories are probably all partly responsible.

But unions are enjoying spectacular success in organizing public-sector employees. Firefighters, police officers, teachers, professors, and civil-service personnel at all levels of government are now forming and joining unions. Although many state laws prohibit or restrict strikes by public employees, the unions often successfully defy these laws.

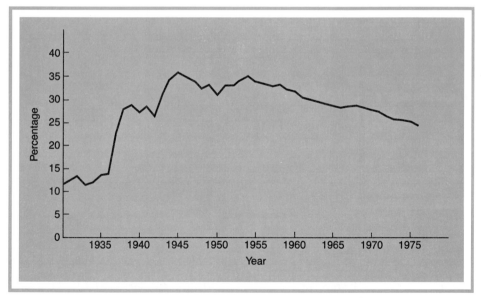

FIGURE 19–4
Union Membership in the United States as a Percentage of Nonagricultural Employment.

Source: U.S. Bureau of Labor Statistics.

Conflict Between Younger and Older Workers

Unions seem to have a generation gap. Nearly half of all union members are under forty, and a third are less than thirty. Yet most of the leaders are over fifty. Although the old guard of labor leaders—John L. Lewis, Walter Reuther, George Meany, and others—are gone, even the new leaders, like Joseph Lane Kirkland, head of the national AFL-CIO, are not as young as most members.

Older workers tend to emphasize the **seniority system**—privileges (such as protection against layoffs) on the basis of years of service. They also favor increases in **fringe benefits**—employer contributions in addition to basic wages and salaries, such as paid holidays, free health and accident insurance, pension plans, and so forth. In contrast, younger workers resent the seniority system, prefer immediate wage increases to additional "fringes," and seek more varied and interesting jobs.

Unions in Politics

Unions have an image problem. With the accomplishment of major victories, such as minimum wage laws and the right to strike, "big labor" has become a powerful force in American politics, and its objectives inevitably clash with the goals of other special-interest groups. Today, over 70 percent of the U.S. population oppose the further growth of unions, and 55 percent believe that unions are already too powerful.

LABOR-MANAGEMENT CONFLICT

Because the goals of employees and unions often conflict with the policies of management, business managers unfamiliar with the sources of these differences are often confronted with severe labor problems. The basic areas of labor–management conflict are examined in this section.

Basic Goals: According to Employees

Unions emphasize five basic goals to employers, goals that often, though not always, reflect the interests of employees. These are (1) higher wages and better fringes, (2) improved working conditions, (3) job security, (4) challenging jobs, and (5) union security.

Wages and Fringes

A key union priority is higher wages and better fringe benefits, such as free health care, pensions, and paid vacations. Even paid dental and legal-aid programs are now included in some "packages," for both private-sector and public employees. Unions have become so successful that the cost of fringe benefits has reached 40 percent of total wage costs. Different methods of employee payment are shown in Figure 19–5.

FIGURE 19-5
Common Methods of Payment to Employees.

METHOD OF PAYMENT	DESCRIPTION
Straight salary	Weekly, monthly, or annual payments are made for the period worked.
Hourly pay	Wages are based on the number of hours worked multiplied by an agreed-on pay rate per hour. Workers record hours worked by punching a time-clock or by signing a time card.
Overtime pay	Overtime rates apply when an employee works beyond the stated minimum number of hours per week. Employees are often paid one and a half times the normal hourly rate for overtime during the work week and double the hourly rate for overtime on weekends.
Shift premiums	Employees often receive higher hourly wages for working evening or early-morning shifts in plants that operate more than eight hours a day.
Piecework	Workers are paid according to their output: for example, five cents for each rim placed on a tire in a tire factory.
Commissions	Often paid to sales personnel, commissions are a fixed percentage of an employee's total sales. The percentage may be increased if the employee performs especially well.
Bonuses	Employees receive extra pay when their work is outstanding or when the business has had a good year. The amount of the bonus varies with the employer.
Profit sharing	Workers receive periodic payments in addition to their regular wages or salary. The amount of the profit-sharing payment is related to the employee's base wage and to the firm's profitability.
Guaranteed annual wage	The firm agrees to pay each worker a stipulated minimum annual income, whether or not there is enough work to keep the employee busy throughout the year.
Cost-of-living escalator	Increases are made in hourly or other wage payments to keep the employee abreast of rising consumer prices. The increase is usually about 80 percent of the year's inflation rate.

Working Conditions

From longer coffee breaks to a full company golf course, unions focus on such working conditions as:

- Amenities for workers, including pleasant surroundings, adequate sanitary facilities, and opportunities for recreation.
- Reasonable schedules for shifts, work crews, working hours and rest periods, and overtime.
- Acceptable assembly-line speed and job definitions.
- Adequate safety.
- Shorter or more flexible work weeks.

Job Security

Rapid technological changes and unemployment in certain industries make workers especially sensitive to the possibility of losing their jobs. Employees

Do Increasing Wages Really Protect You Against Inflation?

The French say, "Salaries go up by the stairs; prices take the elevator." To compensate for inflation, labor unions now include *cost-of-living escalators* in contracts. A typical cost-of-living escalator provides that 80 percent of any increase in prices, as measured by the Consumer Price Index (CPI), be reflected in higher hourly wages. Thus, if the CPI rises by 10 percent in a given year, the annual cost-of-living adjustment will be 8 percent.

Suppose that you earn $10 per hour and that you are protected by a cost-of-living escalator equal to 80 percent of the rise in the CPI. The new union contract provides a 5 percent basic annual wage increase, and the anticipated rate of inflation is 10 percent.

Many people believe that they are better off during periods of inflation, because their monetary wages increase. But they do not consider the steady rise in prices. For example, calculate how much your new pay will be in the above example, then determine how much your real wages will rise after taking into account increased prices and taxes. (The answer appears below.)

ANSWER: Your hourly pay will go up 13 percent to $11.30 per hour, but you would have to earn $11 rather than $10 just to keep up with the 10 percent inflation. Because you must pay taxes on the $1.30 wage increase, you are probably worse off than before the inflation. Your after-tax purchasing power actually decreases, since you must pay some of your additional wages in income tax. Since the federal income tax is progressive, the more rapid the inflation, the higher your tax bracket and the worse off you are!

who spend many years acquiring skills are naturally anxious when they find these skills in danger of becoming obsolete. Job security becomes especially important during periods of high unemployment, when it is harder for displaced workers to find other jobs. American unions have become particularly sensitive to job-security issues, and Figure 19–6 indicates some of the major issues in the conflict over job security between management and labor.

Challenging Jobs

As workers reach a comfortable standard of living, they become more interested in the quality of their jobs. To keep work challenging and avoid worker dissatisfaction, companies are experimenting with worker involvement. One program, a joint effort of the United Auto Workers and Chrysler, allows workers to supervise their own assembly lines and to assemble complete subunits rather than to attach the same part over and over again.

FIGURE 19-6
Job-Security Issues for Workers.

ISSUE	DESCRIPTION
Seniority	Allocates jobs on the basis of years worked. During slack periods, employees with the highest seniority are laid off last.
Subcontracting	Permits employers to hire other firms to produce part or all of a product. To preserve members' jobs, unions often attempt to control the amount of subcontracting.
Introduction of new technology	Frequently enables business to reduce the work force. Unions often try to deflect the new technology by "featherbedding"—requiring an employer to retain workers when they are no longer needed.
Promotion, hiring, dismissals, and transfers	Affect the job security of union members. Unions try to restrict management decisions through veto power or by requiring management to demonstrate legitimate reasons for its actions.
Job reductions	Eliminate union jobs. Job reductions may occur because a plant is unprofitable or because demand is declining. To reduce job losses, unions try to force management to retain existing union employees.
Severance pay	Provides temporary financial protection against job loss. Unions often force employers to pay a year or more in wages to workers laid off permanently.
Apprenticeship programs	Protect workers against competition. Unions protect members' jobs by requiring training programs that few new workers can complete. Apprenticeship programs improve the skills of new workers, but also keep laborers in short supply, safeguarding members' jobs.

Union Security

About 80 percent of all union members are covered by **union security arrangements,** which typically involve (1) some form of compulsory union membership, and (2) checkoff procedures. Under the *closed shop,* a stringent form of compulsory union membership, employers agree to hire only union members. In a *union shop,* management is free to hire whomever it chooses, but all workers must join the established union within a designated period (usually thirty days). In both closed and union shops, remaining a union member is a condition of continued employment. In an *open shop,* employees may decide whether or not they wish to join the union. The main source of economic power for organized labor lies in union security arrangements, since unions are assured that workers will participate in whatever actions they undertake. Workers who oppose union tactics against employers risk losing union membership and their jobs.

Checkoff procedures require that employers deduct union dues from employee paychecks and send these dues directly to the appropriate union. Procedures for the collection of dues are usually specified in the union contract. When compulsory union membership is combined with checkoff procedures, unions are in a powerful bargaining position.

To the extent that workers believe organized labor advances their goals, employees desire union security. But union security arrangements may also force individual workers to join and contribute to organizations in which they prefer not to participate.

Basic Goals: According to Employers

From management's viewpoint, labor is a resource essential to production, and employee wages are an ordinary cost of conducting business. Consequently, a primary goal of management is to obtain the highest possible output from labor at the lowest possible cost. Achieving this goal depends on three key factors: control of unit labor costs, management rights, and worker loyalty.

Control of Unit Labor Costs

Unit labor costs represent the average cost of the labor necessary to produce one unit of a product. Thus, if the unit labor costs of producing a Ford Pinto are $900, that means that Ford spends $900 on wages and fringe benefits to assemble the Pinto. If costs go too high, a company cannot compete, loses profits, and may go bankrupt. So to control unit labor costs, a business manager must (1) pay wages that are reasonable in terms of product prices and competitors' wage and fringe payments, and (2) obtain acceptable levels of production from employees.

Management Rights

To operate efficiently, managers must be able to hire, promote, and dismiss workers; introduce new technology; plan production schedules according to market demand; and close unprofitable plants. These business decisions must be made quickly and with maximum flexibility, without union interference.

Worker Loyalty

The management of a business is capable of controlling and supervising only a fraction of the daily activities of its employees. Highly motivated employees can make invaluable contributions to an efficient business. Thus, management seeks loyal workers who will identify strongly with the firm and act in its best interests. One way a manager can promote loyalty is through a policy of "co-determination." Popular in Germany, this policy involves having workers help in making major operating, production, and financial decisions. Clearly, those who have a hand in setting company goals will be most committed toward accomplishing them.

When Employees' and Employers' Goals Conflict

Inevitably, no matter how cooperative the relationship, there is bound to be conflict between labor and management. Employees want higher wages and fringe benefits, shorter hours, better working conditions, job security, and more control. Employers want lower unit labor costs and sole authority for business decisions. When the two forces clash, each has an arsenal of economic weapons to use against the other (see Figure 19–7 on next page).

How Labor Gets Action: Strikes

A union's most important economic weapon is the **strike,** in which union members refuse to work until their demands are met by management. Business operations are disrupted and employers suffer losses. Although unions generally have *strike funds* with which to compensate striking workers, every-

FIGURE 19-7
Weapons for Labor and Management.

WEAPONS FOR LABOR	WEAPONS FOR MANAGEMENT
1. *Strikes.* Employees refuse to work.	1. *Lockouts.* Employer shuts down operations, forcing workers to lose wages.
2. *Picketing.* Workers march in front of employer's plant to (a) prevent nonstriking workers from entering; (b) get publicity; and (c) discourage suppliers or other union-associated personnel from dealing with the firm.	2. *Strikebreaking.* Employer continues to operate during a strike with nonunion personnel, either supervisors or strikebreakers.
3. *Slowdowns.* Employees refuse to work at a normal pace until the labor dispute is settled.	3. *Court injunctions.* Employer obtains a court order outlawing strikes, picket lines, or slowdowns if there is violence or if the labor contract is violated.
4. *Boycotts.* Workers attempt to stop the purchase of goods or services from an employer in order to gain union recognition or support a strike.	4. *Blacklisting.* Employer attempts to destroy unions by refusing to hire new employees suspected of being union members.
5. *Strike funds.* A portion of union dues is set aside to help workers during long strikes. In some states, striking workers can also collect welfare benefits.	5. *Yellow-dog contracts.* Employees require prospective workers to pledge not to join a union. In most circumstances, this tactic violates federal law.
6. *Selective strikes or negotiations.* Unions focus bargaining efforts on one employer in an industry. For example, the United Auto Workers might strike Ford Motor Company but continue to work at General Motors.	6. *Strike insurance.* Firms in the same industry agree to share profits with any firm that is struck.
7. *Mutual-aid pacts.* Unions help each other financially when one union is on strike.	7. *Joint bargaining or shutdown agreements.* Firms in the same industry negotiate union contracts together or jointly agree to close down if a single firm is struck.
8. *Lobbying.* Unions try to get help from Congress or from the executive branch in securing a settlement.	8. *Lobbying.* Employers try to get help from Congress or from the executive branch in securing a settlement.

one tends to lose during a strike, and this weapon is generally only used as a last resort. Usually, just the threat of a strike is enough to persuade management to make certain concessions. In a *wildcat strike,* employees walk off their jobs without union authorization. In a *sitdown* strike—which is now illegal—employees remain in the plant but refuse to work.

Since work stoppages hurt both sides and benefit foreign competition, they are rarely long or drastic. In 1980, for example, strikes caused direct losses in working time of only 0.4 percent of total hours worked, or less than sixteen minutes per worker per year, as can be seen in Figure 19–8.

How Management Gets Action: Lockouts
Equally as threatening as a strike is business' ultimate weapon, the **lockout,** in which management stops all operations or uses only supervisors or other

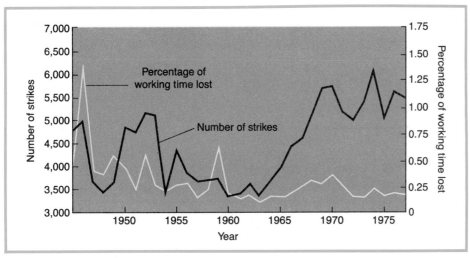

Source: Statistical Abstract of the United States.

FIGURE 19-8
*Modern Strikes
Don't Drain
Much Work Time.*

On the Firing Line:
Between Workers and Management

Ed Hendrix is caught in the middle at Ford Motor Company. As foreman—and one of Ford's 8,000 first-line supervisors—he must carry out management decisions, keep union workers productive, and make sure new cars keep rolling off the assembly line.

Two workers recently claimed that Ford's assembly line was too fast. Their union supported them. Management told Hendrix to hang tough and to threaten the discontented workers with disciplinary action. The workers eventually backed down, but, as Hendrix says, "The foreman is the punching bag. You get your ears beat off from both sides of the fence."

Every day, Hendrix walks the line. He applies enough discipline to get the job done, sometimes calling in the shop steward, but at the same time he must be careful not to dissatisfy the workers and their union. As one worker says, "It's easy to make a foreman look bad. Just screw up."

The job takes its toll. Hendrix has an unlisted phone number and has become a chain smoker. He cannot socialize with his workers. But his salary of $18,000, plus about $5,000 in overtime each year, is more than he could earn on the assembly line. And there's hope for advancement. So he stays on the firing line, says *The Wall Street Journal*.[2]

nonunion personnel. This action places severe economic pressures on union members, who receive no wages or salaries during the lockout. (Some states, however, do provide unemployment compensation during lockouts.)

HOW TO SETTLE LABOR DISPUTES: COLLECTIVE BARGAINING

Well before the strike or lockout phase, most labor–management conflicts are settled through **collective bargaining,** a process of private negotiations between unions and management aimed at settling disputes before they erupt into head-on conflict. This process involves several steps, which are described in the following sections.

Collective Bargaining Comes to Baseball

Pete Rose, Reggie Jackson, Dave Winfield, and Don Sutton are famous names in baseball. They are also millionaires.

The revolution came to baseball in 1967 when Martin Miller's Players Association became the bargaining agent for baseball players. At that time, the average salary of a major-league player was $25,000. By 1980, average salaries reportedly exceeded $75,000. The Association was also responsible for dramatically increasing the amount of baseball owners' contributions to the players' pension fund and for the amount of pay during spring training. The 1976–1979 contract also specified "getaway days," when no games could be scheduled, and limited the number of double-headers the American and National Leagues could schedule. But the major victory for ballplayers was the elimination of the "reserve clause," which allowed club owners to sell or trade a player as they chose. Today, veteran players may become free agents and negotiate with any club they want to play for. Hence, superstars like Pete Rose can switch teams—and become instant multimillionaires in the process.

Will baseball gain or lose through collective bargaining? Will rich teams like the New York Yankees be able to buy pennants by hiring the best free agents? Will baseball fans become disillusioned by the high salaries and financial maneuvering of their heros? Only time will tell. But collective bargaining in organized baseball is definitely here to stay.

Establishing a Negotiating Position

Before formal negotiations begin, management and labor determine their objectives for the period of time to be covered by the contract. Generally, objectives set by both sides are strongly influenced by existing agreements in similar industries. For unions, determining a negotiating position often involves a hired staff of accountants, attorneys, economists, and other experts, who prepare the data, as well as a series of meetings with elected union officials. The union then appoints a bargaining committee to conduct direct negotiations with management.

Management establishes its negotiating position in meetings between general managers and the personnel department, which normally represents management in the collective bargaining process. In large businesses, a specialist, often the vice president of labor relations or the vice president of personnel, handles labor–management negotiations. Since labor contracts are vital to the welfare of the business, negotiators for management are in close contact with top executives.

Negotiating the Contract

Formal negotiations between unions and management begin with expressions of goodwill and hope for a mutually agreeable settlement. Normally, negotiations are conducted at a neutral site (not at the plant or union headquarters). Often they resemble a summit meeting between two major world powers, with labor and management negotiators backed up by extensive technical staffs. The atmosphere at the first negotiating session is usually cool and reserved, since both sides want to appear uncompromising.

During later negotiations, the basic goal of each side is to determine how far the other side is willing to compromise without revealing the degree to which it will make concessions. Less important differences are often settled in various smaller committee meetings prior to the main negotiations.

The toughest stage of negotiations usually occurs shortly before or during the first few days of a possible strike, when both parties have the strongest incentive to settle. Tension is high, bargaining sessions are long, and tempers run short. It is at this eleventh hour that the skills of experienced negotiators are invaluable.

Mediation and Arbitration

Most negotiations result in a solution. But when stalemates occur, labor and management often submit disputes to *mediation* or *arbitration*. **Mediation** is an attempt to settle conflicts through a neutral third party. Mediators may be political leaders, professors, or others who are acceptable to both sides. The Federal Mediation and Conciliation Service, a federal agency, and many state governments maintain lists of available mediators.

Arbitration differs from mediation in that the arbitrator has the power to make binding decisions. In **voluntary arbitration,** labor and management agree to refer any unresolved issues to an arbitrator or to an arbitration panel. Under **compulsory arbitration,** a third party (usually the government) forces labor and management to submit to arbitration. **Last-offer arbitration,** a relatively new intervention device, requires the arbitrator to choose between labor's last offer and management's last offer. This encourages the proposal of reasonable offers.

When mediation and arbitration fail, high public officials—even, at times, the president—often attempt to settle labor–management disputes by private arm twisting, or by appointing a fact-finding panel to outline a reasonable agreement, or by imposing a "cooling-off" period during which strikes and lockouts are legally forbidden while negotiations continue. Intervention at this level is used to prevent national emergencies, such as strikes by postal workers or coal miners.

The Union Contract

The goal of collective bargaining is the **union contract,** a written agreement between labor and management that specifies the rules and procedures to be followed by both parties during the contract period. Violations can result in court actions. A union contract typically includes:

1. Names of the parties, duration of the agreement, provisions for its renewal, and signatures of the parties.
2. Wage rates and fringe benefits, job classifications, shift premiums, and overtime pay.

3. Working conditions, such as hours, timing on shifts, permissible breaks, severance pay, and so on.
4. Union security, like the hiring of new workers and checkoff procedures.
5. Job security, including outside contracting of work, seniority, and so on.
6. Management rights.
7. Procedures for terminating and promoting employees.
8. Limitations on strikes and lockouts during the agreement.
9. Grievance procedures and the appointment of arbitrators.

A union contract at the national level may include several hundred pages of detailed provisions. While the national contract is being negotiated, labor and management at the plant level are usually trying to reach a local agreement. Provisions of the local contracts deal with plant-level labor–management issues, like the classification of jobs and the speed of the assembly line. Local agreements are usually consistent with the provisions of the national contract. Failure to achieve a local agreement may cause the affected plant to remain on strike. If strike-ridden local plants provide components that are essential to a company's production, failure to achieve local contracts may result in the shut-down of the entire business.

Contract Enforcement

Unfortunately, problems between labor and management do not disappear with the signing of national and local contracts. It is not uncommon for disagreements to arise over interpretation of the provisions and over whether the other side is keeping its part of the bargain. So more than 90 percent of all union contracts now include a formal **grievance procedure,** a step-by-step plan for contract-related disputes, or grievances.

A grievance may be initiated by an employee, by the union, or by management. If it is unresolvable at any of the levels shown in Figure 19–9, the grievance eventually reaches an arbitrator or arbitration panel. The arbitrator examines the transcripts of previous negotiations, holds hearings, and listens to presentations by the parties. Arbitration decisions are usually carefully based on the wording in the union contract. The goal is to solve problems well before they become big enough to cause work stoppages.

FIGURE 19-9
A Typical Grievance
Procedure.

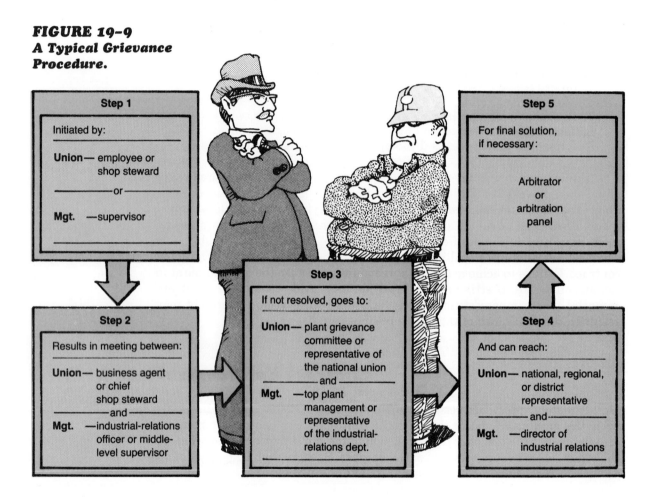

Step 1

Initiated by:
_____

Union— employee or
          shop steward
_____ or _____

Mgt. —supervisor

Step 2

Results in meeting between:
_____

Union— business agent
          or chief
          shop steward
_____ and _____
Mgt. —industrial-relations
          officer or middle-
          level supervisor

Step 3

If not resolved, goes to:
_____

Union— plant grievance
          committee or
          representative of
          the national union
_____ and _____
Mgt. —top plant
          management or
          representative
          of the industrial-
          relations dept.

Step 4

And can reach:
_____

Union— national, regional,
          or district
          representative
_____ and _____
Mgt. —director of
          industrial relations

Step 5

For final solution,
if necessary:
_____

Arbitrator
or
arbitration
panel

GOVERNMENT GROUND RULES
FOR LABOR AND MANAGEMENT

Contemporary collective bargaining procedures did not evolve naturally or even easily out of the long relationship between labor and management.

Rather, they were hammered out bit by bit through a series of legislative acts that today form the ground rules of government policy toward unions and business.

The Norris–LaGuardia Act

Historically, labor was severely handicapped by the willingness of many courts to issue injunctions against its chief economic weapon, the strike. The first major piece of pro-labor legislation, the **Norris–LaGuardia Act** of 1932, substantially strengthened labor's position in contract disputes by preventing employers from utilizing court injunctions, except in cases of violence. The Norris–LaGuardia Act also prevented employers from making yellow-dog contracts, which require prospective workers to pledge not to join a union as a condition of employment. The basic objective of the Norris–LaGuardia Act was to permit labor and management to engage in collective bargaining with a minimum of interference from the courts.

The Wagner Act

The National Labor Relations Act of 1935, popularly known as the **Wagner Act,** forced employers to bargain with unions, required that management abstain from a long list of antiunion practices (including dismissing union leaders unfairly, spying on unions, forming business-dominated unions, and refusing to bargain in good faith with employees), and created the National Labor Relations Board (NLRB), a government agency, to administer its provisions. The NLRB carries out two primary functions. First, on the petition of affected workers, the NLRB conducts *representation elections,* in which employees choose by secret ballot the union they wish to join or vote to remain unaffiliated with any labor group. Second, the NLRB investigates claims by management or by labor that the other side's activities have violated federal law. If the NLRB uncovers an unfair labor practice, it is legally bound to punish the offender. The basic objectives of the Wagner Act were to encourage free collective bargaining between the two equally powerful organizations of management and labor and to establish collective bargaining guidelines.

Industrial-relations managers represent management interests in labor–management negotiations. They prepare briefs for negotiations, interpret contracts for management and union representatives, and help resolve labor grievances. Five years of experience in a lower-level employee-relations job is the normal prerequisite for promotion to industrial-relations manager. A bachelor's or a master's degree in industrial relations, business administration, or labor economics is essential. Actual salaries range widely, beginning at $12,000. Experienced industrial-relations managers may earn more than $50,000. (*Additional information:* contact the industrial-relations department of a local college or university or Director of Personnel; National Labor Relations Board; 1717 Pennsylvania Avenue N.W.; Washington, D.C. 20570.)

General supervisors (or **general foremen**) are "supervisors of supervisors." They usually report to a plant manager and are charged with overseeing 5–20 first-line supervisors (foremen). Education beyond high school is desirable; sometimes promising foremen are promoted to general supervisory positions, in which case additional work in business administration, especially in the principles of management, is essential. Salaries normally range from $20,000 to $40,000, and opportunities are expected to grow in the next ten years. (*Additional information:* contact the personnel department of a local manufacturing company.)

First-line supervisors (or **foremen**) are responsible for the direct supervision of assembly-line or other workers. (See the box "On the Firing Line: Between Workers and Middle Management" for more details.) First-line supervisors normally earn $15,000–$30,000, excluding overtime pay. A college education is not required; workers promoted to first-line supervisory positions are often trained in "principles of supervision" courses. (*Additional information:* contact the personnel department of a local manufacturer.)

Labor-union business agents represent local union interests in labor–management negotiations. They also handle their union's public relations, promote union membership, find jobs for union members, and arrange union meetings. Employee grievances are generally relayed to management by the **shop steward,** who is a company employee as well as a union representative. Competent shop stewards may eventually become the local's business agent. (*Additional information:* contact local unions.)

Labor union leaders at the national level are skilled politicians elected by the union membership. National leaders usually have been the heads of large, influential locals or have obtained the support of previous union leaders. Salaries normally range from $50,000 to $150,000, but the earnings of top union leaders may be $300,000 or more because of the pay they receive for serving on AFL-CIO sponsored committees. (*Additional information:* contact local unions, although information on the total compensation of top union officials may be hard to obtain.)

The Taft-Hartley Act

The third landmark labor law, passed against bitter union opposition in 1947, was the **Taft-Hartley Act,** which attempted to restore a more equitable balance between labor and management through the following provisions:

1. A list of unfair union practices such as secondary boycotts, in which unions induce outside parties to refuse to buy products of companies with which union workers are having a dispute.
2. A procedure under which the president is authorized to stop strikes for an eighty-day cooling-off period if they adversely affect the national interest.
3. Limitations on undesirable union practices such as featherbedding.
4. A method by which individual states can pass right-to-work laws, under which employees cannot be forced to join unions as a condition of employment.

The Landrum-Griffin Act

In the 1950s, a series of dramatic congressional investigations uncovered internal corruption and lack of genuine democracy in some unions. As a result, in 1959, Congress passed the **Landrum-Griffin Act,** which amended the Wagner Act to include provisions designed to protect the financial integrity of the administration of members' funds by union leaders and to ensure that unions genuinely represented their memberships. The act required that every union develop a constitution to be filed with the Secretary of Labor, ordered the fair implementation of union election procedures, established a bill of rights for union members, and defined additional unfair labor practices by unions. The Landrum–Griffin Act attempted to improve the internal operations of organized labor and to make unions responsive to the needs of their members.

Although the Taft–Hartley Act and the Landrum–Griffin Act sharply curtail some union practices, the basic principles laid down in the Wagner Act remain largely intact today. Contemporary labor law encourages the continuance of collective bargaining in private hands; government intervention is considered necessary only when intolerable abuses develop.

Chapter Review & Applications

Key Points to Remember

1. Labor includes craft unions (representing workers in a single profession) and industrial unions (which represent workers in a particular industry, regardless of their occupation).

2. Unions are organized on a local, regional, and national level. The most powerful union is the AFL–CIO, which represents three-fourths of all unionized workers in the United States.

3. Basic goals for employees are better wages and fringe benefits, improved working conditions, job security, more challenging jobs, and union security. From the employer's standpoint, these objectives raise production costs and lessen management's control over the business.

4. The primary goal of management is to obtain the highest possible output from labor at the lowest possible cost. This is achieved through control of unit labor costs, noninterference from unions, and worker loyalty.

5. Labor's major weapon for securing its objectives is the strike. Management gets action by utilizing the lockout.

6. Normally, labor–management disputes are settled through collective bargaining. If these negotiations are unsuccessful, a neutral third party may be called in to mediate or arbitrate. In arbitration, decisions are binding. If mediation and arbitration fail, a public official may intervene.

7. Union contracts specify rules and procedures between employees and employers during a specific time period. Disagreements arising over contract interpretation or adherence are settled by the grievance procedure, a step-by-step plan for settling contract disputes.

8. Four key legislative acts that formed the ground rules for government policy toward unions and management are the Norris–LaGuardia, Wagner, Taft–Hartley, and Landrum–Griffin Acts.

Questions for Discussion

1. What are the main objectives of union members? Of management? Why do they clash?

2. "Wage increases are less important to workers than they used to be." Do you agree with this statement? Why or why not?

3. Describe the structure of a labor union. How are workers represented at each level?

4. Public employee unions are becoming increasingly more militant. Police, teachers, and garbage workers are only three examples. Yet citizens want reduced taxes and good public services. Under what circumstances should public employees be allowed to strike? Why?

5. Suppose that you earn $7.50 per hour and have a cost-of-living escalator equal to 80 percent of the rise in the Consumer Price Index. Your new union contract provides a 5 percent basic annual wage increase, and the anticipated rate of inflation is 7.5 percent. What will you earn next year?

6. Describe the steps in a normal grievance procedure.

Short Cases

1. You represent the management of General Motors in negotiations with the United Auto Workers for a new two-year contract. What factors would you consider in establishing your collective bargaining position?

2. Assume that the language of the labor contract developed between GM and the UAW specifies that "employers may not order workers to undertake unsafe tasks," and that the contract also states that "employees are obligated to follow reasonable orders issued by their supervisors." A union welder has just refused to follow a supervisor's order, claiming that to do so would be hazardous to his safety. Union and management have been unable to agree on the interpretation of the contract. As the assigned mediator, how would you resolve this dispute?

A Critical Business Decision

—made by Charlie Bragg
of the United Automobile Workers

The Situation

The woman at the Ford assembly plant in Warren, Michigan, was upset. The paint in her spray gun was too thin and was squirting over her apron. Complaints to her supervisor had produced no results.

Her solution: to call in Charlie Bragg, officially known as a District Committeeman and a local representative of the United Automobile Workers. As a shop steward, Charlie had been elected by 237 union members in the plant's "trim" department. Notified of the woman's complaint, Bragg acted quickly. He talked with the woman's supervisor and telephoned the person responsible for spray-gun repair. Within minutes, the spray gun was fixed.

Charlie Bragg's work may seem easy to some. Bragg wanders around, talking to union members and occasionally poking his head into unfinished cars. Bragg's duties include fighting disciplinary actions by Ford, arranging vacations and leaves for union workers, supervising the repair of supply racks, and even seeing to it that bathrooms are clean and drinking fountains are unclogged. Because of a provision in the union contract, Bragg's $20,000 salary is paid by Ford, says *The Wall Street Journal*.[3]

Bragg believes that many problems on the shop floor are caused by poor supervision. "A bad foreman," Bragg says, "is a guy who doesn't care about his people. All he cares about is just trying to get that dollar, and he lets his bosses or employees run the area. He's inconsistent. He lets things run rampant for a while, then tries to crack down all at once without being fair."

Charlie Bragg is respected by his co-workers. "He's an outstanding committeeman," says one. "He comes around and talks to you, and when he is paged, he makes it there as quick as he can." Ed Hendrix, a foreman at Ford, views Bragg with grudging enthusiasm. "He's one of the better committeemen," Hendrix comments, "even though he and I don't get along. He's on his side of the fence, and I'm on mine."

The Decision

Work standards are a major source of conflict between Ford Motor Company and the UAW. "Standards men are running our plant," Bragg argues. "In the old days, you had time to go to the bathroom if you wanted. Now you need a relief man for that. You can't even breathe. These standards men went to school, but they didn't take the human factor into account." In Ford's grievance procedure, Bragg represents workers who complain about assembly-line speedups and lack of time to do their work properly. He often gathers evidence by timing union members' on-the-job activities.

Bragg and the UAW face tough problems regarding work standards. Should Charlie Bragg and the UAW defend workers who think they are overworked? Or should Bragg and the UAW cooperate with Ford to improve productivity in order to compete with foreign auto imports, particularly from Japan?

Questions

1. As Charlie Bragg, would you encourage greater productivity from union members by cooperating with Ford? What problems do you foresee if you take this position?
2. Charlie Bragg and Ed Hendrix (see box on page 467) are employed at the same Ford plant. How do their attitudes toward what's important differ? How do these differences reflect the labor–management issues discussed in the chapter?

映画と
音楽と

Pizza PARLOR

SHAKEY'S
PiZZA PARLOR

31

メガネ
TAMAYA

かにのすきや
かに
お2階

International Business

In this chapter you will learn . . .

- why international trade is important for American business.
- how businesses export goods and services to foreign countries.
- how multinational corporations work.
- about the role the United States plays in the international financial community.

20

The benefit of international trade is more efficient employment of the productive forces of the world.

JOHN STEWART MILL

ommunist Chinese slurping Coke? From a $2 million bottling plant in Shanghai? Coca-Cola—practically a symbol of our American life style—hit Peking, Kwanchow, Hangshow, and Shanghai in 1980. It was the first American consumer product to bubble up into the Chinese market. Coca-Cola was willing to start small, offering its product only at tourist hotels. After all, the potential market includes one billion Chinese citizens. And Coke was especially delighted with its exclusive agreement: no Pepsi, Royal Crown, or any other fizzle allowed. (See, also, the color insert that follows this chapter.)

In this chapter we will look at how and why such trade agreements are arranged and what significance they have for the U.S. and world economies and for the corporations that make them.

INTERNATIONAL TRADE

Since World War II, the United States has actively encouraged world trade. Japan needs our lumber, and we need their tape recorders. When both countries benefit, world trade flourishes. The oceans are crisscrossed with boats and planes carrying cargoes between countries: tin from Malaysia, blue jeans from the United States, coffee from Brazil, oil from the Middle East—all going to countries where these resources are scarce. Since the 1970s, our business with communist countries has been especially vigorous.

Why trade? There are three main benefits of world trade: (1) *Locally unavailable goods are exchanged.* In the 1980s and 1990s the United States will import an increasing amount of raw materials and export more technological products and services. Such exchanges benefit everyone. (2) *Low prices result.* Countries that specialize can produce certain products better and less expensively than anyone else can. American farms, for example, help feed the world at economical prices. Japanese cars and electronics are sought the world over. And some nations are blessed with an abundance of oil, coal, or gems. So, ideally, it would be most efficient for us to sell our grain and use the money to buy Japanese television sets and Arabian oil. Unfortunately, the complex nature of international relations often prevents such simple solutions. (3) *Political benefits can result.* Countries that are ideologically at odds with each other often find the door to understanding opened by a mutually beneficial trade arrangement. A good example is the agreement between Coca-Cola and the People's Republic of China described above.

Barriers to Trade

Despite the benefits of trade, most governments restrict international commerce through the use of *tariffs, quotas,* and *exchange controls.*

A **tariff,** or a *customs duty,* is a charge levied by a government on its imports or, less commonly, on its exports. **Protective tariffs** are designed to protect a country's industries against foreign competition by making foreign products more expensive (by, say, 3 percent of their selling price). We now have tariffs on foreign cars, shoes, and many other products. **Revenue tariffs** are lower and are designed only to raise money.

A **quota** is a restriction on the amount of a commodity that can come from a specific nation. For example, there is a U.S. quota on cane sugar. So a Jamaican or Philippine company must secure an *import license,* which states how much sugar it can ship to us in any one year.

Exchange controls are government restrictions on the use of domestic currency to buy foreign products. An American importer of Japanese cameras, for example, needs Japanese currency (yen) to buy cameras before reselling them for dollars. So restricting the number of dollars that can be exchanged for a particular foreign currency also restricts the amount of imports that can come from that country. Nations trying to industrialize frequently impose exchange controls to restrict imports to needed tools and machinery.

Other trade restrictions are *export controls, embargoes,* and *nationalistic buying policies.* **Export controls** put limits on the number of goods that can be sold to foreign nations. One reason for imposing this restriction is to keep domestic prices of those goods at reasonable levels. **Embargoes** restrict or prohibit the flow of a particular good. These are usually imposed for political reasons, as when one nation refuses to supply another with military equipment. **Nationalistic buying policies** encourage government agencies or business firms to use only domestically produced goods and services. For example, as part of a "Buy America" campaign, foreign steel may not be used in the construction of U.S. interstate highways.

Why Restrict Trade?

If international trade is so beneficial, why do we have so many forms of restriction? *Protectionists*—advocates of barriers to trade—cite several reasons:

> NATIONAL DEFENSE   Nations try to be self-sufficient to protect themselves from economic blackmail. A quota on foreign oil, for example, might boost the development of American coal and other energy sources while showing the major oil-exporting countries that we need not be enslaved by demands for higher and higher prices.
>
> WAGE PROTECTION   Labor unions often argue that trade restrictions are needed to protect the wages of American workers. American-made products (shoes, for example) might not sell if they had to compete directly with products made in another country with cheaper labor. High tariffs are supported as a way of making American prices competitive. Unfortunately, this approach creates higher prices for consumers. It also decreases our exports, since foreign countries end up with less money with which to buy our products.
>
> PROTECTION OF INFANT INDUSTRIES   Young, struggling (infant) domestic industries that face powerful competition from abroad may require temporary tariff protection, which can be removed once the industry becomes strong. The trouble with such protection is that the typical industry can end up large and powerful enough to bring political pressure against ever removing the trade restrictions.

TRENDS IN WORLD TRADE

Recently, world trade has been affected by three main factors: international trade agreements, international cartels, and a push toward more commerce with the communist world.

International Trade Agreements

Trade agreements can be as specific as the Coca-Cola deal with the People's Republic of China or as general as the European Economic Community, or "Common Market," in which France, Italy, West Germany, Belgium, Luxembourg, Great Britain, and other European countries agree to drop all tariffs on each other's products. Comecon, the Soviet Union's economic community, organizes trade arrangements among communist countries like Yugoslavia and Romania that are so extensive that Russia imports less than 5 percent of its gross national product from the noncommunist world. The United States has a series of arrangements with numerous other nations to reduce tariffs on each other's products. It is known collectively as the General Agreement on Tariffs and Trade (GATT).

International Cartels

A **cartel** is an international agreement among nations or producers to control the prices and trade flows of a commodity. The most famous international cartel is OPEC, the Organization of Petroleum Exporting Countries. When a commodity like oil is in short supply, producers find it most profitable to band together in setting prices and production output. OPEC is especially effective because it is made up of countries, not businesses, that can better enforce one another's actions. By 1985, as a result of its oil revenues alone, OPEC will have enough money to afford to buy all the stock in all American companies. (The chances of this happening, however, are remote, since only a portion of all stock is normally available for sale.)

Cartels are an extra hardship for less developed countries, which often cannot borrow enough money or export enough of their own products to pay for the products they need from cohesive cartel countries. But even cohesive and powerful cartels like OPEC are subject to internal disagreements that can cause individual producers to lower their prices.

Trade with Communist Countries

U.S. trade with communist nations is booming. Agribusinesses sell grain to Russia and China. High-technology companies ship computers and computer know-how. And soft-drink manufacturers supply Cokes and Pepsis. American business people are counting on communist societies becoming increasingly consumer oriented. They argue that if we don't trade with them, other countries will.

Critics of communist trade, though, believe that political disagreements, such as our protest against the Russian invasion of Afghanistan in 1980, will periodically disrupt trade agreements. And they fear that our technology will be copied or even adapted for military uses. But the communist markets are so large, and all countries so dependent on one another, that expanded international trade will surely continue. To see how a different aspect of international trade works, read the box below.

MULTINATIONAL CORPORATIONS

Products are not the only things that crisscross the oceans. So does money. And a lot of it comes from **multinationals,** businesses that invest in plant and equipment abroad. Multinational corporations can be defined as corporations with plants in at least six countries and with at least 20 percent of their production coming from outside their base country. Multinational investment is increasing rapidly. American investments abroad exceeded $150 billion in 1980. Exxon, for example, one of the very largest "American" corporations, gets two-thirds of its sales from foreign markets. Foreign multinationals are investing in factories in the United States at an unprecedented rate (see Figure 20–1). *Direct foreign investment* in this country, much of it in American businesses, totaled more than $60 billion in 1980.

Portfolio investment in foreign countries, an alternative to direct investment often made by multinationals, is increasing, too, though it is less important for business than direct foreign investment. Most American brokerage

Black-Market Blue Jeans in Red Square

Ivan is a Russian truck driver with a capitalistic flair for entrepreneurship. Employed to drive through Western countries to pick up and deliver regular Soviet goods, Ivan sleeps in his truck to save his "expense account" money. He then exchanges the money for a European currency, which he smuggles back into Russia. He uses the money to buy American blue jeans at one of the special Russian stores stocking popular products that are sold only to people with foreign currency. (The government's purpose for having the special stores is to collect Western currency, which it uses to buy Western imports.) Ivan then turns around and sells the jeans on the Soviet black market for ten times what he paid for them. That's how popular American blue jeans are in Russia. And that's why American companies are so eager to crack communist markets themselves, legally.

FIGURE 20–1
The Fifteen Largest Industrials Outside the U.S. in 1979.

RANK	COMPANY	COUNTRY	INDUSTRY	SALES ($1,000)
1	Royal Dutch/Shell Group	Neth.-Britain	Petroleum	59,416,560
2	British Petroleum	Britain	Petroleum	38,713,496
3	Unilever	Britain-Neth.	Food products	21,748,583
4	ENI	Italy	Petroleum	18,984,960
5	Fiat	Italy	Motor vehicles	18,300,000
6	Française des Pétroles	France	Petroleum	17,305,220
7	Peugeot-Citroën	France	Motor vehicles	17,270,104
8	Volkswagenwerk	Germany	Motor vehicles	16,765,683
9	Philips' Gloeilampenfabrieken	Netherlands	Electronics, appliances	16,576,123
10	Renault	France	Motor vehicles	16,117,376
11	Siemens	Germany	Electronics, appliances	15,069,575
12	Daimler-Benz	Germany	Motor vehicles	14,942,324
13	Hoechst	Germany	Chemicals	14,785,464
14	Bayer	Germany	Chemicals	14,196,027
15	BASF	Germany	Chemicals	14,138,872

Source: *Fortune World Business Directory*, 1980. Reprinted by permission from *Fortune* magazine, © 1980, Time Inc.

firms can help you buy stock in foreign enterprises—from an Australian uranium mine to a West German bank; and they regularly help foreign investors buy stocks and bonds in American businesses.

Advantages of Multinationals

Multinationals (MNCs) can take advantage of national differences to make profits. An MNC may locate its manufacturing in the Far East (because of cheap labor), its research and development in the United States and Western Europe (with their better-educated populations), its storage and marketing in South America and Japan (near major markets), and its base in a country with low business taxes. Multinationals of this type hire financial managers who can pinpoint the best loan in the world for a particular purpose on a particular day. For many MNCs, a national border is of no more importance than a state border is for an American business.

By purchasing resources where they are least costly and selling products where they are most needed, multinationals also contribute to a better world standard of living. And they may bind countries together so tightly that war could become unthinkable. Before the year 2000, about 200 of these giant firms—two-thirds of them American in origin—may well control more than half the output of the free world's private sector.

Disadvantages of Multinationals

But multinationals may be too powerful and could suffer in a politically unstable world.

Their power already exceeds that of some small countries. And there are fears that they may use this power too zealously to protect their investments. In the 1970s, for example, there were allegations that International Telephone and Telegraph (ITT) influenced American foreign policy to help overthrow the existing government in Chile. (The Chilean government was threatening to take over ITT's operations there.) No international law to control this kind of corporate maneuver currently exists nor could one be effectively enforced. Multinationals are also accused of moving investments away from their "home countries" where they may be needed.

But a multinational can also be hurt by a foreign government. As a symbol of foreign power, a multinational can find its operations in a country "nationalized"—taken over—perhaps with no compensation. This happened in Cuba, where Castro's government quickly nationalized all American-owned companies when it came into power. And, on a lesser scale, a multinational can watch a "host" country's currency decline, carrying with it the value of the company's investment.

To minimize these risks, multinationals are employing more managers from the "host" countries themselves. They are also selling more stock and bonds in the countries to create home-based lobbies to fight nationalization. And they sometimes avoid going directly into risky countries—selling, instead, their technology and know-how to a company already located there.

BUILDING AN INTERNATIONAL BUSINESS

Do you want to sell popsicles to Iceland? Distribute Toyotas in Detroit? International business opportunities come in three key forms. A business may: (1) export its products abroad; (2) produce and distribute its products from multinational bases abroad; or, less often, (3) distribute imported products at home or sell only services in foreign countries (usually under a license).

Why Export?

Exports are attractive for four reasons. First, profits in foreign markets are often higher than at home. This can happen when domestic production is not competitive, when the market is growing quickly, or when foreign demand for the product is greater than domestic demand.

Second, exporting can be efficient. In industries whose costs decrease as production volumes expand, the more you manufacture, the lower the unit cost. *Dumping*—selling your surplus abroad below cost—may even be profitable. A business can recover some of its costs without having to lower prices in its own country (which would set a bad precedent). The American steel industry, for example, has accused Japanese steel companies of selling steel in the United States at less than cost.

Third, it may be less expensive to export than to enter a new domestic market. If a business' market share for a product here is as large as it can

Your Next Job
General Tips for Job Hunting

In Chapter 1, we discussed five key steps toward choosing a career. We present here four key steps toward actually getting the job of your choice: (1) job hunting; (2) preparing for the job interview; (3) the job interview; and (4) post-interview follow-up.

Job Hunting

Your purpose is to be granted a personal interview. So schedule meetings with campus recruiters, get lists of prospective employers from the Yellow Pages, Chamber of Commerce publications, and the *College Placement Annual,* and contact the nearest office of your State Employment Service. Talk to friends, faculty, and family. Check the classified section of local newspapers. And don't get discouraged.

Once you have the names of several prospective employers, send your resume (see Chapter 5) and a cover letter to each, requesting an interview. Or pay a direct, personal visit, leaving a copy of your resume.

Interview Preparation

After you have arranged for the interview, find out all you can about the company, so you will be prepared to ask some intelligent questions. Read all published material that is available and check with the Chamber of Commerce or Better Business Bureau for any information they may have.

Specific questions about your prospective job should include: the type of work involved, the company's training program (if any), typical promotional patterns, and company transfer policy. Try to determine your salary requirement and what salary the employer will propose if a job is offered.

You will also have to answer questions. You should be prepared with answers to the following questions commonly asked in a job interview:

1. Why have you chosen this field as a career?
2. Why is this company of interest to you?
3. What are your short-term and your long-term career objectives?
4. What special interests, activities, or qualifications can you contribute to the job?
5. What do you expect of a job?

Obviously, be neat and clean; use good taste in choosing your clothes and know how to pronounce the interviewer's name beforehand. Take along some paper and a pen to make notes to yourself afterward.

The Interview

Common sense is the best guide. Be friendly, honest, and sincere. Sit up in your chair and look interested. Look the interviewer directly in the eye. Judge the length of your answers from cues by the interviewer. Don't answer all questions "yes" or "no." If you find you are doing most of the talking, ask, "Are there any other questions you would like to ask me?"

Remember: (1) you are there to get information about the company and the job, so don't be afraid to ask questions; and (2) you are there to sell yourself, so get your good points across.

Thank the interviewer for the time and consideration taken to interview you. Express your willingness to provide additional information.

Post-Interview Follow-Up

Carefully note any further contacts your interviewer has suggested and follow any instructions he or she has given you. If the interview went well or if the interviewer indicated that you would hear about the job by a specific date, wait at least a week after the interview or the indicated date before checking with the company. Then, briefly remind the interviewer of your previous conversation, express appreciation for the interviewer's time, and explain that you are still interested in the job. Good luck.

realistically become, that firm can either export or begin the costly and risky venture of launching a new product.

Xerox thought that Great Britain was the perfect outlet for one of its most successful copiers, so it formed a joint subsidiary, Rank-Xerox. Five copiers were sent to Great Britain right away, with pride and optimism. But nobody had noticed one small problem: British office doors are narrower than U.S. doors: the copiers wouldn't fit.

British engineers were flown to Rochester, New York, for a collaboration. They managed to reduce the cabinet size, and, finally, Xerox found a home in Great Britain.[1]

Finally, exports can help a business stabilize demand for its products. Sales in one country may drop because of a slight recession, but be strong in another. Seasonal patterns can help, too. Winter sporting goods sales can boom all year long by taking advantage of the fact that winter in Chile, for example, comes in July.

Why Import?

For American business, importing is a much less common practice than exporting. But importing can be just as important. For one thing, there are some commodities and materials that are not as readily available here as elsewhere (copper is one example). Also, it is sometimes cheaper to import some goods (such as hand-knit sweaters) than to make them here. And some foreign goods—such as French wine, Swiss chocolate, and British Rolls Royces—are in big demand for their prestige value. Finally, importing is often just good business. Boeing, for example, buys many aircraft-engine components abroad, then gets huge orders from British Airways and Air France for the Boeing 747s it manufactures here. Business is also booming for importers of electronic games from Japan (see box, at bottom of next page).

The Risks of International Business

Besides tariffs and quotas, there are other problems for international traders:

1. LANGUAGE DIFFERENCES   Misunderstandings can occur even in the translation of brand names. Chevrolet "Nova" in Spanish becomes "no va," or "it doesn't go." And General Motors' "Body by Fisher" is "Corpse by Fisher" in Japanese.
2. CULTURAL DIFFERENCES   Physical and social differences are substantial. The voltages and plugs used in electrical appliances are one example. So is the fact that most Japanese still shop by bus or bicycle—will they want that giant American teddy bear badly enough to carry it home?
3. LEGAL DIFFERENCES   Business, patent, antitrust, tax, and other laws differ substantially. Price fixing, a criminal offense here, is legally acceptable in Europe.
4. EXCHANGE-RATE FLUCTUATIONS   Rapid swings in the relative values of currencies can dramatically change the profit margins of

Space Invaders: From Japan

First they conquered Japan. Then they were sighted in Israel. And now the United States has been invaded. Not by little green men from Mars—but by electronic monsters from Japan. Instead of taking over army bases, they establish themselves in movie theaters, bowling alleys, ski chalets, and campus lounges.

Who are they and what do they want? The electronic invaders are part of a new coin-operated video game craze introduced by Taito Ltd. of Japan. What they want are your quarters. Players all over the world are obsessed with zapping creatures from games like Space Invaders, Asteroids, Galaxian, and Lunar Lander. (An American Company, Cinematronics, has developed its own version of the space video game, aptly called Rip-Off.)

This may be the lighter side of international trade, but the profits are heavy. According to *The Wall Street Journal*,[2] "In a choice location a popular video game grosses about $200 a week and . . . as much as $400 a week in its early stages." Ralph Bender, manager of a game arcade in New York City, calls them "the biggest thing ever to hit the game industry." The size of the coin-operated game market is estimated at $500 million a year. The enormous popularity of the new space games is attributed to superior electronics: noises, colors, and movements that put pinball machines and earlier video games like Pong to shame.

With this kind of success in international trade, can intergalactic commerce be far behind?

FIGURE 20-2
Help for Foreign Trade.

ORGANIZATION	SERVICES OFFERED
Commercial banks	Banks maintain branches throughout the world to provide financial advice and services.
The Export-Import Bank (Exim Bank)	A U.S. government agency, the Exim Bank provides credit to American exporters when banks will not or when foreign governments are providing cheap loans to their exporters.
Bureau of Foreign Commerce, U.S. Department of Commerce	This agency distributes lists of foreign buyers and distributors, credit reports on foreign companies, and information on export opportunities.
The State Department	Commercial attachés, employed by the U.S. State Department, live and work abroad. They provide data on foreign economic developments to the government and to businesses.
Foreign trade zones, U.S. customs	Foreign trade zones are geographic areas in which producers may manufacture, import, process, or store goods without paying customs duties.
The U.S. Tariff Commission	This office determines whether foreign exporters are dumping their products into American markets and whether normally priced foreign imports are damaging an American industry. If so, the industry is eligible for technical assistance, government loans, and tax relief.

internationally minded businesses, which typically produce in one or a few countries and have the bulk of their sales in other countries. Accounting standards now require that foreign exchange earnings or losses be reported each year on financial statements. Thus, the reported earnings of these businesses fluctuate more than the earnings of purely American companies, possibly making internationally oriented businesses less attractive investments for the typical investor. Sources of help for these and other problems are shown in Figure 20–2.

Managing with a Multinational Perspective

International trade creates some challenging managerial problems, ranging from manufacturing to finance. Choosing the right country in which to place production facilities involves consideration of costs, the government regulatory climate, and political stability, among other things. Managers must also decide such questions as: Should we market our own exports abroad with an international sales force, or should we pay to use foreign sales representatives? Should our U.S. divisions produce and market each product separately, or should all of our export activities be combined into a single international division? Should we finance our foreign operations with funds from the U.S. company or with loans from the host country, which may be politically unstable? How should we price our products to maximize our profit in low-tax countries?

International businesses hire many managers to answer questions like these. Lately, these managers tend to be based in this country, while executives for the foreign offices are natives of the host country. The reason is largely because of the decline of the U.S. dollar abroad. Supporting Americans abroad can get very expensive. A small house in Tokyo rents for $3,000 (U.S. currency) a month and McDonald's hamburgers cost more than $3 apiece (again, U.S. currency).

THE UNITED STATES IN THE WORLD ECONOMIC COMMUNITY

Historically, the United States has been a net exporter, meaning that the dollar value of its exports normally exceeds the dollar value of its imports (see Figure 20–3). The difference between the monetary value of a nation's exports and its imports is called that nation's **balance of trade.** When its exports exceed its imports, a nation is said to be enjoying a **surplus** in its balance of trade. When the opposite occurs, the balance of trade is deficient, or has shown a **deficit.**

The **balance of international payments** or, more simply, the **balance of payments** of a nation is a balance sheet representing all of its international economic transactions. As such, the balance of payments includes the balance of trade plus other expenditures like foreign aid and tourist purchases. Since 1950, the United States has had a deficit in its balance of payments, because U.S. dollar outflows have exceeded the dollars spent by foreigners in America. The reason for this deficit is that the surplus in the U.S. balance of payments has been more than offset by federal military and foreign-aid expenditures, by the tendency of American businesses and individuals to invest more funds abroad than foreign businesses and individuals invest in the United States, and by the large amounts of money spent by American tourists compared with that spent by travelers to the United States. Because of huge imports of OPEC

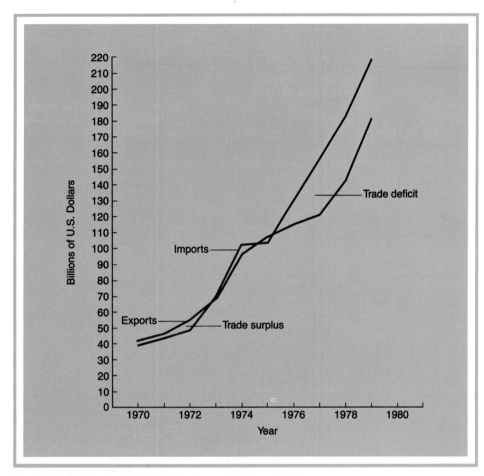

FIGURE 20-3
Trends in the U.S. Balance of Trade.

Source: Statistical Abstract of the United States; International Monetary Fund.

oil and Japanese manufactured goods from 1975 to 1981, the U.S. suffered large deficits in its balance of trade and its balance of payments.

Exchange Rates

An **exchange rate** is the rate at which one country's money is exchanged for another's. These rates fluctuate, as can be seen in Figure 20–4. For example, in July 1980, the exchange rate between the Canadian dollar and the U.S. dollar was 87 cents (U.S.). If the Canadian dollar *depreciates* a bit more, it

FIGURE 20-4
Foreign Exchange Rates.

FOREIGN EXCHANGE
Monday, July 14, 1980

Country	Fgn. currency in dollars Mon.	Fri.	Dollar in fgn. curency Mon.	Fri.	Country	Fgn. currency in dollars Mon.	Fri.	Dollar in fgn. currency Mon.	Fri.
Argentina (Peso)	.0005	.0005	1853.50	1853.50	Japan (Yen)	.004582	.004585	218.23	218.10
Australia (Dollar)	1.1617	1.1625	.8608	.8602	30 day fut	.004565	.004578	219.07	218.45
Austria (Schilling) ...	.0807	.0808	12.39	12.37	60 day fut	.004553	.004564	219.62	219.10
Belgium (Franc)	.0358	.0358	27.95	27.90	90 day fut	.004542	.004555	220.15	219.55
Bolivia (Peso)	.0400	.0400	25.00	25.00	Jordan (Dinar)	3.4364	3.4364	.2910	.2910
Brazil (Cruzeiro)	.0192	.0192	52.21	52.21	Kuwait (Dinar)	3.7538	3.7538	.2664	.2664
Britain (Pound)	2.3787	2.3750	.4204	.4211	Lebanon (Pound)	.2929	.2939	3.4140	3.4020
30 day fut	2.3637	2.3615	.4231	.4235	Mexico (Peso)	.0436	.0436	22.94	22.94
60 day fut	2.3532	2.3485	.4250	.4258	New Zealand (Dollar)	.9900	.9900	1.0101	1.0101
90 day fut	2.3434	2.3386	.4267	.4276	Norway (Krone)	.2081	.2081	4.8045	4.8065
Canada (Dollar)	.8692	.8703	1.1505	1.1490	yPeru (Sol)	.003696	.003696	270.50	270.50
30 day fut	.8678	.8689	1.1523	1.1509	Philippines (Peso) ...	.1333	.1333	7.5035	7.5035
60 day fut	.8663	.8675	1.1544	1.1527	Portugal (Escudo) ...	.0206	.0206	48.55	48.60
90 day fut	.8655	.8660	1.1554	1.1537	Saudi Arabia (Riyal) .	.3014	.3014	3.3175	3.3183
Chile (Peso)	.0256	.0256	39.00	39.00	Singapore (Dollar) ...	.4734	.4747	2.1125	2.1065
Colombia (Peso)	.0212	.0212	47.22	47.22	So. Africa (Rand)	1.3085	1.3085	.7642	.7642
Denmark (Krone)	.1849	.1851	5.4070	5.4035	Spain (Peseta)	.0142	.0141	70.55	70.65
yEgypt (Pound)	1.45	1.45	.6900	.6900	Sweden (Krona)	.2426	.2426	4.1215	4.1225
Ecuador (Sucre).....	.0356	.0356	28.10	28.10	Switzerland (Franc)..	.6236	.6253	1.6035	1.5990
Finland (Mark)	.2774	.2775	3.6050	3.6035	30 day fut	.6258	.6277	1.5980	1.5931
France (Franc)	.2476	.2475	4.0385	4.0400	60 day fut	.6281	.6297	1.5921	1.5881
Greece (Drachma) ...	.0236	.0235	42.45	42.55	90 day fut	.6301	.6316	1.5870	1.5833
Holland (Guilder)	.5244	.5256	1.9070	1.9025	Turkey (Lira)	.0169	.0169	78.00	78.00
Hong Kong (Dollar) ..	.2038	.2038	4.9075	4.9075	Uruguay (Peso)	.1114	.1114	8.9800	8.9800
yIndia (Rupee)	.1299	.1295	7.7000	7.7200	Venezuela (Boliva) ..	.2330	.2330	4.2910	4.2910
Indonesia (Rupiah) ..	.0016	.0016	625.00	625.00	W. Germany (Mark)..	.5737	.5740	1.7430	1.7420
Ireland (Pound)	2.1485	2.1530	.4654	.4645	30 day fut	.5742	.5739	1.7415	1.7424
Israel (Pound)	.0198	.0199	50.52	50.34	60 day fut	.5737	.5739	1.7430	1.7424
Israel (Shekel)	.1980	.1990	5.052	5.034	90 day fut	.5724	.5741	1.7470	.7418
Italy (Lire)	.001205	.001204	830.00	830.25					

Late prices at New York & San Francisco banks, gathered by Bank of America, New York.

y-Official rate.

Prices listed for foreign currencies represent rates quoted in New York by the Bank of America at late afternoon as indicative of market conditions for large business transactions—not the rates available to individual or tourists, which may differ.

Source: *The New York Times* (July 15, 1980).

might be worth 80 cents (U.S.). If the Canadian dollar were to *appreciate* (increase) in value, it might be worth 95 cents in American currency.

Managers watch exchange rates carefully. When the U.S. dollar depreciates relative to the currency of another country, people in that country like American exports better, because they can buy them for less of their own country's money. Exchange rates vary according to the U.S. balance of payments. If we have a deficit, other countries are accumulating more dollars than they can spend on our products. Eventually, this surplus decreases the value of our dollar. Fluctuations in the exchange rate can obviously damage business. Profitable trade can turn unprofitable. Contracts that provide for future sales can become grossly unfair. And foreign investments can lose value quickly.

International Financial Institutions

Governments and businesses have several ways of adjusting to the variations on the international money market. A government that wishes to stabilize its currency may buy or sell it in foreign exchange markets, using gold reserves and foreign currencies to do so. Supply and demand, along with this occasional intervention, has produced a system of *flexible exchange rates* in which national currencies move up and down in value relative to one another. The International Monetary Fund (IMF), originally established by forty-four countries, can also serve as a referee and issue **special drawing rights (SDRs),** a type of world currency used only in transactions between governments.

Businesses also employ international monetary specialists who buy or sell currencies based on their expectations of future currency fluctuations. International monetary specialists also can, for a fee, purchase currency for future delivery on "forward" markets. Thus, an American computer manufacturer that in January of 1981 plans to sell a $1,000,000 computer to Great Britain will be paid in British pounds when the computer is installed in January 1982. To avoid potential losses if the British pound should depreciate in value relative to the U.S. dollar, the computer manufacturer will typically purchase "forward cover" from international currency markets. Forward cover is obtained by buying a contract in January 1981 that guarantees that the British pounds the computer manufacturer receives when the computer is installed in January 1982 will be exchanged for American dollars at the exchange rate specified in the contract. Thus, if the computer is delivered on time, the manufacturer is protected against exchange rate fluctuations.

International monetary specialization, like all areas of international business, is a growing field.

Chapter Review & Applications

Key Points to Remember

1. Three major benefits of world trade are: (1) the exchange of locally unavailable goods; (2) lower prices; and (3) closer political ties between nations.

2. Barriers to trade include tariffs, quotas, exchange controls, export controls, embargoes, and nationalistic buying policies.

3. Three reasons for restriction of trade are: (1) national defense; (2) wage protection; and (3) protection of infant industries.

4. International trade agreements are specific or general arrangements made either between two or more countries or between a business and a country.

5. Multinationals are corporations that invest in plant and equipment in at least six foreign countries with at least 20 percent of their production coming from the outside.

6. Exports are attractive because (1) profits in foreign markets are often higher than at home, (2) they can lower unit cost through large-volume production, (3) they may be less expensive than competing domestically, and (4) they can help a business stabilize demand for its products.

7. Importing is valuable because (1) it supplies goods not available domestically, (2) it is sometimes cheaper than producing the goods at home, and (3) it can stimulate foreign contracts for goods made with imported components.

8. A nation's balance of trade is the difference in value between its exports and imports. When exports exceed imports, there is a surplus in the balance of trade; when imports exceed exports, there is a deficit.

9. A nation's balance of payments is an accounting of all international economic transactions, including the balance of trade, tourist expenditures, foreign aid, and military spending.

10. Exchange rates fluctuate according to a nation's balance of payments. If there is a deficit, the currency decreases in value; if there is a surplus, the currency increases in value.

Questions for Discussion

1. What are the advantages of international trade for individual Americans? What are the potential disadvantages? What advantages and disadvantages exist from the viewpoint of business?

2. Textile imports in the United States have recently risen. What economically powerful special-interest groups would benefit from imposing trade restrictions? What regions of the United States would benefit from such restrictions?

3. If the Arab countries decided to invest $200 billion in the U.S., what might be the consequences for American individuals and businesses?

4. What is a multinational corporation?

Short Cases

1. An American bowling-ball manufacturer spends $2,400,000 (U.S.) to build a plant in Great Britain when the exchange rate is one British pound equals $2.40 (U.S.). One year later, the exchange rate is one British pound equals $2.05. Ignoring depreciation and assuming that the value of the bowling-ball plant has not changed for other business reasons, how much is the plant currently worth in U.S. dollars?

2. When the pound exchanged for $2.40 (U.S.), a bowling ball cost one British pound to manufacture. Bowling-ball production and marketing costs rose 10 percent in Great Britain the following year. Most of the bowling balls in Great Britain are exported to the United States, where bowling-ball production and distribution costs rose only 5 percent the following year. Is the British bowling-ball producer in an improved competitive position compared with the American bowling-ball producer, after the British pound depreciates to $2.05?

A Critical Business Decision

—made by Peter Haas
of Levi Strauss & Company

The Situation

The tough miner paraded through the streets of San Francisco singing the praises of his "Levi's"—a pair of pants made by a shopkeeper named Levi Strauss. Strauss, an unsuccessful gold prospector, had started a small retail business, originally selling dry goods and mining equipment to the prospectors who flocked to California during the 1849 Gold Rush. One day a miner asked Strauss if he had any pants in stock that would stand up to the harsh punishment of the mines. Strauss made the first "Levi's" from the only available material, canvas used for tents and covered wagons. Later, Strauss switched to the familiar blue denim. Cowboys soon discovered that Levi's were comfortable and serviceable in all types of weather, and Levi's blue jeans quickly became a part of Western folklore.

By the 1950s, a century later, Levi Strauss & Company had grown considerably, with annual sales reaching $30 million. But in the 1970s the business really broke loose, and by 1980 company sales exceeded $1 billion.

In the mid 1970s, Levi's jeans were a high-fashion item among Europeans of all ages and incomes. European customers were paying as much as $25 for a pair of used jeans. The demand for Levi's seemed inexhaustible. "Trucks and cars were bashed outside," one executive recalls of the company's main warehouse near Antwerp, Belgium. "We had a table there, and our customers would start fighting over the goods. Pretty soon they'd be sneaking around the table into the warehouse. They'd drive away with pants flapping out the back of the truck." Levi Strauss took advantage of many European fads, incorporating them into new designs. First, it became fashionable to wear jeans in unusual colors and fabrics, like upholstery and velvet. Then patch-pockets caught on, and bell-bottom jeans eventually became popular. So successful was the company that Levi Strauss soon found itself becoming a multinational business with thirteen subsidiaries, nine plants, and twelve warehouses in Europe alone.

Although in the forefront with design, Levi Strauss followed conservative financial policies, building new plants only where existing ones were operating at full capacity. And because it financed its expansion from its own profits, the company remained in sound financial shape during the boom years in blue jean sales.

The Decision

Now, in 1980, Peter Haas, president of Levi Strauss and great-grandnephew of the founder of the company, faces some fundamental decisions. Blue jeans continue to be fashionable around the world in the volatile youth market. As a result, several domestic and foreign producers, backed by heavy advertising budgets, have entered jeans manufacturing on a large scale. In addition, jeans purchasers are showing an increasing interest in designer jeans. In many areas throughout the United States and Europe, specialty jeans shops are becoming popular. And in the United States, large retailers like Sears and Penney's have developed their own line of blue jeans, often pricing them below Levi's. Mainly as a result of the increased output of blue jeans and the greater competition among producers, prices of some lines of jeans have fallen or have increased less than other prices. As Peter Haas considers the future of Levi Strauss, many questions arise. Despite its large size and past success, is the company vulnerable to its new competitors? As a multinational, how should Levi Strauss & Company adjust to changing market conditions throughout the world?[3]

Questions

1. Do you think blue jeans will continue to be popular in the United States? In the rest of the world? Will Levi's continue to be the top product in the blue jeans market?
2. If you were Peter Haas, what actions would you take to reduce Levi's vulnerability to competitors in the jeans market?

The following color insert, titled "The Chronicle of Coca-Cola since 1886," is published by the corporate affairs department of The Coca-Cola Company. We have included it here as a special addendum for the reason that the history and continuing growth of this successful American company exemplify so many of the text's discussions, including such topics as forms of business organization, advertising, marketing, production, government regulation, international business, and so on. The intention is not to endorse or promote Coca-Cola, but rather to illustrate the real-life applications of textbook subjects.

As you read the insert, try to recall—and to relate to it—the business principles you have learned. Also keep in mind the following questions, which you should be able to answer by applying your knowledge of contemporary American business.

1. What do you think are the reasons why Coca-Cola published the booklet?

2. What factors in Coca-Cola's history do you think account for the company's phenomenal success?

3. If you could go back in time, what actions in Coke's history would you change, based on the information and ideas you have gained as you complete an introductory business course?

4. What changes do you think Coca-Cola will need to make to continue to succeed in the 1980s and 1990s in light of the consumers, competitors, and government actions it will be facing?

THE CHRONICLE OF COCA-COLA SINCE 1886

Introduction

Delicious Coca-Cola is called for over 245 million times a day in more than 80 languages and in more than 135 countries around the globe. "The Chronicle of Coca-Cola Since 1886" is the story not only of the phenomenal growth of the beverage from a bubbly brew in an Atlanta backyard to the unprecedented degree of worldwide fame it holds today, but of the people whose work forged the product's reputation for excellence.

Advertisements and artifacts connected with Coca-Cola and its familiar trademark which captured the flavor of the times illustrate this history and are sought by serious collectors as memorabilia.

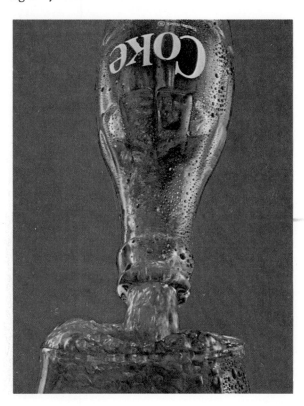

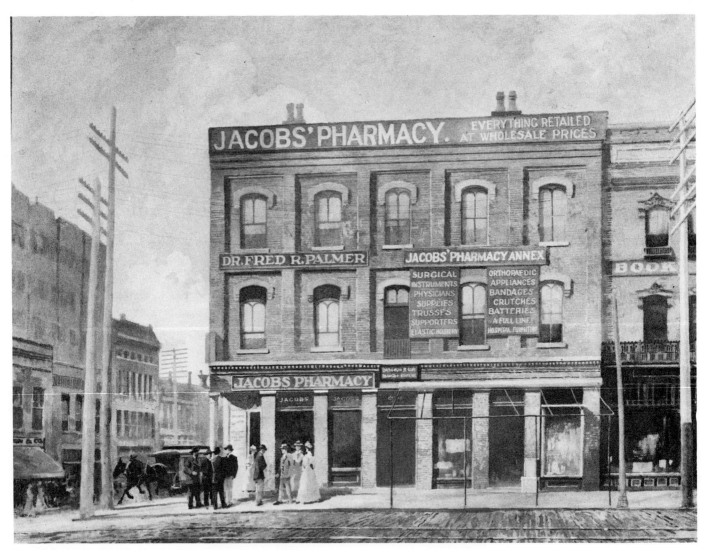

Coca-Cola was first served at Jacobs' Pharmacy in Atlanta in 1886.

BIRTH OF A REFRESHING IDEA

John Pemberton

F. M. Robinson

The pleasant custom of enjoying a crisp Coca-Cola is shared by people from America to Zambia. The familiar shape of the bottle and the flowing script of its trademark are among the most readily recognized symbols known to man.

The product that gave the world its best-known taste originated under modest circumstances in Atlanta, Georgia, on May 8, 1886. According to legend, pharmacist Dr. John Styth Pemberton first produced the syrup for Coca-Cola in a three-legged brass pot in his backyard on Marietta Street.

He carried a jug of the new product down the street to Jacobs' Pharmacy, where it was placed on sale for 5¢ a glass as a soda fountain drink. Whether by design or accident, carbonated water was teamed with the new syrup to produce a drink that was at once "Delicious and Refreshing," a theme that continues to echo today.

Thinking that "the two C's would look well in advertising," Dr. Pemberton's partner and bookkeeper, Frank M. Robinson, suggested the name and calligraphed "Coca-Cola" in the Spencerian script of the day. The first newspaper ad for Coca-Cola soon appeared, on May 29 in *The Atlanta Journal,* inviting thirsty Atlantans to try "the new popular soda fountain drink."

Hand-painted oilcloth signs reading "Coca-Cola" appeared on store awnings, and the suggestion "Drink" was added to the name to tell passersby that the new beverage was for soda fountain enjoyment.

During 1886, sales averaged 13 drinks per day — not a very auspicious beginning for the unique syrup whose production now reaches a billion gallons a year.

However, Dr. Pemberton never fully realized the impact of the beverage he had created. In the next few years, he sold portions of interest in his venture.

In 1888, all of his remaining rights to the product were purchased by Asa G. Candler, an active businessman who proceeded to buy additional rights and acquire complete control.

First calendar featuring advertising for Coca-Cola.

THE CANDLER ERA

On May 1, 1889, Candler published a full page advertisement in *The Atlanta Journal* proclaiming his wholesale and retail drug business as "sole proprietors of Coca-Cola...Delicious. Refreshing. Invigorating." Sole ownership had cost him a total of $2,300.

Asa Candler had a flair for merchandising, and by 1892, sales of Coca-Cola syrup had increased nearly tenfold. He soon disposed of his drug business to devote full time to the soft drink. With his brother, Attorney John S. Candler, Frank Robinson, and two other friends, he formed a Georgia corporation named The Coca-Cola Company, with capital stock of $100,000.

The trademark "Coca-Cola," used in the marketplace since 1886, was registered in the United States Patent Office on January 31, 1893. (Registration has been renewed periodically as required.)

That same year the first dividend was paid to stockholders at $20 per share, which amounted to 20 percent of the book value of a share of stock. Every year since 1893, dividends have been paid on the Company's common stock.

A firm believer in advertising, Candler distributed thousands of coupons for a complimentary glass of Coca-Cola. He maintained a consistent promotional program, giving away souvenir fans, calendars, clocks, urns, and countless novelties, all depicting the trademark design.

While Candler's efforts centered on booming soda fountain sales, other ideas which would spread the enjoyment of Coca-Cola worldwide were developing.

In 1894, in Vicksburg, Mississippi, Joseph A. Biedenharn was so impressed by the growing demand for Coca-Cola at his soda fountain in the Biedenharn Candy Company that he installed bottling machinery in the rear of the store and began to take bottles of Coca-Cola around to plantations and lumber camps up and down the river.

As a result, using syrup shipped from Atlanta, he

B. F. Thomas

Joseph Whitehead

Bottling plants began to appear throughout the country in the early 1900's.

became the first to put Coca-Cola in bottles. His innovation created a new marketing concept which opened the way to wider distribution of Coca-Cola.

That same year, the business had grown to the extent that the first syrup branch manufacturing plant outside of Atlanta was opened in Dallas, Texas. Other branch plants opened in Chicago and Los Angeles the following year.

In 1895, three years after he had launched The Coca-Cola Company, Asa G. Candler announced in his annual report to stockholders: "Coca-Cola is now drunk in every state and territory in the United States."

With the increasing demand for Coca-Cola, the Company quickly outgrew its facilities. A new building erected on Edgewood Avenue at "Coca-Cola Place" in 1898 was the first headquarters building exclusively devoted to the manufacture of syrup and conduct of the business. Candler hailed the new, three-story structure as "sufficient for all our needs for all time to come." It was inadequate in 10 years.

Large-scale bottling of Coca-Cola was made possible when Benjamin F. Thomas and Joseph B. Whitehead of Chattanooga, Tennessee, secured from Candler in 1899 the exclusive rights to bottle and sell Coca-Cola in practically the entire United States.

The contract did exclude the six New England states

Fountain festoons and other displays depicted frequent designs of the early 20's.

Packaging evolved from early syrup jugs and several bottle designs.

where Seth Fowle, a fountain syrup wholesaler, had been given the sole right to sell Coca-Cola syrup in 1892. The Mississippi territory served by the Biedenharns also was excluded temporarily, as well as part of Texas.

The first bottling plant under the new contract was opened in Chattanooga in 1899 and the second in Atlanta the following year.

The two Chattanoogans enlisted the financial assistance of John T. Lupton to assess the situation. Realizing their inability to cover the nation with bottling plants, they began identifying competent individuals to establish community bottling operations. In return, those indivi-

duals received a defined geographic area in which to develop a market for Coca-Cola. This was the genesis of today's locally owned and operated Coca-Cola bottling industry, a significant factor in the global distribution of the beverage.

In the next 30 years, the first two plants increased to number a thousand, with fully 95 percent locally owned and operated. The development of high speed bottling machinery and increasingly efficient transportation reduced this number by consolidations and mergers to more than 550 bottlers in the U.S. today.

1928 Belgian advertisement reflected international availability.

Coca-Cola Goes Overseas

By the first year of the new century, soda fountains in Victoria and Vancouver were convincing western Canadians that "Thirst Knows No Season." Later that same year, Coca-Cola was served at a fountain in London for the first time when Howard Candler, eldest son of the Company's founder, took a jug of syrup along on a vacation trip. An order for five gallons of syrup was mailed back to the States.

Cuba and Puerto Rico were added to the growing list of countries where Coca-Cola could be purchased in 1900, and from such small beginnings the overseas distribution of syrup began.

Today the refreshing taste of Coca-Cola is enjoyed in more than 135 countries, including the reintroduction of the product in Egypt and The People's Republic of China.

People everywhere recognize the distinctive hobble-skirt bottle for Coca-Cola which was developed in the never ending battle against substitution.

The original Hutchinson bottle was designed in 1899 with an iron stopper and rubber washer attached. A variety of straight-sided containers then were used until 1916, when a convention of bottlers approved as standard the unique contour bottle designed by the Root Glass Company of Terre Haute, Indiana.

The now-familiar shape was granted registration as a trademark by the U.S. Patent Office in 1960, an honor accorded to only a handful of other packages. The bottle thus joined the two other trademarks, "Coca-Cola," registered in 1893, and "Coke," first used on labels in 1941 and officially registered in 1945.

In 1919, The Coca-Cola Company was sold by the Candler interests to Atlanta banker Ernest Woodruff and an investor group he had organized. The sale price was $25,000,000. Soon after the sale, the business was reincorporated as a Delaware corporation, and its common stock was put on public sale for $40 per share.

The new owners gained a significant victory in 1920 against imitators and substitutors in one of the few trademark cases ever reviewed by the United States Supreme Court.

Plagued for many years by the trade activities of the Koke Company of America, The Coca-Cola Company won a resounding victory which upheld the trademarks "Coca-Cola" and "Coke." The ruling established that "Coke," when used to denote a beverage, was held to mean Coca-Cola and nothing else.

Mr. Justice Oliver Wendell Holmes, in delivering the opinion of the Court, stated: "The name now characterizes a beverage to be had at almost any soda fountain. It means a single thing coming from a single source and well known to the community."

The new Company also faced another problem. Postwar inflation had caused the price of sugar to rise to 28 cents per pound, four times the average price during the early days of World War I. Negotiations between the Company and bottlers, seeking to readjust the price of syrup, ended in a compromise court decree in 1921 which made adjustments in the price formula and established the perpetuity of bottler contracts.

Legal document representing sale of The Coca-Cola Company in 1919.

A MAN NAMED WOODRUFF

Robert W. Woodruff

Four years after his father purchased the Company, Robert Winship Woodruff was elected president of The Coca-Cola Company in 1923. The vigorous, 33-year-old Georgian had risen from truck salesman to vice president and general manager of White Motor Company before he accepted the presidency from the soft drink firm's Board of Directors. He succeeded Charles Howard Candler, who remained on the Board.

Woodruff envisioned the drink as an international

Early marketing strategy included home visits by Company representatives.

institution. Gathering able associates around him, he instigated a half century of imaginative leadership which carried Coca-Cola to the outposts of civilization.

In 1926, he gave tangible form to his vision by organizing a Foreign Sales Department, later to become a subsidiary known as The Coca-Cola Export Corporation. By changing the syrup distribution method to utilize concentrate for syrup to be processed overseas, transportation costs were reduced and overseas sales began to climb.

The new president put major emphasis on product quality, both fountain and bottle. He established a "Quality Drink" campaign with a staff of trained service men to encourage and assist fountain outlets in correctly serving and aggressively selling Coca-Cola.

With the assistance of leading bottlers, his management defined quality standards for every phase of the bottling operation.

Renewed advertising and marketing force were placed behind the bottle, which could travel anywhere. By the end of 1928, five years after Woodruff became president, the sale of Coca-Cola in bottles had increased 65 percent and, for the first time, bottle sales exceeded sales at the soda fountain.

Robert Woodruff's leadership through the years took the product to unrivaled heights in commercial history.

Concepts accepted as commonplace in modern merchandising were revolutionary when Woodruff took the helm. The Coca-Cola Company developed the innovative 6-bottle carton in the early 20's, making it easier for

Revolutionary merchandisers such as this Glascock cooler
put Coca-Cola "within an arm's reach of desire."

the consumer to bring more Coca-Cola into the home
and family circle. By 1928, when bottle sales topped
fountain sales, the carton was accepted as one of industry's most powerful merchandising tools.

In 1929, the carton was joined by another revolutionary
merchandiser — the metal-top open cooler to serve
Coca-Cola ice-cold in retail outlets. The cooler later was
improved with mechanical refrigeration and automatic
coin control. The factory, office and many other institutions thus became outlets where refreshment could be
enjoyed by workers on the spot by self-service from a
machine which needed little space.

Much like the trademarked bottle, a distinctive fountain glass for Coca-Cola, adopted as standard in 1929,
served to advertise the product. It is now regular equip-

ment at thousands of fountains, and its use has been extended by a large, 12-ounce size.

The Chicago World's Fair of 1933 triggered the introduction of automatic fountain dispensers where syrup and
carbonated water were mixed at the same time the drink
was served. Although soda fountain operators had dispensed Coca-Cola manually since its creation in 1886,
visitors to the fair were amazed to see the attendant
serve a uniform, properly refrigerated drink every time
simply by pulling a handle. By 1937, the automatic dis-
penser had become an important adjunct of the fountain
and similar "post-mix" outlets. It has gone through many
successive models to the current designs in use across the
land. A single unit today can dispense more Coca-Cola
than was served the entire first year of its invention.

Have a Coca-Cola = As you were

...a way to relax on a battleship

Wherever a U. S. battleship may be, the American way of life goes along ... in sports, humor, customs and refreshment. So, naturally, Coca-Cola is there, too, met with frequently at the ship's soda fountain. *Have a "Coke"* is a phrase as common aboard a battle-wagon as it is ashore. It's a signal that spells out *We're pals.* From Atlanta to the Seven Seas, Coca-Cola stands for *the pause that refreshes,* — has become the symbol of happy comradeship.

* * *

Since 1886 Coca-Cola has spread around the world. Its refreshing goodness is welcomed by people around the globe. Despite the fact that many bottling plants are cut off in enemy-occupied lands, Coca-Cola is still being bottled in over 35 allied and neutral nations. So our fighting men can still enjoy it many places overseas.

It's natural for popular names to acquire friendly abbreviations. That's why you hear Coca-Cola called "Coke".

-the global high-sign

FOLLOWING THE TROOPS

World War II caused a severe rationing of sugar in the U.S. The Company's manufacture of syrup for civilian consumption was restricted to 50 percent of pre-war average.

The declaration of war brought forth an order from Robert Woodruff in 1941 "to see that every man in uniform gets a bottle of Coca-Cola for 5¢ wherever he is and whatever it costs the Company." This effort to supply the armed forces with Coke already was underway when an urgent cablegram was sent from General Dwight Eisenhower's Allied Headquarters in North Africa. Dated June 29, 1943, it requested shipment of machinery for operating 10 bottling plants.

Prefaced by the direction that the shipments were not to replace other military cargo, the cablegram also asked for shipment of three million bottles of Coca-Cola and complete equipment for producing the same quantity twice monthly.

An engineer from the Company flew to Algiers and opened the first plant in six months, the forerunner of a total of 64 bottling plants shipped abroad during World War II and set up as close as possible to combat areas in Europe and the Pacific. The best available estimates are that more than five billion bottles of Coke went to military service personnel in addition to that served through dispensers and mobile self-contained units in battle areas.

Out of this worldwide cooperative effort with the Defense Department to maintain the morale of American GI's was born the apt description of Coca-Cola as "The Global High Sign."

Coca-Cola boosted morale during World War II, as shown in this 1944 ad.

While many ads of the 1930's showcased stars such as
Carole Lombard, later advertising reflected the war.

ADVERTISING TAKES OFF

It is unlikely that many commercial slogans will ever create the lasting impact of "The Pause That Refreshes," which first appeared in *The Saturday Evening Post* in February 1929.

It was the descendant of a long line of great slogans which caught public fancy — beginning with the oldest, Dr. Pemberton's "Delicious and Refreshing" in 1886. "Thirst Knows No Season" in 1922, "It Had To Be Good To Get Where It Is" in 1925 and "Around the Corner From Anywhere" in 1927 solidified the product's universal, year-round appeal.

Many more followed, often echoing the refreshing idea: "It's The Refreshing Thing To Do"—1936, "Global High Sign"—1944, "Sign of Good Taste"—1957, "Be Really Refreshed"—1959. The highly successful "Things Go Better With Coke" introduced an easygoing feeling in 1963.

6,000,000 A DAY
In fact, Coca-Cola has an average sale of more than six million drinks for every day in the year ~ It has the charm of purity.

RE-FRESH YOURSELF: FIVE CENTS IS THE PRICE

The famous bellhop appeared in 1925. Works of renowned artists included Haddon Sundblom's beloved Santa Claus and calendar art by Norman Rockwell.

"It's The Real Thing," first used in 1942, was revived in 1969 to support a whole new merchandising stance for the product. In 1971, young people from around the world gathered on a hilltop to sing the memorable "I'd like to buy the world a Coke," a counterpoint to the turbulent times.

In 1976, the reminder that "Coke Adds Life" was introduced. It became the foundation of "Have a Coke and a smile," a campaign of immense popularity resulting from a series of television commercials including the heartwarming spot with 260-pound tackle "Mean" Joe Greene of the Pittsburgh Steelers. This commercial, featuring the game-weary football player tossing his jersey to a sympathetic youngster who offers him a Coke, is among the most popular ever made.

Down through the years, advertising for Coca-Cola has followed the trends of the times, while the overall theme has been refreshment — one of the pleasant things of life, distinctive and acceptable anywhere.

Fine illustrations by top artists including Norman Rockwell have been the hallmark of four-color ads which projected the image of the drink's quality in leading magazines. Noted artist Haddon Sundblom's work even helped mold the national concept of Santa Claus through his popular "portraits" for holiday ads which began in the 1930's.

Famous outdoor poster designs pre-sold the passing customer while phonetic translations of the trademark advertised the product in foreign lands. Ads and news coverage in major American magazines continued to echo the themes of refreshment and availability.

Nationwide use of 24-sheet outdoor posters (billboards) began in 1925 with the appearance of the famous bellhop serving Coca-Cola and the message "6,000,000 a day." The first large electrical signs, or spectaculars, also arose to illuminate the crossroads of the world from London's Piccadilly Circus to Tokyo's Ginza with an indelible and pleasant reminder of Coca-Cola.

In the mid-1920's, radio became an important medium of communication. It continues to be a large segment of the merchandising mix.

In 1950, Edgar Bergen and his sidekick, Charlie McCarthy, appeared on Thanksgiving Day on the first live television network show sponsored by The Coca-Cola Company. Use of this all-powerful new medium swiftly swelled to giant proportions.

In point-of-sale advertising for four million worldwide outlets, Coke is unsurpassed. The quality and quantity of materials designed to identify availability and to assist the dealer in moving product have expanded year after year.

By presenting an internationally unified theme in many languages, combined with locally oriented interpretation, Coke is native wherever it is.

Contemporary campaigns capture warm moments of everyday life, such as the award-winning "Have a Coke and a smile" series featuring the highly popular "Mean" Joe Greene (top).

FROM ONE PACKAGE TO MANY

Until the mid-50's, Coca-Cola was the Company's one product, available in the familiar 6½-ounce bottle or in a glass at the fountain. By 1955, however, changing consumer habits and preferences dictated a wider choice in packaging adaptable to the family's greater mobility, larger rate of consumption and desire for convenience.

To the 6½-ounce bottle were added larger sizes — 10-, 12- and 26-ounce bottles — and, in a few years, a 16-ounce size was filling another market segment.

A new method of dispensing Coca-Cola was put in use in 1954. Called "pre-mix," the finished beverage could be prepared in bulk in the bottling plant and delivered to outlets where equipment refrigerated and dispensed it in cups. Coke was now available in many more types of outlets...where paper cups were more suitable than bottles, or where there was no water connection for "post-mix" dispensing at fountains.

Packaging of Coca-Cola in cans began in 1955, and for several years the armed forces overseas enjoyed this package exclusively. By the end of 1959, however, test marketing was complete, and in 1960 the civilian consumer began to see Coke in 12-ounce, flat-top cans on market shelves.

As consumers showed more desire for greater convenience, the Company began to test market no-deposit, no-return bottles similar in design to the distinctively shaped returnable bottle. That was 1961. Convenience likewise led to the development in 1964 of lift-top cans and lift-top crowns, eliminating the need for the once indispensable opener.

Innovative packaging developments have never ceased. Striving to present Coca-Cola in the most pleasing package consistent with its distinctive quality has become the way of business life for The Coca-Cola Company.

Soft drink history was made with the 1969 announcement of experiments with a plastic bottle for Coke. A larger 16-ounce can appeared. Resealable crowns for bottles boosted the convenience feature during the 70's when bottle sizes grew to 32-, 48-, and 64-ounces and comparable metric sizes. Another new container, a Plasti-Shield bottle, was added, and in late 1977, plastic (Polyethylene Terephthalate) bottles were introduced. The 2-liter plastic size has proven particularly successful.

Citrus beverages, wines and disposable cutlery are among today's products in The Coca-Cola Company's diversified line.

NEW PRODUCTS, NEW HORIZONS

As the Company entered the 1960's and looked back over some 300 billion drinks of Coke, it appeared that the refreshment market of people everywhere had only been lightly touched. There was no saturation point in sight for the world's best loved drink. At the same time, there was room for expansion of other beverage markets.

Following the diversification of packages for Coca-Cola, several new soft drinks were added for distribution by local bottlers. In 1960, the Fanta line of flavored soft drinks was expanded to national markets. Sprite, a lemon-lime specialty drink, arrived nationally the following year.

The Company's first low-calorie beverage, TAB, was introduced in 1963. The low-calorie citrus-flavored drink, Fresca, was added in 1966. By 1970, overseas test marketing of Samson, a protein beverage designed to supplement protein-deficient diets, was developed, followed by a similar beverage called Saci.

During 1972, Mr. PiBB, a spicy cherry beverage, was beginning to enjoy national introduction. The Company now also offers sugar-free formulations of Sprite and Mr. PiBB, a line of sugar-free flavors under the TAB brand name, plus reformulated Fresca and Mr. PiBB.

Dubbed "the world's fastest soft drink," Mello Yello, a lightly carbonated citrus-flavored beverage launched in 1979, has been the most successful new product introduction in soft drink history.

Further attempts to satisfy a variety of palates signaled the introduction of Ramblin' Root Beer in 1979.

A number of trademarked products provide other soft drink brands to markets overseas.

While soft drink products are the backbone of operations, other diversifications took place beginning with the Company's purchase in 1960 of the Minute Maid Corporation.

With this acquisition, the Company entered the citrus beverage market, which encompasses Hi-C products, Bright & Early breakfast drink, Snow Crop orange juice and Five Alive, as well as a variety of fruit juices, ades, blends and lemonade crystals under the well-known Minute Maid name.

Through Tenco, a division of Minute Maid, the Company became one of the world's largest producers of private label coffee and tea. With the merger with Duncan Foods Company in 1964, the Company became one of the leading coffee importing, processing and marketing firms in the country. Today, all of the Company's citrus, coffee and tea business is operated by The Coca-Cola Company Foods Division in Houston, Texas.

Facing the increasing need for energy efficiency, the Company acquired Aqua-Chem, Inc., in 1970. It manufactures water pollution control equipment, seawater desalters and packaged steam and hot water generators.

The subsidiary product line has grown to include disposable plastic straws, bags and cutlery and bottled water. Subsidiaries are Presto Products, Inc., Winkler/Flexible Products, Inc., and Belmont Springs Water Company.

Further acquisitions include Taylor Wine Company and Pleasant Valley Wine Company (Great Western label) of New York, plus Sterling Vineyards and The Monterey Vineyard, both of California. Under an operating unit called The Wine Spectrum, The Coca-Cola Company is a leading U.S. producer of premium still and sparkling wines. The Company also has U.S. distribution rights to some products of Francesco Cinzano, S.P.A.

Dedicated to well-rounded growth, The Coca-Cola Company has matched its expanding product line with increasing social responsibility. Worldwide programs designed to upgrade the quality of life through evolving technological expertise are an ongoing commitment.

With this increasing technological knowledge, milestones in the Company's production come faster with each passing year. To produce the first billion gallons of Coca-Cola syrup required 58 years, 1886-1944. Today The Coca-Cola Company reaches that billion marker every year while providing about eight billion gallons of soft drink products to a thirsty world.

Every day Coca-Cola makes new friends in new places. One of the public's greatest expressions of faith in its continuity lies in applications received by The Coca-Cola Company for bottling franchises on the moon. Apollo astronauts returning from their moonflight were greeted by a Times Square sign flashing, "Welcome Back to Earth, Home of Coca-Cola."

Rising generations with increasingly dynamic lifestyles will demand more refreshment in the 1980's. The Coca-Cola Company is dedicated to meeting the needs of these consumers with vitality and an optimistic attitude based on the fundamentals of quality products, universal availability, innovations in packaging and creative advertising.

As long as people get thirsty, they will need refreshment. The limits are nowhere in sight. The challenges of future markets, lunar or otherwise, lie ahead.

Glossary

A

acceptance An acknowledgment by the party to whom an offer is made that the terms of the offer are satisfactory and that he or she is willing to be bound to a contract.

account The title given to all accounting transactions of a particular type; for example, the sales account includes all sales made by a firm.

accountability Being answerable for results.

account executive The account executive or stockbroker at a brokerage firm who deals directly with investors or financial institutions that purchase securities.

accounting The functional area of business that deals with the collection, organization, analysis, and presentation of financial data.

accounting equation Assets equal liabilities plus owner equity.

accounting transaction Any activity that has an immediate and measurable financial impact on a business, affecting its physical or financial capital or its financial obligation to outsiders.

accounts payable A liability that includes obligations owed to creditors, usually arising from purchases of goods and services on credit; accounts payable are due in less than one year.

accounts receivable An asset that includes obligations owed to the firm, usually arising from its sales; accounts receivable are due within one year.

acturial table A table listing the probabilities of an event (such as the death of an individual); commonly used in the insurance industry to compute risks, premium rates, and so on.

advertising Nonpersonal communication between seller and buyer that is conducted through paid media under clear sponsorship.

advertising agency A firm that specializes in providing promotional services to other businesses for a fee. Services offered include development of advertising copy, selection of advertising media, and placement of the advertisement.

advertising appeal A theme intended to trigger buying decisions or to project a better company image in the target market.

advertising copy The communication that a prospective buyer actually sees or hears.

advertising media The broadcast or print vehicles through which an advertisement is communicated—such as radio, television, magazines, newspapers, and billboards.

affirmative action program EEO (equal employment opportunities) legislation that requires employers who deal with the government to provide equal job opportunities for women and minorities and to demonstrate that they are aggressively seeking to identify and train qualified persons in these categories.

agency A legal relationship in which one party (the agent) is authorized to act on behalf of another (the principal) in transactions with a third party.

agent A person or organization authorized to act on behalf of another.

alternatives The factors over which a decision maker has control in making a decision.

analog computer A machine that solves problems by translating physical variables into related electrical or mechanical quantities.

analytic process A production process in which end products are obtained by breaking down more complex materials.

antitrust laws Laws designed to prevent or control economic concentration.

arbitration An attempt to settle labor–management conflicts through the intervention of a third party neutral to the dispute whose decision is binding. *Voluntary arbitration* takes place when the parties in a dispute agree among themselves to submit the dispute to arbitration. *Compulsory arbitration* takes place when the parties are forced into arbitration by an outside organization, usually the government.

arithmetic-logic unit The device in a computer that performs addition, subtraction, multiplication, and division, compares the relative sizes of two values, and senses positive and negative values.

assets The resources that a business utilizes in attempting to earn a profit.

auditing The process of verifying that an organization has properly recorded and reported its financial data.

authority The right and power to issue orders.

automation The production of goods by self-regulating machines; also the process of making machines automatic.

B

bad debts Uncollectable accounts receivable.

balance of international payments Accounts, usually issued by a government, showing the flow of monies into and from a nation; these accounts are arranged according to certain broad categories such as exports and imports.

balance of trade The accounts that show the values of a nation's exports and imports.

balance sheet A statement of the overall financial condition of a business at a given date.

bank acceptance A draft that is backed (accepted) by a bank. Initially, a commercial bank provides a letter of credit indicating that the bank will accept drafts (in effect, checks) up to a designated amount drawn on the bank by a business. When ordering goods, the business writes a draft on the bank for the required amount.

bankruptcy A condition that exists when a business is unable to continue to operate because it lacks sufficient funds to meet its financial obligations to investors, creditors, employees, the government, and other groups to which it owes money.

batch process A production process in which the manufacturing time for an item is sufficiently short that the tasks of workers and machines can be changed frequently to manufacture different products.

batch processing A method of computer data processing that involves accumulating a volume of work and then processing it as a group.

bidders list A list of vendors believed to be qualified to supply a given item to a firm.

bill of lading A document that lists goods shipped, times of shipment, and the destinations of the goods; it is signed by an agent for a common carrier (for example, the captain of a ship, a railroad or trucking company agent).

binary arithmetic A system of counting that uses only two digits (0 and 1); the binary system is the basis for all present-day designs of electronic digital computers.

board of directors A group appointed by the stockholders of a corporation to assume responsibility for overall direction of the business.

bond A fixed obligation of a business in which it agrees to pay interest plus a specified sum (the principal) to investors.

bonus A form of compensation in which employees are given extra pay when they perform outstanding work or when the business has a good year; the amount of payment may be varied by the firm.

boycott The refusal to use a product by a group acting in concert.

branching The step in a flow diagram or computer operation that involves taking one of two alternate paths.

brand A name, term, symbol, or design (or a combination of them) used by a business firm to identify its goods or services and to distinguish them from those of competitors.

broker The marketing middleman who performs services, such as obtaining and transporting a commodity from one location to another, for a fee.

budget A planning statement that shows the projected revenues and expenses of an organization.

buildings An asset that includes the structures housing the firm's business activities.

business Any privately owned and operated organization primarily devoted to securing profits or other benefits desired by its owners or managers.

business ethics Values relating to what is right, good, or moral in business relationships.

business forecasting The assessment and development of projections of the future that are likely to be of value in corporate decision making.

business interruptions insurance A form of insurance that protects a firm against disruptions in its activities arising from natural disasters like fires and storms.

business law All statutes, codes, rules, regulations, and court actions that regulate business behavior and relationships.

business life insurance A form of insurance that protects a business against the loss of an executive vital to its operations. Also called *key executive insurance*.

buying motives The reasons that consumers buy specific goods or services.

C

callable security A security that may be redeemed before maturity by the issuing organization on terms specified at the time of issue.

capital Funds invested in a business. On a national basis, financial capital refers to the totality of all funds available for business, consumer, and government investment; physical capital refers to the plants, machinery, equipment, residential homes, and governmental installations.

capital budgeting Decisions on the allocations of financial resources that are typically not converted to cash within a year.

capital gain (or loss) A change in the value of an asset. A *capital gain* occurs when an asset appreciates in value over time; a *capital loss* takes place when the asset depreciates in value over time.

capital stock The part of owner equity that includes capital contributed by stockholders.

capitalism See **private enterprise system**

cartel A combination of firms in an industry that agrees to achieve a common objective, usually price fixing.

cash An asset that includes currency, checking and savings deposits in commercial banks, cashier checks, bank and postal money orders, and bank drafts.

cash budget A planning statement that indicates the ability of a business firm to supply those cash needs that must be met on time regardless of sales revenue.

cash flow The total funds available to a business during a given period. Cash flow is approximately equal to the firm's earnings *plus* the depreciation charges included in its accounting statements. Depreciation is included because it is not a "real" expense of a business in the sense that there is an outflow of funds to another party.

caveat emptor A principle in business that holds that without a warranty on a product the buyer assumes all risks; literally, "let the buyer beware."

cease-and-desist order   An order by a government agency, particularly the Federal Trade Commision, requiring an individual or business to terminate a business practice that has been deemed unfair or deceptive.

central processing unit   The portion of a computer that includes the memory or storage unit, the arithmetic-logic unit, and the control unit, plus the operating console.

certified public accountant   A person who has fulfilled all the legal requirements of a state that entitle him or her to obtain an official certificate as an accountant.

channels of distribution   The various ways that goods flow from manufacturers to industrial customers or ultimate consumers.

checkoff procedures   A union requirement that employers deduct union dues from workers' paychecks and send these monies directly to unions.

civil service   A permanent government stall whose positions are based on merit as measured by entrance examinations or recommendations and by periodic examinations for promotion.

closed shop   A stringent form of compulsory union membership in which employers agree to hire only union members.

collateral   Physical or financial assets used as security in obtaining a loan.

collateral trust bond   A bond obtained by securities held in trust by the issuing firm.

collective bargaining   The process of settling disputes between unions and management.

commercial bank   A financial institution that receives checking and savings deposits and other funds from savers and lends funds to businesses, consumers, and governments. Commercial banks are among the financial institutions in the United States that are currently permitted by law to offer checking account services.

commercial paper   Short-term unsecured promissory noted issued by a business, usually in multiples of $25,000.

commission   A form of compensation in which employees are paid a fixed percentage of their total sales.

commodity market   A building or organized meeting place where raw materials and agricultural products are bought and sold, for either present or future delivery.

common law   The unwritten law, consisting of customs and past court decisions that may serve as precedents in future cases.

common stock   Certificates of ownership in a corporation entitling holders to receive any dividends and to exercise other stockholder rights.

communism   A system of central direction of the economy in which the government owns and operates the bulk of economic institutions.

compensation   The total wages, salaries, and fringe benefits received by employees.

competition   The process of determining the price, quality, and available quantity of an item through the impersonal interactions of numerous firms.

computer   Broadly defined, any device that calculates, reckons, or computes. Today, a computer is more narrowly defined as an electronic device that processes data, that is capable of receiving input and producing output, and that stores instructions to solve problems quickly and accurately.

computer hardware   The physical equipment used in a computer system.

computer program   A sequence of instructions used by a computer to solve a problem.

computer programming   The task of writing a computer program.

computer similation   Programming a computer to answer "what if" questions.

computer software   Problem-solving programs plus other computer instructions designed to simplify the programming process.

concentrated marketing   A marketing strategy in which a firm concentrates on one or a few profitable market segments.

conglomerate A firm that produces many types of goods and services.

conglomerate merger The acquisition by a business of one or more firms producing dissimilar products.

consideration In a contractural relationship, the exchange of something of value (usually money, goods, or services) by each participant in the contract.

constraints In a decision-making situation, the restrictions placed on potential solutions to a problem by the nature and importance of the problem; these restrictions usually involve time and costs.

consumer behavior How people make buying decisions.

consumer goods Goods destined for use by ultimate consumers (individuals or households) and available in such a form that they can be used without commercial processing.

consumer movement Activities aimed at giving consumers greater say about the products, prices, and information they receive. Also called *consumerism*.

consumer sovereignty The principle that a private enterprise economy and the business and government institutions in it exist to provide goods and services that consumers want.

containerization Placing goods to be transported into a large box or other container. When the goods are shifted from one type of transportation to another, the entire container is shifted.

continuous process A production process in which the manufacturing operation remains essentially unchanged for extended periods, often months or years.

contract An agreement between two or more parties enforceable by court action.

control unit The portion of a computer that directs the sequence of operations, interprets coded instructions, and initiates proper commands to computer circuits.

controlling The management process by which actual results are compared with plans and corrective action is taken when necessary.

convenience goods Goods that a customer characteristically purchases frequently, immediately, and with a minimum of effort in comparison shopping and buying.

convertible bond A bond that can be exchanged for other securities, usually a specified number of shares of common stock.

convertible preferred stock Preferred stock that can be exchanged for common stock in accordance with terms specified on the stock certificate.

cooperative A business chartered under state law that seeks the economic betterment of its members through the achievement of common goals. A cooperative is owned by its members, each of whom has a single vote; profits are returned to members either in the form of lower prices or as rebates given in proportion to a member's purchases from the cooperative.

corporation A form of a business ownership distinguished by three characteristics: (1) ownership may vary from one individual to several million people who purchase stock in the company; (2) the company is managed according to written principles set forth in the corporate charter; and (3) the owners are exposed to limited liability and at most can lose only their investments in the business.

corrective advertisement An advertisement run by a firm at the request of the Federal Trade Commission to correct misleading statements in the firm's advertisements.

cost of goods sold The direct material costs incurred by a firm in producing its products.

cost-of-living escalator An increase in hourly or other wage payments to keep pace with rising consumer prices.

craft union A labor union that represents a single profession.

credit policy The conditions under which a firm extends credit to its customers.

credit union   A financial institution that collects funds from and lends funds to members.

creditor   A person or organization to whom money is owed.

cumulative security   A security that entitles the holder to recover dividends or interest omitted by an organization in previous years.

current assets   Highly liquid assets that are converted into cash within a one-year period.

current liabilities   Obligations of a business that must be met within one year.

current ratio   Current assets *divided by* current liabilities; the current ratio is one measure of the liquidity of a business.

custom manufacture   The production of goods by a firm according to a customer's specifications.

D

debenture   A long- or intermediate-term fixed obligation of a business.

debt   Any legally binding obligation of a firm to pay a fixed amount of principal or interest for a specified period.

debt financing   Obtaining funds for a business by borrowing from creditors and agreeing to repay a stated amount of principal and interest within a designated time period.

decentralization   A principle of organization that states that decision making should be moved to lower levels of an organization that are independent enough to have their performance measured objectively.

DECIDE process   A process of systematic decision making in which each letter of the word DECIDE represents a specific step in the process (see chapter 6).

decision box   An element in a flow diagram or a computer operation that involves answering "yes" or "no" to a specific question contained within the box; the two alternative answers to the question give rise to branching and looping.

decision factors   The controllable and uncontrollable variables that together determine the outcome of a decision.

decision making   The process of selecting among alternative courses of action.

delayed-action advertising   Advertising that seeks long-range effects such as improved brand awareness, increased product preference, and a more favorable company image.

delegation   Assigning duties to subordinates.

Delphi method   A business forecasting techinque that relies on surveys of experts rather than on the use of past data.

demand curve   A graph showing the relationship between the price of an item and the maximum quantity of the item that customers will buy.

demand deposit   The checking accounts maintained at commercial banks. Such deposits can be withdrawn on demand—that is, at the discretion of the depositor.

demand factors   Determinants of the intensities with which customers desire and are able to pay for goods and services.

departmentation by groups   A principle of organization that states people and activities may be grouped together in an organization when they have similar functions, have the same objectives, or need to be coordinated.

depreciation   The deterioration of plant and equipment over time, whether the production facilities are in use or not. In accounting, the useful life of an asset as well as its original cost and salvage value is estimated; depreciation is then calculated as a normal business expense.

differentiated marketing   A marketing strategy in which a firm designs separate products and marketing programs for each market segment.

digital computer   A machine that processes discrete (as opposed to continuous) values by a sequence of instructions stored internally.

direct-action advertising   Advertising that seeks immediate sales to customers.

direct material The purchased raw materials, semifinished parts, and finished parts that are incorporated in a final product manufactured by a firm.

discount A reduction in the price offered to a customer for prompt payment or for buying in large quantities.

discount rate The rate of interest the Federal Reserve System charges financial institutions that wish to borrow funds from the system.

dissolution In antitrust enforcement, the breaking up of business into smaller units so that it will lack power to reinstitute a violation in restraint of trade.

diversification The development of a multiproduct business in which several products are manufactured in order to moderate the effects of a decline in sales or in profits associated with any single product. In financial investing, the process of purchasing a number of different types of securities in order to moderate the consequences of a decline in value of any specific security.

dividend A cash or stock payment to the owners of a corporation that is based on the number of shares held by the individual owner.

division of functions The division of activities assigned to federal, state, and local governments.

dumping Selling goods, especially in international trade, below their production costs (or, under some international trade laws, below their domestic prices).

E

earnings per share Net income after taxes *divided by* the number of shares of common stock outstanding.

economic concentration Control of an industry by one or a few businesses.

economic growth The expanded production of a nation, as measured by its real gross national product.

electronic data processing The analysis and summarization of data by electronic computers.

embargo The suspension, usually by a government, of trade with another nation or nations.

entering goods Industrial goods like raw materials and parts a firm incorporates in its final products.

equipment loan An extension of credit for which a firm's machinery or equipment is pledged as collateral.

equipment trust bond A bond that uses equipment as collateral. The holder of the bond owns the equipment and leases it to the issuing firm through a trustee. The trustee receives the lease payments from the issuing firm and uses them to pay interest and principal to the bondholder.

equity See **owner equity**

equity financing Issuance of common or preferred stock by a corporation to obtain funds for use in the business. In the case of a sole proprietorship or a partnership, equity financing involves obtaining additional investments from owners or partners.

exception principle A principle of organization that states that decisions on routine problems that recur frequently should be handled by lower-level personnel; only unusual, nonroutine problems should be referred to higher-level managers.

exchange controls Regulations regarding the use of foreign exchange imposed upon nationals under a government's jurisdiction. Exchange controls usually prohibit the use of scarce foreign exchange to purchase consumer goods and luxury goods.

exchange rate The ratio at which a unit of currency of one nation may be traded for that of another.

excise tax A sales tax levied on a selected set of specific products, such as furs, cigarettes, cars, and so on.

expense A cost of doing business.

experimental data Data obtained from experimental studies in which two essentially similar groups are identified and each group is exposed to somewhat different factors, one or more of which is being evaluated.

export controls Government controls regarding the kinds of goods or services that can be sold abroad.

external financing The acquisition of funds through additional contributions by existing or new owners of a business or through borrowing from banks or other financial institutions.

external transaction An accounting transaction that involves an exchange between a firm and an outside party (for example, sales to a customer).

extrapolation The use of information to extend past trends into the future.

F

face value The issue price of a security.

facilitating goods Industrial goods like maintenance, repair, and operating supplies that help an organization perform its functions.

featherbedding The process of attempting to retain unneeded jobs; usually engaged in by labor unions in order to provide job security for their members.

feedback In automation, the process by which information about the output of a machine is repeatedly transmitted (fed back) by an automatic control device so that discrepancies between the machine's actual performance and its desired performance can be corrected; in a flow diagram, a looping step that returns to an earlier stage in the sequence.

fidelity bond A form of insurance issued by bonding companies to protect a business against dishonesty among its employees.

finance The functional area of business that involves obtaining and using funds effectively.

financial institution An organization that receives money from savers and lends funds to consumers, businesses, and governments.

financial intermediary A financial institution that receives savings and makes funds available to consumers, businesses, and governments. Financial intermediaries provide such services as diversification, expert advice on investments, immediate or quick access to funds, and so on, to the saver. In return for these services, the saver accepts a lower interest rate than could be achieved by direct investment.

financial leverage The dollar value of a firm's debt expressed as a percentage of the total investment in the business.

financial ratio A measure of the relationship between two or more financial components of a business that provides insight into the quality and the prospects of the business. Financial ratios discussed in the text include the current ratio, return on equity, return on sales, and earnings per share. Also called *accounting ratio*.

financial structure The specific percentages of external or internal financing and debt or equity financing used by a firm and the maturity dates of its debts.

first-line supervision See **operating management**

fixed assets The property, plants, equipment, and tools owned by a business.

fixed exchange rate The relationship between one currency and another that is kept constant by government intervention in international exchange markets.

flexible exchange rate The demand and the supply of various currencies that establishes the relationships between the prices of currencies. Since demand and supply conditions for currencies (say, American dollars and British pounds) usually vary on a daily basis, the cost of one currency in terms of another also varies frequently.

flow diagram A graphic representation of the sequence of steps required to solve a given problem.

foreign trade zone A geographic area, typically located near a port, to which goods or services may be imported or exported without being subject to tariffs.

foundation goods Industrial goods like plant and equipment purchased by the organization buyer.

franchise Permission granted by a manufacturer or other organization to a retail firm allowing the retailer to sell its products or services in return for a fee; also a document issued by a local government permitting businesses to carry out activities over which the local government can exercise control.

fringe benefits Employer contributions to workers in addition to basic wages or salaries.

functional area A special operating area of a business, such as accounting, finance, or marketing.

futures contract An agreement providing for the delivery or purchase of a commodity at a specified price at some future date.

G

Gantt chart A method of charting and scheduling various kinds of management and production activities.

general partnership A partnership in which each owner is exposed to unlimited liability for all actions of the business.

general-purpose computer A digital computer programmed to process data for a wide variety of applications.

gross national product The money value of all goods and services produced in a nation during one year.

gross profit The difference between a firm's net sales and its cost of goods sold. Also called *gross margin.*

guideline An instruction from management that enables members of an organization to make decisions that achieve objectives more quickly, easily, and consistently.

H

health and accident insurance A form of insurance that protects individuals against illness and accidents; generally includes all or part of hospital, medical, and surgical expenses.

hedging The purchase of a contract for the future delivery of a commodity in order to offset business risk.

horizontal merger The acquisition of a firm by a competing business.

I

income bond A bond that does not pay a guaranteed rate of interest; payment is usually made out of the earnings of the issuing firm.

income statement An accounting statement that indicates the profits or losses sustained by a business during a given period.

indenture A document issued at the time of a bond's initial sale listing the conditions and terms of sale.

indirect material Equipment and supplies that are needed to manage and operate a firm but that are not incorporated in its final products.

industrial goods Goods sold to industrial firms for incorporation in a final product, for producing other goods, or for use in the administrative activities of the firm. Also called *producer goods.*

industrial revolution The replacement of hand tools by machinery and the factory system that began in England around 1760 and in the United States around 1790.

industrial union A labor union that encompasses all workers in a plant, whatever their occupation.

inflation An increase in price levels, often measured by the annual change in consumer or wholesale prices.

inheritance tax A tax on the individual receiving funds from an estate.

injunction A court order decreeing that a person or an organization either take or refrain from taking an action. Those who violate injunctions are held in contempt of court.

inland marine insurance A form of insurance that protects a firm against damages or losses in the shipment of goods by truck, railroad, barge, or air over land.

input device   The unit in a computer designed to bring processable data into a computer.

insurance   A contractual agreement in which for a fee (insurance premium), one party (the insurer) agrees to pay another party (the insured) a sum of money specified in advance if the second party sustains a loss under conditions indicated in the written contract (insurance policy).

intangibles   Assets deriving value from the rights they accord the holder; patents, copyrights, trademarks, and franchises fall in this group.

interchangeable parts   In mass production, parts so similar in physical characteristics as to be indistinguishable.

interest group   An association of persons or organizations that is devoted to promoting common goals, usually by political or educational means.

internal financing   The acquisition of funds through earnings retained in the business (after taxes and dividends are paid) and through monies made available by depreciation.

internal transaction   An accounting transaction that involves an exchange within the firm itself (for example, the consumption of previously purchased supplies).

international reserves   Government-held gold and other assets used in international financial transactions.

international trade   The exchange of goods and services among nations in the form of exports and imports.

inventories   In manufacturing, stockpiles of raw materials used in producing a product and of partially or completely finished goods kept on hand by the firm; in retailing, goods available for sale to consumers.

inventory turnover   Cost of goods sold *divided by* average inventories held; inventory turnover measures the rapidity with which a firm's inventories are depleted and must be replaced during a year.

investment bank   A bank that assists or controls the placement of business securities—particularly the stocks, bonds, and notes—for individual investors or organizations who wish to invest funds. Also known as an *underwriter* or *security house*.

invoice   A document issued by a seller to a buyer indicating the types, quantities, and prices of goods and the total amounts due.

J

job analysis   An evaluation of a position in an organization to determine what detailed tasks the person holding that position should perform.

job description   A written statement describing the duties and responsibilities of a particular position in a firm; the job description is developed by the personnel department in consultation with the manager who supervises the position.

job specification   A written statement describing the skills, work experience, and education that a prospective employee needs in order to perform a given job satisfactorily

L

labor union   A group of workers who join together to achieve common goals related to their employment.

land   An asset that includes land employed in the business.

leading   The management process by which activities of subordinates are guided toward objectives.

legal department   The section of a business that handles routine legal matters and most litigation in which the firm is involved.

liabilities   The financial obligations a business incurs in acquiring resources.

liability insurance   A form of insurance that protects a business or an individual against damages resulting from negligence.

license   A document issued by a local government that gives the holder the right to engage in a designated business or economic activity.

life insurance A form of insurance that provides financial protection against loss of life, with benefits payable to dependents, heirs, or the insured's estate.

limited liability The legal obligation of the owner of a firm to be responsible only for the loss of their individual investments in the business in event of the firm's insolvency.

limited partnership A partnership consisting of one or more general partners who are personally liable for all debts incurred by the business and limited partners who risk only their own investments.

line-and-staff organization A type of formal business organization characterized by (1) unambiguous supervisory authority and (2) specialized technical support from staff personnel.

line-of-credit arrangement An agreement between a financial institution and an individual or organization entitling the latter to borrow up to a specified amount as a matter of right and at the time of the borrower's choice.

line organization The simplest type of formal business organization in which each position has general authority over positions below it in the managerial hierarchy in accomplishing the firm's objectives.

liquid assets Assets that can readily be converted into cash.

liquidity The speed and cost involved in converting assets to cash. Highly liquid assets (for example, U.S. Treasury notes) can be exchanged for cash quickly and at low cost. Illiquid assets (for example, used machinery) may take many months to convert to cash and often must be sold at a considerable loss.

lobbyist A professional who seeks to influence government through personal contacts, information-gathering techniques, political contributions, and letter-writing campaigns.

local The smallest unit of a labor union.

lockout An economic weapon of management in which the firm discontinues all operations until a settlement with a union is reached.

long-term investment Any asset held exclusively for investment (not resale) longer than one year.

long-term liability An obligation of a business that need not be met within one year.

looping The step in a flow diagram or computer operation that involves taking a path that leads back to an earlier stage in the sequence.

M

Machiavellianism A leadership style that justifies using any technique—no matter how deceitful—to manipulate and control people.

machinery and equipment An asset that includes tools used in the business.

main frame See **central processing unit**

make-buy decisions An evaluation by a business of which parts in a final product will be purchased from outside vendors and which will be fabricated by the firm itself.

management A group of people who direct effort toward common goals; also the process of planning, organizing, leading, and controlling an organization's people and resources to achieve its stated goals.

management by objectives A method of management control that seeks to define each person's area of responsibility in terms of the results expected, using observable and measurable job-related criteria.

manager An individual who specializes in knowing how to run a business.

managerial accounting The process of collecting, organizing, and analyzing the financial data of a business in a manner tailored to a particular managerial decision.

manufacturing The process of converting purchased materials into useful products according to plans and specifications developed by the firm and then transporting these products to the buyer.

markdown A reduction in the original retail selling price of an item.

market division An agreement by competitors not to compete in one another's assigned sales territory.

market order An order to buy or sell a security at the existing price. Thus, the investor who orders 100 shares of General Motors at market will pay the going price for GM stock and the brokerage firm's floor trader will obtain the stock at the best price that can be negotiated, keeping in view that the investor's main objective is to acquire or to sell the stock at whatever price can be secured.

market-product grid A diagram used to analyze a market on the basis of the characteristics of potential consumers.

market segment A group of potential customers who are similar in some respect, such as in demographic characteristics or in volume of product use.

market value The price of a good, service, or security as determined by demand and supply.

marketing That area of business that directs the flow of goods and services from producer to consumer in order to satisfy buyers and to achieve company objectives.

marketing channels See **channels of distribution**

marketing concept The principle that stresses shaping products to meet consumer needs rather than attempting to mold those needs to the products.

marketing mix The blend of the four basic marketing activities (product, place, promotion, and price) that a firm employs to reach its target market effectively.

markup See **gross profit**

mass production A system of production that involves (1) the use of specialized machines to make interchangeable parts feasible; (2) the replacement of human and animal energy by mechanical power; and (3) specialization of labor so that workers are assigned a specific set of tasks at which they are skilled.

maturity date The date at which a security be-comes due; at this time, the principal and any remaining interest must be paid in full.

mean The number found by *dividing* the sum of a set of numbers *by* the total number of items in the set. Also called the *arithmetic mean* and the *average*.

measure of central value A number that summarizes a whole set of numbers in a single value.

measure of success A standard used in judging whether a proposed solution to a problem is satisfactory. Also called *criterion*.

median The number located in the exact middle of an entire set of numbers when they are arrayed from lowest to highest. The median is the most typical of all numbers in the set in the sense that half the numbers lie above it and half lie below it.

mediation An attempt to settle labor-management conflicts through the intervention of a third party neutral to the dispute who makes recommendations to unions and management.

memory unit See **storage unit**

merchandise inventory An asset that includes all goods purchased for resale or produced by the firm.

merger The combination of two or more businesses into a single firm.

middle management Managers between top management and operating management in an organization.

middleman A marketing firm (usually a wholesaler or retailer) between the manufacturer and consumer in a channel of distribution.

mixed economy A system of resource allocation that combines elements of several ideologies (for example, capitalism and socialism).

mode The number that occurs most often in a set of numbers.

modes of transportation The basic methods by which goods are moved to customers: air, pipeline, rail, water, and highway.

money GNP The total production of goods and services in an economy, valued at current price levels.

monopoly The domination of an industry by a single firm such that it can control prices and prevent potential competitors from entering the industry.

mortgage bond A bond that is secured by a claim on real assets—land, buildings, equipment, or machinery. In event of default by the issuing firm, the bondholder can sell the pledged assets, using the proceeds to recover the principal or interest due.

mortgages payable A long-term liability against which specific assets are pledged as collateral.

movable assembly line A production process in which incomplete products are carried past workers and machines in fixed positions who perform specified operations on the products before they pass to the next stage.

multinational corporation A corporation, usually owned by citizens of many nations, that produces and sells goods in many major national markets.

municipal bond A bond entitling the owner to receive interest exempt from federal income taxes. If issued by a local government in the same state as the bondholder, the exemption extends to state income taxes as well. Industrial aid, industrial revenue, and in some states pollution control bonds are tax exempt.

mutual fund An organization that pools the contributions of many individuals or organizations for the purposes of investment, often in security markets.

N

natural monopoly The presence of a single seller in an industry where competition would raise the costs of serving customers; natural monopolies are subject to government regulation.

near cash Interest-bearing assets that can easily be converted to cash.

net income The profits that a business realizes from its operations.

net operating income Gross profit *less* operating expenses.

no-fault insurance A form of insurance in which payments for damage are made by the company issuing the insurance according to a fixed schedule of fees established by a government, regardless of which party is responsible for the damage.

noncallable security A security that cannot be redeemed by the issuing organization until it becomes due.

noncumulative security A security that does not entitle the holder to recover dividends or interest once they have been omitted by a firm.

nonpar stocks A stock that does not have a par value printed on the stock certificate.

nonparticipating security A security that does not entitle the holder to receive profits beyond the fixed dividends or interest due him or her as an owner of the security.

nonprofit organization A nongovernmental organization that does not seek profits as a major business objective.

nonvoting security A security that does not entitle the holder to vote on matters of corporate business unless dividend and interest commitments are not met by the firm.

notes payable A liability that includes promissory notes owed by the firm to creditors.

notes receivable An asset that includes promissory notes on monies owed the firm by other individuals or businesses.

nutritional labeling Giving information on the labels of food products in common household units (per bowl, cut, or glass) describing the proportion of recommended daily requirements of vitamins, minerals, and proteins contained in the product; intended to assist consumers in judging food value.

O

objective A goal that a decision maker (or a group) seeks to achieve in a problem-solving situation.

observational data Data collected by watching how people or machines behave, either through mechanical means or through direct personal observation.

ocean marine insurance A form of insurance that protects a firm against damages or losses in the shipment of goods across the seas.

odd pricing A retail strategy of pricing a few pennies below the exact dollar on a low-priced item (for example, $17.95 instead of $18 for a pair of shoes) or a few dollars below an even hundred on a high-priced item (for example, $495 rather than $500 for a sofa).

off-the-job training Job-related instruction obtained by attending courses, seminars, or workshops offered by the firm or by an outside organization educational institution.

offer A proposal by one party (the *offerer*) to enter into a contract with a second party (the *offeree*).

oligopoly The domination of an industry by a few powerful firms.

on-the-job training All instruction given to an employee in the course of the day-to-day job.

online processing A method of computer data processing that involves immediate input–output access to the computer whenever a user wishes to obtain information.

open-account credit A grace period (often ten days) during which a customer may pay for merchandise or services at a discount price. If the supplier's bill is not paid within the grace period, a further period (often 20 days) is extended, during which the customer still receives a discount for payment (although less than during initial grace period). At the end of 30 days, the full bill is due.

open dating Giving the date a retail item was produced by the manufacturer or received by the retailer; intended to assist consumers in judging product freshness.

open-market operations The purchase or sale of U.S. government bonds by the Federal Reserve System in order to alter the money supply.

open shop A shop or business establishment in which employees may voluntarily decide whether to join a union.

operating expenses All nonmaterial costs of conducting a business.

operating management Supervisors whose major job is the immediate direction of people performing clerical or shop work.

operation box An element in a flow diagram or computer operation that involves taking the specific action contained within the box.

organization chart A formal diagram of the authority relationships in a business firm.

organizing The management process by which jobs are structured and qualified people are placed in them.

output device The unit in a computer designed to translate electrical impulses into usable form, such as printed copy or punched cards.

overtime pay A form of compensation in which employees are paid at a rate higher than the normal hourly rate for working more than a minimum number of hours per week, usually 40 hours. A typical arrangement is for employees to be paid one and a half times the normal hourly rate for overtime during the work week and double the hourly rate for overtime on Saturday and Sunday.

owner equity The portion of assets owned outright by the firm.

P

par stock A stock with a par value printed on the stock certificate.

par value The nominal value of a stock at time of issue, as stated on the stock certificate.

participating security A security that entitles the holder to receive returns (in addition to the fixed dividends or interest due him or her as an owner of the security) when the company's earnings rise above an amount specified in advance.

partners' capital In a partnership, the portions of owner equity that include capital contributed by the partners.

partnership A form of business organization in which two or more persons are associated as owners but in which no stock is issued.

pension plan A plan involving contributions by employees or employers that provides income to workers during their retirement years.

per capita Per person; for example, per capita money GNP is the gross national product of a nation *divided by* its population.

peripheral equipment All hardware in a computer not associated directly with the main frame; generally includes the input and output devices plus auxiliary memory or storage units.

personal income Total income from wages, salaries, business, professional, and agricultural receipts, dividends, rent, interest, and government payments to individuals.

personal selling Any personal communication between seller and buyer that is performed by salespeople operating inside or outside the firm.

personnel management The business function that involves (1) recruiting new employees; (2) assisting them while they are employed (for example, by providing on-the-job training); and (3) sometimes assisting them after they leave the company (such as with retirement benefits).

piecework A form of compensation in which workers are paid in accordance with their output (for example, 5¢ for each rim placed on a tire in a tire factory).

place The element of the marketing mix that involves finding appropriate channels of distribution, including retailing and wholesaling institutions, to get the product to the target market at the right time and in the right place.

planning The management process by which a manager sets objectives, assesses the future, and designs a program of action.

plans The means by which an organization's objectives are achieved.

portfolio investment Investment—especially investment abroad—in securities rather than physical plant and equipment.

preemptive placement A method of obtaining funds in which existing owners are given an exclusive opportunity to purchase new securities issued by the firm.

preferred stock Certificate of ownership in a corporation entitling holders to receive specified dividends that are not directly based on the earnings of the firm.

price The element of the marketing mix that involves establishing a monetary value for the product that gives value to the customer and adequate revenue to the producer; also the money and goods exchanged for the ownership or use of some assortment of goods and services.

price discrimination The practice of charging customers different prices for products of like grade and quality.

price fixing An arrangement among competitors to set prices at designated levels.

primary data Data collected for the first time for the immediate purpose or project at hand.

private enterprise system The dominant institution in the American economy, displaying four major characteristics: (1) private ownership of business; (2) private property; (3) freedom of choice; and (4) limited role of government.

private placement A method of obtaining funds in which a firm offers its securities exclusively to a single investor or to a small group of investigators, usually banks, mutual funds, or other financial institutions.

private sector All economic institutions that are not owned by the government—business firms, foundations, cooperatives, and so on.

product The element of the marketing mix that involves developing the right good (or service) for the target market; also a physical item or service that satisfies certain customer needs.

product development An aspect of production that involves generating the designs, models, and prototypes necessary to build final products.

product line The array of products offered for sale by a business.

production The functional area of business in which people and machines design new products, buy and convert materials into finished products, and supply these products to customers; also includes the activities of product development, purchasing, and manufacturing.

production control A manufacturing activity that involves the identification, scheduling, and monitoring of the stages in the production process in order to insure the timely delivery of an item in the right quantity and specified quality.

productivity Real output per worker hour, usually expressed in percentage terms as an annual gain or loss.

profit maximization Achievement of as high a financial return as possible.

profit sharing A form of compensation in which employees receive, in addition to their regular pay, a share in the company's net profits.

profits The difference between the revenues and costs of a business. Profits are available for investment in the business or service to provide dividends and other income for the business owners.

promissory note A signed agreement between two parties (either two individuals or an individual and a financial organization) in which the borrower states in writing that the principal and any outstanding interest due on the loan will be returned to the lender at a designated time.

promotion The element of the marketing mix that includes the use of personal selling and advertising to facilitate sales by communicating information about the product to customers.

property insurance A form of insurance that protects a firm against fire and other natural disasters, usually applied to buildings and equipment.

proprietor's capital In a sole proprietorship, the part of owner equity that includes capital contributed by the sole proprietor.

proprietorship See **sole proprietorship**

prospectus A document describing a new stock issue.

protectionist An advocate of the view that barriers to world trade are desirable.

protective tariff A tariff created with the primary objective of placing domestic industry in a competitively favorable position with regard to foreign competition. This objective is accomplished by taxing imported goods or services.

public offering A method of obtaining funds in which a firm offers new securities to the public.

public sector All government activities, federal, state, or local.

publicity Favorable news coverage of a firm or its products that is obtained without overt initiation or payment by the firm.

publicly owned organization A business established by the federal government or by a state government to achieve goals felt to be for the public good.

purchasing An aspect of production that involves buying the right item in the right quantity at the right price and making it available to the firm at the right time and place.

pure competition An industry in which (1) a large number of firms produce identical products, (2) each firm is free to enter or to leave the industry as it chooses, and (3) government interference is absent.

Q

quality control A manufacturing activity that involves the inspection of an item at various stages in the production process to insure that the final product meets the specifications set for it.

quality of life The economic , social, cultural, and moral welfare of the daily lives of individuals.

R

real GNP The total value of goods and services produced within an economy in a given period of time, valued at the prices that prevailed during a previous base year or years. By valuing GNP at constant (base) prices, the effects of inflation are removed from GNP comparisons.

reference group   A group of people who influence a person's behavior either because he or she is a member of the group or because he or she aspires to be in the group.

register   A listing of all accounting transactions involving a given category.

regulatory agency   A federal, state, or local government unit that is empowered to review the activities of businesses in industries designated by law.

reserve requirements   The proportion of a financial institution's demand and savings deposits that must remain in a Federal Reserve Bank. Raising reserve requirements for these institutions makes less money available for loans and decreases the money supply; lowering reserve requirements produces an increase in the money supply.

resources   All tangible and intangible items used in producing goods and services.

responsibility   Obligation to perform delegated duties.

retailer   An establishment that purchases only consumer goods from manufacturers or wholesalers and sells them to ultimate consumers.

retained earnings   The part of owner equity that includes all profits that have been kept for use by the business.

return on investment   The total return, or profit, obtained from a project *divided by* the amount of money invested in it.

revenue   The financial receipts of a business.

revenue tariff   A tariff or tax on imports primarily designed to raise funds to finance governmental activities.

right-to-work laws   State laws that give an employee the right to join or not to join a union. Under right-to-work laws, unions cannot require union membership to obtain employment or force an employee to pay union dues.

risk management   The functional area of business concerned with controlling unexpected variations in the outcomes of business decisions.

risk-return relationship   The connection between the amount of risk involved in an investment and expected profits. Normally, the greater the risk associated with a business activity, the higher the return on investment that can be anticipated.

S

salary   A form of compensation in which employees are given regular weekly or monthly payments for each period worked.

savings and loan association   A financial institution that receives savings accounts and checking accounts from individuals and organizations and largely places the resulting funds in home mortgages and other real-estate investments.

savings bank   A financial institution that receives savings and checking accounts but not demand deposits, from individuals and organizations and makes the resulting funds available as business, consumer, or government loans.

scalar principle   A principle of organization that states that authority and responsibility should flow in a continuous line from the highest person in an organization to the lowest.

scientific management   A school of management thought developed by Fredrick W. Taylor that emphasizes ways to increase productivity through careful planning.

secondary data   Data pertinent to a current problem that have been collected by another individual or group for some other purpose or project.

secured loan   A loan for which some physical or financial asset is pledged as collateral.

security market   A building or organized meeting place where stocks and bonds are bought and sold.

self-insurance   A form of business protection in which a firm meets risks by absorbing losses itself, rather than seeking insurance coverage.

seniority system A reward system that assigns employees important work privileges (such as protection against layoffs) on the basis of their years of service.

shift premium A form of compensation in which employees are paid more than the normal hourly wage for working the evening or early morning shift.

shop steward The union member designated to represent a small group of workers within a plant. Also called *business agent*.

shopping goods Goods that the customer, in the process of selection and purchase, characteristically compares on such bases as suitability, quality, price, and style; these goods are frequently unbranded or, if branded, the names are not very important to the consumer.

shrinkage Losses of a business firm due to theft, spoilage, or breakage.

social security The Old Age, Survivors, and Disability Insurance System, commonly known as social security, that provides retirement benefits, disability benefits, and makes other insurance-related payments to recipients. The program is administered by the federal government and financed by taxes paid by both employee and employer.

socialism The view of traditional socialism is that government should own the basic industries in the economy, such as automobiles, iron and steel, and the railroads. An alternative view of socialism is the welfare state, in which large tax collections finance such programs as social security, medical care, unemployment compensation, and welfare benefits; these programs are made available by the government either free of charge or at a nominal cost.

sole proprietorship A business owned by one person who often manages it as well.

span of control A principle of organization that states that there is a limit to the number of subordinates who should report to one superior, since a supervisor has only a certain amount of time, energy, and attention to devote to supervision.

special-purpose computer A digital computer tailored to a specific application.

specialization The division of labor in which each employee concentrates on a specific task or set of tasks in the production of a product instead of on the production of an individual finished product. As employees become skilled at their specialities, their output increases.

specialty goods Goods with unique characteristics and/or brand identification for which a significant group of buyers is habitually willing to make a special purchasing effort; such goods are generally branded, and the brands are important in the consumer's buying decision.

specific duty A tax on imports brought into a country that is based on a designated monetary charge for each physical unit of the goods imported.

specifications A detailed description of the materials, dimensions, and performance requirements of all items comprising a finished product.

staffing The process by which managers select, train, promote, and retire subordinates.

standard manufacture The production of items by a firm in accordance with its own specifications.

standard parts See **interchangeable parts**

standards In mass production, tolerances or limits from which a given part cannot deviate.

statutory law Written constitutions, codes, statutes, and regulations enacted by the people or their elected representatives.

stock dividends A payment to the existing owners of a corporation of stock that is normally newly issued by the corporation; this payment is either made in lieu of or in addition to any cash dividend paid by the corporation.

stock right A document that entitles the holder to purchase shares of the common stock of a firm according to terms specified on the document.

stockholder A holder or owner of stock in a corporation. Also called *shareholder*.

storage unit The device in a computer in which

data are stored and from which they are obtained when needed.

straight-line depreciation   A formula for calculating depreciation that allocates the difference between the purchase price of an asset *minus* its salvage value equally over the number of years of the asset's estimated life. The annual estimated depreciation is then treated as a business cost, even though the firm has not experienced a direct cash payment to any person or organization.

strategic planning   Planning to achieve general organizational goals over a long-range period (two years or more).

strike   An economic weapon of organized labor in which union members collectively refuse to work until their demands are met by management.

subordinated debenture   A bond that is an unsecured obligation of a business; in the event of liquidation, general creditors and holders of debentures must be paid in full before claims of owners of subordinated debentures are recognized.

substitute product   A product that may be used in place of another product to perform substantially the same function; an example is the wide line of copiers offered by the Xerox Corporation.

supplies inventory   An asset that includes accumulated supplies purchased for use in production.

supply curve   The relationship (in graph form) that indicates what quantities of a good or a service suppliers in an industry will produce at various selling prices.

supply factors   Determinants of the quantities of goods or services that producers will place on the market.

surety bond   A form of insurance issued by bonding companies that protects a business against nonperformance by an employee or by a party with which the firm has entered into contract.

survey data   Data obtained by asking people questions, through either personal interviews, telephone interviews, or self-administered questionnaires.

synthetic process   A production process in which final products are built up or assembled from basic parts.

T

tactical planning   Planning to acheive organizational subgoals over a short-range period (less than two years).

target market   The specific group or groups of customers to whom a company wishes to sell its products or services.

tariff   A tax or a fee paid on imports; usually paid at the import's point of entry into a country.

tax-exempt bond   See **municipal bond**

term life policy   A form of life insurance that provides protection for a designated period, after which the insurer can refuse to insure or charge higher rates.

term loan   An extension of credit by a bank or an insurance company for a period of more than one year.

time sharing   A method of computer utilization that involves linking many remote input–output terminals (usually teletypewriters) to a central computer with a large storage capacity.

top management   The president and vice presidents of a firm.

trade acceptance   A draft (in effect, a check) drawn on the buyer for the amount of the buyer's purchase and signed by the buyer; the trade acceptance typically designates the bank or other financial institution to which the draft is to be presented.

trade credit   An extension of credit in which a supplier allows customers several weeks or months to make payment.

trading area   The geographic region from which a business draws most of its customers and obtains most of its sales revenue.

transfer payment   A government expenditure for which no goods or services are received in return;

social security and welfare payments fall into this category.

transportation   A manufacturing activity that provides for the inbound movement of raw materials and parts and the outbound shipment of finished products.

trustee   A person, usually a representative of a financial institution, who is responsible for protecting the rights of the bondholders of a business; the trustee also carries out much of the paperwork involved in paying interest and repaying principal on the bond.

tying contract   The sale of a product to customers only in combination with another product; tying contracts are prohibited by federal law.

U

uncertainties   The factors over which a decision maker has no control in making a decision.

underwriter   A firm or group of firms, usually representing the investment banking community, that is responsible for pricing, promoting, and selling a new stock or bond issue.

undifferentiated marketing   A marketing strategy in which a firm manufactures only a single product and attempts to attract all buyers with a single marketing program.

union contract   A written agreement between labor and management that specifies in detail the rules and procedures to be followed by both parties.

union shop   A shop or business establishment in which management is free to hire nonunion workers provided that they join the established union within a designated period, usually 30 days.

unit pricing   Giving retail price information on a cents-per-ounce or cents-per-pound basis; intended to assist consumers in making price comparisons.

unity of command   A principle of organization that states that no member of an organization should report to more than one superior.

unlimited liability   A legal obligation of the owner of a firm to use his or her entire business and personal wealth to pay off any accumulated debts of the firm.

unsecured loan   A loan that does not involve the use of collateral.

V

value analysis   Systematic appraisal of the design, quality, and performance requirements of an item in order to reduce purchasing and manufacturing costs.

vertical merger   The acquisition by a firm of one of its suppliers or customers.

voting security   A security that entitles the holder to vote on matters of corporate business, such as election of the board of directors.

W

wages   A form of compensation in which employees are paid at a fixed hourly rate or in accordance with the number of units (or parts) of commodity produced.

whole life policy   A form of life insurance in which premiums are paid throughout a person's lifetime, with the full amount of the policy payable upon death.

wholesaler   An establishment that sells to retailers, other middlemen, or industrial users, but that does not sell in significant amounts to ultimate consumers.

worker compensation insurance   A form of insurance required by state law and paid for by employers that protects employees while they are engaged in the employer's business; the amount of the claim is stipulated by law.

working capital management   Decisions about the uses of current assets and short-term debt.

References

Chapter 1

1. "Alternative Pioneers," *Corporate Report,* Oct. 1979, pp. 73–74; personal interviews with company personnel.
2. John H. Dessauer, *My Years with Xerox* (Garden City, N.Y.: Doubleday, 1971), pp. 21–87.
3. John Brooks, "Annals of Business—A Friendly Product," *New Yorker,* 12 Nov. 1979, pp. 58–94.
4. Ibid.
5. "P & G's New Product Onslought," *Business Week,* 1 Oct. 1979, pp. 76–82; John A. Prestbo, "At Procter and Gamble, Success Is Largely Due to Heeding Consumer," *The Wall Street Journal,* 29 April 1980, p. 1; Peter Vanderwicken, "P & G's Secret Ingredient," *Fortune,* July 1974, pp. 75ff.
6. Ibid.
7. "Alternative Pioneers," pp. 73–74.

Chapter 2

1. Marshall Loeb, "The Strength of Samson," *Time,* 30 July 1979, p. 62; Elizabeth Cronin, "But Is It the Real Thing?" *Forbes,* 18 Sept. 1978, p. 124; Joyce Levaton, "J. Paul Austin, First over the Wall, Prepares to Teach China What Things Go Better with," *People,* 8 Jan. 1979, pp. 18–19.
2. Ralph Vartabedian, "Inventor Passes Go, Collects Garbage," *The Minneapolis Star,* 23 Jan. 1980, p. 1.
3. Jim Montgomery, "A Secret Life," *The Wall Street Journal,* 21 Jan. 1980, p. 1. Reprinted by permission of The Wall Street Journal, © Dow Jones & Company, Inc. 1980. All rights reserved.
4. Kermit Vandiver, "Why Should My Conscience Bother Me?" from *In the Name of Profit* by Robert L. Heilbroner and others. Copyright © 1972 by Doubleday & Company, Inc. Used by permission of publisher.

Chapter 3

1. "The Glamour Business That Really Wasn't," *Rainbow Magazine* (Fall 1979), pp. 40–42.
2. Adapted from Don Larson, *Land of the Giants: A History of Minnesota Business* (Minneapolis: Dorn Books, 1979), pp. 130–32.
3. Margaret Rudkin, "The First Twenty-Five Years," *The Pepperidge Farm Conveyor–25th Anniversary Issue* (1962). Copyright © 1962 by Margaret Rudkin. Used by permission.
4. Adapted from Larson, pp. 56–73.
5. Berry Gordy, Jr., "What's an Entrepreneur?" *The New York Times,* 14 Jan. 1979, p. F7.
6. Herschel Johnson, "Motown: The Sound of Success," *Black Enterprise* (June 1974), pp. 71–80. Copyright 1974 Earl G. Graves Publishing Co., Inc., 295 Madison Avenue, New York, N.Y. 10017. All rights reserved.

Chapter 4

1. The definition of management is adapted from James A. F. Stoner, *Management* (Englewood Cliffs, N.J.: Prentice-Hall, 1978), p. 7.
2. The definitions of the four functions of management are adapted from Joseph L. Massie, *Essentials of Management,* 2nd ed. (Englewood Cliffs, N.J.: Prentice-Hall, 1971), pp. 6–7.
3. The examples of economic indicators are taken in part from "Economic Indicators: Turtles, Butterflies, Monks and Waiters," *The Wall Street Journal,* 27 Aug. 1979, p. 1. Reprinted by permission of The Wall Street Journal, © Dow Jones & Company, Inc. 1979. All rights reserved.
4. Max Ways, "Hall of Fame for Business Leadership," *Fortune,* Jan. 1975, p. 72.
5. "Fotomat Focuses on Videotape," *Business Week,*

29 Jan. 1979, pp. 58–63; Jacques Nehr, "New Focus for Photo Finishes," *Advertising Age,* 9 April 1979, p. 20; "Fotomat Develops Storefront Locations, Refocuses Its Logo," *Chain Store Age Executive,* Nov. 1979, pp. 69–70.

6. Allan C. Filley and Robert J. House, *Managerial Process and Organizational Behavior* (Glenwood, Ill.: Scott, Foresman, and Company, 1969), p. 12. Copyright © 1969 by Scott, Foresman and Company. Reprinted by permission.

7. "Josten's: A School Supplier Stays with Basics as Enrollment Declines," *Business Week,* 21 April 1980, pp. 124–29; personal interviews with company personnel.

Chapter 5

1. The information on Henry Ford and on Alfred P. Sloan, Jr., is based on Peter F. Drucker, *Management: Tasks, Responsibilities, Practices* (New York: Harper and Row, 1973), pp. 380–84 and 520–23; and Max Ways, "Hall of Fame for Business Leadership," *Fortune,* Jan. 1975, pp. 66–68.

2. Jeremy Main, "Terrific Companies to Work for," *Money,* Nov. 1976, pp. 44–48.

3. J. Patrick Wright, *On a Clear Day You Can See General Motors* (Gross Pointe, Mich.: Wright Enterprises, 1979), pp. 158–70.

4. The discussion of the traditional principles of organization is based on Allan C. Filley and Robert J. House, *Managerial Process and Organizational Behavior,* p. 12, Copyright © 1969 by Scott, Foresman and Company. Reprinted by permission; W. Warren Haynes and Joseph L. Massie, *Management: Analysis Concepts and Cases,* 2nd ed. (Englewood Cliffs, N.J.: Prentice-Hall, 1969), pp. 91–110; and Joseph L. Massie, *Essentials of Management,* 2nd ed. (Englewood Cliffs, N.J.: Prentice-Hall, 1971), pp. 64–72.

5. "Personal Management Styles," *Business Week,* 4 May 1974, pp. 43–51; Fred Bayles, "Polaroid's 'Chief Intellectual' to Retire," *Minneapolis Tribune,* 20 April 1980, p. 70; Dan Cordtz, "How Polaroid Bet Its Future on the SX-70," *Fortune,* Jan. 1974, pp. 82ff.

6. Roy Rowan, "Watch Out for Chemical Reactions at the Top," *Fortune,* 25 Sept. 1978, pp. 92–95.

7. Max Ways, "Hall of Fame for Business Leadership," *Fortune,* Jan. 1975, pp. 66–68.

8. Barbara Lorenheim, "A Test to Uncover Managerial Skills," *The New York Times,* 21 Jan. 1979; "How RPI Helps Locate Talent," *Business Week,* 18 Sept. 1978, pp. 129–31; James A. F. Stoner, *Management* (Englewood Cliffs, N.J.: Prentice-Hall, 1978), pp. 510–11.

9. From Judith Furrer, Inver Hills Community College.

10. Laurence J. Peter and Raymond Hull, *The Peter Principle* (New York: William Morrow, 1969), pp. 9–36. Adapted by permission of William Morrow & Company and Souvenir Press.

11. Rush Loving, Jr., "Bob Six's Long Search for a Successor," *Fortune,* June 1975, p. 92ff. Reprinted by permission from *Fortune* magazine; © 1975 Time Inc.

Chapter 6

1. F. J. Roethlisberger, *Management and Morale* (Cambridge, Mass.: Harvard Univ. Press, 1941), pp. 10–11; and Allan C. Filley and Robert J. House, *Managerial Process and Organizational Behavior* (Glenwood, Ill.: Scott, Foresman and Company, 1969), pp. 18–23. Copyright © 1969 by Scott, Foresman and Company. Reprinted by permission.

2. Joe Blade, "Bell Employees Protest Job Pressures," *Minneapolis Star,* 15 June 1979, p. 1, Section D.

3. Dennis McGrath, "Behind the Scenes at Valleyfair," *Minneapolis Tribune,* 29 July 1979, p. 4, Section D.

4. The bases of effective communication are based on William F. Keefe, *Listen, Management!* (New York: McGraw-Hill, 1971), p. 44.

5. "Coping with Anxiety at AT&T," *Business Week,* 28 May 1979, pp. 95–106.

6. The information on barriers to communication is based on Herbert J. Chruden and Arthur W. Sherman, Jr., *Personnel Management,* 4th ed. (Cincinnati, Ohio: South-Western, 1972), pp. 363–70; and Joseph L. Massie, *Essentials of Management,* 2nd ed. (Englewood Cliffs, N.J.: Prentice-Hall, 1971), pp. 97–98.

7. Robert Townsend, *Up the Organization* (New York: Alfred A. Knopf, 1970), p. 99.

8. Albert Henry Smith, *The Writings of Benjamin Franklin* (New York: The MacMillan Company, 1905).

9. Robert Payne, *The Great Man* (New York: Coward, McCann & Geoghegan, Inc., 1974).

10. C. Northcote Parkinson, *Parkinson's Law* (Boston: Houghton Mifflin, 1971), pp. 3–8.

11. "Women Finally Get Mentors of Their Own," *Business Week,* 23 Oct. 1978, p. 74.

12. "Young Top Management: The New Goals, Rewards, Lifestyles," *Business Week,* 6 Oct. 1975, pp. 56–67.

13. "Xerox Goes Retail," *Advertising Age,* 14, April 1980. "The Office of the Future Gets a Common Voice," *Business Week,* 26 May 1980, pp. 57–58; "How Not to Exploit the Hardware," *Business Week,* 24 March 1979, pp. 90–92; "Xerox's Bid to Unlock the Office of the Future," *Business Week,* 24 Dec. 1979, p. 47.

Chapter 7

1. "Texas Instruments Shows U.S. Business How to Survive in the 1980's," *Business Week,* 18 Sept. 1978, p. 89; Gene Bylinsky, "Those Smart Young Robots on the Production Line," *Fortune,* 17 Dec. 1979, pp. 90–96; Josephine Marcotty, "Robots: They're Still Rather Stupid, But Useful," *Minneapolis Tribune,* 20 Jan. 1980, p. 13 Dff.

2. Marshall Loeb, "Ideas Are All We Have," *Time,* 3 Dec. 1979, p. 89; lecture by Bud Grossman to students at the College of Business Administration, University of Minnesota, February 27, 1980.

3. Charles Chamberlain, "Sears Told to Pay Millions for Wrench," *The Minneapolis Tribune,* 1 June 1979, p. 1.

4. The sequence of purchasing steps is described in Dean S. Ammer, *Materials Management,* 3rd ed. (Homewood, Ill.: Richard D. Irwin, 1974), pp. 44–66.

5. Edward Meadows, "How Three Companies Increased Their Productivity," *Fortune,* 10 March 1980, pp. 92–101.

6. Dennis J. McGrath, "General Mills Turns Indoors to Grow Produce," *Minneapolis Tribune,* 24 February 1980, p. 1 Dff.

7. Roy Rowan, "Business Triumphs of the Seventies," *Fortune,* 31 Dec. 1979, p. 34.

8. David Lewin, "New Woman Movie Boss 'Comfortable' at Top," *Minneapolis Tribune,* 3 Feb. 1980, p. G1 ff; Earl C. Gottschalk, "Fox Film's Fortunes Soaring on the Wings of 'Star Wars' Movie," *The Wall Street Journal,* 1 Jan. 1978, p. 1; "Ladd News Tied to Nosedive in Fox Stock Price," *Broadcasting,* 9 July 1979, pp. 36–37.

Chapter 8

1. John R. Emshwiller, "John DeLorean Says He'll Show Industry 'How to Build Cars,'" *The Wall Street Journal,* 12 Jan. 1979, p. 1. Reprinted by permission of The Wall Street Journal, © Dow Jones & Company, Inc. 1979. All rights reserved.

2. The four P's and their definitions are adapted from E. Jerome McCarthy, *Basic Marketing: A Managerial Approach,* 6th ed. (Homewood, Ill.: Richard D. Irwin, Inc., 1978), pp. 38–45.

3. "Tom Swift and His Electric Hamburger Cooker," *Forbes,* 15 Oct. 1977, p. 112.

4. "What Makes the New Consumer Buy," *Business Week,* 24 April 1971, p. 58.

5. The discussion of undifferentiated, differentiated, and concentrated marketing is adapted from Philip Kotler, *Marketing Management,* 4th ed. (Englewood Cliffs, N.J.: Prentice-Hall, 1980), pp. 206–209.

6. Peter W. Bernstein, "Polaroid Struggles to Get Back in Focus," *Fortune,* 7 April 1980, pp. 66–70.

7. John Koten, "Mixing with Coke over Trademarks

Is Always a Fizzle," *The Wall Street Journal,* 10 March 1978, p. 1.
8. Interviews with company personnel.

Chapter 9
1. "Panacea, Placebo, Nostrum, Amen," *Forbes,* 15 Oct. 1977, pp. 83–90.
2. Reprinted from "L'Eggs Success Grew from a Rumpled Piece of Cloth," *Marketing News,* 29 Dec. 1978, p. 9; published by the American Marketing Association.
3. William Robbins, "Moving Sears toward Its Old Ways," *The New York Times,* 11 March 1979, p. F7, "Sears' New 5-Year Plan: To Serve Middle America," *Advertising Age,* 4 Dec. 1978, p. 3ff.; Wyndham Robertson, "How Sears' Retailing Strategy Backfired," *Fortune,* 8 May 1978, pp. 103–104; "Sears' Strategic About-Face," *Business Week,* 8 Jan. 1979, pp. 80–83; "J.C. Penney's Fashion Gamble," *Business Week,* 16 Jan. 1978, pp. 66–74; "Retailers Shake Out a Staid Old Image," *U.S. News & World Report,* 23 Oct. 1978, pp. 83–88.
4. "Mars: Behind Its Chocolate Curtain Is a Sweet Performer," *Business Week,* 14 Aug. 1978, pp. 52–57.
5. "Student Sells $1 Million of Magazine Subscriptions," *The New York Times,* 1 Aug. 1971, pp. 41 ff.

Chapter 10
1. From Marty Olmstead, "Man of a Thousand Designs," *PSA Magazine,* March 1980, pp. 80–83; carried aboard Pacific Southwest Airlines. © 1980 East/West Network, Inc.
2. Arthur M. Louis, "How One Man Makes $120,000 a Year Selling Insurance," *Fortune,* July 1974, pp. 131–40.
3. Ibid.
4. Personal interviews with company personnel.

Chapter 11
1. H. Gordon Garbedian, *Thomas A. Edison: Builder of Civilization* (New York: John Messner, 1947), pp. 52–53.

2. "The Troubles That Are Taxing H & R Block," *Business Week,* 8 Dec. 1973, pp. 112–13.
3. "The Touche Ross Manual for Spotting Fraud," *Business Week,* 17 Feb. 1975, p. 52.
4. Thomas Hayes, "Emerson Electric's Profit Push," *The New York Times,* 10 Dec. 1979.

Chapter 12
1. Charles J. V. Murphy, "Jack Simplot and His Private Conglomerate," *Fortune,* Aug. 1968, pp. 122ff.
2. Susie Nazem, "A Penny-Pinching Strategy Pays Off at the Gas Pumps," *Fortune,* 5 June 1978, pp. 140ff.

Chapter 13
1. Dick Youngblood, "Schaak Taking Steps to Stop the Flow of Red Ink," *Minneapolis Tribune,* 8 Sept. 1974, p. C13.
2. "Dunner's Delight: More Firms Pay Bills Slowly, Spurring Boom in Collectors' Business," *The Wall Street Journal,* 31 July 1979, p. 1. Reprinted by permission of The Wall Street Journal, © Dow Jones & Company, Inc. 1979. All rights reserved.
3. Jeffrey Tannenbaum, "Uncalculated Risk: At Firm, a Record Loss Looms on Computer Policies," *The Wall Street Journal,* 10 July 1979, p. 1; "Computer Lease Losses Continue to Mount," *Business Insurance,* 13 (Dec. 24, 1979), 4; "Computer Leasing Nearly Floors Lloyd's," *Business Week,* 24 Dec. 1979, p. 48.
4. " 'Free Agent' Gary Fink Proves You Needn't Be Gray to Sell Life Insurance," *The Wall Street Journal,* 3 Oct. 1978, p. 1. Reprinted by permission of The Wall Street Journal, © Dow Jones & Company, Inc. 1978. All rights reserved.
5. Winston Williams, "The Airline and the Astronaut: Can Borman Pull It Off?" *The New York Times,* 18 Nov. 1979, p. F3.

Chapter 14
1. David McClintick, "How Did Home-Stake Spend All That Money That Investors Put in?" *The Wall*

Street Journal, 29 Aug. 1974, p. 1; "Gulling the Beautiful People," *Time,* 8 July 1974, p. 45.

2. Barry Newman, "Moving Money: In the Back Office of a Bunk, 'Blipping' Is Not Appreciated," *The Wall Street Journal,* 6 June 1975, p. 1. Reprinted by permission of The Wall Street Journal, © Dow Jones & Co., Inc. 1975. All rights reserved.

3. Jim Powell, "Where to Turn if Ruff Times," *The New York Times,* 11 Nov. 1979, p. F3.

Chapter 15

1. Bernard Wysocki, Jr., "Executives Discover Computers Can Help Them in Daily Routine," *The Wall Street Journal,* 6 July 1979, p. 1. Reprinted by permission of The Wall Street Journal, © Dow Jones & Company, Inc. 1979. All rights reserved.

2. The quotation is from "Shiny Apple," *Time,* 5 Nov. 1979, pp. 84–87. Other sources for the box are: Dan Dorfman, "Move over, Horatio Alger—Little Apple out West," *Esquire,* 6 June 1978, p. 9; "The Hot New Computer Companies," *Dun's Review,* Jan. 1979, p. 55; "Public Might Get a Crack at Apple," *The Wall Street Journal,* 30 June 1980, p. 15, Richard A. Shaffer, "U.S. Personnel—Computer Makers Face Fierce Rivalry from Japan," *The Wall Street Journal,* 27 June 1980, p. 21

3. Material in this box and the section "How Businesses Misuse Computers" are based on " 'The Nagging Feeling' of Undetected Fraud," *U.S. News & World Report,* 19 Dec. 1977, p. 42; Robin L. Friedman, "The Latest in Larceny: Computer-Aided Crimes," *Business Week,* 3 July 1978, pp. 10–11; and Hal Lancaster, "Rise of Minicomputers, Ease of Running Them Facilitate New Frauds," *The Wall Street Journal,* 5 Oct. 1977, p. 1. Reprinted by permission of The Wall Street Journal, © Dow Jones & Company, Inc. 1977. All rights reserved.

4. Jim Hyatt, "At One Toy Company, the Guys in Research Are Three and Four Years Old," *The Wall Street Journal,* 20 Dec. 1971, p. 1. Reprinted by permission of The Wall Street Journal, © Dow Jones & Company, Inc. 1971. All rights reserved.

5. "Shiny Apple," pp. 84–87; Dorfman, "Move over, Horatio Alger—Little Apple out West," p. 9; "The Hot New Computer Companies," p. 55; "Public Might Get a Crack at Apple," p. 15; Schaffer, "U.S. Personnel—Computer Makers Face Fierce Rivalry from Japan," p. 21.

Chapter 16

1. "The Fast-Food Stores: Three Strategies for Fast Growth," *Business Week,* 11 July 1977, pp. 56–68.

2. The attractions and drawbacks of small businesses are cited in Wendell O. Metcalf, *Starting and Managing a Small Business of Your Own,* 2nd ed. (Washington, D.C.: U.S. Small Business Administration, 1962), pp. 1–2.

3. Everett Groseclose, "You Have Problems? Consider the Plight of the Nation's SOBs," *The Wall Street Journal,* 20 March 1975, p. 1.

4. Frederick C. Klein, "Launching a Business in These Risky Times Is a Frustrating Task," *The Wall Street Journal,* 6 Nov. 1974, pp. 1 ff. Reprinted by permission of The Wall Street Journal © Dow Jones & Company, Inc. 1971. All rights reserved.

5. Jerome L. Fels and Lewis G. Rudnick, "Investigate Before Investing: Guidance for Prospective Franchisees" (Washington: International Franchise Association, 1979, $2.50 prepaid).

6. Based on general information supplied by McDonald's Corporation (Oak Brook, Ill.: McDonald's Corporation, 1980).

7. Jim Montgomery, "Low Pay, Bossy Bosses Kill Kids' Enthusiasm for Food Service Jobs," *The Wall Street Journal,* 15 March 1979, p. 1. Reprinted by permission of The Wall Street Journal, © Dow Jones & Company, Inc. 1979. All rights reserved.

8. J. Anthony Lukas, "As American as McDonald's Hamburger on the Fourth of July," *The New York Times Magazine,* 4 July 1971.

Chapter 17

1. Barth David Schwartz, "How to Make a Million Doing Your Own Thing," *Fortune,* 4 June 1979, p. 141.

2. The case study of Greco's small business failure appears in Kurt B. Mayer and Sidney Goldstein, *The First Two Years: Problems of Small Firms' Growth and Survival* (Washington, D.C.: U.S. Small Business Administration, 1961), pp. 118–33

3. The case study of estimating a shoe store's sales revenue is adapted from William Rudelius et al., "Assessing Retail Opportunities in Low-Income Areas," *Journal of Retailing* (Fall 1972), pp. 96–114. The general method is adapted from *Retail Location Manual–Small Business in Low-Income Areas* (Chicago: Real Estate Research Corporation, 1967), Vol. I.

4. Much of the material in the section of running a small business is based on Wendell O. Metcalf, *Starting and Managing a Small Business of Your Own,* 2nd ed. (Washington, D.C.: U.S. Small Business Administration, 1962), pp. 25–32.

5. Frank E. Emerson, "The Biomedical Businessman," *Black Enterprise,* Feb. 1980, pp. 91–94. Copyright 1980, The Earl G. Graves Publishing Co., Inc., 295 Madison Avenue, New York, N.Y. 10017. All rights reserved.

Chapter 18

1. "Stretched Thin: Civic Duties Become a More Beastly Burden for Chief Executives," *The Wall Street Journal,* 11 June 1980, p. 1. Reprinted by permission of The Wall Street Journal, © Dow Jones & Company, Inc. 1980. All rights reserved.

Chapter 19

1. Ed Townsend, "Unions Look to Women for '80s Growth," *The Christian Science Monitor,* 20 Dec. 1979. Reprinted by permission from *The Christian Science Monitor* © 1979. The Christian Science Publishing Society. All rights reserved.

2. Lawrence G. O'Donnell, "As a Ford Foreman, Ed Hendrix Finds He Is Man in the Middle," *The Wall Street Journal,* 25 July 1973, p. 1. Reprinted by permission of The Wall Street Journal, © Dow Jones & Company, Inc. 1973. All rights reserved.

3. Walter Mossberg, "A Union Man at Ford, Charlie Bragg Deals in Problems, Gripes," *The Wall Street Journal,* 26 July 1973, p. 1. Reprinted by permission of The Wall Street Journal, © Dow Jones & Company, Inc. 1973. All rights reserved.

Chapter 20

1. From John H. Dessauer, *My Years with Xerox* (Garden City, N.Y.: Doubleday, 1971), pp. 141–56.

2. Julie Salamon, "Watch Out, Earth! Invaders from Space Are Coming for You," *The Wall Street Journal,* 13 Aug. 1980, p. 1. Reprinted by permission of The Wall Street Journal, © Dow Jones & Company, Inc. 1980. All rights reserved.

3. Peter Vanderwicken, "When Levi Strauss Burst Its Britches," *Fortune,* April 1971, pp. 130ff; "Back to Basic Bottoms," *Forbes,* 15 March 1975, p. 80; and Milton Moskowitz, "The Levi Lifestyle," *The New York Times,* 6 Aug. 1972, Business Section, p. 1ff.

Sources of illustrations:

Chapter 1: p. 4, © Richard Frieman/Photo Researchers, Inc.; p. 6, Courtesy of Alternative Pioneering Systems, Inc.; p. 7, © Ewing Galloway; p. 10, Photo Courtesy of Xerox Corporation; p. 12, Courtesy Levi Strauss and Co.; p. 13 Courtesy Levi Strauss and Co.; pp. 16–17, Illustration by Abe Gurvin; p. 22, © Culver Pictures; p. 23, Courtesy of Procter & Gamble; p. 25, © Mark Perlstein/Black Star.

Chapter 2: p. 28, © Donald C. Dietz/Stock, Boston; p. 32, © James Pickerill/Black Star; p. 34, Sybil Shelton/© Peter Arnold, Inc.; p. 36, *Dunagin's People* by Ralph Dunagin © 1979 Field Enterprises, Inc. Courtesy of Field Newspaper Syndicate; p. 45, © Charles Gatewood; p. 46, U.S. Bureau of Labor Statistics; p. 48, © Charles Gatewood; p. 49, Michael Crummett/© Black Star.

Chapter 3: p. 56, © David Attie; p. 60, Copyright Fred Forbes 1980/Humbird Hopkins; p. 66, Pepperidge Farm; p. 67, Courtesy of Digital Equipment Corporation; p. 68, © James H. Karales/Peter Arnold, Inc.; p. 71, Charles Harbutt/© Magnum Photos, Inc.; p. 75, Courtesy Land O' Lakes, Inc.

Chapter 4: p. 80, © Ellis Herwig/Stock, Boston; p. 87, Illustration by Joe Argenziano for *Fortune Magazine* 1976; p. 90, © Billy E. Barnes; p. 98, © 1980 Fotomat Corporation; p. 101, © Martin Adler Levick/Black Star.

Chapter 5: p. 108, © Charles Schneider; p. 116, Courtesy of Beetleboards International, 7777 Sunset Blvd., Los Angeles, CA 90046; p. 117, General Motors; p. 128, By permission of Johnny Hart and Field Enterprises, Inc.; p. 130, *top*, U.S. Department of the Interior. National Park Service. Edison National Historic Site; p. 130, *bot.* © Cecil Beaton; p. 133, © Owen Franken/Stock, Boston.

Chapter 6: p. 136, © Marjorie Pickens; p. 140, © Ken Light/Black Star; p. 142, Data (for diagram) based on Hierarchy of Needs in "A Theory of Human Motivation" in *Motivation and Personality*, 2nd Edition by Abraham H. Maslow. Copyright © 1970 by Abraham H. Maslow; p. 145, © 1978 Laimute E. Druskis/Taurus Photos; p. 148, United Technologies; p. 149, Copyright, © 1979, G.B.Trudeau. Reprinted

with permission of Universal Press Syndicate. All rights reserved; p. 150, Reprinted by permission of the Harvard Business Review. Exhibit adapted from "How to Choose a Leadership Pattern" by Robert Tannenbaum and Warren H. Schmidt (March-April 1958). Copyright © 1958 by the President and Fellows of Harvard College; all rights reserved.

Chapter 7: p. 160, © Peter Menzel; p. 162, Photo by Texas Instruments, Inc.; p. 167, Logo courtesy of General Foods Corporation; p. 170, © Bill Owens/ Jeroboam, Inc.; p. 176, © Steven Lewis/The Picture Cube.

Chapter 8: p. 188, © Jozef Vissel/Freelance Photographer's Guild; p. 190, Logo courtesy DeLorean Motor Company; p. 198, © Bill Owens/Jeroboam, Inc.; p. 202, *l.,* Courtesy of Procter & Gamble; p. 202, *c.,* Colgate Palmolive Company; p. 202, *r.,* Lever Brothers; p. 213, © Mark Mellett/Taurus Photos; p. 217, Printed with permission of Yoplait U.S.A. ® Yoplait is a registered trademark of Sodima.

Chapter 9: p. 218, © John Oldenkamp; p. 222, James H. Karales/© Peter Arnold, Inc; p. 227, Illustration by Abe Gurvin; p. 229, © Dennis Brack/ Black Star; p. 233, © Harvey Barad/Monkmeyer Press Photo Service; p. 236, © Richard Faverty/ NYT Pictures; p. 239, Courtesy Educational Subscription Service, Inc.

Chapter 10: p. 240, Courtesy of Beetleboards International, 7777 Sunset Blvd., Los Angeles, CA 90046; p. 242, Courtesy of Beetleboards International, 7777 Sunset Blvd., Los Angeles, CA 90046; p. 243, © Stephen J. Potter/Stock, Boston; p. 247, *top,* Reprinted with the permission of General Motors Corporation; p. 247, *bot.,* Chevrolet Motor Division; p.

Index